Avizandum Statutes on

Scots Family Law
2010–2011

Eighth edition

Avizandum Statutes on

Scots Family Law
2010–2011

Eighth edition

Editor

Jane Mair LLM, PhD
Senior Lecturer in Law, University of Glasgow

Avizandum Publishing Ltd
Edinburgh
2010

Avizandum Publishing Ltd
58 Candlemaker Row
Edinburgh EH1 2QE

First published   2002
Reprinted   2003
2nd Edition   2004
3rd Edition   2005
Reprinted   2006
4th edition   2006
5th edition   2007
6th edition   2008
7th edition   2009
Reprinted   2010
8th edition   2010

ISBN 978-1-904968-42-9

Parliamentary material is reproduced with the permission of the Controller of
HMSO on behalf of Parliament and of the Office of the Queen's Printer for
Scotland on behalf of the Scottish Parliament.

British Library Cataloguing in Publication Data
A catalogue record for this book is available from the British Library

Typeset by AFS Image Setters Ltd, Glasgow
Printed and bound by Thomson Litho, East Kilbride, Scotland

EDITOR'S PREFACE

This volume is intended primarily as a resource for undergraduate students of child and family law and the provisions which have been included reflect the content of undergraduate courses. In selecting provisions to include I have considered a number of factors. Most important of these is relevancy – this volume aims to reflect the content of undergraduate courses and, although the final selection of materials was mine, it was made following consultation with fellow teachers of family law. As with previous editions, statutory instruments have not been included. This decision was made partly on the basis that students are unlikely to refer to these on a frequent basis and, when they need to do so, statutory instruments are now readily accessible on the internet.

Unlike recent years, there has been very little new family law legislation since the previous edition although new material included last year, in particular the Adoption and Children (Scotland) Act 2007, has continued to come into force. One area of Scots family law which remains in a relatively unsettled state is that relating to child support. Amendments to the Child Support Act 1991 as a result of the Child Maintenance and Other Payments Act 2008 have been made but relatively few provisions from these Acts are included. As with all of the material included in this volume, our aim is to reflect what is taught in Scottish law schools and we welcome feedback, in particular as to other sections of both the 1991 and 2008 Acts which would be useful.

I have endeavoured to update the materials to the end of June 2010. Material which was not included in the statute as originally enacted has been identified by the use of square brackets.

Jane Mair
Glasgow University
July 2010

CONTENTS

PART I

STATUTES

REGISTRATION OF BIRTHS, DEATHS AND MARRIAGES (SCOTLAND)
ACT 1965
(1965, c 49)

PART II
REGISTRATION OF BIRTHS

13   Particulars of births to be registered

[(1)   The prescribed particulars of the birth of every child born in Scotland shall be registered in accordance with this Part of this Act and for that purpose each district registrar for each registration district shall keep—
   (a)   a register of births, and
   (b)   a register of still-births.]
   [. . .]
(4)   Where a child is born (whether within or out of Scotland) in a ship, aircraft or land vehicle in the course of a journey, and that child is brought by such ship, aircraft or land vehicle to any place in Scotland, the birth shall, unless the Registrar General [of Births, Deaths and Marriages for Scotland] otherwise directs, be deemed for the purposes of this section to have occurred at that place.

14   Duty to give information of particulars of birth

(1)   Subject to the subsequent provisions of this Part of this Act, in the case of every birth it shall be the duty of—
   (a)   the [child's father or mother (whether or not they have attained the age of sixteen years)], or
   (b)   in the case of the death or inability of the father and mother, each other person who under the next following subsection is qualified to give information concerning the birth,
within twenty-one days from the date of the birth, [to give to the district registrar for a registration district information of the prescribed particulars concerning the birth]:
   Provided that the giving of that information [. . .] by the father or the mother or by any one of those persons shall constitute a discharge of any duty imposed by this subsection on any other person.
   [(1A)   For the purposes of subsection (1) above, a person shall give information of the prescribed particulars concerning a birth to the district registrar for a registration district by—
   (a)   attending personally at the registration office for that district and—
      (i)   giving to the registrar information of the particulars required to be registered concerning the birth, and
      (ii)   attesting, in the prescribed manner, the prescribed form (in this Part, the 'birth registration form') concerning the birth in the presence of the registrar, or
   (b)   submitting to the registrar by a prescribed means a birth registration form concerning the birth which has been completed by the person and attested by him in the prescribed manner.]
(2)   The following persons, in addition to the father and mother, shall be qualified to give information concerning the birth of a child, that is to say—

(a)   any relative of either parent of the child, being a relative who has knowledge of the birth;

(b)   the occupier of the premises in which the child was, to the knowledge of that occupier, born;

(c)   any person present at the birth;

(d)   any person having charge of the child.

(3)   Nothing in this [. . .] section shall authorise the registration of the particulars of any birth in two or more registers, or more than once in any one register.

(4)   If it appears to the Registrar General that the particulars of the birth of any child have been registered in two or more registers, or more than once in any one register, he may give directions for the cancellation of all those registrations except such one of them as may be specified in the directions.

[(4A)   In the case of a child who has a parent by virtue of section 42 of the Human Fertilisation and Embryology Act 2008, the references in subsections (1) and (2) to the father of the child are to be read as references to the woman who is a parent by virtue of that section.]

[(5)   In this section, any reference to the father or parent of the child shall not include a reference to a father who is not married to the mother and has not been married to her since the child's conception.]

18   Births of children born out of wedlock

[(1)   Subject to section 18ZA of this Act no person who is not married to the mother of a child and has not been married to her since the child's conception shall be required, as father of the child, to give information concerning the birth of the child and, save as provided in section 20 of this Act, the [district registrar for the registration district] shall not enter in the [birth registration form concerning the birth] the name and surname of any such person as father of the child except—

(a)   at the joint request of the mother and the person acknowledging himself to be the father of the child (in which case that person shall [attest, in the prescribed manner, the birth registration form] together with the mother); or

(b)   at the request of the mother—

(i)   on the production of—

(aa)   a declaration in the prescribed form made by the mother stating that that person is the father of the child; and

(bb)   a statutory declaration made by that person acknowledging himself to be the father of the child; or

(ii)   on production of a decree by a competent court finding or declaring that person to be the father of the child; or

(c)   at the request of that person on production of—

(i)   a declaration in the prescribed form by that person acknowledging himself to be the father of the child; and

(ii)   a statutory declaration made by the mother stating that that person is the father of the child.]

[(1A)   Where a person acknowledging himself to be the father of a child makes a request to the [district registrar for the registration district] in accordance with paragraph (c) of subsection (1) of this section, he shall be treated as a qualified informant concerning the birth of the child for the purposes of this Act; and the giving of information concerning the birth of the child by that person and the [attesting of the birth registration form concerning the birth] by him in the presence of the registrar shall act as a discharge of any duty of any other qualified informant under section 14 of this Act.]

(2)   In any case where the name and surname of the father of a [. . .] child has not been entered in the [birth registration form concerning the birth], the Registrar General may record that name and surname by causing an appropriate entry to be made in the Register of Corrections Etc—

(a)   if a decree of paternity has been granted by a competent court; or

(b) if there is produced to him [a declaration and a statutory declaration such as are mentioned in paragraph (b) or (c) of subsection 1 of this section]; or

(c) if, where the mother is dead [or cannot be found or is incapable of making a request under subsection (1)(b) of this section, or a declaration under subsection (1)(b)(i)(aa) of this section, or a statutory declaration under subsection (1)(c)(ii) of this section] he is ordered so to do by the sheriff upon application made to the sheriff [. . .] by the person acknowledging himself to be the father of the child.

Where a decree of paternity has been granted by any court the clerk of court shall, where no appeal has been made against such decree, on the expiration of the time within which such an appeal may be made, or where an appeal has been made against such a decree, on the conclusion of any appellate proceedings, notify the import of such decree in the prescribed form to the Registrar General.

[(3) A person under the age of sixteen years has legal capacity—

(a) to make a request, declaration or statutory declaration under subsection (1) or (2)(b) above if, in the opinion of the registrar; or

(b) to make an application under subsection (2)(c) above if, in the opinion of the sheriff,

that person understands the nature of the request or, as the case may be, of the declaration, statutory declaration or application; and without prejudice to the generality of this subsection a person twelve years of age or more shall be presumed to be of sufficient age and maturity to have such understanding.]

[**18ZA Registration of father or second female parent by virtue of certain provisions of the Human Fertilisation and Embryology Act 2008**

(1) The registrar shall not enter in the register—

(a) as the father of a child the name of a man who is to be treated for that purpose as the father of the child by virtue of section 39(1) or 40(1) or (2) of the Human Fertilisation and Embryology Act 2008 (circumstances in which man to be treated as father of child for purpose of registration of birth where fertility treatment undertaken after his death); or

(b) as a parent of the child, the name of a woman who is to be treated for that purpose as a parent of the child by virtue of section 46(1) or (2) of that Act (circumstances in which woman to be treated as parent of child for purposes of registration of birth where fertility treatment undertaken after her death),

unless the condition in subsection (2) below is satisfied.

(2) The condition in this subsection is satisfied if—

(a) the mother requests the registrar to make such an entry in the register and produces the relevant documents; or

(b) in the case of the death or inability of the mother, the relevant documents are produced by some other person who is a qualified informant.

(3) In this section 'the relevant documents' means—

(a) the consent in writing and election mentioned in section 39(1), 40(1) or (2) or 46(1) or (2) (as the case requires) of the Human Fertilisation and Embryology Act 2008;

(b) a certificate of a registered medical practitioner as to the medical facts concerned; and

(c) such other documentary evidence (if any) as the registrar considers appropriate.]

[**18A Decrees of parentage and non-parentage**

(1) Where a decree of parentage or non-parentage has been granted by any court the clerk of court shall—

(a) where no appeal has been made against such decree, on the expiration of the time within which such an appeal may be made, or

(b) where an appeal has been made against such a decree, on the conclusion of any appellate proceedings, notify the import of such decree in the prescribed form to the Registrar General.

(2) Where it appears to the Registrar General that the import of a decree notified to him under subsection (1) above does not correspond with the entry in the register of births in respect of any person to whom the decree relates he shall cause an appropriate entry to be made in the Register of Corrections Etc.]

[18B   Births of children where second female parent by virtue of section 43 of the Human Fertilisation and Embryology Act 2008

(1) No woman shall as a parent of a child by virtue of section 43 of the Human Fertilisation and Embryology Act 2008 ('the woman concerned') be required, as a parent of the child, to give information concerning the birth of the child and, save as provided in section 20 of this Act, the district registrar for the registration district shall not enter in the birth registration form concerning the birth the name and surname of any woman as a parent of the child by virtue of section 43 of that Act of 2008 except—

(a) at the joint request of the mother and the woman concerned (in which case the woman concerned shall attest, in the prescribed manner, the birth registration form together with the mother); or

(b) at the request of the mother on production of—

(i) a declaration in the prescribed form made by the mother stating that the woman concerned is a parent of the child by virtue of section 43 of the Human Fertilisation and Embryology Act 2008; and

(ii) a statutory declaration made by the woman concerned acknowledging herself to be a parent of the child by virtue of section 43 of that Act; or

(c) at the request of the mother on production of a decree by a competent court finding or declaring the woman concerned to be a parent of the child by virtue of section 43 of that Act; or

(d) at the request of the woman concerned on production of—

(i) a declaration in the prescribed form made by the woman concerned acknowledging herself to be a parent of the child by virtue of section 43 of that Act; and

(ii) a statutory declaration made by the mother stating that the woman concerned is a parent of the child by virtue of section 43 of that Act.

(2) Where a person acknowledging herself to be a parent of the child by virtue of section 43 of the Human Fertilisation and Embryology Act 2008 makes a request to the district registrar for the registration district in accordance with paragraph (d) of subsection (1) of this section, she shall be treated as a qualified informant concerning the birth of the child for the purposes of this Act; and the giving of information concerning the birth of the child by that person and the attesting of the birth registration form concerning the birth by her in the presence of the registrar shall act as a discharge of any duty of any other qualified informant under section 14 of this Act.

(3) In any case where the name and surname of a woman who is a parent of a child by virtue of section 43 of the Human Fertilisation and Embryology Act 2008 has not been entered in the birth registration form concerning the birth, the Registrar General may record that name and surname by causing an appropriate entry to be made in the Register of Corrections Etc—

(a) if there is produced to him a declaration and a statutory declaration such as are mentioned in paragraph (b) or (d) of subsection (1) of this section; or

(b) if, where the mother is dead or cannot be found or is incapable of making a request under subsection (1)(b) or (c) of this section, or a declaration under subsection (1)(b)(i) or a statutory declaration under subsection (1)(d)(ii) of this section, the Registrar General is ordered so to do by the sheriff upon application made to the sheriff by the person acknowledging herself to be a parent of the child by virtue of section 43 of the Human Fertilisation and Embryology Act 2008.]

[. . .]

20 Re-registration in certain cases

(1) In the case of any person, if—

(a) the entry relating to him in the register of births is affected by any matter contained in the Register of Corrections Etc respecting his status [parentage or non-parentage], or

(b) the entry relating to him in the register of births has been so made as to imply that he was found exposed, or

(c) the entry relating to him in the register of births [has been so made as to imply that his parents were not then married to one another and his parents have subsequently married one another and subject to subsection (1B) below] [; or

(d) the entry relating to the child in the register of births has been made so as to imply that the person, other than the mother, recorded as a parent of the child is so by virtue of section 43 of the Human Fertilisation and Embryology Act 2008 and the mother and that person have subsequently become parties to a civil partnership with each other and subject to subsection (1B) below,]

the [birth may, where subsection (1A) below applies, be re-registered], and any such re-registration shall be effected in such manner as may be prescribed:

[(1A) This subsection applies—

(a) where the Registrar-General authorises the re-registration, and

(b) in such other cases or classes of case as may be prescribed.

(1B) A birth may not be re-registered] in pursuance of paragraph (c) [or (d)] [. . .], in a case where the paternity [or parentage] of the person has not been entered in the register of births or in the Register of Corrections Etc in accordance with section 18 [or 18B] of this Act, or any corresponding enactment in force before the commencement of this Act, save with the sanction of the sheriff granted upon the application—

(i) of both parents of the person jointly, or

(ii) where one of the parents is dead, of the surviving parent, or

(iii) where both parents are dead, of or on behalf of the person,

after such intimation as the sheriff may direct, and after due inquiry, and a hearing of any party having interest who may appear to oppose such application.

(2) In this section any reference to the register of births includes a reference to any register of births kept under any enactment in force at any time before the commencement of this Act.

[. . .]

43 Recording of baptismal name or change of name or surname

(1) The following provisions of this section, except subsection 6(b), shall apply only to persons whose births are registered in Scotland, and, without prejudice to the provisions of section 24 of the Adoption Act 1958 relating to the giving or taking of a new name, to persons in respect of whom there is an entry in the Adopted Children Register maintained by the Registrar General under section 22 of that Act.

(2) In this section 'change' in relation to a name or surname includes any change by way of substitution, addition, omission, spelling or hyphenation.

(3) Where, within twelve months from the date of the birth of any child, the name by which it was registered is changed or, if it was registered without a name, a name is given to the child, the Registrar General [. . .], shall [, where within two years from the date of the birth of the child, an application in the prescribed form is made to the Registrar General in respect of that matter by the qualified applicant,] cause an entry containing the name mentioned in the [application] to be made in the Register of Corrections Etc, and only one such entry may be made under this subsection in respect of any one child. [. . .]

(4) Where an application in the prescribed form is made to the Registrar General by the qualified applicant in respect of the change of name or surname of a child under sixteen years of age the Registrar General may record that change of

name or surname by causing an appropriate entry to be made in the Register of Corrections Etc.

[. . .]

Only one change of name and one change of surname in respect of any one child may be recorded under this subsection, but no change of name shall be recorded under this subsection in the case of a child in respect of whom a change of name has been recorded by virtue of the last foregoing subsection.

(5) Where an application in the prescribed form is made to the Registrar General in respect of a change of name or surname, in the case of a person over sixteen years of age [. . .] by that person, the Registrar General may record that change of name or surname by causing an appropriate entry to be made in the Register of Corrections Etc.

[. . .]

Only one change of name and three changes of surname in respect of any one person may be recorded under this subsection, and a period of five years must elapse after one change of surname is recorded before another such change may be recorded.

(6) Notwithstanding the foregoing provisions of this section, where an application is made to the Registrar General in respect of a change of name or surname—

(a)   in the case of a child under sixteen years of age, by the [qualified applicant] of that child, in the case of a person over sixteen years of age [. . .] by that person, and there is produced to the Registrar General—

(i) a decree or certificate of change of name or surname pronounced or, as the case may be, granted by or on behalf of the Lyon King of Arms, or

(ii) a certified copy of a will, settlement, or deed of trust containing a condition that the person concerned shall take a name or surname different from that in which his birth was registered, together with evidence to the satisfaction of the Registrar General that the name or surname has thereafter been so changed, or

(b)   in the case of a male person who has married in Scotland and who has changed his name or surname following his marriage, by that person, and there is produced to the Registrar General a decree or certificate as described in the foregoing paragraph,

the Registrar General may record that change of name or surname by causing an appropriate entry to be made in the Register of Corrections Etc.

(7) Where an application is made to the Registrar General in respect of the recording of an alternative name, being the English equivalent of a non-English name, in the case of a child under sixteen years of age, by the [qualified applicant] of that child, in the case of a person over sixteen years of age [. . .] by that person the Registrar General may record that name as an alternative name by causing an appropriate entry to be made in the Register of Corrections Etc.

(8) On making an application under any of the provisions of this section the applicant shall pay such fees as may be prescribed.

(9) Nothing in this section shall affect any rule of law as respects change of name or surname, and in particular, without prejudice to that generality, the validity as evidence of change of name or surname of a decree or certificate pronounced or, as the case may be, granted by or on behalf of the Lyon King of Arms.

[(9A) In this section 'qualified applicant' means—

(a)   where only one parent has parental responsibilities in relation to the child, that parent;

(b)   where both parents have such responsibilities in relation to the child, both parents; and

(c)   where neither parent has such responsibilities, any other person who has such responsibilities.

(9B) A person may be a qualified applicant for the purposes of this section whether or not he has attained the age of sixteen years].

ABORTION ACT 1967
(1967, c 87)

1 Medical termination of pregnancy
(1) Subject to the provisions of this section, a person shall not be guilty of an offence under the law relating to abortion when a pregnancy is terminated by a registered medical practitioner if two registered medical practitioners are of the opinion, formed in good faith—
[(a) that the pregnancy has not exceeded its twenty-fourth week and that the continuance of the pregnancy would involve risk, greater than if the pregnancy were terminated, of injury to the physical or mental health of the pregnant woman or any existing children of her family; or
(b) that the termination is necessary to prevent grave permanent injury to the physical or mental health of the pregnant woman; or
(c) that the continuance of the pregnancy would involve risk to the life of the pregnant woman, greater than if the pregnancy were terminated; or
(d) that there is a substantial risk that if the child were born it would suffer from such physical or mental abnormalities as to be seriously handicapped.]
(2) In determining whether the continuance of a pregnancy would involve such risk of injury to health as is mentioned in paragraph (a) [or (b)] of subsection (1) of this section, account may be taken of the pregnant woman's actual or reasonably foreseeable environment.
(3) Except as provided by subsection (4) of this section, any treatment for the termination of pregnancy must be carried out in a hospital vested in [. . .] the Secretary of State [. . .] for the purposes of [his functions under the National Health Service Act 2006 or the National Health Service (Scotland) Act 1978 or in a hospital vested in a Primary Care Trust or in a National Health Service Trust [or an NHS foundation trust] or in a place approved for the purposes of this section by the Secretary of State.]
[(3A) The power under subsection (3) of this section to approve a place includes power, in relation to treatment consisting primarily in the use of such medicines as may be specified in the approval and carried out in such manner as may be so specified, to approve a class of places.]
(4) Subsection (3) of this section, and so much of subsection (1) as relates to the opinion of two registered medical practitioners, shall not apply to the termination of a pregnancy by a registered medical practitioner in a case where he is of the opinion, formed in good faith, that the termination is immediately necessary to save the life or to prevent grave permanent injury to the physical or mental health of the pregnant woman.

SOCIAL WORK (SCOTLAND ACT 1968
(1968, s 49)

PART I
ADMINISTRATION

5 Powers of the Secretary of State
(1) Local authorities shall perform their functions under this Act [and Part II of the Children (Scotland) Act 1995] under the general guidance of the Secretary of State.
[(1A) Without prejudice to subsection (1) above, the Secretary of State may issue directions to local authorities, either individually or collectively, as to the manner in which they are to exercise any of their functions under this Act or any of the enactments mentioned in [subsection (1B) below] and a local authority shall comply with any direction made under this subsection.]
[(1B) The enactments referred to in subsection (1A) above are—

(a)   this Act as read with sections 1 and 2(1) of the Chronically Sick and Disabled Persons Act 1970 and the Disabled Persons (Services, Consultation and Representation) Act 1986;

(b)   Part IV of the Children and Young Persons (Scotland) Act 1937;

(c)   section 22(2) to (5A), (7) and (8), section 26(2) to (4) and sections 43, 45, 47 and 48 of the National Assistance Act 1948;

(d)   the Disabled Persons (Employment) Act 1958;

(e)   sections 10 to 12 of the Matrimonial Proceedings (Children) Act 1958, and sections 11 and 12 of the Guardianship Act 1973;

(f)   [section 51 of the Criminal Procedure (Scotland) Act 1995;]

(g)   the Children Act 1975;

(h)   the Adoption Act 1976;

[. . .]

(j)   sections 21 to 23 of the Health and Social Services and Social Security Adjudications Act 1983;

(k)   [the Mental Health (Care and Treatment) (Scotland) Act 2003];

(l)   the Foster Children (Scotland) Act 1984;

(m)   sections 38(6) and 235 of the Housing (Scotland) Act 1987;

(n)   the Access to Personal Files Act 1987; [. . .] and

[. . .]

(p)   Part II of the Children (Scotland) Act 1995;

[(q)   the Adoption and Children (Scotland) Act 2007 (asp 4).]]

[(2)   The Secretary of State may make regulations in relation to—

(a)   the performance of the functions assigned to local authorities by this Act;

(b)   the activities of voluntary organisations in so far as those activities are concerned with the like purposes;

[(c)   the performance of the functions of local authorities under any of the enactments mentioned in paragraphs (b), (d), (e), (g), (h), (i), (1), (o), [(p) and (q)] of subsection (1B) above.

[. . .]

(3)   Without prejudice to the generality of subsection (2) above, regulations under this section may make such provision as is mentioned in subsection (4) of this section as regards—

(a)   the boarding out of persons other than children by local authorities and voluntary organisations, whether under any enactment or otherwise; and

(b)   the placing of children under paragraph (a), or the making of arrangements in respect of children under paragraph (c), of section 26(1) of the Children (Scotland) Act 1995, by local authorities.

(4)   The provision referred to in subsection (3) of this section is—

(a)   for the recording—

(i) by local authorities and voluntary organisations, of information relating to those with whom persons are so boarded out, or who are willing to have persons so boarded out with them; and

(ii) by local authorities, of information relating to those with whom children are so placed or with whom such arrangements are made or who are willing to have children so placed with them or to enter into such arrangements,

(b)   for securing that—

(i) persons are not so boarded out in any household unless it is for the time being approved by such local authority or voluntary organisation as may be prescribed by the regulations; and

(ii) children are not so placed or, in accordance with such arrangements, provided with accommodation, in any household unless it is for the time being approved by the local authority placing the child or as the case may be making the arrangements;

(c)   for securing that, where possible, the person with whom a child is so placed or with whom such arrangements are made is either of the same religious persuasion as the child or gives an undertaking that the child shall be brought up in that persuasion;

(d)   for securing—

(i)   that a person who is, and the place in which he is, so boarded out by a local authority or voluntary organisation is supervised and inspected by that authority or organisation; and

(ii)   that a child who is, and the place in which he is, so placed or, in accordance with such arrangements, provided with accommodation, by a local authority is supervised and inspected by that authority,

and that he shall be removed from the place in question if his welfare appears to require it.

(5)   In subsections (3) and (4) of this section, 'child' [means a person who is under the age of 18].]

[5A   Local authority plans for community care services

(1)   Within such period after the day appointed for the coming into force of this section as the Secretary of State may direct, and in accordance with the provisions of this section, each local authority shall prepare and publish a plan for the provision of community care services in their area.

(2)   Each local authority shall from time to time review any plan prepared by them under subsection (1) above, and shall, in the light of any such review, prepare and publish—

(a)   any modifications to the plan under review; or

(b)   if the case requires, a new plan.

(3)   In preparing any plan or carrying out any review under subsection (1) or, as the case may be, subsection (2) above the authority shall consult—

(a)   any Health Board providing services under the National Health Service (Scotland) Act 1978 in the area of the authority;

[. . .]

(c)   such voluntary organisations as appear to the authority to represent the interests of persons who use or are likely to use any community care services within the area of the authority or the interests of private carers who, within that area, provide care to persons for whom, in the exercise of their functions under this Act or any of the enactments mentioned in [section 5(1B)] of this Act, the local authority have a power or a duty to provide, or to secure the provision of, a service;

(d)   such voluntary housing agencies and other bodies as appear to the authority to provide housing or community care services in their area; and

(e)   such other persons as the Secretary of State may direct.

(4)   In this section—

'community care services' means services, other than services for children, which a local authority are under a duty or have a power to provide, or to secure the provision of, under Part II of this Act or [section 25 (provision of care and support services for persons who have or have had a mental disorder), 26 (provision of services designed to promote well-being and social development of such persons) or 27 (assistance with travel in connection with such services) of the Mental Health (Care and Treatment) (Scotland) Act 2003]; and

'private carer' means a person who is not employed to provide the care in question by any body in the exercise of its functions under any enactment.]

[5B   Complaints procedure

(1)   Subject to the provisions of this section, the Secretary of State may by order require local authorities to establish a procedure whereby a person, or anyone acting on his behalf, may make representations (including complaints) in relation to the authority's discharge of, or failure to discharge, any of their functions under this Act, or any of the enactments [mentioned in section 5(1B)] of this Act, in respect of that person.

(2)   For the purposes of subsection (1) of this section, 'person' means any person for whom the local authority have a power or a duty to provide, or to secure the provision of, a service, and whose need or possible need for such a service has (by whatever means) come to the attention of the authority.

(3)   An order under subsection (1) of this section may be commenced at different times in respect of such different classes of person as may be specified in the order.

(4)   In relation to a child, representations may be made by virtue of subsection (1) above by the child, or on his behalf by—

(a)   his parent;

(b)   any person having parental [responsibilities and parental rights (within the meaning of section 1(3) and section 2(4) respectively of the Children (Scotland) Act 1995 in relation to him];

(c)   any local authority foster parent; or

(d)   any other person appearing to the authority to have a sufficient interest in the child's wellbeing to warrant his making representations on the child's behalf.

(5)   In this section—

'child' means a child under the age of 18 years; [. . .]

(6)   A local authority shall comply with any directions given by the Secretary of State as to the procedure to be adopted in considering representations made as mentioned in subsection (1) of this section and as to the taking of such action as may be necessary in consequence of such representations.

(7)   Every local authority shall give such publicity to the procedure established under this section as they consider appropriate.]

[. . .]

[6A   Inquiries

(1)   Without prejudice to section 6B(1) of this Act, the Secretary of State may cause an inquiry to be held into—

(a)   the functions of a local authority under this Act or any of the enactments mentioned in section 5(1B) of this Act;

(b)   the functions of an adoption society, within the meaning of [section 119(1) of the Adoption and Children (Scotland) Act 2007 (asp 4)];

[. . .]

(d)   the detention of a child under—

(i)   section 57 of the Children and Young Persons (Scotland) Act 1937; or

(ii)   section 44 or 208 of the Criminal Procedure (Scotland) Act 1995;

(e)   the functions of the Principal Reporter under Part III of the Local Government (Scotland) Act 1994, the Children (Scotland) Act 1995 or any other enactment.

(2)   The Secretary of State may, before an inquiry is commenced, direct that it shall be held in private, but where no such direction has been given the person holding the inquiry may if he thinks fit hold it or any part of it in private.

(3)   Subsections (2) to (8) of section 210 of the Local Government (Scotland) Act 1973 (powers in relation to local inquiries) shall apply in relation to an inquiry under this section as they apply in relation to a local inquiry under that section.]

[6B   Local authority inquiries into matters affecting children

(1)   Without prejudice to section 6A(1) of this Act, a local authority may cause an inquiry to be held into their functions under this Act, or any of the enactments mentioned in section 5(1B) of this Act, in so far as those functions relate to children.

(2)   The local authority may, before an inquiry under this section is commenced, direct that it be held in private; but where no such direction is given, the person holding the inquiry may if he thinks fit hold it, or any part of it, in private.

(3)   Subsections (2) to (6) of section 210 of the Local Government (Scotland) Act 1973 (powers in relation to local inquiries) shall apply in relation to an inquiry

under this section as they apply in relation to a local inquiry under that section, so however that, for the purposes of the application, any reference in those subsections to a Minister shall be construed as a reference to the local authority and any reference to an officer of his Department as a reference to an officer of that authority.

(4)   The expenses incurred by a local authority in relation to an inquiry under this section (including such reasonable sum as the authority may determine for the services of any of their officers engaged in the inquiry) shall, unless the authority are of the opinion that those expenses should be defrayed in whole or in part by them, be paid by such party to the inquiry as they may direct; and the authority may certify the amount of the expenses so incurred.

(5)   Any sum certified under subsection (4) above and to be defrayed in accordance with a direction under that subsection shall be a debt due by the party directed and shall be recoverable accordingly.

(6)   The local authority may make an award as to the expenses of the parties at the inquiry and as to the parties by whom such expenses shall be paid.]

PART II
PROMOTION OF SOCIAL WELFARE BY LOCAL AUTHORITIES

General

12   General social welfare services of local authorities

(1)   It shall be the duty of every local authority to promote social welfare by making available advice, guidance and assistance on such a scale as may be appropriate for their area, and in that behalf to make arrangements and to provide or secure the provision of such facilities (including the provision or arranging for the provision of residential and other establishments) as they may consider suitable and adequate, and such assistance may, [subject to subsections (3) to (5) of this section, be given in kind or in cash on, or in respect of, any relevant person.

(2)   A person is a relevant person for the purposes of this section if, not being less than eighteen years of age, he is] in need requiring assistance in kind or, in exceptional circumstances constituting an emergency, in cash, where the giving of assistance in either form would avoid the local authority being caused greater expense in the giving of assistance in another form, or where probable aggravation of the person's need would cause greater expense to the local authority on a later occasion.

[(2A)   A person to whom section 115 of the Immigration and Asylum Act 1999 (exclusion from benefits) applies is not to receive assistance under subsection (1) of this section (whether by way of residential accommodation or otherwise) if his need for assistance has arisen solely—

(a)   because he is destitute; or

(b)   because of the physical effects, or anticipated physical effects, of his being destitute.

(2B)   Subsections (3) and (5) to (8) of section 95 of the Immigration and Asylum Act 1999, and paragraph 2 of Schedule 8 to that Act, apply for the purposes of subsection (2A) as they apply for the purposes of that section, but for the references in subsections (5) and (7) of that section and in that paragraph to the Secretary of State substitute references to a local authority.]

(3)   Before giving assistance to, or in respect of, a person in cash under subsection (1) of this section a local authority shall have regard to his eligibility for receiving assistance from any other statutory body and, if he is so eligible, to the availability to him of that assistance in his time of need.

[(3A)   In determining, for the purposes of this section, whether to make available assistance by providing, or securing the provision of, residential accom-

modation to a person, a local authority shall disregard so much of the person's
resources—

    (a)   as may be prescribed; or

    (b)   as is determined by them in such a way as may be prescribed,

and any order made by virtue of this subsection may make different provision for
different cases and for different persons.

    (3B) An order made by virtue of paragraph (a) of subsection (3A) of this sec-
tion may prescribe circumstances in which assistance such as is mentioned in that
subsection is to be made available disregarding entirely a person's resources.

    (3C) In subsections (3A) and (3B) of this section, references to a person's
resources are to resources within the meaning of the order prescribing the amount,
or as the case may be the way, in question.

    (3D) A statutory instrument made in exercise of the power conferred by para-
graph (a) or (b) of subsection (3A) of this section shall be subject to annulment in
pursuance of a resolution of the Scottish Parliament.]

    (4) Assistance given in kind or in cash to, or in respect of, persons under this
section may be given unconditionally or subject to such conditions as to the repayment of the assistance, or of its value, whether in whole or in part, as the local
authority may consider reasonable having regard to the means of the person
receiving the assistance and to the eligibility of the person for assistance from any
other statutory body.

    (5) Nothing in the provisions of this section shall affect the performance by a
local authority of their functions under any other enactment.

    [(6) For the purposes of subsection (2) of this section 'person in need' includes
a person who is in need of care and attention arising out of drug or alcohol dependency or release from prison or other form of detention.]

[12A Duty of local authority to assess needs

    (1) Subject to the provisions of this section, where it appears to a local
authority that any person for whom they are under a duty or have a power to
provide, or to secure the provision of, community care services may be in need of
any such services, the authority—

    (a)   shall make an assessment of the needs of that person for those services;
and

    [(b)   shall then decide, having regard to the results of that assessment, and
taking account—

        (i)   where it appears to them that a person ('the carer') provides a sub-
stantial amount of care on a regular basis for that person, of such care as is
being so provided; and

        (ii) in so far as it is reasonable and practicable to do so, both of the views
of the person whose needs are being assessed and of the views of the carer
(provided that, in either case, there is a wish, or as the case may be a capacity,
to express a view),

whether the needs of the person being assessed call for the provision of any such
services.]

    (2) Before deciding, under subsection (1)(b) of this section, that the needs of
any person call for the provision of nursing care, a local authority shall consult a
medical practitioner.

    (3) If, while they are carrying out their duty under subsection (1) of this sec-
tion, it appears to a local authority that there may be a need for the provision to
any person to whom that subsection applies—

    (a)   of any services under the National Health Service (Scotland) Act 1978 by
the Health Board— (i) in whose area he is ordinarily resident; or (ii) in whose
area the services to be supplied by the local authority are, or are likely, to be
provided; or

    (b)   of any services which fall within the functions of a housing authority

(within the meaning of section 130 (housing) of the Local Government (Scotland) Act 1973) which is not the local authority carrying out the assessment,
the local authority shall so notify that Health Board or housing authority, and shall request information from them as to what services are likely to be made available to that person by that Health Board or housing authority; and, thereafter, in carrying out their said duty, the local authority shall take into account any information received by them in response to that request.

(4)   Where a local authority are making an assessment under this section and it appears to them that the person concerned is a disabled person, they shall—

    (a)   proceed to make such a decision as to the services he requires as is mentioned in section 4 of the Disabled Persons (Services, Consultation and Representation) Act 1986 without his requesting them to do so under that section; and

    (b)   inform him that they will be doing so and of his rights under that Act.

(5)   Nothing in this section shall prevent a local authority from providing or arranging for the provision of community care services for any person without carrying out a prior assessment of his needs in accordance with the preceding provisions of this section if, in the opinion of the authority, the condition of that person is such that he requires those services as a matter of urgency.

(6)   If, by virtue of subsection (5) of this section, community care services have been provided for any person as a matter of urgency, then, as soon as practicable thereafter, an assessment of his needs shall be made in accordance with the preceding provisions of this section.

(7)   This section is without prejudice to section 3 of the said Act of 1986.

(8)   In this section—

'community care services' has the same meaning as in section 5A of this Act;

'disabled person' has the same meaning as in the said Act of 1986; and

'medical practitioner' means a fully registered person within the meaning of section 55 (interpretation) of the Medical Act 1983.]

[12AA   Assessment of ability to provide care

(1)   A person ('the carer') who provides, or intends to provide, a substantial amount of care on a regular basis for another person aged eighteen or over ('the person cared for') may, whether or not the carer is a child, request a local authority to make an assessment ('the carer's assessment') of the carer's ability to provide or to continue to provide such care for that person.

(2)   The local authority to whom the request is made shall—

    (a)   comply with the request where it appears to them that the person cared for is a person for whom they must or may provide, or secure the provision of, community care services; and

    (b)   if they then or subsequently make an assessment under subsection (1)(a) of section 12A of this Act of the needs of the person cared for, have regard to the results of the carer's assessment—

        (i)   in the assessment of the person cared for; and

        (ii)   in making their decision under subsection (1)(b) of that section as respects that person.

(3)   Subsection (1) above does not apply as respects a carer who provides, or will provide, the care in question—

    (a)   by virtue of a contract of employment or other contract; or

    (b)   as a volunteer for a voluntary organisation.

(4)   Section 8 of the Disabled Persons (Services, Consultation and Representation) Act 1986 (c 33) (duty of local authority to take into account abilities of carer in deciding whether to provide certain services to disabled person) shall not apply in a case where a local authority make an assessment, by virtue of subsection (2)(a) above, in respect of a carer of a disabled person.

(5)   Subsections (4) to (7) of section 12A of this Act apply to a local authority making an assessment by virtue of subsection (2)(a) of this section as they apply

to a local authority making an assessment under subsection (1)(a) of that section.

(6)   In this section, 'community care services', 'disabled person' and 'person' have the same meanings as in section 12A of this Act.]

[12AB   Duty of local authority to provide information to carer

(1)   Where it appears to a local authority both that—

(a)   a person aged eighteen or over ('the person cared for') is a person for whom the authority are under a duty or have a power to provide community care services; and

(b)   another person ('the carer') provides, or intends to provide, a substantial amount of care on a regular basis for the person cared for the local authority shall notify the carer that he may be entitled under section 12AA of this Act to request an assessment of his ability to provide, or continue to provide, care for the person cared for.

(2)   In this section, 'community care services' and 'person' have the same meanings as in section 12A of this Act.]

[12B   Direct payments in respect of community care services

(1)   Where, as respects [any person] in need—

(a)   a local authority

[(i)   have decided under section 12A of this Act that his needs call for the provision of any service which is a community care service; or

(ii)   have a duty to provide a service to him under section 22(1) of the Children (Scotland) Act 1995 (c 36) (promotion of welfare of children in need) other than a service which comprises giving assistance in cash;]

(b)   the person is [not] of a description which is specified for the purposes of this subsection by regulations, the authority [shall, if and while (the payment having been offered by the authority) either the person consents or consent is duly given on his behalf,], make to him, in respect of his securing the provision of the service, a payment of such amount as, subject to subsection (2) below, they [determine to be appropriate].

[(1A)   The amount of any payment made, under subsection (1) above, with or without first assessing the person's ability to contribute to securing the provision of the service in question, may be determined on the supposition that he has no such ability; but this subsection is subject to subsection (5A) below.

(1B)   Consent is duly given as mentioned in subsection (1) above if—

(a)   the authority are satisfied that the person on whose behalf it is given is himself incapable of giving it; and

(b)   the person who gives it is of a category specified for the purposes of that subsection by regulations,

and such regulations may authorise the person so consenting to intromit with the payment and to do anything requisite to secure the provision of the service.

(1C)   The reference in subsections (1) to (1B) above to securing the provision of the service is to securing its provision by any person, including the authority themselves (provided that both they and the consenting person so wish) or any other local authority.]

(2)   If—

(a)   an authority pay under subsection (1) above at a rate below their estimate of the reasonable cost of securing the provision of the service concerned, and

(b)   the person to whom the payment is made satisfies the authority that his means are insufficient for it to be reasonably practicable for him to make up the difference,

the authority shall so adjust the payment to him under that subsection as to avoid there being a greater difference than that which appears to them to be reasonably practicable for him to make up.

(3)   A payment under subsection (1) above shall be subject to the condition that the person to whom it is made shall not secure the provision of the service to which it relates by a person who is of a description specified for the purposes of this subsection by regulations.

(4)   Regulations may

[(a)   provide that the [duty imposed by subsection (1) above shall not apply] in relation to the provision of residential accommodation for any person for a period in excess of such period as may be specified in the regulations;

[(b)   impose preconditions which must be fulfilled if the service concerned is, by virtue of that subsection, to be provided by the authority by whom the payment under that subsection is made and special conditions which shall apply as respects a service so provided by them;

(c)   specify circumstances in which the authority are not required to make payments under that subsection (whether circumstances relating to the person in question or to the service in question or to both);

(d)   specify circumstances in which the authority may or must terminate the making of such payments; and

(e)   authorise such payments to be made, on behalf of the payee, to some other person of a category specified, for the purposes of this subsection, by regulations.]

(5)   If the authority by whom a payment under subsection (1) above is made are not satisfied, in relation to the whole or any part of the payment—

(a)   that it has been used to secure the provision of the service to which it relates, or

(b)   that the condition imposed by subsection (3) above, or any condition properly imposed by them, has been met in relation to its use,

they may require the payment or, as the case may be, the part of the payment to be repaid.

[(5A)   An authority who have made a determination by virtue of subsection (1A) above in respect of a payment—

(a)   having first assessed the recipient's ability to contribute to securing the provision of the service in question, may; or

(b)   other than is mentioned in paragraph (a) above, shall thereafter make such an assessment and may,

having regard to the assessment, require from him such repayment as appears to them appropriate.

(5B)   If the person from whom a repayment is required under subsection (5A) above satisfies the authority that, notwithstanding the assessment to which regard was had in making the requirement, his means are insufficient for it to be reasonably practicable for him to make that repayment, the authority shall adjust the requirement so that the amount to be repaid becomes an amount which appears to them to be reasonably practical for him to repay.]

(6)   Regulations under this section shall be made by the Secretary of State and may—

[(za)   make provision for the delegation of functions to local authorities;]

(a)   make different provision for different cases; and

(b)   include such supplementary, incidental, consequential and transitional provisions and savings as the Secretary of State thinks fit.

[(7)   The definition of 'community care services' in section 5A of this act shall, with the modification mentioned in subsection (8) below, apply for the purposes of this section as that definition applies for the purposes of that section.

(8)   The modification is that the words ', other than services for children,' in the definition shall be disregarded.]

[12C   Further provisions relating to direct payments

(1)   Except as provided by subsection (2) below, the fact that a local authority make a payment under [subsection (1) of section 12B] of this Act shall not affect

their functions with respect to the provision of the service to which the payment relates.

(2)   Subject to subsection (3) below, where an authority make a payment under [subsection (i) of section 12B(1)] of this Act they shall not be under any obligation to the person to whom it is made with respect to the provision of the service to which it relates [(except in so far as it is provided by them by virtue of that subsection)] as long as they are satisfied that the need which calls for the provision of that service will be met by virtue of [that subsection].

(3)   The fact that an authority make a payment under section 12B(1) of this Act shall not affect their functions under section 12 of this Act in relation to the provision, to the person to whom the payment is made, of assistance, in exceptional circumstances constituting an emergency, in cash in respect of the service to which the payment under section 12B(1) relates.]

13   Power of local authorities to assist persons in need in disposal of produce of their work

Where, by virtue of [section 12 of this Act], a local authority make arrangements or provide or secure the provision of facilities for the engagement of persons in need (whether under a contract of service or otherwise) in suitable work, that local authority may assist such persons in disposing of the produce of their work.

[13ZA   Provision of services to incapable adults

(1)   Where—

(a)   a local authority have decided under section 12A of this Act that an adult's needs call for the provision of a community care service; and

(b)   it appears to the local authority that the adult is incapable in relation to decisions about the service,

the local authority may take any steps which they consider would help the adult to benefit from the service.

(2)   Without prejudice to the generality of subsection (1) above, steps that may be taken by the local authority include moving the adult to residential accommodation provided in pursuance of this Part.

(3)   The principles set out in subsections (2) to (4) of section 1 of the 2000 Act apply in relation to any steps taken under subsection (1) above as they apply to interventions in the affairs of an adult under or in pursuance of that Act.

(4)   Subsection (1) does not authorise a local authority to take steps if they are aware that—

(a)   there is a guardian or welfare attorney with powers relating to the proposed steps;

(b)   an intervention order has been granted relating to the proposed steps; or

(c)   an application has been made (but not yet determined) for an intervention order or guardianship order under Part 6 of the 2000 Act relating to the proposed steps.

(5)   In this section—

(a)   'the 2000 Act' means the Adults with Incapacity (Scotland) Act 2000 (asp 4);

(b)   'adult' has the meaning given in section 1(6) of the 2000 Act;

(c)   'community care service' has the meaning given in section 5A of this Act;

(d)   'incapable' has the meaning given in section 1(6) of the 2000 Act;

(e)   'intervention order' is to be construed in accordance with section 53 of the 2000 Act;

(f)   the reference to a guardian includes a reference to—

(i)   a guardian appointed under the 2000 Act; and

(ii)   a guardian (however called) appointed under the law of any country to, or entitled under the law of any country to act for, an adult during his incapacity, if the guardianship is recognised by the law of Scotland;

(g)   the reference to a welfare attorney includes a reference to—

(i)   a welfare attorney within the meaning of section 16 of the 2000 Act; and
(ii)   a person granted, under a contract, grant or appointment governed by
the law of any country, powers (however expressed) relating to the granter's
personal welfare and having effect during the granter's incapacity.]

Residential accommodation with nursing

[13A   Residential accommodation with nursing
(1)   Without prejudice to section 12 of this Act, a local authority shall—
   [(a)   provide and maintain, or
   (b)]   make such arrangements as they consider appropriate and adequate for
the provision of
suitable residential accommodation where nursing is provided for persons who
appear to them to be in need of such accommodation by reason of infirmity, age,
illness or mental disorder, dependency on drugs or alcohol or being substantially
handicapped by any deformity or disability.
   [(2)   [A]rrangements made by virtue of subsection (1) above shall be made with
a voluntary or other organisation or other person, being an organisation or person
providing—
   (a)   an independent health care service which is a private psychiatric hospital; or
   (b)   a care home service.
   (2A)   Expressions used in subsection (2) above have the same meanings as in
the Regulation of Care (Scotland) Act 2001 (asp 8).]
   (3)   The provisions of section 6 of this Act apply in relation to premises where
accommodation is provided for the purposes of this section as they apply in relation to establishments provided for the purposes of this Act.
   [(4)   No arrangements under subsection (1) above may be given effect to in relation to a person to whom section 115 of the Immigration and Asylum Act 1999
(exclusion from benefits) applies solely—
   (a)   because he is destitute; or
   (b)   because of the physical effects, or anticipated physical effects, of his
being destitute.
   (5)   Subsections (3) and (5) to (8) of section 95 of the Immigration and Asylum
Act 1999, and paragraph 2 of Schedule 8 to that Act, apply for the purposes of
subsection (4) above as they apply for the purposes of that section, but for the
references in subsections (5) and (7) of that section and in that paragraph to the
Secretary of State substitute references to a local authority.]

Provision of care and after-care

[13B   Provision of care and after-care
(1)   Subject to subsection (2) below, a local authority may, with the approval of
the Secretary of State, and shall, if and to the extent that the Secretary of State so
directs, make arrangements for the purpose of the prevention of illness, the care of
persons suffering from illness, and the after-care of such persons.
   (2)   The arrangements which may be made under subsection (1) above do not
include arrangements in respect of medical, dental or nursing care, or health visit-
ing.
   [(3)   No arrangements under subsection (1) above may be given effect to in relation to a person to whom section 115 of the Immigration and Asylum Act 1999
(exclusion from benefits) applies solely—
   (a)   because he is destitute; or
   (b)   because of the physical effects, or anticipated physical effects, of his
being destitute.
   (4)   Subsections (3) and (5) to (8) of section 95 of the Immigration and Asylum
Act 1999, and paragraph 2 of Schedule 8 to that Act, apply for the purposes of

subsection (3) above as they apply for the purposes of that section, but for the references in subsections (5) and (7) of that section and in that paragraph to the Secretary of State substitute references to a local authority.]]

PART IV
RESIDENTIAL AND OTHER ESTABLISHMENTS

Provision of residential and other establishments

59 Provision of residential and other establishments by local authorities, and maximum period for repayment of sums borrowed for such provision

(1) [Without prejudice to their duties under sections 12 and 13A of this Act it] shall be the duty of a local authority to provide and maintain such residential and other establishments as may be required for their functions under this Act [or under Part II of the Children (Scotland) Act 1995] or arrange for the provision of such establishments.

(2) For the purpose of discharging their duty under the foregoing subsection a local authority may—

(a)   themselves provide such establishments as aforesaid; or

(b)   join with another local authority in providing those establishments; or

(c)   secure the provision of such establishments by voluntary organisations or other persons including other local authorities.

(3)   The maximum period for the repayment of sums borrowed by a local authority for the purposes of this section shall be such period not exceeding sixty years as may be sanctioned by the Secretary of State; and accordingly in Schedule 6 to the Local Government (Scotland) Act 1947, at the end, there shall be added the following entry, that is to say—

Section 59 of the Social Work (Scotland) Act 1968.	Such period not exceeding sixty years as may be sanctioned by the Secretary of State.

PART VI
CONTRIBUTIONS IN RESPECT OF CHILDREN IN CARE ETC

78 Duty to make contributions in respect of children in care etc

(1) Where a child [is being looked after by a local authority] or a supervision requirement to which this Part of this Act applies has been made in respect of him, contributions in respect of the child (hereinafter in this Part of this Act referred to as the 'maintainable child') shall be payable—

(a)   while the maintainable child is under sixteen years of age, by [any natural person who has parental responsibilities (within the meaning of section 1(3) of the Children (Scotland) Act 1995)] in relation to him;

(b)   if he is over sixteen years of age [. . .] by the maintainable child himself.

[(2)   This Part of this Act applies to any supervision requirement which, under paragraph (a) of section 70(3) of the Children (Scotland) Act 1995, requires the child concerned to reside in a place or places other than his own home.]

[(2A)   No contributions shall be payable under subsection 1(a) of this section by a contributor during a period when he is in receipt of income support, an income-based jobseeker's allowance (payable under the Jobseekers Act 1995) [, an income-related allowance under Part I of the Welfare Reform Act 2007 (employment and support allowance)] or family credit.]

(3)   In this Part of this Act 'contributor' means a person liable to make contributions by virtue of subsection (1) of this section in respect of a maintainable child.

[78A   Recovery of contributions

(1)   Section 87 of this Act (charges for services and accommodation) shall not apply to the provision of services (including accommodation) under this Act in

respect of maintainable children, and the provisions of this section shall apply thereto.

(2)   A local authority providing such services may recover from a contributor a contribution (if any) of such amount as is reasonable and, subject to that, may recover—

(a)   a standard contribution determined by them in respect of maintainable children who are [looked after by them]; or

(b)   such other contribution as they consider reasonable in the circumstances.]

79   Recipients of contributions

(1)   Subject to the provisions of the following subsection, contributions payable under the last foregoing section shall be payable to the local authority within whose area the contributor is residing, and shall, in the case of contributions paid in respect of a maintainable child [looked after by] a local authority, other than the authority to whom the contributions are payable as aforesaid, be paid over by the last-mentioned authority to that other authority, but subject to such deductions in respect of services rendered by the local authority to whom the contributions were payable as may be agreed between the authorities concerned or as, in default of agreement, may be determined by the Secretary of State.

(2)   Where a contributor is for the time being residing in England or Wales or Northern Ireland contributions payable by him under the last foregoing section shall be payable to the local authority [looking after the child].

80   Enforcement of duty to make contributions

(1)   Where a child becomes a maintainable child by virtue of being [looked after by a local authority] any court of summary jurisdiction, having jurisdiction in the place where the contributor is for the time being residing, may, on the application of the local authority, at any time make an order on any contributor, hereinafter in this Act referred to as a contribution order, for weekly contributions in respect of the child of such amount as the court thinks proper.

[. . .]

(4)   Subject to the following provisions of this section, a contribution order in respect of a maintainable child shall remain in force [throughout the period during which he is looked after by a local authority].

(5)   No contribution shall be payable, by virtue of a contribution order by a contributor who, [being a natural person, has parental responsibilities (within the meaning of section 1(3) of the Children (Scotland) Act 1995) in relation to the maintainable child], in respect of any period after the maintainable child becomes sixteen.

(6)   A contribution order may be revoked or varied by any court of summary jurisdiction having jurisdiction in the place where the contributor is for the time being residing and shall be enforceable in like manner as a decree for aliment.

(7)   Where a contributor resides in England or Wales or Northern Ireland this section shall have effect as if for any reference to a court of summary jurisdiction having jurisdiction in a place where the contributor is for the time being residing there were substituted a reference to a court of summary jurisdiction having jurisdiction in any place within the area of the local authority [looking after] the child.

81   Provisions as to decrees for ailment

(1)   [. . .]

(2)   Where [. . .] a decree for aliment [of a maintainable child] is in force, on the application of the local authority concerned, any court of summary jurisdiction having jurisdiction in the place where the [person liable under the decree] is for the time being residing may, at any time, or order the payments under the decree [. . .] to be paid to the local authority who are from time to time entitled under

either of the last two foregoing sections to receive contributions in respect of the child.

(3)   Where [. . .] an order made under this section in respect to a decree for aliment is in force any sums received under the decree for aliment shall be applied in like manner as if they were contributions received under a contribution order.

(4)(a)   In this section the local authority concerned means the local authority which may make application for a contribution order in respect of a child under the last foregoing section;

   (b)   where the [person liable to pay aliment for a child under a decree] is resident in England or Wales or Northern Ireland, subsection (2) of this section shall have effect as if for the reference to a court of summary jurisdiction having jurisdiction in the place where [that person] is for the time being residing, there were substituted a reference to a court of summary jurisdiction having jurisdiction in any place within the area of the local authority concerned.

82   Recovery of arrears of contributions

(1)   Where, by virtue of an order or decree made under either of the last two foregoing sections, any sum is payable to a local authority, the local authority in whose area the person liable under the order or decree is for the time being residing, or, as the case may be, the local authority [looking after] the child to whom the order or decree relates, shall be entitled to receive and give a discharge for, and, if necessary, enforce payment of, any arrears accrued due under the order or decree, notwithstanding that those arrears may have accrued at a time when he was not resident in that area or, as the case may be, when the authority were not entitled to sums payable under the order or decree.

(2)   In any proceedings under either of the last two foregoing sections, a certificate purporting to be signed by the clerk to a local authority for the time being entitled to receive contributions, or by some other officer of the authority duly authorised in that behalf, and stating that any sum due to the authority under an order or decree is overdue and unpaid, shall be sufficient evidence of the facts stated therein.

83   Variation of trusts

(1)   Where a child is by virtue of a supervision requirement removed from the care of any person and that person is entitled under any trust to receive any sum of money in respect of the maintenance of the child, on the application of the local authority concerned any court of summary jurisdiction, having jurisdiction in the place where that person is for the time being residing, may at any time order the whole or any part of the sums so payable under the trust to be paid to the local authority, to be applied by the authority for the benefit of the child in such manner as, having regard to the terms of the trust, the court may direct.

(2)   Where the person in whose care a child has been residing is for the time being residing in England or Wales or Northern Ireland the foregoing subsection shall have effect as if for the reference to a court having jurisdiction in the place where that person is residing there were substituted a reference to a court of summary jurisdiction having jurisdiction in any place within the area of the local authority [looking after] the child.

[83A   References in this Part of this Act to child being looked after

In this Part of this Act, references to a child being looked after by a local authority shall be construed in accordance with section 17(6) of the Children (Scotland) Act 1995.]

PART VII
MISCELLANEOUS AND GENERAL

General

84   Transfer of assets and liabilities

Where any functions are transferred to a local authority by virtue of this Act all property, rights, liabilities and obligations relating to the performance of those functions which immediately before the date of transfer were the property, rights, liabilities and obligations of the body or person from which the functions are transferred shall on that date be transferred to and vest in the local authority or, as the case may be, the local authorities to which the functions have been transferred, and the provisions of Schedule 6 to this Act shall have effect for the purposes of this section.

86   Adjustments between authority providing accommodation etc, and authority of area of residence

(1)   Any expenditure which apart from this [subsection] would fall to be borne by a local authority—

(a)   in the provision under this Act [or under section 25 of the Children (Scotland) Act 1995] of accommodation for a person ordinarily resident in the area of another local authority, or

(b)   in the provision under Part II of this Act [, or under or by virtue of Part II of the said Act of 1995, of services and facilities for a person ordinarily so resident (including, in the case of a child, any expenses incurred after he has ceased to be a child, and, in the event of another local authority taking over, under section 24(4) of that Act, the provision of accommodation for him,] including also any travelling or other expenses incurred in connection with the taking over), or

[(ba)   in making a payment under section 12B of this Act in relation to the provision of a service for a person ordinarily so resident; or]

(c)   for the conveyance of a person ordinarily resident as aforesaid, or

(d)   in administering a supervision requirement in respect of a person ordinarily resident as aforesaid, [or

(e)   in the provision, for persons ordinarily so resident, of services under section 25 (care and support services for persons who have or who have had a mental disorder), 26 (services designed to promote well-being and social development of such persons) or 27 (assistance with travel in connection with such services) of the Mental Health (Care and Treatment) (Scotland) Act 2003;]

shall be recoverable from the other local authority, and in this subsection any reference to another local authority includes a reference to a local authority in England and Wales.

(2)   Any question arising under this section as to the ordinary residence of a person shall be determined by the Secretary of State, and the Secretary of State may determine that a person has no ordinary residence.

(3)   In determining for the purposes of subsection (1) of this section the ordinary residence of any person or child [any period during which he is provided with accommodation under this Act or under sections 25 to 27 of the Mental Health (Care and Treatment) (Scotland) Act 2003 (asp 13),] any period during which he was a patient in a [health service hospital (within the meaning of section 108(1) of the National Health Service (Scotland) Act 1978 (c 29) [or in a hospital managed by a National Health Service trust established under the National Health Service Act 2006, the National Health Service (Wales) Act 2006 or section 12A of the National Health Service (Scotland) Act 1978]] or, in the case of a child, any period during which he resided in any place as an inmate of a school or other institution, or in accordance with the requirements of a supervision requirement, supervision order [, youth rehabilitation order] or probation order or the condi-

tions of a recognizance, or while boarded out under this Act or under [. . .] the Children and Young Persons (Scotland) Act 1937 by a local authority or education authority [or placed with local authority foster parents under the Children Act 1989, or provided with accommodation under paragraph (4) of, or by virtue of paragraph (c) of section 26(1) of the Children (Scotland) Act 1995] shall be disregarded.

[(4)   This subsection applies where a local authority ('the responsible authority') performs a function under—

(a)   this Act;

(b)   Part II of the Children (Scotland) Act 1995 (c 36); or

(c)   section 25 to 27 of the Mental Health (Care and Treatment) (Scotland) Act 2003 (asp 13), by making arrangements with a person ('the provider') in terms of which the provider undertakes to accommodate, or to secure accommodation for, another person.

(5)   Where subsection (4) applies—

(a)   any expenditure incurred under the arrangements by a provider which is a local authority is recoverable from the responsible authority; and

(b)   any period during which the person is accommodated under the arrangements is to be disregarded in determining the person's ordinary residence for the purposes of subsection (1) of this section.

(6)   The Scottish Ministers may make regulations specifying circumstances in which a local authority ('the providing authority') may recover from another local authority ('the other authority') expenditure which the providing authority incurs in the provision of services or facilities under arrangements made with the other authority for the purpose of enabling that other authority to perform a function under—

(a)   this Act;

(b)   Part II of the Children (Scotland) Act 1995 (c 36); or

(c)   section 25 to 27 of the Mental Health (Care and Treatment) (Scotland) Act 2003 (asp 13).

(7)   The Scottish Ministers may make regulations specifying circumstances which must be taken into account, or disregarded, when determining a person's ordinary residence for the purposes of subsection (1) of this section (and such regulations may modify subsection (2), (3) and (5)(b) of this section).

(8)   Regulations made under subsection (6) or (7) of this section may—

(a)   make different provision for different cases and for different persons;

(b)   include such supplementary, incidental, consequential and transitional provisions and savings as the Scottish Ministers think fit.

(9)   Despite section 90(2) of this Act, no statutory instrument containing regulations made under subsection (7) of this section which includes provisions which modify this section may be made unless a draft of the instrument has been laid before, and approved by a resolution of, the Scottish Parliament.

(10)   References in subsections (4) to (6) of this section to a local authority which is providing accommodation, service or facilities include references to a local authority in England or Wales.]

[. . .]

87   Charges that may be made for services and accommodation

(1)   [Subject to sections 78 and 78A of this Act (contributions in respect of maintainable children) and to the following provisions of this section, a local authority providing a service under this Act [or section 25 (care and support services for persons who have or have had a mental disorder), 26 (services designed to promote well-being and social development of such persons) or 27 (assistance with travel in connection with such services) of the Mental Health (Care and Treatment) (Scotland) Act 2003 (asp 13)] or under or by virtue of Part II of the Children (Scot-

land) Act 1995] may recover such charge (if any) for it as they consider reasonable.]

[(1A)   If a person—

(a)   avails himself of a service provided under this Act [or section 25, 26 or 27 of the Mental Health (Care and Treatment) (Scotland) Act 2003 (asp 13)] or under or by virtue of Part II of the Children (Scotland) Act 1995]; and

(b)   satisfies the authority providing the service that his means are insufficient for it to be reasonably practicable for him to pay for the service the amount which he would otherwise be obliged to pay for it,

the authority shall not require him to pay more for it than it appears to them that it is reasonably practicable for him to pay.]

[(1B)   Subsections (1) and (1A) above do not apply as respects any amount required not to be charged by subsection (1) of section 1 of the Community Care and Health (Scotland) Act 2002 (asp 5) (charging and not charging for social care) or required to be charged or not to be charged by virtue of subsection (4) of that section.]

(2)   Persons, other than maintainable children, for whom accommodation is provided under this Act [or section 25 of the Mental Health (Care and Treatment) (Scotland) Act 2003 (asp 13)]; shall be required to pay for that accommodation in accordance with the subsequent provisions of this section.

(3)   Subject to the following provisions of this section, accommodation provided under this Act [or section 25 of the Mental Health (Care and Treatment) (Scotland) Act 2003 (asp 13)] shall be regarded as accommodation provided under Part III of the National Assistance Act 1948, and [sections 22(2) to (8) and 26(2) to (4) (as amended by any enactment within the meaning of the Scotland Act 1998 (c 46)) of the said Act of 1948] shall apply accordingly.

(4)   In the application of the said section 22, for any reference to the Minister there shall be substituted a reference to the Secretary of State, and in the application of the said section 26, any references to arrangements under a scheme for the provision of accommodation shall be construed as references to arrangements made by a local authority with a voluntary organisation [or any other person or body] for the provision of accommodation under this Act [or section 25 of the Mental Health (Care and Treatment) (Scotland) Act 2003 (asp 13)].

(5)   The Secretary of State may, with the consent of the Treasury, make regulations for modifying or adjusting the rates at which payments under this section are made, where such a course appears to him to be justified, and any such regulations may provide for the waiving of any such payment in whole or in part in such circumstances as may be specified in the regulations.

[. . .]

[. . .]

90   Orders, regulations etc

(1)   Any power to make regulations or orders [. . .] or to make rules conferred on the Secretary of State by this Act shall be exercisable by statutory instrument.

(2)   Any statutory instrument made in the exercise of any power to make regulations conferred by this Act shall be subject to annulment in pursuance of a resolution of either House of Parliament.

(3)   Any power conferred by this Act to make orders shall include a power, exercisable in the like manner and subject to the same conditions, to vary or revoke any such order.

[(4)   A statutory instrument containing an order under section 27(1D) or 27A(1A)(c) of this Act is not made unless a draft of the instrument has been laid before, and approved by resolution of, the Scottish Parliament.]

91   Expenses

There shall be defrayed out of moneys provided by Parliament—

(a)   any sums required for the payment of grants under this Act or any other expenses of the Secretary of State under this Act, and

(b)   any increase attributable to the provisions of this Act in the sums payable out of such money under any other Act.

92   Effect of Act on rate support grant

(1)   The Secretary of State shall have power, by an order made in the like manner and subject to the like provisions as a rate support grant order, to vary the provisions of any rate support grant order made before the commencement of this Act for a grant period ending after the commencement of this Act.

(2)   Any order made by virtue of this section may be made for all or any of the years comprised in the said rate support grant period, as may be specified in the order, and in respect of the year or years so specified shall increase the annual aggregate amount of the rate support grants to such extent as may appear to the Secretary of State to be appropriate having regard to any additional expenditure incurred or likely to be incurred by councils of counties or of large burghs in consequence of the passing of this Act.

(3)   The provisions of this section shall have effect without prejudice to the exercise of any power conferred by section 4 of the Local Government (Scotland) Act 1966 (which confers power to vary rate support grant orders in consequence of unforeseen increases in the level of prices, costs or remuneration).

(4)   In this section the expressions 'rate support grant order' and 'grant period' have the meanings respectively assigned to them by subsection (1) and subsection (3) of section 3 of the Local Government (Scotland) Act 1966.

[92A   Power of the Secretary of State to make grants

The Secretary of State may, with the approval of the Treasury, make grants out of money provided by Parliament towards any expenses of local authorities in respect to their functions under—

(a)   Part II of this Act; and

(b)   [sections 25 to 31 of the Mental Health (Care and Treatment) (Scotland) Act 2003],

in relation to persons suffering from mental illness.]

Supplementary

93   Transitional provisions

The transitional provisions set out in Schedule 7 to this Act shall have effect for the purposes of the transition to the provisions of this Act from the law in force before the commencement of this Act.

94   Interpretation

(1)   In this Act, except where otherwise expressly provided or the context otherwise requires, the following expressions have the meanings hereby respectively assigned to them—

'approved school' means a school approved by the Secretary of State under section 79 of the Children and Young Persons Act 1933,

'approved school order' has the meaning assigned to it by section 107(1) of the Children and Young Persons Act 1933,

[. . .]

'constable' means a constable of a police force within the meaning of the Police (Scotland) Act 1967,

'contribution' and 'contribution order' have the meanings respectively assigned to them by sections 78 and 80 of this Act,

'domiciliary services' means any services, being services provided in the home, which appear to a local authority to be necessary for the purpose of enabling a person to maintain as independent an existence as is practicable in his home,] 'establishment' means an establishment managed by a local authority, voluntary organisation or any other person, which provides non-residential accommodation for the purposes of this Act, [or of Part II of the Children (Scotland) Act 1995] whether for reward or not,

'functions' shall include powers and duties,

'hospital' [has the meaning assigned to it by section 329 of the Mental Health (Care and Treatment) (Scotland) Act 2003,]

'local authority', in relation to Scotland, has the meaning assigned to it by section 1(2) of this Act,

'maintainable child' has the meaning assigned to it by section 78 of this Act,

'mental disorder' has the meaning assigned to it by [section 328 of the Mental Health (Care and Treatment) (Scotland) Act 2003],

['mental health officer' means a person appointed under subsection (1) of section 32 of the Mental Health (Care and Treatment) (Scotland) Act 2003 and includes a person deemed, by virtue of subsection (3) of that section, to be so appointed,]

'parent' means either parent or both parents, except that where the child was born out of wedlock and the parents have not subsequently married each other it means the natural mother but not the natural father,]

'performance', in relation to functions, includes the exercise of powers as well as the performance of duties, and 'perform' shall be construed accordingly,

'persons in need' means persons who,

(a) are in need of care and attention arising out of infirmity, youth or age; or

(b) suffer from illness or mental disorder or are substantially handicapped by any deformity or disability; or

[. . .]

(d) being persons prescribed by the Secretary of State who have asked for assistance, are, in the opinion of a local authority, persons to whom the authority may appropriately make available the services and facilities provided by them under this Act,

'prescribed' means

(a) in section 3 prescribed by regulations; and

(b) [. . .]

[(c) in sections 12(3A), 27A, 27B, 62(2), 64A(3), 66(1) and (2), 94, paragraphs 2(2) and (3), 4(3) and (4) of Schedule 7, prescribed by order, and 'prescribe' shall be construed accordingly.]

['probation order'—

(a) in relation to an order imposed by a court in England or Wales, means a [community order within the meaning of Part 12 of the Criminal Justice Act 2003],

(b) in relation to an order imposed by a court in Northern Ireland, has the same meaning as in the Criminal Justice (Northern Ireland) Order 1996;]

'residential establishment' means an establishment managed by a local authority, voluntary organisation or any other person, which provides residential accommodation for the purposes of this Act [or of Part II of the Children (Scotland) Act 1995], whether for reward or not,

'supervision order', in relation to an order imposed by a court in England or Wales, [means a supervision order under the Powers of Criminal Courts (Sentencing) Act 2000 or the Children Act 1989], and in relation to an order imposed by a court in Northern Ireland [means a supervision order under the Children and Young Persons Act (Northern Ireland) 1968 or the Children (Northern Ireland) Order 1995],

'supervision requirement' has the meaning assigned to it by [section 70(1) of the Children (Scotland) Act 1995],

'training school' has the meaning assigned to it by section 180(1) of the Children and Young Persons Act (Northern Ireland) 1968,] 'training school order' means an order made by a court in Northern Ireland sending a child or young person to a training school,

'voluntary organisation' means a body the activities of which are carried on otherwise than for profit, but does not include any public or local authority,

'welfare authority' means a welfare authority constituted under the Public Health and Local Government (Administrative Provisions) Act (Northern Ireland) 1946.

(2)   Unless the context otherwise requires, any reference in this Act to any other enactment is a reference thereto as amended, and includes a reference thereto as extended or applied by or under any other enactment including this Act.

(3)   Without prejudice to the last foregoing subsection, any reference in this Act to an enactment of the Parliament of Northern Ireland, or to an enactment which that Parliament has power to amend, shall be construed, in relation to Northern Ireland, as a reference to that enactment as amended by any Act of that Parliament, whether passed before or after this Act, and to any enactment of that Parliament passed after this Act and re-enacting the said enactment with or without modifications.

97   Extension of certain provisions of Act to England and Wales, Northern Ireland and the Channel Islands

(1)   The following provisions of this Act shall extend to England and Wales, that is to say—

[. . .]

sections 86 and 87

section 98(3)

Schedule 2, paragraphs 7 and 13

Schedule 8

Part II of Schedule 9.

[. . .]

(4)   Save as aforesaid, and except in so far as it relates to the interpretation or commencement of the provisions, this Act shall extend only to Scotland.

98   Commencement

(1)   This Act (except this section) shall come into operation on such date as the Secretary of State may by order appoint.

(2)   Different dates may be appointed by order under this section for different purposes of this Act; and any reference in any provision of this Act to the commencement of this Act shall, unless otherwise provided by any such order, be construed as a reference to the date on which that provision comes into operation.

(3)   An order under this section may make such transitional provisions as appear to the Secretary of State to be necessary or expedient in connection with the provisions thereby brought into force, including such adaptations of those provisions or of any provision of this Act then in force as appear to the Secretary of State necessary or expedient for the purposes or in consequence of the operation of any provision of this Act before the coming into force of any other provision of this Act or of the Children and Young Persons Act 1969.

99   Short title

This Act may be cited as the Social Work (Scotland) Act 1968.

DOMICILE AND MATRIMONIAL PROCEEDINGS ACT 1973
(1973, c 45)

PART I
DOMICILE

Husband and wife

1　Abolition of wife's dependent domicile

(1)　Subject to subsection (2) below, the domicile of a married woman as at any time after the coming into force of this section shall, instead of being the same as her husband's by virtue only of marriage, be ascertained by reference to the same factors as in the case of any other individual capable of having an independent domicile.

(2)　Where immediately before this section came into force a woman was married and then had her husband's domicile by dependence, she is to be treated as retaining that domicile (as a domicile of choice, if it is not also her domicile of origin) unless and until it is changed by acquisition or revival of another domicile either on or after the coming into force of this section.

(3)　This section extends to England and Wales, Scotland and Northern Ireland.

[. . .]

PART III
JURISDICTION IN CONSISTORIAL CAUSES (SCOTLAND)

7　Jurisdiction of Court of Session

(1)　Subsections [(2A) to (10)] below shall have effect, subject to section 12(6) of this Act, with respect to the jurisdiction of the Court of Session to entertain—

(a)　an action for divorce, separation, declarator of nullity of marriage, declarator of marriage; [or

(aa)　an action for declarator of recognition, or non-recognition, of a relevant foreign decree.]

[. . .]

[(2A)　The Court shall have jurisdiction to entertain an action for divorce or separation if (and only if)—

(a)　the Scottish courts have jurisdiction under the Council Regulation; or

(b)　the action is an excluded action and either of the parties to the marriage in question is domiciled in Scotland on the date when the action is begun.]

(3)　The Court shall have jurisdiction to entertain an action for declarator of marriage . . . if (and only if) either of the parties to the marriage—

(a)　is domiciled in Scotland on the date when the action is begun; or

(b)　was habitually resident in Scotland throughout the period of one year ending with that date; or

(c)　died before that date and either—

(i)　was at death domiciled in Scotland, or

(ii)　had been habitually resident in Scotland throughout the period of one year ending with the date of death.

[(3A)　The Court shall have jurisdiction to entertain an action for declarator of nullity of marriage or for declarator of recognition, or non-recognition, of a relevant foreign decree if (and only if)—

(a)　the Scottish courts have jurisdiction under the Council Regulation; or

(b)　the action is one to which subsection (3B) below applies and either of the parties to the marriage—

(a)　is domiciled in Scotland on the date when the action is begun, or

(b)　died before that date and either—

(i)　was at death domiciled in Scotland; or

(ii)   had been habitually resident in Scotland throughout the period of
one year ending with the date of death.
(3B)   This subsection applies to an action—
(a)   which is an excluded action; or
(b)   where one of the parties to the marriage died before the date when the
action is begun.]
[. . .]
(5)   The Court shall, at any time when proceedings are pending in respect of
which it has jurisdiction by virtue of subsection (2) [(2A), (3) or (3A)] above (or
of this subsection), also have jurisdiction to entertain other proceedings, in
respect of the same marriage, for divorce, separation or declarator of marriage
[or] declarator of nullity of marriage [. . .] notwithstanding that jurisdiction
would not be exercisable [under any of those subsections].
[(5A)   Subsection (5) does not give the Court jurisdiction to entertain proceedings in contravention of Article 6 of the Council Regulation.]
(6)   Nothing in this section affects the rules governing the jurisdiction of the
Court of Session to entertain, in an action for divorce, an application for payment
by a co-defender of damages or expenses.
(7)   The foregoing provisions of this section are without prejudice to any rule of
law whereby the Court of Session has jurisdiction in certain circumstances to
entertain actions for separation as a matter of necessity and urgency.
(8)   No action for divorce in respect of a marriage shall be entertained by the
Court of Session by virtue of [this section] while proceedings for divorce or nullity
of marriage, begun before the commencement of this Act, are pending (in respect
of the same marriage) in England and Wales, Northern Ireland, the Channel
Islands or the Isle of Man; and provision may be made by rules of court as to
when, for the purposes of this subsection, proceedings are to be treated as begun
or pending in any of those places.
[(9)   In this section, 'relevant foreign decree' means a decree of divorce, nullity
or separation granted outwith a member state of the European Union.
(10)   References in subsection (3A) to a marriage shall, in the case of an action
for declarator of recognition, or non-recognition, of a relevant foreign decree, be
construed as references to the marriage to which the relevant foreign decree
relates.]

8   Jurisdiction of sheriff court in respect of actions for separation

(1)   Subsections (2) to [(6)] below shall have effect, subject to section 12(6) of
this Act, with respect to the jurisdiction of the sheriff court to entertain—
[(a)] an action for separation [or divorce.]; [and
(b)   an action for declarator of recognition, or non-recognition, of a relevant
foreign decree.]
(2)   The court shall have jurisdiction to entertain an action for separation [or
divorce or for declarator of recognition, or non-recognition, of a relevant foreign
decree] if (and only if)—
[(a)   either—
(i)   the Scottish courts have jurisdiction under the Council Regulation; or
(ii)   the action is an excluded action where either party to the marriage in
question is domiciled in Scotland at the date when the action is begun;]
(b)   either party to the marriage—
(i)   was resident in the sheriffdom for a period of forty days ending with
that date, or
(ii)   had been resident in the sheriffdom for a period of not less than forty
days ending not more than forty days before the said date, and has no known
residence in Scotland at that date.
(3)   In respect of any marriage, the court shall have jurisdiction to entertain an
action for separation [or divorce] (notwithstanding that jurisdiction would not be

exercisable under subsection (2) above) if it is begun at a time when an original action is pending in respect of the marriage; and for this purpose 'original action' means an action in respect of which the court has jurisdiction by virtue of subsection (2), or of this subsection.

[(3A)   Subsection (3) does not give the Court jurisdiction to entertain an action in contravention of Article 6 of the Council Regulation.]

(4)   The foregoing provisions of this section are without prejudice to any jurisdiction of a sheriff court to entertain an action of separation [or divorce] remitted to it in pursuance of any enactment or rule of court, [provided that entertaining the action would not contravene Article 6 of the Council Regulation].

[(5)   In this section, 'relevant foreign decree' has the meaning given by section 7(9).

(6)   References in subsection (2) to a marriage shall, in the case of an action for declarator of recognition, or non-recognition, of a relevant foreign decree, be construed as references to the marriage to which the relevant foreign decree relates.]

10   Ancillary and collateral orders

(1)   [Where after the commencement of this Act, an application is competently made to the Court of Session or to a sheriff court for the making, or the variation or recall, of an order which is ancillary or collateral to] an action for any of the following remedies, namely, divorce, separation, declarator of marriage and declarator of nullity of marriage (whether the application is made in the same proceedings or in other proceedings and whether it is made before or after the pronouncement of a final decree in the action), then, if the court has or, as the case may be, had by virtue of this Act or of any enactment or rule of law in force before the commencement of this Act jurisdiction to entertain the action, it shall have jurisdiction to entertain the application [. . .] whether or not it would have jurisdiction to do so apart from this subsection.

[(1A)   For the purposes of subsection (1) above, references to an application for the making, or the variation or recall, of an order are references to the making, or the variation or recall, of an order relating to children, aliment, financial provision on divorce, judicial separation, nullity of marriage or expenses.]

[(1B)   Subsection (1) above does not give the Court of Session or a sheriff court jurisdiction to entertain an application in proceedings where—
(a)   the court is exercising jurisdiction in the proceedings by virtue of Article 2 of the Council Regulation; and
(b)   the making or variation of an order in consequence of the application would contravene Article 6 of the Council Regulation.]

(2)   It is hereby declared that where—
(a)   the Court of Session has jurisdiction by virtue of this section to entertain an application for the variation or recall as respects any person of an order made by it, and
(b)   the order is one to which section 8 (variation and recall by the sheriff of certain orders made by the Court of Session) of the Law Reform (Miscellaneous Provisions) (Scotland) Act 1966 applies,
then, for the purposes of any application under the said section 8 for the variation or recall of the order in so far as it relates to that person, the sheriff, as defined in that section, has jurisdiction as respects that person to exercise the power conferred on him by that section.

11   Sisting of certain actions

[(1)]   The provisions of Schedule 3 to this Act shall have effect with respect to the sisting of actions for any of the following remedies, namely, divorce, separation, declarator of marriage or declarator of nullity of marriage, and with respect to the other matters mentioned in that Schedule; but nothing in that Schedule—
(a)   requires or authorises a sist of an action which is pending when this Act comes into force; or

(b)   prejudices any power to sist an action which is exercisable by any court apart from the Schedule.

[(2)   Subsection (1) above and Schedule 3 to this Act and any power mentioned in subsection (1)(b) are subject to Article 19 of the Council Regulation.]

12   Supplementary

(1)   In relation to any action for any of the following three remedies, namely, declarator of marriage, declarator of nullity of marriage, and declarator of freedom and putting to silence, references in this Part of this Act to the marriage shall be construed as including references to the alleged, or, as the case may be, the purported, marriage.

(2)   References in this Part of this Act to an action for a particular remedy shall be construed, in relation to a case where the remedy is sought along with other remedies in one action, as references to so much of the proceedings in the action as relates to the particular remedy.

(3)   References in this Part of this Act to the remedy of separation shall be construed, in relation to an action in a sheriff court, as references to the remedy of separation and aliment.

(4)   For the purposes of this Act the period during which an action in the Court of Session or a sheriff court is pending shall be regarded as including any period while the taking of an appeal is competent and the period while any proceedings on appeal are pending; and in this subsection references to an appeal include references to a reclaiming motion.

(5)   In this Part of this Act—

(a)   any reference to an enactment shall, unless the contrary intention appears, be construed as a reference to that enactment as amended or extended, and as including a reference thereto as applied, by or under any other enactment (including this Act);

[(b)   'Contracting State' means Belgium, Germany, Greece, Spain, France Ireland, Italy, Luxembourg, the Netherlands, Austria, Portugal, Finland, Sweden, and the United Kingdom;

(c)   'the Council Regulation' means Council Regulation (EC) No 2201/2003 of 27th November 2003 concerning] jurisdiction and the recognition and enforcement of judgments in matrimonial matters and in matters of parental responsibility [. . .]; and

(d)   'excluded action' means an action in respect of which no court of a Contracting State has jurisdiction under the Council Regulation and the defender is not a person who is—

(i)   a national of a Contracting State (other than the United Kingdom or Ireland); or

(ii)   domiciled in Ireland.]

(6)   Nothing in this Part of this Act affects any court's jurisdiction to entertain any proceedings begun before the commencement of this Act.

(7)   Subject to subsection (6) above, the enactments described in Schedule 4 to this Act shall have effect subject to the amendments therein specified, being amendments consequential on the provisions of this Part of this Act.

DAMAGES (SCOTLAND) ACT 1976
(1976, c 13)

1   Rights of relatives of a deceased person

(1)   Where a person dies in consequence of personal injuries sustained by him as a result of an act or omission of another person, being an act or omission giving rise to liability to pay damages to the injured person or his executor, then, subject to the following provisions of this Act, the person liable to pay those damages (in this section referred to as 'the responsible person') shall also be liable to pay

damages in accordance with this section to any relative of the deceased, being a relative within the meaning of Schedule 1 to this Act.

(2)   No liability shall arise under this section if the liability to the deceased or his executor in respect of the act or omission has been excluded or discharged (whether by antecedent agreement or otherwise) by the deceased before his death, or is excluded by virtue of any enactment.

[(2A)   Where subsection (2B) below applies—

(a)   liability arises under this section even though the liability to the deceased or the deceased's executor mentioned in subsection (2) above has been discharged as mentioned in that subsection; but

(b)   that liability is limited to the payment of such sum of damages as is awarded under subsection (4) below.

(2B)   This subsection applies where—

(a)   the personal injury in consequence of which the deceased died is mesothelioma; and

(b)   the discharge of liability and the death each occurred on or after 20 December 2006 (and whether before, on or after the date on which section 1 of the Rights of Relatives to Damages (Mesothelioma) (Scotland) Act 2007 (asp 18) came into force).]

(3)   The damages which the responsible person shall be liable to pay to a relative of a deceased under this section shall (subject to the provisions of this Act) be such as will compensate the relative for any loss of support suffered by him since the date of the deceased's death or likely to be suffered by him as a result of the act or omission in question, together with any reasonable expense incurred by him in connection with the deceased's funeral.

(4)   [Subject to subsection (4A),] if the relative is a member of the deceased's immediate family (within the meaning of section 10(2) of this Act) there shall be awarded, without prejudice to any claim under subsection (3) above, such sum of damages, if any, as the court thinks just by way of compensation for [all or any of the following—

(a)   distress and anxiety endured by the relative in contemplation of the suffering of the deceased before his death;

(b)   grief and sorrow of the relative caused by the deceased's death;

(c)   the loss of such non-patrimonial benefit as the relative might have been expected to derive from the deceased's society and guidance if the deceased had not died,

and the court in making an award under this subsection shall not be required to ascribe specifically any part of the award to any of paragraphs (a), (b) and (c) above.]

[(4A)   Notwithstanding section 10(2) of, and Schedule 1 to, this Act, no award of damages under subsection (4) above shall be made to a person related by affinity to the deceased.

(4B)   In subsection (4A), a 'person related by affinity to the deceased' includes—

(a)   a stepchild, step-parent, stepbrother or stepsister of the deceased; and

(b)   any person who was an ascendant or descendant of any of the step-relatives mentioned in paragraph (a).]

(5)   [Subject to subsection (5A) below] in assessing for the purposes of this section the amount of any loss of support suffered by a relative of a deceased no account shall be taken of—

(a)   any patrimonial gain or advantage which has accrued or will or may accrue to the relative from the deceased or from any other person by way of succession or settlement;

(b)   any insurance money, benefit, pension or gratuity which has been, or will be or may be, paid as a result of the deceased's death;

and in this subsection—

'benefit' means benefit under the Social Security Act 1975 or the Social Security (Northern Ireland) Act 1975, and any payment by a friendly society or trade union for the relief or maintenance of a member's dependants;

'insurance money' includes a return of premiums; and

'pension' includes a return of contributions and any payment of a lump sum in respect of a person's employment.

[(5A)　Where a deceased has been awarded a provisional award of damages under section 12(2) of the Administration of Justice Act 1982, the making of that award does not prevent liability from arising under this section but in assessing for the purposes of this section the amount of any loss of support suffered by a relative of the deceased the court shall take into account such part of the provisional award relating to future patrimonial loss as was intended to compensate the deceased for a period beyond the date on which he died.]

(6)　In order to establish loss of support for the purposes of this section it shall not be essential for a claimant to show that the deceased was, or might have become, subject to a duty in law to provide or contribute to the support of the claimant; but if any such fact is established it may be taken into account in determining whether, and if so to what extent, the deceased, if he had not died, would have been likely to provide or contribute to such support.

(7)　Except as provided in this section [or in Part II of the Administration of Justice Act 1982 or under regulation 3 of the Railways (Convention on International Carriage by Rail) Regulations 2005] no person shall be entitled by reason of relationship to damages (including damages by way of solatium) in respect of the death of another person.

[1A　Transmissibility to executor of rights of deceased relative

Any right to damages under any provision of section 1 of this Act which is vested in the relative concerned immediately before his death shall be transmitted to the relative's executor; but, in determining the amount of damages payable to an executor by virtue of this section, the court shall have regard only to the period ending immediately before the relative's death.]

[2　Rights transmitted to executor in respect of deceased person's injuries

(1)　Subject to the following provisions of this section, there shall be transmitted to the executor of a deceased person the like rights to damages in respect of personal injuries (including a right to damages by way of solatium) sustained by the deceased as were vested in him immediately before his death.

(2)　There shall not be transmitted to the executor under this section a right to damages by way of compensation for patrimonial loss attributable to any period after the deceased's death.

(3)　In determining the amount of damages by way of solatium payable to an executor by virtue of this section, the court shall have regard only to the period ending immediately before the deceased's death.

(4)　In so far as a right to damages vested in the deceased comprised a right to damages (other than for patrimonial loss) in respect of injury resulting from defamation or any other verbal injury or other injury to reputation sustained by the deceased, that right shall be transmitted to the deceased's executor only if an action to enforce that right had been brought by the deceased before his death and had not been concluded by then within the meaning of section 2A(2) of this Act.]

[2A　Enforcement by executor of rights transmitted to him

(1)　For the purpose of enforcing any right transmitted to an executor under section 1A or 2 of this Act the executor shall be entitled—

(a)　to bring an action; or

(b)　if an action for that purpose had been brought by the deceased but had not been concluded before his death, to be sisted as pursuer in that action.

(2)　For the purpose of subsection (1) above, an action shall not be taken to be concluded while any appeal is competent or before any appeal taken has been disposed of.]

[. . .]

4 Executor's claim not to be excluded by relatives' claim: and *vice versa*

A claim by the executor of a deceased person for damages under section 2 of this Act is not excluded by the making of a claim by a relative of the deceased for damages under section 1 of this Act [or by a decreased relative's executor under section 1A of this Act; nor is a claim by a relative of a deceased person or by a deceased relative's executor for damages under the said section 1 or (as the case may be) the said section 1A] excluded by the making of a claim by the deceased's executor or damages under the said section 2.

[. . .]

6 Limitation of total amount of liability

(1) Where in any action to which [this section] of this Act applies, so far as directed against any defender, it is shown that by antecedent agreement, compromise or otherwise, the liability arising in relation to that defender from the personal injuries in question had, before the deceased's death, been limited to damages of a specified or ascertainable amount, or where that liability is so limited by virtue of any enactment, nothing in this Act shall make the defender liable to pay damages exceeding that amount; and accordingly where in such an action there are two or more pursuers any damages to which they would respectively be entitled under this Act apart from the said limitation shall, if necessary, be reduced *pro rata*.

(2) Where two or more such actions are conjoined, the conjoined actions shall be treated for the purposes of this section as if they were a single action.

[(3) This section applies to any action in which, following the death of any person from personal injuries, damages are claimed—

(a) by the executor of the deceased, in respect of the injuries from which the deceased died;

(b) in respect of the death of the deceased, by any relative of his or if the relative has died, by the relative's executor.]

7 Amendment of references in other Acts

In any Act passed before this Act, unless the context otherwise requires, any reference to solatium in respect of the death of any person (however expressed) shall be construed as a reference to a loss of society award within the meaning of section 1 of this Act; and any reference to a dependant of a deceased person, in relation to an action claiming damages in respect of the deceased person's death, shall be construed as including a reference to a relative of the deceased person within the meaning of this Act.

8 Abolition of right of assythment

After the commencement of this Act no person shall in any circumstances have a right to assythment, and accordingly any action claiming that remedy shall (to the extent that it does so) be incompetent.

9 Damages due to injured person for patrimonial loss caused by personal injuries whereby expectation of life is diminished

(1) This section applies to any action for damages in respect of personal injuries sustained by the pursuer where his expected date of death is earlier than it would have been if he had not sustained the injuries.

(2) In assessing, in any action to which this section applies, the amount of any patrimonial loss in respect of the period after the date of decree—

(a) it shall be assumed that the pursuer will live until the date when he would have been expected to die if he had not sustained the injuries (hereinafter referred to as the 'notional date of death');

(b)   the court may have regard to any amount, whether or not it is an amount related to earnings by the pursuer's own labour or other gainful activity, which in its opinion the pursuer, if he had not sustained the injuries in question, would have received in the period up to his notional date of death by way of benefits in money or money's worth, being benefits derived from sources other than the pursuer's own estate;

(c)   the court shall have regard to any diminution of any such amount as aforesaid by virtue of expenses which in the opinion of the court the pursuer, if he had not sustained the injuries in question, would reasonably have incurred in the said period by way of living expenses.

[9A   Solatium for loss of expectation of life

(1)   In assessing, in an action for damages in respect of personal injuries, the amount of damages by way of solatium, the court shall, if—

(a)   the injured person's expectation of life has been reduced by the injuries; and

(b)   the injured person is, was at any time or is likely to become, aware of that reduction,

have regard to the extent that, in consequence of that awareness, he has suffered or is likely to suffer.

(2)   Subject to subsection (1) above, no damages by way of solatium shall be recoverable in respect of loss of expectation of life.

(3)   The court in making an award of damages by way of solatium shall not be required to ascribe specifically any part of the award to loss of expectation of life.]

10   Interpretation

(1)   In this Act, unless the context otherwise requires—

[. . .]

'personal injuries' includes any disease or an impairment of a person's physical or mental condition [and injury resulting from defamation or any other verbal injury or other injury to reputation, or injury resulting from harassment actionable under section 8 of the Protection from Harassment Act 1997];

'relative', in relation to a deceased person, has the meaning assigned to it by Schedule 1 to this Act.

(2)   References in this Act to a member of a deceased person's immediate family are references to any relative of his who falls within [any of sub-paragraphs (a) to (cc)] of paragraph 1 of Schedule 1 to this Act.

(3)   References in this Act to any other Act are references to that Act as amended, extended or applied by any other enactment, including this Act.

12   Citation, application to Crown, commencement and extent

(1)   This Act may be cited as the Damages (Scotland) Act 1976.

(2)   This Act binds the Crown.

(5)   This Act extends to Scotland only.

SCHEDULES

SCHEDULE 1
DEFINITION OF 'RELATIVE'

(1)   In this Act 'relative' in relation to a deceased person includes—

(a)   any person who immediately before the deceased's death was the spouse [or civil partner] of the deceased;

[(aa)   any person, not being the spouse [or civil partner] of the deceased, who was, immediately before the deceased's death, living with the deceased as husband or wife or in a relationship which had the characteristics of the relationship between civil partners;]

(b)   any person who was a parent or child of the deceased;

(c)   any person not falling within sub-paragraph (b) above who was accepted by the deceased as a child of his family;

[(ca)   any person not falling within sub-paragraph (b) above who accepted the deceased as a child of the person's family;

(cb)   any person who—

(i)   was the brother or sister of the deceased; or

(ii)   was brought up in the same household as the deceased and who was accepted as a child of the family in which the deceased was a child;

(cc)   any person who was a grandparent or grandchild of the deceased;]

(d)   any person [not falling within sub-paragraph (b) or (cc) above] who was an ascendant or descendant [. . .] of the deceased;

(e)   any person [not falling within sub-paragraph (cb)(i) above] who was, or was the issue of, a brother, sister, uncle or aunt of the deceased;

(f)   any person who, having been a spouse of the deceased, had ceased to be so by virtue of a divorce; [and

(g)   any person who, having been a civil partner of the deceased, had ceased to be so by virtue of the dissolution of the civil partnership,]

but does not include any other person.

(2)   In deducing any relationship for the purposes of the foregoing paragraph—

(a)   any relationship by affinity shall be treated as a relationship by consanguinity; any relationship of the half blood shall be treated as a relationship of the whole blood; and the stepchild of any person shall be treated as his child; and

(b)   section 1(1) of the Law Reform (Parent and Child) (Scotland) Act 1986 shall apply; and any reference (however expressed) in this Act to a relative shall be construed accordingly.

DIVORCE (SCOTLAND) ACT 1976
(1976, c 39)

Divorce

1   [Grounds of divorce]

(1)   In an action for divorce the court may grant decree of divorce if, but only if, it is established in accordance with the following provisions of this Act that—

[(a)]   the marriage has broken down irretrievably [, or

(b)   an interim gender recognition certificate under the Gender Recognition Act 2004 has, after the date of the marriage, been issued to either party to the marriage.]

References in this Act (other than in sections 5(1) and 13 of this Act) to an action for divorce are to be construed as references to such an action brought after the commencement of this Act.

(2)   The irretrievable breakdown of a marriage shall, subject to the following provisions of this Act, be taken to be established in an action for divorce if—

(a)   since the date of the marriage the defender has committed adultery; or

(b)   since the date of the marriage the defender has at any time behaved (whether or not as a result of mental abnormality and whether such behaviour has been active or passive) in such a way that the pursuer cannot reasonably be expected to cohabit with the defender; or

[. . .]

(d)   there has been no cohabitation between the parties at any time during a continuous period of [one year] after the date of the marriage and immediately preceding the bringing of the action and the defender consents to the granting of decree of divorce; or

(e)   there has been no cohabitation between the parties at any time during a continuous period of [two] years after the date of the marriage and immediately preceding the bringing of the action.

(3)   The irretrievable breakdown of a marriage shall not be taken to be established in an action for divorce by reason of subsection (2)(a) of this section if the adultery mentioned in the said subsection (2)(a) has been connived at in such a way as to raise the defence of *lenocinium* or has been condoned by the pursuer's cohabitation with the defender in the knowledge or belief that the defender has committed the adultery.

(4)   Provision shall be made by act of sederunt—

(a)   for the purpose of ensuring that, where in an action for divorce to which subsection (2)(d) of this section relates the defender consents to the granting of decree, he has been given such information as will enable him to understand—

(i)   the consequences to him of his consenting as aforesaid; and

(ii)   the steps which he must take to indicate his consent; and

(b)   prescribing the manner in which the defender in such an action shall indicate his consent, and any withdrawal of such consent, to the granting of decree;

and where the defender has indicated (and not withdrawn) his consent in the prescribed manner, such indication shall be sufficient evidence of such consent.

[. . .]

(6)   In an action for divorce the standard of proof required to establish the ground of the action shall be on balance of probability.

2   Encouragement of reconciliation

(1)   At any time before granting decree [under paragraph (a) of section 1(1)], if it appears to the court that there is a reasonable prospect of a reconciliation between the parties, it shall continue, or further continue, the action for such period as it thinks proper to enable attempts to be made to effect such a reconciliation; and if during any such continuation the parties cohabit with one another, no account shall be taken of such cohabitation for the purposes of that action.

(2)   Adultery shall not be held to have been condoned within the meaning of section 1(3) of this Act by reason only of the fact that after the commission of the adultery the pursuer has continued or resumed cohabitation with the defender, provided that the pursuer has not cohabited with the defender at any time after the end of the period of three months from the date on which such cohabitation as is referred to in the said section 1(3) was continued or resumed as aforesaid.

[. . .]

(4)   In considering whether any period mentioned in paragraph [. . .], (d), or (e) of section 1(2) of this Act has been continuous no account shall be taken of any period or periods not exceeding six months in all during which the parties cohabited with one another; but no such period or periods during which the parties cohabited with one another shall count as part of the period of non-cohabitation required by any of those paragraphs.

3   Action for divorce following on decree of separation

(1)   The court may grant decree in an action for divorce notwithstanding that decree of separation has previously been granted to the pursuer on the same, or substantially the same, facts as those averred in support of the action for divorce; and in any such action (other than an action for divorce by reason of section 1(2)(a) of this Act) the court may treat an extract decree of separation lodged in process as sufficient proof of the facts upon which such decree was granted.

(2)   Nothing in this section shall entitle the court to grant decree of divorce without receiving evidence from the pursuer.

[3A Postponement of decree of divorce where religious impediment to remarry exists

(1) Notwithstanding that irretrievable breakdown of a marriage has been established in an action for divorce, the court may—

    (a) on the application of a party ('the applicant'); and

    (b) if satisfied—

        (i) that subsection (2) applies; and

        (ii) that it is just and reasonable to do so,

postpone the grant of decree in the action until it is satisfied that the other party has complied with subsection (3).

(2) This subsection applies where—

    (a) the applicant is prevented from entering into a religious marriage by virtue of a requirement of the religion of that marriage; and

    (b) the other party can act so as to remove, or enable or contribute to the removal of, the impediment which prevents that marriage.

(3) A party complies with this subsection by acting in the way described in subsection (2)(b).

(4) The court may, whether or not on the application of a party and notwithstanding that subsection (2) applies, recall a postponement under subsection (1).

(5) The court may, before recalling a postponement under subsection (1), order the other party to produce a certificate from a relevant religious body confirming that the other party has acted in the way described in subsection (2)(b).

(6) For the purposes of subsection (5), a religious body is 'relevant' if the applicant considers the body competent to provide the confirmation referred to in that subsection.

(7) In this section—

'religious marriage' means a marriage solemnised by a marriage celebrant of a prescribed religious body, and 'religion of that marriage' shall be construed accordingly;

'prescribed' means prescribed by regulations made by the Scottish Ministers.

(8) Any reference in this section to a marriage celebrant of a prescribed religious body is a reference to—

    (a) a minister, clergyman, pastor or priest of such a body;

    (b) a person who has, on the nomination of such a body, been registered under section 9 of the Marriage (Scotland) Act 1977 as empowered to solemnise marriages; or

    (c) any person who is recognised by such a body as entitled to solemnise marriages on its behalf.

(9) Regulations under subsection (7) shall be made by statutory instrument; and any such instrument shall be subject to annulment in pursuance of a resolution of the Scottish Parliament.]

Actions for separation

4 Actions for separation

(1) Sections 1, 2 and 11 of this Act shall apply to an action for separation or separation and aliment brought after the commencement of this Act and decree in such action as those sections apply to an action for divorce and decree therein subject to—

    (a) the modification that any reference to irretrievable breakdown of a marriage shall be construed as a reference to grounds justifying decree of separation of the parties to a marriage; and

    (b) all other necessary modifications.

(2) In an action for separation or separation and aliment brought after the commencement of this Act, decree of separation shall not be pronounced except in accordance with the provisions of this section.

    [. . .]

Supplemental

[. . .]

10 Right of husband to cite paramour as a co-defender and to sue for damages abolished

(1) After the commencement of this Act the following rights of a husband shall be abolished, that is to say—

(a) the right to cite a paramour of his wife as a co-defender in an action for divorce, and

(b) the right to claim or to obtain damages (including solatium) from a paramour by way of reparation.

(2) Nothing in the provisions of the foregoing subsection shall preclude the court from awarding the expenses of the action for or against the paramour or alleged paramour in accordance with the practice of the court.

[. . .]

11 Curator *ad litem* to be appointed in certain cases

Provision shall be made by act of sederunt for the purpose of securing that, where in an action for divorce the defender is suffering from mental illness, the court shall appoint a curator *ad litem* to the defender.

12 Amendments, repeals and transitional provisions

[. . .]

(3) Subject to the following provisions of this section and without prejudice to the operation of section 38 of the Interpretation Act 1889 (effect of repeals), nothing in this section shall affect any proceedings brought, anything done, or the operation of any order made, under any enactment repealed by this section; nor shall anything in this Act be taken to revive any rule of law superseded by any enactment repealed by this section.

(4) Anything which, prior to the commencement of this Act, could have been done under section 2 of the Divorce (Scotland) Act 1938 or section 26 or 27 of the Succession (Scotland) Act 1964 may, after the commencement of this Act, be done under the corresponding provision of section 5 or 6 of this Act.

(5) An order under section 2 of the Divorce (Scotland) Act 1938 for the payment of an annual or periodical allowance to or for the behoof of a child of the marriage may, after the commencement of this Act, be varied or recalled by a subsequent order under subsection (2) of that section as if that section had not been repealed by this Act.

(6) Subsection (5) of section 5 of this Act shall apply in relation to an order for the payment of an annual or periodical allowance under section 2 of the Divorce (Scotland) Act 1938 or of a periodical allowance under section 26 of the Succession (Scotland) Act 1964 as it applies in relation to an order for the payment of a periodical allowance under the said section 5.

13 Interpretation

(1) In this Act, unless the context otherwise requires—

'action for divorce' has the meaning assigned to it by section 1(1) of this Act;

'the court' means in relation to an action [. . .] the Court of Session or the sheriff [court] as the case may require.

(2) For the purposes of this Act, the parties to a marriage shall be held to cohabit with one another only when they are in fact living together as man and wife; and 'cohabitation' shall be construed accordingly.

(3) References in this Act to any enactment are references to that enactment as amended, and include references thereto as applied, by any other enactment, including, except where the context otherwise requires, this Act.

14 Citation, commencement and extent
(1) This Act may be cited as the Divorce (Scotland) Act 1976.

(2) This Act except section 8 shall come into operation on 1st

(3) So much of section 12 of, and Schedule 1 to, this Act as af

of section 16 of the Maintenance Orders Act 1950 shall exten‹
Wales and to Northern Ireland as well as Scotland, but save as
shall extend to Scotland only.

MARRIAGE (SCOTLAND) ACT 1977
(1977, c 15)

Minimum age for marriage

1 Minimum age for marriage
(1) No person domiciled in Scotland may marry before he attains the age of 16.

(2) A marriage solemnised in Scotland between persons either of whom is
under the age of 16 shall be void.

Forbidden degrees

2 Marriage of related persons
(1) [Subject to subsection (1A) [. . .] below,] a marriage between a man and any
woman related to him in a degree specified in column 1 of Schedule 1 to this Act,
or between a woman and any man related to her in a degree specified in column 2
of that Schedule shall be void if solemnised—

    (a) in Scotland; or

    (b) at a time when either party is domiciled in Scotland.

[(1A) Subsection (1) above does not apply to a marriage between a man and
any woman related to him in a degree specified in column 1 of paragraph 2 of
Schedule 1 to this Act, or between a woman and any man related to her in a
degree specified in column 2 of that paragraph, if—

    (a) both parties have attained the age of 21 at the time of the marriage; and

    (b) the younger party has not at any time before attaining the age of 18 lived
in the same household as the other party and been treated by the other party as
a child of his family.

    [. . .]

(2) For the purposes of this section a degree of relationship exists—

    (a) in the case of a degree specified in paragraph 1 of Schedule 1 to this Act,
whether it is of the full blood or the half blood.

    [. . .]

(3) Where a person is related to another person in a degree not specified in
Schedule 1 to this Act that degree of relationship shall not, in Scots law, bar a valid
marriage between them; but this subsection is without prejudice to—

    (a) the effect which a degree of relationship not so specified may have under
the provisions of a system of law other than Scots law in a case where such provisions apply as the law of the place of celebration of a marriage or as the law of
a person's domicile; or

    (b) any rule of law that a marriage may not be contracted between persons
either of whom is married to a third person.

[(4) References in this section and in Schedule 1 to this Act to relationships and
degrees of relationship shall be construed in accordance with section 1(1) of the
Law Reform (Parent and Child) (Scotland) Act 1986.

(5) Where the parties to an intended marriage are related in a degree specified
in paragraph 2 of Schedule 1 to this Act, either party may (whether or not an
objection to the marriage has been submitted in accordance with section 5(1) of
this Act) apply to the Court of Session for a declarator that the conditions specified

paragraphs (a) and (b) of subsection (1A) above are fulfilled in relation to the intended marriage.]

[(6) Subsection (1A) [. . .] above and paragraph 2 [. . .] of Schedule 1 to this Act have effect subject to the following modifications in the case of a party to a marriage whose gender has become the acquired gender under the Gender Recognition Act 2004 ('the relevant person').

(7) Any reference in those provisions to a former wife or former husband of the relevant person includes (respectively) any former husband or former wife of the relevant person.

[(7A) This section and Schedule 1 to this Act have effect as if any reference in paragraphs 1 and 2 of that Schedule to a mother within any of the degrees of relationship specified in either column included a woman who is a parent of a child by virtue of section 42 or 43 of the Human Fertilisation and Embryology Act 2008 (c 22).]

[. . .]

Preliminaries to regular marriage

3 Notice of intention to marry

(1) Subject to subsections (2) to (4) below, each of the parties to a marriage intended to be solemnised in Scotland shall submit to the district registrar a notice, in the prescribed form, of intention to marry (in this Act referred to as a 'marriage notice') [and] the prescribed fee, his birth certificate and—

(a) if he has previously been married and the marriage has been dissolved, a copy of the decree of divorce, dissolution or annulment;

[(aa) if he has previously been in civil partnership and the civil partnership has been dissolved, a copy of the decree of dissolution or annulment;]

(b) in the case of a widow or widower, the death certificate of the former spouse;

(c) in any case where a certificate is required under subsection (5) below, that certificate;

[(d) where he is related to the other party in a degree specified in paragraph 2 of Schedule 1 to this Act, a declaration in the prescribed form stating—

(i) the degree of relationship; and

(ii) that the younger party has not at any time before attaining the age of 18 lived in the same household as the other party and been treated by the other party as a child of his family.]

(2) If a party is unable to submit his birth certificate or any document referred to in paragraph (a) [, (aa)] or (b) of subsection (1) above, he may in lieu thereof make a declaration stating that for reasons specified in that declaration it is impracticable for him to submit that certificate or document; and he shall provide the district registrar with such—

(a) information in respect of the matters to which such certificate or document would have related; and

(b) documentary evidence in support of that information, as the district registrar may require.

(3) If any document submitted under subsection (1) above is written in a language other than English, the party submitting it shall [also submit] a translation of it in English certified by the translator as a correct translation.

[(3A) A person submitting a notice under subsection (1) above shall make and attest in the prescribed manner the necessary declaration (the form for which shall be included in any form prescribed for the notice).

(3B) The necessary declaration is a declaration that the person submitting the notice believes that the parties to the marriage are eligible to be married to each other.]

(4)   Where a party to a marriage intended to be solemnised in Scotland is residing in another part of the United Kingdom, he may submit to the district registrar
a valid certificate for marriage (in this Act referred to as an 'approved certificate')
issued in that other part: and where that party so submits an approved certificate,
he need not, unless the Registrar General so directs, comply with the other provisions of this section.

(5)   A party to a marriage intended to be solemnised in Scotland who is not
domiciled in any part of the United Kingdom is required, if practicable, to submit
under subsection (1)(c) above a certificate, issued by a competent authority in the
state in which the party is domiciled, to the effect that he is not known to be subject to any legal incapacity (in terms of the law of that state) which would prevent
his marrying:

Provided that such a party—

(i)   may, where under the law of the state in which he is domiciled his
personal law is that of another foreign state, submit in lieu of the said certificate
a like certificate issued by a competent authority in that other state;

(ii)   need not submit a certificate under paragraph (c) of subsection (1)
above—

(a)   if he has been resident in the United Kingdom for a period of 2 or
more years immediately before the date on which he submits a marriage
notice under that subsection in respect of the said marriage; or

[(b)   if no such certificate has been issued only by reason of the fact that the
validity of a divorce or annulment granted by a court of civil jurisdiction in
Scotland or entitled to recognition in Scotland under section 44 or 45 of the
Family Law Act 1986 is not recognised in the state in which the certificate
would otherwise have been issued.]

[(6)   In this section, 'the district registrar' means—

(a)   where the marriage is to be solemnised in a registration district, the district registrar for that district;

(b)   where the marriage is to be solemnised in Scottish waters—

(i)   in the case where the marriage is to be solemnised by an approved
celebrant, the district registrar for any registration district;

(ii)   in the case where the marriage is to be solemnised by an authorised
registrar, the district registrar for the registration district of the proposed
authorised registrar.]

4   Marriage notice book and list of intended marriages

(1)   On receipt of a marriage notice or an approved certificate in respect of a
party to an intended marriage, the district registrar shall forthwith enter such particulars, extracted from such notice or certificate, as may be prescribed, together
with the date of receipt by him of such notice or certificate, in a book (in this Act
referred to as 'the marriage notice book') supplied to him for that purpose by the
Registrar General.

[(2)   The district registrar shall maintain a list of the intended marriages in
respect of which he has received a marriage notice or an approved certificate (the
'district list').

(2A)   Subject to subsection (2B) below, the district list shall be displayed in a
conspicuous place at the registration office.

(2B)   If the registration office comprises more than one set of premises, it shall
be sufficient for the purpose of subsection (2A) above if the district registrar dis-
plays the list in a conspicuous place at the principal premises only.

(2C)   The district registrar shall, as soon as practicable after he has received a
marriage notice or an approved certificate in relation to an intended marriage—

(a)   make an entry in the district list containing the relevant particulars of the
marriage; and

(b)   provide (in such form and by such means as the Registrar General thinks fit) the relevant particulars of the marriage to the Registrar General.

(2D)   The Registrar General shall maintain a list of proposed marriages in Scotland (the 'Scottish list').

(2E)   The Registrar General shall make the Scottish list available for public inspection (at such locations, by such means and in such forms as the Registrar General thinks fit).

(2F)   The Registrar General shall, as soon as practicable after the relevant particulars of a marriage are provided to him under subsection (2C)(b) above, make an entry in the Scottish list containing those particulars.

(2G)   An entry in a district list or the Scottish list shall remain in that list until the proposed date of the marriage to which it relates has elapsed.]

(3)   Any person claiming that he may have reason to submit an objection to an intended marriage, or to the issue of a certificate under section 7 of this Act to a party to such marriage, may, free of charge and at any time when the registration office is open for public business, inspect any entry relating to the marriage in the marriage notice book.

[(4)   For the purpose of this section, the relevant particulars of a marriage are such particulars, extracted from the marriage notice book, as may be prescribed.

(5)   In this section and sections 5 and 6 of this Act, 'the district registrar' means—

(a)   where the marriage is to be solemnised in a registration district, the district registrar for that district;

(b)   where the marriage is to be solemnised in Scottish waters—

(i)   in the case where the marriage is to be solemnised by an approved celebrant, the district registrar to whom the marriage notices or approved certificates in respect of the marriage were submitted;

(ii)   in the case where the marriage is to be solemnised by an authorised registrar, the district registrar for the registration district of the proposed authorised registrar.]

5   Objections to marriage

(1)   Any person may at any time before the solemnisation of a marriage in Scotland submit an objection in writing thereto to the district registrar:

Provided that where the objection is on the ground mentioned in subsection (4)(d) below, it shall [not be treated as submitted until there has also been produced to the registrar] a supporting certificate [attested in the prescribed manner] by a registered medical practitioner.

[(1A)   For the purpose of subsection (1) above, an objection which is submitted to the registrar by electronic means is to be treated as in writing if it is received in a form which is legible and capable of being used for subsequent reference.]

(2)   Where the district registrar receives an objection in accordance with subsection (1) above he shall—

(a)   in any case where he is satisfied that the objection relates to no more than a misdescription or inaccuracy in the marriage notice or approved certificate, notify the parties to the marriage of the nature of the objection and make such enquiries into the matter mentioned in it as he thinks fit; and thereafter he shall, subject to the approval of the Registrar General, make any necessary correction to any document relating to the marriage;

(b)   in any other case—

(i)   forthwith notify the Registrar General of the objection;

(ii)   pending consideration of the objection by the Registrar General, suspend the completion or issue of the Marriage Schedule in respect of the marriage;

(iii)   where, in the case of a marriage to be solemnised by an approved celebrant, the Marriage Schedule has already been issued to the parties, if possible notify that celebrant of the objection and advise him not to solemnise the marriage pending the said consideration.

(3) [Subject to subsection (3A) below,] if the Registrar General is satisfied, on consideration of an objection of which he has received notification under subsection (2)(b)(i) above, that—

(a)   there is a legal impediment to the marriage, he shall direct the district registrar to take all reasonable steps to ensure that the marriage does not take place and shall notify, or direct the district registrar to notify, the parties to the intended marriage accordingly;

(b)   there is no legal impediment to the marriage, he shall inform the district registrar to that effect.

[(3A)   Where—

(a)   an objection of which the Registrar General has received notification under subsection (2)(b)(i) above is on the ground that—

(i)   the parties are related in a degree specified in paragraph 2 of Schedule 1 to this Act; and

(ii)   the conditions specified in paragraphs (a) and (b) of section 2(1A) of this Act are not satisfied; and

(b)   an extract decree of declarator that those conditions are satisfied, granted on an application under section 2(5) of this Act, is produced to the Registrar General,

the Registrar General shall inform the district registrar that there is no legal impediment to the marriage on that ground.

(4)   For the purposes of [this section] and section 6 of this Act, there is a legal impediment to a marriage where—

(a)   that marriage would be void by virtue of section 2(1) of this Act;

(b)   one of the parties is, or both are, already married [or in civil partnership];

(c)   one or both of the parties will be under the age of 16 on the date of solemnisation of the intended marriage;

(d)   one or both of the parties is or are incapable of understanding the nature of a marriage ceremony or of consenting to marriage;

(e)   both parties are of the same sex; or

(f)   one or both of the parties is, or are, not domiciled in Scotland and, on a ground other than one mentioned in paragraphs (a) to (e) above, a marriage in Scotland between the parties would be void *ab initio* according to the law of the domicile of the party or parties as the case may be.

(5)   A person who has submitted an objection in accordance with subsection (1) above may at any time withdraw it:

Provided that the Registrar General shall be entitled to have regard to that objection notwithstanding such withdrawal.

6   The Marriage Schedule

(1)   Where the district registrar has received a marriage notice or approved certificate in respect of each of the parties to a marriage intended to be solemnised in Scotland and is satisfied that there is no legal impediment to the marriage or, as the case may be, is informed by the Registrar General under section 5(3)(b) [or (3A)] of this Act that there is no such legal impediment, he shall, subject to subsection (2) below, complete a Marriage Schedule in the prescribed form.

(2)   If a period of more than 3 months has elapsed since the date of receipt (as entered by the district registrar in the marriage notice book) of a marriage notice or an approved certificate in respect of a party to the marriage, the Registrar General may direct that the district registrar shall not complete the Marriage Schedule unless that party submits a new marriage notice or approved certificate to the district registrar.

(3)   Subject to subsection (4) below, in the case of a marriage to be solemnised

by an approved celebrant, the Marriage Schedule completed in accordance with subsection (1) above shall be issued by the district registrar at the registration office to one or both of the parties to the intended marriage.

(4)   The district registrar shall not issue a Marriage Schedule under subsection (3) above—

(a)   within 14 days of the date of receipt (as entered by him in the marriage notice book) of a marriage notice in respect of the marriage to which the Marriage Schedule relates, except where—

(i)   he has received a written request from one or both of the parties for the issue of the Marriage Schedule on a specified date within the said 14 days stating the reason for the request; and

(ii)   he has been authorised to issue the Marriage Schedule on that specified date by the Registrar General;

(b)   on a date earlier than 7 days before the date of the intended marriage unless he has been authorised to issue the Marriage Schedule on that earlier date by the Registrar General.

[(4A)   For the purpose of subsection (4)(a)(i) above, a request which is made by electronic means is to be treated as being written if it is received in a form which is legible and capable of being used for subsequent reference.]

(5)   Subject to subsections (6) and (7) below and section [23A] of this Act, a re-ligious marriage may be solemnised only on the date and at the place specified in the Marriage Schedule

(6)   Subject to subsection (7) below, if, for any reason, the marriage cannot be solemnised on the date or at the place so specified and a new date or place is fixed for the marriage, the district registrar shall—

(a)   issue another Marriage Schedule under subsection (3) above, in lieu of that already issued, specifying that new date or place; or

(b)   substitute, or direct the approved celebrant to substitute, that new date or place in the Marriage Schedule already issued.

(7)   Subsection (6) above shall not apply in a case where the new date fixed for the marriage is more than 3 months after the date for the marriage as specified in the Marriage Schedule already issued or where the new place so fixed is in a dif-ferent registration district, [is in Scottish waters instead of a registration district or is in a registration district instead of Scottish waters,] but in such a case the Regis-trar General may, according to the circumstances, direct—

(a)   the district registrar [. . .] to proceed as in paragraph (a) or (b) (which-ever the Registrar General considers the more appropriate) of subsection (6) above; or

(b)   each party to the marriage to submit to the said district registrar a new marriage notice or approved certificate.

7   Marriage outside Scotland where a party resides in Scotland

(1)   Where a person residing in Scotland is a party to a marriage intended to be solemnised in—

(a)   England or Wales with a party residing in England or Wales and desires; or

(b)   any country, territory or place outside Great Britain, and, for the purpose of complying with the law in force in that country, territory or place, is required to obtain from a competent authority in Scotland,

a certificate in respect of his legal capacity to marry, he may submit, in the form and with the fee and documents specified in section 3(1)(a), (b) [and (d)] of this Act, notice of intention to marry to the district registrar for the district in which he resides (the said registrar being in this section referred to as the 'appropriate regis-trar') as if it were intended that the marriage should be solemnised in that district, and sections 3(2) and (3) and 4 of this Act shall apply accordingly.

(2)   The appropriate registrar shall, if satisfied (after consultation, if the appro-

priate registrar considers it necessary, with the Registrar General) that a person who has by virtue of subsection (1) above submitted a marriage notice to him is not subject to any legal incapacity (in terms of Scots law) which would prevent his marrying, issue to that person a certificate in the prescribed form that he is not known to be subject to any such incapacity:

Provided that the certificate shall not be issued earlier than 14 days after the date of receipt (as entered by the appropriate registrar in the marriage notice book) of the marriage notice.

(3)   Any person may, at any time before a certificate is issued under subsection (2) above, submit to the appropriate registrar an objection in writing to such issue; and the objection shall be taken into account by the appropriate registrar in deciding whether, in respect of the person to whom the certificate would be issued, he is satisfied as mentioned in the said subsection (2).

[(4)   For the purpose of subsection (3) above, an objection which is submitted by electronic means is to be treated as in writing if it is received in a form which is legible and capable of being used for subsequent reference.]

Persons who may solemnise marriage

8   Persons who may solemnise marriage

(1)   [Subject to section 23A of this Act,] a marriage may be solemnised by and only by—

(a)   a person who is—

(i)   a minister of the Church of Scotland; or

(ii)   a minister, clergyman, pastor, or priest of a religious body prescribed by regulations made by the Secretary of State, or who, not being one of the foregoing, is recognised by a religious body so prescribed as entitled to solemnise marriages on its behalf; or

(iii)   registered under section 9 of this Act; or

(iv)   temporarily authorised under section 12 of this Act; or

(b)   a person who is a district registrar or assistant registrar appointed under section 17 of this Act.

(2)   In this Act—

(a)   any such person as is mentioned in subsection (1)(a) above is referred to as an 'approved celebrant', and a marriage solemnised by an approved celebrant is referred to as a 'religious marriage';

(b)   any such person as is mentioned in subsection (1)(b) above is referred to as an 'authorised registrar', and a marriage solemnised by an authorised registrar is referred to as a 'civil marriage'.

Religious marriages

9   Registration of nominated persons as celebrants

(1)   A religious body, not being—

(a)   the Church of Scotland; or

(b)   prescribed by virtue of section 8(1)(a)(ii) of this Act,

may nominate to the Registrar General any of its members who it desires should be registered under this section as empowered to solemnise marriages:

[. . .]

(2)   The Registrar General shall reject a nomination made under subsection (1) above if in his opinion—

(a)   the nominating body is not a religious body; or

(b)   the marriage ceremony used by that body is not of an appropriate form; or

(c)   the nominee is not a fit and proper person to solemnise a marriage; or

(d)   there are already registered under this section sufficient members of the same religious body as the nominee to meet the needs of that body.

(3)   For the purposes of subsection (2)(b) above, a marriage ceremony is of an appropriate form if it includes, and is in no way inconsistent with—

(a)   a declaration by the parties, in the presence of each other, the celebrant and two witnesses, that they accept each other as husband and wife; and

(b)   a declaration by the celebrant, after the declaration mentioned in paragraph (a) of this subsection, that the parties are then husband and wife,

and the Registrar General may, before deciding whether to accept or reject a nomination, require the nominating body to produce to him in writing the form of words used at its marriage ceremonies.

(4)   Where the Registrar General accepts a nomination made to him under subsection (1) above, he—

(a)   shall determine the period during which the nominee shall be empowered to solemnise marriages, being a period of not more than 3 years; and

(b)   may determine that the nominee shall be empowered to solemnise marriages only in such area as the Registrar General may specify,

and may make his acceptance subject to such other conditions as he thinks fit:

Provided that nothing in paragraph (a) above shall preclude the Registrar General from accepting a further nomination of that nominee, in accordance with this section, to take effect at any time after the end of the period determined by the Registrar General under the said paragraph (a).

(5)   The Registrar General shall—

(a)   where he accepts a nomination made to him under subsection (1) above—

(i)   so inform the nominee and the nominating body, specifying the period during which the acceptance shall have effect and any condition to which the acceptance is subject;

(ii)   enter the name of the nominee, the nominating body and such other particulars as he deems appropriate in a register which he shall establish and maintain and which shall be made available for public inspection at all reasonable times without charge;

(b)   where he rejects the nomination, by notice in writing inform the nominating body of the reasons for that rejection.

[(5A)   For the purpose of subsection (5)(b) above, notice which is given by electronic means is to be treated as in writing if it is received in a form which is legible and capable of being used for subsequent reference.]

(6)   The nominating body may, if aggrieved by a rejection under this section, within 28 days of receiving notice of that rejection, appeal to the Secretary of State, and on any such appeal the Secretary of State may direct the Registrar General to accept the nomination or may confirm its rejection and shall inform the nominating body of his direction or confirmation, as the case may be, and the reason for it; and such direction or confirmation shall be final:

Provided that if a reason given for a confirmation of the rejection of a nomination is that the nominating body is not a religious body, that body may, within 42 days of receiving notice of the confirmation, appeal against the confirmation to the Court of Session and seek the determination of that court as to whether the body is a religious body; and if—

(a)   the court determine that the nominating body is a religious body; and

(b)   the said reason was the only reason given for the confirmation,

that determination shall be given effect to by the Registrar General as if it were a direction under this subsection to accept the nomination.

10   Removal of celebrant's name from registers

(1)   Subject to the provisions of this section, the Registrar General may remove the name of a person registered under section 9 of this Act from the register on the ground that—

(a)   that person has requested that his name should be so removed; or

(b)   the body which nominated that person under section 9(1) of this Act no longer desires that he should be so registered; or

(c)   the marriage ceremony used by the said body is no longer of an appropriate form within the meaning of section 9(3) of this Act; or

(d)   that person—

(i)   has, while registered as an approved celebrant, been convicted of an offence under this Act; or

(ii)   has, for the purpose of profit or gain, been carrying on a business of solemnising marriages; or

(iii)   is not a fit and proper person to solemnise marriages; or

(iv)   for any other reason, should not be so registered.

(2)   The Registrar General shall not remove the name of a person from the register on any ground mentioned in subsection (1)(d) above unless he has given to that person at least 21 days notice in writing of his intention to do so.

[(2A)   For the purpose of subsection (2) above, notice which is given by electronic means is to be treated as in writing if it is received in a form which is legible and capable of being used for subsequent reference.]

(3)   The Registrar General shall—

(a)   in the notice given under subsection (2) above, specify the ground of removal and call upon the said person to show cause, within the period specified in the notice, why his name should not be removed from the register; and

(b)   consider any representations made to him within the said period by that person.

(4)   Where a person's name has been removed from the register on any of the grounds mentioned in paragraphs (c) and (d) of subsection (1) above, that person or the body which nominated him under section 9(1) of this Act may, if aggrieved by the removal, within 28 days of receiving notice of the removal appeal to the Secretary of State, and on any such appeal the Secretary of State may give such direction as he thinks proper to the Registrar General as to the removal from, or restoration to, the register of that name; and such direction shall be final.

(5)   Where a person has received a notice in pursuance of subsection (2) above, he shall not solemnise a marriage unless and until his name is restored to the register or, as the case may be, the Registrar General has decided not to remove his name from the register.

11   Alterations to register maintained under s 9

A body registered in pursuance of section 9(5)(a)(ii) of this Act shall notify the Registrar General of any of the following events (if practicable, within 21 days of its occurrence)—

(a)   any change in the name or the address of the body or any amalgamation with any other religious body, giving the name and address of any approved celebrant who is a member of the body so registered;

(b)   the death of an approved celebrant who is a member of the body so registered;

(c)   any change of name, address or designation of an approved celebrant who is a member of the body so registered;

(d)   the cessation of an approved celebrant who is a member of the body so registered from exercising the functions of an approved celebrant, giving his name and address;

and the Registrar General shall, on receipt of any such notification, make whatever alteration to the register maintained by him under section 9 of this Act as he considers necessary or desirable.

12   Temporary authorisation of celebrants

[(1)]   The Registrar General may, in accordance with such terms and conditions as may be specified in the authorisation, grant to any person a temporary written authorisation to solemnise—

    (a)   a marriage or marriages specified in the authorisation, or
    (b)   marriages during such period as shall be specified in the authorisation:
    [. . .]
    [(2)   For the purposes of subsection (1) above, an authorisation which is issued
by electronic means is to be treated as written if it is received in a form which is
legible and capable of being used for subsequent reference.]

13   Preliminaries to solemnisation of religious marriages
    (1)   A marriage shall not be solemnised by an approved celebrant unless
    (a)   the parties produce to him before the marriage ceremony a Marriage
Schedule, in respect of the marriage, issued in accordance with this Act;
    (b)   both parties to the marriage are present; and
    (c)   two persons professing to be 16 years of age or over are present as wit-
nesses.
    [. . .]

14   Form of ceremony to be used by approved celebrant
An approved celebrant who is a person specified—
    (a)   in section 8(1)(a)(i) or (ii) of this Act shall not solemnise a marriage
except in accordance with a form of ceremony recognised by the religious body
to which he belongs as sufficient for the solemnisation of marriages;
    (b)   in section 8(1)(a)(iii) or (iv) of this Act shall not solemnise a marriage
except in accordance with a form of ceremony which includes and is in no way
inconsistent with the declarations specified in section 9(3) of this Act.

15   Registration of religious marriages
    (1)   Immediately after the solemnisation of the marriage the Marriage Schedule
shall be signed by the parties contracting the marriage, by both witnesses present
thereat and by the approved celebrant.
    (2)   The parties to the marriage shall, within 3 days thereafter, deliver the Mar-
riage Schedule, or send it by post or arrange that it is delivered, to the district
registrar.
    (3)   As soon as possible after receipt of the Marriage Schedule, the district regis-
trar shall cause the particulars as set forth in that Schedule to be entered in the
register of marriages kept by him; and subject to subsection (4) below, he shall not
register a religious marriage unless and until he receives a duly signed Marriage
Schedule in respect of that marriage.
    (4)   Where the Registrar General is satisfied that a marriage has been properly
solemnised and that the Marriage Schedule in respect of the marriage has been
duly signed but has been lost or destroyed, he may direct the district registrar to
complete an exact copy of the original Marriage Schedule and, so far as practicable, to arrange for its signature by those persons who signed the original
Schedule; and as soon as possible thereafter, the district registrar shall cause the
particulars as set forth in that copy to be entered in the register of marriages kept
by him.
    [(5)   In this section and section 16 of this Act, 'the district registrar' means—
    (a)   where the marriage has been solemnised in a registration district, the dis-
trict registrar for that district;
    (b)   where the marriage has been solemnised in Scottish waters, the district
registrar who issued the Marriage Schedule in respect of the marriage.]

16   Registrar's power to require delivery of Marriage Schedule
    (1)   Where after the expiration of 21 days from the date of marriage as entered
in the Marriage Schedule that Schedule has not been delivered to the district registrar, he may serve a notice in the prescribed form on either of the parties to the
marriage requiring that party within 8 days from the date of service of the notice
to deliver the said Schedule, or send it by post, to the district registrar.
    (2)   If any party on whom a notice has been served in pursuance of subsection

(1) above fails to comply with the notice, the district registrar may serve on that party a second notice in the prescribed form requiring that party to attend personally at the registration office of the district registrar, within 8 days from the date of service of the second notice, for the purpose of delivering the Marriage Schedule to the district registrar to enable him to register the marriage.

Civil marriages

17 Appointment of authorised registrars

For the purpose of affording reasonable facilities for the solemnisation of civil marriages throughout Scotland, the Registrar General—

(a) shall appoint such number of district registrars as he thinks necessary; and

(b) may, in respect of any district for which he has appointed a district registrar under paragraph (a) above, appoint one or more assistant registrars, as persons who may solemnise marriages:

[. . .]

18 Places at which civil marriages may be solemnised

(1) Subject to the provisions of this section, an authorised registrar shall solemnise a civil marriage—

[(a)] in his registration office;

(b) at an approved place in his registration district; or

(c) on or in an approved vessel, while in Scottish waters.]

(2) An authorised registrar may, with the approval of the Registrar General, solemnise a civil marriage—

[(a)] in the registration office of another authorised registrar [; or

(b) at an approved place in the district of another authorised registrar.]

(3) If either of the parties to an intended civil marriage is unable to attend the registration office of an authorised registrar for the solemnisation of the marriage, an authorised registrar may, subject to the following provisions of this section and on reimbursement of any additional expenditure incurred by him by virtue of this subsection, solemnise the marriage—

(a) at any place in his registration district other than his registration office; or

(b) with the approval of the Registrar General, at any place in any registration district in respect of which there is no authorised registrar.

(4) The authorised registrar shall not solemnise a marriage at any such place as is described in subsection (3)(a) or (b) above unless—

(a) application has been made to him by either of the parties to the intended marriage requesting him to solemnise the marriage at such a place and stating the reason why one of the parties is unable to attend a registration office; and

(b) subject to subsection (5) below, he is satisfied on consideration of the application that the party is unable to attend a registration office by reason of serious illness or serious bodily injury and that there is good reason why the marriage cannot be delayed until the party is able to attend a registration office.

(5) If the authorised registrar is not satisfied as mentioned in subsection (4)(b) above, he shall consult the Registrar General who may direct him to solemnise the marriage in accordance with the application made under subsection (4)(a) above or to refuse so to solemnise it.

[(6) For the purposes of this section 'approved place' means any place approved by virtue of regulations made under section 18A of this Act.

(7) For the purposes of this section, 'approved vessel' means a vessel approved by virtue of regulations made under section 18A of this Act, by the home local authority.

(8)   In subsection (7) above, the 'home local authority' means the local authority which is the local registration authority for the authorised registrar's registration district.]

[18A   Approved places
(1)   The Scottish Ministers may by regulations make provision for or in connection with the approval by local authorities [—

(a)] of places in their areas in which civil marriages may be solemnised;

[(b) of vessels on or in which, while they are in Scottish waters, their authorised registrars may solemnise marriages.

(1A)   For the purposes of subsection (1)(b) above, a local authority's authorised registrars are the authorised registrars for whose registration district the local authority is the local registration authority.]

(2)   Regulations under subsection (1) above may in particular include provision as to—

(a)   the kinds of place [or vessel] in respect of which approvals may be granted;

(b)   the procedure to be followed in relation to applications for approval;

(c)   the considerations to be taken into account by a local authority in determining whether to approve any places [or vessels];

(d)   the duration and renewal of approvals;

(e)   the conditions that shall or may be imposed by a local authority on granting or renewing an approval;

(f)   the determination and charging by local authorities of fees in respect of—

(i)   applications for the approval of places [or vessels];

(ii)   the renewal of approvals; and

(iii)   the attendance by authorised registrars at places approved under the regulations;

(g)   the circumstances in which a local authority shall or may revoke or suspend an approval or vary any of the conditions imposed in relation to an approval;

(h)   the notification to the Registrar General of all approvals granted, renewed, revoked, suspended or varied;

(i)   the notification to the district registrar for the district in which a place approved under the regulations is situated of all approvals relating to such a place which are granted, renewed, revoked, suspended or varied;

(j)   the keeping by the Registrar General, district registrars and local authorities of registers of places [and vessels] approved under the regulations; and

(k)   the issue by the Registrar General of guidance supplementing the provision made by the regulations.

(3)   A person who has made an application under regulations made under subsection (1) above may appeal, by summary application, to the sheriff against any decision made by a local authority in relation to the application (including any decision to revoke or suspend, or to vary any of the conditions imposed in relation to, an approval granted in pursuance of that application).

(4)   An appeal under subsection (3) above may be made only on one or more of the following grounds—

(a)   that the local authority's decision was based on an error of law;

(b)   that the local authority's decision was based on an incorrect material fact;

(c)   that the local authority has acted contrary to natural justice; or

(d)   that the local authority has acted unreasonably in the exercise of its discretion.

(5)   An appeal under subsection (3) above shall not, unless on good cause shown, be considered by the sheriff unless lodged with the sheriff clerk within 28 days of the date on which the local authority made the decision being appealed against.

(6)   In upholding an appeal under subsection (3) above, the sheriff may—

(a)   remit the case with the reasons for the sheriff's decision to the local authority for reconsideration by the local authority of its decision; or

(b)   reverse or modify the local authority's decision.

(7)   A party to an appeal under subsection (3) above may appeal, on a point of law only, against the decision of the sheriff to the Court of Session within 28 days of the date of that decision.

(8)   Regulations under subsection (1) above may make different provision for different cases or circumstances.

(9)   [Subject to subsection (10) below, a statutory instrument containing regulations made under subsection (1) above] shall be subject to annulment in pursuance of a resolution of the Scottish Parliament.

(10)   A statutory instrument containing the first regulations under subsection (1) above shall not be made unless a draft of the instrument has been laid before, and approved by a resolution of, the Scottish Parliament.]

19   Marriage ceremony and registration of marriage

(1)   An authorised registrar shall not solemnise a marriage within 14 days of the date of receipt (as entered in the marriage notice book) of a marriage notice in respect of that marriage, unless—

(a)   he has received a written request from one or both of the parties to solemnise the marriage on a specified earlier date stating the reason for the request, and

(b)   he has been authorised to solemnise the marriage on that earlier date by the Registrar General.

[(1A)   For the purpose of subsection (1) above, a request which is made by electronic means is to be treated as written if it is received in a form which is legible and capable of being used for subsequent reference.]

(2)   A marriage shall not be solemnised by an authorised registrar unless—

(a)   he has available to him at the time of the ceremony a Marriage Schedule, in respect of the marriage, completed in accordance with this Act and the prescribed fee for the marriage has been paid;

(b)   both parties to the marriage are present; and

(c)   two persons professing to be 16 years of age or over are present as witnesses.

(3)   Immediately after the solemnisation of the marriage the Marriage Schedule shall be signed by the parties contracting the marriage, by both witnesses present thereat and by the authorised registrar who solemnised it.

(4)   As soon as possible after the Marriage Schedule has been signed in accordance with subsection (3) above—

[(a)   in a case where the marriage has been solemnised by the authorised registrar—

(i)   in his registration office;

(ii)   in any such place as is mentioned in section 18(3) of this Act;

(iii)   at an approved place in his district; or

(iv)   in or on an approved vessel in Scottish waters,

that authorised registrar;

(b)   in a case where the marriage has been solemnised by the authorised registrar—

(i)   in the registration office of another authorised registrar; or

(ii)   at an approved place in the district of another authorised registrar,

that other authorised registrar,]

shall cause the particulars as set forth in that Schedule to be entered in the register of marriages kept by him.

[(5)   In this section, 'approved place' and 'approved vessel' have the meanings given to those expressions, respectively, by subsections (6) and (7) of section 18 of this Act.]

20 Second marriage ceremony

(1) Where two persons have gone through a marriage ceremony with each other outside the United Kingdom, whether before or after the commencement of this Act, but they are not, or are unable to prove that they are, validly married to each other in Scots law, an authorised registrar, on an application made to him by those persons, may, subject to the approval of the Registrar General and to subsection (2) below, solemnise their marriage as if they had not already gone through a marriage ceremony with each other.

(2) Sections 3 to 6 and 18 and 19 of this Act shall apply for the purpose of solemnising a marriage under this section except that—

(a) there shall be submitted to the authorised registrar a statutory declaration by both parties—

(i) stating that they have previously gone through a marriage ceremony with each other; and

(ii) specifying the date and place at which, and the circumstances in which, they went through that ceremony;

(b) section 5(4)(b) of this Act shall not apply in respect of the parties already being married to each other;

(c) the Marriage Schedule shall contain such modifications as the Registrar General may direct to indicate that the parties have previously gone through a marriage ceremony with each other; and

(d) after the Marriage Schedule has been signed in accordance with section 19(3) of this Act, the authorised registrar shall make an endorsement on it in the following terms—

'The ceremony of marriage between the parties mentioned in this Schedule was performed in pursuance of section 20 of the Marriage (Scotland) Act 1977, following a statutory declaration by them that they had gone through a ceremony of marriage with each other on the   day of   19   , at

Dated the   day of   19   ,

(Signature of authorised registrar)'.

[Void marriages

20A Grounds on which marriage void

(1) Where subsection (2) or (3) applies in relation to a marriage solemnised in Scotland, the marriage shall be void.

(2) This subsection applies if at the time of the marriage ceremony a party to the marriage who was capable of consenting to the marriage purported to give consent but did so by reason only of duress or error.

(3) This subsection applies if at the time of the marriage ceremony a party to the marriage was incapable of—

(a) understanding the nature of marriage; and

(b) consenting to the marriage.

(4) If a party to a marriage purported to give consent to the marriage other than by reason only of duress or error, the marriage shall not be void by reason only of that party's having tacitly withheld consent to the marriage at the time when it was solemnised.

(5) In this section 'error' means—

(a) error as to the nature of the ceremony; or

(b) a mistaken belief held by a person ('A') that the other party at the ceremony with whom A purported to enter into a marriage was the person whom A had agreed to marry.]

Irregular marriages

21 Registration of irregular marriages
Where decree of declarator establishing—
    (a) a marriage by cohabitation with habit and repute; or
    (b) a marriage contracted before 1st July 1940 by declaration *de praesenti* or
by promise *subsequente copula,*
has been granted in the Court of Session, the principal clerk of Session shall forthwith cause the decree, the names, designations and addresses of the parties, and
the date, as determined by the Court, on which the marriage was constituted to be
intimated to the Registrar General, and on receipt of such intimation the Registrar
General shall cause the marriage to be registered.

General

22 Interpreters at marriage ceremony
    (1) Where the person by whom a marriage is to be solemnised under this Act
considers that it is necessary or desirable, he may use the services of an interpreter
(not being a party or a witness to the marriage) at the marriage ceremony.
    (2) The interpreter shall—
    (a) before the marriage ceremony, sign a written statement that he under-
stands, and is able to converse in, any language in respect of which he is to act
as interpreter at that ceremony; and
    (b) immediately after the marriage ceremony, furnish the person solemn-
ising the marriage with a certificate written in English and signed by the interpreter that he has faithfully acted as interpreter at that ceremony.
    (3) Any fee for the services of the interpreter shall be paid by the parties to the
marriage.

23 Cancellation of entry in register of marriages
If a marriage in respect of which an entry has been made in a register of marriages
is found or declared to be void, the Registrar General shall direct the cancellation
of the entry.

[23A Validity of registered marriage
    (1) Subject to sections 1 and 2 of, and without prejudice to section 24(1) of, this
Act, where the particulars of any marriage at the ceremony in respect of which
both parties were present are entered in a register of marriages by or at the behest
of an appropriate registrar, the validity of that marriage shall not be questioned, in
any legal proceedings whatsoever, on the ground of failure to comply with a
requirement or restriction imposed by, under or by virtue of this Act.
    (2) In subsection (1) above, 'appropriate registrar' means
    (a) in the case of a civil marriage, an authorised registrar; and
    (b) in any other case, a district registrar.]

24 Offences
    (1) Any person who—
    (a) falsifies or forges any Marriage Schedule, certificate or declaration issued
or made, or purporting to be issued, or made, under this Act;
    (b) knowingly uses, or gives or sends to any person as genuine, any false or
forged Marriage Schedule, certificate, declaration or other document issued or
made, or purporting to be issued or made, or required, under this Act;
    (c) being an approved celebrant, solemnises a marriage without a Marriage
Schedule in respect of the marriage, issued in accordance with this Act, being
available to him at the time of the marriage ceremony;
    (d) not being an approved celebrant or an authorised registrar, conducts a
marriage ceremony in such a way as to lead the parties to the marriage to
believe that he is solemnising a valid marriage;

(e)   being an approved celebrant or an authorised registrar, solemnises a
marriage without both parties to the marriage being present,
shall be guilty of an offence and shall be liable—
    (i)   on conviction on indictment, to a fine or to imprisonment for a term not
exceeding 2 years or to both;
    (ii)   on summary conviction, to a fine not exceeding £100 or to imprison-
ment for a term not exceeding 3 months or to both [; or
(f)   being an authorised registrar, solemnises a marriage in a place otherwise
than in accordance with section 18(1) of this Act.]
(2)   Any person who—
    (a)   solemnises a marriage in an area in which by virtue of section 9(4)(b) of
this Act he is not permitted to solemnise a marriage;
    (b)   solemnises a marriage in contravention of section 10(5) of this Act;
    (c)   being a person temporarily authorised under section 12(a) of this Act,
solemnises a marriage not specified in that authorisation;
    (d)   solemnises a marriage in contravention of section 14 of this Act; or
    (e)   being a party to a marriage, fails to comply with a notice served under
section 16(2) of this Act,
shall be guilty of an offence and shall be liable on summary conviction to a fine
not exceeding £100.
(3)   Summary proceedings for an offence under this Act or, in relation to information supplied under or for the purposes of this Act, section 53(1)(a) of the Registration of Births, Deaths and Marriages (Scotland) Act 1965, may be commenced at
any time within the period of 3 months from the date on which evidence sufficient
in the opinion of the Lord Advocate to justify the proceedings comes to his knowledge or within the period of 12 months from the commission of the offence,
whichever period last expires; and subsection (3) of [section 136 of the Criminal
Procedure (Scotland) Act 1995] (date of commencement of summary proceedings)
shall have effect for the purposes of this section as it has effect for the purposes of
that section.

[24A   Form, and manner of attestation, of documents

(1)   Regulations prescribing the form of a document may, unless the document
requires to be signed, make provision for the document to be electronic rather than
paper-based.
(2)   Regulations prescribing the manner in which a document requires to be
attested may make different provision for different cases or circumstances.]

25   Regulations

(1)   Any power to make regulations conferred by this Act shall be exercisable
by statutory instrument and no such regulations shall be made by the Registrar
General except with the approval of the Secretary of State.
(2)   Any statutory instrument containing regulations which prescribe fees for
the purposes of this Act shall be subject to annulment in pursuance of a resolution
of either House of Parliament.
(3)   The Statutory Instruments Act 1946 shall apply to a statutory instrument
containing regulations made for the purposes of this Act by the Registrar General
as if the regulations had been made by a Minister of the Crown.

26   Interpretation

(1)   Except where the context otherwise requires and subject to [subsections (2)
and (2A)] below, expressions used in this Act and in the Registration of Births,
Deaths, and Marriages (Scotland) Act 1965 have the same meanings in this Act
as in that Act.
(2)   In this Act, except where the context otherwise requires—
    'annulment' includes any decree or declarator of nullity of marriage, however
expressed;

'approved celebrant' has the meaning assigned to it by section 8(2)(a) of this Act;

'authorised registrar' has the meaning assigned to it by section 8(2)(b) of this Act;

[. . .]

'name' includes surname;

'prescribed' means prescribed by regulations made by the Registrar General;

'religious body' means an organised group of people meeting regularly for common religious worship.

['Scottish waters' means the area comprising such of the internal waters and territorial sea of the United Kingdom as are within Scotland ('Scotland' having the meaning given by section 126(1) and (2) of the Scotland Act 1998 (c 46)), other than any area which is part of a registration district;

'vessel' includes any—

(a)   vehicle; or

(b)   other structure.

(2A)   For the purposes of this Act—

(a)   the seaward boundary of a registration district which extends into the sea shall, subject to paragraph (b) below, be the low water mark of the ordinary spring tide;

(b)   a vessel which is below the low water mark of the ordinary spring tide is to be regarded as within a registration district if it is—

(i)   positioned adjacent to land which is within the district;

(ii)   affixed to the land for the purpose of maintaining its position; and

(iii)   so positioned for the purpose of enabling access to and from the land;

(c)   a jetty or similar structure which is partly above the low water mark of the ordinary spring tide and partly below that mark is to be regarded as being wholly above that mark.]

(3)   Except where the context otherwise requires, any reference in this Act to any other enactment shall be construed as a reference to that enactment as amended by or under any other enactment, including this Act.

27   Transitional and saving provisions

(1)   Where, before the commencement of this Act—

(a)   proclamation of banns or publication of notice has been applied for by one or both of the parties to; or

(b)   a licence has been granted by a sheriff in respect of,

an intended marriage in accordance with an enactment repealed by this Act, then the marriage shall proceed in accordance with the enactments repealed by this Act as if they had not been so repealed:

Provided that this subsection shall cease to have effect in respect of the marriage if—

(i)   a certificate of proclamation of banns or publication of notice issued in respect of the said application; or

(ii)   the said licence,

ceases to be valid in accordance with any enactment so repealed.

(2)   Any form used, and any requirement as to the particulars to be entered in any form used, for the purposes of any enactment repealed by this Act shall continue in force as though prescribed under this Act until other forms or particulars are so prescribed.

(3)   Nothing in this Act shall affect the validity of any marriage solemnised or contracted before 1st January 1978.

(4)   Nothing in the foregoing provisions of this section shall be taken as prejudicing the operation of section 38 of the Interpretation Act 1889 (which relates to the effect of repeals).

29 Short title, commencement and extent

(1) This Act may be cited as the Marriage (Scotland) Act 1977.

(2) This Act, except this section, shall come into force on 1st January 1978.

(3) This Act, except this section and, in so far as relating to the Marriage with Foreigners Act 1906, the Marriage Act 1939, the Marriage Act 1949 and the Marriage (Scotland) Act 1956, section 28, shall extend to Scotland only.

SCHEDULES

SCHEDULE 1
DEGREES OF RELATIONSHIP

Column 1   *Column 2*

1.—Relationships by consanguinity

Mother;	Father;
Daughter;	Son;
Father's mother;	Father's father;
Mother's mother;	Mother's father;
Son's daughter;	Son's son;
Daughter's daughter;	Daughter's son;
Sister;	Brother;
Father's sister;	Father's brother;
Mother's sister;	Mother's brother;
Brother's daughter;	Brother's son;
Sister's daughter;	Sister's son;
Father's father's mother;	Father's father's father;
Father's mother's mother;	Father's mother's father;
Mother's father's mother;	Mother's father's father;
Mother's mother's mother;	Mother's mother's father;
Son's son's daughter;	Son's son's son;
Son's daughter's daughter;	Son's daughter's son;
Daughter's son's daughter;	Daughter's son's son;
Daughter's daughter's daughter;	Daughter's daughter's son.

[2.—Relationships by affinity referred to in section 2(1A)

Daughter of former wife;	Son of former husband;
Daughter of former civil partner;	Son of former civil partner;
Former wife of father;	Former husband of mother;
Former civil partner of mother;	Former civil partner of father;
Former wife of father's father;	Former husband of father's mother;
Former civil partner of mother's mother;	Former civil partner of mother's father;
Former wife of mother's father;	Former husband of mother's mother;
Former civil partner of father's mother;	Former civil partner of father's father;
Daughter of son of former wife;	Son of son of former husband;
Daughter of former civil partner;	Son of former civil partner;
Daughter of daughter of former wife;	Son of daughter of former husband;
Daughter of daughter of former civil partner;	Son of daughter of former civil partner.

[. . .]

3.—Relationships by adoption

Adoptive mother or former
    adoptive mother;
Adopted daughter or former
    adopted daughter;

Adoptive father or former
    adoptive father;
Adopted son or former
    adopted son.

ADOPTION (SCOTLAND) ACT 1978
(1978, c 28)

PART IV
STATUS OF ADOPTED CHILDREN

38 Meaning of 'adoption order' in Part IV

(1) In this Part 'adoption order' means—

(a) an adoption order within the meaning of section 65(1);

(b) an adoption order under the Children Act 1975, the Adoption Act 1958, the Adoption Act 1950 or any enactment repealed by the Adoption Act 1950;

(c) an order effecting an adoption made in England, Wales, Northern Ireland, the Isle of Man or any of the Channel Islands;

[(cc) a Convention adoption;]

(d) an 'overseas adoption' within the meaning of section 65(2); or

(e) any other adoption recognised by the law of Scotland; and cognate expressions shall be construed accordingly.

(2) The definition of adoption order includes, where the context admits, an adoption order which took effect before the commencement of the Children Act 1975.

39 Status conferred by adoption

[(1) A child who is the subject of an adoption order shall be treated in law—

(a) where the adopters are a married couple, as if—

(i) he had been born as a [. . .] child of the marriage (whether or not he was in fact born after the marriage was constituted); and

(ii) [subject to subsection (2A)] he were not the child of any person other than the adopters;

(b) where the adoption order is made by virtue of section 15(1)(aa) as if—

(i) he had been born as a [. . .] child of the marriage between the adopter and the natural parent to whom the adopter is married (whether or not he was in fact born after the marriage was constituted); and

(ii) [subject to subsection (2A)] he were not the child of any person other than the adopter and that natural parent; and

(c) in any other case, as if—

(i) he had been born as a [. . .] child of the adopter; and

(ii) [subject to subsection (2A)] he were not the child of any person other than the adopter.]

(2) Where [a] child has been adopted by one of his natural parents as sole adoptive parent and the adopter thereafter marries the other natural parent, subsection (1) shall not affect any enactment or rule of law whereby, by virtue of the marriage, the child is rendered the [. . .] child of both natural parents.

[(2A) Where, in the case of a child adopted under a Convention adoption, the Court of Session is satisfied, on an application under this subsection—

(a)   that under the law of the country in which the adoption was effected the adoption is not a full adoption;

(b)   that the consents referred to in Article 4(c) and (d) of the Convention have not been given for a full adoption, or that the United Kingdom is not the receiving State (within the meaning of Article 2 of the Convention); and

(c)   that it would be more favourable to the child for a direction to be given under this subsection,

the Court may direct that sub-paragraph (ii) of, as the case may be, paragraph (a), (b) or (c) of subsection (1) shall not apply, or shall not apply to such extent as may be specified in the direction: and in this subsection 'full adoption' means an adoption by virtue of which the child falls to be treated in law as if he were not the child of any person other than the adopters or adopter.]

(3)   This section has effect—

(a)   in the case of an adoption before 1st January 1976, from that date, and

(b)   in the case of any other adoption, from the date of the adoption.

(4)   Subject to the provisions of this Part, this section—

(a) applies for the construction of enactments or instruments passed or made before or after the commencement of this Act so far as the context admits; and

(b) does not affect things done or events occurring before the adoption or, where the adoption took place before 1st January 1976, before that date.

(5)   This section has effect subject to the provisions of section 44.

[. . .]

41   Miscellaneous enactments

(1)   Section 39 does not apply in determining the forbidden degrees of consanguinity and affinity in respect of the law relating to marriage [, to the eligibility of persons to register as civil partners of each other] or in respect of the crime of incest, except that, on the making of an adoption order, the adopter and the child shall be deemed, for all time coming, to be within the said forbidden degrees in respect of the law relating to marriage and incest [, to such eligibility and to incest].

(2)   [S]ection 39 does not apply for the purposes of any provision of—

(a)   [the British Nationality Act 1981],

(b)   the Immigration Act 1971,

(c)   any instrument having effect under an enactment within paragraph (a) or (b), or

(d)   any other law for the time being in force which determines [British citizenship, British Overseas Territories citizenship, the status of a British National (Overseas) or British Overseas citizenship].

42   Pensions

Section 39(1) does not affect entitlement to a pension which is payable to or for the benefit of a child and is in payment at the time of his adoption.

43   Insurance

Where a child is adopted whose natural parent has effected an insurance with a friendly society or a collecting society or an industrial insurance company for the payment on the death of the child of money for funeral expenses, the rights and liabilities under the policy shall by virtue of the adoption be transferred to the adoptive parents who shall for the purposes of the enactments relating to such societies and companies be treated as the person who took out the policy.

44   Effect of s 39 on succession and *inter vivos* deed

Section 39 (status conferred by adoption) does not affect the existing law relating to adopted persons in respect of—

(a)   the succession to a deceased person (whether testate or intestate), and

(b)   the disposal of property by virtue of any *inter vivos* deed.

MATRIMONIAL HOMES (FAMILY PROTECTION) (SCOTLAND) ACT 1981
(1981, c 59)

Protection of occupancy rights of one spouse against the other

1 Right of spouse without title to occupy matrimonial home

(1) Where, apart from the provisions of this Act, one spouse is entitled, or permitted by a third party, to occupy a matrimonial home (an 'entitled spouse') and the other spouse is not so entitled or permitted (a 'non-entitled spouse'), the non-entitled spouse shall, subject to the provisions of this Act, have the following rights—

(a) if in occupation, a right [. . .] to [continue to occupy] the matrimonial home or any part of it by the entitled spouse;

(b) if not in occupation, a right to enter into and occupy the matrimonial home.

[(1A) The rights conferred by subsection (1) above to continue to occupy or, as the case may be, to enter and occupy the matrimonial home include, without prejudice to their generality, the right to do so together with any child of the family.]

(2) In subsection (1) above, an 'entitled spouse' includes a spouse who is entitled, or permitted by a third party, to occupy a matrimonial home along with an individual who is not the other spouse only if that individual has waived his or her right of occupation in favour of the spouse so entitled or permitted.

(3) If the entitled spouse refuses to allow the non-entitled spouse to exercise the right conferred by subsection (1)(b) above, the non-entitled spouse may exercise that right only with the leave of the court under section 3(3) or (4) of this Act.

(4) In this Act, the rights mentioned in paragraphs (a) and (b) of subsection (1) above are referred to as occupancy rights.

(5) A non-entitled spouse may renounce in writing his or her occupancy rights only—

(a) in a particular matrimonial home; or

(b) in a particular property which it is intended by the spouses will become a matrimonial home.

(6) A renunciation under subsection (5) above shall have effect only if at the time of making the renunciation, the non-entitled spouse has sworn or affirmed before a notary public that it was made freely and without coercion of any kind. [In this subsection, 'notary public' includes any person duly authorised by the law of the country (other than Scotland) in which the swearing or affirmation takes place to administer oaths or receive affirmations in that other country.]

[(7) Subject to subsection (5), if—

(a) there has been no cohabitation between an entitled spouse and a non-entitled spouse during a continuous period of two years; and

(b) during that period the non-entitled spouse has not occupied the matrimonial home,

the non-entitled spouse shall, on the expiry of that period, cease to have occupancy rights in the matrimonial home.

(8) A non-entitled spouse who has ceased to have occupancy rights by virtue of subsection (7) may not apply to the court for an order under section 3(1).]

2 Subsidiary and consequential rights

(1) For the purpose of securing the occupancy rights of a non-entitled spouse, that spouse shall, in relation to a matrimonial home, be entitled without the consent of the entitled spouse—

(a) to make any payment due by the entitled spouse in respect of rent, rates, secured loan instalments, interest or other outgoings (not being outgoings on repairs or improvements);

(b) to perform any other obligation incumbent on the entitled spouse (not being an obligation in respect of non-essential repairs or improvements);

(c)   to enforce performance of an obligation by a third party which that third party has undertaken to the entitled spouse to the extent that the entitled spouse may enforce such performance;

(d)   to carry out such essential repairs as the entitled spouse may carry out;

(e)   to carry out such non-essential repairs or improvements as may be authorised by an order of the court, being such repairs or improvements as the entitled spouse may carry out and which the court considers to be appropriate for the reasonable enjoyment of the occupancy rights;

(f)   to take such other steps, for the purpose of protecting the occupancy rights of the non-entitled spouse, as the entitled spouse may take to protect the occupancy rights of the entitled spouse.

(2)   Any payment made under subsection (1)(a) above or any obligation performed under subsection (1)(b) above shall have effect in relation to the rights of a third party as if the payment were made or the obligation were performed by the entitled spouse; and the performance of an obligation which has been enforced under subsection (1)(c) above shall have effect as if it had been enforced by the entitled spouse.

(3)   Where there is an entitled and a non-entitled spouse, the court, on the application of either of them, may, having regard in particular to the respective financial circumstances of the spouses, make an order apportioning expenditure incurred or to be incurred by either spouse—

(a)   without the consent of the other spouse, on any of the items mentioned in paragraphs (a) and (d) of subsection (1) above;

(b)   with the consent of the other spouse, on anything relating to a matrimonial home.

(4)   Where both spouses are entitled, or permitted by a third party, to occupy a matrimonial home—

(a)   either spouse shall be entitled, without the consent of the other spouse, to carry out such non-essential repairs or improvements as may be authorised by an order of the court, being such repairs or improvements as the court considers to be appropriate for the reasonable enjoyment of the occupancy rights;

(b)   the court, on the application of either spouse, may, having regard in particular to the respective financial circumstances of the spouses, make an order apportioning expenditure incurred or to be incurred by either spouse, with or without the consent of the other spouse, on anything relating to the matrimonial home.

(5)   Where one spouse owns or hires, or is acquiring under a hire-purchase or conditional sale agreement, furniture and plenishings in a matrimonial home—

(a)   the other spouse may, without the consent of the first mentioned spouse—

(i) make any payment due by the first mentioned spouse which is necessary, or take any other step which the first mentioned spouse is entitled to take to secure the possession or use of any such furniture and plenishings (and any such payment shall have effect in relation to the rights of a third party as if it were made by the first mentioned spouse); or

(ii) carry out such essential repairs to the furniture and plenishings as the first mentioned spouse is entitled to carry out;

(b)   the court, on the application of either spouse, may, having regard in particular to the respective financial circumstances of the spouses, make an order apportioning expenditure incurred or to be incurred by either spouse—

(i) without the consent of the other spouse, in making payments under a hire, hire-purchase or conditional sale agreement, or in paying interest charges in respect of the furniture and plenishings, or in carrying out essential repairs to the furniture and plenishings; or

(ii) with the consent of the other spouse, on anything relating to the furniture and plenishings.

(6) An order under subsection (3), (4)(b) or (5)(b) above may require one spouse to make a payment to the other spouse in implementation of the apportionment.

(7) Any application under subsection (3), (4)(b) or (5)(b) above shall be made within five years of the date on which any payment in respect of such incurred expenditure was made.

(8) Where—
(a) the entitled spouse is a tenant of a matrimonial home; and
(b) possession thereof is necessary in order to continue the tenancy; and
(c) the entitled spouse abandons such possession,
the tenancy shall be continued by such possession by the non-entitled spouse.

(9) In this section 'improvements' includes alterations and enlargement.

3 Regulation by court of rights of occupancy of matrimonial home

(1) [Subject to section 1(7) of this Act,] where there is an entitled and a non-entitled spouse, or where both spouses are entitled, or permitted by a third party, to occupy a matrimonial home, either spouse may apply to the court for an order—
(a) declaring the occupancy rights of the applicant spouse;
(b) enforcing the occupancy rights of the applicant spouse;
(c) restricting the occupancy rights of the non-applicant spouse;
(d) regulating the exercise by either spouse of his or her occupancy rights;
(e) protecting the occupancy rights of the applicant spouse in relation to the other spouse.

(2) Where one spouse owns or hires, or is acquiring under a hire-purchase or conditional sale agreement, furniture and plenishings in a matrimonial home, the other spouse, if he or she has occupancy rights in that home, may apply to the court for an order granting to the applicant the possession or use in the matrimonial home of any such furniture and plenishings; but, subject to section 2 of this Act, an order under this subsection shall not prejudice the rights of any third party in relation to the non-performance of any obligation under such hire-purchase or conditional sale agreement.

(3) The court shall grant an application under subsection (1)(a) above if it appears to the court that the application relates to a matrimonial home; and, on an application under any of paragraphs (b) to (e) of subsection (1) or under subsection (2) above, the court may make such order relating to the application as appears to it to be just and reasonable having regard to all the circumstances of the case including—
(a) the conduct of the spouses in relation to each other and otherwise;
(b) the respective needs and financial resources of the spouses;
(c) the needs of any child of the family;
(d) the extent (if any) to which—
(i) the matrimonial home; and
(ii) in relation only to an order under subsection (2) above, any item of furniture and plenishings referred to in that subsection,
is used in connection with a trade, business or profession of either spouse; and
(e) whether the entitled spouse offers or has offered to make available to the non-entitled spouse any suitable alternative accommodation.

(4) Pending the making of an order under subsection (3) above, the court, on the application of either spouse, may make such interim order as it may consider necessary or expedient in relation to—
(a) the residence of either spouse in the home to which the application relates;
(b) the personal effects of either spouse or of any child of the family; or
(c) the furniture and plenishings:

Provided that an interim order may be made only if the non-applicant spouse has been afforded an opportunity of being heard by or represented before the court.

(5) The court shall not make an order under subsection (3) or (4) above if it appears that the effect of the order would be to exclude the non-applicant spouse from the matrimonial home.

(6) If the court makes an order under subsection (3) or (4) above which requires the delivery to one spouse of anything which has been left in or removed from the matrimonial home, it may also grant a warrant authorising a messenger-at-arms or sheriff officer to enter the matrimonial home or other premises occupied by the other spouse and to search for and take possession of the thing required to be delivered, if need be by opening shut and lockfast places, and to deliver the thing in accordance with the said order:

Provided that a warrant granted under this subsection shall be executed only after expiry of the period of a charge, being such period as the court shall specify in the order for delivery.

(7) Where it appears to the court—

(a) on the application of a non-entitled spouse, that that spouse has suffered a loss of occupancy rights or that the quality of the non-entitled spouse's occupation of a matrimonial home has been impaired; or

(b) on the application of a spouse who has been given the possession or use of furniture and plenishings by virtue of an order under subsection (3) above, that the applicant has suffered a loss of such possession or use or that the quality of the applicant's possession or use of the furniture and plenishings has been impaired,

in consequence of any act or default on the part of the other spouse which was intended to result in such loss or impairment, it may order that other spouse to pay to the applicant such compensation as the court in the circumstances considers just and reasonable in respect of that loss or impairment.

(8) A spouse may renounce in writing the right to apply under subsection (2) above for the possession or use of any item of furniture and plenishings.

4 Exclusion orders

(1) Where there is an entitled and a non-entitled spouse, or where both spouses are entitled, or permitted by a third party, to occupy a matrimonial home, either spouse [whether or not that spouse is in occupation at the time of the application] may apply to the court for an order (in this Act referred to as 'an exclusion order') suspending the occupancy rights of the other spouse ('the non-applicant spouse') in a matrimonial home.

(2) Subject to subsection (3) below, the court shall make an exclusion order if it appears to the court that the making of the order is necessary for the protection of the applicant or any child of the family from any conduct or threatened or reasonably apprehended conduct of the non-applicant spouse which is or would be injurious to the physical or mental health of the applicant or child.

(3) The court shall not make an exclusion order if it appears to the court that the making of the order would be unjustified or unreasonable—

(a) having regard to all the circumstances of the case including the matters specified in paragraphs (a) to (e) of section 3(3) of this Act; and

(b) where the matrimonial home—

(i) is or is part of an agricultural holding within the meaning of section 1 of the [Agricultural Holdings (Scotland) Act 1991]; or

(ii) is let, or is a home in respect of which possession is given, to the non-applicant spouse or to both spouses by an employer as an incident of employment,

subject to a requirement that the non-applicant spouse or, as the case may be, both spouses must reside in the matrimonial home, having regard to that requirement and the likely consequences of the exclusion of the non-applicant spouse from the matrimonial home.

(4) In making an exclusion order the court shall, on the application of the applicant spouse,—

(a) grant a warrant for the summary ejection of the non-applicant spouse from the matrimonial home;

(b) grant an interdict prohibiting the non-applicant spouse from entering the matrimonial home without the express permission of the applicant;

(c) grant an interdict prohibiting the removal by the non-applicant spouse, except with the written consent of the applicant or by a further order of the court, of any furniture and plenishings in the matrimonial home;

unless, in relation to paragraph (a) or (c) above, the non-applicant spouse satisfies the court that it is unnecessary for it to grant such a remedy.

(5) In making an exclusion order the court may—

(a) grant an interdict prohibiting the non-applicant spouse from entering or remaining in a specified area in the vicinity of the matrimonial home;

(b) where the warrant for the summary ejection of the non-applicant spouse has been granted in his or her absence, give directions as to the preservation of the non-applicant spouse's goods and effects which remain in the matrimonial home;

(c) on the application of either spouse, make the exclusion order or the warrant or interdict mentioned in paragraph (a), (b) or (c) of subsection (4) above or paragraph (a) of this subsection subject to such terms and conditions as the court may prescribe;

(d) on application as aforesaid, make such other order as it may consider necessary for the proper enforcement of an order made under subsection (4) above or paragraph (a), (b) or (c) of this subsection.

(6) Pending the making of an exclusion order, the court may, on the application of the applicant spouse, make an interim order suspending the occupancy rights of the non-applicant spouse in the matrimonial home to which the application for the exclusion order relates; and subsections (4) and (5) above shall apply to such interim order as they apply to an exclusion order:

Provided that an interim order may be made only if the non-applicant spouse has been afforded an opportunity of being heard by or represented before the court.

(7) Without prejudice to subsections (1) and (6) above, where both spouses are entitled, or permitted by a third party, to occupy a matrimonial home, it shall be incompetent for one spouse to bring an action of ejection from the matrimonial home against the other spouse.

5   Duration of orders under ss 3 and 4

(1) The court may, on the application of either spouse, vary or recall any order made by it under section 3 or 4 of this Act, but, subject to subsection (2) below, any such order shall, unless previously so varied or recalled, cease to have effect—

(a) on the termination of the marriage; or

(b) subject to section 6(1) of this Act, where there is an entitled and a non-entitled spouse, on the entitled spouse ceasing to be an entitled spouse in respect of the matrimonial home to which the order relates; or

(c) where both spouses are entitled, or permitted by a third party, to occupy the matrimonial home, on both spouses ceasing to be so entitled or permitted.

(2) Without prejudice to the generality of subsection (1) above, an order under section 3(3) or (4) of this Act which grants the possession or use of furniture and plenishings shall cease to have effect if the furniture and plenishings cease to be permitted by a third party to be retained in the matrimonial home.

Occupancy rights in relation to dealings with third parties

6   Continued exercise of occupancy rights after dealing

(1)   Subject to subsection (3) below—

(a)   the continued exercise of the rights conferred on a non-entitled spouse by the provisions of this Act in respect of a matrimonial home shall not be prejudiced by reason only of any dealing of the entitled spouse relating to that home; and

(b)   a third party shall not by reason only of such a dealing be entitled to occupy that matrimonial home or any part of it.

[(1A)   The occupancy rights of a non-entitled spouse in relation to a matrimonial home shall not be exercisable in relation to the home where, following a dealing of the entitled spouse relating to the home—

(a)   a person acquires the home, or an interest in it, in good faith and for value from a person other than the person who is or, as the case may be, was the entitled spouse; or

(b)   a person derives title to the home from a person who acquired title as mentioned in paragraph (a).]

(2)   In this section and section 7 of this Act—

'dealing' includes the grant of a heritable security and the creation of a trust but does not include a conveyance under section 80 of the Lands Clauses Consolidation (Scotland) Act 1845;

'entitled spouse' does not include a spouse who, apart from the provisions of this Act,—

(a)   is permitted by a third party to occupy a matrimonial home; or

(b)   is entitled to occupy a matrimonial home along with an individual who is not the other spouse, whether or not that individual has waived his or her right of occupation in favour of the spouse so entitled;

and 'non-entitled spouse' shall be construed accordingly.

(3)   This section shall not apply in any case where—

(a)   the non-entitled spouse in writing either—

(i)   consents or has consented to the dealing, and any consent shall be in such form as the Secretary of State may, by regulations made by statutory instrument, prescribe; or

(ii)   renounces or has renounced his or her occupancy rights in relation to the matrimonial home or property to which the dealing relates;

(b)   the court has made an order under section 7 of this Act dispensing with the consent of the non-entitled spouse to the dealing;

(c)   the dealing occurred, or implements, a binding obligation entered into by the entitled spouse before his or her marriage to the non-entitled spouse;

(d)   the dealing occurred, or implements, a binding obligation entered into before the commencement of this Act; . . .

(e)   the dealing comprises [a transfer for value to] a third party who has acted in good faith if, [. . .] there is produced to the third party by the [transferor—

(i)   a written declaration signed by the transferor, or a person acting on behalf of the transferor under a power of attorney or as a guardian (within the meaning of the Adults with Incapacity (Scotland) Act 2000 (asp 4)), that the subjects of the transfer are not, or were not at the time of the dealing, a matrimonial home in relation to which a spouse of the transferor has or had occupancy rights; or

(ii)   a renunciation of occupancy rights or consent to the dealing which bears to have been properly made or given by the non-entitled spouse or a person acting on behalf of the non-entitled spouse under a power of attorney or as a guardian (within the meaning of the Adults with Incapacity (Scotland) Act 2000 (asp 4))]; or

(f)   the entitled spouse has permanently ceased to be entitled to occupy the matrimonial home, and at any time thereafter a continuous period of [2] years has elapsed, during which the non-entitled spouse has not occupied the matrimonial home.]

(4)   [*Amends Land Registration (Scotland) Act 1979.*]

7   Dispensation by court with spouse's consent to dealing

(1)   [Subject to subsections (1A) to (1D) below the] court may, on the application of an entitled spouse or any other person having an interest, make an order dispensing with the consent of a non-entitled spouse to a dealing which has taken place or a proposed dealing, if—

(a)   such consent is unreasonably withheld;

(b)   such consent cannot be given by reason of physical or mental disability;

(c)   the non-entitled spouse cannot be found after reasonable steps have been taken to trace him or her; or

(d)   the non-entitled spouse is [under legal disability by reason of nonage].

[(1A)   Subsection (1B) applies if, in relation to a proposed sale—

(a)   negotiations with a third party have not begun; or

(b)   negotiations have begun but a price has not been agreed.

(1B)   An order under subsection (1) dispensing with consent may be made only if—

(a)   the price agreed for the sale is no less than such amount as the court specifies in the order; and

(b)   the contract for the sale is concluded before the expiry of such period as may be so specified.

(1C)   Subsection (1D) applies if the proposed dealing is the grant of a heritable security.

(1D)   An order under subsection (1) dispensing with consent may be made only if—

(a)   the heritable security is granted for a loan of no more than such amount as the court specifies in the order; and

(b)   the security is executed before the expiry of such period as may be so specified.]

(2)   For the purposes of subsection (1)(a) above, a non-entitled spouse shall have unreasonably withheld consent to a dealing which has taken place or a proposed dealing, where it appears to the court—

(a)   that the non-entitled spouse has led the entitled spouse to believe that he or she would consent to the dealing and that the non-entitled spouse would not be prejudiced by any change in the circumstances of the case since such apparent consent was given; or

(b)   that the entitled spouse has, having taken all reasonable steps to do so, been unable to obtain an answer to a request for consent.

(3)   The court, in considering whether to make an order under subsection (1) above, shall have regard to all the circumstances of the case including the matters specified in paragraphs (a) to (e) of section 3(3) of this Act.

[(3A)   If the court refuses an application for an order under subsection (1), it may make an order requiring a non-entitled spouse who is or becomes the occupier of the matrimonial home—

(a)   to make such payments to the owner of the home in respect of that spouse's occupation of it as may be specified in the order;

(b)   to comply with such other conditions relating to that spouse's occupation of the matrimonial home as may be so specified.]

(4)   Where—

(a)   an application is made for an order under this section; and

(b)   an action is or has been raised by a non-entitled spouse to enforce occupancy rights,

the action shall be sisted until the conclusion of the proceedings on the application.
[. . .]

8   Interests of heritable creditors

(1)   The rights of a third party with an interest in the matrimonial home as a creditor under a secured loan in relation to the non-performance of any obligation under the loan shall not be prejudiced by reason only of the occupancy rights of the non-entitled spouse; but where a non-entitled spouse has or obtains occupation of a matrimonial home and—

(a)   the entitled spouse is not in occupation; and

(b)   there is a third party with such an interest in the matrimonial home,

the court may, on the application of the third party, make an order requiring the non-entitled spouse to make any payment due by the entitled spouse in respect of the loan.

(2)   This section shall not apply [to secured loans in respect of which the security was granted prior to the commencement of section 13 of the Law Reform (Miscellaneous Provisions) (Scotland) Act 1985] unless the third party in granting the secured loan acted in good faith and . . . there was produced to the third party by the entitled spouse—

(a)   [a written declaration signed] by the entitled spouse declaring that there is no non-entitled spouse; or

(b)   a renunciation of occupancy rights or consent to the taking of the loan which bears to have been properly made or given by the non-entitled spouse.

[(2A)   This section shall not apply to secured loans in respect of which the security was granted after the commencement of section 13 of the Law Reform (Miscellaneous Provisions) (Scotland) Act 1985 unless the third party in granting the secured loan acted in good faith and [. . .] there was produced to the third party by the grantor—

(a)   [a written declaration signed] by the grantor declaring that the security subjects are not or were not at the time of the granting of the security a matrimonial home in relation to which a spouse of the grantor has or had occupancy rights; or

(b)   a renunciation of occupancy rights or consent to the granting of the security which bears to have been properly made or given by the non-entitled spouse.

(2B)   for the purposes of subsections (2) and (2A) above, the time of granting a security, in the case of a heritable security, is the date of delivery of the deed creating the security.]

9   Provisions where both spouses have title

(1)   Subject to subsection (2) below, where, apart from the provisions of this Act, both spouses are entitled to occupy a matrimonial home—

(a)   the rights in that home of one spouse shall not be prejudiced by reason only of any dealing of the other spouse; and

(b)   a third party shall not by reason only of such a dealing be entitled to occupy that matrimonial home or any part of it.

(2)   The definition of 'dealing' in section 6(2) of this Act and sections 6(3) and 7 of this Act shall apply for the purposes of subsection (1) above as they apply for the purposes of section 6(1) of this Act subject to the following modifications—

(a)   any reference to the entitled spouse and to the non-entitled spouse shall be construed as a reference to a spouse who has entered into or, as the case may be, proposes to enter into a dealing and to the other spouse respectively; and

(b)   in paragraph (b) of section 7(4) the reference to occupancy rights shall be construed as a reference to any rights in the matrimonial home.

[Reckoning of non-cohabitation periods in sections 1 and 6]

[9A   Effect of court action under section 3, 4 or 5 on reckoning of periods in sections 1 and 6

(1)   Subsection (2) applies where an application is made under section 3(1), 4(1) or 5(1) of this Act.

(2)   In calculating the period of two years mentioned in section 1(7)(a) or 6(3)(f) of this Act, no account shall be taken of the period mentioned in subsection (3) below.

(3)   The period is the period beginning with the date on which the application is made and—

(a)   in the case of an application under section 3(1) or 4(1) of this Act, ending on the date on which—

(i)   an order under section 3(3) or, as the case may be, 4(2) of this Act is made; or

(ii)   the application is otherwise finally determined or abandoned;

(b)   in the case of an application under section 5(1) of this Act, ending on the date on which—

(i)   the order under section 3(3) or, as the case may be, 4(2) is varied or recalled; or

(ii)   the application is otherwise finally determined or abandoned.]

[. . .]

11   Poinding

Where [an attachment] has been executed of furniture and plenishings of which the debtor's spouse has the possession or use by virtue of an order under section 3(3) or (4) of this Act, the sheriff, on the application of that spouse within 40 days of the date of execution of [the attachment], may—

(a)   declare that [the attachment] is null; or

(b)   make such order as he thinks appropriate to protect such possession or use by that spouse,

if he is satisfied that the purpose of the diligence was wholly or mainly to prevent such possession or use.

12   Adjudication

(1)   Where a matrimonial home of which there is an entitled spouse and a non-entitled spouse is adjudged, the Court of Session, on the application of the non-entitled spouse within 40 days of the date of the decree of adjudication, may—

(a)   order the reduction of the decree; or

(b)   make such order as it thinks appropriate to protect the occupancy rights of the non-entitled spouse,

if it is satisfied that the purpose of the diligence was wholly or mainly to defeat the occupancy rights of the non-entitled spouse.

(2)   In this section, 'entitled spouse' and 'non-entitled spouse' have the same meanings respectively as in section 6(2) of this Act.

Transfer of tenancy

13   Transfer of tenancy

(1)   The court may, on the application of a non-entitled spouse, make an order transferring the tenancy of a matrimonial home to that spouse and providing, subject to subsection (11) below, for the payment by the non-entitled spouse to the entitled spouse of such compensation as seems just and reasonable in all the circumstances of the case.

[(2)   In an action—

(a)   for divorce, the Court of Session or a sheriff;

(b)   for nullity of marriage, the Court of Session,

may, on granting decree or within such period as the court may specify on granting decree, make an order granting an application under subsection (1) above.]

(3) In determining whether to grant an application under subsection (1) above, the court shall have regard to all the circumstances of the case including the matters specified in paragraphs (a) to (e) of section 3(3) of this Act and the suitability of the applicant to become the tenant and the applicant's capacity to perform the obligations under the lease of the matrimonial home.

(4) The non-entitled spouse shall serve a copy of an application under subsection (1) above on the landlord and, before making an order under subsection (1) above, the court shall give the landlord an opportunity of being heard by it.

(5) On the making of an order granting an application under subsection (1) above, the tenancy shall vest in the non-entitled spouse without intimation to the landlord, subject to all the liabilities under the lease (other than any arrears of rent for the period before the making of the order, which shall remain the liability of the original entitled spouse).

(6) The clerk of court shall notify the landlord of the making of an order granting an application under subsection (1) above.

(7) It shall not be competent for a non-entitled spouse to apply for an order under subsection (1) above where the matrimonial home—

    (a) is let to the entitled spouse by his or her employer as an incident of employment, and the lease is subject to a requirement that the entitled spouse must reside therein;

    (b) [is on or pertains to land comprised in an agricultural lease];

    (c) is on or pertains to a croft or the subject of a cottar or the holding of a landholder or a statutory small tenant;

    (d) is let on a long lease;

    (e) is part of the tenancy land of a tenant-at-will.

(8) In subsection (7) above—

['agricultural lease' means a lease constituting a 1991 Act tenancy within the meaning of the Agricultural Holdings (Scotland) Act 2003 (asp 11) or a lease constituting a limited duration tenancy or a short limited duration tenancy (within the meaning of that Act);]

'cottar' has the same meaning as in section 28(4) of the [Crofters (Scotland) Act 1993];

'croft' has the same meaning as in the [Crofters (Scotland) Act 1993];

'holding', in relation to a landholder and a statutory small tenant, 'landholder' and 'statutory small tenant' have the same meanings respectively as in sections 2(1), 2(2) and 32(1) of the Small Landholders (Scotland) Act 1911;

'long lease' has the same meaning as in section 28(1) of the Land Registration (Scotland) Act 1979;

'tenant-at-will' has the same meaning as in section 20(8) of the Land Registration (Scotland) Act 1979.

(9) Where both spouses are joint or common tenants of a matrimonial home, the court may, on the application of one of the spouses, make an order vesting the tenancy in that spouse solely and providing, subject to subsection (11) below, for the payment by the applicant to the other spouse of such compensation as seems just and reasonable in the circumstances of the case.

(10) Subsections (2) to (8) above shall apply for the purposes of an order under subsection (9) above as they apply for the purposes of an order under subsection (1) above subject to the following modifications—

    (a) in subsection (3) for the word 'tenant' there shall substituted the words 'sole tenant';

    (b) in subsection (4) for the words 'non-entitled' there should be substituted the word 'applicant';

    (c) in subsection (5) for the words 'non-entitled' and 'liability of the original entitled spouse' there shall substituted respectively the words 'applicant' and 'joint and several liability of both spouses';

    (d) in subsection (7)—

        (i) for the words 'a non-entitled' there shall substituted the words 'an applicant';

        (ii) for paragraph (a) there shall be substituted the following paragraph—

        '(a) is let to both spouses by their employer as an incident of employment, and the lease is subject to a requirement that both spouses must reside there;';

        (iii) paragraphs (c) and (e) shall be omitted.

(11) Where the matrimonial home is a [Scottish secure tenancy within the meaning of the Housing (Scotland) Act 2001 (asp 10)] no account shall be taken, in assessing the amount of any compensation to be awarded under subsection (1) or (9) above, of the loss, by virtue of the transfer of the tenancy of the home, of a right to purchase the home under [Part III of the Housing (Scotland) Act 1987 (c 26)].

(12) In the Tenants' Rights, Etc (Scotland) Act 1980—

    (a) paragraph 6 of Part I of Schedule 2 is repealed.

[. . .]

Matrimonial interdicts

14 Interdict competent where spouses live together

(1) It shall not be incompetent for the court to entertain an application by a spouse for a matrimonial interdict by reason only that the spouses are living together as man and wife.

(2) In this section [. . .] of this Act—

'matrimonial interdict' means an interdict including an interim interdict which—

    (a) restrains or prohibits any conduct of one spouse towards the other spouse or a child of the family, or

    [(b) subject to subsection (3), prohibits a spouse from entering or remaining in—

        (i) a matrimonial home;

        (ii) any other residence occupied by the applicant spouse;

        (iii) any place of work of the applicant spouse;

        (iv) any school attended by a child in the permanent or temporary care of the applicant spouse.]

[(3) Subsection (4) applies if in relation to a matrimonial home the non-applicant spouse—

    (a) is an entitled spouse; or

    (b) has occupancy rights.

(4) Except where subsection (5) applies, the court may not grant a matrimonial interdict prohibiting the non-applicant spouse from entering or remaining in the matrimonial home.

(5) This subsection applies if—

    (a) the interdict is ancillary to an exclusion order; or

    (b) by virtue of section 1(3), the court refuses leave to exercise occupancy rights.

(6) In this section [. . .], 'applicant spouse' means the spouse who has applied for the interdict; and 'non-applicant spouse' shall be construed accordingly.]

[. . .]

Cohabiting couples

18 Occupancy rights of cohabiting couples

(1) If a man and a woman are living with each other as if they were man and wife [or two persons of the same sex are living together as if they were civil

partners] ('[in either case] a cohabiting couple') in a house which, apart from the provisions of this section—

(a)   one of them (an 'entitled partner') is entitled, or permitted by a third party, to occupy; and

(b)   the other (a 'non-entitled partner') is not so entitled or permitted to occupy,

the court may, on the application of the non-entitled partner, if it appears that the [entitled partner and the non-entitled partner] are a cohabiting couple in that house, grant occupancy rights therein to the applicant for such period, not exceeding [6] months, as the court may specify:

Provided that the court may extend the said period for a further period or periods, no such period exceeding 6 months.

(2)   In determining whether for the purpose of subsection (1) above [two persons] are a cohabiting couple the court shall have regard to all the circumstances of the case including—

(a)   the time for which it appears they have been living together; and

(b)   whether there [is any child—

(i)   of whom they are the parents; or

(ii)   who they have treated as a child of theirs.].

(3)   While an order granting an application under subsection (1) above or an extension of such an order is in force, or where both partners of a cohabiting couple are entitled, or permitted by a third party, to occupy the house where they are cohabiting, the following provisions of this Act shall subject to any necessary modifications—

(a)   apply to the cohabiting couple as they apply to parties to a marriage; and

(b)   have effect in relation to any child residing with the cohabiting couple as they have effect in relation to a child of the family,

section 2;

section 3, except subsection (1)(a);

section 4;

in section 5(1), the words from the beginning to 'Act' where it first occurs;

[section 13]; and

section 22,

and any reference in these provisions to a matrimonial home shall be construed as a reference to a house.

(4)   Any order under section 3 or 4 of this Act as applied to a cohabiting couple by subsection (3) above shall have effect—

(a)   if one of them is a non-entitled partner, for such a period, not exceeding the period or periods which from time to time may be specified in any order under subsection (1) above for which occupancy rights have been granted under that subsection, as may be specified in the order;

(b)   if they are both entitled, or permitted by a third party, to occupy the house, until a further order of the court.

(5)   Nothing in this section shall prejudice the rights of any third party having an interest in the house referred to in subsection (1) above.

(6)   In this section—

'house' includes a caravan, houseboat or other structure in which the couple are cohabiting and any garden or other ground or building attached to, and usually occupied with, or otherwise required for the amenity or convenience of, the house, caravan, houseboat or other structure;

'occupancy rights' means the following rights of a non-entitled partner—

(a)   if in occupation, a right to [continue to occupy] the house [and, without prejudice to the generality of these rights, includes the right to continue to occupy or, as the case may be, to enter and occupy the house together with any child residing with the cohabiting couple];

(b)   if not in occupation, a right to enter into and occupy the house;

'entitled partner' includes a partner who is entitled, or permitted by a third party, to occupy the house along with an individual who is not the other partner only if that individual has waived his or her right of occupation in favour of the partner so entitled or permitted.

[Domestic interdicts]

[18A   Meaning of 'domestic interdict'
    (1)   In section 18B, 'domestic interdict' means—
        (a)   an interdict granted on the application of a person ('A') who is (or was) living with another person ('B') as if they were husband and wife against B for any of the purposes mentioned in subsection (2); or
        (b)   an interdict granted on the application of a person ('C') who is (or was) living with another person ('D') as if they were civil partners against D for any of the purposes mentioned in subsection (2).
    (2)   Those purposes are—
        (a)   restraining or prohibiting such conduct of the defender towards—
            (i)   the pursuer; or
            (ii)   any child in the permanent or temporary care of the pursuer,
as the court may specify;
        (b)   prohibiting the defender from entering or remaining in—
            (i)   a family home occupied by the pursuer and the defender;
            (ii)   any other residence occupied by the pursuer;
            (iii)   any place of work of the pursuer;
            (iv)   any school attended by a child in the permanent or temporary care of the pursuer.
    (3)   In this section and in section 18B—
'family home' means, subject to subsection (4), any house, caravan, houseboat or other structure which has been provided or has been made available by the pursuer or the defender (or both of them) as (or has become) a family residence for them and includes any garden or other ground or building usually occupied with, or otherwise required for the amenity or convenience of, the house, caravan, houseboat or other structure; but does not include a residence provided or made available by any person for the pursuer or, as the case may be, the defender to reside in (whether or not with any child of the pursuer and the defender) separately from the defender or, as the case may be, the pursuer; and
'interdict' includes interim interdict.
    (4)   If the tenancy of a family home is transferred from a pursuer to a defender (or, as the case may be, from a defender to a pursuer) by agreement or under any enactment, the home shall, on such transfer, cease to be a family home.
    (5)   In subsection (3), 'child of the pursuer and the defender' includes any child or grandchild of the pursuer or the defender, and any person who has been brought up or treated by the pursuer or the defender as if the person were a child of the pursuer or, as the case may be, the defender, whatever the age of such a child, grandchild or person.]

[18B   Domestic interdicts: further provision
    (1)   Subsection (2) applies if the defender—
        (a)   is entitled to occupy a family home;
        (b)   is permitted by a third party to occupy it; or
        (c)   has, by virtue of section 18(1), occupancy rights in it.
    (2)   Except where subsection (3) applies, the court may not grant a domestic interdict prohibiting the defender from entering or remaining in the family home.
    (3)   This subsection applies if—
        (a)   the interdict is ancillary to an exclusion order; or
        (b)   an order under section 18(1) granting or extending occupancy rights is recalled.]

Miscellaneous and general

19 Rights of occupancy in relation to division and sale

Where a spouse brings an action for the division and sale of a matrimonial home which the spouses own in common, the court, after having regard to all the circumstances of the case including—

(a) the matters specified in paragraphs (a) to (d) of section 3(3) of this Act; and

(b) whether the spouse bringing the action offers or has offered to make available to the other spouse any suitable alternative accommodation,

may refuse to grant decree in that action or may postpone the granting of decree for such period as it may consider reasonable in the circumstances or may grant decree subject to such conditions as it may prescribe.

[. . .]

22 Interpretation

[(1)] In this Act—

'caravan' means a caravan which is mobile or affixed to the land;

'child of the family' includes any child or grandchild of either spouse, and any person who has been brought up or [treated] by either spouse as if he or she were a child of that spouse, whatever the age of such a child, grandchild or person may be;

'the court' means the Court of Session or the sheriff;

'furniture and plenishings' means any article situated in a matrimonial home which—

(a) is owned or hired by either spouse or is being acquired by either spouse under a hire-purchase agreement or conditional sale agreement; and

(b) is reasonably necessary to enable the home to be used as a family residence,

but does not include any vehicle, caravan or houseboat, or such other structure as is mentioned in the definition of 'matrimonial home';

'matrimonial home' means [subject to subsection (2)] any house, caravan, houseboat or other structure which has been provided or has been made available by one or both of the spouses as, or has become, a family residence and includes any garden or other ground or building [. . .] usually occupied with, or otherwise required for the amenity or convenience of, the house, caravan, houseboat or other structure [but does not include a residence provided or made available by [a person for one] spouse to reside in, whether with any child of the family or not, separately from the other spouse];

'occupancy rights' has, subject to section 18(6) of this Act, the meaning assigned by section 1(4) of this Act;

'the sheriff' includes the sheriff having jurisdiction in the district where the matrimonial home is situated;

'tenant' includes sub-tenant and a statutory tenant as defined in section 3 of the Rent (Scotland) Act [1984 and a statutory assured tenant as defined in section 16(1) of the Housing (Scotland) Act 1988] and 'tenancy' shall be construed accordingly;

'entitled spouse' and 'non-entitled spouse', subject to sections 6(2) and 12(2) of this Act, have the meanings respectively assigned to them by section 1 of this Act.

(2) If—

(a) the tenancy of a matrimonial home is transferred from one spouse to the other by agreement or under any enactment; and

(b) following the transfer, the spouse to whom the tenancy was transferred occupies the home but the other spouse does not,

the home shall, on such transfer, cease to be a matrimonial home.

23   Short title, commencement and extent

(1)   This Act may be cited as the Matrimonial Homes (Family Protection) (Scotland) Act 1981.

(2)   This Act (except this section) shall come into operation on such day as the Secretary of State may by order made by statutory instrument appoint, and different days may be so appointed for different provisions and for different purposes.

(3)   This Act extends to Scotland only.

ADMINISTRATION OF JUSTICE ACT 1982
(1982, c 53)

PART I
DAMAGES FOR PERSONAL INJURIES ETC

Abolition of certain claims for damages etc

1   Abolition of right to damages for loss of expectation of life

(1)   In an action under the law of England and Wales or the law of Northern Ireland for damages for personal injuries—

(a)   no damages shall be recoverable in respect of any loss of expectation of life caused to the injured person by the injuries; but

(b)   if the injured person's expectation of life has been reduced by the injuries, the court, in assessing damages in respect of pain and suffering caused by the injuries, shall take account of any suffering caused or likely to be caused to him by awareness that his expectation of life has been so reduced.

(2)   The reference in subsection (1)(a) above to damages in respect of loss of expectation of life does not include damages in respect of loss of income.

PART II
DAMAGES FOR PERSONAL INJURIES ETC—SCOTLAND

7   Damages in respect of services

Where a person (in this Part of this Act referred to as 'the injured person')—

(a)   has sustained personal injuries, or

(b)   has died in consequence of personal injuries sustained,

as a result of an act or omission of another person giving rise to liability in any person (in this Part of this Act referred to as 'the responsible person') to pay damages, the responsible person shall also be liable to pay damages in accordance with the provisions of sections 8 and 9 of this Act.

8   Services rendered to injured person

(1)   Where necessary services have been rendered to the injured person by a relative in consequence of the injuries in question, then, unless the relative has expressly agreed in the knowledge that an action for damages has been raised or is in contemplation that no payment should be made in respect of those services, the responsible person shall be liable to pay to the injured person by way of damages such sum as represents reasonable remuneration for those services and repayment of reasonable expenses incurred in connection therewith.

[(2)   The injured person shall be under an obligation to account to the relative for any damages recovered from the responsible person under subsection (1) above.

(3)   Where, at the date of an award of damages in favour of the injured person, it is likely that necessary services will, after that date, be rendered to him by a relative in consequence of the injuries in question, then, unless the relative has expressly agreed that no payment shall be made in respect of those services, the responsible person shall be liable to pay to the injured person by way of damages such sum as represents—

(a) reasonable remuneration for those services; and

(b) reasonable expenses which are likely to be incurred in connection there-with.

(4) The relative shall have no direct right of action in delict against the responsible person in respect of any services or expenses referred to in this section.]

9 Services to injured person's relative

(1) The responsible person shall be liable to pay to the injured person a reasonable sum by way of damages in respect of the inability of the injured person to render the personal services referred to in subsection (3) below.

(2) Where the injured person has died, any relative of his entitled to damages in respect of loss of support under section 1(3) of the Damages (Scotland) Act 1976 shall be entitled to include as a head of damage under that section a reasonable sum in respect of the loss to him of the personal services mentioned in subsection (3) below.

(3) The personal services referred to in subsections (1) and (2) above are personal services—

(a) which were or might have been expected to have been rendered by the injured person before the occurrence of the act or omission giving rise to liability,

(b) of a kind which, when rendered by a person other than a relative, would ordinarily be obtainable on payment, and

(c) which the injured person but for the injuries in question might have been expected to render gratuitously to a relative.

(4) Subject to subsection (2) above, the relative shall have no direct right of action in delict against the responsible person in respect of the personal services mentioned in subsection (3) above.

10 Assessment of damages for personal injuries

Subject to any agreement to the contrary, in assessing the amount of damages payable to the injured person in respect of personal injuries there shall not be taken into account so as to reduce that amount—

(a) any contractual pension or benefit (including any payment by a friendly society or trade union);

(b) any pension or retirement benefit payable from public funds other than any pension or benefit to which section 2(1) of the Law Reform (Personal Injuries) Act 1948 applies;

(c) any benefit payable from public funds, in respect of any period after the date of the award of damages, designed to secure to the injured person or any relative of his a minimum level of subsistence;

(d) any redundancy payment under the [Employment Rights Act 1996], or any payment made in circumstances corresponding to those in which a right to a redundancy payment would have accrued if [section 135] of that Act had applied;

(e) any payment made to the injured person or to any relative of his by the injured person's employer following upon the injuries in question where the recipient is under an obligation to reimburse the employer in the event of damages being recovered in respect of those injuries;

(f) subject to paragraph (iv) below, any payment of a benevolent character made to the injured person or to any relative of his by any person following upon the injuries in question;

but there shall be taken into account—

(i) any remuneration or earnings from employment;

(ii) any [contribution-based jobseeker's allowance (payable under the Jobseekers' Act 1995);]

(iii) any benefit referred to in paragraph (c) above payable in respect of any period prior to the date of the award of damages;

(iv) any payment of a benevolent character made to the injured person or to any relative of his by the responsible person following on the injuries in question, where such a payment is made directly and not through a trust or other fund from which the injured person or his relatives have benefited or may benefit.

13 Supplementary

(1) In this Part of this Act, unless the context otherwise requires—

'personal injuries' includes any disease or any impairment of a person's physical or mental condition [and injury resulting from defamation or any other verbal injury or other injury to reputation];

'relative', in relation to the injured person, means—

(a) the spouse or divorced spouse;

[(aa) the civil partner or former civil partner;]

(b) any person, not being the spouse of the injured person, who was, at the time of the act or omission giving rise to liability in the responsible person, living with the injured person as husband or wife;

[(ba) any person, not being the civil partner of the injured person, who was, at the time of the act or omission giving rise to liability in the responsible person, living with the injured person as the civil partner of the injured person;]

(c) any ascendant or descendant;

(d) any brother, sister, uncle or aunt; or any issue of any such person;

(e) any person accepted by the injured person as a child of his family.

In deducing any relationship for the purposes of the foregoing definition—

(a) any relationship by affinity shall be treated as a relationship by consanguinity; any relationship of the half blood shall be treated as a relationship of the whole blood; and the stepchild of any person shall be treated as his child; and

(b) [section 1(1) of the Law Reform (Parent and Child) (Scotland) Act 1986 shall apply; and any reference (however expressed) in this Act to a relative shall be construed accordingly].

(2) Any reference in this Part of this Act to a payment, benefit or pension shall be construed as a reference to any such payment, benefit or pension whether in cash or in kind.

(3) This Part of this Act binds the Crown.

LAW REFORM (HUSBAND AND WIFE) (SCOTLAND) ACT 1984
(1984, c 15)

Abolition of actions of breach of promise of marriage, adherence and enticement

1 Promise of marriage not an enforceable obligation

(1) No promise of marriage or agreement between two persons to marry one another shall have effect under the law of Scotland to create any rights or obligations; and no action for breach of any such promise or agreement may be brought in any court in Scotland, whatever the law applicable to the promise or agreement.

(2) This section shall have effect in relation to any promise made or agreement entered into before it comes into force, but shall not affect any action commenced before it comes into force.

2 Actions of adherence and enticement abolished

(1) No spouse shall be entitled to apply for a decree from any court in Scotland ordaining the other spouse to adhere.

(2) No person shall be liable in delict to any person by reason only of having induced the spouse of that person to leave or remain apart from that person.

(3)   This section shall not affect any action commenced before this Act comes into force.

Abolition of miscellaneous rules relating to husband and wife

3   Curatory after marriage
(1)   No married person shall, by reason only of minority, be subject to the curatory of his parent or of any person appointed by his parent.
[. . .]
(3)   Section 2 of the Married Women's Property (Scotland) Act 1920 (husband to be curator to his wife during her minority) is repealed.

4   Abolition of husband's right to choose matrimonial home
Any rule of law entitling the husband, as between husband and wife, to determine where the matrimonial home is to be, shall cease to have effect.

5   Abolition of certain rules relating to antenuptial marriage contracts
(1)   In relation to an antenuptial contract of marriage entered into after this Act comes into force—
    (a)   any rule of law enabling a woman to create an alimentary right in her own favour in respect of any property provided by her shall cease to have effect;
    (b)   any rule of law whereby the marriage is onerous consideration for any provision of the contract, shall cease to have effect.
(2)   Nothing in paragraph (b) of subsection (1) above shall affect the operation of any enactment relating to gifts in consideration of marriage.

6   Abolition of husband's remaining liability for wife's debts incurred before marriage
(1)   A husband shall not be liable, by reason only of being her husband, for any debts incurred by his wife before marriage.
(2)   Subsection (1) above shall have effect in relation to any such debts, whether incurred before or after this Act comes into force.
(3)   Section 4 of the Married Women's Property (Scotland) Act 1877 (liability of husband for wife's antenuptial debts limited to amount of property received through her) is repealed.

7   Abolition of *praepositura*
(1)   For the purpose of determining a husband's liability for any obligation incurred by his wife after this Act comes into force, a married woman shall not be presumed as a matter of law to have been placed by her husband in charge of his domestic affairs, and any rule of law to the contrary shall cease to have effect.
(2)   No warrant of inhibition or inhibition in whatever form may be granted at the instance of a husband for the purpose of cancelling his wife's authority to incur any obligation on his behalf.
(3)   No such inhibition granted before the date this Act comes into force shall be registered on or after that date, and any such inhibition registered before that date shall be treated as discharged on that date.

CHILD ABDUCTION ACT 1984
(1984, c 37)

PART II
OFFENCE UNDER LAW OF SCOTLAND

6   Offence in Scotland of parent, etc taking or sending child out of United Kingdom

(1)   Subject to subsections (4) and (5) below, a person connected with a child under the age of sixteen years commits an offence if he takes or sends the child out of the United Kingdom—

(a)   without the appropriate consent if there is in respect of the child—

(i)   an order of a court in the United Kingdom awarding custody of the child to any person [or naming any person as the person with whom the child is to live; or]

(ii)   an order of a court in England, Wales or Northern Ireland making the child a ward of court;

(b)   if there is in respect of the child an order of a court in the United Kingdom prohibiting the removal of the child from the United Kingdom or any part of it.

(2)   A person is connected with a child for the purposes of this section if—

(a)   he is a parent or guardian of the child; or

(b)   there is in force an order of a court in the United Kingdom awarding custody of the child to him [or naming him as the person with whom the child is to live] (whether solely or jointly with any other person); or

(c)   in the case of [a child whose parents are not and have never been married to one another], there are reasonable grounds for believing that he is the father of the child.

(3)   In this section, the 'appropriate consent' means—

(a)   in relation to a child to whom subsection (1)(a)(i) above applies—

(i)   the consent of each person

(a)   who is a parent or guardian of the child; or

(b)   to whom custody of the child has been awarded [or who is named as the person with whom the child is to live (whether the award is made, or the person so named is named] solely or jointly with any other person) by an order of a court in the United Kingdom; or

(ii)   the leave of that court;

(b)   in relation to a child to whom subsection (1)(a)(ii) above applies, the leave of the court which made the child a ward of court;

Provided that, in relation to a child to whom more than one order referred to in subsection (1)(a) above applies, the appropriate consent may be that of any court which has granted an order as referred to in the said subsection (1)(a); and where one of these orders is an order referred to in the said subsection (1)(a)(ii) no other person as referred to in paragraph (a)(i) above shall be entitled to give the appropriate consent.

(4)   In relation to a child to whom subsection (1)(a)(i) above applies, a person does not commit an offence by doing anything without the appropriate consent if—

(a)   he does it in the belief that each person referred to in subsection (3)(a)(i) above—

(i)   has consented; or

(ii)   would consent if he was aware of all the relevant circumstances; or

(b)   he has taken all reasonable steps to communicate with such other person but has been unable to communicate with him.

(5)   In proceedings against any person for an offence under this section it shall be a defence for that person to show that at the time of the alleged offence he had

no reason to believe that there was in existence an order referred to in subsection (1) above.

(6) For the purposes of this section—

(a)   a person shall be regarded as taking a child if he causes or induces the child to accompany him or any other person, or causes the child to be taken; and

(b)   a person shall be regarded as sending a child if he causes the child to be sent.

(7) In this section 'guardian' means a person appointed by deed or will or by order of a court of competent jurisdiction to be the guardian of a child.

7 Power of arrest
A constable may arrest without warrant any person whom he reasonably suspects of committing or having committed an offence under this Part of this Act.

8 Penalties and prosecutions
A person guilty of an offence under this Part of this Act shall be liable—

(a)   on summary conviction, to imprisonment for a term not exceeding three months or to a fine not exceeding the statutory maximum . . ., or both; or

(b)   on conviction on indictment, to imprisonment for a term not exceeding two years or to a fine, or both.

9 Proof and admissibility of certain documents
(1) For the purposes of this Part of this Act, a document duly authenticated which purports to be—

(a)   an order or other document issued by a court of the United Kingdom (other than a Scottish court) shall be sufficient evidence of any matter to which it relates;

(b)   a copy of such an order or other document shall be deemed without further proof to be a true copy unless the contrary is shown, and shall be sufficient evidence of any matter to which it relates.

(2) A document is duly authenticated for the purposes of—

(a)   subsection (1)(a) above if it purports to bear the seal of that court;

(b)   subsection (1)(b) above if it purports to be certified by any person in his capacity as a judge, magistrate or officer of that court to be a true copy.

10 Evidence
In any proceedings in relation to an offence under this Part of this Act it shall be presumed, unless the contrary is shown, that the child named in the order referred to in section 6(1) above, or in any copy thereof, is the child in relation to whom the proceedings have been taken.

MATRIMONIAL AND FAMILY PROCEEDINGS ACT 1984
(1984, c 42)

PART IV
FINANCIAL PROVISION IN SCOTLAND AFTER OVERSEAS DIVORCE ETC

28   Circumstances in which a Scottish court may entertain application for financial provision

(1)   Where parties to a marriage have been divorced in an overseas country, then, subject to subsection (4) below, if the jurisdictional requirements and the conditions set out in subsections (2) and (3) below respectively are satisfied, the court may entertain an application by one of the parties for an order for financial provision.

(2)   The jurisdictional requirements mentioned in subsection (1) above are that—

(a)   the applicant was domiciled or habitually resident in Scotland on the date when the application was made; and

(b)   the other party to the marriage—

(i)   was domiciled or habitually resident in Scotland on the date when the application was made; or

(ii)   was domiciled or habitually resident in Scotland when the parties last lived together as husband and wife; or

(iii)   on the date when the application was made, was an owner or tenant of, or had a beneficial interest in, property in Scotland which had at some time been a matrimonial home of the parties; and

(c)   where the court is the sheriff court, either—

(i)   one of the parties was, on the date when the application was made, habitually resident in the sheriffdom; or

(ii)   paragraph (b)(iii) above is satisfied in respect of property wholly or partially within the sheriffdom.

(3)   The conditions mentioned in subsection (1) above are that—

(a)   the divorce falls to be recognised in Scotland;

(b)   the other party to the marriage initiated the proceedings for divorce;

(c)   the application was made within five years after the date when the divorce took effect;

(d)   a court in Scotland would have had jurisdiction to entertain an action for divorce between the parties if such an action had been brought in Scotland immediately before the foreign divorce took effect;

(e)   the marriage had a substantial connection with Scotland; and

(f)   both parties are living at the time of the application.

(4)   Where the jurisdiction of the court to entertain proceedings under this Part of this Act would fall to be determined by reference to the jurisdictional requirements imposed by virtue of Part I of the Civil Jurisdiction and Judgments Act 1982 (implementation of certain European conventions) [or by virtue of Council Regulation (EC) No 44/2001 of 22nd December 2000 on jurisdiction and the recognition and enforcement of judgments in civil and commercial matters, as amended from time to time and as applied by the Agreement made on 19th October 2005 between the European Community and the Kingdom of Denmark on jurisdiction and the recognition and enforcement of judgments in civil and commercial matters (OJ No L 299 16.11.2005 at p 62)] then—

(a)   satisfaction of the requirements of subsection (2) above shall not obviate the need to satisfy the requirements imposed by virtue of [that Regulation or] Part I of that Act; and

(b)   satisfaction of the requirements imposed by virtue of [that Regulation or] Part I of that Act shall obviate the need to satisfy the requirements of subsection (2) above;

and the court shall entertain or not entertain the proceedings accordingly.

29   Disposal of application in Scotland

(1)   Subject to subsections (2) to (5) below, Scots law shall apply, with any necessary modifications, in relation to an application under section 28 above as it would apply if the application were being made in an action for divorce in Scotland.

(2)   In disposing of an application entertained by it under the said section 28, the court shall exercise its powers so as to place the parties, in so far as it is reasonable and practicable to do so, in the financial position in which they would have been if the application had been disposed of, in an action for divorce in Scotland, on the date on which the foreign divorce took effect.

(3)   In determining what is reasonable and practicable for the purposes of subsection (2) above, the court shall have regard in particular to—

(a)   the parties' resources, present and foreseeable at the date of disposal of the application;

(b)   any order made by a foreign court in or in connection with the divorce proceedings for the making of financial provision in whatever form, or the transfer of property, by one of the parties to the other; and

(c)   subsection (5) below.

(4)   Except where subsection (5) below applies, the court may make an order for an interim award of a periodical allowance where—

(a)   it appears from the applicant's averments that in the disposal of the application an order for financial provision is likely to be made; and

(b)   the court considers that such an interim award is necessary to avoid hardship to the applicant.

(5)   Where but for section 28(2)(b)(iii) above the court would not have jurisdiction to entertain the application, the court may make an order—

(a)   relating to the former matrimonial home or its furniture and plenishings; or

(b)   that the other party to the marriage shall pay to the applicant a capital sum not exceeding the value of that other party's interest in the former matrimonial home and its furniture and plenishings,

but shall not be entitled to make any other order for financial provision.

[29A   Application of Part IV to annulled marriages

This Part of this Act shall apply to an annulment, of whatever nature, of a purported marriage, as it applies to a divorce, and references to marriage and divorce shall be construed accordingly.]

30   Interpretation of Part IV

(1)   In the foregoing provisions of this Part of this Act unless the context otherwise requires—

'the court' means the Court of Session or the sheriff court;

'furniture and plenishings' has the meaning assigned by section 22 of the Matrimonial Homes (Family Protection) (Scotland) Act 1981;

'matrimonial home' has the meaning assigned by the said section 22;

'order for financial provision' means any one or more of the orders specified in [section 8(1) of the Family Law (Scotland) Act 1985] (financial provision) or an order under section 13 of the Matrimonial Homes (Family Protection) (Scotland) Act 1981 (transfer of tenancy of matrimonial home);

'overseas country' means a country or territory outside the British Islands; and

'tenant' has the meaning assigned by the said section 22.

(2)   Any reference in the foregoing provisions of this Part of this Act to a party to a marriage shall include a reference to a party to a marriage which has been terminated.

Aliment

1 Obligation of aliment

(1) From the commencement of this Act, an obligation of alimei by, and only by—

    (a)   a husband to his wife;

    (b)   a wife to her husband;

    [(bb) a partner in a civil partnership to the other partner,]

    (c)   a father or mother to his or her child;

    (d)   a person to a child (other than a child who has been boarded out with him by a local or other public authority or a voluntary organisation) who has been accepted by him as a child of his family.

(2) For the purposes of this Act, an obligation of aliment is an obligation to provide such support as is reasonable in the circumstances, having regard to the matters to which a court is required or entitled to have regard under section 4 of this Act in determining the amount of aliment to award in an action for aliment.

(3) Any obligation of aliment arising under a decree or by operation of law and subsisting immediately before the commencement of this Act shall, except insofar as consistent with this section, cease to have effect as from the commencement of this Act.

(4) Nothing in this section shall affect any arrears due under a decree at the date of termination or cessation of an obligation of aliment, nor any rule of law by which a person who is owed an obligation of aliment may claim aliment from the executor of a deceased person or from any person enriched by the succession to the estate of a deceased person.

(5) In subsection (1) above—

'child' means a person—

    (a)   under the age of 18 years; or

    (b)   over that age and under the age of 25 years who is reasonably and appropriately undergoing instruction at an educational establishment, or training for employment or for a trade, profession or vocation;

'husband' and 'wife' include the parties to a valid polygamous marriage.

2 Actions for aliment

(1) A claim for aliment only (whether or not expenses are also sought) may be made, against any person owing an obligation of aliment, in the Court of Session or the sheriff court.

(2) Unless the court considers it inappropriate in any particular case, a claim for aliment may also be made, against any person owing an obligation of aliment, in proceedings—

    (a)   for divorce, separation, declarator of marriage or declarator of nullity of marriage;

    [(aa) for dissolution of a civil partnership, separation of civil partners or declarator of nullity of a civil partnership,]

    (b)   relating to orders for financial provision;

    [(c)   concerning parental responsibilities or parental rights (within the meaning of sections 1(3) and 2(4) respectively of the Children (Scotland) Act 1995) or guardianship in relation to children;]

    (d)   concerning parentage or legitimacy;

    (e)   of any other kind, where the court considers it appropriate to include a claim for aliment.

(3) In this Act 'action for aliment' means a claim for aliment in proceedings referred to in subsection (1) or (2) above.

(4) An action for aliment may be brought—

(a)   by a person (including a child) to whom the obligation of aliment is owed;

(b)   by the curator bonis of an incapax;

(c)   on behalf of a child under the age of 18 years, by—

    (i)   the [parent or guardian] of the child;

    [. . .]

[(iii)   a person with whom the child lives or who is seeking a residence order (within the meaning of section 11(2)(c) of the Children (Scotland) Act 1995) in respect of the child.]

(5)   A woman (whether married or not) may bring an action for aliment on behalf of her unborn child as if the child had been born, but no such action shall be heard or disposed of prior to the birth of the child.

(6)   It shall be competent to bring an action for aliment, notwithstanding that the person for or on behalf of whom aliment is being claimed is living in the same household as the defender.

(7)   It shall be a defence to an action for aliment brought by virtue of subsection (6) above that the defender is fulfilling the obligation of aliment, and intends to continue doing so.

(8)   It shall be a defence to an action for aliment by or on behalf of a person other than a child under the age of 16 years that the defender is making an offer, which it is reasonable to expect the person concerned to accept, to receive that person into his household and to fulfil the obligation of aliment.

(9)   For the purposes of subsection (8) above, in considering whether it is reasonable to expect a person to accept an offer, the court shall have regard among other things to any conduct, decree or other circumstances which appear to the court to be relevant: but the fact that a husband and wife [or the partners in a civil partnership] have agreed to live apart shall not of itself be regarded as making it unreasonable to expect a person to accept such an offer.

(10)   A person bringing an action for aliment under subsection (4)(c) above may give a good receipt for aliment paid under the decree in the action.

3   Powers of court in action for aliment

(1)   The court may, if it thinks fit, grant decree in an action for aliment, and in granting such decree shall have power—

(a)   to order the making of periodical payments, whether for a definite or an indefinite period or until the happening of a specified event;

(b)   to order the making of alimentary payments of an occasional or special nature, including payments in respect of inlying, funeral or educational expenses;

(c)   to backdate an award of aliment under this Act—

    (i)   to the date of the bringing of the action or to such later date as the court thinks fit; or

    (ii)   on special cause shown, to a date prior to the bringing of the action;

(d)   to award less than the amount claimed even if the claim is undisputed.

(2)   Nothing in subsection (1) above shall empower the court to substitute a lump sum for a periodical payment.

4   Amount of aliment

(1)   In determining the amount of aliment to award in an action for aliment, the court shall, subject to subsection (3) below, have regard—

(a)   to the needs and resources of the parties;

(b)   to the earning capacities of the parties;

(c)   generally to all the circumstances of the case.

(2)   Where two or more parties owe an obligation of aliment to another person, there shall be no order of liability, but the court, in deciding how much, if any, aliment to award against any of those persons, shall have regard, among the other circumstances of the case, to the obligation of aliment owed by any other person.

(3)   In having regard under subsection (1)(c) above generally to all the circumstances of the case, the court—

(a)   may, if it thinks fit, take account of any support, financial or otherwise, given by the defender to any person whom he maintains as a dependant in his household, whether or not the defender owes an obligation of aliment to that person; and

(b)   shall not take account of any conduct of a party unless it would be manifestly inequitable to leave it out of account.

[(4)   Where a court makes an award of aliment in an action brought by or on behalf of a child under the age of 16 years, it may include in that award such provision as it considers to be in all the circumstances reasonable in respect of the expenses incurred wholly or partly by the person having care of the child for the purpose of caring for the child.]

5   Variation or recall of decree of aliment

(1)   A decree granted in an action for aliment brought before or after the commencement of this Act may, on an application by or on behalf of either party to the action, be varied or recalled by an order of the court if since the date of the decree there has been a material change of circumstances.

[(1A)   Without prejudice to the generality of subsection (1) above, the making of a [maintenance calculation] with respect to a child for whom the decree of aliment was granted is a material change of circumstances for the purposes of that subsection.]

(2)   The provisions of this Act shall apply to applications and orders under subsection (1) above as they apply to actions for aliment and decrees in such actions, subject to any necessary modifications.

(3)   On an application under subsection (1) above, the court may, pending determination of the application, make such interim order as it thinks fit.

(4)   Where the court backdates an order under subsection (1) above, the court may order any sums paid under the decree to be repaid.

6   Interim aliment

(1)   A claim for interim aliment shall be competent—

(a)   in an action for aliment, by the [person] who claims aliment against the other [person];

(b)   in an action for divorce, separation, declarator of marriage or declarator of nullity of marriage, by either party against the other party,

[(c)   in an action for dissolution of a civil partnership, separation of civil partners or declarator of nullity of a civil partnership, by either partner against the other partner,]

on behalf of the claimant and any person on whose behalf he is entitled to act under section 2(4) of this Act.

(2)   Where a claim under subsection (1) above has been made, then, whether or not the claim is disputed, the court may award by way of interim aliment the sum claimed or any lesser sum or may refuse to make such an award.

(3)   An award under subsection (2) above shall consist of an award of periodical payments payable only until the date of the disposal of the action in which the award was made or such earlier date as the court may specify.

(4)   An award under [this section] may be varied or recalled by an order of the court; and the provisions of this section shall apply to an award so varied and the claim therefor as they applied to the original award and the claim therefor.

7   Agreements on aliment

(1)   Any provision in an agreement which purports to exclude future liability for aliment or to restrict any right to bring an action for aliment shall have no effect unless the provision was fair and reasonable in all the circumstances of the agreement at the time it was entered into.

(2)   Where a person who owes an obligation of aliment to another person has entered into an agreement to pay aliment to or for the benefit of the other person,

on a material change of circumstances application may be made to the court by or on behalf of either person for variation of the amount payable under the agreement or for termination of the agreement.

[(2ZA)   On an application under subsection (2) above, the court may—

(a)   pending determination of the application, make such interim order as it thinks fit;

(b)   make an order backdating a variation of the amount payable under the agreement to—

(i)   the date of the application or such later date as the court thinks fit; or

(ii)   on special cause shown, a date prior to the date of the application.

(2ZB)   Where the court makes an order under subsection (2ZA)(b) above, it may order any sums paid under the agreement to be repaid on such terms (including terms relating to repayment by instalments) as the court thinks fit.

(2ZC)   Nothing in subsection (2ZA) shall empower the court to substitute a lump sum for a periodical payment.]

[(2A)   Without prejudice to the generality of subsection (2) above, the making of a [maintenance calculation] with respect to a child to whom or for whose benefit aliment is payable under such an agreement is a material change of circumstances for the purposes of that subsection.]

(3)   Subsections (8) and (9) of section 2 of this Act (which afford a defence to an action for aliment in certain circumstances) shall apply to an action to enforce such an agreement as is referred to in subsection (2) above as they apply to an action for aliment.

(4)   In [this section] 'the court' means the court which would have jurisdiction and competence to entertain an action for aliment between the parties to the agreement to which the application under that subsection relates.

(5)   In this section 'agreement' means an agreement entered into before or after the commencement of this Act and includes a unilateral voluntary obligation.

Financial provision on divorce, etc

8   Orders for financial provision

(1)   In an action for divorce, either party to the marriage [and in an action for dissolution of a civil partnership, either partner] may apply to the court for one or more of the following orders—

(a)   an order for the payment of a capital sum [. . .] to him by the other party to the marriage;

[(aa)   an order for the transfer of property to him by the other party to the marriage;]

(b)   an order for the making of a periodical allowance to him by the other party to the marriage;

[(ba)   an order under section 12A(2) or (3) of this Act;

(baa)   a pension sharing order;]

(c)   an incidental order within the meaning of section 14(2) of this Act.

(2)   Subject to sections 12 to 15 of this Act, where an application has been made under subsection (1) above, the court shall make such order, if any, as is—

(a)   justified by the principles set out in section 9 of this Act; and

(b)   reasonable having regard to the resources of the parties.

(3)   An order under subsection (2) above is in this Act referred to as an 'order for financial provision'.

[(4)   The court shall not, in the same proceedings, make both a pension sharing order and an order under section 12A(2) or (3) of this Act in relation to the same pension arrangement.

[(4A)   The court shall not make a pension sharing order, or an order under section 12A(2) or (3) of this Act, in relation to matrimonial property, or partnership property, consisting of compensation such as is mentioned in section 10(5A).]

(5)   Where, as regards a pension arrangement, the parties to a marriage [or the partners in a civil partnership] have in effect a qualifying agreement which contains a term relating to pension sharing, the court shall not—

(a)   make an order under section 12A(2) or (3) of this Act; or

(b)   make a pension sharing order,

relating to the arrangement unless it also sets aside the agreement or term under section 16(1)(b) of this Act.

(6)   The court shall not make a pension sharing order in relation to the rights of a person under a pension arrangement if there is in force an order under section 12A(2) or (3) of this Act which relates to benefits or future benefits to which he is entitled under the pension arrangement.

(7)   In subsection (5) above—

(a)   'term relating to pension sharing' shall be construed in accordance with section 16(2A) of this Act; and

(b)   'qualifying agreement' has the same meaning as in section 28(3) of the Welfare Reform and Pensions Act 1999.]

[8A   Pension sharing orders: apportionment of charges

If a pension sharing order relates to rights under a pension arrangement, the court may include in the order provision about the apportionment between the parties of any charge under section 41 of the Welfare Reform and Pensions Act 1999 (charges in respect of pension sharing costs) or under corresponding Northern Ireland legislation.]

9   Principles to be applied

(1)   The principles which the court shall apply in deciding what order for financial provision, if any, to make are that—

(a)   the net value of the matrimonial property should be shared fairly between the parties to the marriage [or as the case may be the net value of the partnership property should be so shared between the partners in the civil partnership];

(b)   fair account should be taken of any economic advantage derived by either [person] from contributions by the other, and of any economic disadvantage suffered by either [person] in the interests of the other [person] or of the family;

(c)   any economic burden of caring should be shared fairly between the [persons]—

[(i)]   after divorce, for a child of the marriage under the age of 16 years;

[(ii)   after dissolution of the civil partnership, for a child under that age who has been accepted by both partners as a child of the family [or in respect of whom they are, by virtue of sections 33 and 42 of the Human Fertilisation and Embryology Act 2008, the parents],]

(d)   a [person] who has been dependent to a substantial degree on the financial support of the other [person] should be awarded such financial provision as is reasonable to enable him to adjust, over a period of not more than three years from—

[(i)]   the date of the decree of divorce, to the loss of that support on divorce;

[(ii)   the date of the decree of dissolution of the civil partnership, to the loss of that support on dissolution,]

(e)   a [person] who at the time of the divorce [or of the dissolution of the civil partnership] seems likely to suffer serious financial hardship as a result of the divorce [or dissolution] should be awarded such financial provision as is reasonable to relieve him of hardship over a reasonable period.

(2)   In subsection (1)(b) above and section 11(2) of this Act—

'economic advantage' means advantage gained whether before or during the marriage [or civil partnership] and includes gains in capital, in income and in earning capacity, and 'economic disadvantage' shall be construed accordingly;

'contributions' means contributions made whether before or during the marriage [or civil partnership]; and includes indirect and non-financial contributions and, in particular, any such contribution made by looking after the family home or caring for the family.

10 Sharing of value of matrimonial property [or partnership property]

(1)   In applying the principle set out in section 9(1)(a) of this Act, the net value of the matrimonial property [or partnership property] shall be taken to be shared fairly between the [persons] when it is shared equally or in such other proportions as are justified by special circumstances.

(2)   [Subject to subsection (3A) below,] the net value of the [. . .] property shall be the value of the property at the relevant date after deduction of any debts incurred by [one or both of the parties to the marriage or as the case may be of the partners]—

(a)   before the marriage so far as they relate to the matrimonial property [or before the registration of the partnership so far as they relate to the partnership property], and

(b)   during the marriage [or partnership],

which are outstanding at that date.

(3)   In this section 'the relevant date' means whichever is the earlier of—

(a)   subject to subsection (7) below, the date on which the [persons] ceased to cohabit;

(b)   the date of service of the summons in the action for divorce [or for dissolution of the civil partnership].

[(3A)   In its application to property transferred by virtue of an order under section 8(1)(aa) of this Act this section shall have effect as if—

(a)   in subsection (2) above, for 'relevant date' there were substituted 'appropriate valuation date';

(b)   after that subsection there were inserted—

'(2A)   Subject to subsection (2B), in this section the "appropriate valuation date" means—

(a)   where the parties to the marriage or, as the case may be, the partners agree on a date, that date;

(b)   where there is no such agreement, the date of the making of the order under section 8(1)(aa).

(2B)   If the court considers that, because of the exceptional circumstances of the case, subsection (2A)(b) should not apply, the appropriate valuation date shall be such other date (being a date as near as may be to the date referred to in subsection (2A)(b)) as the court may determine.'; and

(c)   subsection (3) did not apply.]

(4)   Subject to [subsections (5) and (5A)] below, in this section and in section 11 of this Act 'the matrimonial property' means all the property belonging to the parties or either of them at the relevant date which was acquired by them or him (otherwise than by way of gift or succession from a third party)—

(a)   before the marriage for use by them as a family home or as furniture or plenishings for such home; or

(b)   during the marriage but before the relevant date.

[(4A)   Subject to [subsections (5) and (5A)] below, in this section and in section 11 of this Act 'the partnership property' means all the property belonging to the partners or either of them at the relevant date which was acquired by them or by one of them (otherwise than by way of gift or succession from a third party)—

(a)   before the registration of the partnership for use by them as a family home.or as furniture or plenishings for such a home, or

(b)   during the partnership but before the relevant date.]

(5)   The proportion of any rights or interests of either [person]—

[(a)]   under a life policy [. . .] or similar arrangement [; and

(b)   in any benefits under a pension arrangement which either [person] has or may have (including such benefits payable in respect of the death of either [person]),

[. . .]

which is] referable to the period to which subsection (4)(b) [or (4A)(b)] above refers shall be taken to form part of the matrimonial property [or partnership property].

[(5A)   Where either person is entitled to compensation payable under Chapter 3 of Part 2 of the Pensions Act 2004 or any provision in force in Northern Ireland corresponding to that Chapter, the proportion of the compensation which is referable to the period to which subsection (4)(b) or (4A)(b) above refers shall be taken to form part of the matrimonial property or partnership property.]

(6)   In subsection (1) above 'special circumstances', without prejudice to the generality of the words, may include—

(a)   the terms of any agreement between the [persons] on the ownership or division of any of the matrimonial property [or partnership property];

(b)   the source of the funds or assets used to acquire any of the matrimonial property [or partnership property] where those funds or assets were not derived from the income or efforts of the [persons] during the marriage [or partnership];

(c)   any destruction, dissipation or alienation of property by either [person];

(d)   the nature of the [family] property [or partnership property], the use made of it (including use for business purposes or as a [family] home) and the extent to which it is reasonable to expect it to be realised or divided or used as security;

(e)   the actual or prospective liability for any expenses of valuation or transfer of property in connection with the divorce [or the dissolution of the civil partnership].

(7)   For the purposes of subsection (3) above no account shall be taken of any cessation of cohabitation where the [persons] thereafter resumed cohabitation, except where the [persons] ceased to cohabit for a continuous period of 90 days or more before resuming cohabitation for a period or periods of less than 90 days in all.

[(8)   The Secretary of State may by regulations make provision about calculation and verification in relation to the valuation for the purposes of this Act of benefits under a pension arrangement or relevant state scheme rights.]

[(8A)   Regulations under subsection (8) above may include—

(a)   provision for calculation or verification in accordance with guidance from time to time prepared by a prescribed person; and

(b)   provision by reference to regulations under section 30 or 49(4) of the Welfare Reform and Pensions Act 1999.]

[(8B)   The Scottish Ministers may by regulations make provision for the purposes of this Act about—

(a)   calculation and verification of PPF compensation;

(b)   apportionment of PPF compensation.

(8C)   Regulations under subsection (8B) may include provision—

(a)   for calculation of verification in a manner approved by a prescribed person,

(b)   by reference to regulations under section 112 of the Pensions Act 2008.]

(9)   Regulations under subsection (8) [or (8B)] above [may make different provision for different purposes and] shall be made by statutory instrument which shall be subject to annulment in pursuance of a resolution of either House of Parliament.

11 Factors to be taken into account

(1)   In applying the principles set out in section 9 of this Act, the following provisions of this section shall have effect.

(2)   For the purposes of section 9(1)(b) of this Act, the court shall have regard to the extent to which—

(a)   the economic advantages or disadvantages sustained by either [person] have been balanced by the economic advantages or disadvantages sustained by the other [person], and

(b)   any resulting imbalance has been or will be corrected by a sharing of the value of the matrimonial property [or the partnership property] or otherwise.

(3)   For the purposes of section 9(1)(c) of this Act, the court shall have regard to—

(a)   any decree or arrangement for aliment for the child;

(b)   any expenditure or loss of earning capacity caused by the need to care for the child;

(c)   the need to provide suitable accommodation for the child;

(d)   the age and health of the child;

(e)   the educational, financial and other circumstances of the child;

(f)   the availability and cost of suitable child-care facilities or services;

(g)   the needs and resources of the [persons]; and

(h)   all the other circumstances of the case.

(4)   For the purposes of section 9(1)(d) of this Act, the court shall have regard to—

(a)   the age, health and earning capacity of the [person] who is claiming the financial provision;

(b)   the duration and extent of the dependence of that [person prior to divorce or to the dissolution of the civil partnership];

(c)   any intention of that [person] to undertake a course of education or training;

(d)   the needs and resources of the [persons]; and

(e)   all the other circumstances of the case.

(5)   For the purposes of section 9(1)(e) of this Act, the court shall have regard to—

(a)   the age, health and earning capacity of the [person] who is claiming the financial provision;

(b)   the duration of the marriage [or of the civil partnership];

(c)   the standard of living of the [persons] during the marriage [or civil partnership];

(d)   the needs and resources of the [persons]; and

(e)   all the other circumstances of the case.

(6)   In having regard under subsections (3) to (5) above to all the other circumstances of the case, the court may, if it thinks fit, take account of any support, financial or otherwise, given by the [person] who is to make the financial provision to any person whom he maintains as a dependant in his household whether or not he owes an obligation of aliment to that person.

(7)   In applying the principles set out in section 9 of this Act, the court shall not take account of the conduct of either party [to the marriage or as the case may be of either partner] unless—

(a)   the conduct has adversely affected the financial resources which are relevant to the decision of the court on a claim for financial provision; or

(b)   in relation to section 9(1)(d) or (e), it would be manifestly inequitable to leave the conduct out of account.

12 Orders for payment of capital sum or transfer of property

(1)   An order under section 8(2) of this Act for payment of a capital sum or transfer of property may be made—

    (a)   on granting decree of divorce [or of dissolution of a civil partnership]; or

    (b)   within such period as the court on granting [the decree] may specify.

    (2)   The court, on making an order referred to in subsection (1) above, may stipulate that it shall come into effect at a specified future date.

    (3)   The court, on making an order under section 8(2) of this Act for payment of a capital sum, may order that the capital sum shall be payable by instalments.

    (4)   Where an order referred to in subsection (1) above has been made, the court may, on an application by—

    [(a)]   either party to the marriage;

    [(b)   either partner,]

on a material change of circumstances, vary the date or method of payment of the capital sum or the date of transfer of property.

[12A   Orders for payment of capital sum: pensions lump sums

    (1)   This section applies where the court makes an order under section 8(2) of this Act for payment of a capital sum (a 'capital sum order') by a party to the marriage [or a partner in a civil partnership ('the liable person')] in circumstances where—

    (a)   the matrimonial property [or the partnership property] within the meaning of section 10 of this Act includes any rights or interests in benefits under a pension [arrangement] which the liable [person] has or may have (whether such benefits are payable to him or in respect of his death); and

    (b)   those benefits include a lump sum payable to him or in respect of his death.

    (2)   Where the benefits referred to in subsection (1) above include a lump sum payable to the liable [person] the court, on making the capital sum order, may make an order requiring the [person responsible for the pension arrangement] in question to pay the whole or part of that sum, when it becomes due, to the other party to the marriage [or as the case may be to the other partner ('the other person')].

    (3)   Where the benefits referred to in subsection (1) above include a lump sum payable in respect of the death of the liable [person], the court, on making the capital sum order, may make an order—

    (a)   if the [person responsible for the pension arrangement in question has] power to determine the person to whom the sum, or any part of it, is to be paid, requiring them to pay the whole or part of that sum, when it becomes due, to the other [person];

    (b)   if the liable [person] has power to nominate the person to whom the sum, or any part of it, is to be paid, requiring the liable [person] to nominate the other [person] in respect of the whole or part of that sum;

    (c)   in any other case, requiring the [person responsible for the pension arrangement] in question to pay the whole or part of that sum, when it becomes due, to the other [person] instead of to the person to whom, apart from the order, it would be paid.

    (4)   Any payment by the [person responsible for the pension agreement] under an order under subsection (2) or (3) above—

    (a)   shall discharge so much of the [liability of the person responsible for the pension arrangement] to or in respect of the liable [person] as corresponds to the amount of the payment; and

    (b)   shall be treated for all purposes as a payment made by the liable [person] in or towards the discharge of his liability under the capital sum order.

    (5)   Where the liability of the liable [person] under the capital sum order has been discharged in whole or in part, other than by a payment by the [person responsible for the pension arrangement] under an order under subsection (2) or (3) above, the court may, on an application by any person having an interest, recall any order under either of those subsections or vary the amount specified in such an order, as appears to the court appropriate in the circumstances.

(6)   Where—

(a)   an order under subsection (2) or (3) above imposes any requirement on the [person responsible for a pension arrangement] ('the first [arrangement]') and the liable [person] acquires transfer credits under another [arrangement] ('the new [arrangement]') which are derived (directly or indirectly) from a transfer from the first [arrangement] of all his accrued rights under that [arrangement]; and

(b)   [the person responsible for the new arrangement has] been given notice in accordance with regulations under subsection (8) below,

the order shall have effect as if it had been made instead in respect of the [person responsible for the new arrangement]; and in this subsection 'transfer credits' has the same meaning as in the Pension Schemes Act 1993.

(7)   Without prejudice to subsection (6) above, any court may, on an application by any person having an interest, vary an order under subsection (2) or (3) above by substituting for [the person responsible for the pension arrangement] specified in the order [person responsible for any other pension arrangement] under which any lump sum referred to in subsection (1) above is payable to the liable [person] or in respect of his death.

[(7ZA)   Subsection (7ZB) applies where a right under an occupational pension scheme to payment of a lump sum in respect of death would, but for the provisions of Chapter 3 of Part 2 of the Pensions Act 2004 (c 35), arise during an assessment period (within the meaning of section 132 of that Act).

(7ZB)   An order under subsection (3) shall not take effect until the assessment period comes to an end for a reason other than the giving of a transfer notice under section 160 of that Act.

(7ZC)   Notwithstanding the provisions of section 8(4A), for the purpose only of giving effect to subsection (7), the court may deal with an order under subsection (2) so that it—

(a)   is addressed to the Board of the Pension Protection Fund instead of the person responsible for a pension arrangement; and

(b)   takes effect in respect of an entitlement to compensation payable under Chapter 3 of Part 2 of the Pensions Act 2004 or the Northern Ireland provision, instead of rights in relation to any lump sum referred to in subsection (1) which is payable to the liable party.

(7A)   Where—

(a)   the court makes an order under subsection (3); and

(b)   after the making of the order the Board gives the trustees or managers of the scheme a notice under section 160 of the Pensions Act 2004 ('the 2004 Act'), or the Northern Ireland provision, in relation to the scheme,

the order shall, on the giving of such notice, be recalled.

(7B)   Subsection (7C) applies where—

(a)   the court makes an order under subsection (2) imposing requirements on the trustees or managers of an occupational pension scheme; and

(b)   after the making of the order the Board gives the trustees or managers of the scheme a notice under section 160 of the 2004 Act, or the Northern Ireland provision, in relation to the scheme.

(7C)   The order shall have effect from the time when the notice is given—

(a)   as if—

(i)   references to the trustees or managers of the scheme were references to the Board; and

(ii)   references to any lump sum to which the person with benefits under a pension arrangement is or might become entitled under the scheme were references to the amount of any compensation payable under that Chapter of the 2004 Act, or the Northern Ireland provision, to which that person is or might become entitled in respect of the lump sum; and

(b)   subject to such other modifications as may be prescribed by regulations by the Scottish Ministers.]

(8)   The Secretary of State may by regulations—

(a)   require notices to be given in respect of changes of circumstances relevant to orders under subsection (2) or (3) above.

[. . .]

(9)   Regulations under [subsections (7C)(b) and] (8) above shall be made by statutory instrument which shall be subject to annulment in pursuance of a resolution of either House of Parliament.

[(10)   The definition of 'benefits under a pension scheme' in section 27 of this Act does not apply to this section.

(11)   In subsections (7A) to (7C) 'the Northern Ireland provision', in relation to a provision of the 2004 Act, means any provision in force in Northern Ireland corresponding to the provision of that Act.]

13   Orders for periodical allowance

(1)   An order under section 8(2) of this Act for a periodical allowance may be made—

(a)   on granting decree of divorce [or of dissolution of a civil partnership];

(b)   within such period as the court on granting [the decree] may specify; or

(c)   after [such decree] where—

(i)   no such order has been made previously;

(ii)   application for the order has been made after the date of decree; and

(iii)   since the date of decree there has been a change of circumstances.

(2)   The court shall not make an order for a periodical allowance under section 8(2) of this Act unless—

(a)   the order is justified by a principle set out in paragraph (c), (d) or (e) of section 9(1) of this Act; and

(b)   it is satisfied that an order for payment of a capital sum or for transfer of property [or a pension sharing order] under that section would be inappropriate or insufficient to satisfy the requirements of the said section 8(2).

(3)   An order under section 8(2) of this Act for a periodical allowance may be for a definite or an indefinite period or until the happening of a specified event.

(4)   Where an order for a periodical allowance has been made under section 8(2) of this Act, and since the date of the order there has been a material change of circumstances, the court shall, on an application by or on behalf of either party to the marriage or his executor [, or as the case may be either partner or his executor], have power by subsequent order—

(a)   to vary or recall the order for a periodical allowance;

(b)   to backdate such variation or recall to the date of the application therefor or, on cause shown, to an earlier date;

(c)   to convert the order into an order for payment of a capital sum or for a transfer of property.

[(4A)   Without prejudice to the generality of subsection (4) above, the making of a maintenance [calculation] with respect to a child who has his home with a person to whom the periodical allowance is made (being a child to whom the person making the allowance has an obligation of aliment) is a material change of circumstances for the purposes of that subsection.]

(5)   The provisions of this Act shall apply to applications and orders under subsection (4) above as they apply to applications for periodical allowance and orders on such applications.

(6)   Where the court backdates an order under subsection (4)(b) above, the court may order any sums paid by way of periodical allowance to be repaid.

(7)   An order for a periodical allowance made under section 8(2) of this Act—

(a)   shall, if subsisting at the death of the [person] making the payment, continue to operate against that [person's] estate, but without prejudice to the making of an order under subsection (4) above;

[(b)   shall cease to have effect on the person receiving payment—
        (i)   marrying,
        (ii)   entering into a civil partnership,
        (iii)   dying,]
except in relation to any arrears due under it.

14   Incidental orders

(1)   Subject to subsection (3) below, an incidental order may be made under section 8(2) of this Act before, on or after the granting or refusal of decree of divorce [or of dissolution of a civil partnership].

(2)   In this Act, 'an incidental order' means one or more of the following orders—

(a)   an order for the sale of property;

(b)   an order for the valuation of property;

(c)   an order determining any dispute between the parties to the marriage [or as the case may be the partners] as to their respective property rights by means of a declarator thereof or otherwise;

(d)   an order regulating the occupation of—
        [(i)]   the matrimonial home; or
        [(ii)   the family home of the partnership,]
or the use of furniture and plenishings therein or excluding either [person] from such occupation;

(e)   an order regulating liability, as between the [persons], for outgoings in respect of—
        [(i)]   the matrimonial home; or
        (ii)   the family home of the partnership,]
or furniture or plenishings therein;

(f)   an order that security shall be given for any financial provision;

(g)   an order that payments shall be made or property transferred to any curator bonis or trustee or other person for the benefit of the [person] by whom or on whose behalf application has been made under section 8(1) of this Act for an incidental order;

(h)   an order setting aside or varying any term in an antenuptial or postnuptial marriage settlement [or in any corresponding settlement in respect of the civil partnership];

(j)   an order as to the date from which any interest on any amount awarded shall run;

[(ja)   in relation to a deed relating to moveable property, an order dispensing with the execution of the deed by the grantor and directing the sheriff clerk to execute the deed;]

(k)   any ancillary order which is expedient to give effect to the principles set out in section 9 of this Act or to any order made under section 8(2) of this Act.

(3)   An incidental order referred to in subsection (2)(d) or (e) above may be made only on or after the granting of [the decree].

(4)   An incidental order may be varied or recalled by subsequent order on cause shown.

(5)   So long as an incidental order granting a party to a marriage the right to occupy a matrimonial home or the right to use furniture and plenishings therein remains in force then—

(a)   section 2(1), (2), (5)(a) and (9) of the Matrimonial Homes (Family Protection) (Scotland) Act 1981 (which confer certain general powers of management on a spouse in relation to a matrimonial home), and

(b)   subject to section 15(3) of this Act, section 12 of the said Act of 1981 and

section [41 of the Bankruptcy (Scotland) Act 1985] (which protect the occupancy rights of a spouse against arrangements intended to defeat them),
shall, except to the extent that the order otherwise provides, apply in relation to the order—

    (i)   as if that party were a non-entitled spouse and the other party were an entitled spouse within the meaning of section 1(1) or 6(2) of the said Act of 1981 as the case may require;

    (ii)   as if the right to occupy a matrimonial home under that order were 'occupancy rights' with the meaning of the said Act of 1981; and

    (iii)   with any other necessary modifications; and

subject to section 15(3) of this Act, section 11 of the said Act of 1981 (protection of spouse in relation to furniture and plenishings) shall apply in relation to the order as if that party were a spouse within the meaning of the said section 11 and the order were an order under section 3(3) or (4) of the said Act of 1981.

[(5A)   So long as an incidental order granting a partner in a civil partnership the right to occupy a family home or the right to use furnishings and plenishings therein remains in force then—

    (a)   section 102(1), (2), (5)(a) and (9) of the Civil Partnership Act 2004, and

    (b)   subject to section 15(3) of this Act, section 111 of that Act,

shall, except to the extent that the order otherwise provides, apply in relation to the order in accordance with subsection (5B).

(5B)   Those provisions apply—

    (a) as if that partner were a non-entitled partner and the other partner were an entitled partner within the meaning of section 101 or 106(2) of that Act as the case may require,

    (b)   as if the right to occupy a family home under that order were a right specified in paragraph (a) or (b) of section 101(1) of that Act, and

    (c)   with any other necessary modification.]

(6)   In subsection (2)(h) above, 'settlement' includes a settlement by way of a policy of assurance to which section 2 of the Married Women's Policies of Assurance (Scotland) Act 1880 relates.

(7)   Notwithstanding subsection (1) above, the Court of Session may by Act of Sederunt make rules restricting the categories of incidental order which may be made under section 8(2) of this Act before the granting of decree of divorce.

15 Rights of third parties

(1)   The court shall not make an order under section 8(2) of this Act for the transfer of property if the consent of a third party which is necessary under any obligation, enactment or rule of law has not been obtained.

(2)   The court shall not make an order under section 8(2) of this Act for the transfer of property subject to security without the consent of the creditor unless he has been given an opportunity of being heard by the court.

(3)   Neither an incidental order, nor any rights conferred by such an order, shall prejudice any rights of any third party insofar as those rights existed immediately before the making of the order.

16 Agreements on financial provision

(1)   Where the parties to a marriage [or the partners in a civil partnership] have entered into an agreement as to financial provision to be made on divorce [or on dissolution of the civil partnership], the court may make an order setting aside or varying—

    (a)   any term of the agreement relating to a periodical allowance where the agreement expressly provides for the subsequent setting aside or variation by the court of that term; or

    (b)   the agreement or any term of it where the agreement was not fair and reasonable at the time it was entered into.

(2)   The court may make an order—

(a)   under subsection (1)(a) above at any time after granting decree of divorce; and

[(b)   under subsection (1)(b) above, if the agreement does not contain a term relating to pension sharing, on granting decree of divorce [or of dissolution of the civil partnership] or within such time as the court may specify, on granting decree of divorce [or of dissolution of the civil partnership]; or

(c)   under subsection (1)(b) above, if the agreement contains a term relating to pension sharing—

(i)   where the order sets aside the agreement or sets aside or varies the term relating to pension sharing, on granting decree of divorce; and

(ii)   where the order sets aside or varies any other term of the agreement, on granting decree of divorce or within such time thereafter as the court may specify on granting decree of divorce.]

[(2A)   In subsection (2) above, a term relating to pension sharing is a term corresponding to provision which may be made in a pension sharing order and satisfying the requirements set out in section 28(1)(f) or 48(1)(f) of the Welfare Reform and Pensions Act 1999.

(2B)   Subsection (2C) applies where—

(a)   the parties to a marriage or the partners in a civil partnership have entered into an agreement as to financial provision to be made on divorce or on dissolution of the civil partnership; and

(b)   the agreement includes provision in respect of a person's rights or interests or benefits under an occupational pension scheme.

(2C)   The Board of the Pension Protection Fund's subsequently assuming responsibility for the occupational pension scheme in accordance with Chapter 3 of Part 2 of the Pension Act 2004 or any provision in force in Northern Ireland corresponding to that Chapter shall not affect—

(a)   the power of the court under subsection (1)(b) to make an order setting aside or varying the agreement or any term of it;

(b)   on an appeal, the powers of the appeal court in relation to the order.]

(3)   Without prejudice to subsections (1) and (2) above, where the parties to a marriage [or the partners in a civil partnership] have entered into an agreement as to financial provision to be made on divorce [or on dissolution of the civil partnership] and—

(a)   the estate of the [person] by whom any periodical allowance is payable under the agreement has, since the date when the agreement was entered into, been sequestrated, the award of sequestration has not been recalled and the [person] has not been discharged;

(b)   an analogous remedy within the meaning of section 10(5) of the Bankruptcy (Scotland) Act 1985 has, since that date, come into force and remains in force in respect of that [person's] estate;

(c)   that [person's] estate is being administered by a trustee acting under a voluntary trust deed granted since that date by the [person] for the benefit of his creditors generally or is subject to an analogous arrangement [; or

(d)   by virtue of the making of a maintenance calculation, child support maintenance has become payable by either party to the agreement with respect to a child to whom or for whose benefit periodical allowance is paid under that agreement,]

the court may, on or at any time after granting decree of divorce [or of dissolution of the civil partnership], make an order setting aside or varying any term of the agreement relating to the periodical allowance.

(4)   Any term of an agreement purporting to exclude the right to apply for an order under subsection (1)(b) or (3) above shall be void.

(5)   In this section, 'agreement' means an agreement entered into before or after the commencement of this Act.

17   Financial provision on declarator of nullity of marriage

(1)   Subject to the following provisions of this section, the provisions of this Act shall apply to actions for declarator of nullity of marriage [or of a civil partnership] as they apply to actions for divorce [or for dissolution of a civil partnership]; and in this Act, unless the context otherwise requires, 'action for divorce' includes an action for declarator of nullity of marriage [and 'action for dissolution of a civil partnership' includes an action for declarator of nullity of a civil partnership] and, in relation to such an action, 'decree' [, 'divorce' and dissolution of a civil partnership] shall be construed accordingly.

(2)   In an action for declarator of nullity of marriage [or of nullity of a civil partnership], it shall be competent for either party to claim interim aliment under section 6(1) of this Act notwithstanding that he denies the existence of the marriage [or civil partnership].

(3)   Any rule of law by virtue of which either party to an action for declarator of nullity of marriage may require restitution of property upon the granting of such declarator shall cease to have effect.

Supplemental

18   Orders relating to avoidance transactions

(1)   Where a claim has been made (whether before or after the commencement of this Act), being—

    (a)   an action for aliment,

    (b)   a claim for an order for financial provision, or

    (c)   an application for variation or recall of a decree in such an action or of an order for financial provision,

the [person] making the claim may, not later than one year from the date of the disposal of the claim, apply to the court for an order—

    (i)   setting aside or varying any transfer of, or transaction involving, property effected by the other [person] not more than 5 years before the date of the making of the claim; or

    (ii)   interdicting the other [person] from effecting any such transfer or transaction.

(2)   Subject to subsection (3) below, on an application under subsection (1) above for an order the court may, if it is satisfied that the transfer or transaction had the effect of, or is likely to have the effect of, defeating in whole or in part any claim referred to in subsection (1) above, make the order applied for or such other order as it thinks fit.

(3)   An order under subsection (2) above shall not prejudice any rights of a third party in or to the property where that third party—

    (a)   has in good faith acquired the property or any of it or any rights in relation to it for value; or

    (b)   derives title to such property or rights from any person who has done so.

(4)   Where the court makes an order under subsection (2) above, it may include in the order such terms and conditions as it thinks fit and may make any ancillary order which it considers expedient to ensure that the order is effective.

[. . .]

20   Provision of details of resources

In an action—

    (a)   for aliment;

    (b)   which includes a claim for an order for financial provision; or

    (c)   which includes a claim for interim aliment,

the court may order either party to provide details of his resources or those relating to a child or incapax on whose behalf he is acting.

21   Award of aliment or custody where divorce or separation refused

A court which refuses a decree of divorce [, separation or dissolution of a civil partnership] shall not, by virtue of such refusal, be prevented from making an order for aliment [. . .] or an incidental order determining any dispute between the [persons] as to their respective property rights.

22   Expenses of action

The expenses incurred by a [person] in pursuing or defending—

    (a)   an action for aliment brought [—

       (i)] by either party to the marriage or

    [(ii) by either party in a civil partnership,]

on his own behalf against the other party;

    (b)   an action for divorce, separation [(whether of the parties to a marriage or the civil partners in a civil partnership)], declarator of marriage or declarator of nullity of marriage;

    [(bb) an action for dissolution of a civil partnership, declarator that a civil partnership exists or declarator of nullity of a civil partnership,]

    (c)   an application made after the commencement of this Act for variation or recall of a decree of aliment or an order for financial provision in an action brought before or after the commencement of this Act,

shall not be regarded as necessaries for which the other party to the marriage [or the other partner in a civil partnership] is liable.

23   [*Amends Sheriff Courts (Civil Jurisdiction and Procedure) (Scotland) Act 1963*]

Matrimonial property, etc

24   Marriage not to affect property rights or legal capacity

    (1)   Subject to the provisions of any enactment (including this Act), marriage [or civil partnership] shall not of itself affect—

    (a)   the respective rights of the parties to the marriage [or as the case may be the partners in a civil partnership] in relation to their property;

    (b)   the legal capacity of [those parties or partners].

    (2)   Nothing in subsection (1) above affects the law of succession.

25   Presumption of equal shares in household goods

    (1)   If any question arises (whether during or after a marriage [or civil partnership]) as to the respective rights of ownership of the parties to a marriage [or the partners in a civil partnership] in any household goods obtained in prospect of or during the marriage [or civil partnership] other than by gift or succession from a third party, it shall be presumed, unless the contrary is proved, that each has a right to an equal share in the goods in question.

    (2)   For the purposes of subsection (1) above, the contrary shall not be treated as proved by reason only that while [—

    (a)] the parties were married;

    [(b) the partners were in a civil partnership],

and living together the goods in question were purchased from a third party by either party alone or by both in unequal shares.

    (3)   In this section 'household goods' means any goods (including decorative or ornamental goods) kept or used at any time during the marriage [or civil partnership in any family] home for the joint domestic purposes of the parties to the marriage [or the partners], other than—

    (a)   money or securities;

    (b)   any motor car, caravan or other road vehicle;

    (c) any domestic animal.

26 Presumption of equal shares in money and property derived from housekeeping allowance

If any question arises (whether during or after a marriage [or civil partnership]) as to the right of a party to a marriage [or as the case may be of a partner in a civil partnership] to money derived from any allowance made by either party [or partner] for their joint household expenses or for similar purposes, or to any property acquired out of such money, the money or property shall, in the absence of any agreement between them to the contrary, be treated as belonging to each party [or partner] in equal shares.

General

27 Interpretation

(1) In this Act, unless the context otherwise requires—

'action' means an action brought after the commencement of this Act;

'action for aliment' has the meaning assigned to it by section 2(3) of this Act;

'aliment' does not include aliment pendente lite or interim aliment under section 6 of this Act;

['benefits under a pension arrangement' includes any benefits by way of pension, including relevant state scheme rights, whether under a pension arrangement or note;]

'caravan' means a caravan which is mobile or affixed to the land;

'child' includes [a child whether or not his parents have ever been married to one another], and any reference to the child of a marriage (whether or not subsisting) includes a child (other than a child who has been boarded out with the parties, or one of them, by a local or other public authority or a voluntary organisation) who has been accepted by the parties as a child of the family;

['child support maintenance' has the meaning assigned to it by section 3(6) of the Child Support Act 1991;]

['civil partnership', in relation to an action for declarator of nullity of a civil partnership, means purported civil partnership;]

'the court' means the Court of Session or the sheriff, as the case may require;

'decree' in an action for aliment includes an order of the court awarding aliment;

'family' includes a one-parent family [and in relation to a civil partnership means the members of the civil partnership together with any child accepted by them both as a child of the family [or in respect of whom they are, by virtue of sections 33 and 42 of the Human Fertilisation and Embryology Act 2008, the parents]];

'incidental order' has the meaning assigned to it by section 14(2) of this Act;

['maintenance calculation' has the meaning assigned to it by section 54 of the Child Support Act 1991;]

'marriage', in relation to an action for declarator of nullity of marriage, means purported marriage;

'matrimonial home' has the meaning assigned to it by section 22 of the Matrimonial Homes (Family Protection) (Scotland) Act 1981 [as amended by section 13(10) of the Law Reform (Miscellaneous Provisions) (Scotland) Act 1985];

'needs' means present and foreseeable needs;

'obligation of aliment' shall be construed in accordance with section 1(2) of this Act;

'order for financial provision' means an order under section 8(2) of this Act and, in sections 18(1) and 22(c) of this Act, also includes an order under section 5(2) of the Divorce (Scotland) Act 1976;

['partner', in relation to a civil partnership, includes a person who [was] a partner in a civil partnership which has been terminated and an ostensible partner in a civil partnership which has been annulled;]

'party to a marriage' and 'party to the marriage' include a party to a marriage which has been terminated or annulled;

['pension arrangement' means—

(a)   any occupational pension scheme within the meaning of the Pension Schemes Act 1993;

(b)   a personal pension scheme within the meaning of that Act;

(c)   a retirement annuity contract;

(d)   an annuity or insurance policy purchased or transferred for the purpose of giving effect to rights under an occupational pension scheme or a personal pension scheme;

(e)   an annuity purchased or entered into for the purpose of discharging liability in respect of a pension credit under section 29(1)(b) of the Welfare Reform and Pensions Act 1999 or under corresponding Northern Ireland legislation;]

['pension sharing order' is an order which—

(a)   provides that one party's—

(i)   shareable rights under a specified pension arrangement, or

(ii)   shareable state scheme rights,

be subject to pension sharing for the benefit of the other party, and

(b)   specifies the percentage value, or the amount, to be transferred;]

['person responsible for a pension arrangement' means—

(a)   in the case of an occupational pension scheme or a personal pension scheme, the trustees or managers of the scheme;

(b)   in the case of a retirement annuity contract or an annuity falling within paragraph (d) or (e) of the definition of 'pension arrangement' above, the provider of their annuity;

(c)   in the case of an insurance policy falling within paragraph (d) of the definition of that expression, the insurer;]

'property' in sections 8, 12, 13 and 15 of this Act does not include a tenancy transferable under section 13 of the Matrimonial Homes (Family Protection) (Scotland) Act 1981;

['relevant state scheme rights' means—

(a)   entitlement, or prospective entitlement, to a Category A retirement pension by virtue of section 44(3)(b) of the Social Security Contributions and Benefits Act 1992 or under corresponding Northern Ireland legislation; and

(b)   entitlement, or prospective entitlement, to a pension under section 55A of the Social Security Contributions and Benefits Act 1992 (shared additional pension) or under corresponding Northern Ireland legislation;]

'resources' means present and foreseeable resources;

['retirement annuity contract' means a contract or scheme approved under Chapter III of Part XIV of the Income and Corporation Taxes Act 1988;]

['trustees or managers' in relation to an occupational pension scheme or a personal pension scheme means—

(a)   in the case of a scheme established under a trust, the trustees of the scheme; and

(b)   in any other case, the managers of the scheme;]

'voluntary organisation' means a body, other than a local or other public authority, the activities of which are not carried on for profit.

[(1A)   In subsection (1), in the definition of 'pension sharing order'—

(a)   the reference to shareable rights under a pension arrangement is to rights in relation to which pension sharing is available under Chapter I of Part IV of the Welfare Reform and Pensions Act 1999, or under corresponding Northern Ireland legislation, and

(b)   the reference to shareable state scheme rights is to rights in relation to which pension sharing is available under Chapter II of Part IV of the Welfare Reform and Pensions Act 1999, or under corresponding Northern Ireland legislation.]

(2)　For the purposes of this Act, the parties to a marriage shall be held to cohabit with one another only when they are in fact living together as man and wife.

29　Citation, commencement and extent

(1)　This Act may be cited as the Family Law (Scotland) Act 1985.

(2)　This Act shall come into operation on such day as the Secretary of State may appoint by order made by statutory instrument, and different days may be appointed for different purposes.

(3)　An order under subsection (2) above may contain such transitional provisions and savings as appear to the Secretary of State necessary or expedient in connection with the provisions brought into force (whether wholly or partly) by the order.

(4)　So much of section 28 of, and Schedule 1 to, this Act as affects the operation of the Maintenance Orders Act 1950 and the Maintenance Orders (Reciprocal Enforcement) Act 1972 shall extend to England and Wales and to Northern Ireland as well as to Scotland, but save as aforesaid this Act shall extend to Scotland only.

CHILD ABDUCTION AND CUSTODY ACT 1985
(1985, c 60)

PART I
INTERNATIONAL CHILD ABDUCTION

1　The Hague Convention

(1)　In this Part of this Act 'the Convention' means the Convention on the Civil Aspects of International Child Abduction which was signed at The Hague on 25th October 1980.

(2)　Subject to the provisions of this Part of this Act, the provisions of that Convention set out in Schedule 1 to this Act shall have the force of law in the United Kingdom.

[(3)　But—

(a)　those provisions of the Convention;

(b)　this Part of this Act; and

(c)　rules of court under section 10 of this Act,

are subject to Article 60 of the Council Regulation (by virtue of which the Regulation takes precedence over the Convention, in so far as it concerns matters governed by the Regulation).

(4)　The 'Council Regulation' means Council Regulation (EC) No 2201/2003 of 27th November 2003 concerning jurisdiction and the recognition and enforcement of judgments in matrimonial matters and matters of parental responsibility.]

2　Contracting States

(1)　For the purposes of the Convention as it has effect under this Part of this Act the Contracting States other than the United Kingdom shall be those for the time being specified by an Order in Council under this section.

(2)　An Order in Council under this section shall specify the date of the coming into force of the Convention as between the United Kingdom and any State specified in the Order; and, except where the Order otherwise provides, the Convention shall apply as between the United Kingdom and that State only in relation to wrongful removals or retentions occurring on or after that date.

(3)　Where the Convention applies, or applies only, to a particular territory or particular territories specified in a declaration made by a Contracting State under Article 39 or 40 of the Convention references to that State in subsections (1) and (2) above shall be construed as references to that territory or those territories.

3 Central Authorities

(1) Subject to subsection (2) below, the functions under the Convention of a Central Authority shall be discharged—

    (a) in England and Wales and in Northern Ireland by the Lord Chancellor; and

    (b) in Scotland by the Secretary of State.

(2) Any application made under the Convention by or on behalf of a person outside the United Kingdom may be addressed to the Lord Chancellor as the Central Authority in the United Kingdom,

(3) Where any such application relates to a function to be discharged under subsection (1) above by the Secretary of State it shall be transmitted by the Lord Chancellor to the Secretary of State and where such an application is addressed to the Secretary of State but relates to a function to be discharged under subsection (1) above by the Lord Chancellor the Secretary of State shall transmit it to the Lord Chancellor.

4 Judicial authorities

The courts having jurisdiction to entertain applications under the Convention shall be—

    (a) in England and Wales or in Northern Ireland the High Court; and

    (b) in Scotland the Court of Session.

5 Interim powers

Where an application has been made to a court in the United Kingdom under the Convention, the court may, at any time before the application is determined, give such interim directions as it thinks fit for the purpose of securing the welfare of the child concerned or of preventing changes in the circumstances relevant to the determination of the application.

6 Reports

Where the Lord Chancellor or the Secretary of State is requested to provide information relating to a child under Article 7(d) of the Convention he may—

    (a) request a local authority or [an officer of the service] to make a report to him in writing with respect to any matter which appears to him to be relevant;

    (b) request the Department of Health and Social Services for Northern Ireland to arrange for a suitably qualified person to make such a report to him;

    (c) request any court to which a written report relating to the child has been made to send him a copy of the report;

and such a request shall be duly complied with.

7 Proof of documents and evidence

(1) For the purposes of Article 14 of the Convention a decision or determination of a judicial or administrative authority outside the United Kingdom may be proved by a duly authenticated copy of the decision or determination; and any document purporting to be such a copy shall be deemed to be a true copy unless the contrary is shown.

(2) For the purposes of subsection (1) above a copy is duly authenticated if it bears the seal, or is signed by a judge or officer, of the authority in question.

(3) For the purposes of Articles 14 and 30 of the Convention any such document as is mentioned in Article 8 of the Convention, or a certified copy of any such document, shall be sufficient evidence of anything stated in it.

8 Declarations by United Kingdom courts

The High Court or Court of Session may, on an application made for the purposes of Article 15 of the Convention by any person appearing to the court to have an interest in the matter, make a declaration or declarator that the removal of any child from, or his retention outside, the United Kingdom was wrongful within the meaning of Article 3 of the Convention.

9   Suspension of court's powers in cases of wrongful removal

The reference in Article 16 of the Convention to deciding on the merits of rights of custody shall be construed as a reference to—

(a)   making, varying or revoking a custody order, or [a supervision order under section 31 of the Children Act 1989 or Article 50 of the Children (Northern Ireland) Order 1995]

[(aa) enforcing under section 29 of the Family Law Act 1986 a custody order within the meaning of Chapter V of Part I of that Act;]

(b)   registering or enforcing a decision under Part II of this Act;

[. . .]

[(d)   making, varying or discharging an order under section 86 of the Children (Scotland) Act 1995].

[. . .]

10   Rules of court

(1)   An authority having power to make rules of court may make such provision for giving effect to this Part of this Act as appears to that authority to be necessary or expedient.

(2)   Without prejudice to the generality of subsection (1) above, rules of court may make provision—

(a)   with respect to the procedure on applications for the return of a child and with respect to the documents and information to be furnished and the notices to be given in connection with any such application;

(b)   for the transfer of any such application between the appropriate courts in the different parts of the United Kingdom;

(c)   for the giving of notices by or to a court for the purposes of the provisions of Article 16 of the Convention and section 9 above and generally as respects proceedings to which those provisions apply;

(d)   for enabling a person who wishes to make an application under the Convention in a Contracting State other than the United Kingdom to obtain from any court in the United Kingdom an authenticated copy of any decision of that court relating to the child to whom the application is to relate.

11   Cost of applications

The United Kingdom having made such a reservation as is mentioned in the third paragraph of Article 26 of the Convention, the costs mentioned in that paragraph shall not be borne by any Minister or other authority in the United Kingdom except so far as they fall to be so borne [by virtue of—

(a)   the provision of any service funded by the Legal Services Commission as part of the Community Legal Service, or

(b)   the grant of legal aid or legal advice and assistance under] the Legal Aid (Scotland) Act 1967, Part I of the Legal Advice and Assistance Act 1972 or the Legal Aid Advice and Assistance (Northern Ireland) Order 1981.

PART II

RECOGNITION AND ENFORCEMENT OF CUSTODY DECISIONS

12   The European Convention

(1)   In this Part of this Act 'the Convention' means the European Convention on Recognition and Enforcement of Decisions concerning Custody of Children and on the Restoration of Custody of Children which was signed in Luxembourg on 20th May 1980.

(2)   Subject to the provisions of this Part of this Act, the provisions of that Convention set out in Schedule 2 to this Act (which include Articles 9 and 10 as they have effect in consequence of a reservation made by the United Kingdom under Article 17) shall have the force of law in the United Kingdom.

[(3)   But—

(a)   those provisions of the Convention;

(b)   this Part of this Act; and

(c)   rules of court under section 24 of this Act,

are subject to Article 60 of the Council Regulation (by virtue of which the Regulation takes precedence over the Convention, in so far as it concerns matters governed by the Regulation).

(4)   The 'Council Regulation' means Council Regulation (EC) No 2201/2003 of 27th November 2003 concerning jurisdiction and the recognition and enforcement of judgments in matrimonial matters and matters of parental responsibility.]

13   Contracting States

(1)   For the purposes of the Convention as it has effect under this Part of this Act the Contracting States other than the United Kingdom shall be those for the time being specified by an Order in Council under this section.

(2)   An Order in Council under this section shall specify the date of the coming into force of the Convention as between the United Kingdom and any State specified in the Order.

(3)   Where the Convention applies, or applies only, to a particular territory or particular territories specified by a Contracting State under Article 24 or 25 of the Convention references to that State in subsections (1) and (2.) above shall be construed as references to that territory or those territories.

14   Central Authorities

(1)   Subject to subsection (2) below, the functions under the Convention of a Central Authority shall be discharged—

(a)   in England and Wales and in Northern Ireland by the Lord Chancellor; and

(b)   in Scotland by the Secretary of State.

(2)   Any application made under the Convention by or on behalf of a person outside the United Kingdom may be addressed to the Lord Chancellor as the Central Authority in the United Kingdom.

(3)   Where any such application relates to a function to be discharged under subsection (1) above by the Secretary of State it shall be transmitted by the Lord Chancellor to the Secretary of State and where such an application is addressed to the Secretary of State but relates to a function to be discharged under subsection (1) above by the Lord Chancellor the Secretary of State shall transmit it to the Lord Chancellor.

15   Recognition of decisions

(1)   Articles 7 and 12 of the Convention shall have effect in accordance with this section.

(2)   A decision to which either of those Articles applies which was made in a Contracting State other than the United Kingdom shall be recognised in each part of the United Kingdom as if made by a court having jurisdiction to make it in that part but—

(a)   the appropriate court in any part of the United Kingdom may, on the application of any person appearing to it to have an interest in the matter, declare on any of the grounds specified in Article 9 or 10 of the Convention that the decision is not to be recognised in any part of the United Kingdom; and

(b)   the decision shall not be enforceable in any part of the United Kingdom unless registered in the appropriate court under section 16 below.

(3)   The references in Article 9(1)(c) of the Convention to the removal of the child are to his improper removal within the meaning of the Convention.

16   Registration of decisions

(1)   A person on whom any rights are conferred by a decision relating to custody made by an authority in a Contracting State other than the United King-

dom may make an application for the registration of the decision in an appropriate court in the United Kingdom.

(2) The Central Authority in the United Kingdom shall assist such a person in making such an application if a request for such assistance is made by him or on his behalf by the Central Authority of the Contracting State in question.

(3) An application under subsection (1) above or a request under subsection (2) above shall be treated as a request for enforcement for the purposes of Articles 10 and 13 of the Convention.

(4) The High Court or Court of Session shall refuse to register a decision if—

(a) the court is of the opinion that on any of the grounds specified in Article 9 or 10 of the Convention the decision should not be recognised in any part of the United Kingdom;

(b) the court is of the opinion that the decision is not enforceable in the Contracting State where it was made and is not a decision to which Article 12 of the Convention applies; or

(c) an application in respect of the child under Part I of this Act is pending.

(5) Where the Lord Chancellor is requested to assist in making an application under this section to the Court of Session he shall transmit the request to the Secretary of State and the Secretary of State shall transmit to the Lord Chancellor any such request to assist in making an application to the High Court.

(6) In this section 'decision relating to custody' has the same meaning as in the Convention.

17 Variation and revocation of registered decisions

(1) Where a decision which has been registered under section 16 above is varied or revoked by an authority in the Contracting State in which it was made, the person on whose behalf the application for registration of the decision was made shall notify the court in which the decision is registered of the variation or revocation.

(2) Where a court is notified under subsection (1) above of the revocation of a decision, it shall—

(a) cancel the registration, and

(b) notify such persons as may be prescribed by rules of court of the cancellation,

(3) Where a court is notified under subsection (1) above of the variation of a decision, it shall—

(a) notify such persons as may be prescribed by rules of court of the variation, and

(b) subject to any conditions which may be so prescribed, vary the registration.

(4) The court in which a decision is registered under section 16 above may also, on the application of any person appearing to the court to have an interest in the matter, cancel or vary the registration if it is satisfied that the decision has been revoked or, as the case may be, varied by an authority in the Contracting State in which it was made.

18 Enforcement of decisions

Where a decision relating to custody has been registered under section 16 above, the court in which it is registered shall have the same powers for the purpose of enforcing the decision as if it had been made by that court; and proceedings for or with respect to enforcement may be taken accordingly.

19 Interim powers

Where an application has been made to a court for the registration of a decision under section 16 above or for the enforcement of such a decision, the court may, at any time before the application is determined, give such interim directions as it thinks fit for the purpose of securing the welfare of the child concerned or of preventing changes in the circumstances relevant to the determination of the application or, in the case of an application for registration, to the determination of any subsequent application for the enforcement of the decision.

20 Suspension of court's powers

(1)   Where it appears to any court in which such proceedings as are mentioned in subsection (2) below are pending in respect of a child that—

(a)   an application has been made for the registration of a decision in respect of the child under section 16 above (other than a decision mentioned in subsection (3) below) or that such a decision is registered; and

(b)   the decision was made in proceedings commenced before the proceedings which are pending,

the powers of the court with respect to the child in those proceedings shall be restricted as mentioned in subsection (2) below unless, in the case of an application for registration, the application is refused.

(2)   Where subsection (1) above applies the court shall not—

(a)   in the case of custody proceedings, make, vary or revoke any custody order, or [a supervision order under section 31 of the Children Act 1989 or article 50 of the Children (Northern Ireland) Order 1995; or

(aa)   in the case of proceedings under section 29 of the Family Law Act 1986 for the enforcement of a custody order within the meaning of Chapter V of Part I of that Act, enforce that order.]

[. . .]

[(d)   in the case of proceedings for, or for the variation or discharge of, a parental responsibilities order under section 86 of the Children (Scotland) Act 1995, make, vary or discharge any such order;]

[. . .]

[(2A)   Where it appears to the Secretary of State—

(a)   that an application has been made for the registration of a decision in respect of a child under section 16 above (other than a decision mentioned in subsection (3) below); or

(b)   that such a decision is registered,

the Secretary of State shall not make, vary or revoke any custody order in respect of the child unless, in the case of an application for registration, the application is refused.]

(3)   The decision referred to in subsection (1) [or (2A)] above is a decision which is only a decision relating to custody within the meaning of section 16 of this Act by virtue of being a decision relating to rights of access.

(4)   Paragraph (b) of Article 10(2) of the Convention shall be construed as referring to custody proceedings within the meaning of this Act.

(5)   This section shall apply to a children's hearing [(as defined in section 93(1) of the Children (Scotland) Act 1995)].

21 Reports

Where the Lord Chancellor or the Secretary of State is requested to make enquiries about a child under Article 15(1)(b) of the Convention he may—

(a)   request a local authority or [an officer of the service] to make a report to him in writing with respect to any matter relating to the child concerned which appears to him to be relevant;

(b)   request the Department of Health and Social Services for Northern Ireland to arrange for a suitably qualified person to make such a report to him;

(c)   request any court to which a written report relating to the child has been made to send him a copy of the report;

and any such request shall be duly complied with.

22 Proof of documents and evidence

(1)   In any proceedings under this Part of this Act a decision of an authority

outside the United Kingdom may be proved by a duly authenticated copy of the decision; and any document purporting to be such a copy shall be deemed to be a true copy unless the contrary is shown.

(2) For the purposes of subsection (1) above a copy is duly authenticated if it bears the seal, or is signed by a judge or officer, of the authority in question.

(3) In any proceedings under this Part of this Act any such document as is mentioned in Article 13 of the Convention, or a certified copy of any such document, shall be sufficient evidence of anything stated in it.

23 Decisions of United Kingdom courts

(1) Where a person on whom any rights are conferred by a decision relating to custody made by a court in the United Kingdom makes an application to the Lord Chancellor or the Secretary of State under Article 4 of the Convention with a view to securing its recognition or enforcement in another Contracting State, the Lord Chancellor or the Secretary of State may require the court which made the decision to furnish him with all or any of the documents referred to in Article 13(1)(b), (c) and (d) of the Convention.

(2) Where in any custody proceedings a court in the United Kingdom makes a decision relating to a child who has been removed from the United Kingdom, the court may also, on an application made by any person for the purposes of Article 12 of the Convention, declare the removal to have been unlawful if it is satisfied that the applicant has an interest in the matter and that the child has been taken from or sent or kept out of the United Kingdom without the consent of the person (or, if more than one, all the persons) having the right to determine the child's place of residence under the law of the part of the United Kingdom in which the child was habitually resident.

(3) In this section 'decision relating to custody' has the same meaning as in the Convention.

24 Rules of court

(1) An authority having power to make rules of court may make such provision for giving effect to this Part of this Act as appears to that authority to be necessary or expedient.

(2) Without prejudice to the generality of subsection (1) above, rules of court may make provision—

(a) with respect to the procedure on applications to a court under any provision of this Part of this Act and with respect to the documents and information to be furnished and the notices to be given in connection with any such application;

(b) for the transfer of any such application between the appropriate courts in the different parts of the United Kingdom;

(c) for the giving of directions requiring the disclosure of information about any child who is the subject of proceedings under this Part of this Act and for safeguarding its welfare.

[24A Power to order disclosure of child's whereabouts

(1) Where—

(a) in proceedings for the return of a child under Part I of this Act; or

(b) on an application for the recognition, registration or enforcement of a decision in respect of a child under Part II of this Act,

there is not available to the court adequate information as to where the child is, the court may order any person who it has reason to believe may have relevant information to disclose it to the court.

(2) A person shall not be excused from complying with an order under subsection (1) above by reason that to do so may incriminate him or his spouse [or civil partner] of an offence; but a statement or admission made in compliance with

such an order shall not be admissible in evidence against either of them in proceedings for any offence other than perjury.]

PART III
SUPPLEMENTARY

25 Termination of existing custody orders, etc
(1) Where—
    (a) an order is made for the return of a child under Part I of this Act; or
    (b) a decision with respect to a child (other than a decision mentioned in subsection (2) below) is registered under section 16 of this Act,
any custody order relating to him shall cease to have effect.

(2) The decision referred to in subsection (1)(b) above is a decision which is only a decision relating to custody within the meaning of section 16 of this Act by virtue of being a decision relating to rights of access.

    [. . .]

26 Expenses
There shall be paid out of money provided by Parliament—
    (a) any expenses incurred by the Lord Chancellor or the Secretary of State by virtue of this Act; and
    (b) any increase attributable to this Act in the sums so payable under any other Act.

27 Interpretation
(1) In this Act 'custody order' means [(unless the contrary intention appears)] any such order or authorisation as is mentioned in Schedule 3 to this Act and 'custody proceedings' means proceedings in which an order within paragraphs 1, 2, 5, 6, 8 or 9 of that Schedule may be made [. . .] varied or revoked.

(2) For the purposes of this Act 'part of the United Kingdom' means England and Wales, Scotland or Northern Ireland and 'the appropriate court', in relation to England and Wales or Northern Ireland means the High Court and, in relation to Scotland, the Court of Session.

(3) In this Act 'local authority' means—
    (a) in relation to England and Wales, the council of a non-metropolitan county, a metropolitan district, a London borough or the Common Council of the City of London; and
    (b) in relation to Scotland, a [. . .] council [constituted under section 2 of the Local Government Etc (Scotland) Act 1994].

[(4) In this Act a decision relating to rights of access in England and Wales or Scotland or Northern Ireland means a decision as to the contact which a child may, or may not, have with any person.

(5) In this Act 'officer of the service' has the same meaning as in the Criminal Justice and Court Services Act 2000.]

28 Application as respects British Islands and colonies
(1) Her Majesty may by Order in Council direct that any of the provisions of this Act specified in the Order shall extend, subject to such modifications as may be specified in the Order, to—
    (a) the Isle of Man,
    (b) any of the Channel Islands, and
    (c) any colony.

(2) Her Majesty may by Order in Council direct that this Act shall have effect in the United Kingdom as if any reference in this Act, or in any amendment made by this Act, to any order which may be made, or any proceedings which may be brought or any other thing which may be done in, or in any part of, the United Kingdom included a reference to any corresponding order which may be made or,

as the case may be, proceedings which may be brought or other thing which may be done in any of the territories mentioned in subsection (1) above.

(3)   An Order in Council under this section may make such consequential, incidental and supplementary provision as Her Majesty considers appropriate.

(4)   An Order in Council under this section shall be subject to annulment in pursuance of a resolution of either House of Parliament.

29   Short title, commencement and extent

(1)   This Act may be cited as the Child Abduction and Custody Act 1985.

(2)   This Act shall come into force on such day as may be appointed by an order made by statutory instrument by the Lord Chancellor and the Lord Advocate; and different days may be so appointed for different provisions.

(3)   This Act extends to Northern Ireland.

SCHEDULES

SCHEDULE 1
CONVENTION ON THE CIVIL ASPECTS OF INTERNATIONAL CHILD ABDUCTION

Section 1(2)

CHAPTER 1—SCOPE OF THE CONVENTION

Article 3

The removal or the retention of a child is to be considered wrongful where—

(a)   it is in breach of rights of custody attributed to a person, an institution or any other body, either jointly or alone, under the law of the State in which the child was habitually resident immediately before the removal or retention; and

(b)   at the time of removal or retention those rights were actually exercised, either jointly or alone, or would have been so exercised but for the removal or retention.

The rights of custody mentioned in sub-paragraph (a) above may arise in particular by operation of law or by reason of a judicial or administrative decision, or by reason of an agreement having legal effect under the law of that State.

Article 4

The Convention shall apply to any child who was habitually resident in a Contracting State immediately before any breach of custody or access rights. The Convention shall cease to apply when the child attains the age of sixteen years.

Article 5

For the purposes of this Convention—

(a)   'rights of custody' shall include rights relating to the care of the person of the child and, in particular, the right to determine the child's place of residence;

(b)   'rights of access' shall include the right to take a child for a limited period of time to a place other than the child's habitual residence.

CHAPTER II—CENTRAL AUTHORITIES

Article 7

Central Authorities shall co-operate with each other and promote co-operation amongst the competent authorities in their respective States to secure the prompt return of children and to achieve the other objects of this Convention.

In particular, either directly or through any intermediary, they shall take all appropriate measures—

(a) to discover the whereabouts of a child who has been wrongfully removed or retained;

(b) to prevent further harm to the child or prejudice to interested parties by taking or causing to be taken provisional measures;

(c) to secure the voluntary return of the child or to bring about an amicable resolution of the issues;

(d) to exchange, where desirable, information relating to the social background of the child;

(e) to provide information of a general character as to the law of their State in connection with the application of the Convention;

(f) to initiate or facilitate the institution of judicial or administrative proceedings with a view to obtaining the return of the child and, in a proper case, to make arrangements for organizing or securing the effective exercise of rights of access;

(g) where the circumstances so require, to provide or facilitate the provision of legal aid and advice, including the participation of legal counsel and advisers;

(h) to provide such administrative arrangements as may be necessary and appropriate to secure the safe return of the child;

(i) to keep each other informed with respect to the operation of this Convention and, as far as possible, to eliminate any obstacles to its application.

CHAPTER III—RETURN OF CHILDREN

Article 8

Any person, institution or other body claiming that a child has been removed or retained in breach of custody rights may apply either to the Central Authority of the child's habitual residence or to the Central Authority of any other Contracting State for assistance in securing the return of the child.

The application shall contain—

(a) information concerning the identity of the applicant, of the child and of the person alleged to have removed or retained the child;

(b) where available, the date of birth of the child;

(c) the grounds on which the applicant's claim for return of the child is based;

(d) all available information relating to the whereabouts of the child and the identity of the person with whom the child is presumed to be.

The application may be accompanied or supplemented by—

(e) an authenticated copy of any relevant decision or agreement;

(f) a certificate or an affidavit emanating from a Central Authority, or other competent authority of the State of the child's habitual residence, or from a qualified person, concerning the relevant law of that State;

(g) any other relevant document.

Article 9

If the Central Authority which receives an application referred to in Article 8 has reason to believe that the child is in another Contracting State, it shall directly and without delay transmit the application to the Central Authority of that Contracting State and inform the requesting Central Authority, or the applicant, as the case may be.

Article 10

The Central Authority of the State where the child is shall take or cause to be taken all appropriate measures in order to obtain the voluntary return of the child.

Article 11

The judicial or administrative authorities of Contracting States shall act expeditiously in proceedings for the return of children.

If the judicial or administrative authority concerned has not reached a decision within six weeks from the date of commencement of the proceedings, the applicant or the Central Authority of the requested State, on its own initiative or if asked by the Central Authority of the requesting State, shall have the right to request a statement of the reasons for the delay. If a reply is received by the Central Authority of the requested State, that Authority shall transmit the reply to the Central Authority of the requesting State, or to the applicant, as the case may be.

Article 12

Where a child has been wrongfully removed or retained in terms Article 3 and, at the date of the commencement of the proceedings before the judicial or administrative authority of the Contracting State where the child is, a period of less than one year has elapsed from the date of the wrongful removal or retention, the authority concerned shall order the return of the child forthwith.

The judicial or administrative authority, even where the proceedings have been commenced after the expiration of the period of one year referred to in the preceding paragraph, shall also order the return of the child, unless it is demonstrated that the child is now settled in its new environment.

Where the judicial or administrative authority in the requested state has reason to believe that the child has been taken to another State, it may stay the proceedings or dismiss the application for the return of the child.

Article 13

Notwithstanding the provisions of the preceding Article, the judicial or administrative authority of the requested State is not bound to order the return of the child if the person, institution or other body which opposes its return establishes that—

(a) the person, institution or other body having the care of the person of the child was not actually exercising the custody rights at the time of removal or retention, or had consented to or subsequently acquiesced in the removal or retention; or

(b) there is a grave risk that his or her return would expose the child to physical or psychological harm or otherwise place the child in an intolerable situation.

The judicial or administrative authority may also refuse to order the return of the child if it finds that the child objects to being returned and has attained an age and degree of maturity at which it is appropriate to take account of its views.

In considering the circumstances referred to in this Article, the judicial and administrative authorities shall take into account the information relating to the social background of the child provided by the Central Authority or other competent authority of the child's habitual residence.

Article 14

In ascertaining whether there has been a wrongful removal or retention within the meaning of Article 3, the judicial or administrative authorities of the requested State may take notice directly of the law of, and of judicial or administrative decisions, formally recognised or not in the State of the habitual residence of the child, without recourse to the specific procedures for the proof of that law or for the recognition of foreign decisions which would otherwise be applicable.

Article 15

The judicial or administrative authorities of a Contracting State may, prior to the making of an order for the return of the child request that the applicant obtain from the authorities of the State of the habitual residence of the child a decision or other determination that the removal or retention was wrongful within the meaning of Article 3 of the Convention, where such a decision or determination may be obtained in that State. The Central Authorities of the Contracting States shall so far as practicable assist applicants to obtain such a decision or determination.

Article 16

After receiving notice of a wrongful removal or retention of a child in the sense of Article 3, the judicial or administrative authorities of the Contracting State to which the child has been removed or in which it has been retained shall not decide on the merits of rights of custody until it has been determined that the child is not to be returned under this Convention or unless an application under this Convention is not lodged within a reasonable time following receipt of the notice.

Article 17

The sole fact that a decision relating to custody has been given in or is entitled to recognition in the requested State shall not be a ground for refusing to return a child under this Convention, but the judicial or administrative authorities of the requested State may take account of the reasons for that decision in applying this Convention.

Article 18

The provisions of this Chapter do not limit the power of a judicial or administrative authority to order the return of the child at any time.

Article 19

A decision under this Convention concerning the return of the child shall not be taken to be a determination on the merits of any custody issue.

CHAPTER IV—RIGHTS OF ACCESS

Article 21

An application to make arrangements for organising or securing the effective exercise of rights of access may be presented to the Central Authorities of the Contracting States in the same way as an application for the return of a child.

The Central Authorities are bound by the obligations of co-operation which are set forth in Article 7 to promote the peaceful enjoyment of access rights and the fulfilment of any conditions to which the exercise of those rights may be subject. The Central Authorities shall take steps to remove, as far as possible, all obstacles to the exercise of such rights. The Central Authorities, either directly or through intermediaries, may initiate or assist in the institution of proceedings with a view to organising or protecting these rights and securing respect for the conditions to which the exercise of these rights may be subject.

CHAPTER V—GENERAL PROVISIONS

Article 22

No security, bond or deposit, however described, shall be required to guarantee the payment of costs and expenses in the judicial or administrative proceedings falling within the scope of this Convention.

Article 24

Any application, communication or other document sent to the Central Authority of the requested State shall be in the original language, and shall be accompanied by a translation into the official language or one of the official languages of the requested State or, where that is not feasible, a translation into French or English.

Article 26

Each Central Authority shall bear its own costs in applying this Convention.

Central Authorities and other public services of Contracting States shall not impose any charges in relation to applications submitted under this Convention. In particular, they may not require any payment from the applicant towards the costs and expenses of the proceedings or, where applicable, those arising from the participation of legal counsel or advisers. However, they may require the payment of the expenses incurred or to be incurred in implementing the return of the child.

However, a Contracting State may, by making a reservation in accordance with Article 42, declare that it shall not be bound to assume any costs referred to in the preceding paragraph resulting from the participation of legal counsel or advisers or from court proceedings, except insofar as those costs may be covered by its system of legal aid and advice.

Upon ordering the return of a child or issuing an order concerning rights of access under this Convention, the judicial or administrative authorities may, where appropriate, direct the person who removed or retained the child, or who prevented the exercise of rights of access, to pay necessary expenses incurred by or on behalf of the applicant, including travel expenses, any costs incurred or payments made for locating the child, the costs of legal representation of the applicant, and those of returning the child.

Article 27

When it is manifest that the requirements of this Convention are not fulfilled or that the application is otherwise not well founded, a Central Authority is not bound to accept the application. In that case, the Central Authority shall forthwith inform the applicant or the Central Authority through which the application was submitted, as the case may be, of its reasons.

Article 28

A Central Authority may require that the application be accompanied by a written authorisation empowering it to act on behalf of the applicant, or to designate a representative so to act.

Article 29

This Convention shall not preclude any person, institution or body who claims that there has been a breach of custody or access rights within the meaning of Article 3 or 21 from applying directly to the judicial or administrative authorities of a Contracting State, whether or not under the provisions of this Convention.

Article 30

Any application submitted to the Central Authorities or directly to the judicial or administrative authorities of a Contracting State in accordance with the terms of this Convention, together with documents and any other information appended thereto or provided by a Central Authority, shall be admissible in the courts or administrative authorities of the Contracting States.

Article 31

In relation to a State which in matters of custody of children has two or more systems of law applicable in different territorial units—

(a) any reference to habitual residence in that State shall be construed as referring to habitual residence in a territorial unit of that State;

(b) any reference to the law of the State of habitual residence shall be construed as referring to the law of the territorial unit in that State where the child habitually resides.

Article 32

In relation to a State which in matters of custody of children has two or more systems of law applicable to different categories of persons, any reference to the law of that State shall be construed as referring to the legal system specified by the law of that State.

SCHEDULE 2
EUROPEAN CONVENTION ON RECOGNITION AND ENFORCEMENT ON DECISIONS CONCERNING CUSTODY OF CHILDREN

Section 12(2)

Article 1

For the purposes of this Convention:

(a) 'child' means a person of any nationality, so long as he is under 16 years of age and has not the right to decide on his own place of residence under the law of his habitual residence, the law of his nationality or the internal law of the State addressed;

(b) 'authority' means a judicial or administrative authority;

(c) 'decision relating to custody' means a decision of an authority in so far as it relates to the care of the person of the child, including the right to decide on the place of his residence, or to the right of access to him.

(d) 'improper removal' means the removal of a child across an international frontier in breach of a decision relating to his custody which has been given in a Contracting State and which is enforceable in such a State; 'improper removal' also includes:

(i) the failure to return a child across an international frontier at the end of a period of the exercise of the right of access to this child or at the end of any other temporary stay in a territory other than that where the custody is exercised;

(ii) a removal which is subsequently declared unlawful within the meaning of Article 12.

Article 4

(1) Any person who has obtained in a Contracting State a decision relating to the custody of a child and who wishes to have that decision recognised or enforced in another Contracting State may submit an application for this purpose to the central authority in any Contracting State.

(2) The application shall be accompanied by the documents mentioned in Article 13.

(3) The central authority receiving the application, if it is not the central authority in the State addressed, shall send the documents directly and without delay to that central authority.

(4) The central authority receiving the application may refuse to intervene where it is manifestly clear that the conditions laid down by this Convention are not satisfied.

(5)   The central authority receiving the application shall keep the applicant informed without delay of the progress of his application.

Article 5

(1)   The central authority in the State addressed shall take or cause to be taken without delay all steps which it considers to be appropriate, if necessary by instituting proceedings before its competent authorities, in order:
(a)   to discover the whereabouts of the child;
(b)   to avoid, in particular by any necessary provisional measures, prejudice to the interests of the child or of the applicant;
(c)   to secure the recognition or enforcement of the decision;
(d)   to secure the delivery of the child to the applicant where enforcement is granted;
(e)   to inform the requesting authority of the measures taken and their results.
(2)   Where the central authority in the State addressed has reason to believe that the child is in the territory of another Contracting State it shall send the documents directly and without delay to the central authority of that State.
(3)   With the exception of the cost of repatriation, each Contracting State undertakes not to claim any payment from an applicant in respect of any measures taken under paragraph (1) of this Article by the central authority of that State on the applicant's behalf, including the costs of proceedings and, where applicable, the costs incurred by the assistance of a lawyer.
(4)   If recognition or enforcement is refused, and if the central authority of the State addressed considers that it should comply with a request by the applicant to bring in that State proceedings concerning the substance of the case, that authority shall use its best endeavours to secure the representation of the applicant in the proceedings under conditions no less favourable than those available to a person who is resident in and a national of that State and for this purpose it may, in particular, institute proceedings before its competent authorities.

Article 7

A decision relating to custody given in a Contracting State shall be recognised and, where it is enforceable in the State of origin, made enforceable in every other Contracting State.

Article 9

(1)   [Recognition and enforcement may be refused] if:
(a)   in the case of a decision given in the absence of the defendant or his legal representative, the defendant was not duly served with the document which instituted the proceedings or an equivalent document in sufficient time to enable him to arrange his defence; but such a failure to effect service cannot constitute a ground for refusing recognition or enforcement where service was not effected because the defendant had concealed his whereabouts from the person who instituted the proceedings in the State of origin;
(b)   in the case of a decision given in the absence of the defendant or his legal representative, the competence of the authority giving the decision was not founded:
(i)   on the habitual residence of the defendant; or
(ii)   on the last common habitual residence of the child's parents, at least one parent being still habitually resident there; or
(iii)   on the habitual residence of the child;
(c)   the decision is incompatible with a decision relating to custody which became enforceable in the State addressed before the removal of the child,

unless the child has had his habitual residence in the territory of the requesting State for one year before his removal.

(3) In no circumstances may the foreign decision be reviewed as to its substance.

Article 10

(1) [Recognition and enforcement may also be refused] on any of the following grounds:

(a) if it is found that the effects of the decision are manifestly incompatible with the fundamental principles of the law relating to the family and children in the State addressed;

(b) if it is found that by reason of a change in the circumstances including the passage of time but not including a mere change in the residence of the child after an improper removal, the effects of the original decision are manifestly no longer in accordance with the welfare of the child;

(c) if at the time when the proceedings were instituted in the State of origin:

(i) the child was a national of the State addressed or was habitually resident there and no such connection existed with the State of origin;

(ii) the child was a national both of the State of origin and of the State addressed and was habitually resident in the State addressed;

(d) if the decision is incompatible with a decision given in the State addressed or enforceable in that State after being given in a third State, pursuant to proceedings begun before the submission of the request for recognition or enforcement, and if the refusal is in accordance with the welfare of the child.

(2) Proceedings for recognition or enforcement may be adjourned on any of the following grounds:

(a) if an ordinary form of review of the original decision has been commenced;

(b) if proceedings relating to the custody of the child, commenced before the proceedings in the State of origin were instituted, are pending in the State addressed;

(c) if another decision concerning the custody of the child is the subject of proceedings for enforcement or of any other proceedings concerning the recognition of the decision.

Article 11

(1) Decisions on rights of access and provisions of decisions relating to custody which deal with the rights of access shall be recognised and enforced subject to the same conditions as other decisions relating to custody.

(2) However, the competent authority of the State addressed may fix the conditions for the implementation and exercise of the right of access taking into account, in particular, undertakings given by the parties on this matter.

(3) Where no decision on the right of access has been taken or where recognition or enforcement of the decision relating to custody is refused, the central authority of the State addressed may apply to its competent authorities for a decision on the right of access if the person claiming a right of access so requests.

Article 12

Where, at the time of the removal of a child across an international frontier, there is no enforceable decision given in a Contracting State relating to his custody, the provisions of this Convention shall apply to any subsequent decision, relating to the custody of that child and declaring the removal to be unlawful, given in a Contracting State at the request of any interested person.

Article 13

(1)   A request for recognition or enforcement in another Contracting State of a decision relating to custody shall be accompanied by:

(a)   a document authorising the central authority of the State addressed to act on behalf of the applicant or to designate another representative for that purpose;

(b)   a copy of the decision which satisfies the necessary conditions of authenticity;

(c)   in the case of a decision given in the absence of the defendant or his legal representative, a document which establishes that the defendant was duly served with the document which instituted the proceedings or an equivalent document;

(d)   if applicable, any document which establishes that, in accordance with the law of the State of origin, the decision is enforceable;

(e)   if possible, a statement indicating the whereabouts or likely whereabouts of the child in the State addressed;

(f)   proposals as to how the custody of the child should be restored.

Article 15

(1)   Before reaching a decision under paragraph (1)(b) of Article 10, the authority concerned in the State addressed:

(a)   shall ascertain the child's views unless this is impracticable having regard in particular to his age and understanding; and

(b)   may request that any appropriate enquiries be carried out.

(2)   The cost of enquiries in any Contracting State shall be met by the authorities of the State where they are carried out.

Requests for enquiries and the results of enquiries may be sent to the authority concerned through the central authorities.

Article 16

(1)   In relation to a State which has in matters of custody two or more systems of law of territorial application:

(a)   reference to the law of a person's habitual residence or to the law of a person's nationality shall be construed as referring to the system of law determined by the rules in force in that State or, if there are no such rules, to the system of law with which the person concerned is most closely connected;

(b)   reference to the State of origin or to the State addressed shall be construed as referring, as the case may be, to the territorial unit where the decision was given or to the territorial unit where recognition or enforcement of the decision or restoration of custody is requested.

(2)   Paragraph (1)(a) of this Article also applies mutatis mutandis to States which have in matters of custody two or more systems of law of personal application.

SCHEDULE 3
CUSTODY ORDER   Section 27(1)

PART II
SCOTLAND

5.   An order made by a court of civil jurisdiction in Scotland under any enactment or rule of law with respect to the [residence,] custody, care or control of a
child [or contact with,] or access to a child, excluding—
          (i)   an order placing a child under the supervision of a local authority;
          [. . .]
          (iii)   an order relating to the [guardianship] of a child;
          (iv)   an order made under section [86 of the Children (Scotland) Act 1995];
          (v)   [an order made, or warrant or authorisation granted, under or by virtue
of Chapter 2 or 3 of Part II of the Children (Scotland) Act 1995 to remove the
child to a place of safety or to secure accommodation, to keep him at such a
place or in such accommodation, or to prevent his removal from a place where
he is being accommodated (or an order varying or discharging any order,
warrant or authorisation so made or granted);]
          (vi)   an order made in proceedings under this Act;
          [(vii)   an adoption order (as defined in section 28(1) of the Adoption and
Children (Scotland) Act 2007 (asp 4));
          (viii)   a permanence order (as defined in subsection (2) of section 80 of that
Act) which includes provision such as is mentioned in paragraph (c) of that
subsection.]
          [6.   A supervision requirement made by a children's hearing under section 70
of the Children (Scotland) Act 1995 (whether or not continued under section 73 of
that Act) or made by the sheriff under section 51(5)(c)(iii) of that Act and any
order made by a court in England and Wales or in Northern Ireland if it is an
order which, by virtue of section 33(1) of that Act, has effect as if it were such a
supervision requirement.]
          [. . .]

LAW REFORM (PARENT AND CHILD) (SCOTLAND) ACT 1986
(1986, c 9)

1   [Abolition of status of illegitimacy]
(1)   [No person whose status is governed by Scots law shall be illegitimate; and
accordingly the fact that a person's parents are not or have not been married to
each other shall be left out of account in—
          (a)   determining the person's legal status; or
          (b)   establishing the legal relationship between the person and any other
person.]
(2)   [. . .] Any reference (however expressed) in any enactment or deed to any
relative shall, unless the contrary intention appears in the enactment or deed, be
construed in accordance with subsection (1) above.
          [. . .]
(4)   Nothing in this section shall apply to the construction or effect of—
          (a)   any enactment passed or made before the commencement of section 21
of the Family Law (Scotland) Act 2006 (asp 2);
          (b)   any deed executed before such commencement.
          [. . .]
[(5)   In subsection (4), 'enactment' includes an Act of the Scottish Parliament.]
(6)   It shall no longer be competent to bring an action for declarator of legitimacy, legitimation or illegitimacy.]

[. . .]

5 Presumptions

(1) A man shall be presumed to be the father of a child—

(a) if he was married to the mother of the child at any ti beginning with the conception and ending with the birth of the

(b) where paragraph (a) above does not apply, if both he a the child have acknowledged that he is the father and he has such in any register kept under section 13 (register of births and still-births) or section 44 (register of corrections, etc) of the Registration of Births, Deaths and Marriages (Scotland) Act 1965 or in any corresponding register kept under statutory authority in any part of the United Kingdom other than Scotland.

(2) Subsection (1)(a) above shall apply in the case of a void, voidable or irregular marriage as it applies in the case of a valid and regular marriage.

(3) Without prejudice to the effect under any rule of law which a decree of declarator in an action to which section 7 of this Act applies may have in relation to the parties, a decree of declarator in such an action shall give rise to a presumption to the same effect as the decree; and any such presumption shall displace any contrary presumption howsoever arising.

(4) Any presumption under this section may be rebutted by proof on a balance of probabilities.

6 Determination of parentage by blood sample

(1) This section applies where, for the purpose of obtaining evidence relating to the determination of parentage in civil proceedings, a [sample of blood or other body fluid or of body tissue] is sought by a party to the proceedings or by a curator *ad litem*.

(2) Where [such] a sample is sought from a child [under the age of 16 years], consent to the taking of the sample may be given by [any person having parental responsibilities (within the meaning of section 1(3) of the Children (Scotland) Act 1995) in relation to him or having] care and control of him.

(3) Where [such] a sample is sought from any person who is incapable of giving consent, the court may consent to the taking of the sample where—

(a) there is no person who is entitled to give such consent, or

(b) there is such a person, but it is not reasonably practicable to obtain his consent in the circumstances, or he is unwilling to accept the responsibility of giving or withholding consent.

(4) The court shall not consent under subsection (3) above to the taking of [such] a sample from any person unless the court is satisfied that the taking of the sample would not be detrimental to the person's health.

7 Actions for declarator

(1) An action for declarator of parentage [or non-parentage] may be brought in the Court of Session or the sheriff court.

(2) Such an action may be brought in the Court of Session if and only if the child was born in Scotland or the alleged or presumed parent or the child—

(a) is domiciled in Scotland on the date when the action is brought;

(b) was habitually resident in Scotland for not less than one year immediately preceding that date; or

(c) died before that date and either—

(i) was at the date of death domiciled in Scotland; or

(ii) had been habitually resident in Scotland for not less than one year immediately preceding the date of death.

(3) Such an action may be brought in the sheriff court if and only if—

(a) the child was born in the sheriffdom, or

(b) an action could have been brought in the Court of Session under subsection (2) above and the alleged or presumed parent or the child was habitually resident in the sheriffdom on the date when the action is brought or on the date of his death.

[. . .]

(5) Nothing in any rule of law or enactment shall prevent the court making in any proceedings an incidental finding as to parentage [or non-parentage] for the purposes of those proceedings.

(6) In this section 'the alleged or presumed parent' includes a person who claims or is alleged to be or not to be the parent.

8 Interpretation

In this Act, unless the context otherwise requires, the following expressions shall have the following meanings respectively assigned to them—

'action for declarator' includes an application for declarator contained in other proceedings [but does not include an appeal under section 20(1)(a) or (b) (Appeals) of the Child Support Act 1991 made to the court by virtue of an order made under section 45 (Jurisdiction of the courts in certain proceedings) of that Act];

[. . .]

'the court' means the Court of Session or the sheriff;

[. . .]

'deed' means any disposition, contract, instrument or writing whether *inter vivos* or *mortis causa*;

'non-parentage' means that a person is not or was not the parent, or is not or was not the child, of another person;

'parent' includes natural parent;

'parentage' means that a person is or was the parent, or is or was the child, of another person;

[. . .]

9 Savings and supplementary provisions

(1) Nothing in this Act shall—

(a) affect any rule of law whereby a child born out of wedlock takes the domicile of his mother as a domicile of origin or dependence;

(b) [subject to subsection (1A) below,] except to the extent that Schedules 1 and 2 to this Act otherwise provide, affect the law relating to adoption of children;

(c) apply to any title, coat of arms, honour or dignity transmissible on the death of the holder thereof or affect the succession thereto or the devolution thereof [(including, in particular, the competence of bringing an action of declarator of legitimacy, legitimation or illegitimacy in connection with such succession or devolution);

(ca) affect the functions of the Lord Lyon King of Arms so far as relating to the granting of arms;]

(d) affect the right of legitim out of, or the right of succession to, the estate of any person who died before the commencement of this Act.

[(1A) Subsections (1) and (2) of section 1 of this Act shall apply in relation to adopted children.]

(2) The court may at any time vary or recall any order made under section 3 of this Act or consent given by it under section 6 of this Act.

HUMAN FERTILISATION AND EMBRYOLOGY ACT 1990
(1990, c 37)

Principal terms used

1 Meaning of 'embryo', 'gamete' and associated expressions

(1) In this Act (except in section 4A or in the term 'human admixed embryo')—

(a) embryo means a live human embryo and does not include a human admixed embryo (as defined by section 4A(6)), and

(b) references to an embryo include an egg that is in the process of fertilisation or is undergoing any other process capable of resulting in an embryo.]

(2) This Act, so far as it governs bringing about the creation of an embryo, applies only to bringing about the creation of an embryo outside the human body; and in this Act—

[(a) references to embryos the creation of which was brought about in vitro (in their application to those where fertilisation or any other process by which an embryo is created is complete) are to those where fertilisation or any other process by which the embryo was created began outside the human body whether or not it was completed there, and]

(b) references to embryos taken from a woman do not include embryos whose creation was brought about *in vitro*.

(3) This Act, so far as it governs the keeping or use of an embryo, applies only to keeping or using an embryo outside the human body.

(4) [In this Act (except in section 4A)—

(a) references to eggs are to live human eggs, including cells of the female germ line at any stage of maturity, but (except in subsection (1)(b)) not including eggs that are in the process of fertilisation or are undergoing any other process capable of resulting in an embryo,

(b) references to sperm are to live human sperm, including cells of the male germ line at any stage of maturity, and

(c) references to gametes are to be read accordingly.]

[(5) For the purposes of this Act, sperm is to be treated as partner-donated sperm if the donor of the sperm and the recipient of the sperm declare that they have an intimate physical relationship.]

[(6) If it appears to the Secretary of State necessary or desirable to do so in the light of developments in science or medicine, regulations may provide that in this Act (except in section 4A) 'embryo', 'eggs', 'sperm' or 'gametes' includes things specified in the regulations which would not otherwise fall within the definition.

(7) Regulations made by virtue of subsection (6) may not provide for anything containing any nuclear or mitochondrial DNA that is not human to be treated as an embryo or as eggs, sperm or gametes.]

[1A Reference to Directives

In this Act—

'the first Directive' means Directive 2004/23/EC of the European Parliament and of the Council of 31 March 2004 on setting standards of quality and safety for the donation, procurement, testing, processing, preservation, storage and distribution of human tissues and cells,

'the second Directive' means Commission Directive 2006/17/EC of 8 February 2006 implementing Directive 2004/23/EC of the European Parliament and of the Council as regards certain technical requirements for the donation, procurement and testing of human tissues and cells, and

'the third Directive' means Commission Directive 2006/86/EC of 24 October 2006 implementing Directive 2004/23/EC of the European Parliament and of the Council as regards traceability requirements, notification of serious adverse reactions and events and certain technical requirements for the coding, processing, preservation, storage and distribution of human tissues and cells.]

2   Other terms

(1)   In this Act—

'the Authority' means the Human Fertilisation and Embryology Authority established under section 5 of this Act,

['basic partner treatment services' means treatment services that are provided for a woman and a man together without using—

(a)   the gametes of any other person, or

(b)   embryos created outside the woman's body,

'competent authority', in relation to an EEA state other than the United Kingdom or in relation to Gibraltar, means an authority designated in accordance with the law of that state or territory as responsible for implementing the requirements of the first, second and third Directives,]

'directions' means directions under section 23 of this Act,

['distribution', in relation to gametes or embryos intended for human application, means transportation or delivery, and related terms are to be interpreted accordingly,

'human application' means use in a human recipient,]

'licence' means a licence under Schedule 2 to this Act and, in relation to a licence, 'the person responsible' has the meaning given by section 17 of this Act,

'non-medical fertility services' means any services that are provided, in the course of a business, for the purpose of assisting women to carry children, but are not medical, surgical or obstetric services,

['nuclear DNA', in relation to an embryo, includes DNA in the pronucleus of the embryo,]

'processing', in relation to gametes or embryos intended for human application, means any operation involved in their preparation, manipulation or packaging, and related terms are to be interpreted accordingly,

['procurement', in relation to gametes or embryos intended for human application, means any process by which they are made available, and related terms are to be interpreted accordingly,]

'serious adverse event' means—

(a)   any untoward occurrence which may be associated with the procurement, testing, processing, storage or distribution of gametes or embryos intended for human application and which, in relation to a donor of gametes or a person who receives treatment services or non-medical fertility services—

(i)   might lead to the transmission of a communicable disease, to death, or life-threatening, disabling or incapacitating conditions, or

(ii)   might result in, or prolong, hospitalisation or illness, or

(b)   any type of gametes or embryo misidentification or mix-up,

'serious adverse reaction' means an unintended response, including a communicable disease, in a donor of gametes intended for human application or a person who receives treatment services or non-medical fertility services, which may be associated with the procurement or human application of gametes or embryos and which is fatal, life-threatening, disabling, incapacitating or which results in, or prolongs, hospitalisation or illness,

'store', in relation to gametes or embryos, means preserve, whether by cryopreservation or in any other way, and 'storage' and 'stored' are to be interpreted accordingly, and

'traceability' means the ability—

(a)   to identify and locate gametes and embryos during any step from procurement to use for human application or disposal,

(b)   to identify the donor and recipient of particular gametes, embryos [or human admixed embryos],

. (c)   to identify any person who has carried out any activity in relation to particular gametes or embryos, and

(d)   to identify and locate all relevant data relating to products and materials coming into contact with particular gametes or embryos and which can affect their quality or safety,]

'treatment services' means medical, surgical or obstetric services provided to the public or a section of the public for the purpose of assisting women to carry children.

(2) References in this Act to keeping, in relation to embryos [, gametes or human admixed embryos] include keeping while preserved [in storage].

[(2A) For the purposes of this Act, a person who, from any premises, controls the provision of services for transporting gametes or embryos is to be taken to distribute gametes or embryos on those premises.

(2B) In this Act, any reference to a requirement of a provision of the first, second or third Directive is a reference to a requirement which that provision requires to be imposed.]

(3) For the purposes of this Act, a woman is not to be treated as carrying a child until the embryo has become implanted.

[2A   Third party agreements

(1) For the purposes of this Act, a 'third party agreement' is an agreement in writing between a person who holds a licence and another person which is made in accordance with any licence conditions imposed by the Authority for the purpose of securing compliance with the requirements of Article 24 of the first Directive (relations between tissue establishments and third parties) and under which the other person—

(a)   procures, tests or processes gametes or embryos (or both), on behalf of the holder of the licence, or

(b)   supplies to the holder of the licence any goods or services (including distribution services) which may affect the quality or safety of gametes or embryos.

(2)   In this Act—

'relevant third party premises', in relation to a licence, means any premises (other than premises to which the licence relates)—

(a)   on which a third party procures, tests, processes or distributes gametes or embryos on behalf of any person in connection with activities carried out by that person under a licence, or

(b)   from which a third party provides any goods or services which may affect the quality or safety of gametes or embryos to any person in connection with activities carried out by that person under a licence;

'third party' means a person with whom a person who holds a licence has a third party agreement.

(3)   References in this Act to the persons to whom a third party agreement applies are to—

(a)   the third party,

(b)   any person designated in the third party agreement as a person to whom the agreement applies, and

(c)   any person acting under the direction of a third party or of any person so designated.]

Activities governed by the Act

3   Prohibitions in connection with embryos

(1) [No person shall bring about the creation of an embryo except in pursuance of a licence].

[(1A) No person shall keep or use an embryo except—

(a)   in pursuance of a licence, or

(b)   in the case of—

(i)   the keeping, without storage, of an embryo intended for human application, or

(ii)   the processing, without storage, of such an embryo, in pursuance of a third party agreement.

(1B)   No person shall procure or distribute an embryo intended for human application except in pursuance of a licence or a third party agreement.]

[(2)   No person shall place in a woman—

(a)   an embryo other than a permitted embryo (as defined by section 3ZA), or

(b)   any gametes other than permitted eggs or permitted sperm (as so defined).]

(3)   A licence cannot authorise—

(a)   keeping or using an embryo after the appearance of the primitive streak,

(b)   placing an embryo in any animal, [or]

(c)   keeping or using an embryo in any circumstances in which regulations prohibit its keeping or use

[. . .]

(4)   For the purposes of subsection (3)(a) above, the primitive streak is to be taken to have appeared in an embryo not later than the end of the period of 14 days beginning with [the day on which the process of creating the embryo began], not counting any time during which the embryo is stored.

[3ZA   Permitted eggs, permitted sperm and permitted embryos

(1)   This section has effect for the interpretation of section 3(2).

(2)   A permitted egg is one—

(a)   which has been produced by or extracted from the ovaries of a woman, and

(b)   whose nuclear or mitochondrial DNA has not been altered.

(3)   Permitted sperm are sperm—

(a)   which have been produced by or extracted from the testes of a man, and

(b)   whose nuclear or mitochondrial DNA has not been altered.

(4)   An embryo is a permitted embryo if—

(a)   it has been created by the fertilisation of a permitted egg by permitted sperm,

(b)   no nuclear or mitochondrial DNA of any cell of the embryo has been altered, and

(c)   no cell has been added to it other than by division of the embryo's own cells.

(5)   Regulations may provide that—

(a)   an egg can be a permitted egg, or

(b)   an embryo can be a permitted embryo,

even though the egg or embryo has had applied to it in prescribed circumstances a prescribed process designed to prevent the transmission of serious mitochondrial disease.

(6)   In this section—

(a)   'woman' and 'man' include respectively a girl and a boy (from birth), and

(b)   'prescribed' means prescribed by regulations.]

[3A   Prohibition in connection with germ cells

(1)   No person shall, for the purpose of providing fertility services for any woman, use female germ cells taken or derived from an embryo or a foetus or use embryos created by using such cells.

(2)   In this section—

'female germ cells' means cells of the female germ line and includes such cells at any stage of maturity and accordingly includes eggs; and

'fertility services' means medical, surgical or obstetric services provided for the purpose of assisting women to carry children.]

4   Prohibitions in connection with gametes
  (1)   No person shall—
    (a)   store any gametes, or
    (b)   [in the course of providing treatment services for any woman, use—
      (i)   any sperm, other than partner-donated sperm which has been neither processed nor stored,
      (ii)   the woman's eggs after processing or storage, or
      (iii)   the eggs of any other woman.
    [. . .]
  [(1A)   No person shall procure, test, process or distribute any gametes intended for human application except in pursuance of a licence or a third party agreement.]
  (2)   A licence cannot authorise storing or using gametes in any circumstances in which regulations prohibit their storage or use.
  (3)   No person shall place sperm and eggs in a woman in any circumstances specified in regulations except in pursuance of a licence.
  (4)   Regulations made by virtue of subsection (3) above may provide that, in relation to licences only to place sperm and eggs in a woman in such circumstances, sections 12 to 22 of this Act shall have effect with such modifications as may be specified in the regulations.
  (5)   Activities regulated by this section or section 3 [or 4A] of this Act are referred to in this Act as 'activities governed by this Act'.

[4A   Prohibitions in connection with genetic material not of human origin
  (1)   No person shall place in a woman—
    (a)   a human admixed embryo,
    (b)   any other embryo that is not a human embryo, or
    (c)   any gametes other than human gametes.
  (2)   No person shall—
    (a)   mix human gametes with animal gametes,
    (b)   bring about the creation of a human admixed embryo, or
    (c)   keep or use a human admixed embryo,
except in pursuance of a licence.
  (3)   A licence cannot authorise keeping or using a human admixed embryo after the earliest of the following—
    (a)   the appearance of the primitive streak, or
    (b)   the end of the period of 14 days beginning with the day on which the process of creating the human admixed embryo began, but not counting any time during which the human admixed embryo is stored.
  (4)   A licence cannot authorise placing a human admixed embryo in an animal.
  (5)   A licence cannot authorise keeping or using a human admixed embryo in any circumstances in which regulations prohibit its keeping or use.
  (6)   For the purposes of this Act a human admixed embryo is—
    (a)   an embryo created by replacing the nucleus of an animal egg or of an animal cell, or two animal pronuclei, with—
      (i)   two human pronuclei,
      (ii)   one nucleus of a human gamete or of any other human cell, or
      (iii)   one human gamete or other human cell,
    (b)   any other embryo created by using—
      (i)   human gametes and animal gametes, or
      (ii)   one human pronucleus and one animal pronucleus,
    (c)   a human embryo that has been altered by the introduction of any sequence of nuclear or mitochondrial DNA of an animal into one or more cells of the embryo,
    (d)   a human embryo that has been altered by the introduction of one or more animal cells, or

(e)   any embryo not falling within paragraphs (a) to (d) which contains both nuclear or mitochondrial DNA of a human and nuclear or mitochondrial DNA of an animal ('animal DNA') but in which the animal DNA is not predominant.

(7)   In subsection (6)—

(a)   references to animal cells are to cells of an animal or of an animal embryo, and

(b)   references to human cells are to cells of a human or of a human embryo.

(8)   For the purposes of this section an 'animal' is an animal other than man.

(9)   In this section 'embryo' means a live embryo, including an egg that is in the process of fertilisation or is undergoing any other process capable of resulting in an embryo.

(10)   In this section—

(a)   references to eggs are to live eggs, including cells of the female germ line at any stage of maturity, but (except in subsection (9)) not including eggs that are in the process of fertilisation or are undergoing any other process capable of resulting in an embryo, and

(b)   references to gametes are to eggs (as so defined) or to live sperm, including cells of the male germ line at any stage of maturity.

(11)   If it appears to the Secretary of State necesssary or desirable to do so in the light of developments in science or medicine, regulations may—

(a)   amend (but not repeal) paragraphs (a) to (e) of subsection (6);

(b)   provide that in this section 'embryo', 'eggs' or 'gametes' includes things specified in the regulations which would not otherwise fall within the definition.

(12)   Regulations made by virtue of subsection (11)(a) may make any amendment of subsection (7) that appears to the Secretary of State to be appropriate in consequence of any amendment of subsection (6).]

Status

27   Meaning of 'mother'

(1)   The woman who is carrying or has carried a child as a result of the placing in her of an embryo or of sperm and eggs, and no other woman, is to be treated as the mother of the child.

(2)   Subsection (1) above does not apply to any child to the extent that the child is treated by virtue of adoption as not being the [woman's child].

(3)   Subsection (1) above applies whether the woman was in the United Kingdom or elsewhere at the time of the placing in her of the embryo or the sperm and eggs.

28   Meaning of 'father'

(1)   [Subject to subsections (5A) to (5I) below, this] section applies in the case of a child who is being or has been carried by a woman as the result of the placing in her of an embryo or of sperm and eggs or her artificial insemination.

(2)   If—

(a)   at the time of the placing in her of the embryo or the sperm and eggs or of her insemination, the woman was a party to a marriage, and

(b)   the creation of the embryo carried by her was not brought about with the sperm of the other party to the marriage,

then, subject to subsection (5) below, the other party to the marriage shall be treated as the father of the child unless it is shown that he did not consent to the placing in her of the embryo or the sperm and eggs or to her insemination (as the case may be).

(3)   If no man is treated, by virtue of subsection (2) above, as the father of the child but—

(a)   the embryo or the sperm and eggs were placed in the woman, or she was artificially inseminated, in the course of treatment services provided for her and a man together by a person to whom a licence applies, and

(b)   the creation of the embryo carried by her was not brought about with the sperm of that man,

then, subject to subsection (5) below, that man shall be treated as the father of the child.

(4)   Where a person is treated as the father of the child by virtue of subsection (2) or (3) above, no other person is to be treated as the father of the child.

(5)   Subsections (2) and (3) above do not apply—

(a)   in relation to England and Wales and Northern Ireland, to any child who, by virtue of the rules of common law, is treated as the legitimate child of the parties to a marriage,

(b)   in relation to Scotland, to any child who, by virtue of any enactment or other rule of law, is treated as the child of the parties to a marriage, or

(c)   to any child to the extent that the child is treated by virtue of adoption as not being the [man's child].

[(5A)   If—

(a)   a child has been carried by a woman as the result of the placing in her of an embryo or of sperm and eggs or her artificial insemination,

(b)   the creation of the embryo carried by her was brought about by using the sperm of a man after his death, or the creation of the embryo was brought about using the sperm of a man before his death but the embryo was placed in the woman after his death,

(c)   the woman was a party to a marriage with the man immediately before his death,

(d)   the man consented in writing (and did not withdraw the consent)—

(i)   to the use of his sperm after his death which brought about the creation of the embryo carried by the woman or (as the case may be) to the placing in the woman after his death of the embryo which was brought about using his sperm before his death, and

(ii)   to being treated for the purpose mentioned in subsection (5I) below as the father of any resulting child,

(e)   the woman has elected in writing not later than the end of the period of 42 days from the day on which the child was born for the man to be treated for the purpose mentioned in subsection (5I) below as the father of the child, and

(f)   no-one else is to be treated as the father of the child by virtue of sub-section (2) or (3) above or by virtue of adoption or the child being treated as mentioned in paragraph (a) or (b) of subsection (5) above,

then the man shall be treated for the purpose mentioned in subsection (5I) below as the father of the child.

(5B)   If—

(a)   a child has been carried by a woman as the result of the placing in her of an embryo or of sperm and eggs or her artificial insemination,

(b)   the creation of the embryo carried by her was brought about by using the sperm of a man after his death, or the creation of the embryo was brought about using the sperm of a man before his death but the embryo was placed in the woman after his death,

(c)   the woman was not a party to a marriage with the man immediately before his death but treatment services were being provided for the woman and the man together before his death either by a person to whom a licence applies or outside the United Kingdom,

(d)   the man consented in writing (and did not withdraw the consent)—

(i)   to the use of his sperm after his death which brought about the creation of the embryo carried by the woman or (as the case may be) to the placing in the woman after his death of the embryo which was brought about using his sperm before his death, and

(ii)   to being treated for the purpose mentioned in subsection (5I) below as the father of any resulting child,

(e)   the woman has elected in writing not later than the end of the period of 42 days from the day on which the child was born for the man to be treated for the purpose mentioned in subsection (5I) below as the father of the child, and

(f)   no-one else is to be treated as the father of the child by virtue of subsection (2) or (3) above or by virtue of adoption or the child being treated as mentioned in paragraph (a) or (b) of subsection (5) above,

then the man shall be treated for the purpose mentioned in subsection (5I) below as the father of the child.

(5C)   If—

(a)   a child has been carried by a woman as the result of the placing in her of an embryo,

(b)   the embryo was created at a time when the woman was a party to a marriage,

(c)   the creation of the embryo was not brought about with the sperm of the other party to the marriage,

(d)   the other party to the marriage died before the placing of the embryo in the woman,

(e)   the other party to the marriage consented in writing (and did not withdraw the consent)—

(i)   to the placing of the embryo in the woman after his death, and

(ii)   to being treated for the purpose mentioned in subsection (5I) below as the father of any resulting child,

(f)   the woman has elected in writing not later than the end of the period of 42 days from the day on which the child was born for the other party to the marriage to be treated for the purpose mentioned in subsection (5I) below as the father of the child, and

(g)   no-one else is to be treated as the father of the child by virtue of subsection (2) or (3) above or by virtue of adoption or the child being treated as mentioned in paragraph (a) or (b) of subsection (5) above,

then the other party to the marriage shall be treated for the purpose mentioned in subsection (5I) below as the father of the child.

(5D)   If—

(a)   a child has been carried by a woman as the result of the placing in her of an embryo,

(b)   the embryo was not created at a time when the woman was a party to a marriage but was created in the course of treatment services provided for the woman and a man together either by a person to whom a licence applies or outside the United Kingdom,

(c)   the creation of the embryo was not brought about with the sperm of that man,

(d)   the man died before the placing of the embryo in the woman,

(e)   the man consented in writing (and did not withdraw the consent)—

(i)   to the placing of the embryo in the woman after his death, and

(ii)   to being treated for the purpose mentioned in subsection (5I) below as the father of any resulting child,

(f)   the woman has elected in writing not later than the end of the period of 42 days from the day on which the child was born for the man to be treated for the purpose mentioned in subsection (5I) below as the father of the child, and

(g)   no-one else is to be treated as the father of the child by virtue of subsection (2) or (3) above or by virtue of adoption or the child being treated as mentioned in paragraph (a) or (b) of subsection (5) above,

then the man shall be treated for the purpose mentioned in subsection (5I) below as the father of the child.

(5E)   In the application of subsections (5A) to (5D) above to Scotland, for any reference to a period of 42 days there shall be substituted a reference to a period of 21 days.

(5F)   The requirement under subsection (5A), (5B), (5C) or (5D) above as to the making of an election (which requires an election to be made either on or before the day on which the child was born or within the period of 42 or, as the case may be, 21 days from that day) shall nevertheless be treated as satisfied if the required election is made after the end of that period but with the consent of the Registrar General under subsection (5G) below.

(5G)   The Registrar General may at any time consent to the making of an election after the end of the period mentioned in subsection (5F) above if, on an application made to him in accordance with such requirements as he may specify, he is satisfied that there is a compelling reason for giving his consent to the making of such an election.

(5H)   In subsections (5F) and (5G) above 'the Registrar General' means the Registrar General for England and Wales, the Registrar General of Births, Deaths and Marriages for Scotland or (as the case may be) the Registrar General for Northern Ireland.

(5I)   The purpose referred to in subsections (5A) to (5D) above is the purpose of enabling the man's particulars to be entered as the particulars of the child's father in (as the case may be) a register of live-births or still-births kept under the Births and Deaths Registration Act 1953 or the Births and Deaths Registration (Northern Ireland) Order 1976 or a register of births or still-births kept under the Registration of Births, Deaths and Marriages (Scotland) Act 1965.]

(6)   Where—

(a)   the sperm of a man who had given such consent as is required by paragraph 5 of Schedule 3 to this Act was used for a purpose for which such consent was required, or

(b)   the sperm of a man, or any embryo the creation of which was brought about with his sperm, was used after his death,

he is not [, subject to subsections (5A) and (5B) above,] to be treated as the father of the child.

(7)   The references in subsection (2) above [and subsections (5A) to (5D) above] to the parties to a marriage at the time there referred to—

(a)   are to the parties to a marriage subsisting at that time, unless a judicial separation was then in force, but

(b)   include the parties to a void marriage if either or both of them reasonably believed at that time that the marriage was valid; and for the purposes of this subsection it shall be presumed, unless the contrary is shown, that one of them reasonably believed at that time that the marriage was valid.

(8)   This section applies whether the woman was in the United Kingdom or elsewhere at the time of the placing in her of the embryo or the sperm and eggs or her artificial insemination.

(9)   In subsection (7)(a) above, 'judicial separation' includes a legal separation obtained in a country outside the British Islands and recognised in the United Kingdom.

29   Effect of sections 27 and 28

(1)   Where by virtue of section 27 or 28 of this Act a person is to be treated as the mother or father of a child, that person is to be treated in law as the mother or, as the case may be, father of the child for all purposes.

(2)   Where by virtue of section 27 or 28 of this Act a person is not to be treated as the mother or father of a child, that person is to be treated in law as not being the mother or, as the case may be, father of the child for any purpose.

(3)   Where subsection (1) or (2) above has effect, references to any relationship between two people in any enactment, deed or other instrument or document (whenever passed or made) are to be read accordingly.

[(3A)   Subsections (1) to (3) above do not apply in relation to the treatment in law of a deceased man in a case to which section 28(5A), (5B), (5C) or (5D) of this Act applies.

(3B)   Where subsection (5A), (5B), (5C) or (5D) of section 28 of this Act applies, the deceased man—

(a)   is to be treated in law as the father of the child for the purpose referred to in that subsection, but

(b)   is to be treated in law as not being the father of the child for any other purpose.

(3C)   Where subsection (3B) above has effect, references to any relationship between two people in any enactment, deed or other instrument or document (whenever passed or made) are to be read accordingly.

(3D)   In subsection (3C) above 'enactment' includes an enactment comprised in, or in an instrument made under, an Act of the Scottish Parliament or Northern Ireland legislation.]

(4)   In relation to England and Wales and Northern Ireland, nothing in the provisions of section 27(1) or 28(2) to (4) [or (5A) to (5I)], read with this section, affects—

(a)   the succession to any dignity or title of honour or renders any person capable of succeeding to or transmitting a right to succeed to any such dignity or title, or

(b)   the devolution of any property limited (expressly or not) to devolve (as nearly as the law permits) along with any dignity or title of honour.

(5)   In relation to Scotland—

(a)   those provisions do not apply to any title, coat of arms, honour or dignity transmissible on the death of the holder thereof or affect the succession thereto or the devolution thereof, and

(b)   where the terms of any deed provide that any property or interest in property shall devolve along with a title, coat of arms, honour or dignity, nothing in those provisions shall prevent that property or interest from so devolving.

[. . .]

Information

[31   Register of information

(1)   The Authority shall keep a register which is to contain any information which falls within subsection (2) and which—

(a)   immediately before the coming into force of section 24 of the Human Fertilisation and Embryology Act 2008, was contained in the register kept under this section by the Authority, or

(b)   is obtained by the Authority.

(2)   Subject to subsection (3), information falls within this subsection if it relates to—

(a)   the provision for any identifiable individual of treatment services other than basic partner treatment services,

(b)   the procurement or distribution of any sperm, other than sperm which is partner-donated sperm and has not been stored, in the course of providing non-medical fertility services for any identifiable individual,

(c)   the keeping of the gametes of any identifiable individual or of an embryo taken from any identifiable woman,

(d)   the use of the gametes of any identifiable individual other than their use for the purpose of basic partner treatment services, or

(e)   the use of an embryo taken from any identifiable woman,

or if it shows that any identifiable individual is a relevant individual.

(3)   Information does not fall within subsection (2) if it is provided to the

Authority for the purposes of any voluntary contact register as defined by section 31ZF(1).

(4) In this section 'relevant individual' means an individual who was or may have been born in consequence of—

(a) treatment services, other than basic partner treatment services, or

(b) the procurement or distribution of any sperm (other than partner-donated sperm which has not been stored) in the course of providing non-medical fertility services.]

[31ZA Request for information as to genetic parentage etc

(1) A person who has attained the age of 16 ('the applicant') may by notice to the Authority require the Authority to comply with a request under subsection (2).

(2) The applicant may request the Authority to give the applicant notice stating whether or not the information contained in the register shows that a person ('the donor') other than a parent of the applicant would or might, but for the relevant statutory provisions, be the parent of the applicant, and if it does show that—

(a) giving the applicant so much of that information as relates to the donor as the Authority is required by regulations to give (but no other information), or

(b) stating whether or not that information shows that there are other persons of whom the donor is not the parent but would or might, but for the relevant statutory provisions, be the parent and if so—

(i) the number of those other persons,

(ii) the sex of each of them, and

(iii) the year of birth of each of them.

(3) The Authority shall comply with a request under subsection (2) if—

(a) the information contained in the register shows that the applicant is a relevant individual, and

(b) the applicant has been given a suitable opportunity to receive proper counselling about the implications of compliance with the request.

(4) Where a request is made under subsection (2)(a) and the applicant has not attained the age of 18 when the applicant gives notice to the Authority under subsection (1), regulations cannot require the Authority to give the applicant any information which identifies the donor.

(5) Regulations cannot require the Authority to give any information as to the identity of a person whose gametes have been used or from whom an embryo has been taken if a person to whom a licence applied was provided with the information at a time when the Authority could not have been required to give information of the kind in question.

(6) The Authority need not comply with a request made under subsection (2)(b) by any applicant if it considers that special circumstances exist which increase the likelihood that compliance with the request would enable the applicant—

(a) to identify the donor, in a case where the Authority is not required by regulations under subsection (2)(a) to give the applicant information which identifies the donor, or

(b) to identify any person about whom information is given under subsection (2)(b).

(7) In this section—

'relevant individual' has the same meaning as in section 31;

'the relevant statutory provisions' means sections 27 to 29 of this Act and sections 33 to 47 of the Human Fertilisation and Embryology Act 2008.]

[31ZB Request for information as to intended spouse etc

(1) Subject to subsection (4), a person ('the applicant') may by notice to the Authority require the Authority to comply with a request under subsection (2).

(2) The applicant may request the Authority to give the applicant notice stating

whether or not information contained in the register shows that, but for the relevant statutory provisions, the applicant would or might be related to a person specified in the request ('the specified person') as—

(a)   a person whom the applicant proposes to marry,

(b)   a person with whom the applicant proposes to enter into a civil partnership, or

(c)   a person with whom the applicant is in an intimate physical relationship or with whom the applicant proposes to enter into an intimate physical relationship.

(3)   Subject to subsection (5), the Authority shall comply with a request under subsection (2) if—

(a)   the information contained in the register shows that the applicant is a relevant individual,

(b)   the Authority receives notice in writing from the specified person consenting to the request being made and that notice has not been withdrawn, and

(c)   the applicant and the specified person have each been given a suitable opportunity to receive proper counselling about the implications of compliance with the request.

(4)   A request may not be made under subsection (2)(c) by a person who has not attained the age of 16.

(5)   Where a request is made under subsection (2)(c) and the specified person has not attained the age of 16 when the applicant gives notice to the Authority under subsection (1), the Authority must not comply with the request.

(6)   Where the Authority is required under subsection (3) to comply with a request under subsection (2), the Authority must take all reasonable steps to give the applicant and the specified person notice stating whether or not the information contained in the register shows that, but for the relevant statutory provisions, the applicant and the specified person would or might be related.

(7)   In this section—

'relevant individual' has the same meaning as in section 31;

'the relevant statutory provisions' has the same meaning as in section 31ZA.]

[31ZC   Power of Authority to inform donor of request for information

(1)   Where—

(a)   the Authority has received from a person ('the applicant') a notice containing a request under subsection (2)(a) of section 31ZA, and

(b)   compliance by the Authority with its duty under that section has involved or will involve giving the applicant information relating to a person other than the parent of the applicant who would or might, but for the relevant statutory provisions, be a parent of the applicant ('the donor'),

the Authority may notify the donor that a request under section 31ZA(2)(a) has been made, but may not disclose the identity of the applicant or any information relating to the applicant.

(2)   In this section 'the relevant statutory provisions' has the same meaning as in section 31ZA.]

[31ZD   Provision to donor of information about resulting children

(1)   This section applies where a person ('the donor') has consented under Schedule 3 (whether before or after the coming into force of this section) to—

(a)   the use of the donor's gametes, or an embryo the creation of which was brought about using the donor's gametes, for the purposes of treatment services provided under a licence, or

(b)   the use of the donor's gametes for the purposes of non-medical fertility services provided under a licence.

(2)   In subsection (1)—

(a)   'treatment services' do not include treatment services provided to the donor, or to the donor and another person together, and

(b)   'non-medical fertility services' do not include any services involving partner-donated sperm.

(3)   The donor may by notice request the appropriate person to give the donor notice stating—

(a)   the number of persons of whom the donor is not a parent but would or might, but for the relevant statutory provisions, be a parent by virtue of the use of the gametes or embryos to which the consent relates,

(b)   the sex of each of those persons, and

(c)   the year of birth of each of those persons.

(4)   Subject to subsections (5) to (7), the appropriate person shall notify the donor whether the appropriate person holds the information mentioned in subsection (3) and, if the appropriate person does so, shall comply with the request.

(5)   The appropriate person need not comply with a request under subsection (3) if the appropriate person considers that special circumstances exist which increase the likelihood that compliance with the request would enable the donor to identify any of the persons falling within paragraphs (a) to (c) of subsection (3).

(6)   In the case of a donor who consented as described in subsection (1)(a), the Authority need not comply with a request made to it under subsection (3) where the person who held the licence referred to in subsection (1)(a) continues to hold a licence under paragraph 1 of Schedule 2, unless the donor has previously made a request under subsection (3) to the person responsible and the person responsible—

(a)   has notified the donor that the information concerned is not held, or

(b)   has failed to comply with the request within a reasonable period.

(7)   In the case of a donor who consented as described in subsection (1)(b), the Authority need not comply with a request made to it under subsection (3) where the person who held the licence referred to in subsection (1)(b) continues to hold a licence under paragraph 1A of Schedule 2, unless the donor has previously made a request under subsection (3) to the person responsible and the person responsible—

(a)   has notified the donor that the information concerned is not held, or

(b)   has failed to comply with the request within a reasonable period.

(8)   In this section 'the appropriate person' means—

(a)   in the case of a donor who consented as described in paragraph (a) of subsection (1)—

(i)   where the person who held the licence referred to in that paragraph continues to hold a licence under paragraph 1 of Schedule 2, the person responsible, or

(ii)   the Authority, and

(b)   in the case of a donor who consented as described in paragraph (b) of subsection (1)—

(i)   where the person who held the licence referred to in that paragraph continues to hold a licence under paragraph 1A of Schedule 2, the person responsible, or

(ii)   the Authority.

(9)   In this section 'the relevant statutory provisions' has the same meaning as in section 31ZA.]

[31ZE   Provision of information about donor-conceived genetic siblings

(1)   For the purposes of this section two relevant individuals are donor-conceived genetic siblings of each other if a person ('the donor') who is not the parent of either of them would or might, but for the relevant statutory provisions, be the parent of both of them.

(2)   Where—

(a)   the information on the register shows that a relevant individual ('A') is the donor-conceived genetic sibling of another relevant individual ('B'),

(b)   A has provided information to the Authority ('the agreed information') which consists of or includes information which enables A to be identified with the request that it should be disclosed to—
>   (i)   any donor-conceived genetic sibling of A, or
>   (ii)   such siblings of A of a specified description which includes B, and
(c)   the conditions in subsection (3) are satisfied,
then, subject to subsection (4), the Authority shall disclose the agreed information to B.

(3)   The conditions referred to in subsection (2)(c) are—
>   (a)   that each of A and B has attained the age of 18,
>   (b)   that B has requested the disclosure to B of information about any donor-conceived genetic sibling of B, and
>   (c)   that each of A and B has been given a suitable opportunity to receive proper counselling about the implications of disclosure under subsection (2).

(4)   The Authority need not disclose any information under subsection (2) if it considers that the disclosure of information will lead to A or B identifying the donor unless—
>   (a)   the donor has consented to the donor's identity being disclosed to A or B, or
>   (b)   were A or B to make a request under section 31ZA(2)(a), the Authority would be required by regulations under that provision to give A or B information which would identify the donor.

(5)   In this section—
'relevant individual' has the same meaning as in section 31;
'the relevant statutory provisions' has the same meaning as in section 31ZA.]

[31ZF   Power of Authority to keep voluntary contact register
(1)   In this section and section 31ZG, a 'voluntary contact register' means a register of persons who have expressed their wish to receive information about any person to whom they are genetically related as a consequence of the provision to any person of treatment services in the United Kingdom before 1 August 1991.

(2)   The Authority may—
>   (a)   set up a voluntary contact register in such manner as it thinks fit,
>   (b)   keep a voluntary contact register in such manner as it thinks fit,
>   (c)   determine criteria for eligibility for inclusion on the register and the particulars that may be included,
>   (d)   charge a fee to persons who wish their particulars to be entered on the register,
>   (e)   arrange for samples of the DNA of such persons to be analysed at their request,
>   (f)   make such arrangements as it thinks fit for the disclosure of information on the register between persons who appear to the Authority to be genetically related, and
>   (g)   impose such conditions as it thinks fit to prevent a person ('A') from disclosing information to a person to whom A is genetically related ('B') where that information would identify any person who is genetically related to both A and B.

(3)   The Authority may make arrangements with any person by whom a voluntary contact register is kept before the commencement of this section for the supply by that person to the Authority of the information contained in the register maintained by that person.]

[31ZG   Financial assistance for person setting up or keeping voluntary contact register
(1)   The Authority may, instead of keeping a voluntary contact register, give financial assistance to any person who sets up or keeps a voluntary contact register.

(2) Financial assistance under subsection (1) may be given in any form, and in particular, may be given by way of—
  (a) grants,
  (b) loans,
  (c) guarantees, or
  (d) incurring expenditure for the person assisted.
(3) Financial assistance under subsection (1) may be given on such terms and conditions as the Authority considers appropriate.
(4) A person receiving assistance under subsection (1) must comply with the terms and conditions on which it is given, and compliance may be enforced by the Authority.]

[31A The Authority's register of licences

(1) The Authority shall keep a register recording the grant, suspension or revocation of—
  (a) every licence under paragraph 1 or 2 of Schedule 2 authorising activities in relation to gametes or embryos intended for use for human application,
  (b) every licence under paragraph 1A of Schedule 2 [, and]
  [(c) every licence under paragraph 3 of Schedule 2 authorising activities in connection with the derivation from embryos of stem cells that are intended for human application.]
(2) The register shall specify, in relation to each such licence—
  (a) the activities authorised,
  (b) the address of the premises to which the licence relates,
  (c) the name of the person responsible and [the name of the holder of the licence (if different)], and
  (d) any variations made.
(3) The Authority shall make such of the information included in the register as it considers appropriate available to the public in such manner as it considers appropriate.]

[31B The Authority's register of serious adverse events and serious adverse reactions

(1) The Authority shall keep a register containing information provided to it under this Act about any serious adverse event or serious adverse reaction.
(2) The Authority shall make such of the information included in the register as it considers appropriate available to the public in such manner as it considers appropriate.]

32 Information to be provided to Registrar General

(1) This section applies where a claim is made before the Registrar General that a [person] is or is not the [parent] of a child and it is necessary or desirable for the purpose of any function of the Registrar General to determine whether the claim is or may be well-founded.
(2) The Authority shall comply with any request made by the Registrar General by notice to the Authority to disclose whether any information on the register kept in pursuance of section 31 of this Act tends to show [that the person may be a parent of the child by virtue of any of the statutory provisions] and, if it does, disclose that information.
  [(2A) In subsection (2) 'the relevant statutory provisions' means—
  (a) section 28 of this Act, and
  (b) sections 35 to 47 of the Human Fertilisation and Embryology Act 2008.]
(3) In this section and section [33A] of this Act, 'the Registrar General' means the Registrar General for England and Wales, the Registrar General of Births, Deaths and Marriages for Scotland or the Registrar General for Northern Ireland, as the case may be.

[33A   Disclosure of information

(1)   No person shall disclose any information falling within section 31(2) which the person obtained (whether before or after the coming into force of section 24 of the Human Fertilisation and Embryology Act 2008) in the person's capacity as—

(a)   a member or employee of the Authority,

(b)   any person exercising functions of the Authority by virtue of section 8B or 8C of this Act (including a person exercising such functions by virtue of either of those sections as a member of staff or as an employee),

(c)   any person engaged by the Authority to provide services to the Authority,

(d)   any person employed by, or engaged to provide services to, a person mentioned in paragraph (c),

(e)   a person to whom a licence applies,

(f)   a person to whom a third party agreement applies, or

(g)   a person to whom directions have been given.

(2)   Subsection (1) does not apply where—

(a)   the disclosure is made to a person as a member or employee of the Authority or as a person exercising functions of the Authority as mentioned in subsection (1)(b),

(b)   the disclosure is made to or by a person falling within subsection (1)(c) for the purpose of the provision of services which that person is engaged to provide to the Authority,

(c)   the disclosure is made by a person mentioned in subsection (1)(d) for the purpose of enabling a person falling within subsection (1)(c) to provide services which that person is engaged to provide to the Authority,

(d)   the disclosure is made to a person to whom a licence applies for the purpose of that person's functions as such,

(e)   the disclosure is made to a person to whom a third party agreement applies for the purpose of that person's functions under that agreement,

(f)   the disclosure is made in pursuance of directions given by virtue of section 24,

(g)   the disclosure is made so that no individual can be identified from the information,

(h)   the disclosure is of information other than identifying donor information and is made with the consent required by section 33B,

(i)   the disclosure—

(i) is made by a person who is satisfied that it is necessary to make the disclosure to avert an imminent danger to the health of an individual ('P'),

(ii) is of information falling within section 31(2)(a) which could be disclosed by virtue of paragraph (h) with P's consent or could be disclosed to P by virtue of subsection (5), and

(iii) is made in circumstances where it is not reasonably practicable to obtain P's consent,

(j)   the disclosure is of information which has been lawfully made available to the public before the disclosure is made,

(k)   the disclosure is made in accordance with sections 31ZA to 31ZE,

(l)   the disclosure is required or authorised to be made—

(i) under regulations made under section 33D, or

(ii) in relation to any time before the coming into force of the first regulations under that section, under regulations made under section 251 of the National Health Service Act 2006,

(m)   the disclosure is made by a person acting in the capacity mentioned in subsection (1)(a) or (b) for the purpose of carrying out the Authority's duties under section 8A,

(n)   the disclosure is made by a person acting in the capacity mentioned in subsection (1)(a) or (b) in pursuance of an order of a court under section 34 or 35,

(o)   the disclosure is made by a person acting in the capacity mentioned in subsection (1)(a) or (b) to the Registrar General in pursuance of a request under section 32,

(p)   the disclosure is made by a person acting in the capacity mentioned in subsection (1)(a) or (b) to any body or person discharging a regulatory function for the purpose of assisting that body or person to carry out that function,

(q)   the disclosure is made for the purpose of establishing in any proceedings relating to an application for an order under subsection (1) of section 54 of the Human Fertilisation and Embryology Act 2008 whether the condition specified in paragraph (a) or (b) of that subsection is met,

(r)   the disclosure is made under section 3 of the Access to Health Records Act 1990,

(s)   the disclosure is made under Article 5 of the Access to Health Records (Northern Ireland) Order 1993, or

(t)   the disclosure is made necessarily for—

(i)   the purpose of the investigation of any offence (or suspected offence), or

(ii)   any purpose preliminary to proceedings, or for the purposes of, or in connection with, any proceedings.

(3)   Subsection (1) does not apply to the disclosure of information in so far as—

(a)   the information identifies a person who, but for sections 27 to 29 of this Act or sections 33 to 47 of the Human Fertilisation and Embryology Act 2008, would or might be a parent of a person who instituted proceedings under section 1A of the Congenital Disabilities (Civil Liability) Act 1976, and

(b)   the disclosure is made for the purpose of defending such proceedings, or instituting connected proceedings for compensation against that parent.

(4)   Paragraph (t) of subsection (2), so far as relating to disclosure for the purpose of the investigation of an offence or suspected offence, or for any purpose preliminary to, or in connection with proceedings, does not apply—

(a)   to disclosure of identifying donor information, or

(b)   to disclosure, in circumstances in which subsection (1) of section 34 of this Act applies, of information relevant to the determination of the question mentioned in that subsection, made by any person acting in a capacity mentioned in any of paragraphs (c) to (g) of subsection (1).

(5)   Subsection (1) does not apply to the disclosure to any individual of information which—

(a)   falls within subsection (2) of section 31 of this Act by virtue of any of paragraphs (a) to (e) of that subsection, and

(b)   relates only to that individual or, in the case of an individual who is treated together with, or gives a notice under section 37 or 44 of the Human Fertilisation and Embryology Act 2008 in respect of, another, only to that individual and that other.

(6)   In subsection (2)—

(a)   in paragraph (p) 'regulatory function' has the same meaning as in section 32 of the Legislative and Regulatory Reform Act 2006, and

(b)   in paragraph (t) references to 'proceedings' include any formal procedure for dealing with a complaint.

(7)   In this section 'identifying donor information' means information enabling a person to be identified as a person whose gametes were used in accordance with consent given under paragraph 5 of Schedule 3 for the purposes of treatment services or non-medical fertility services in consequence of which an identifiable individual was, or may have been, born.]

[33B   Consent required to authorise certain disclosures

(1)   This section has effect for the purposes of section 33A(2)(h).

(2)   Subject to subsection (5), the consent required by this section is the consent of each individual who can be identified from the information.

(3)   Consent in respect of a person who has not attained the age of 18 years ('C') may be given—

(a)   by C, in a case where C is competent to deal with the issue of consent, or

(b)   by a person having parental responsibility for C, in any other case.

(4)   Consent to disclosure given at the request of another shall be disregarded unless, before it is given, the person requesting it takes reasonable steps to explain to the individual from whom it is requested the implications of compliance with the request.

(5)   In the case of information which shows that any identifiable individual ('A') was, or may have been, born in consequence of treatment services, the consent required by this section does not include A's consent if the disclosure is necessarily incidental to the disclosure of information falling within section 31(2)(a).

(6)   The reference in subsection (3) to parental responsibility is—

(a)   in relation to England and Wales, to be read in accordance with the Children Act 1989;

(b)   in relation to Northern Ireland, to be read in accordance with the Children (Northern Ireland) Order 1995;

(c)   in relation to Scotland, to be read as a reference to parental responsibilities and parental rights within the meaning of the Children (Scotland) Act 1995.]

[33C   Power to provide for additional exceptions from section 33A(1)

(1)   Regulations may provide for additional exceptions from section 33A(1).

(2)   No exception may be made under this section for—

(a)   disclosure of a kind mentioned in paragraph (a) or (b) of subsection (4) of section 33A, or

(b)   disclosure in circumstances in which section 32 of this Act applies of information having the tendency mentioned in subsection (2) of that section, made by any person acting in a capacity mentioned in any of paragraphs (c) to (g) of subsection (1) of section 33A.]

[33D   Disclosure for the purposes of medical or other research

(1)   Regulations may—

(a)   make such provision for and in connection with requiring or regulating the processing of protected information for the purposes of medical research as the Secretary of State considers is necessary or expedient in the public interest or in the interests of improving patient care, and

(b)   make such provision for and in connection with requiring or regulating the processing of protected information for the purposes of any other research as the Secretary of State considers is necessary or expedient in the public interest.

(2)   Regulations under subsection (1) may, in particular, make provision—

(a)   for requiring or authorising the disclosure or other processing of protected information to or by persons of any prescribed description subject to compliance with any prescribed conditions (including conditions requiring prescribed undertakings to be obtained from such persons as to the processing of such information),

(b)   for securing that, where prescribed protected information is processed by a person in accordance with the regulations, anything done by that person in so processing the information must be taken to be lawfully done despite any obligation of confidence owed by the person in respect of it,

(c)   for requiring fees of a prescribed amount to be paid to the Authority in prescribed circumstances by persons in relation to the disclosure to those persons of protected information under those regulations,

(d)   for the establishment of one or more bodies to exercise prescribed functions in relation to the processing of protected information under those regulations,

(e)   as to the membership and proceedings of any such body, and

(f)   as to the payment of remuneration and allowances to any member of any such body and the reimbursement of expenses.

(3)   Where regulations under subsection (1) require or regulate the processing of protected information for the purposes of medical research, such regulations may enable any approval given under regulations made under section 251 of the National Health Service Act 2006 (control of patient information) to have effect for the purposes of the regulations under subsection (1) in their application to England and Wales.

(4)   Subsections (1) to (3) are subject to subsections (5) to (8).

(5)   Regulations under subsection (1) may not make any provision requiring or authorising the disclosure or other processing, for any purpose, of protected information, where that information is information from which an individual may be identified, if it would be reasonably practicable to achieve that purpose otherwise than pursuant to such regulations, having regard to the cost of and technology available for achieving that purpose.

(6)   Regulations under this section may not make provision for or in connection with the processing of protected information in a manner inconsistent with any provision made by or under the Data Protection Act 1998.

(7)   Subsection (6) does not affect the operation of provisions made under subsection (2)(b).

(8)   Before making any regulations under this section the Secretary of State shall consult such bodies appearing to the Secretary of State to represent the interests of those likely to be affected by the regulations as the Secretary of State considers appropriate.

(9)   In this section—

'prescribed' means prescribed by regulations made by virtue of this section,

'processing', in relation to information, means the use, disclosure, or obtaining of the information or the doing of such other things in relation to it as may be prescribed for the purposes of this definition, and

'protected information' means information falling within section 31(2).]

34   Disclosure in interests of justice

(1)   Where in any proceedings before a court the question whether a person is or is not the parent of a child by virtue of sections 27 to 29 of this Act [or sections 33 to 47 of the Human Fertilisation and Embryology Act 2008] falls to be determined, the court may on the application of any party to the proceedings make an order requiring the Authority—

(a)   to disclose whether or not any information relevant to that question is contained in the register kept in pursuance of section 31 of this Act, and

(b)   if it is, to disclose so much of it as is specified in the order,

but such an order may not require the Authority to disclose any information falling within section 31(2) [(c) to (e)] of this Act.

(2)   The court must not make an order under subsection (1) above unless it is satisfied that the interests of justice require it to do so, taking into account—

(a)   any representations made by any individual who may be affected by the disclosure, and

(b)   the welfare of the child, if under 18 years old, and of any other person under that age who may be affected by the disclosure.

(3)   If the proceedings before the court are civil proceedings, it—

(a)   may direct that the whole or any part of the proceedings on the application for an order under subsection (2) above shall be heard in camera, and

(b)   if it makes such an order, may then or later direct that the whole or any part of any later stage of the proceedings shall be heard in camera.

(4)   An application for a direction under subsection (3) above shall be heard in camera unless the court otherwise directs.

35   Disclosure in interests of justice: congenital disabilities, etc

(1)   Where for the purpose of instituting proceedings under section 1 of the Congenital Disabilities (Civil Liability) Act 1976 (civil liability to child born disabled) it is necessary to identify a person who would or might be the parent of a child but for [the relevant statutory provisions], the court may, on the application of the child, make an order requiring the Authority to disclose any information contained in the register kept in pursuance of section 31 of this Act identifying that person.

(2)   Where, for the purposes of any action for damages in Scotland (including any such action which is likely to be brought) in which the damages claimed consist of or include damages or solatium in respect of personal injury (including any disease and any impairment of physical or mental condition), it is necessary to identify a person who would or might be the parent of a child but for [the relevant statutory provisions], the court may, on the application of any party to the action or, if the proceedings have not been commenced, the prospective pursuer, make an order requiring the Authority to disclose any information contained in the register kept in pursuance of section 31 of this Act identifying that person.

[(2A)   In subsections (1) and (2) 'the relevant statutory provisions' means—

(a)   sections 27 to 29 of this Act, and

(b)   sections 33 to 47 of the Human Fertilisation and Embryology Act 2008.]

(3)   Subsections (2) to (4) of section 34 of this Act apply for the purposes of this section as they apply for the purposes of that.

[. . .]

Conscientious objection

38   Conscientious objection

(1)   No person who has a conscientious objection to participating in any activity governed by this Act shall be under any duty, however arising, to do so.

(2)   In any legal proceedings the burden of proof of conscientious objection shall rest on the person claiming to rely on it.

(3)   In any proceedings before a court in Scotland, a statement on oath by any person to the effect that he has a conscientious objection to participating in a particular activity governed by this Act shall be sufficient evidence of that fact for the purpose of discharging the burden of proof imposed by subsection (2) above.47#-Index

The expressions listed in the left-hand column below are respectively defined or (as the case may be) are to be interpreted in accordance with the provisions of this Act listed in the right-hand column in relation to those expressions.

Expression	Relevant provision
Activities governed by this Act	Section 4(5)
[Appeals committee	Section 20A(2)]
Authority	Section 2(1)
[Basic partner treatment services	Section 2(1)]
Carry, in relation to a child	Section 2(3)
[Competent authority	Section 2(1)]

Expression	Relevant provision
Directions	Section 2(1)
[Distribution, in relation to gametes or embryos intended for human application	Section 2(1)]
Embryo [(except in section 4A or in the term 'human admixed embryo')]	Section 1
[First Directive	Section 1A]
Gametes, eggs or sperm [(except in section 4A)]	Section 1
[Human admixed embryo]	Section 4A(6)]
[Human application	Section 2(1)]
Keeping, in relation to embryos or gametes	Section 2(2)
Licence	Section 2(1)
[. . .]	[. . .]
[Non-medical fertility services	Section 2(1)]
[Nuclear DNA (in relation to an embryo)	Section 2(1)]
[Partner-donated sperm	Section 1(5)]
Person responsible	Section 17(1)
Person to whom a licence applies	Section 17(2)
[Person to whom a third party agreement applies	Section 2A(3)]
[Processing, in relation to gametes or embryos intended for human application	Section 2(1)]
[Procurement, in relation to gametes or embryos intended for human application	Section 2(1)]
[Relevant third party premises, in relation to a licence	Section 2A(2)]
[Second Directive	Section 1A]
[Serious adverse event	Section 2(1)]
[Serious adverse reaction	Section 2(1)]
Statutory storage period	Section 14(3) to (5)
Store, and similar expressions, in relation to embryos [, human admixed embryos] or gametes	[Section 2(1)]
[Third Directive	Section 1A]
[Third party	Section 2A(2)]
[Third party agreement	Section 2A(1)]
[Traceability	Section 2(1)]
Treatment services	Section 2(1)

49 Short title, commencement, etc

(1)   This Act may be cited as the Human Fertilisation and Embryology Act 1990.

(2)   This Act shall come into force on such day as the Secretary of State may by order made by statutory instrument appoint and different days may be appointed for different provisions and for different purposes.

(3)   Sections 27 to 29 of this Act shall have effect only in relation to children carried by women as a result of the placing in them of embryos or of sperm and eggs, or of their artificial insemination (as the case may be), after the commencement of those sections.

(4) Section 27 of the Family Law Reform Act 1987 (artificial insemination) does not have effect in relation to children carried by women as the result of their artificial insemination after the commencement of sections 27 to 29 of this Act.

(5) Schedule 4 to this Act (which makes minor and consequential amendments) shall have effect.

(6) An order under this section may make such transitional provision as the Secretary of State considers necessary or desirable and, in particular, may provide that where activities are carried on under the supervision of a particular individual, being activities which are carried on under the supervision of that individual at the commencement of sections 3 and 4 of this Act, those activities are to be treated, during such period as may be specified in or determined in accordance with the order, as authorised by a licence (having, in addition to the conditions required by this Act, such conditions as may be so specified or determined) under which that individual is the person responsible.

(7) Her Majesty may by Order in Council direct that any of the provisions of this Act shall extend, with such exceptions, adaptations and modifications (if any) as may be specified in the Order, to any of the Channel Islands.

LAW REFORM (MISCELLANEOUS PROVISIONS) (SCOTLAND) ACT 1990
(1990, c 40)

Blood and other samples in civil proceedings

70 Blood and other samples in civil proceedings

(1) In any civil proceedings to which this section applies, the court may (whether or not on application made to it) request a party to the proceedings—

(a) to provide a sample of blood or other body fluid or of body tissue for the purpose of laboratory analysis;

(b) to consent to the taking of such a sample from a child in relation to whom the party has power to give such consent.

(2) Where a party to whom a request under subsection (1) above has been made refuses or fails—

(a) to provide or, as the case may be, to consent to the taking of, a sample as requested by the court, or

(b) to take any step necessary for the provision or taking of such a sample,

the court may draw from the refusal or failure such adverse inference, if any, in relation to the subject matter of the proceedings as seems to it to be appropriate.

(3) In section 6 of the Law Reform (Parent and Child) (Scotland) Act 1986 (determination of parentage by blood sample)—

(a) in subsection (1), for the words 'blood sample' there shall be substituted 'sample of blood or other body fluid or of body tissue'; and

(b) in each of subsections (2), (3) and (4), for the words 'a blood' there shall be substituted 'such a'.

(4) This section applies to any civil proceedings brought in the Court of Session or the sheriff court—

(a) on or after the date of the commencement of this section; or

(b) before the said date in a case where the proof has not by that date begun.

CHILD SUPPORT ACT 1991
(1991, c 48)

The basic principles

1   The duty to maintain

(1)   For the purposes of this Act, each parent of a qualifying chi,
for maintaining him.

(2)   For the purposes of this Act, [a non-resident parent] shall be taken to have
met his responsibility to maintain any qualifying child of his by making periodical
payments of maintenance with respect to the child of such amount, and at such
intervals, as may be determined in accordance with the provisions of this Act.

(3)   Where a maintenance [calculation] made under this Act requires the
making of periodical payments, it shall be the duty of the [non-resident] parent
with respect to whom the [calculation] was made to make those payments.

2   Welfare of children: the general principle

Where, in any case which falls to be dealt with under this Act, the [Commission]
[. . .] is considering the exercise of any discretionary power conferred by this
Act, [it] shall have regard to the welfare of any child likely to be affected by [its]
decision.

3   Meaning of certain terms used in this Act

(1)   A child is a 'qualifying child' if—

   (a)   one of his parents is, in relation to him, [a non-resident parent]; or

   (b)   both of his parents are, in relation to him, [non-resident] parents.

(2)   The parent of any child is a '[non-resident parent'], in relation to him, if—

   (a)   that parent is not living in the same household with the child; and

   (b)   the child has his home with a person who is, in relation to him, a person
with care.

(3)   A person is a 'person with care', in relation to any child, if he is a person—

   (a)   with whom the child has his home;

   (b)   who usually provides day to day care for the child (whether exclusively
or in conjunction with any other person); and

   (c)   who does not fall within a prescribed category of person.

(4)   The Secretary of State shall not, under subsection (3)(c), prescribe as a
category—

   (a)   parents;

   (b)   guardians;

   (c)   persons in whose favour residence orders under section 8 of the Children
Act 1989 are in force;

   (d)   in Scotland, persons [with whom a child is to live by virtue of a residence order under section 11 of the Children (Scotland) Act 1995].

(5)   For the purposes of this Act there may be more than one person with care
in relation to the same qualifying child.

(6)   Periodical payments which are required to be paid in accordance with a
[maintenance calculation] are referred to in this Act as 'child support maintenance'.

(7)   Expressions are defined in this section only for the purposes of this Act.

4   Child support maintenance

(1)   A person who is, in relation to any qualifying child or any qualifying
children, either the person with care or the [non-resident] parent may apply to the
[Commission] for a [maintenance calculation] to be made under this Act with
respect to that child, or any of those children.

(2)   Where a maintenance [calculation] has been made in response to an application under this section the [Commission] may, if the person with care or [non-

dent] parent with respect to whom the [calculation] was made applies to [it] inder this subsection, arrange for—

(a) the collection of the child support maintenance payable in accordance with the [calculation];

(b) the enforcement of the obligation to pay child support maintenance in accordance with the [calculation].

(3) Where an application under subsection (2) for the enforcement of the obligation mentioned in subsection (2)(b) authorises the [Commission] to take steps to enforce that obligation whenever [it] considers it necessary to do so, the [Commission] may act accordingly.

(4) A person who applies to the [Commission] under this section shall, so far as that person reasonably can, comply with such regulations as may be made by the Secretary of State with a view to the [Commission] [. . .] being provided with the information which is required to enable—

(a) the [non-resident parent to be identified or] traced (where that is necessary);

(b) the amount of child support maintenance payable by the [non-resident] parent to be [calculated]; and

(c) that amount to be recovered from the [non-resident] parent.

(5) Any person who has applied to the [Commission] under this section may at any time request [it] to cease acting under this section.

(6) It shall be the duty of the [Commission] to comply with any request made under subsection (5) (but subject to any regulations made under subsection (8)).

(7) The obligation to provide information which is imposed by subsection (4)—

(a) shall not apply in such circumstances as may be prescribed; and

(b) may, in such circumstances as may be prescribed, be waived by the [Commission].

(8) The Secretary of State may by regulations make such incidental, supplemental or transitional provision as he thinks appropriate with respect to cases in which he is requested to cease to act under this section.

[. . .]

[(10) No application may be made at any time under this section with respect to a qualifying child or any qualifying children if—

(a) there is in force a written maintenance agreement made before 5th April 1993, or a maintenance order [made before a prescribed date] in respect of that child or those children and the person who is, at that time, the [non-resident] parent; or

[(aa) a maintenance order made on or after the date prescribed for the purposes of paragraph (a) is in force in respect of them, but has been so for less than the period of one year beginning with the date on which it was made;]

[(ab) a maintenance agreement—

(i) made on or after the date prescribed for the purposes of paragraph (a); and

(ii) registered for execution in the Books of Council and Session or the sheriff court books,

is in force in respect of them, but has been so for less than the period of one year beginning with the date on which it was made.]

[. . .]

5 Child support maintenance: supplemental provisions

(1) Where—

(a) there is more than one person with care of a qualifying child; and

(b) one or more, but not all, of them have parental responsibility for . . . the child;

no application may be made for a maintenance [calculation] with respect to the child by any of those persons who do not have parental responsibility for . . . the child.

(2)   Where more than one application for a maintenance [calculation] is made with respect to the child concerned, only one of them may be proceeded with.

(3)   The Secretary of State may by regulations make provision as to which of two or more applications for a maintenance [calculation] with respect to the same child is to be proceeded with.

[. . .]

7   Right of child in Scotland to apply for [calculation]

(1)   A qualifying child who has attained the age of 12 years and who is habitually resident in Scotland may apply to the [Commission] for a maintenance [calculation] to be made with respect to him if—

(a)   no such application has been made by a person who is with respect to that child, a person with care or a [non-resident] parent. [. . .]

(2)   An application made under subsection (1) shall authorise the [Commission] to make a maintenance [calculation] with respect to any other children of the [non-resident] parent who are qualifying children in the care of the same person as the child making the application.

(3)   Where a maintenance [calculation] has been made in response to an application under this section the [Commission] may, if the person with care, the [non-resident] parent with respect to whom the [calculation] was made or the child concerned applies to [it] under this subsection, arrange for—

(a)   the collection of the child support maintenance payable in accordance with the [calculation].

(b)   the enforcement of the obligation to pay child support maintenance in accordance with the [calculation].

(4)   Where an application under subsection (3) for the enforcement of the obligation mentioned in subsection (3)(b) authorises the [Commission] to take steps to enforce that obligation whenever [it] considers it necessary to do so, the [Commission] may act accordingly.

(5)   Where a child has asked the [Commission] to proceed under this section, the person with care of the child, the [non-resident] parent and the child concerned shall, so far as they reasonably can, comply with such regulations as may be made by the Secretary of State with a view to the [Commission] [. . .] being provided with the information which is required to enable—

(a)   the [non-resident] parent to be traced (where that is necessary);

(b)   the amount of child support maintenance payable by the [non-resident] parent to be [calculated]; and

(c)   that amount to be recovered from the [non-resident] parent.

(6)   The child who has made the application (but not the person having care of him) may at any time request the [Commission] to cease acting under this section.

(7)   It shall be the duty of the [Commission] to comply with any request made under subsection (6) (but subject to any regulations made under subsection (9)).

(8)   The obligation to provide information which is imposed by subsection (5)—

(a)   shall not apply in such circumstances as may be prescribed by the Secretary of State; and

(b)   may, in such circumstances as may be so prescribed, be waived by the [Commission].

(9)   The Secretary of State may by regulations make such incidental, supplemental or transitional provision as he thinks appropriate with respect to cases in which he is requested to cease to act under this section.

(10)   No application may be made at any time under this section by a qualifying child if—

[(a)] there is in force a written maintenance agreement made before 5th April 1993, or a maintenance order [made before a prescribed date] in respect of that child and the person who is, at that time, the [non-resident parent; or

(b)   a maintenance order made on or after the date prescribed for the purposes of paragraph (a) is in force in respect of them, but has been so for less than the period of one year beginning with the date on which it was made.]

[(c)   a maintenance agreement—
    (i)   made on or after the date prescribed for the purposes of paragraph (a); and
    (ii)   registered for execution in the Books of Council and Session or the sheriff court books,

is in force in respect of them, but has been so for less than the period of one year beginning with the date on which it was made.]

8   Role of the courts with respect to maintenance for children

(1)   This subsection applies in any case where [the Commission] would have jurisdiction to make a maintenance [calculation] with respect to a qualifying child and [a non-resident parent] of his on an application duly made by a person entitled to apply for such [a calculation] with respect to that child.

(2)   Subsection (1) applies even though the circumstances of the case are such that [the Commission] would not make [a calculation] if it were applied for.

(3)   [Except as provided in subsection (3A)] in any case where subsection (1) applies, no court shall exercise any power which it would otherwise have to make, vary, or revive any maintenance order in relation to the child and [non-resident parent] concerned.

[(3A)   Unless a maintenance calculation has been made with respect to the child concerned, subsection (3) does not prevent a court from varying a maintenance order in relation to that child and the non-resident parent concerned—
    (a)   if the maintenance order was made on or after the date prescribed for the purposes of section 4(10)(a) or 7(10)(a); or
    (b)   where the order was made before then, in any case in which section 4(10) or 7(10) prevents the making of an application for a maintenance calculation with respect to or by that child.]

(4)   Subsection (3) does not prevent a court from revoking a maintenance order.

(5)   The Lord Chancellor or in relation to Scotland the Lord Advocate may by order provide that, in such circumstances as may be specified by the order, this section shall not prevent a court from exercising any power which it has to make a maintenance order in relation to a child if—
    (a)   a written agreement (whether or not enforceable) provides for the making, or securing, by [a non-resident parent] of the child of periodical payments to or for the benefit of the child; and
    (b)   the maintenance order which the court makes is, in all material respects, in the same terms as that agreement.

[(5A)   The Lord Chancellor may make an order under subsection (5) only with the concurrence of the Lord Chief Justice.]

(6)   This section shall not prevent a court from exercising any power which it has to make a maintenance order in relation to a child if—
    (a)   a maintenance [calculation] is in force with respect to the child;
    [(b)   the non-resident parent's [gross] weekly income exceeds the figure referred to in paragraph 10(3) of Schedule 1 (as it has effect from time to time pursuant to regulations made under paragraph 10A(1)(b));]
    (c)   the court is satisfied that the circumstances of the case make it appropriate for the [non-resident] parent to make or secure the making of periodical payments under a maintenance order in addition to the child support maintenance payable by him in accordance with the maintenance [calculation].

(7)   This section shall not prevent a court from exercising any power which it has to make a maintenance order in relation to a child if—
    (a)   the child is, will be or (if the order were to be made) would be receiving instruction at an educational establishment or undergoing training for a trade, profession or vocation (whether or not while in gainful employment); and

(b)   the order is made solely for the purposes of requiring the person making or securing the making of periodical payments fixed by the order to meet some or all of the expenses incurred in connection with the provision of the instruction or training.

(8)   This section shall not prevent a court from exercising any power which it has to make a maintenance order in relation to a child if—

(a)   a disability living allowance is paid to or in respect of him; or

(b)   no such allowance is paid but he is disabled,

and the order is made solely for the purpose of requiring the person making or securing the making of periodical payments fixed by the order to meet some or all of any expenses attributable to the child's disability.

(9)   For the purposes of subsection (8), a child is disabled if he is blind, deaf or dumb or is substantially and permanently handicapped by illness, injury, mental disorder or congenital deformity or such other disability as may be prescribed.

(10)   This section shall not prevent a court from exercising any power which it has to make a maintenance order in relation to a child if the order is made against a person with care of the child.

(11)   In this Act 'maintenance order', in relation to any child, means an order which requires the making or securing of periodical payments to or for the benefit of the child and which is made under—

(a)   Part II of the Matrimonial Causes Act 1973;

(b)   the Domestic Proceedings and Magistrates' Courts Act 1978;

(c)   Part III of the Matrimonial and Family Proceedings Act 1984;

(d)   the Family Law (Scotland) Act 1985;

(e)   Schedule 1 to the Children Act 1989;

[(ea) Schedule 5, 6 or 7 to the Civil Partnership Act 2004; or]

(f)   any other prescribed enactment,

and includes any order varying or reviving such an order.

[(12)   The Lord Chief Justice may nominate a judicial office holder (as defined in section 109(4) of the Constitutional Reform Act 2005) to exercise his functions under this section.]

9   Agreements about maintenance

(1)   In this section 'maintenance agreement' means any agreement for the making, or for securing the making, of periodical payments by way of maintenance, or in Scotland aliment, to or for the benefit of any child.

(2)   Nothing in this Act shall be taken to prevent any person from entering into a maintenance agreement.

(3)   [Subject to section 4(10)(a) [and (ab)] and section 7(10),] the existence of a maintenance agreement shall not prevent any party to the agreement or any other person, from applying for a maintenance [calculation] with respect to any child to or for whose benefit periodical payments are to be made or secured under the agreement.

(4)   Where any agreement contains a provision which purports to restrict the right of any person to apply for a maintenance [calculation] that provision shall be void.

(5)   Where section 8 would prevent any court from making a maintenance order in relation to a child and [non-resident] parent of his, no court shall exercise any power that it has to vary any agreement so as—

(a)   to insert a provision requiring that [non-resident] parent to make or secure the making of periodical payments by way of maintenance, or in Scotland aliment, to or for the benefit of that child; or

(b)   to increase the amount payable under such a provision.

[(6)   In any case in which section 4(10) or 7(10) prevents the making of an application for a maintenance [calculation] [. . .] subsection (5) shall have effect with the omission of paragraph (b).]

10   Relationship between maintenance assessments and certain court orders and related matters

(1)   Where an order of a kind prescribed for the purposes of this subsection is in force with respect to any qualifying child with respect to whom a maintenance [calculation] is made, the order—

(a)   shall, so far as it relates to the making or securing of periodical payments, cease to have effect to such extent as may be determined in accordance with regulations made by the Secretary of State; or

(b)   where the regulations so provide, shall, so far as it so relates, have effect subject to such modifications as may be so determined.

(2)   Where an agreement of a kind prescribed for the purposes of this subsection is in force with respect to any qualifying child with respect to whom a maintenance [calculation] is made, the agreement—

(a)   shall, so far as it relates to the making or securing of periodical payments, be unenforceable to such extent as may be determined in accordance with regulations made by the Secretary of State; or

(b)   where the regulations so provide, shall, so far as it so relates, have effect subject to such modifications as may be so determined.

(3)   Any regulations under this section may, in particular, make such provision with respect to—

(a)   any case where any person with respect to whom an order or agreement of a kind prescribed for the purposes of subsection (1) or (2) has effect applies to the prescribed court, before the end of the prescribed period, for the order or agreement to be varied in the light of the maintenance [calculation] and of the provisions of this Act;

(b)   the recovery of any arrears under the order or agreement which fell due before the coming into force of the maintenance [calculation]

as the Secretary of State considers appropriate and may provide that, in prescribed circumstances, an application to any court which is made with respect to an order of a prescribed kind relating to the making or securing of periodical payments to or for the benefit of a child shall be treated by the court as an application for the order to be revoked.

(4)   The Secretary of State may by regulations make provision for—

(a)   notification to be given by [the Commission] to the prescribed person in any case where [it] considers that the making of a maintenance [calculation] has affected, or is likely to affect, any order of a kind prescribed for the purposes of this subsection;

(b)   notification to be given by the prescribed person to the [Commission] in any case where a court makes an order which it considers has affected, or is likely to affect, a maintenance [calculation].

(5)   Rules may be made under section 144 of the Magistrates' Courts Act 1980 (rules of procedure) requiring any person who, in prescribed circumstances, makes an application to a magistrates' court for a maintenance order to furnish the court with a statement in a prescribed form, and signed by [an officer of the Commission] as to whether or not, at the time when the statement is made, there is a maintenance [calculation] in force with respect to that person or the child concerned.

In this subsection—

'maintenance order' means an order of a prescribed kind for the making or securing of periodical payments to or for the benefit of a child; and

'prescribed' means prescribed by the rules.

Special cases

42 Special cases

(1) The Secretary of State may by regulations provide that in prescribed circumstances a case is to be treated as a special case for the purposes of this Act.

(2) Those regulations may, for example, provide for the following to be special cases—

(a)   each parent of a child is [a non-resident] parent in relation to the child;

(b)   there is more than one person who is a person with care in relation to the same child;

(c)   there is more than one qualifying child in relation to the same [non-resident] parent but the person who is the person with care in relation to one of those children is not the person who is the person with care in relation to all of them;

(d)   a person is [a non-resident] parent in relation to more than one child and the other parent of each of those children is not the same person;

(e)   the person with care has care of more than one qualifying child and there is more than one [non-resident] parent in relation to those children;

(f)   a qualifying child has his home in two or more separate households.

(3) The Secretary of State may by regulations make provision with respect to special cases.

(4) Regulations made under subsection (3) may, in particular—

(a)   modify any provision made by or under this Act, in its application to any special case or any special case falling within a prescribed category;

(b)   make new provision for any such case; or

(c)   provide for any prescribed provision made by or under this Act not to apply to any such case.

43 Recovery of child support maintenance by deduction from benefit

[(1) This section applies where—

(a)   a non-resident parent is liable to pay a flat rate of child support maintenance (or would be so liable but for a variation having been agreed to), and that rate applies (or would have applied) because he falls within paragraph 4(1)(b) or (c) or 4(2) of Schedule 1; and

(b)   such conditions as may be prescribed for the purposes of this section are satisfied.

(2) The power of the Secretary of State to make regulations under section 5 of the Social Security Administration Act 1992 by virtue of subsection (1)(p) (deductions from benefits) may be exercised in relation to cases to which this section applies with a view to securing that payments in respect of child support maintenance are made or that arrears of child support maintenance are recovered.

(3) For the purposes of this section, the benefits to which section 5 of the 1992 Act applies are to be taken as including war disablement pensions and war widows' pensions (within the meaning of section 150 of the Social Security Contributions and Benefits Act 1992 (interpretation)).]

Jurisdiction

44 Jurisdiction

(1) [The Commission] shall have jurisdiction to make a maintenance [calculation] with respect to a person who is—

(a)   a person with care;

(b)   a [non-resident] parent; or

(c)   a qualifying child,

only if that person is habitually resident in the United Kingdom [except in the case of a non-resident parent who falls within subsection (2A)].

(2)   Where the person with care is not an individual subsection (1) shall have effect as if paragraph (a) were omitted,

[(2A)   A non-resident parent falls within this subsection if he is not habitually resident in the United Kingdom, but is—

(a)   employed in the civil service of the Crown, including Her Majesty's Diplomatic Service and Her Majesty's Overseas Civil Service;

(b)   a member of the naval, military or air forces of the Crown, including any person employed by an association established for the purposes of Part XI of the Reserve Forces Act 1996;

(c)   employed by a company of a prescribed description registered under the Companies Act 1985 in England and Wales or in Scotland, or under the Companies (Northern Ireland) Order 1986; or

(d)   employed by a body of a prescribed description.]

[. . .]

45   Jurisdiction of courts in certain proceedings under this Act

(1)   The Lord Chancellor or, in relation to Scotland, the Lord Advocate may by order make such provision as he considers necessary to secure that appeals, or such class of appeals as may be specified in the order—

(a)   shall be made to a court instead of being made to [the First-tier Tribunal]; or

(b)   shall be so made in such circumstances as may be so specified.

(2)   In subsection (1), 'court' means—

(a)   in relation to England and Wales and subject to any provision made under Schedule 11 to the Children Act 1989 (jurisdiction of courts with respect to certain proceedings relating to children) the High Court, a county court or a magistrates' court; and

(b)   in relation to Scotland, the Court of Session or the sheriff.

(3)–(5)   [Amend the Children Act 1989.]

[. . .]

(7)   Any order under subsection (1) [. . .] may make—

(a)   such modifications of any provision of this Act or of any other enactment; and

(b)   such transitional provision,

as the Minister making the order considers appropriate in consequence of any provision made by the order.

Miscellaneous and supplemental

. . .

54   Interpretation

[(1)]   In this Act—

['application for a variation' means an application under section 28A or 28G;]

'Benefits Acts' means the [Social Security Contributions and Benefits Act 1992 and the Social Security Administration Act 1992];

[. . .]

['charging order' has the same meaning as in section 1 of the Charging Orders Act 1979;]

'child benefit' has the same meaning as in the Child Benefit Act 1975;

[. . .]

'child support maintenance' has the meaning given in section 3(6);

[. . .]

['Commission' means the Child Maintenance and Enforcement Commission;]

'deduction from earnings order' has the meaning given in section 31(2);

['default maintenance decision' has the meaning given in section 12;]

['deposit-taker' means a person who, in the course of a business, may lawfully accept deposits in the United Kingdom;]

'disability living allowance' has the same meaning as in the [Benefit Acts];

[. . .]

'general qualification' shall be construed in accordance with section 71 of the Courts and Legal Services Act 1990 (qualification for judicial appointments);

['income-based jobseeker's allowance' has the same meaning as in the Jobseeker's Act 1995;]

['income-related employment and support allowance' means an income-related allowance under Part 1 of the Welfare Reform Act 2007 (employment and support allowance);]

'income support' has the same meaning as in the Benefit Acts;

'interim maintenance [decision]' has the meaning given in section 12;

'liability order' has the meaning given in [section 32M(2)];

'maintenance agreement' has the meaning given in section 9(1);

'maintenance [calculation]' means [a calculation] of maintenance made under this Act and, except in prescribed circumstances, includes [a default maintenance decision and an interim maintenance decision];

'maintenance order' has the meaning given in section 8(11);

[. . .]

'non-resident parent', has the meaning given in section 3(2);

'parent', in relation to any child, means any person who is in law the mother or father of the child;

[. . .]

'parent with care' means a person who is, in relation to a child, both a parent and a person with care;]

['parental responsibility', in the application of this Act—(a) to England and Wales, has the same meaning as in the Children Act 1989; and (b) to Scotland, shall be construed as a reference to 'parental responsibilities' within the meaning given by section 1(3) of the Children (Scotland) Act 1995;]

'person with care' has the meaning given in section 3(3);

'prescribed' means prescribed by regulations made by the Secretary of State;

'qualifying child' has the meaning given in section 3(1);

['voluntary payment' has the meaning given in section 28J.]

[(2)   The definition of 'deposit-taker' in subsection (1) is to be read with—
   (a)   section 22 of the Financial Services and Markets Act 2000;
   (b)   any relevant order under that section; and
   (c)   Schedule 2 to that Act.]

55   Meaning of 'child'

(1)   For the purposes of this Act a person is a child if—
   (a)   he is under the age of 16;
   (b)   he is under the age of 19 and receiving full-time education (which is not advanced education)—
       (i)   by attendance at a recognised educational establishment; or
       (ii)   elsewhere, if the education is recognised by the Secretary of State; or
   (c)   he does not fall within paragraph (a) or (b) but—
       (i)   he is under the age of 18, and
       (ii)   prescribed conditions are satisfied with respect to him.

(2)   A person is not a child for the purposes of this Act if he—
   (a)   is or has been married;
   (b)   has celebrated a marriage which is void; or
   (c)   has celebrated a marriage in respect of which a decree of nullity has been granted [or has been a party to a civil partnership in respect of which a nullity order has been made].

(3)   In this section—

'advanced education' means education of a prescribed description; and

'recognised educational establishment' means an establishment recognised by the Secretary of State for the purposes of this section as being, or as comparable to, a university, college or school.

re a person has reached the age of 16, the Secretary of State may recog-
ion provided for him otherwise than at a recognised educational estab-
nly if the Secretary of State is satisfied that education was being so
r him immediately before he reached the age of 16.

Secretary of State may provide that in prescribed circumstances education is or is not to be treated for the purposes of this section as being full-time.

(6) In determining whether a person falls within subsection (1)(b), no account
shall be taken of such interruptions in his education as may be prescribed.

(7) The Secretary of State may by regulations provide that a person who ceases
to fall within subsection (1) shall be treated as continuing to fall within that subsection for a prescribed period.

(8) No person shall be treated as continuing to fall within subsection (1) by
virtue of regulations made under subsection (7) after the end of the week in which
he reaches the age of 19.

AGE OF LEGAL CAPACITY (SCOTLAND) ACT 1991
(1991, c 50)

1 Age of legal capacity

(1) As from the commencement of this Act—

(a) a person under the age of 16 years shall, subject to section 2 below, have
no legal capacity to enter into any transaction;

(b) a person of or over the age of 16 years shall have legal capacity to enter
into any transaction.

(2) Subject to section 8 below, any reference in any enactment to a pupil (other
than in the context of education or training) or to a person under legal disability or
incapacity by reason of nonage shall, insofar as it relates to any time after the commencement of this Act, be construed as a reference to a person under the age of 16
years.

(3) Nothing in this Act shall—

(a) apply to any transaction entered into before the commencement of this Act;

(b) confer any legal capacity on any person who is under legal disability or
incapacity other than by reason of nonage;

(c) affect the delictual or criminal responsibility of any person;

(d) affect any enactment which lays down an age limit expressed in years for
any particular purpose;

(e) prevent any person under the age of 16 years from receiving or holding
any right, title or interest;

(f) affect any existing rule of law or practice whereby—

(i) any civil proceedings may be brought or defended, or any step in civil
proceedings may be taken in the name of a person under the age of 16 years
[in relation to whom there is no person entitled to act as his legal representative (within the meaning of Part I of the Children (Scotland) Act 1995), or
where there is such a person] is unable (whether by reason of conflict of
interest or otherwise) or refuses to bring or defend such proceedings or take
such step;

(ii) the court may, in any civil proceedings, appoint a curator *ad litem* to a
person under the age of 16 years;

(iii) the court may, in relation to the approval of an arrangement under
section 1 of the Trusts (Scotland) Act 1961, appoint a curator *ad litem* to a
person of or over the age of 16 years but under the age of 18 years;

(iv) the court may appoint a curator bonis to any person;

(g) prevent any person under the age of 16 years from [exercising
parental responsibilities and parental rights (within the meaning of sections
1(3) and 2(4) respectively of the Children (Scotland) Act 1995) in relation to any
child of his].

(4)   Any existing rule of law relating to the legal capacity of minors and pupils which is inconsistent with the provisions of this Act shall cease to have effect.

(5)   Any existing rule of law relating to reduction of a transaction on the ground of minority and lesion shall cease to have effect.

2   Exceptions to general rule

(1)   A person under the age of 16 years shall have legal capacity to enter into a transaction—

(a)   of a kind commonly entered into by persons of his age and circumstances, and

(b)   on terms which are not unreasonable.

(2)   A person of or over the age of 12 years shall have testamentary capacity, including legal capacity to exercise by testamentary writing any power of appointment.

(3)   A person of or over the age of 12 years shall have legal capacity to consent to the making of an adoption order in relation to him. [. . .]

(4)   A person under the age of 16 years shall have legal capacity to consent on his own behalf to any surgical, medical or dental procedure or treatment where, in the opinion of a qualified medical practitioner attending him, he is capable of understanding the nature and possible consequences of the procedure or treatment.

[(4ZA)   For the purposes of subsection (4), the storage of gametes in accordance with the Human Fertilisation and Embryology Act 1990 is to be treated as a medical procedure.

(4ZB)   A person under the age of 16 years shall have legal capacity to consent to the use of the person's human cells in accordance with Schedule 3 to the Human Fertilisation and Embryology Act 1990 for the purposes of a project of research where the person is capable of understanding the nature of the research; and in this subsection 'human cells' has the same meaning as in that Schedule.]

[(4A)   A person under the age of 16 years shall have legal capacity to instruct a solicitor, in connection with any civil matter, where that person has a general understanding of what it means to do so; and without prejudice to the generality of this subsection a person 12 years of age or more shall be presumed to be of sufficient age and maturity to have such understanding.

(4B)   A person who by virtue of subsection (4A) above has legal capacity to instruct a solicitor shall also have legal capacity to sue, or to defend, in any civil proceedings.

(4C)   Subsections (4A) and (4B) above are without prejudice to any question of legal capacity arising in connection with any criminal matter.]

(5)   Any transaction—

(a)   which a person under the age of 16 years purports to enter into after the commencement of this Act, and

(b)   in relation to which that person does not have legal capacity by virtue of this section,

shall be void.

3   Setting aside of transactions

(1)   A person under the age of 21 years ('the applicant') may make application to the court to set aside a transaction which he entered into while he was of or over the age of 16 years but under the age of 18 years and which is a prejudicial transaction.

(2)   In this section 'prejudicial transaction' means a transaction which—

(a)   an adult, exercising reasonable prudence, would not have entered into in the circumstances of the applicant at the time of entering into the transaction, and

(b)   has caused or is likely to cause substantial prejudice to the applicant.

(3)   Subsection (1) above shall not apply to—

(a)   the exercise of testamentary capacity;
(b)   the exercise by testamentary writing of any power of appointment;
(c)   the giving of consent to the making of an adoption order;
(d)   the bringing or defending of, or the taking of any step in, civil proceedings;
(e)   the giving of consent to any surgical, medical or dental procedure or treatment;
(f)   a transaction in the course of the applicant's trade, business or profession;
(g)   a transaction into which any other party was induced to enter by virtue of any fraudulent misrepresentation by the applicant as to age or other material fact;
(h)   a transaction ratified by the applicant after he attained the age of 18 years and in the knowledge that it could be the subject of an application to the court under this section to set it aside; or
(j)   a transaction ratified by the court under section 4 below.

(4)   Where an application to set aside a transaction can be made or could have been made under this section by the person referred to in subsection (1) above, such application may instead be made by that person's executor, trustee in bankruptcy, trustee acting under a trust deed for creditors or curator bonis at any time prior to the date on which that person attains or would have attained the age of 21 years.

(5)   An application under this section to set aside a transaction may be made—
(a)   by an action in the Court of Session or the sheriff court, or
(b)   by an incidental application in other proceedings in such court,
and the court may make an order setting aside the transaction and such further order, if any, as seems appropriate to the court in order to give effect to the rights of the parties.

4   Ratification by court of proposed transaction

(1)   Where a person of or over the age of 16 years but under the age of 18 years proposes to enter into a transaction which, if completed, could be the subject of an application to the court under section 3 above to set aside, all parties to the proposed transaction may make a joint application to have it ratified by the court.

(2)   The court shall not grant an application under this section if it appears to the court that an adult, exercising reasonable prudence and in the circumstances of the person referred to in subsection (1) above, would not enter into the transaction.

(3)   An application under this section shall be made by means of a summary application—
(a)   to the sheriff of the sheriffdom in which any of the parties to the proposed transaction resides, or
(b)   where none of the said parties resides in Scotland, to the sheriff at Edinburgh,
and the decision of the sheriff on such application shall be final.

5   Guardians of persons under 16

(1)   Except insofar as otherwise provided in Schedule 1 to this Act, as from the commencement of this Act any reference in any rule of law, enactment or document to the tutor of a pupil child shall be construed as a reference to [a person entitled to act as a child's legal representative (within the meaning of Part I of the Children (Scotland) Act 1995), and any reference to the tutory of such a child shall be construed as a reference to the entitlement to act as a child's legal representative enjoyed by a person by, under or by virtue of the said Part I].

(2)   Subject to section 1(3)(f) above, as from the commencement of this Act no guardian of a person under the age of 16 years shall be appointed as such except under [section 7 of the Children (Scotland) Act 1995].

(3)   As from the commencement of this Act, no person shall, by reason of age alone, be subject to the curatory of another person.

(4)   As from the commencement of this Act, no person shall be appointed as *factor loco tutoris*.

6   Attainment of age

(1)   The time at which a person attains a particular age expressed in years shall be taken to be the beginning of the relevant anniversary of the date of his birth.

(2)   Where a person has been born on 29th February in a leap year, the relevant anniversary in any year other than a leap year shall be taken to be 1st March.

(3)   The provisions of this section shall apply only to a relevant anniversary which occurs after the commencement of this Act.

[. . .]

8   Transitional provision

Where any person referred to in section 6(4)(b), 17(3), 18(3) or 18A(2) of the Prescription and Limitation (Scotland) Act 1973 as having been under legal disability by reason of nonage was of or over the age of 16 years but under the age of 18 years immediately before the commencement of this Act, any period prior to such commencement shall not be reckoned as, or as part of, the period of 5 years, or (as the case may be) 3 years, specified respectively in section 6, 17, 18 or 18A of that Act.

9   Interpretation

In this Act, unless the context otherwise requires—

'existing' means existing immediately before the commencement of this Act;

[. . .]

'transaction' means a transaction having legal effect, and includes—

(a)   any unilateral transaction;

(b)   the exercise of testamentary capacity;

(c)   the exercise of any power of appointment;

(d)   the giving by a person of any consent having legal effect;

(e)   the bringing or defending of, or the taking of any step in, civil proceedings;

(f)   acting as arbiter or trustee;

(g)   acting as an instrumentary witness.

10   Amendments and repeals

(1)   The enactments mentioned in Schedule 1 to this Act shall have effect subject to the amendments therein specified.

(2)   The enactments specified in Schedule 2 to this Act are repealed to the extent specified in the third column of that Schedule.

11   Short title, commencement and extent

(1)   This Act may be cited as the Age of Legal Capacity (Scotland) Act 1991.

(2)   This Act shall come into force at the end of the period of two months beginning with the date on which it is passed.

(3)   This Act shall extend to Scotland only.

CIVIL EVIDENCE (FAMILY MEDIATION) (SCOTLAND) ACT 1995
(1995, c 6)

1   Inadmissibility in civil proceedings of information as to what occurred during family mediation

(1)   Subject to section 2 of this Act, no information as to what occurred during family mediation to which this Act applies shall be admissible as evidence in any civil proceedings.

(2)   This Act applies to family mediation—

(a)   between two or more individuals relating to—

(i)   the residence of a child;

(ii)   the regulation of personal relations and direct contact between a child and any other person;

(iii)   the control, direction or guidance of a child's upbringing;

(iv)   the guardianship or legal representation of a child; or

(v)   any other matter relating to a child's welfare;

(b)   between spouses or former spouses concerning matters arising out of the breakdown or termination of their marriage;

(c)   between parties to a purported marriage concerning matters arising out of the breakdown or annulment of their purported marriage;

[(cc)   between partners in a civil partnership or persons in a purported civil partnership concerning matters arising out of the breakdown or termination of their relationship;]

(d)   between co-habitants or former co-habitants concerning matters arising out of the breakdown or termination of their relationship; or

(e)   of such other description as the Secretary of State may prescribe,

which is conducted by a person accredited as a mediator in family mediation to an organisation which is concerned with such mediation and which is approved for the purposes of this Act by the Lord President of the Court of Session.

(3)   The Lord President of the Court of Session may—

(a)   in approving an organisation under subsection (2) above, specify the period for which the approval is granted;

(b)   if he thinks fit, withdraw the approval at any time.

(4)   A certificate by the Lord President approving an organisation under subsection (2) above shall be—

(a)   in such form as may be prescribed by Act of Sederunt; and

(b)   admissible as evidence in any civil proceedings and sufficient evidence of the matters contained therein.

(5)   A document purporting to be a certificate by the Lord President for the purposes of this Act shall be accepted by the court as such unless the contrary is proved.

(6)   The Lord President may, in connection with the performance of any of his functions under this Act, require an organisation which is seeking, or has been granted, approval under subsection (2) above to provide him with such information as he thinks fit.

(7)   For the purposes of subsection (2)(d) above, 'co-habitants' means—

[(a)]   a man and a woman who are not married to each other but who are living together as if they were husband and wife [, or

(b)   two persons who are not civil partners of each other but are living together as if they were civil partners.]

(8)   In this Act, 'civil proceedings' does not include an arbitration or proceedings before a tribunal or inquiry.

(9)   In this section and section 2 of this Act, any reference to what occurred during family mediation shall include a reference to what was said, written or observed during such mediation.

2 Exceptions to general rule of inadmissibility

(1)   Nothing in section 1 of this Act shall prevent the admissibility as evidence in civil proceedings—

(a)   of information as to any contract entered into during family mediation or of the fact that no contract was entered into during such mediation;

(b)   where any contract entered into as a result of family mediation is challenged in those civil proceedings, of information as to what occurred during family mediation which relates to the subject matter of that challenge;

(c)   of information as to what occurred during family mediation if every participant (other than the mediator) in that mediation agrees that the information should be admitted as evidence; or

(d)   of information as to what occurred during family mediation if those civil proceedings are proceedings—

(i)   (whether under any enactment or otherwise) relating to a child's care or protection to which a local authority or a voluntary organisation is a party;

(ii)   Under [Chapter 2 or 3 of Part II of the Children (Scotland) Act 1995] before, or relating to, a children's hearing, [before a sheriff or before a justice of the peace];

[(iia)   on any appeal from such proceedings as are mentioned in subparagraph (ii) above];

(iii)   [for the making of an adoption order (as defined in section 28(1) of the Adoption and Children (Scotland) Act 2007)];

[. . .]

(v)   against one of the participants, or the mediator, in a family mediation in respect of damage to property, or personal injury, alleged to have been caused by that participant or, as the case may be, mediator during family mediation; or

(vi)   arising from the family mediation and to which the mediator is a party.

(2)   For the purposes of this section—

(a)   an individual, spouse, former spouse, party to a purported marriage, or co-habitant referred to in section 1(2) of this Act; and

(b)   insofar as the family mediation includes any of the matters mentioned in section 1(2)(a) of this Act, a child who—

(i)   is the subject of such a family mediation; and

(ii)   at the time the family mediation took place was capable of understanding the nature and significance of the matters to which the information which is sought to be admitted as evidence relates,

shall be regarded as a participant in the family mediation.

(3)   Notwithstanding anything in the Age of Legal Capacity (Scotland) Act 1991, any child who is regarded as a participant in family mediation by virtue of subsection (2) above shall have legal capacity to agree that information should be admitted as evidence.

(4)   The Secretary of State may prescribe other persons or classes of person who shall be regarded for the purposes of this section as participants in a family mediation.

3 Short title, construction, commencement and extent

(1)   This Act may be cited as the Civil Evidence (Family Mediation) (Scotland) Act 1995.

(2)   In this Act, 'prescribe', except in relation to an Act of Sederunt, means prescribe by regulations made by statutory instrument subject to annulment in pursuance of a resolution of either House of Parliament.

(3)   This Act shall come into force on such day as the Lord Advocate may by order made by statutory instrument appoint; and such order may include such transitional or incidental provisions as appear to him to be necessary or expedient.

(4)   This Act extends to Scotland only.

CHILDREN (SCOTLAND) ACT 1995
(1995, c 36)

PART I
PARENTS, CHILDREN AND GUARDIANS

Parental responsibilities and parental rights

1 Parental responsibilities

(1) Subject to section 3(1)(b) [and (d)] and (3) of this Act, a parent has in relation to his child the responsibility—

(a) to safeguard and promote the child's health, development and welfare;

(b) to provide, in a manner appropriate to the stage of development of the child—

(i) direction;

(ii) guidance,

to the child;

(c) if the child is not living with the parent, to maintain personal relations and direct contact with the child on a regular basis; and

(d) to act as the child's legal representative,

but only in so far as compliance with this section is practicable and in the interests of the child.

(2) 'Child' means for the purposes of—

(a) paragraphs (a), (b)(i), (c) and (d) of subsection (1) above, a person under the age of sixteen years;

(b) paragraph (b)(ii) of that subsection, a person under the age of eighteen years.

(3) The responsibilities mentioned in paragraphs (a) to (d) of subsection (1) above are in this Act referred to as 'parental responsibilities'; and the child, or any person acting on his behalf, shall have title to sue, or to defend, in any proceedings as respects those responsibilities.

(4) The parental responsibilities supersede any analogous duties imposed on a parent at common law; but this section is without prejudice to any other duty so imposed on him or to any duty imposed on him by, under or by virtue of any other provision of this Act or of any other enactment.

2 Parental rights

(1) Subject to section 3(1)(b) [and (d)] and (3) of this Act, a parent, in order to enable him to fulfil his parental responsibilities in relation to his child, has the right—

(a) to have the child living with him or otherwise to regulate the child's residence;

(b) to control, direct or guide, in a manner appropriate to the stage of development of the child, the child's upbringing;

(c) if the child is not living with him, to maintain personal relations and direct contact with the child on a regular basis; and

(d) to act as the child's legal representative.

(2) Subject to subsection (3) below, where two or more persons have a parental right as respects a child, each of them may exercise that right without the consent of the other or, as the case may be, of any of the others, unless any decree or deed conferring the right, or regulating its exercise, otherwise provides.

(3) Without prejudice to any court order, no person shall be entitled to remove a child habitually resident in Scotland from, or to retain any such child outwith, the United Kingdom without the consent of a person described in subsection (6) below.

(4) The rights mentioned in paragraphs (a) to (d) of subsection (1) above are in this Act referred to as 'parental rights'; and a parent, or any person acting on his

behalf, shall have title to sue, or to defend, in any proceedings as respects those rights.

(5)   The parental rights supersede any analogous rights enjoyed by a parent at common law; but this section is without prejudice to any other right so enjoyed by him or to any right enjoyed by him by, under or by virtue of any other provision of this Act or of any other enactment.

(6)   The description of a person referred to in subsection (3) above is a person (whether or not a parent of the child) who for the time being has and is exercising in relation to him a right mentioned in paragraph (a) or (c) of subsection (1) above; except that, where both the child's parents are persons so described, the consent required for his removal or retention shall be that of them both.

(7)   In this section, 'child' means a person under the age of sixteen years.

3   Provisions relating both to parental responsibilities and to parental rights

(1)   Notwithstanding section 1(1) of the Law Reform (Parent and Child) (Scotland) Act 1986 (provision for disregarding whether a person's parents are not, or have not been, married to one another in establishing the legal relationship between him and any other person)—

(a)   a child's mother has parental responsibilities and parental rights in relation to him whether or not she is or has been married to his father; and

(b)   without prejudice to any arrangements which may be made under subsection (5) below and subject to any agreement which may be made under section 4 of this Act, his father has such responsibilities and rights in relation to him only if—

[(i)] married to the mother at the time of the child's conception or subsequently [; or

(ii)   where not married to the mother at that time or subsequently, the father is registered as the child's father under any of the enactments mentioned in subsection (1A).]

[(c)   without prejudice to any arrangements which may be made under subsection (5) below, where a child has a parent by virtue of section 42 of the Human Fertilisation and Embryology Act 2008, that parent has parental responsibilities and parental rights in relation to the child;

(d)   without prejudice to any arrangements which may be made under subsection (5) below and subject to any agreement which may be made under section 4A(1) of this Act, where a child has a parent by virtue of section 43 of the Human Fertilisation and Embryology Act 2008, that parent has parental responsibilities and parental rights in relation to the child if she is registered as a parent of the child under any of the enactments mentioned in subsection (3A).]

[(1A)   Those enactments are—

(a)   section 18(1)(a), (b)(i) and (c) and (2)(b) of the Registration of Births, Deaths and Marriages (Scotland) Act 1965;

(b)   sections 10(1)(a) to (e) and 10A(1)(a) to (e) of the Births and Deaths Registration Act 1953; and

(c)   article 14(3)(a) to (e) of the Births and Deaths Registration (Northern Ireland) Order 1976.]

(2)   For the purposes of subsection (1)(b) above, the father shall be regarded as having been married to the mother at any time when he was a party to a purported marriage with her which was—

(a)   voidable; or

(b)   void but believed by them (whether by error of fact or of law) in good faith at that time to be valid.

(3)   Subsection (1) above is without prejudice to any order made under section 11 of this Act or section 3(1) of the said Act of 1986 (provision analogous to the said section 11 but repealed by this Act) or to any other order, disposal or resolu-

tion affecting parental responsibilities or parental rights; and nothing in subsection (1) above or in this Part of this Act shall affect any other—

(a)   enactment (including any other provision of this Act or of that Act); or

(b)   rule of law,

by, under or by virtue of which a person may have imposed on him (or be relieved of) parental responsibilities or may be granted (or be deprived of) parental rights.

[(3A)   Those enactments are—

(a)   paragraphs (a), (b) and (d) of section 18B(1) and section 18B(3)(a) of the Registration of Births, Deaths and Marriages (Scotland) Act 1965;

(b)   paragraphs (a), (b) and (c) of section 10(1B) and of section 10A(1B) of the Births and Deaths Registration Act 1953;

(c)   sub-paragraphs (a), (b) and (c) of Article 14ZA(3) of the Births and Deaths Registration (Northern Ireland) Order 1976.]

(4)   The fact that a person has parental responsibilities or parental rights in relation to a child shall not entitle that person to act in any way which would be incompatible with any court order relating to the child or the child's property, or with any supervision requirement made under section 70 of this Act.

(5)   Without prejudice to [sections 4(1) and 4A(1)] of this Act, a person who has parental responsibilities or parental rights in relation to a child shall not abdicate those responsibilities or rights to anyone else but may arrange for some or all of them to be fulfilled or exercised on his behalf, and without prejudice to that generality any such arrangement may be made with a person who already has parental responsibilities or parental rights in relation to the child concerned.

(6)   The making of an arrangement under subsection (5) above shall not affect any liability arising from a failure to fulfil parental responsibilities; and where any arrangements so made are such that the child is a foster child for the purposes of the Foster Children (Scotland) Act 1984, those arrangements are subject to the provisions of that Act.

4   Acquisition of parental rights and responsibilities by natural father

(1)   Where a child's mother has not been deprived of some or all of the parental responsibilities and parental rights in relation to him and, by virtue of subsection (1)(b) of section 3 of this Act, his father has no parental responsibilities or parental rights in relation to him, the father and mother, whatever age they may be, may by agreement provide that, as from the appropriate date, the father shall have the parental responsibilities and parental rights which (in the absence of any order under section 11 of this Act affecting those responsibilities and rights) he would have if married to the mother.

(2)   No agreement under subsection (1) above shall have effect unless—

(a)   in a form prescribed by the Secretary of State; and

(b)   registered in the Books of Council and Session while the mother still has the parental responsibilities and parental rights which she had when the agreement was made.

(3)   The date on which such registration as is mentioned in subsection (2)(b) above takes place shall be the 'appropriate date' for the purposes of subsection (1) above.

(4)   An agreement which has effect by virtue of subsection (2) above shall, subject only to section 11(11) of this Act, be irrevocable.

[4A   Acquisition of parental responsibilities and parental rights by second female parent by agreement with mother

(1)   Where—

(a)   a child's mother has not been deprived of some or all of the parental responsibilities and parental rights in relation to the child; and

(b)   the child has a parent by virtue of section 43 of the Human Fertilisation and Embryology Act 2008 and that parent is not registered as such under any of the enactments mentioned in section 3(3A),

the mother and the other parent may by agreement provide that, as from the appropriate date, the other parent shall have the parental responsibilities and rights (in the absence of any order under section 11 of this Act affecting responsibilities and rights) as if the other parent were treated as a parent by virtue of section 42 of that Act of 2008.

(2)   Section 4(2), (3) and (4) applies in relation to an agreement under subsection (1) of this section as it applies in relation to an agreement under subsection (1) of section 4.]

5   Care or control of child by person without parental responsibilities or parental rights

(1)   Subject to subsection (2) below, it shall be the responsibility of a person who has attained the age of sixteen years and who has care or control of a child under that age, but in relation to him either has no parental responsibilities or parental rights or does not have the parental responsibility mentioned in section 1(1)(a) of this Act, to do what is reasonable in all the circumstances to safeguard the child's health, development and welfare; and in fulfilling his responsibility under this section the person may in particular, even though he does not have the parental right mentioned in section 2(1)(d) of this Act, give consent to any surgical, medical or dental treatment or procedure where—

(a)   the child is not able to give such consent on his own behalf, and

(b)   it is not within the knowledge of the person that a parent of the child would refuse to give the consent in question.

(2)   Nothing in this section shall apply to a person in so far as he has care or control of a child in a school ('school' having the meaning given by section 135(1) of the Education (Scotland) Act 1980).

6   Views of children

(1)   A person shall, in reaching any major decision which involves—

(a)   his fulfilling a parental responsibility or the responsibility mentioned in section 5(1) of this Act; or

(b)   his exercising a parental right or giving consent by virtue of that section,

have regard so far as practicable to the views (if he wishes to express them) of the child concerned, taking account of the child's age and maturity, and to those of any other person who has parental responsibilities or parental rights in relation to the child (and wishes to express those views); and without prejudice to the generality of this subsection a child twelve years of age or more shall be presumed to be of sufficient age and maturity to form a view.

(2)   A transaction entered into in good faith by a third party and a person acting as legal representative of a child shall not be challengeable on the ground only that the child, or a person with parental responsibilities or parental rights in relation to the child, was not consulted or that due regard was not given to his views before the transaction was entered into.

Guardianship

7   Appointment of guardians

(1)   A child's parent may appoint a person to be guardian of the child in the event of the parent's death; but—

(a)   such appointment shall be of no effect unless—

(i)   in writing and signed by the parent; and

(ii)   the parent, at the time of death, was entitled to act as legal representative of the child (or would have been so entitled if he had survived until after the birth of the child); and

(b)   any parental responsibilities or parental rights (or the right to appoint a further guardian under this section) which a surviving parent has in relation to the child shall subsist with those which, by, under or by virtue of this Part of this Act, the appointee so has.

(2)   A guardian of a child may appoint a person to take his place as guardian in the event of the guardian's death; but such appointment shall be of no effect unless in writing and signed by the person making it.

(3)   An appointment as guardian shall not take effect until accepted, either expressly or impliedly by acts which are not consistent with any other intention.

(4)   If two or more persons are appointed as guardians, any one or more of them shall, unless the appointment expressly provides otherwise, be entitled to accept office even if both or all of them do not accept office.

(5)   Subject to any order under section 11 or 86 of this Act, a person appointed as a child's guardian under this section shall have, in respect of the child, the responsibilities imposed, and the rights conferred, on a parent by sections 1 and 2 of this Act respectively; and sections 1 and 2 of this Act shall apply in relation to a guardian as they apply in relation to a parent.

(6)   Without prejudice to the generality of subsection (1) of section 6 of this Act, a decision as to the appointment of a guardian under subsection (1) or (2) above shall be regarded for the purposes of that section (or of that section as applied by subsection (5) above) as a major decision which involves exercising a parental right.

8   Revocation and other termination of appointment

(1)   An appointment made under section 7(1) or (2) of this Act revokes an earlier such appointment (including one made in an unrevoked will or codicil) made by the same person in respect of the same child, unless it is clear (whether as a result of an express provision in the later appointment or by any necessary implication) that the purpose of the later appointment is to appoint an additional guardian.

(2)   Subject to subsections (3) and (4) below, the revocation of an appointment made under section 7(1) or (2) of this Act (including one made in an unrevoked will or codicil) shall not take effect unless the revocation is in writing and is signed by the person making the revocation.

(3)   An appointment under section 7(1) or (2) of this Act (other than one made in a will or codicil) is revoked if, with the intention of revoking the appointment, the person who made it—

(a)   destroys the document by which it was made; or

(b)   has some other person destroy that document in his presence.

(4)   For the avoidance of doubt, an appointment made under section 7(1) or (2) of this Act in a will or codicil is revoked if the will or codicil is revoked.

(5)   Once an appointment of a guardian has taken effect under section 7 of this Act, then, unless the terms of the appointment provide for earlier termination, it shall terminate only by virtue of—

(a)   the child concerned attaining the age of eighteen years;

(b)   the death of the child or the guardian; or

(c)   the termination of the appointment by a court order under section 11 of this Act.

Administration of child's property

9   Safeguarding of child's property

(1)   Subject to section 13 of this Act, this section applies where—

(a)   property is owned by or due to a child;

(b)   the property is held by a person other than a parent or guardian of the child; and

(c)   but for this section, the property would be required to be transferred to a parent having parental responsibilities in relation to the child or to a g⟨…⟩ for administration by that parent or guardian on behalf of the child.

(2) Subject to subsection (4) below, where this section applies and the perso⟨n⟩ holding the property is an executor or trustee, then—

(a) if the value of the property exceeds £20,000, he shall; or

(b) if that value is not less than £5,000 and does not exceed £20,000, he may,

apply to the Accountant of Court for a direction as to the administration of the property.

(3) Subject to subsection (4) below, where this section applies and the person holding the property is a person other than an executor or trustee, then, if the value of the property is not less than £5,000, that person may apply to the Accountant of Court for a direction as to the administration of the property.

(4) Where the parent or guardian mentioned in subsection (1)(c) above has been appointed a trustee under a trust deed to administer the property concerned, subsections (2) and (3) above shall not apply, and the person holding the property shall transfer it to the parent or guardian.

(5) On receipt of an application under subsection (2) or (3) above, the Accountant of Court may do one, or (in so far as the context admits) more than one, of the following—

(a) apply to the court for the appointment of a judicial factor (whether or not the parent or guardian mentioned in subsection (1)(c) above) to administer all or part of the property concerned and in the event of the court making such an appointment shall direct that the property, or as the case may be part, concerned be transferred to the factor;

(b) direct that all or part of the property concerned be transferred to himself;

(c) direct that all or, in a case where the parent or guardian so mentioned has not been appointed by virtue of paragraph (a) above, part of the property concerned be transferred to the parent or guardian,

to be administered on behalf of the child.

(6) A direction under subsection (5)(c) above may include such conditions as the Accountant of Court considers appropriate, including in particular a condition—

(a) that in relation to the property concerned no capital expenditure shall be incurred without his approval; or

(b) that there shall be exhibited annually to him the securities and bank books which represent the capital of the estate.

(7) A person who has applied under subsection (2) or (3) above for a direction shall not thereafter transfer the property concerned except in accordance with a direction under subsection (5) above.

(8) The Secretary of State may from time to time prescribe a variation in any sum referred to in subsections (2) and (3) above.

(9) In this section 'child' means a person under the age of sixteen years who is habitually resident in Scotland.

10 Obligations and rights of person administering child's property

(1) A person acting as a child's legal representative in relation to the administration of the child's property—

(a) shall be required to act as a reasonable and prudent person would act on his own behalf, and

(b) subject to any order made under section 11 of this Act, shall be entitled to do anything which the child, if of full age and capacity, could do in relation to that property;

and subject to subsection (2) below, on ceasing to act as legal representative, shall be liable to account to the child for his intromissions with the child's property.

(2) No liability shall be incurred by virtue of subsection (1) above in respect of funds which have been used in the proper discharge of the person's responsibility to safeguard and promote the child's health, development and welfare.

Court orders

ating to parental responsibilities etc
nt circumstances in proceedings in the Court of Session or
ier those proceedings are or are not independent of any other
ay be made under this subsection in relation to—
 responsibilities;
 l rights;
 anship; or

(a)   :t to section 14(1) and (2) of this Act, the administration of a child's
property.

(2)   The court may make such order under subsection (1) above as it thinks fit;
and without prejudice to the generality of that subsection may in particular so
make any of the following orders—

(a)   an order depriving a person of some or all of his parental responsibilities
or parental rights in relation to a child;

(b)   an order—
(i)   imposing upon a person (provided he is at least sixteen years of age or
is a parent of the child) such responsibilities; and
(ii)   giving that person such rights;

(c)   an order regulating the arrangements as to—
(i)   with whom; or
(ii)   if with different persons alternately or periodically, with whom during
what periods,
a child under the age of sixteen years is to live (any such order being known as a
'residence order');

(d)   an order regulating the arrangements for maintaining personal relations
and direct contact between a child under that age and a person with whom the
child is not, or will not be, living (any such order being known as a 'contact
order');

(e)   an order regulating any specific question which has arisen, or may arise,
in connection with any of the matters mentioned in paragraphs (a) to (d) of subsection (1) of this section (any such order being known as a 'specific issue
order');

(f)   an interdict prohibiting the taking of any step of a kind specified
in the interdict in the fulfillment of parental responsibilities or the exercise
of parental rights relating to a child or in the administration of a child's
property;

(g)   an order appointing a judicial factor to manage a child's property or
remitting the matter to the Accountant of Court to report on suitable arrangements for the future management of the property; or

(h)   an order appointing or removing a person as guardian of the child.

(3)   The relevant circumstances mentioned in subsection (1) above are—

(a)   that application for an order under that subsection is made by a person
who—
(i)   not having, and never having had, parental responsibilities or parental
rights in relation to the child, claims an interest;
(ii)   has parental responsibilities or parental rights in relation to the child;
[. . .]

[(aa)   that application for a contact order is made with the leave of the court
by a person whose parental responsibilities or parental rights in relation to the
child were extinguished on the making of an adoption order;

(ab)   that application for an order under subsection (1) above (other than a
contact order) is made by a person who has had, but for a reason other than is
mentioned in subsection (4) below, no longer has, parental responsibilities or
parental rights in relation to the child;]

(b)   that although [no application for an order under subsection (1) above] has been made, the court (even if it declines to make any other order) considers it should make such an order.

(4)   The reasons referred to in subsection (3)[ab] above are that the parental responsibilities or parental rights have been—

(a)   extinguished on the making of an adoption order;

[. . .]

(c)   extinguished by virtue of [section 55(1) of the Human Fertilisation and Embryology Act 2008 (parental orders: supplementary provision)] on the making of a parental order under [section 54 of that Act].

[. . .]

(5)   In subsection (3)(a) [and (ab)] above 'person' includes (without prejudice to the generality of that subsection) the child concerned; but it does not include a local authority.

(6)   In subsection (4) above—

[. . .] 'adoption order' [has the meaning given by section 119 of the Adoption and Children (Scotland) Act 2007] [. . .].

(7)   Subject to subsection (8) below, in considering whether or not to make an order under subsection (1) above and what order to make, the court—

(a)   shall regard the welfare of the child concerned as its paramount consideration and shall not make any such order unless it considers that it would be better for the child that the order be made than that none should be made at all, and

(b)   taking account of the child's age and maturity, shall so far as practicable—

(i)   give him an opportunity to indicate whether he wishes to express his views;

(ii)   if he does so wish, give him an opportunity to express them; and

(iii)   have regard to such views as he may express.

[(7A)   In carrying out the duties imposed by subsection (7)(a) above, the court shall have regard in particular to the matters mentioned in subsection (7B) below.

(7B)   Those matters are—

(a)   the need to protect the child from—

(i)   any abuse; or

(ii)   the risk of any abuse,

which affects, or might affect, the child;

(b)   the effect such abuse, or the risk of such abuse, might have on the child;

(c)   the ability of a person—

(i)   who has carried out abuse which affects or might affect the child; or

(ii)   who might carry out such abuse,

to care for, or otherwise meet the needs of, the child; and

(d)   the effect any abuse, or the risk of any abuse, might have on the carrying out of responsibilities in connection with the welfare of the child by a person who has (or, by virtue of an order under subsection (1), would have) those responsibilities.

(7C)   In subsection (7B) above—

'abuse' includes—

(a)   violence, harassment, threatening conduct and any other conduct giving rise, or likely to give rise, to physical or mental injury, fear, alarm or distress;

(b)   abuse of a person other than the child; and

(c)   domestic abuse;

'conduct' includes—

(a)   speech; and

(b)   presence in a specified place or area.

(7D)   Where—

(a)   the court is considering making an order under subsection (1) above; and

(b)   in pursuance of the order two or more relevant persons would have to co-operate with one another as respects matters affecting the child,

the court shall consider whether it would be appropriate to make the order.

(7E)   In subsection (7D) above, 'relevant person', in relation to a child, means—

(a)   a person having parental responsibilities or parental rights in respect of the child; or

(b)   where a parent of the child does not have parental responsibilities or parental rights in respect of the child, a parent of the child.]

(8)   The court shall, notwithstanding subsection (7) above, endeavour to ensure that any order which it makes, or any determination by it not to make an order, does not adversely affect the position of a person who has, in good faith and for value, acquired any property of the child concerned, or any right or interest in such property.

(9)   Nothing in paragraph (b) of subsection (7) above requires a child to be legally represented, if he does not wish to be, in proceedings in the course of which the court implements that paragraph.

(10)   Without prejudice to the generality of paragraph (b) of subsection (7) above, a child twelve years of age or more shall be presumed to be of sufficient age and maturity to form a view for the purposes both of that paragraph and of subsection (9) above.

(11)   An order under subsection (1) above shall have the effect of depriving a person of a parental responsibility or parental right only in so far as the order expressly so provides and only to the extent necessary to give effect to the order; but in making any such order as is mentioned in paragraph (a) or (b) of subsection (2) above the court may revoke any agreement which, in relation to the child concerned, has effect by virtue of section 4(2) [or 4A(2)] of this Act.

(12)   Where the court makes a residence order which requires that a child live with a person who, immediately before the order is made does not have in relation to the child all the parental responsibilities mentioned in paragraphs (a), (b) and (d) of section 1(1), and the parental rights mentioned in paragraphs (b) and (d) of section 2(1), of this Act (those which he does not so have being in this subsection referred to as the 'relevant responsibilities and rights') that person shall, subject to the provisions of the order or of any other order made under subsection (1) above, have the relevant responsibilities and rights while the residence order remains in force.

(13)   Any reference in this section to an order includes a reference to an interim order or to an order varying or discharging an order.

[11A   Restriction on making of orders under section 11

(1)   Subsection (2) applies where a permanence order (as defined in section 80(2) of the Adoption and Children (Scotland) Act 2007 (asp 4)) is in force in respect of a child.

(2)   The court may not, under subsection (1) of section 11 of this Act, make an order such as is mentioned in any of paragraphs (a) to (e) of subsection (2) of that section.]

12   Restrictions on decrees for divorce, separation or annulment affecting children

(1)   In any action for—

[(a)]   divorce, judicial separation or declarator of nullity of marriage, [or

(b)   dissolution or declarator of nullity of a civil partnership or separation of civil partners,]

the court shall, where this section applies, consider (in the light of such information as is before the court as to the arrangements which have been, or are proposed to be, made for the upbringing of each child by virtue of which it applies) whether to exercise with respect to him the powers conferred by section 11 or 54 of this Act.

(2) Where, in any case to which this section applies, the court is of the opinion that—

(a) the circumstances of the case require, or are likely to require, it to exercise any power under section 11 or 54 of this Act with respect to the child concerned;

(b) it is not in a position to exercise that power without giving further consideration to the case; and

(c) there are exceptional circumstances which make it desirable in the interests of that child that it should not grant decree in the action until it is in a position to exercise such a power,

it shall postpone its decision on the granting of decree in the action until it is in such a position.

(3) This section applies where a child of the family has not reached the age of sixteen years at the date when the question first arises as to whether the court should give such consideration as is mentioned in subsection (1) above.

(4) In this section 'child of the family', in relation to—

(a) the parties to a marriage, means—

[(i)] a child of both of them; or

[(ii)] any other child, not being a child who is placed with them as foster parents by a local authority or voluntary organisation, who has been treated by both of them as a child of their family; [or

(b) the partners in a civil partnership, means a child who [—

(i)] has been treated by both partners as a child of the family which their partnership constitutes; [or

(ii) whose parents are the partners (being parents by virtue of sections 33 and 42 of the Human Fertilisation and Embryology Act 2008).]

13   Awards of damages to children

(1) Where in any court proceedings a sum of money becomes payable to, or for the benefit of, a child under the age of sixteen years, the court may make such order relating to the payment and management of the sum for the benefit of the child as it thinks fit.

(2) Without prejudice to the generality of subsection (1) above, the court may in an order under this section—

(a) appoint a judicial factor to invest, apply or otherwise deal with the money for the benefit of the child concerned;

(b) order the money to be paid—

(i) to the sheriff clerk or the Accountant of Court; or

(ii) to a parent or guardian of that child,

to be invested, applied or otherwise dealt with, under the directions of the court, for the benefit of that child; or

(c) order the money to be paid directly to that child.

(3) Where payment is made to a person in accordance with an order under this section, a receipt given by him shall be a sufficient discharge of the obligation to make the payment.

Jurisdiction and choice of law

14   Jurisdiction and choice of law in relation to certain matters

(1) The Court of Session shall have jurisdiction to entertain an application for an order relating to the administration of a child's property if the child is habitually resident in, or the property is situated in, Scotland.

(2) A sheriff shall have jurisdiction to entertain such an application if the child is habitually resident in, or the property is situated in, the sheriffdom.

(3)   Subject to subsection (4) below, any question arising under this Part of this Act—

    (a)   concerning—
        (i)   parental responsibilities or parental rights; or
        (ii)   the responsibilities or rights of a guardian,
in relation to a child shall, in so far as it is not also a question such as is mentioned in paragraph (b) below, be determined by the law of the place of the child's habitual residence at the time when the question arises;

    (b)   concerning the immediate protection of a child shall be determined by the law of the place where the child is when the question arises; and

    (c)   as to whether a person is validly appointed or constituted guardian of a child shall be determined by the law of the place of the child's habitual residence on the date when the appointment was made (the date of death of the testator being taken to be the date of appointment where an appointment was made by will), or the event constituting the guardianship occurred.

(4)   Nothing in any provision of law in accordance with which, under subsection (3) above, a question which arises in relation to an application for, or the making of, an order under subsection (1) of section 11 of this Act falls to be determined, shall affect the application of subsection (7) of that section.

[(5)   The provisions of sections 9, 11, 13 and this section are subject to Sections 2 and 3 of Chapter II of Council Regulation (EC) No 2201/2003 of 27th November 2003 concerning jurisdiction and the recognition and enforcement of judgments in matrimonial matters and matters of parental responsibility.]

Interpretation

15   Interpretation of Part I
    (1)   In this Part of this Act—
'child' means, where the expression is not otherwise defined, a person under the age of eighteen years;
    'contact order' has the meaning given by section 11(2)(d) of this Act;
    'parent', in relation to any person, means, subject to [Chapter 3 of Part 1 of the Adoption and Children (Scotland) Act 2007] and sections 27 to 30 of the Human Fertilisation and Embryology Act 1990 [and Part 2 of the Human Fertilisation and Embryology Act 2008] and any regulations made under [section 55(1) of that Act of 2008], someone, of whatever age, who is that person's genetic father or mother;
    'parental responsibilities' has the meaning given by section 1(3) of this Act;
    'parental rights' has the meaning given by section 2(4) of this Act;
    'residence order' has the meaning given by section 11(2)(c) of this Act;
    'specific issue order' has the meaning given by section 11(2)(e) of this Act; and
    'transaction' has the meaning given by section 9 of the Age of Legal Capacity (Scotland) Act 1991 (except that, for the purposes of subsection (5)(b) below, paragraph (d) of the definition in question shall be disregarded).

    (2)   No provision in this Part of this Act shall affect any legal proceedings commenced, or any application made to a court, before that provision comes into effect; except that where, before section 11 of this Act comes into force, there has been final decree in a cause in which, as respects a child, an order for custody or access, or an order which is analogous to any such order as is mentioned in subsection (2) of that section, has been made, any application on or after the date on which the section does come into force for variation or recall of the order shall proceed as if the order had been made under that section.

    (3)   In subsection (2) above, the reference to final decree is to a decree or interlocutor which, taken by itself or along with previous interlocutors, disposes of the whole subject matter of the cause.

    (4)   Any reference in this Part of this Act to a person—
        (a)   having parental rights or responsibilities;

(b)   acting as a legal representative; or
(c)   being appointed a guardian,
is to a natural person only.

(5)   Any reference in this Part of this Act to a person acting as the legal representative of a child is a reference to that person, in the interests of the child—

(a)   administering any property belonging to the child; and
(b)   acting in, or giving consent to, any transaction where the child is incapable of so acting or consenting on his own behalf.

(6)   Where a child has legal capacity to sue, or to defend, in any civil proceedings, he may nevertheless consent to be represented in those proceedings by any person who, had the child lacked that capacity, would have had the responsibility to act as his legal representative.

[(7)   No provision in this Part of this Act shall permit a person to give a consent to the storage of gametes under the Human Fertilisation and Embryology Act 1990 on behalf of a child.]

PART II
PROMOTION OF CHILDREN'S WELFARE BY LOCAL AUTHORITIES AND BY CHILDREN'S HEARINGS ETC

CHAPTER 1
SUPPORT FOR CHILDREN AND THEIR FAMILIES

Introductory

16   Welfare of child and consideration of his views

(1)   Where under or by virtue of this Part of this Act, a children's hearing decide, or a court determines, any matter with respect to a child the welfare of that child throughout his childhood shall be their or its paramount consideration.

(2)   In the circumstances mentioned in subsection (4) below, a children's hearing or as the case may be the sheriff, taking account of the age and maturity of the child concerned, shall so far as practicable—

(a)   give him an opportunity to indicate whether he wishes to express his views;
(b)   if he does so wish, give him an opportunity to express them; and
(c)   have regard to such views as he may express;

and without prejudice to the generality of this subsection a child twelve years of age or more shall be presumed to be of sufficient age and maturity to form a view.

(3)   In the circumstances mentioned in subsection (4)(a)(i) or (ii) or (b) of this section, no requirement or order so mentioned shall be made with respect to the child concerned unless the children's hearing consider, or as the case may be the sheriff considers, that it would be better for the child that the requirement or order be made than that none should be made at all.

(4)   The circumstances to which subsection (2) above refers are that—

(a)   the children's hearing—

(i)   are considering whether to make, or are reviewing, a supervision requirement;
(ii)   are considering whether to grant a warrant under subsection (1) of section 66, or subsection (4) or (7) of section 69, of this Act or to provide under subsection (5) of the said section 66 for the continuation of a warrant;
(iii)   are engaged in providing advice under section 60(10) of this Act; or
(iv)   are drawing up a report under section 73(13) of this Act;

(b)   the sheriff is considering—

(i)   whether to make, vary or discharge [. . .] a child assessment order or an exclusion order;

(ii)   whether to vary or discharge a child protection order;

(iii)   whether to grant a warrant under section 67 of this Act; or

(iv)   on appeal, whether to make such substitution as is mentioned in section 51(5)(c)(iii) of this Act; or

(c)   the sheriff is otherwise disposing of an appeal against a decision of a children's hearing.

(5)   If, for the purpose of protecting members of the public from serious harm (whether or not physical harm)—

(a)   a children's hearing consider it necessary to make a decision under or by virtue of this Part of this Act which (but for this paragraph) would not be consistent with their affording paramountcy to the consideration mentioned in subsection (1) above, they may make that decision; or

(b)   a court considers it necessary to make a determination under or by virtue of Chapters 1 to 3 of this Part of this Act which (but for this paragraph) would not be consistent with its affording such paramountcy, it may make that determination.

17   Duty of local authority to child looked after by them

(1)   Where a child is looked after by a local authority they shall, in such manner as the Secretary of State may prescribe—

(a)   safeguard and promote his welfare (which shall, in the exercise of their duty to him be their paramount concern);

(b)   make such use of services available for children cared for by their own parents as appear to the authority reasonable in his case; and

(c)   take such steps to promote, on a regular basis, personal relations and direct contact between the child and any person with parental responsibilities in relation to him as appear to them to be, having regard to their duty to him under paragraph (a) above, both practicable and appropriate.

(2)   The duty under paragraph (a) of subsection (1) above includes, without prejudice to that paragraph's generality, the duty of providing advice and assistance with a view to preparing the child for when he is no longer looked after by a local authority.

(3)   Before making any decision with respect to a child whom they are looking after, or proposing to look after, a local authority shall, so far as is reasonably practicable, ascertain the views of—

(a)   the child;

(b)   his parents;

(c)   any person who is not a parent of his but who has parental rights in relation to him; and

(d)   any other person whose views the authority consider to be relevant, regarding the matter to be decided.

(4)   In making any such decision a local authority shall have regard so far as practicable—

(a)   to the views (if he wishes to express them) of the child concerned, taking account of his age and maturity;

(b)   to such views of any person mentioned in subsection (3)(b) to (d) above as they have been able to ascertain; and

(c)   to the child's religious persuasion, racial origin and cultural and linguistic background.

(5)   If, for the purpose of protecting members of the public from serious harm (whether or not physical harm) a local authority consider it necessary to exercise, in a manner which (but for this paragraph) would not be consistent with their duties under this section, their powers with respect to a child whom they are looking after, they may do so.

(6)   Any reference in this Chapter of this Part to a child who is 'looked after' by a local authority, is to a child—

(a)   for whom they are providing accommodation under section 25 of this Act;

(b)   who is subject to a supervision requirement and in respect of whom they are the relevant local authority;

(c)   who is subject to an order made, or authorisation or warrant granted, by virtue of Chapter 2, 3 or 4 of this Part of this Act, being an order, authorisation or warrant in accordance with which they have responsibilities as respects the child;

(d)   who is subject to an order in accordance with which, by virtue of regulations made under section 33(1) of this Act, they have such responsibilities [; or

(e)   in respect of whom a permanence order has, on an application by them under section 80 of the Adoption and Children (Scotland) Act 2007 (asp 4), been made and has not ceased to have effect.]

(7)   Regulations made by the Secretary of State under subsection (1) above may, without prejudice to the generality of that subsection, include—

(a)   provision as to the circumstances in which the child may be cared for by the child's own parents; and

(b)   procedures which shall be followed in the event of the child's death.

18   Duty of persons with parental responsibilities to notify change of address to local authority looking after child

(1)   Where a child is being looked after by a local authority, each natural person who has parental responsibilities in relation to the child shall, without unreasonable delay, inform that authority whenever the person changes his address.

(2)   A person who knowingly fails to comply with the requirement imposed by subsection (1) above shall be liable on summary conviction to a fine of level 1 on the standard scale; but in any proceedings under this section it shall be a defence that—

(a)   the change was to the same address as that to which another person who at that time had parental responsibilities in relation to the child was changing; and

(b)   the accused had reasonable cause to believe that the other person had informed the authority of the change of address of them both.

Provision of services

19   Local authority plans for services for children

(1)   Within such period after the coming into force of this section as the Secretary of State may direct, each local authority shall prepare and publish a plan for the provision of relevant services for or in respect of children in their area.

(2)   References to 'relevant services' in this section are to services provided by a local authority under or by virtue of—

(a)   this Part of this Act; or

(b)   any of the enactments mentioned in section 5(1B)(a) to (o) of the Social Work (Scotland) Act 1968 (enactments in respect of which Secretary of State may issue directions to local authorities as to the exercise of their functions).

(3)   A local authority shall from time to time review the plan prepared by them under subsection (1) above (as modified, or last substituted, under this subsection) and may, having regard to that review, prepare and publish—

(a)   modifications (or as the case may be further modifications) to the plan reviewed; or

(b)   a plan in substitution for that plan.

(4)   The Secretary of State may, subject to subsection (5) below, issue directions as to the carrying out by a local authority of their functions under subsection (3) above.

(5)   In preparing any plan, or carrying out any review, under this section a local authority shall consult—

(a)   every Health Board and National Health Service trust providing services under the National Health Service (Scotland) Act 1978 in the area of the authority;

(b)   such voluntary organisations as appear to the authority—

(i)   to represent the interests of persons who use or are likely to use relevant services in that area; or

(ii)   to provide services in that area which, were they to be provided by the authority, might be categorised as relevant services;

(c)   the Principal Reporter appointed under section 127 of the Local Government etc (Scotland) Act 1994;

(d)   the chairman of the children's panel for that area;

(e)   such housing associations, voluntary housing agencies and other bodies as appear to the authority to provide housing in that area; and

(f)   such other persons as the Secretary of State may direct.

20   Publication of information about services for children

(1)   A local authority shall, within such period after the coming into force of this section as the Secretary of State may direct, and thereafter from time to time, prepare and publish information—

(a)   about relevant services which are provided by them for or in respect of children (including, without prejudice to that generality, services for or in respect of disabled children or children otherwise affected by disability) in their area or by any other local authority for those children; and

(b)   where they consider it appropriate, about services which are provided by voluntary organisations and by other persons for those children, being services which the authority have power to provide and which, were they to do so, they would provide as relevant services.

(2) In subsection (1) above, 'relevant services' has the same meaning as in section 19 of this Act.

21   Co-operation between authorities

(1)   Where it appears to a local authority that an appropriate person could, by doing certain things, help in the exercise of any of their functions under this Part of this Act, they may, specifying what those things are, request the help of that person.

(2)   For the purposes of subsection (1) above, persons who are appropriate are—

(a)   any other local authority;

(b)   a health board constituted under section 2 of the National Health Service (Scotland) Act 1978;

(c)   a national health service trust established under section 12A of that Act; and

(d)   any person authorised by the Secretary of State for the purposes of this section;

and an appropriate person receiving such a request shall comply with it provided that it is compatible with their own statutory or other duties and obligations and (in the case of a person not a natural person) does not unduly prejudice the discharge of any of their functions.

22   Promotion of welfare of children in need

(1)   A local authority shall—

(a)   safeguard and promote the welfare of children in their area who are in need; and

(b) so far as is consistent with that duty, promote the upbringing of such children by their families,
by providing a range and level of services appropriate to the children's needs.

(2) In providing services under subsection (1) above, a local authority shall have regard so far as practicable to each child's religious persuasion, racial origin and cultural and linguistic background.

(3) Without prejudice to the generality of subsection (1) above—
(a) a service may be provided under that subsection—
(i) for a particular child;
(ii) if provided with a view to safeguarding or promoting his welfare, for his family; or
(iii) if provided with such a view, for any other member of his family; and
(b) the services mentioned in that subsection may include giving assistance in kind or, in exceptional circumstances, in cash.

(4) Assistance such as is mentioned in subsection (3)(b) above may be given unconditionally or subject to conditions as to the repayment, in whole or in part, of it or of its value; but before giving it, or imposing such conditions, the local authority shall have regard to the means of the child concerned and of his parents and no condition shall require repayment by a person at any time when in receipt of—
(a) income support or [working families tax] credit payable under the Social Security Contributions and Benefits Act 1992; or
[(aa) any element of child tax credit other than the family element or working tax credit; or]
(b) an income-based jobseeker's allowance payable under the Jobseekers Act 1995 [; or
(c) an income-related allowance under Part 1 of the Welfare Reform Act 2007 (employment and support allowance).]

23 Children affected by disability

(1) Without prejudice to the generality of subsection (1) of section 22 of this Act, services provided by a local authority under that subsection shall be designed—
(a) to minimise the effect on any—
(i) disabled child who is within the authority's area, of his disability; and
(ii) child who is within that area and is affected adversely by the disability of any other person in his family, of that other person's disability; and
(b) to give those children the opportunity to lead lives which are as normal as possible.

(2) For the purposes of this Chapter of this Part a person is disabled if he is chronically sick or disabled or suffers from mental disorder (within the meaning of the Mental Health (Scotland) Act 1984).

(3) [Where requested to do so by—
(a) a child's parent or guardian; or
(b) a mental health officer (as defined in section 329 of the Mental Health (Care and Treatment) (Scotland) Act 2003 (asp 13)) who—
(i) has responsibility under that Act or the Criminal Procedure (Scotland) Act 1995 (c 46) for a child's case; and
(ii) makes the request for the purposes of either of those Acts,
a local authority shall, for the purpose of facilitating the discharge of such duties as the authority may have under section 22(1) of this Act (whether or not by virtue of subsection (1) above) as respects the child, carry out an assessment of the child, or of any other person in the child's family, to determine the needs of the child, or of any other person in the child's family, to determine the needs of the child in so far as attributable to his disability or to that of the other person.]

[(4) In determining the needs of a child under subsection (3) above, the local authority shall take account—

(a) where it appears to them that a person ('the carer') provides a substantial amount of care on a regular basis for the child, or for another person in the child's family who is being assessed under that subsection, of such care as is being so provided; and

(b) in so far as it is reasonable and practicable to do so, of—

(i) the views of the parent or guardian of the child, and the child; and

(ii) the views of the carer,

provided that the parent, guardian, child or carer in question has a wish, or as the case may be, a capacity, to express a view.]

24 Assessment of ability of carers to provide care for disabled children

[(1) Subject to subsection (2) below, a person ('the carer') who provides, or intends to provide, a substantial amount of care on a regular basis for a disabled child may, whether or not the carer is a child, request a local authority to make an assessment ('the carer's assessment') of the carer's ability to provide or to continue to provide such care for the child.

(1A) The local authority to whom the request is made shall—

(a) comply with the request where it appears to them that the child, or another person in the child's family, is a person for whom they must or may provide services under section 22(1) of this Act; and

(b) if they then or subsequently make an assessment under section 23(3) of this Act to determine the needs of the child, have regard to the results of the carer's assessment—

(i) in the assessment of the child; or

(ii) in making a decision as to the discharge by them of any duty they may have as respects the child under section 2(1) of the Chronically Sick and Disabled Persons Act 1970 (c 44) or under section 22(1) of this Act.]

(2) No request may be made under subsection (1) above by a person who provides or will provide the care in question—

(a) under or by virtue of a contract of employment or other contract; or

(b) as a volunteer for a voluntary organisation.

(3) Where an assessment of a carer's ability to continue to provide, or as the case may be to provide, care for a child is carried out under subsection (1) above, there shall, as respects the child, be no requirement under section 8 of the Disabled Persons (Services, Consultation and Representation) Act 1986 (carer's ability to continue to provide care to be considered in any decision as respects provision of certain services for disabled persons) to have regard to that ability.

(4) In this section 'person' means a natural person.

[24A Duty of local authority to provide information to carer of disabled child

Where it appears to a local authority both that—

(a) a child is a disabled child for whom they must or may provide services under section 22(1) of this Act; and

(b) a person ('the carer') provides, or intends to provide, a substantial amount of care on a regular basis for the child,

the local authority shall notify the carer that he may be entitled under section 24(1) of this Act to request an assessment of his ability to provide, or to continue to provide, care for the child.]

25 Provision of accommodation for children, etc

(1) A local authority shall provide accommodation for any child who, residing or having been found within their area, appears to them to require such provision because—

(a) no-one has parental responsibility for him;

(b)   he is lost or abandoned; or

(c)   the person who has been caring for him is prevented, whether or not permanently and for whatever reason, from providing him with suitable accommodation or care.

(2)   Without prejudice to subsection (1) above, a local authority may provide accommodation for any child within their area if they consider that to do so would safeguard or promote his welfare.

(3)   A local authority may provide accommodation for any person within their area who is at least eighteen years of age but not yet twenty-one, if they consider that to do so would safeguard or promote his welfare.

(4)   A local authority providing accommodation under subsection (1) above for a child who is ordinarily resident in the area of another local authority shall notify the other authority, in writing, that such provision is being made; and the other authority may at any time take over the provision of accommodation for the child.

(5)   Before providing a child with accommodation under this section, a local authority shall have regard, so far as practicable, to his views (if he wishes to express them), taking account of his age and maturity; and without prejudice to the generality of this subsection a child twelve years of age or more shall be presumed to be of sufficient age and maturity to form a view.

(6)   Subject to subsection (7) below—

(a)   a local authority shall not provide accommodation under this section for a child if any person who—

(i)   has parental responsibilities in relation to him and the parental rights mentioned in section 2(1)(a) and (b) of this Act; and

(ii)   is willing and able either to provide, or to arrange to have provided, accommodation for him,

objects; and

(b)   any such person may at any time remove the child from accommodation which has been provided by the local authority under this section.

(7)   Paragraph (a) of subsection (6) above does not apply—

(a)   as respects any child who, being at least sixteen years of age, agrees to be provided with accommodation under this section; or

(b)   where a residence order has been made in favour of one or more persons and that person has, or as the case may be those persons have, agreed that the child should be looked after in accommodation provided by, or on behalf of, the local authority;

and paragraph (b) of that subsection does not apply where accommodation has been provided for a continuous period of at least six months (whether by a single local authority or, by virtue of subsection (4) above, by more than one local authority), unless the person removing the child has given the local authority for the time being making such provision at least fourteen days' notice in writing of his intention to remove the child.

(8)   In this Part of this Act, accommodation means, except where the context otherwise requires, accommodation provided for a continuous period of more than twenty-four hours.

26   Manner of provision of accommodation to child looked after by local authority

(1)   A local authority may provide accommodation for a child looked after by them by—

(a)   placing him with—

(i)   a family (other than such family as is mentioned in paragraph (a) or (b) of the definition of that expression in section 93(1) of this Act);

(ii)   a relative of his; or

(iii)   any other suitable person. [. . .]

(b)   maintaining him in a residential establishment; or

(c)   making such other arrangements as appear to them to be appropriate, including (without prejudice to the generality of this paragraph) making use of such services as are referred to in section 17(1)(b) of this Act.

(2)   A local authority may arrange for a child whom they are looking after—

(a)   to be placed, under subsection (1)(a) above, with a person in England and Wales or in Northern Ireland; or

(b)   to be maintained in any accommodation in which—

(i)   a local authority in England and Wales could maintain him by virtue of section 23(2)(b) to (e) of the Children Act 1989; or

(ii)   an authority within the meaning of the Children (Northern Ireland) Order 1995 could maintain him by virtue of Article 27(2)(b) to (e) of that Order.

27   Day care for pre-school and other children

(1)   Each local authority shall provide such day care for children in need within their area who—

(a)   are aged five or under; and

(b)   have not yet commenced attendance at a school,

as is appropriate; and they may provide such day care for children within their area who satisfy the conditions mentioned in paragraphs (a) and (b) but are not in need.

(2)   A local authority may provide facilities (including training, advice, guidance and counselling) for those—

(a)   caring for children in day care; or

(b)   who at any time accompany such children while they are in day care.

(3)   Each local authority shall provide for children in need within their area who are in attendance at a school such care—

(a)   outside school hours; or

(b)   during school holidays,

as is appropriate; and they may provide such care for children within their area who are in such attendance but are not in need.

(4)   In this section—

'day care' means any form of care provided for children during the day, whether or not it is provided on a regular basis; and

'school' has the meaning given by section 135(1) of the Education (Scotland) Act 1980.

28   Removal of power to arrange for emigration of children

Section 23 of the Social Work (Scotland) Act 1968 (which provides a power for local authorities and voluntary associations, with the consent of the Secretary of State, to make arrangements for the emigration of children in their care) shall cease to have effect.

Advice and assistance for young persons formerly looked after by local authorities

29   After-care

(1)   A local authority shall, unless they are satisfied that his welfare does not require it, advise, guide and assist any person in their area over school age but not yet nineteen years of age who, at the time when he ceased to be of school age or at any subsequent time was, but who is no longer, looked after by a local authority.

(2)   If a person within the area of a local authority is at least nineteen, but is less than twenty-one, years of age and is otherwise a person such as is described in subsection (1) above, he may by application to the authority request that they provide him with advice, guidance and assistance; and they may, unless they are satisfied that his welfare does not require it, grant that application.

(3) [Subject to section 73(2) of the Regulation of Care (Scotland) Act 2001 (asp 8)], assistance given under subsection (1) or (2) above may include assistance in kind or in cash.

(4) Where a person—

(a) over school age ceases to be looked after by a local authority; or

(b) described in subsection (1) above is being provided with advice, guidance or assistance by a local authority,

they shall, if he proposes to reside in the area of another local authority, inform that other local authority accordingly provided that he consents to their doing so.

[(5) It is the duty of each local authority, in relation to any person to whom they have a duty under subsection (1) above or who makes an application under subsection (2) above, to carry out an assessment of the person's needs.

(6) Each local authority shall establish a procedure for considering representations (including complaints) made to them by any person mentioned in subsection (1) or (2) above about the discharge of their functions under the provisions of subsections (1) to (5) above.

(7) In subsection (1) above, the reference to having been 'looked after by a local authority' shall be construed as including having been looked after by a local authority in England and Wales, and subsection (4) of section 105 of the Children Act 1989 (c 41) (construction of references to a child looked after by a local authority) shall apply for the purposes of this subsection as it applies for the purposes of that Act ('local authority in England and Wales' being construed in accordance with subsection (1) of that section).]

30 Financial assistance towards expenses of education or training and removal of power to guarantee indentures etc

(1) Without prejudice to section 12 of the Social Work (Scotland) Act 1968 (general social welfare services of local authorities), a local authority may make—

(a) grants to any relevant person in their area to enable him to meet expenses connected with his receiving education or training; and

(b) contributions to the accommodation and maintenance of any such person in any place near where he may be—

(i) employed, or seeking employment; or

(ii) receiving education or training.

(2) Subject to subsection (3) below, a person is a relevant person for the purposes of subsection (1) above if—

(a) he is over school age but not yet twenty-one years of age; and

(b) at the time when he ceased to be of school age or at any subsequent time he was, but he is no longer, looked after by a local authority.

(3) A local authority making grants under paragraph (a), or contributions under paragraph (b)(ii), of subsection (1) above to a person may continue to make them, though he has in the meantime attained the age of twenty-one years, until he completes the course of education or training in question; but if, after he has attained that age, the course is interrupted by any circumstances they may only so continue if he resumes the course as soon as is practicable.

(4) Section 25 of the Social Work (Scotland) Act 1968 (which empowers a local authority to undertake obligations by way of guarantee under any indentures or other deed of apprenticeship or articles of clerkship entered into by a person in their care or under supplemental deeds or articles) shall cease to have effect.

Miscellaneous and general

31   Review of case of child looked after by local authority

(1)   Without prejudice to their duty under section 17(1)(a) of this Act, it shall be the duty of a local authority who are looking after a child to review his case at such intervals as may be prescribed by the Secretary of State.

(2)   The Secretary of State may prescribe—

(a)   different intervals in respect of the first such review and in respect of subsequent reviews;

(b)   the manner in which cases are to be reviewed under this section;

(c)   the considerations to which the local authority are to have regard in reviewing cases under this section.

32   Removal of child from residential establishment

A local authority, notwithstanding any agreement made in connection with the placing of a child in a residential establishment under this Chapter, or Chapter 4, of this Part of this Act by them—

(a)   may, at any time; and

(b)   shall, if requested to do so by the person responsible for the establishment,

remove a child so placed.

33   Effect of orders etc made in different parts of the United Kingdom

(1)   The Secretary of State may make regulations providing for a prescribed order which is made by a court in England and Wales or in Northern Ireland, if that order appears to him to correspond generally to an order of a kind which may be made under this Part of this Act or to a supervision requirement, to have effect in prescribed circumstances and for prescribed purposes of the law of Scotland as if it were an order of that kind or, as the case may be, as if it were a supervision requirement.

(2)   The Secretary of State may make regulations providing—

(a)   for a prescribed order made under this Part of this Act by a court in Scotland; or

(b)   for a supervision requirement,

if that order or requirement appears to him to correspond generally to an order of a kind which may be made under any provision of law in force in England and Wales or in Northern Ireland, to have effect in prescribed circumstances and for prescribed purposes of the law of England and Wales, or as the case may be of Northern Ireland, as if it were an order of that kind.

(3)   Regulations under subsection (1) or (2)(a) above may provide for the order given effect for prescribed purposes to cease to have effect for those purposes, or for the purposes of the law of the place where the order was made, if prescribed conditions are satisfied.

(4)   Where a child who is subject to a supervision requirement is lawfully taken to live in England and Wales or in Northern Ireland, the requirement shall cease to have effect if prescribed conditions are satisfied.

(5)   Regulations under this section may modify any provision of—

(a)   the Social Work (Scotland) Act 1968 or this Act in any application which the Acts may respectively have, by virtue of the regulations, in relation to an order made otherwise than in Scotland;

(b)   the Children Act 1989 or the Children and Young Persons Act 1969 [or sections 63 to 67 of and Schedules 6 and 7 to the Powers of Criminal Courts (Sentencing) Act 2000] in any application which those Acts may respectively have, by virtue of the regulations, in relation to an order prescribed under subsection (2)(a) above or to a supervision requirement; or

(c)   the Children (Northern Ireland) Order 1995 or the Children and Young Persons Act (Northern Ireland) 1968 in any application which they may respectively have, by virtue of the regulations, in relation to an order so prescribed or to a supervision requirement.

[. . .]

35 [*Amends Education (Scotland) Act 1980*]

36 Welfare of certain children in hospitals and nursing homes etc
(1) Where a child is provided with residential accommodation by a person mentioned in subsection (3) below and it appears to the person that the child either—
    (a) has had no parental contact for a continuous period of three months or more; or
    (b) is likely to have no parental contact for a period which, taken with any immediately preceding period in which the child has had no such contact, will constitute a continuous period of three months or more,
the person shall (whether or not the child has been, or will be, so accommodated throughout the continuous period) so notify the local authority in whose area the accommodation is provided.
(2) A local authority receiving notification under subsection (1) above shall—
    (a) take such steps as are reasonably practicable to enable them to determine whether the child's welfare is adequately safeguarded and promoted while he is so accommodated; and
    (b) consider the extent to which (if at all) they should exercise any of their functions under this Act with respect to the child.
(3) The persons are—
    (a) any health board constituted under section 2 of the National Health Service (Scotland) Act 1978;
    (b) any national health service trust established under section 12A of that Act;
    (c) any person carrying on a private hospital registered under Part IV of the Mental Health (Scotland) Act 1984;
    [(d) any person providing a care home service (as defined by section 2(3) of the Regulation of Care (Scotland) Act 2001 (asp 8)).]
(4) For the purposes of subsection (1) above, a child has parental contact only when in the presence of a person having parental responsibilities in relation to him.
(5) A person duly authorised by a local authority may in the area of that authority, at all reasonable times, enter for the purposes of subsection (2) above or of determining whether there has been compliance with subsection (1) above any such place as is mentioned in sub-paragraph (i) or (ii) of subsection (3)(c) above and may for those purposes inspect any records or registers relating to that place; and subsections (2A) to (2D) and (4) of section 6 of the Social Work (Scotland) Act 1968 (exercise of powers of entry and inspection) [(as in force immediately prior to their repeal by section 8 of the Joint Inspection of Children's Services and Inspection of Social Work Services (Scotland) Act 2006)] shall apply in respect of a person so authorised as they [applied] in respect of a person duly authorised under subsection (1) of that section.

[. . .]

38 Short-term refuges for children at risk of harm
(1) Where a child appears—
    (a) to a local authority to be at risk of harm, they may at the child's request—
        (i) provide him with refuge in a residential establishment both controlled or managed by them and designated by them for the purposes of this paragraph; or

(ii)   arrange for a person whose household is approved by virtue of section 5(3)(b) of the Social Work (Scotland) Act 1968 (provision for securing that persons are not placed in any household unless the household has prescribed approval) and is designated by them for the purposes of this paragraph to provide him with refuge in that household,

for a period which does not exceed the relevant period;

(b)   to a person who [provides a care home service (as defined by section 2(3) of the Regulation of Care (Scotland) Act 2001 (asp 8))] or to any person for the time being employed in the management of the accommodation in question, to be at risk of harm, the person to whom the child so appears may at the child's request provide him with refuge, for a period which does not exceed the relevant period, in the accommodation but shall do so only if and to the extent that the local authority within whose area the accommodation is situated have given their approval to the use of the accommodation (or a part of the accommodation) for the purposes of this paragraph.

(2)   The Secretary of State may by regulations make provision as to—

(a)   designation, for the purposes of paragraph (a) of subsection (1) above, of establishments and households;

(b)   application for, the giving of and the withdrawal of, approval under paragraph (b) of subsection (1) above;

(c)   requirements (if any) which must be complied with while any such approval remains in force;

(d)   the performance by a person mentioned in the said paragraph (b) of anything to be done by him under that paragraph;

(e)   the performance by a local authority of their functions under this section; and

(f)   the giving, to such persons or classes of person as may be specified in the regulations, of notice as to the whereabouts of a child provided with refuge under this section,

and regulations made under this subsection may include such incidental and supplementary provisions as he thinks fit.

(3)   While a child is being provided with refuge under, and in accordance with regulations made under, this section, none of the enactments mentioned in subsection (4) below shall apply in relation to him unless the commencement of the period of refuge has followed within two days of the termination of a prior period of refuge so provided to him by any person.

(4)   The enactments are—

(a)   section 89 of this Act and, so far as it applies in relation to anything done in Scotland, section 83 of this Act; and

(b)   section 32(3) of the Children and Young Persons Act 1969 (compelling, persuading, inciting or assisting any person to be absent from detention etc), so far as it applies in relation to anything done in Scotland.

(5)   References in this section to the relevant period shall be construed as references either to a period which does not exceed seven days or, in such exceptional circumstances as the Secretary of State may prescribe, to a period which does not exceed fourteen days.

(6)   A child who is provided with refuge for a period by virtue of such arrangements as are mentioned in subsection (1)(a) above shall not be regarded as a foster child for the purposes of the Foster Children (Scotland) Act 1984 by reason only of such provision.

CHAPTER 2
CHILDREN'S HEARINGS

Constitution of children's hearings

39 Formation of children's panel and children's hearings

(1) For every local government area there shall be a children's panel for the purposes of this Act, and any other enactment conferring powers on a children's hearing (or on such a panel).

(2) Schedule 1 to this Act shall have effect with respect to the recruitment, appointment, training and expenses of members of a children's panel and the establishment of Children's Panel Advisory Committees and joint advisory committees.

(3) Sittings of members of the children's panel (to be known as 'children's hearings') shall be constituted from the panel in accordance with subsection (5) below.

(4) A children's hearing shall be constituted for the performance of the functions given to such a hearing by or by virtue of—

(a)   this Act; or

(b)   any other enactment conferring powers on a children's hearing.

(5) A children's hearing shall consist of three members, one of whom shall act as chairman; and shall not consist solely of male, or solely of female, members.

Qualifications, employment and duties of reporters

40 Qualification and employment of reporters

(1) The qualifications of a reporter shall be such as the Secretary of State may prescribe.

(2) A reporter shall not, without the consent of the Scottish Children's Reporter Administration, be employed by a local authority.

(3) The Secretary of State may make regulations in relation to the functions of any reporter under this Act and the Criminal Procedure (Scotland) Act [1995].

(4) The Secretary of State [. . .] may—

(a)   by regulations empower a reporter, whether or not he is an advocate or solicitor, to conduct before a sheriff any proceedings which under this Chapter or Chapter 3 of this Part of this Act are heard by the sheriff;

(b)   prescribe such requirements as they think fit as to qualifications, training or experience necessary for a reporter to be so empowered.

(5) In this section, 'reporter' means—

(a)   the Principal Reporter; or

(b)   any officer of the Scottish Children's Reporter Administration to whom there is delegated, under section 131(1) of the Local Government etc (Scotland) Act 1994, any of the functions which the Principal Reporter has under this or any other enactment.

Safeguards for children

41 Safeguarding child's interests in proceedings

(1) Subject to subsection (2) below, in any proceedings under this Chapter or Chapter 3 of this Part of this Act either at a children's hearing or before the sheriff, the hearing or, as the case may be, the sheriff—

(a)   shall consider if it is necessary to appoint a person to safeguard the interests of the child in the proceedings; and

(b)   if they, or he, so consider, shall make such an appointment, on such terms and conditions as appear appropriate.

(2) Subsection (1) above shall not apply in relation to proceedings under section 57 of this Act.

(3)   Where a children's hearing make an appointment under subsection (1)(b) above, they shall state the reasons for their decision to make that appointment.

(4)   The expenses of a person appointed under subsection (1) above shall—

(a)   in so far as reasonably incurred by him in safeguarding the interests of the child in the proceedings, and

(b)   except in so far as otherwise defrayed in terms of regulations made under section 101 of this Act,

be borne by the local authority—

(i)   for whose area the children's panel from which the relevant children's hearing has been constituted is formed;

(ii)   where there is no relevant children's hearing, within whose area the child resides.

(5)   For the purposes of subsection (4) above, 'relevant children's hearing' means, in the case of proceedings—

(a)   at a children's hearing, that hearing;

(b)   under section 68 of this Act, the children's hearing who have directed the application;

(c)   on an appeal under section 51 of this Act, the children's hearing whose decision is being appealed against.

Conduct of proceedings at and in connection with children's hearing

42   Power of Secretary of State to make rules governing procedure at children's hearing etc

(1)   Subject to the following provisions of this Act, the Secretary of State may make rules for constituting and arranging children's hearings and other meetings of members of the children's panel and for regulating their procedure.

(2)   Without prejudice to the generality of subsection (1) above, rules under that subsection may make provision with respect to—

(a)   the conduct of, and matters which shall or may be determined by, a business meeting arranged under section 64 of this Act;

(b)   notification of the time and place of a children's hearing to the child and any relevant person in relation to the child and to such other persons as may be prescribed;

(c)   how the grounds for referring the case to a children's hearing under section 65(1) of this Act are to be stated, and the right of the child and any such relevant person to dispute those grounds;

(d)   the making available by the Principal Reporter, subject to such conditions as may be specified in the rules, of reports or information received by him to—

(i)   members of the children's hearing;

(ii)   the child concerned;

(iii)   any relevant person; and

(iv)   any other person or class of persons so specified;

(e)   the procedure in relation to the disposal of matters arising under section 41(1) of this Act;

(f)   the functions of any person appointed by a children's hearing under section 41(1) of this Act and any right of that person to information relating to the proceedings in question;

(g)   the recording in writing of any statement given under section 41(3) of this Act;

(h)   the right to appeal to the sheriff under section 51(1)(a) of this Act against a decision of the children's hearing and notification to such persons as may be prescribed of the proceedings before him;

(i)   the right of the child and of any such relevant person to be represented at a children's hearing;

(j)   the entitlement of the child, of any such relevant person and of any person who acts as the representative of the child or of any such relevant person to the refund of such expenses, incurred by the child or as the case may be the person or representative, as may be prescribed in connection with a children's hearing and with any proceedings arising from the hearing;

 (k) persons whose presence shall be permitted at a children's hearing.

43 Privacy of proceedings at and right to attend children's hearing

 (1) Subject to subsection (3) below, a children's hearing shall be conducted in private, and, subject to any rules made under section 42 of this Act, no person other than a person whose presence is necessary for the proper consideration of the case which is being heard, or whose presence is permitted by the chairman, shall be present.

 (2) The chairman shall take all reasonable steps to ensure that the number of persons present at a children's hearing at any one time is kept to a minimum.

 (3) The following persons have the right to attend a children's hearing—

 (a) a member of the Council on Tribunals, or of the Scottish Committee of that Council, in his capacity as such; and

 (b) subject to subsection (4) below, a *bona fide* representative of a newspaper or news agency.

 (4) A children's hearing may exclude a person described in subsection (3)(b) above from any part or parts of the hearing where, and for so long as, they are satisfied that—

 (a) it is necessary to do so, in the interests of the child, in order to obtain the child's views in relation to the case before the hearing; or

 (b) the presence of that person is causing, or is likely to cause, significant distress to the child.

 (5) Where a children's hearing have exercised the power conferred by subsection (4) above to exclude a person, the chairman may, after that exclusion has ended, explain to the person the substance of what has taken place in his absence.

44 Prohibition of publication of proceedings at children's hearing

 (1) No person shall publish [any matter in respect of a case about which the Principal Reporter has from any source received information or] any matter in respect of proceedings at a children's hearing, or before a sheriff on an application under section 57, section 60(7), section 65(7) or (9), section 76(1) or section 85(1) of this Act, or on any appeal under this Part of this Act, which is intended to, or is likely to, identify—

 (a) [the child concerned in, or any child connected (in any way) with, the case,] proceedings or appeal; or

 (b) an address or school as being that of any such child.

 (2) Any person who contravenes subsection (1) above shall be guilty of an offence and shall be liable on summary conviction to a fine not exceeding level 4 on the standard scale in respect of each such contravention.

 (3) It shall be a defence in proceedings for an offence under this section for the accused to prove that he did not know, and had no reason to suspect, that the published matter was intended, or was likely, to identify the child or, as the case may be, the address or school.

 (4) In this section 'to publish' includes, without prejudice to the generality of that expression,—

 (a) to publish matter in a programme service, as defined by section 201 of the Broadcasting Act 1990 (definition of programme service); and

 (b) to cause matter to be published.

 (5) The requirements of subsection (1) above may, in the interests of justice, be dispensed with by—

 (a) the sheriff in any proceedings before him;

 (b) the Court of Session in any appeal under section 51(11) of this Act; or

(c)   the Secretary of State in relation to any proceedings at a children's hearing,
to such extent as the sheriff, the Court or the Secretary of State as the case may be considers appropriate.

[(6)   The requirements of subsection (1) do not apply in relation to the publication by or on behalf of a local authority or an adoption agency (within the meaning of the Adoption and Children (Scotland) Act 2007 (asp 4)) of information about a child for the purposes of making arrangements in relation to the child under this Act or that Act.]

45   Attendance of child and relevant person at children's hearing

(1)   Where a child has been notified in accordance with rules made under subsection (1) of section 42 of this Act by virtue of subsection (2)(b) of that section that his case has been referred to a children's hearing, he shall—

(a)   have the right to attend at all stages of the hearing; and

(b)   subject to subsection (2) below, be under an obligation to attend those stages in accordance with the notice.

(2)   Without prejudice to subsection (1)(a) above and section 65(4) of this Act, where a children's hearing are satisfied—

(a)   in a case concerned with an offence mentioned in Schedule 1 to the Criminal Procedure (Scotland) Act [1995] that the attendance of the child is not necessary for the just hearing of that case; or

(b)   in any case, that it would be detrimental to the interests of the child for him to be present at the hearing of his case,
they may release the child from the obligation imposed by subsection (1)(b) above.

(3)   Subject to subsection (2) above, the Principal Reporter shall be responsible for securing the attendance of the child at the hearing of his case by a children's hearing (and at any subsequent hearing to which the case is continued under section 69(1)(a) of this Act).

(4)   On the application of the Principal Reporter, a children's hearing, if satisfied on cause shown that it is necessary for them to do so, may issue, for the purposes of subsection (3) above, a warrant under this subsection to find the child, to keep him in a place of safety and to bring him before a children's hearing.

(5)   Where a child has failed to attend a children's hearing in accordance with such notice as is mentioned in subsection (1) above, they may, either on the application of the Principal Reporter or of their own motion, issue a warrant under this subsection, which shall have the same effect as a warrant under subsection (4) above.

(6)   A child who has been taken to a place of safety under a warrant granted under this section shall not be kept there after whichever is the earlier of—

(a)   the expiry of seven days beginning on the day he was first so taken there; or

(b)   the day on which a children's hearing first sit to consider his case in accordance with subsection (7) below.

(7)   Where a child has been found in pursuance of a warrant under this section and he cannot immediately be brought before a children's hearing, the Principal Reporter shall, wherever practicable, arrange a children's hearing to sit on the first working day after the child was so found.

(8)   Subject to section 46 of this Act, a person who is a relevant person as respects a child shall, where a children's hearing are considering the case of the child—

(a)   have the right to attend at all stages of the hearing; and

(b)   be obliged to attend at all stages of the hearing unless the hearing are satisfied that it would be unreasonable to require his attendance or that his attendance is unnecessary for the proper consideration of the case.

(9)   Any person who fails to attend a hearing which, under subsection (8)(b) above, he is obliged to attend shall be guilty of an offence and shall be liable on summary conviction to a fine not exceeding level 3 on the standard scale.

46   Power to exclude relevant person from children's hearing
(1)   Where a children's hearing are considering the case of a child in respect of whom a person is a relevant person, they may exclude that person, or that person and any representative of his, or any such representative, from any part or parts of the hearing for so long as is necessary in the interests of the child, where they are satisfied that—

(a)   they must do so in order to obtain the views of the child in relation to the case before the hearing; or

(b)   the presence of the person or persons in question is causing, or is likely to cause, significant distress to the child.

(2)   Where a children's hearing exercise the power conferred by subsection (1) above, the chairman of the hearing shall, after that exclusion has ended, explain to any person who was so excluded the substance of what has taken place in his absence.

47   Presumption and determination of age
(1)   Where a children's hearing has been arranged in respect of any person, the hearing—

(a)   shall, at the commencement of the proceedings, make inquiry as to his age and shall proceed with the hearing only if he declares that he is a child or they so determine; and

(b)   may, at any time before the conclusion of the proceedings, accept a declaration by the child, or make a fresh determination, as to his age.

(2)   The age declared to, or determined by, a children's hearing to be the age of a person brought before them shall, for the purposes of this Part of this Act, be deemed to be the true age of that person.

(3)   No decision reached, order continued, warrant granted or requirement imposed by a children's hearing shall be invalidated by any subsequent proof that the age of a person brought before them had not been correctly declared to the hearing or determined by them.

Transfer etc of cases

48   Transfer of case to another children's hearing
(1)   Where a children's hearing are satisfied, in relation to a case which they are hearing, that it could be better considered by a children's hearing constituted from a children's panel for a different local government area, they may at any time during the course of the hearing request the Principal Reporter to arrange for such other children's hearing to dispose of the case.

(2)   Where a case has been transferred in pursuance of subsection (1) above, the grounds of referral accepted or established for the case shall not require to be further accepted or established for the purposes of the children's hearing to which the case has been transferred.

[. . .]

50   Treatment of child's case on remission by court
(1)   Where a court has, under [section 49 of the Criminal Procedure (Scotland) Act 1995], remitted a case to a children's hearing for disposal, a certificate signed by the clerk of the court stating that the child or person concerned has pled guilty to, or has been found guilty of, the offence to which the remit relates shall be conclusive evidence for the purposes of the remit that the offence has been committed by the child or person.

(2)   Where a court has under [subsection (7) of the said section 49] remitted a

case to a children's hearing for disposal, the provisions of this Act shall apply to the person concerned as if he were a child.

Appeals

51 Appeal against decision of children's hearing or sheriff

(1)   Subject to subsection (15) below, a child or a relevant person (or relevant persons) or both (or all)—

(a)   may, within a period of three weeks beginning with the date of any decision of a children's hearing, appeal to the sheriff against that decision; and

(b)   where such an appeal is made, shall be heard by the sheriff.

(2)   The Principal Reporter shall, in respect of any appeal under subsection (1) above, ensure that all reports and statements available to the hearing, along with the reports of their proceedings and the reasons for the decision, are lodged with the sheriff clerk.

(3)   The sheriff may, on appeal under subsection (1) above, hear evidence from, or on behalf of, the parties in relation to the decision; and, without prejudice to that generality, the sheriff may—

(a)   examine the Principal Reporter;

(b)   examine the authors or compilers of any reports or statements; and

(c)   call for any further report which he considers may assist him in deciding the appeal.

(4)   Where the sheriff decides that an appeal under this section has failed, he shall confirm the decision of the children's hearing.

(5)   Where the sheriff is satisfied that the decision of the children's hearing is not justified in all the circumstances of the case he shall allow the appeal, and—

(a)   where the appeal is against a warrant to find and keep or, as the case may be, to keep a child in a place of safety, he shall recall the warrant;

(b)   where the child is subject to a supervision requirement containing a [movement restriction condition imposed under subsection (3)(b) of section 70 of this Act or a condition imposed under subsection (9) of that section], he shall direct that the condition shall cease to have effect; and

(c)   in any case, he may, as he thinks fit—

(i)   remit the case with reasons for his decision to the children's hearing for reconsideration of their decision; or

(ii)   discharge the child from any further hearing or other proceedings in relation to the grounds for the referral of the case; or

(iii)   substitute for the disposal by the children's hearing any requirement which could be imposed by them under section 70 of this Act.

(6)   Where a sheriff imposes a requirement under subsection (5)(c)(iii) above, that requirement shall for the purposes of this Act, except of this section, be treated as a disposal by the children's hearing.

(7)   Where the sheriff is satisfied that an appeal under subsection (1) above against the decision of a children's hearing arranged under section 73(8) of this Act is frivolous, he may order that no subsequent appeal against a decision to continue (whether with or without any variation) the supervision requirement in question shall lie until the expiration of twelve months beginning with the date of the order.

(8)   An appeal under subsection (1) above in respect of the issue of a warrant by a children's hearing shall be disposed of within three days of the lodging of the appeal; and failing such disposal the warrant shall cease to have effect at the end of that period.

(9)   Where a child or a relevant person appeals under subsection (1) above against a decision of a children's hearing in relation to a supervision requirement, the child or the relevant person may make application to a children's hearing for the suspension of the requirement appealed against.

(10)   It shall be the duty of the Principal Reporter forthwith to arrange a

children's hearing to consider the application under subsection (9
hearing may grant or refuse the application.

(11)   Subject to subsections (13) and (15) below, an appeal shal
stated case either on a point of law or in respect of any irregularity
of the case—

    (a)   to the sheriff principal from any decision of the sheriff—

        (i)   on an appeal under subsection (1) of this section;

        (ii)   on an application made under section 65(7) or (9) of this Aci

        (iii)   on an application made under section 85(1) of this Act; and

    (b)   to the Court of Session from any decision of the sheriff such as is men-
tioned in sub-paragraphs (i) to (iii) of paragraph (a) above and, with leave of the
sheriff principal, from any decision of the sheriff principal on an appeal under
that paragraph; and the decision of the Court of Session in the matter shall be
final.

(12)   An appeal under subsection (11) above may be made at the instance of—

    (a)   the child or any relevant person, either alone or together; or

    (b)   the Principal Reporter on behalf of the children's hearing.

(13)   An application to the sheriff, or as the case may be the sheriff principal, to
state a case for the purposes of an appeal under subsection (11)(a) or (b) above
shall be made within a period of twenty-eight days beginning with the date of the
decision appealed against.

(14)   On deciding an appeal under subsection (11) above the sheriff principal or
as the case may be the Court of Session shall remit the case to the sheriff for disposal in accordance with such directions as the court may give.

(15)   No appeal shall lie under this section in respect of—

    (a)   a decision of the sheriff on an application under section 57 of this Act; or

    (b)   a decision of a children's hearing continuing a child protection order
under section 59(4) of this Act.

CHAPTER 3
PROTECTION AND SUPERVISION OF CHILDREN

Children requiring compulsory measures of supervision

52   Children requiring compulsory measures of supervision

(1)   The question of whether compulsory measures of supervision are necessary
in respect of a child arises if at least one of the conditions mentioned in subsection
(2) below is satisfied with respect to him.

(2)   The conditions referred to in subsection (1) above are that the child—

    (a)   is beyond the control of any relevant person;

    (b)   is falling into bad associations or is exposed to moral danger;

    (c)   is likely—

        (i)   to suffer unnecessarily; or

        (ii)   be impaired seriously in his health or development,
due to a lack of parental care;

    (d)   is a child in respect of whom any of the offences mentioned in [Schedule
1 to the Criminal Procedure (Scotland) Act 1995] (offences against children to
which special provisions apply) has been committed;

    (e)   is, or is likely to become, a member of the same household as a child in
respect of whom any of the offences referred to in paragraph (d) above has been
committed;

    (f)   is, or is likely to become, a member of the same household as a person
who has committed any of the offences referred in paragraph (d) above;

    (g)   is, or is likely to become, a member of the same household as a
person in respect of whom an offence under [sections 1 and 3 of the Criminal
Law (Consolidation) (Scotland) Act 1995] (incest and intercourse with a child

by step-parent or person in position of trust) has been committed by a member of that household;

(h) has failed to attend school regularly without reasonable excuse;

(i) has committed an offence;

(j) has misused alcohol or any drug, whether or not a controlled drug within the meaning of the Misuse of Drugs Act 1971;

(k) has misused a volatile substance by deliberately inhaling its vapour, other than for medicinal purposes;

(l) is being provided with accommodation by a local authority under section 25 [of this Act], or is the subject of a [permanence order made under section 80, of the Adoption and Children (Scotland) Act 2007] and, in either case, his behaviour is such that special measures are necessary for his adequate supervision in his interest or the interest of others.

[(m) is a child to whom subsection (2A) below applies.

(2A) This subsection applies to a child where—

(a) a requirement is made of the Principal Reporter under section 11(1) of the Antisocial Behaviour etc (Scotland) Act 2004 (asp 8) (power of sheriff to require Principal Reporter to refer case to children's hearing) in respect of the child's case; and

(b) the child is not subject to a supervision requirement.]

(3) In this Part of this Act, 'supervision' in relation to compulsory measures of supervision may include measures taken for the protection, guidance, treatment or control of the child.

Preliminary and investigatory measures

53 Provision of information to the Principal Reporter

(1) Where information is received by a local authority which suggests that compulsory measures of supervision may be necessary in respect of a child, they shall—

(a) cause inquiries to be made into the case unless they are satisfied that such inquiries are unnecessary; and

(b) if it appears to them after such inquiries, or after being satisfied that such inquiries are unnecessary, that such measures may be required in respect of the child, give to the Principal Reporter such information about the child as they have been able to discover.

(2) A person, other than a local authority, who has reasonable cause to believe that compulsory measures of supervision may be necessary in respect of a child—

(a) shall, if he is a constable, give to the Principal Reporter such information about the child as he has been able to discover;

(b) in any other case, may give the Principal Reporter that information.

(3) A constable shall make any report required to be made under paragraph (b) of section 17(1) of the Police (Scotland) Act 1967 (duty to make reports in relation to commission of offences) in relation to a child to the Principal Reporter as well as to the appropriate prosecutor.

(4) Where an application has been made to the sheriff—

(a) by the Principal Reporter in accordance with a direction given by a children's hearing under section 65(7) or (9) of this Act; or

(b) by any person entitled to make an application under section 85 of this Act,

the Principal Reporter may request any prosecutor to supply him with any evidence lawfully obtained in the course of, and held by the prosecutor in connection with, the investigation of a crime or suspected crime, being evidence which may assist the sheriff in determining the application; and, subject to subsection (5) below, it shall be the duty of the prosecutor to comply with such a request.

(5) A prosecutor may refuse to comply with a request issued under subsection

(4) above where he reasonably believes that it is necessary to retain the evidence for the purposes of any proceedings in respect of a crime, whether the proceedings have been commenced or are to be commenced by him.

(6) The Lord Advocate may direct that in any specified case or class of cases any evidence lawfully obtained in the course of an investigation of a crime or suspected crime shall be supplied, without the need for a request under subsection (4) above, to the Principal Reporter.

(7) In subsections (3), (4) and (5) above 'crime' and 'prosecutor' have the same meanings respectively given by section [307 of the Criminal Procedure (Scotland) Act 1995].

54 Reference to the Principal Reporter by court

(1) Where in any relevant proceedings it appears to the court that any of the conditions in section 52(2)(a) to (h), (j), (k) or (1) of this Act is satisfied with respect to a child, it may refer the matter to the Principal Reporter, specifying the condition.

(2) In this section 'relevant proceedings' means—

(a) an action for divorce or judicial separation or for declarator of marriage, nullity of marriage, parentage or non-parentage;

[(aa) an action for dissolution or declarator of nullity of a civil partnership or separation of civil partners;]

(b) proceedings relating to parental responsibilities or parental rights within the meaning of Part I of this Act;

(c) proceedings for an adoption order under the [Adoption and Children (Scotland) Act 2007];

[(ca) proceedings for the making, variation or revocation of a permanence order under that Act in respect of a child who is not subject to a supervision requirement;]

(d) proceedings for an offence against section 35 (failure by parent to secure regular attendance by his child at a public school), 41 (failure to comply with attendance order) or 42(3) (failure to permit examination of child) of the Education (Scotland) Act 1980.

(3) Where the court has referred a matter to the Principal Reporter under subsection (1) above, he shall—

(a) make such investigation as he thinks appropriate; and

(b) if he considers that compulsory measures of supervision are necessary, arrange a children's hearing to consider the case of the child under section 69 of this Act; and subsection (1) of that section shall apply as if the condition specified by the court under subsection (1) above were a ground of referral established in accordance with section 68 of this Act.

55 Child assessment orders

(1) A sheriff may grant an order under this section for an assessment of the state of a child's health or development, or of the way in which he has been treated (to be known as a 'child assessment order'), on the application of a local authority if he is satisfied that—

(a) the local authority have reasonable cause to suspect that the child in respect of whom the order is sought is being so treated (or neglected) that he is suffering, or is likely to suffer, significant harm;

(b) such assessment of the child is required in order to establish whether or not there is reasonable cause to believe that the child is so treated (or neglected); and

(c) such assessment is unlikely to be carried out, or be carried out satisfactorily, unless the order is granted.

(2) Where—

(a) an application has been made under subsection (1) above; and

(b)   the sheriff considers that the conditions for making a child protection order under section 57 of this Act are satisfied,

he shall make such an order under that section as if the application had been duly made by the local authority under that section rather than this section.

(3)   A child assessment order shall—

(a)   specify the date on which the assessment is to begin;

(b)   have effect for such period as is specified in the order, not exceeding seven days beginning with the date specified by virtue of paragraph (a) above;

(c)   require any person in a position to produce the child to—

(i)   produce him to any authorised person;

(ii)   permit that person or any other authorised person to carry out an assessment in accordance with the order; and

(iii)   comply with any other conditions of the order; and

(d)   be carried out by an authorised person in accordance with the terms of the order.

(4)   A child assessment order may—

(a)   where necessary, permit the taking of the child concerned to any place for the purposes of the assessment; and

(b)   authorise the child to be kept at that place, or any other place, for such period of time as may be specified in the order.

(5)   Where a child assessment order makes provision under subsection (4) above, it shall contain such directions as the sheriff considers appropriate as to the contact which the child shall be allowed to have with any other person while the child is in any place to which he has been taken or in which he is being kept under a child assessment order.

(6)   In this section 'authorised person' means any officer of the local authority, and any person authorised by the local authority to perform the assessment, or perform any part of it.

56   Initial investigation by the Principal Reporter

(1)   Where the Principal Reporter receives information from any source about a case which may require a children's hearing to be arranged he shall, after making such initial investigation as he thinks necessary, proceed with the case in accordance with subsection (4) or (6) below.

(2)   For the purposes of making any initial investigation under subsection (1) above, the Principal Reporter may request from the local authority a report on the child and on such circumstances concerning the child as appear to him to be relevant; and the local authority shall supply the report which may contain such information, from any person whomsoever, as the Principal Reporter thinks, or the local authority think, fit.

(3)   A report requested under subsection (2) above may contain information additional to that given by the local authority under section 53 of this Act.

(4)   The Principal Reporter may decide, after an initial investigation under subsection (1) above, that a children's hearing does not require to be arranged; and where he so decides—

(a)   he shall inform the child, any relevant person and the person who brought the case to his notice, or any of those persons, that he has so decided;

(b)   he may, if he considers it appropriate, refer the case to a local authority with a view to their making arrangements for the advice, guidance and assistance of the child and his family in accordance with Chapter 1 of this Part of this Act [; and

(c)   he may, where it appears to him that—

(i)   an education authority have a duty under section 14(3) of the Education (Scotland) Act 1980 (c 44) in relation to the child; and

(ii)   the authority are not complying with that duty,

refer the matter to the Scottish Ministers.

(4A)   A reference made under subsection (4)(c) above shall be in writing.

(4B)   A copy of a reference made under subsection (4)(c) above shall be sent by the Principal Reporter to the education authority in respect of which the reference is made.]

(5)   Where the Principal Reporter has decided under subsection (4) above that a children's hearing does not require to be arranged, he shall not at any other time, on the basis solely of the information obtained during the initial investigation referred to in that subsection, arrange a children's hearing under subsection (6) below.

(6)   Where it appears to the Principal Reporter that compulsory measures of supervision are necessary in respect of the child, he shall arrange a children's hearing to which he shall refer the case for consideration and determination.

(7)   Where the Principal Reporter has arranged a children's hearing in accordance with subsection (6) above, he—

(a)   shall, where he has not previously done so, request a report under subsection (2) above;

(b)   may request from the local authority such information, supplementary or additional to a report requested under subsection (2) above, as he thinks fit;

and the local authority shall supply that report, or as the case may be information, and any other information which they consider to be relevant.

Measures for the emergency protection of children

57   Child protection orders

(1)   Where the sheriff, on an application by any person, is satisfied that—

(a)   there are reasonable grounds to believe that a child—

(i)   is being so treated (or neglected) that he is suffering significant harm; or

(ii)   will suffer such harm if he is not removed to and kept in a place of safety, or if he does not remain in the place where he is then being accommodated (whether or not he is resident there); and

(b)   an order under this section is necessary to protect that child from such harm (or such further harm),

he may make an order under this section (to be known as a 'child protection order').

(2)   Without prejudice to subsection (1) above, where the sheriff on an application by a local authority is satisfied—

(a)   that they have reasonable grounds to suspect that a child is being or will be so treated (or neglected) that he is suffering or will suffer significant harm;

(b)   that they are making or causing to be made enquiries to allow them to decide whether they should take any action to safeguard the welfare of the child; and

(c)   that those enquiries are being frustrated by access to the child being unreasonably denied, the authority having reasonable cause to believe that such access is required as a matter of urgency,

he may make a child protection order.

(3)   Without prejudice to any additional requirement imposed by rules made by virtue of section 91 of this Act, an application for a child protection order shall—

(a)   identify—

(i)   the applicant; and

(ii)   in so far as practicable, the child in respect of whom the order is sought;

(b)   state the grounds on which the application is made; and

(c)   be accompanied by such supporting evidence, whether in documentary form or otherwise, as will enable the sheriff to determine the application.

(4)   A child protection order may, subject to such terms and conditions as the sheriff considers appropriate, do any one or more of the following—

(a)   require any person in a position to do so to produce the child to the applicant;

(b)   authorise the removal of the child by the applicant to a place of safety, and the keeping of the child at that place;

(c)   authorise the prevention of the removal of the child from any place where he is being accommodated;

(d)   provide that the location of any place of safety in which the child is being kept should not be disclosed to any person or class of person specified in the order.

(5)   Notice of the making of a child protection order shall be given forthwith by the applicant to the local authority in whose area the child resides (where that authority is not the applicant) and to the Principal Reporter.

(6)   In taking any action required or permitted by a child protection order or by a direction under section 58 of this Act the applicant shall only act where he reasonably believes that to do so is necessary to safeguard or promote the welfare of the child.

(7)   Where by virtue of a child protection order a child is removed to a place of safety provided by a local authority, they shall, subject to the terms and conditions of that order and of any direction given under section 58 of this Act, have the like duties in respect of the child as they have under section 17 of this Act in respect of a child looked after by them.

58   Directions in relation to contact and exercise of parental responsibilities and parental rights

(1)   When the sheriff makes a child protection order, he shall at that time consider whether it is necessary to give a direction to the applicant for the order as to contact with the child for—

(a)   any parent of the child;

(b)   any person with parental responsibilities in relation to the child; and

(c)   any other specified person or class of persons;

and if he determines that there is such a necessity he may give such a direction.

(2)   Without prejudice to the generality of subsection (1) above, a direction under that subsection may—

(a)   prohibit contact with the child for any person mentioned in paragraphs (a) to (c) of that subsection;

(b)   make contact with the child for any person subject to such conditions as the sheriff considers appropriate to safeguard and promote the welfare of the child.

(3)   A direction under subsection (1) above may make different provision in relation to different persons or classes of person.

(4)   A person applying for a child protection order under section 57(1) or (2) of this Act may at the same time apply to the sheriff for a direction in relation to the exercise or fulfilment of any parental responsibilities or parental rights in respect of the child concerned, if the person considers such a direction necessary to safeguard or promote the welfare of the child.

(5)   Without prejudice to the generality of subsection (4) above, a direction under that subsection may be sought in relation to—

(a)   any examination as to the physical or mental state of the child;

(b)   any other assessment or interview of the child; or

(c)   any treatment of the child arising out of such an examination or assessment,

which is to be carried out by any person.

(6)   The sheriff may give a direction sought under subsection (4) above where he considers there is a necessity such as is mentioned in that subsection; and such a direction may be granted subject to such conditions, if any, as the sheriff (having regard in particular to the duration of the child protection order to which it relates) considers appropriate.

(7)   A direction under this section shall cease to have effect when—
  (a)   the sheriff, on an application under section 60(7) of this Act, directs that it is cancelled; or
  (b)   the child protection order to which it is related ceases to have effect.

59   Initial hearing of case of child subject to child protection order

(1)   This section applies where—
  (a)   a child in respect of whom a child protection order has been made—
    (i)   has been taken to a place of safety by virtue of section 57(4)(b) of this Act; or
    (ii)   is prevented from being removed from any place by virtue of section 57(4)(c) of this Act;
  (b)   the Principal Reporter has not exercised his powers under section 60(3) of this Act to discharge the child from the place of safety; and
  (c)   the Principal Reporter has not received notice, in accordance with section 60(9) of this Act, of an application under subsection (7) of that section.

(2)   Where this section applies, the Principal Reporter shall arrange a children's hearing to conduct an initial hearing of the child's case in order to determine whether they should, in the interests of the child, continue the child protection order under subsection (4) below.

(3)   A children's hearing arranged under subsection (2) above shall take place on the second working day after that order is implemented.

(4)   Where a children's hearing arranged under subsection (2) above are satisfied that the conditions for the making of a child protection order under section 57 of this Act are established, they may continue the child protection order and any direction given under section 58 of this Act (whether with or without variation of the order or, as the case may be, the direction) until the commencement of a children's hearing in relation to the child arranged in accordance with section 65(2) of this Act.

(5)   In subsection (3) above, section 60 and section 65(2) of this Act any reference, in relation to the calculation of any period, to the time at which a child protection order is implemented shall be construed as a reference—
  (a)   in relation to such an order made under paragraph (b) of subsection (4) of section 57 of this Act, to the day on which the child was removed to a place of safety in accordance with the order; and
  (b)   in relation to such an order made under paragraph (c) of that subsection, to the day on which the order was made,
and 'implement' shall be construed accordingly.

60   Duration, recall or variation of child protection order

(1)   Where, by the end of twenty-four hours of a child protection order being made (other than by virtue of section 57(4)(c) of this Act), the applicant has made no attempt to implement the order it shall cease to have effect.

(2)   Where an application made under subsection (7) below has not been determined timeously in accordance with subsection (8) below, the order to which the application relates shall cease to have effect.

(3)   A child shall not be—
  (a)   kept in a place of safety under a child protection order;
  (b)   prevented from being removed from any place by such an order; or
  (c)   subject to any term or condition contained in such an order or a direction given under section 58 of this Act,
where the Principal Reporter, having regard to the welfare of the child, considers that, whether as a result of a change in the circumstances of the case or of further information relating to the case having been received by the Principal Reporter, the conditions for the making of a child protection order in respect of the child are no longer satisfied or that the term, condition or direction is no

longer appropriate and notifies the person who implemented the order that he so considers.

(4)   The Principal Reporter shall not give notice under subsection (3) above where—

(a)   proceedings before a children's hearing arranged under section 59(2) of this Act in relation to the child who is subject to the child protection order have commenced; or

(b)   the hearing of an application made under subsection (7) of this section has begun.

(5)   Where the Principal Reporter has given notice under subsection (3) above, he shall also, in such manner as may be prescribed, notify the sheriff who made the order.

(6)   A child protection order shall cease to have effect—

(a)   where an initial hearing arranged under section 59(2) of this Act does not continue the order under subsection (4) of that section;

(b)   where an application is made to the sheriff under subsection (7) below, on the sheriff recalling such order under subsection (13) below;

(c)   on the person who implemented the order receiving notice from the Principal Reporter that he has decided not to refer the case of a child who is subject to the order to a children's hearing arranged in accordance with section 65(2) of this Act;

(d)   on the Principal Reporter giving notice in accordance with subsection (3) above in relation to the order that he considers that the conditions for the making of it are no longer satisfied; or

(e)   where such order is continued under section 59(4) of this Act or subsection (12)(d) below, on the commencement of a children's hearing arranged under section 65(2) of this Act.

(7)   An application to the sheriff to set aside or vary a child protection order made under section 57 of this Act or a direction given under section 58 of this Act or such an order or direction continued (whether with or without variation) under section 59(4) of this Act, may be made by or on behalf of—

(a)   the child to whom the order or direction relates;

(b)   a person having parental rights over the child;

(c)   a relevant person;

(d)   any person to whom notice of the application for the order was given by virtue of rules; or

(e)   the applicant for the order made under section 57 of this Act.

(8)   An application under subsection (7) above shall be made—

(a)   in relation to a child protection order made under section 57, or a direction given under section 58, of this Act, before the commencement of a children's hearing arranged in accordance with section 59(2) of this Act; and

(b)   in relation to such an order or direction continued (whether with or without variation) by virtue of subsection (4) of the said section 59, within two working days of such continuation,

and any such application shall be determined within three working days of being made.

(9)   Where an application has been made under subsection (7) above, the applicant shall forthwith give notice, in a manner and form prescribed by rules, to the Principal Reporter.

(10)   At any time which is—

(a)   after the giving of the notice required by subsection (9) above; but

(b)   before the sheriff has determined the application in accordance with subsection (11) below,

the Principal Reporter may arrange a children's hearing the purpose of which shall be to provide any advice they consider appropriate to assist the sheriff in his determination of the application.

(11) The sheriff shall, after hearing the parties to the application and, if he wishes to make representations, the Principal Reporter, determine whether—

(a)   the conditions for the making of a child protection order under section 57 of this Act are satisfied; or

(b)   where the application relates only to a direction under section 58 of this Act, the direction should be varied or cancelled.

(12)   Where the sheriff determines that the conditions referred to in subsection (11)(a) above are satisfied, he may—

(a)   confirm or vary the order, or any term or condition on which it was granted;

(b)   confirm or vary any direction given, in relation to the order, under section 58 of this Act;

(c)   give a new direction under that section; or

(d)   continue in force the order and any such direction until the commencement of a children's hearing arranged in accordance with section 65(2) of this Act.

(13)   Where the sheriff determines that the conditions referred to in subsection (11)(a) above are not satisfied he shall recall the order and cancel any direction given under section 58 of this Act.

61   Emergency protection of children where child protection order not available

(1)   Where, on the application of any person, a justice of the peace is satisfied—

(a)   both that the conditions laid down for the making of a child protection order in section 57(1) of this Act are satisfied and that it is probable that any such order, if made, would contain an authorisation in terms of paragraph (b) or (c) of subsection (4) of that section; but

(b)   that it is not practicable in the circumstances for an application for such an order to be made to the sheriff or for the sheriff to consider such an application,

he may grant to the applicant an authorisation under this section.

(2)   Where on the application of a local authority a justice of the peace is satisfied—

(a)   both that the conditions laid down for the making of a child protection order in section 57(2) of this Act are satisfied and that it is probable that any such order, if made, would contain an authorisation in terms of paragraph (b) or (c) of subsection (4) of that section; but

(b)   that it is not practicable in the circumstances for an application for such an order to be made to the sheriff or for the sheriff to consider such an application,

he may grant an authorisation under this section.

(3)   An authorisation under this section may—

(a)   require any person in a position to do so to produce the child to the applicant;

(b)   prevent any person from removing a child from a place where he is then being accommodated;

(c)   authorise the applicant to remove the child to a place of safety and to keep him there until the expiration of the authorisation.

(4)   An authorisation under this section shall cease to have effect—

(a)   twelve hours after being made, if within that time—

(i)   arrangements have not been made to prevent the child's removal from any place specified in the authorisation; or

(ii)   he has not been, or is not being, taken to a place of safety; or

(b)   where such arrangements have been made or he has been so taken when—

(i)   twenty-four hours have expired since it was so given; or

(ii) an application for a child protection order in respect of the child is disposed of,

whichever is the earlier.

(5) Where a constable has reasonable cause to believe that—

(a) the conditions for the making of a child protection order laid down in section 57(1) are satisfied;

(b) that it is not practicable in the circumstances for him to make an application for such an order to the sheriff or for the sheriff to consider such an application; and

(c) that, in order to protect the child from significant harm (or further such harm), it is necessary for him to remove the child to a place of safety,

he may remove the child to such a place and keep him there.

(6) The power conferred by subsection (5) above shall not authorise the keeping of a child in a place of safety for more than twenty-four hours from the time when the child is so removed.

(7) The authority to keep a child in a place of safety conferred by subsection (5) above shall cease on the disposal of an application in relation to the child for a child protection order.

(8) A child shall not be—

(a) kept in a place of safety; or

(b) prevented from being removed from any place,

under this section where the Principal Reporter considers that the conditions for the grant of an authorisation under subsection (1) or (2) above or the exercise of the power conferred by subsection (5) above are not satisfied, or that it is no longer in the best interests of the child that he should be so kept.

62 Regulations in respect of emergency child protection measures

(1) The Secretary of State may make regulations concerning the duties in respect of a child of any person removing him to, and keeping him in, a place of safety under section 61 above.

(2) Regulations under this section may make provision requiring—

(a) notification of the removal of a child to be given to a person specified in the regulations;

(b) intimation to be given to any person of the place of safety at which a child is being kept;

(c) notification to be given to any person of the ceasing to have effect, under section 61(4)(a) of this Act, of an authorisation.

Children arrested by the police

63 Review of case of child arrested by police

(1) Where the Principal Reporter has been informed by a constable, in accordance with section [43(5) of the Criminal Procedure (Scotland) Act 1995], that charges are not to be proceeded with against a child who has been detained in a place of safety in accordance with that section, the Principal Reporter shall, unless he considers that compulsory measures of supervision are not required in relation to the child, arrange a children's hearing to which he shall refer the case.

(2) A children's hearing arranged under subsection (1) above shall begin not later than the third day after the Principal Reporter received the information mentioned in that subsection.

(3) Where the Principal Reporter considers that a child of whose detention he has been informed does not require compulsory measures of supervision, he shall direct that the child shall no longer be kept in the place of safety.

(4) Subject to subsection (3) above, a child who has been detained in a place of safety may continue to be kept at that place until the commencement of a children's hearing arranged under subsection (1) above.

(5) Subject to subsection (6) below, a children's hearing arranged under subsection (1) above may—

(a) if they are satisfied that the conditions mentioned in subsection (2) of section 66 of this Act are satisfied, grant a warrant to keep the child in a place of safety; and

(b) direct the Principal Reporter to arrange a children's hearing for the purposes of section 65(1) of this Act, and subsections (3) to (8) of the said section 66 shall apply to a warrant granted under this subsection as they apply to a warrant granted under subsection (1) of the said section 66.

(6) A child shall not be kept in a place of safety in accordance with a warrant granted under subsection (5) above where the Principal Reporter, having regard to the welfare of the child, considers that, whether as a result of a change in the circumstances of the case or of further information relating to the case having been received by the Principal Reporter—

(a) the conditions mentioned in section 66(2) of this Act are no longer satisfied in relation to the child; or

(b) the child is not in need of compulsory measures of supervision,

and where he does so consider he shall give notice to that effect to the person who is keeping the child in that place in accordance with the warrant.

Business meeting preparatory to children's hearing

64 Business meeting preparatory to children's hearing

(1) At any time prior to the commencement of proceedings at the children's hearing, the Principal Reporter may arrange a meeting with members of the children's panel from which the children's hearing is to be constituted under section 39(4) of this Act for those proceedings (any such meeting being, in this Part of this Act referred to as a 'business meeting').

(2) Where a business meeting is arranged under subsection (1) above, the Principal Reporter shall give notice to the child in respect of whom the proceedings are to be commenced and any relevant person in relation to the child—

(a) of the arrangement of the meeting and of the matters which may be considered and determined by the meeting;

(b) of their right to make their views on those matters known to the Principal Reporter; and

(c) of the duty of the Principal Reporter to present those views to the meeting.

(3) A business meeting, subject to subsection (4) below—

(a) shall determine such procedural and other matters as may be prescribed by rules under subsection (1) of section 42 of this Act by virtue of subsection (2)(a) of that section; and

(b) may give such direction or guidance to the Principal Reporter in relation to the performance of his functions in relation to the proceedings as they think appropriate.

(4) Before a business meeting makes such a determination or gives such direction or guidance to the Principal Reporter, the Principal Reporter shall present, and they shall consider, any views expressed to him by virtue of subsection (2)(b) above.

(5) Subject to any rules made under section 42(1) of this Act by virtue of subsection (2)(a) of that section and with the exception of sections 44 and, as regards any determination made by the business meeting under subsection (3)(a) above, 51, the provisions of this Act which relate to a children's hearing shall not apply to a business meeting.

Referral to, and disposal of case by, children's hearing

65 Referral to, and proceedings at, children's hearing

(1) The Principal Reporter shall refer to the children's hearing, for consideration and determination on the merits, the case of any child in respect of whom he is satisfied that—

(a) compulsory measures of supervision are necessary, and

(b) at least one of the grounds specified in section 52(2) of this Act is established;

and he shall state such grounds in accordance with rules made under section 42(1) of this Act by virtue of subsection (2)(c) of that section.

[(1A) Where the Principal Reporter is satisfied that the ground specified in section 52(2)(m) of this Act is established in respect of any child, he shall be taken to be satisfied as to the matter mentioned in section 65(1)(a) in respect of the child.]

(2) Where a referral is made in respect of a child who is subject to a child protection order made under section 57, and that order is continued under section 59(4) or 60(12)(d), of this Act, the Principal Reporter shall arrange for the children's hearing under subsection (1) above to take place on the eighth working day after the order was implemented.

(3) Where a referral is made in respect of a child who is subject to a supervision requirement, the children's hearing shall, before disposing of the referral in accordance with section 69(1)(b) or (c) of this Act, review that requirement in accordance with subsections (9) to (12) of section 73 of this Act.

(4) Subject to subsections (9) and (10) below, it shall be the duty of the chairman of the children's hearing to whom a child's case has been referred under subsection (1) above to explain to the child and the relevant person, at the opening of proceedings on the referral, the grounds stated by the Principal Reporter for the referral in order to ascertain whether these grounds are accepted in whole or in part by them.

(5) Where the chairman has given the explanation required by subsection (4) above and the child and the relevant person accept the grounds for the referral, the children's hearing shall proceed in accordance with section 69 of this Act.

(6) Where the chairman has given the explanation required by subsection (4) above and the child and the relevant person accept the grounds in part, the children's hearing may, if they consider it appropriate to do so, proceed in accordance with section 69 of this Act with respect to those grounds which are accepted.

(7) Where the chairman has given the explanation required under subsection (4) above and either or both of the child and the relevant person—

(a) do not accept the grounds for the referral; or

(b) accept the grounds in part, but the children's hearing do not consider it appropriate to proceed with the case under subsection (6) above,

the hearing shall either direct the Principal Reporter to make an application to the sheriff for a finding as to whether such grounds for the referral as are not accepted by the child and the relevant person are established or shall discharge the referral.

(8) Subject to subsection (10) below, it shall be the duty of the chairman to explain to the child and to the relevant person the purpose for which the application to the sheriff is being made and to inform the child that he is under an obligation to attend the hearing before the sheriff.

(9) Where a children's hearing are satisfied that the child—

(a) for any reason will not be capable of understanding the explanation of the grounds for the referral required under subsection (4) above; or

(b) has not understood an explanation given under that subsection,

they shall either direct the Principal Reporter to make an application to the sheriff for a finding as to whether any of the grounds of the referral are established or discharge the referral.

(10)   The acceptance by the relevant person of the grounds of the referral shall not be a requirement for a children's hearing proceeding under this section to consider a case where that person is not present.

66 Warrant to keep child where children's hearing unable to dispose of case

(1)   Without prejudice to any other power enjoyed by them under this Part of this Act and subject to subsection (5) below, a children's hearing—

(a)   arranged to consider a child's case under this Part of this Act; and

(b)   unable to dispose of the case,

may, if they are satisfied that one of the conditions mentioned in subsection (2) below is met, grant a warrant under this subsection.

(2)   The conditions referred to in subsection (1) above are—

(a)   that there is reason to believe that the child may—

(i)   not attend at any hearing of his case; or

(ii)   fail to comply with a requirement under section 69(3) of this Act; or

(b)   that it is necessary that the child should be kept in a place of safety in order to safeguard or promote his welfare.

(3)   A warrant under subsection (1) above may require any person named in the warrant—

(a)   to find and to keep or, as the case may be, to keep the child in a place of safety for a period not exceeding twenty-two days after the warrant is granted;

(b)   to bring the child before a children's hearing at such times as may be specified in the warrant.

(4)   A warrant under subsection (1) above may contain such conditions as appear to the children's hearing to be necessary or expedient, and without prejudice to that generality may—

(a)   subject to section 90 of this Act, require the child to submit to any medical or other examination or treatment; and

(b)   regulate the contact with the child of any specified person or class of persons.

(5)   Subject to subsection (8) below, at any time prior to its expiry, a warrant granted under this section may, on an application to the children's hearing, on cause shown by the Principal Reporter, be continued in force, whether with or without variation of any condition imposed by virtue of subsection (4) above, by the children's hearing for such further period, not exceeding twenty-two days, as appears to them to be necessary.

(6)   Where a children's hearing are satisfied—

[(a)   that one of the conditions mentioned in section 70(10) of this Act is met; and

(b)   that it is necessary to do so],

they may order that, pending the disposal of his case, the child shall be liable to be placed and kept in secure accommodation within a residential establishment at such times as the person in charge of that establishment, with the agreement of the chief social work officer of the relevant local authority, considers necessary.

(7)   Where a children's hearing grant a warrant under subsection (1) above or continue such a warrant under subsection (5) above, they may order that the place of safety at which the child is to be kept shall not be disclosed to any person or class of persons specified in the order.

(8)   A child shall not be kept in a place of safety or secure accommodation by virtue of this section for a period exceeding sixty-six days from the day when he was first taken to a place of safety under a warrant granted under subsection (1) above.

67 Warrant for further detention of child

(1)   Where a child is being kept in a place of safety by virtue of a warrant granted under section 66 of this Act or under this subsection, the Principal Re-

porter at any time prior to the expiry of that warrant may apply to the sheriff for a warrant to keep the child in that place after the warrant granted under the said section 66 or, as the case may be, this subsection has expired.

(2)   A warrant under subsection (1) above shall only be granted on cause shown and—

(a)   shall specify the date on which it will expire; and

(b)   may contain any such requirement or condition as may be contained in a warrant granted under the said section 66.

(3)   Where the sheriff grants a warrant under subsection (1) above, he may also make an order under this subsection in such terms as are mentioned in subsection (6) or (7) of the said section 66; and any order under this subsection shall cease to have effect when the warrant expires.

(4)   An application under subsection (1) above may be made at the same time as, or during the hearing of, an application which the Principal Reporter has been directed by a children's hearing to make under section 65(7) or (9) of this Act.

68   Application to sheriff to establish grounds of referral

(1)   This section applies to applications under subsections (7) and (9) of section 65 of this Act and a reference in this section (except in subsection (8)) to 'an application' is a reference to an application under either of those subsections.

(2)   An application shall be heard by the sheriff within twenty-eight days of its being lodged.

(3)   Where one of the grounds for the referral to which an application relates is the condition referred to in section 52(2)(i)—

(a)   the application shall be made to the sheriff who would have jurisdiction if the child were being prosecuted for that offence; and

(b)   in hearing the application in relation to that ground, the standard of proof required in criminal proceedings shall apply.

(4)   A child shall—

(a)   have the right to attend the hearing of an application; and

(b)   subject to subsection (5) below, be under an obligation to attend such hearing;

and without prejudice to the right of each of them to be legally represented, the child and the relevant person may be represented by a person other than a legally qualified person at any diet fixed by the sheriff for the hearing of the application.

(5)   Without prejudice to subsection (4)(a) above, the sheriff may dispense with the obligation imposed by subsection (4)(b) above where he is satisfied—

(a)   in an application in which the ground of referral to be established is a condition mentioned in section 52(2)(d), (e), (f) or (g) of this Act, that the obligation to attend of the child is not necessary for the just hearing of that application; and

(b)   in any application, that it would be detrimental to the interests of the child for him to be present at the hearing of the application.

(6)   Where the child fails to attend the hearing of an application at which his attendance has not been dispensed with under subsection (5) above, the sheriff may grant an order to find and keep the child; and any order under this subsection shall be authority for bringing the child before the sheriff and, subject to subsection (7) below, for keeping him in a place of safety until the sheriff can hear the application.

(7)   The child shall not be kept in a place of safety by virtue of subsection (6) above after whichever is the earlier of—

(a)   the expiry of fourteen days beginning with the day on which the child is found; or

(b)   the disposal of the application by the sheriff.

(8)   Where in the course of the hearing of an application—

(a)   under section 65(7) of this Act, the child and the relevant person accept any of the grounds for referral to which the application relates, the sheriff shall; or

(b)   under section 65(9) of this Act, the relevant person accepts any of the grounds for referral to which the application relates, the sheriff may, if it appears to him reasonable to do so,

dispense with the hearing of evidence relating to that ground and deem the ground to be established for the purposes of the application, unless he is satisfied that, in all the circumstances of the case, the evidence should be heard.

(9)   Where a sheriff decides that none of the grounds for referral in respect of which an application has been made are established, he shall dismiss the application, discharge the referral to the children's hearing in respect of those grounds and recall, discharge or cancel any order, warrant, or direction under this Chapter of this Act which relates to the child in respect of those grounds.

(10)   Where the sheriff, after the hearing of any evidence or on acceptance in accordance with subsection (8) above, finds that any of the grounds for the referral to which the application relates is, or should be deemed to be, established—

(a)   he shall remit the case to the Principal Reporter to make arrangements for a children's hearing to consider and determine the case; and

(b)   he may if he is satisfied that—

(i)   keeping the child in a place of safety is necessary in the child's best interests; or

(ii)   there is reason to believe that the child will run away before the children's hearing sit to consider the case,

issue an order requiring, subject to subsection (12) below, that the child be kept in a place of safety until the children's hearing so sit.

(11)   An order issued under subsection (10) above may, if the sheriff is satisfied—

[(a)   that one of the conditions mentioned in section 70(10) of this Act is met; and

(b)   that it is necessary for the order to do so],

provide that the child shall be liable to be placed and kept in secure accommodation within a residential establishment at such times as the person in charge of the establishment, with the agreement of the chief social work officer of the relevant local authority, considers necessary.

(12)   A child shall not be kept in a place of safety by virtue of subsection (10)(b) above after whichever is the earlier of the following—

(a)   the expiry of three days beginning with the day on which he is first so kept; or

(b)   the consideration of his case by the children's hearing arranged under subsection (10)(a) above.

[68A   Restrictions on evidence in certain cases involving sexual abuse

(1)   This section applies in relation to—

(a)   an application under section 65(7) or (9) of this Act in which the ground of referral to be established is a condition mentioned in—

(i)   paragraph (b) of subsection (2) of section 52 of this Act where that condition is alleged to be satisfied by reference to sexual behaviour engaged in by any person,

(ii)   paragraph (d), (e) or (f) of that subsection where that condition is alleged to be satisfied by reference to a relevant offence, or

(iii)   paragraph (g) of that subsection, or

(b)   an application under section 85 of this Act for a review of a finding that any such ground of referral is established.

(2)   In hearing the application, the sheriff shall not admit, or allow questioning

designed to elicit, evidence which shows or tends to show that the child who is the subject of the application or any other witness giving evidence at the hearing (such child or other witness being referred to in this section and section 68B of this Act as 'the witness')—

(a)   is not of good character (whether in relation to sexual matters or otherwise),

(b)   has, at any time, engaged in sexual behaviour not forming part of the subject matter of the ground of referral,

(c)   has, at any time (other than shortly before, at the same time as or shortly after the acts which form part of the subject matter of the ground of referral), engaged in such behaviour, not being sexual behaviour, as might found the inference that the witness is not a credible or reliable witness, or

(d)   has, at any time, been subject to any such condition or predisposition as might found the inference referred to in paragraph (c) above.

(3)   In subsection (1)(a)(ii) above, 'relevant offence' means—

(a)   an offence mentioned in paragraph 1 or 4 of Schedule 1 (offences against children under the age of 17 to which special provisions apply) to the Criminal Procedure (Scotland) Act 1995 (c 46), or

(b)   any other offence mentioned in that Schedule where there is a substantial sexual element in the alleged commission of the offence.

(4)   In subsection (2)(b) and (c) above—

(a)   'the subject matter of the ground of referral' means—

(i)   in the case of an application in which the ground of referral to be established is the condition referred to in paragraph (a)(i) of subsection (1) above, the sexual behaviour referred to in that paragraph,

(ii)   in the case of any other application, the acts or behaviour constituting the offence by reference to which the ground of referral is alleged to be established, and

(b)   the reference to engaging in sexual behaviour includes a reference to undergoing or being made subject to any experience of a sexual nature.]

[68B   Exceptions to restrictions under section 68A

(1)   The sheriff hearing an application referred to in subsection (1) of section 68A of this Act may, on an application by any party to the proceedings, admit such evidence or allow such questioning as is referred to in subsection (2) of that section if satisfied that—

(a)   the evidence or questioning will relate only to a specific occurrence or occurrences of sexual or other behaviour or to specific facts demonstrating—

(i)   the character of the witness, or

(ii)   any condition or predisposition to which the witness is or has been subject,

(b)   that occurrence or those occurrences of behaviour or facts are relevant to establishing the ground of referral, and

(c)   the probative value of the evidence sought to be admitted or elicited is significant and is likely to outweigh any risk of prejudice to the proper administration of justice arising from its being admitted or elicited.

(2)   In subsection (1) above—

(a)   the reference to an occurrence or occurrences of sexual behaviour includes a reference to undergoing or being made subject to any experience of a sexual nature,

(b)   'the proper administration of justice' includes—

(i)   appropriate protection of the witness's dignity and privacy, and

(ii)   ensuring the facts and circumstances of which the sheriff is made aware are relevant to an issue to be put before the sheriff and commensurate with the importance of that issue to the sheriff's decision on the question whether the ground of referral is established.

(3)   In this section, 'the witness' means the child who is the subject of the application referred to in section 68A(1) or other witness in respect of whom the evidence is sought to be admitted or elicited.]

69   Continuation or disposal of referral by children's hearing

(1)   Where the grounds of referral of the child's case stated by the Principal Reporter are accepted or are established in accordance with section 68 or section 85 of this Act, the children's hearing shall consider those grounds, any report obtained under section 56(7) of this Act and any other relevant information available to them and shall—

(a)   continue the case to a subsequent hearing in accordance with subsection (2) below;

(b)   discharge the referral of the case in accordance with subsection (12) below; or

(c)   make a supervision requirement under section 70 of this Act.

(2)   The children's hearing may continue the case to a subsequent hearing under this subsection where they are satisfied that, in order to complete their consideration of the case, it is necessary to have a further investigation of the case.

(3)   Where a children's hearing continue the case under subsection (2) above, they may, for the purposes of the investigation mentioned by that subsection, require the child to attend, or reside at, any clinic, hospital or other establishment during a period not exceeding twenty-two days.

(4)   Where a child fails to fulfil a requirement made under subsection (3) above, the children's hearing may, either on an application by the Principal Reporter or of their own motion, grant a warrant under this subsection.

(5)   A warrant under subsection (4) above shall be authority—

(a)   to find the child;

(b)   to remove the child to a place of safety and keep him there; and

(c)   where the place of safety is not the clinic, hospital or other establishment referred to in the requirement made under subsection (3) above, to take the child from the place of safety to such clinic, hospital or other establishment for the purposes of the investigation mentioned in subsection (2) above.

(6)   A warrant under subsection (4) above shall be granted for such period as appears to the children's hearing to be appropriate, provided that no warrant shall permit the keeping of a child in a place of safety after whichever is the earlier of—

(a)   the expiry of twenty-two days after the warrant is granted; or

(b)   the day on which the subsequent hearing of the child's case by a children's hearing begins.

(7)   Where a child's case has been continued under subsection (2) above and the children's hearing are satisfied that—

(a)   keeping the child in a place of safety is necessary in the interests of safeguarding or promoting the welfare of the child; or

(b)   there is reason to believe that the child may not attend the subsequent hearing of his case,

they may grant a warrant requiring that the child be taken to and kept in a place of safety.

(8)   A warrant under subsection (7) above shall cease to have effect on whichever is the earlier of—

(a)   the expiry of twenty-two days after the warrant is granted; or

(b)   the day on which the subsequent hearing of the child's case by a children's hearing begins.

(9)   A warrant under subsection (4) or (7) above may contain such conditions as appear to the children's hearing to be necessary or expedient, and without prejudice to that generality may—

(a) subject to section 90 of this Act, require the child to submit to any medical or other examination or treatment;

(b) regulate the contact with the child of any specified person or class of persons.

(10) Where a child is to be kept at a place of safety under a warrant granted under this section or is to attend, or reside at, any place in accordance with a requirement made under subsection (3) above, the children's hearing may order that such place shall not be disclosed to any person or class of persons specified in the order.

(11) Where a child is to reside in a residential establishment by virtue of a requirement made or warrant granted under this section, the children's hearing may, if satisfied—

[(a) that one of the conditions mentioned in section 70(10) of this Act is met; and

(b) that it is necessary to do so,]

order that while the requirement or warrant remains in effect he shall be liable to be placed in secure accommodation within that establishment at such times as the person in charge of the establishment, with the agreement of the chief social work officer of the relevant local authority, considers necessary.

(12) Where a children's hearing decide not to make a supervision requirement under section 70 of this Act they shall discharge the referral.

(13) On the discharge of the referral of the child's case any order, direction, or warrant under Chapter 2, or this Chapter, of this Act in respect of the child's case shall cease to have effect.

70 Disposal of referral by children's hearing: supervision requirements, including residence in secure accommodation

(1) Where the children's hearing to whom a child's case has been referred under section 65(1) of this Act are satisfied that compulsory measures of supervision are necessary in respect of the child they may make a requirement under this section (to be known as a 'supervision requirement').

(2) A children's hearing, where they decide to make such a requirement, shall consider whether to impose any condition such as is described in subsection (5)(b) below.

(3) A supervision requirement may require the child—

(a) to reside at any place or places specified in the requirement; and

(b) to comply with any condition contained in the requirement.

[(3B) A children's hearing may, for the purpose of enabling a child to comply with a supervision requirement, impose such duties on the relevant local authority as may be specified in the supervision requirement.

(3C) The duties imposed under subsection (3B) above may include that of securing or facilitating the provision for the child of services of a kind other than that provided by the relevant local authority.]

(4) The place or, as the case may be, places specified in a requirement under subsection (3)(a) above may, without prejudice to the generality of that subsection, be a place or places in England or Wales; and a supervision requirement shall be authority for the person in charge of such a place to restrict the child's liberty to such extent as that person may consider appropriate, having regard to the terms of the requirement.

(5) A condition imposed under subsection (3)(b) above may, without prejudice to the generality of that subsection—

(a) subject to section 90 of this Act, require the child to submit to any medical or other examination or treatment;

(b) regulate the contact with the child of any specified person or class of persons.

(6) A children's hearing may require, when making a supervision requirement,

that any place where the child is to reside in accordance with the supervision requirement shall not be disclosed to any person specified in the requirement under this subsection or class of persons so specified.

(7) A children's hearing who make a supervision requirement may determine that the requirement shall be reviewed at such time during the duration of the requirement as they determine.

[(7A) Where, on a review under subsection (7) above, it appears to the children's hearing that the relevant local authority are in breach of a duty imposed on them under section 71 of this Act, the hearing may direct the Principal Reporter to give the authority notice of an intended application under section 71A(2) of this Act.

(7B) The Principal Reporter shall, at the same time as giving the notice of an intended application under section 71A(2) of this Act, send a copy of the notice to—

(a) the child to whom the duty referred to in subsection (7A) above relates;

(b) any person who, in relation to the child, is a relevant person;

(c) any person appointed under section 41 of this Act to safeguard the interests of the child in any proceedings which are taking place when the notice is given.

(7C) Notice of an intended application under section 71A(2) of this Act is a written notice—

(a) setting out the respects in which the relevant local authority are in breach of the duty imposed on them under section 71 of this Act; and

(b) stating that if the authority do not comply with that duty within the period of 21 days beginning with the day on which they received the notice, the Principal Reporter may make an application under section 71A(2) of this Act.

(7D) Where a children's hearing have made a direction under subsection (7A) above, they shall determine that a further review under subsection (7) above take place on or as soon as is reasonably practicable after the expiry of the period of 28 days beginning with the day on which notice was given in pursuance of that direction.

(7E) Where on a further review under subsection (7) above which takes place by virtue of subsection (7D) above, it appears to the children's hearing that the relevant local authority continues to be in breach of the duty referred to in subsection (7A) above, the hearing may authorise the Principal Reporter to make an application under section 71A(2) of this Act.]

(8) A supervision requirement shall be in such form as the Secretary of State may prescribe by rules.

[(9) A children's hearing may exercise a power mentioned in subsection (9A) below in relation to a child if they are satisfied—

(a) that one of the conditions mentioned in subsection (10) below is met; and

(b) that it is necessary to exercise the power concerned.

(9A) The powers are—

(a) that the children's hearing may specify in the supervision requirement that the child shall be liable to be placed and kept in secure accommodation in a residential establishment specified, under subsection (3)(a) above, in the requirement during such period as the person in charge of that establishment, with the agreement of the chief social work officer of the relevant local authority, considers necessary; and

(b) that the children's hearing may impose, under subsection (3)(b) above, a movement restriction condition.

(10) The conditions are—

(a) that the child, having previously absconded, is likely to abscond and, if he absconds, it is likely that his physical, mental or moral welfare will be at risk; and

(b) that the child is likely to injure himself or some other person.

(11)   In this section, 'movement restriction condition' means a condition—

(a)   restricting the child's movements in such way as may be specified in the supervision requirement; and

(b)   requiring the child to comply with such arrangements for monitoring compliance with the restriction mentioned in paragraph (a) above as may be so specified.

(12)   Where a children's hearing impose a condition such as is mentioned in subsection (9A)(b) above, they shall also impose under subsection (3)(b) above such of the conditions prescribed by the Scottish Ministers for the purposes of this section as they consider necessary in the child's case.

(13)   The Scottish Ministers may by regulations make provision as to the arrangements mentioned in subsection (11)(b) above.

(14)   Regulations under subsection (13) above may in particular include provision—

(a)   prescribing what method or methods of monitoring compliance with the restriction mentioned in paragraph (a) of subsection (11) above may be specified in a supervision requirement;

(b)   specifying the devices which may be used for the purpose of that monitoring;

(c)   prescribing the person who may be designated by a children's hearing to carry out that monitoring or the class or description of person from which that person may be drawn;

(d)   requiring a children's hearing who have designated a person in pursuance of paragraph (c) above who is no longer within the provision made under that paragraph to vary the designation accordingly and notify the child of the variation.

(15)   The Scottish Ministers may, by contract or otherwise, secure the services of such persons as they think fit to carry out the monitoring mentioned in subsection (11)(b) above and may do so in a way in which those services are provided differently in relation to different areas or different forms of that monitoring.

(16)   Nothing in any enactment or rule of law prevents the disclosure to a person providing services in pursuance of subsection (15) above of information relating to a child where the disclosure is made for the purposes only of the full and proper provision of the monitoring mentioned in subsection (11)(b) above.

(17)   A children's hearing may include in a supervision requirement a movement restriction condition only if the hearing is constituted from the children's panel for a local government area which is prescribed for the purposes of this section by the Scottish Ministers.]

71 Duties of local authority with respect to supervision requirements

(1)   The relevant local authority shall, as respects a child subject to a supervision requirement, give effect to the requirement.

[(1A)   Where a supervision requirement imposes, under section 70(3A) of this Act, duties on the relevant local authority, the authority shall perform those duties.]

(2)   Where a supervision requirement provides that the child shall reside—

(a)   in relevant accommodation; or

(b)   in any other accommodation not provided by a local authority,

the relevant local authority shall from time to time investigate whether, while the child is so resident, any conditions imposed by the supervision requirement are being fulfilled; and may take such steps as they consider reasonable if they find that such conditions are not being fulfilled.

(3)   In this section, 'relevant accommodation' means accommodation provided by the parents or relatives of the child or by any person associated with them or with the child.

[71A   Enforcement of local authorities' duties under section 71

(1)   The sheriff principal may, on an application under subsection (2) below, make an order requiring a relevant local authority in breach of a duty imposed on them under section 71 of this Act to perform that duty.

(2)   The Principal Reporter, having been so authorised by a children's hearing under section 70(7E) of this Act, may apply for an order under subsection (1) above.

(3)   No such application shall be competent unless—

(a)   the Principal Reporter has, on a direction of the children's hearing made under section 70(7A) of this Act, given the relevant local authority the notice referred to in that provision; and

(b)   the authority have failed to comply, within the period stipulated in the notice, with the duty there referred to.

(4)   In deciding whether to apply under subsection (2) above, the Principal Reporter shall not take into account any factor relating to the adequacy of the means available to the relevant local authority to enable it to comply with the duty.

(5)   An application under subsection (2) above shall be made by summary application.

(6)   The sheriff principal having jurisdiction under this section is the sheriff principal of the sheriffdom in which is situated the principal office of the relevant local authority in breach of the duty referred to in subsection (1) above.

(7)   An order under subsection (1) above shall be final.]

72   Transfer of child subject to supervision requirement in case of necessity

(1)   In any case of urgent necessity, where it is in the interests of—

(a)   a child who is required by a supervision requirement imposed under section 70(3)(a) of this Act to reside in a specific residential establishment or specific other accommodation; or

(b)   other children in that establishment or accommodation,

the chief social work officer of the relevant local authority may direct that, notwithstanding that requirement, the child be transferred to another place.

(2)   Any child transferred under subsection (1) above shall have his case reviewed, in accordance with section 73(8) of this Act, by a children's hearing within seven days of his transfer.

73   Duration and review of supervision requirement

(1)   No child shall continue to be subject to a supervision requirement for any period longer than is necessary in the interests of promoting or safeguarding his welfare.

(2)   Subject to any variation or continuation of a supervision requirement under subsection (9) below, no supervision requirement shall remain in force for a period longer than one year.

(3)   A supervision requirement shall cease to have effect in respect of a child not later than on his attaining the age of eighteen years.

(4)   A relevant local authority shall refer the case of a child who is subject to a supervision requirement to the Principal Reporter where they are satisfied that—

(a)   the requirement in respect of the child ought to cease to have effect or be varied;

(b)   a condition contained in the requirement is not being complied with; or

(c)   the best interests of the child would be served by their—

[(i)   applying under section 80 of the Adoption and Children (Scotland) Act 2007 (asp 4) ('the 2007 Act') for a permanence order;

(ii)   applying under section 92 of the 2007 Act for variation of such an order;

(iii)   applying under section 93 of the 2007 Act for amendment of such an order;

(iv) applying under section 98 of the 2007 Act for revocation of such an order; or

(v) placing the child for adoption,
and they intend to make any such application or to place the child for adoption.]

[(4A) The Scottish Ministers may make regulations specifying by reference to the occurrence of an event or events described in the regulations the period of time during which a referral under subsection (4)(c) is to be made.]

(5) Where the relevant local authority are aware that an application has been made and is pending, or is about to be made, under [section 29 or 30 of the 2007 Act] for an adoption order in respect of a child who is subject to a supervision requirement, they shall forthwith refer his case to the Principal Reporter.

(6) A child or any relevant person may require a review of a supervision requirement in respect of the child at any time at least three months after—

(a) the date on which the requirement is made; or

(b) the date of the most recent continuation, or variation, by virtue of this section of the requirement.

(7) Where a child is subject to a supervision requirement and, otherwise than in accordance with that requirement or with an order under section 11 of this Act, a relevant person proposes to take the child to live outwith Scotland, the person shall, not later than twenty-eight days before so taking the child, give notice of that proposal in writing to the Principal Reporter and to the relevant local authority.

(8) The Principal Reporter shall—

(a) arrange for a children's hearing to review any supervision requirement in respect of a child where—

(i) the case has been referred to him under subsection (4) or (5) above;

(ii) the review has been required under subsection (6) above;

(iii) the review is required by virtue of section 70(7) or section 72(2) of this Act;

(iv) he has received in respect of the child such notice as is mentioned in subsection (7) above; or

[(iva) the case has been referred to him under section 96(3) or 106 of the Adoption and Children (Scotland) Act 2007 (asp 4);]

(v) in any other case, the supervision requirement will expire within three months;

[(aa) where—

(i) a requirement is made of the Principal Reporter under section 11(1) of the Antisocial Behaviour etc (Scotland) Act 2004 (asp 8) (power of sheriff to require Principal Reporter to refer case to children's hearing) in respect of the child's case; and

(ii) the child is subject to a supervision requirement,
arrange for a children's hearing to review the supervision requirement;]; and

(b) make any arrangements incidental to [any such] review.

(9) Where a supervision requirement is reviewed by a children's hearing arranged under subsection (8) above, they may—

(a) where they are satisfied that in order to complete the review of the supervision requirement it is necessary to have a further investigation of the child's case, continue the review to a subsequent hearing;

(b) terminate the requirement;

(c) vary the requirement;

(d) insert in the requirement any requirement which could have been imposed by them under section 70(3) of this Act; or

(e) continue the requirement, with or without such variation or insertion.

(10) Subsections (3) to (10) of section 69 of this Act shall apply to a continuation under paragraph (a) of subsection (9) above of a review of a supervision requirement as they apply to the continuation of a case under subsection (1)(a) of that section.

(11)   Where a children's hearing vary or impose a requirement under sub-section (9) above which requires the child to reside in any specified place or places, they may order that such place or places shall not be disclosed to any person or class of persons specified in the requirement.

(12)   Where a children's hearing is arranged under subsection (8)(a)(v) above, they shall consider whether, if the supervision requirement is not continued, the child still requires supervision or guidance; and where a children's hearing consider such supervision or guidance is necessary, it shall be the duty of the local authority to provide such supervision or guidance as the child is willing to accept.

(13)   Where a children's hearing is arranged by virtue of subsection (4)(c) or (5) above, then irrespective of what the hearing do under subsection (9) above they shall draw up a report which shall provide advice in respect of, as the case may be, the proposed application under [section 80 of the 2007 Act], or the proposed placing for adoption or the application, or prospective application, under [. . .] that Act, for any court which may subsequently require to come to a decision, in relation to the child concerned, such as is mentioned in subsection (14) below.

[(13A)   A report drawn up under subsection (13) shall be in such form as may be prescribed by the Scottish Ministers.]

(14)   A court which is considering whether, in relation to a child, to grant an application under [section 29, 30 or 80 of the 2007 Act] and which, by virtue of subsection (13) above, receives a report as respects that child, shall consider the report before coming to a decision in the matter.

74   Further provision as respects children subject to supervision requirements

The Secretary of State may by regulations provide—

(a)   for the transmission of information regarding a child who is subject to a supervision requirement to any person who, by virtue of that requirement, has, or is to have, control over the child;

(b)   or the temporary accommodation, where necessary, of a child so subject; and

(c)   for the conveyance of a child so subject—

(i)   to any place in which, under the supervision requirement, he is to reside;

(ii)   to any place to which he falls to be taken under subsection (1) or (5) of section 82 of this Act; or

(iii)   to any person to whom he falls to be returned under subsection (3) of that section.

75   Powers of Secretary of State with respect to secure accommodation

(1)   The Secretary of State may by regulations make provision with respect to the placing in secure accommodation of any child—

(a)   who is subject to a requirement imposed under section 70(3)(a) of this Act but not subject to a requirement under subsection (9) of that section; or

(b)   who is not subject to a supervision requirement but who is being looked after by a local authority in pursuance of such enactments as may be specified in the regulations.

(2)   Regulations under subsection (1) above may—

(a)   specify the circumstances in which a child may be so placed under the regulations;

(b)   make provision to enable a child who has been so placed or any relevant person to require that the child's case be brought before a children's hearing within a shorter period than would apply under regulations made under subsection (3) below; and

(c)   specify different circumstances for different cases or classes of case.

(3)   Subject to subsection (4) below and without prejudice to subsection (2)(b) above, the Secretary of State may prescribe—

(a)   the maximum period during which a child may be kept under this Act in secure accommodation without the authority of a children's hearing or of the sheriff;

(b)   the period within which a children's hearing shall be arranged to consider the case of a child placed in secure accommodation by virtue of regulations made under this section (and different periods may be so prescribed in respect of different cases or classes of case).

(4)   Subsection (8) of section 66 of this Act shall apply in respect of a child placed in secure accommodation under regulations made under this section as if such placing took place by virtue of that section.

(5)   The Secretary of State may by regulations vary the period within which a review of a condition imposed under section 70(9) of this Act shall be reviewed under section 73 of this Act.

(6)   The Secretary of State may by regulations make provision for the procedures to be applied in placing children in secure accommodation; and without prejudice to the generality of this subsection, such regulations may—

(a)   specify the duties of the Principal Reporter in relation to the placing of children in secure accommodation;

(b)   make provision for the referral of cases to a children's hearing for review; and

(c)   make provision for any person with parental responsibilities in relation to the child to be informed of the placing of the child in secure accommodation.

[Parenting orders

75A   Requirement on Principal Reporter to apply for parenting order
(1)   Subsection (2) below applies where it appears to—

(a)   the children's hearing to whom a child's case has been referred under section 65(1) of this Act; or

(b)   a children's hearing arranged, under section 73(8) of this Act, to review a supervision requirement in respect of a child,

that it might be appropriate for a parenting order to be made in respect of a parent of the child under section 102 of the Antisocial Behaviour etc (Scotland) Act 2004 (asp 8) (the '2004 Act').

(2)   The hearing may require the Principal Reporter to consider whether to apply, under subsection (3) of that section of the 2004 Act, for such an order.

(3)   A requirement under subsection (2) above shall specify—

(a)   the parent in respect of whom it might be appropriate for the order to be made; and

(b)   by reference to subsections (4) to (6) of that section of the 2004 Act, the condition in respect of which the application might be made.

(4)   In subsection (1) above, 'parent' and 'child' have the same meanings as in section 117 of the 2004 Act.]

[Failure to provide education for excluded pupils

75B   Failure to provide education for excluded pupils: reference to Scottish Ministers
(1)   Where it appears to the children's hearing to whom a child's case has been referred under section 65(1) of this Act that—

(a)   an education authority have a duty under section 14(3) of the Education (Scotland) Act 1980 (c 44) in relation to the child; and

(b)   the authority are not complying with that duty,
they may require the Principal Reporter to refer the matter to the Scottish Ministers.

(2)   The Principal Reporter shall comply with any requirement made under subsection (1) above.

(3)   A reference made by virtue of subsection (1) above shall be in writing.

(4)   A copy of a reference made by virtue of subsection (1) above shall be sent by the Principal Reporter to the education authority in respect of which the reference is made.]

Exclusion orders

76   Exclusion orders

(1)   Subject to subsections (3) to (9) below, where on the application of a local authority the sheriff is satisfied, in relation to a child, that the conditions mentioned in subsection (2) below are met, he may grant an order under this section (to be known as 'an exclusion order') excluding from the child's family home any person named in the order (in this Part of this Act referred to as the 'named person').

(2)   The conditions are—

(a)   that the child has suffered, is suffering, or is likely to suffer, significant harm as a result of any conduct, or any threatened or reasonably apprehended conduct, of the named person;

(b)   that the making of an exclusion order against the named person—

(i)   is necessary for the protection of the child, irrespective of whether the child is for the time being residing in the family home; and

(ii)   would better safeguard the child's welfare than the removal of the child from the family home; and

(c)   that, if an order is made, there will be a person specified in the application who is capable of taking responsibility for the provision of appropriate care for the child and any other member of the family who requires such care and who is, or will be, residing in the family home (in this section, sections 77 to 79 and section 91(3)(f) of this Act referred to as an 'appropriate person').

(3)   No application under subsection (1) above for an exclusion order shall be finally determined under this section unless—

(a)   the named person has been afforded an opportunity of being heard by, or represented before, the sheriff, and

(b)   the sheriff has considered any views expressed by any person on whom notice of the application has been served in accordance with rules making such provision as is mentioned in section 91(3)(d) of this Act.

(4)   Where, on an application under subsection (1) above, the sheriff—

(a)   is satisfied as mentioned in that subsection; but

(b)   the conditions mentioned in paragraphs (a) and (b) of subsection (3) above for the final determination of the application are not fulfilled,
he may grant an interim order, which shall have effect as an exclusion order pending a hearing by the sheriff under subsection (5) below held within such period as may be specified in rules made by virtue of section 91(3)(e) of this Act.

(5)   The sheriff shall conduct a hearing under this subsection within such period as may be specified in rules made by virtue of section 91(3)(e) of this Act, and, if satisfied at that hearing as mentioned in subsection (1) above, he may, before finally determining the application, confirm or vary the interim order, or any term or condition on which it was granted, or may recall such order.

(6)   Where the conditions mentioned in paragraphs (a) and (b) of subsection (3) above have been fulfilled, the sheriff may, at any point prior to the final determination of the application, grant an interim order.

(7)   An order under subsection (5) or (6) above shall have effect as an exclusion order pending the final determination of the application.

(8)   Where—

(a)   an application is made under subsection (1) above; and

(b)   the sheriff considers that the conditions for making a child protection order under section 57 of this Act are satisfied,

he may make an order under that section as if the application had been duly made by the local authority under that rather than under this section.

(9)   The sheriff shall not make an exclusion order if it appears to him that to do so would be unjustifiable or unreasonable, having regard to—

(a)   all the circumstances of the case, including without prejudice to the generality of this subsection the matters specified in subsection (10) below; and

(b)   any requirement such as is specified in subsection (11) below and the likely consequences in the light of that requirement of the exclusion of the named person from the family home.

(10)   The matters referred to in subsection (9)(a) above are—

(a)   the conduct of the members of the child's family (whether in relation to each other or otherwise);

(b)   the respective needs and financial resources of the members of that family;

(c)   the extent (if any) to which—

(i)   the family home; and

(ii)   any relevant item in that home,

is used in connection with a trade, business or profession by any member of the family.

(11)   The requirement referred to in subsection (9)(b) above is a requirement that the named person (whether alone or with any other person) must reside in the family home, where that home—

(a)   [is on or comprised in a lease constituting a 1991 Act tenancy within the meaning of the Agricultural Holdings (Scotland) Act 2003 (asp 11) or in a lease constituting a short limited duration tenancy or a limited duration tenancy (within the meaning of that Act)]; or

(b)   is let, or is a home in respect of which possession is given, to the named person (whether alone or with any other person) by an employer as an incident of employment.

(12)   In this Part of this Act—

'caravan' has the meaning given to it by section 29(1) of the Caravan Sites and Control of Development Act 1960;

'exclusion order', includes an interim order granted under subsection (4) above and such an order confirmed or varied under subsection (5) above and an interim order granted under subsection (6) above; except that in subsection (3) above and in section 79 of this Act, it does not include an interim order granted under sub-section (4) above;

'family' has the meaning given in section 93(1) of this Act;

'family home' means any house, caravan, houseboat or other structure which is used as a family residence and in which the child ordinarily resides with any person described in subsection (13) below and the expression includes any garden or other ground or building attached to and usually occupied with, or otherwise required for the amenity or convenience of, the house, caravan, houseboat or other structure.

(13)   The description of person referred to in the definition of 'family home' in subsection (12) above, is a person who has parental responsibilities in relation to the child, or who ordinarily (and other than by reason only of his employment) has charge of, or control over him.

77 Effect of, and orders etc ancillary to, exclusion order

(1)   An exclusion order shall, in respect of the home to which it relates, have the effect of suspending the named person's rights of occupancy (if any) and shall prevent him from entering the home, except with the express permission of the local authority which applied for the order.

(2)   The sheriff, on the application of the local authority, may, if and in so far as he thinks fit, when making an exclusion order do any of the things mentioned in subsection (3) below.

(3)   The things referred to in subsection (2) above are—

(a)   grant a warrant for the summary ejection of the named person from the home;

(b)   grant an interdict prohibiting the named person from entering the home without the express permission of the local authority;

(c)   grant an interdict prohibiting the removal by the named person of any relevant item specified in the interdict from the home, except either—

(i)   with the written consent of the local authority, or of an appropriate person; or

(ii)   by virtue of a subsequent order of the sheriff,

(d)   grant an interdict prohibiting the named person from entering or remaining in a specified area in the vicinity of the home;

(e)   grant an interdict prohibiting the taking by the named person of any step of a kind specified in the interdict in relation to the child;

(f)   make an order regulating the contact between the child and the named person,

and the sheriff may make any other order which he considers is necessary for the proper enforcement of a remedy granted by virtue of paragraph (a), (b) or (c) of this subsection.

(4)   No warrant, interdict or order (except an interdict granted by virtue of paragraph (b) of subsection (3) above) shall be granted or made under subsection (2) above if the named person satisfies the sheriff that it is unnecessary to do so.

(5)   Where the sheriff grants a warrant of summary ejection under subsection (2) above in the absence of the named person, he may give directions as to the preservation of any of that person's goods and effects which remain in the family home.

(6)   The sheriff may make an order of the kind specified in subsection (3)(f) above irrespective of whether there has been an application for such an order.

(7)   On the application of either the named person or the local authority, the sheriff may make the exclusion order, or any remedy granted under subsection (2) above, subject to such terms and conditions as he considers appropriate.

(8)   In this Part of this Act references to a 'relevant item' are references to any item within the home which both—

(a)   is owned or hired by any member of the family concerned or an appropriate person or is being acquired by any such member or person under a hire purchase agreement or conditional sale agreement; and

(b)   is reasonably necessary to enable the home to be used as a family residence,

but does not include any such vehicle, caravan or houseboat or such other structure so used as is mentioned in the definition of 'family home' in section 76(12) of this Act.

78 Powers of arrest etc in relation to exclusion order

(1)   The sheriff may, whether or not on an application such as is mentioned in subsection (2) below, attach a power of arrest to any interdict granted under section 77(2) of this Act by virtue of subsection (3) of that section.

(2)   A local authority may at any time while an exclusion order has effect apply for such attachment of a power of arrest as is mentioned in subsection (1) above.

(3)   A power of arrest attached to an interdict by virtue of subsection (1) above shall not have effect until such interdict, together with the attached power of arrest, is served on the named person.

(4)   If, by virtue of subsection (1) above, a power of arrest is attached to an interdict, the local authority shall, as soon as possible after the interdict, together with the attached power of arrest, is served on the named person, ensure that there is delivered—

(a)   to the chief constable of the police area in which the family home is situated; and

(b)   where the interdict was granted by virtue of section 77(3)(e) of this Act, to the chief constable of the area in which the step or conduct which is prevented by the interdict may take place,

a copy of the application for the interdict and of the interlocutor granting the interdict together with a certificate of service of the interdict and, where the application to attach the power of arrest was made after the interdict was granted, a copy of that application and of the interlocutor above granting it and a certificate of service of the interdict together with the attached power of arrest.

(5)   Where any interdict to which a power of arrest is attached by virtue of subsection (1) above is varied or recalled, the person who applied for the variation or recall shall ensure that there is delivered to each chief constable specified in subsection (4) above a copy of the application for such variation or recall and of the interlocutor granting the variation or recall.

(6)   A constable may arrest without warrant the named person if he has reasonable cause for suspecting that person to be in breach of an interdict to which a power of arrest has been attached by virtue of subsection (1) above.

(7)   Where a person has been arrested under subsection (6) above, the constable in charge of a police station may—

(a)   if satisfied there is no likelihood of that person further breaching the interdict to which the power of arrest was attached under subsection (1) above, liberate him unconditionally; or

(b)   refuse to liberate that person.

(8)   Such a refusal to liberate an arrested person as is mentioned in subsection (7)(b) above, and the detention of that person until his appearance in court by virtue of either subsection (11) below, or any provision of the Criminal Procedure (Scotland) Act [1995], shall not subject that constable to any claim whatsoever.

(9)   Where a person has been liberated under subsection (7)(a) above, the facts and circumstances which gave rise to the arrest shall be reported to the procurator fiscal forthwith.

(10)   Subsections (11) to (13) below apply only where—

(a)   the arrested person has not been released under subsection (7)(a) above; and

(b)   the procurator fiscal decides that no criminal proceedings are to be taken in respect of the facts and circumstances which gave rise to the arrest.

(11)   A person arrested under subsection (6) above shall, wherever practicable, be brought before the sheriff sitting as a court of summary criminal jurisdiction for the district in which he was arrested not later than in the course of the first day after the arrest such day not being a Saturday, a Sunday or a court holiday prescribed for that court under [section 8 of the said Act of 1995], on which the sheriff is not sitting for the disposal of criminal business.

(12)   Subsections (1), [(2) and (4) of section 15 of the said Act of 1995] (intimation to a person named by the person arrested) shall apply to a person arrested under subsection (6) above as they apply to a person who has been arrested in respect of an offence.

(13)   Where a person is brought before the sheriff under subsection (11) above—

(a)   the procurator fiscal shall present to the court a petition containing—

(i)   a statement of the particulars of the person arrested under subsection (6) above;

(ii)   a statement of the facts and circumstances which gave rise to that arrest; and

(iii)   a request that the person be detained for a further period not exceeding two days;

(b)   the sheriff, if it appears to him that—

(i)   the statement referred to in paragraph (a)(ii) above discloses a *prima facie* breach of interdict by the arrested person;

(ii)   proceedings for breach of interdict will be taken; and

(iii)   there is a substantial risk of violence by the arrested person against any member of the family, or an appropriate person, resident in the family home,

may order the arrested person to be detained for a period not exceeding two days; and

(c)   the sheriff shall, in any case in which paragraph (b) above does not apply, order the release of the arrested person from custody (unless that person is in custody in respect of some other matter);

and in computing the period of two days referred to in paragraphs (a) and (b) above, no account shall be taken of a Saturday, a Sunday or any holiday in the court in which proceedings for breach of interdict will require to be raised.

(14)   Where a person—

(a)   is liberated under subsection (7)(a) above; or

(b)   is to be brought before the sheriff under subsection (11) above,

the procurator fiscal shall at the earliest opportunity, and, in the case of a person to whom paragraph (b) above applies, before that person is brought before the sheriff, take all reasonable steps to intimate to—

(i)   the local authority which made the application for the interdict;

(ii)   an appropriate person who will reside in, or who remains in residence in, the family home mentioned in the order; and

(iii)   any solicitor who acted for the appropriate person when the interdict was granted or to any other solicitor who the procurator fiscal has reason to believe acts for the time being for that person,

that he has decided that no criminal proceedings should be taken in respect of the facts and circumstances which gave rise to the arrest of the named person.

79   Duration, variation and recall of exclusion order

(1)   Subject to subsection (2) below, an exclusion order shall cease to have effect on a date six months after being made.

(2)   An exclusion order shall cease to have effect on a date prior to the date mentioned in subsection (1) above where—

(a)   the order contains a direction by the sheriff that it shall cease to have effect on that prior date;

(b)   the sheriff, on an application under subsection (3) below, recalls the order before the date so mentioned; or

(c)   any permission given by a third party to the spouse or partner of the named person, or to an appropriate person, to occupy the home to which the order relates is withdrawn.

(3)   The sheriff may, on the application of the local authority, the named person, an appropriate person or the spouse or partner of the named person, if that spouse or partner is not excluded from the family home and is not an appropriate person, vary or recall an exclusion order and any warrant, interdict, order or direction granted or made under section 77 of this Act.

(4)   For the purposes of this section, partners are persons who live together in a family home as if they were husband and wife.

80   Exclusion orders: supplementary provisions

(1)   The Secretary of State may make regulations with respect to the powers, duties and functions of local authorities in relation to exclusion orders.

(2)   An application for an exclusion order, or under section 79(3) of this Act for the variation or recall of such an order or of any thing done under section 77(2) of this Act, shall be made to the sheriff for the sheriffdom within which the family home is situated.

Offences in connection with orders etc for protection of children

81   Offences in connection with orders etc for protection of children

A person who intentionally obstructs—
   (a)   any person acting under a child protection order;
   (b)   any person acting under an authorisation granted under section 61(1) or (2) of this Act; or
   (c)   a constable acting under section 61(5) of this Act,
shall, subject to section 38(3) and (4) of this Act, be guilty of an offence and shall be liable on summary conviction to a fine not exceeding level 3 on the standard scale.

Fugitive children and harbouring

82   Recovery of certain fugitive children

(1)   A child who absconds—
   (a)   from a place of safety in which he is being kept under or by virtue of this Part of this Act;
   (b)   from a place (in this section referred to as a 'relevant place') which, though not a place of safety such as is mentioned in paragraph (a) above, is a residential establishment in which he is required to reside by virtue of section 70(3)(a) of this Act or a hospital or other institution in which he is temporarily residing while subject to such a requirement; or
   (c)   from a person who, by virtue of a supervision requirement or of section 74 of this Act, has control over him while he is being taken to, is awaiting being taken to, or (whether or not by reason of being on leave) is temporarily away from, such place of safety or relevant place,
may be arrested without warrant in any part of the United Kingdom and taken to the place of safety or as the case may be the relevant place; and a court which is satisfied that there are reasonable grounds for believing that the child is within any premises may, where there is such power of arrest, grant a warrant authorising a constable to enter those premises and search for the child using reasonable force if necessary.

(2)   Without prejudice to the generality of subsection (1) above, a child who at the end of a period of leave from a place of safety or relevant place fails to return there shall, for the purposes of this section, be taken to have absconded.

(3)   A child who absconds from a person who, not being a person mentioned in paragraph (c) of subsection (1) above, is a person who has control over him by virtue of a supervision requirement may, subject to the same provisions as those to which an arrest under that subsection is subject, be arrested as is mentioned in that subsection and returned to that person; and the provision in that subsection for a warrant to be granted shall apply as respects such a child as it applies as respects a child mentioned in that subsection.

(4)   If a child—
   (a)   is taken under subsection (1) above to a place of safety or relevant place; or
   (b)   is returned under subsection (3) above to a person,

but the occupier of that place of safety or of that relevant place, or as the case may be that person, is unwilling or unable to receive him, that circumstance shall be intimated forthwith to the Principal Reporter.

(5)   Where intimation is required by subsection (4) above as respects a child, he shall be kept in a place of safety until—

(a)   in a case where he is subject to a supervision requirement, he can be brought before a children's hearing for that requirement to be reviewed; or

(b)   in any other case, the Principal Reporter has, in accordance with section 56(6) of this Act, considered whether compulsory measures of supervision are required in respect of him.

83   Harbouring

A person who—

(a)   knowingly assists or induces a child to abscond in circumstances which render the child liable to arrest under subsection (1) or (3) of section 82 of this Act;

(b)   knowingly and persistently attempts to induce a child so to abscond;

(c)   knowingly harbours or conceals a child who has so absconded; or

(d)   knowingly prevents a child from returning—

(i)   to a place mentioned in paragraph (a) or (b) of the said subsection (1);

(ii)   to a person mentioned in paragraph (c) of that subsection, or in the said subsection (3),

shall, subject to section 38(3) and (4) of this Act, to section 51(5) and (6) of the Children Act 1989 and to Article 70(5) and (6) of the Children (Northern Ireland) Order 1995 (analogous provision for England and Wales and for Northern Ireland), be guilty of an offence and liable on summary conviction to a fine not exceeding level 5 on the standard scale or to imprisonment for a term not exceeding six months or to both such fine and such imprisonment.

Implementation of authorisations etc

84   Implementation of authorisations etc

Where an order, authorisation or warrant under this Chapter or Chapter 2 of this Part of this Act grants power to find a child and to keep him in a place of safety, such order, authorisation or warrant may be implemented as if it were a warrant for the apprehension of an accused person issued by a court of summary jurisdiction; and any enactment or rule of law applying to such a warrant shall, subject to the provisions of this Act, apply in like manner to the order, authorisation or warrant.

New evidence: review of establishment of grounds of referral

85   Application for review of establishment of grounds of referral

(1)   Subject to subsections (3) and (4) below, where subsection (2) below applies an application may be made to the sheriff for a review of a finding such as is mentioned in section 68(10) of this Act.

(2)   This subsection applies where the sheriff, on an application made by virtue of subsection (7) or (9) of section 65 of this Act (in this section referred to as the 'original application'), finds that any of the grounds of referral is established.

(3)   An application under subsection (1) above may only be made where the applicant claims—

(a)   to have evidence which was not considered by the sheriff on the original application, being evidence the existence or significance of which might materially have affected the determination of the original application;

(b)   that such evidence—
  (i)   is likely to be credible and reliable; and
  (ii)   would have been admissible in relation to the ground of referral which was found to be established on the original application; and
(c)   that there is a reasonable explanation for the failure to lead such evidence on the original application.

(4)   An application under subsection (1) above may only be made by—
(a)   the child in respect of whom the ground of referral was found to be established; or
(b)   any person who is a relevant person in relation to that child.

(5)   Where the sheriff on an application under subsection (1) above is not satisfied that any of the claims made in the application are established he shall dismiss the application.

(6)   Where the sheriff is satisfied on an application under subsection (1) above that the claims made in the application are established, he shall consider the evidence and if, having considered it, he is satisfied that—
(a)   none of the grounds of referral in the original application to which the application relates is established, he shall allow the application, discharge the referral to the children's hearing in respect of those grounds and proceed in accordance with subsection (7) below in relation to any supervision requirement made in respect of the child (whether or not varied under section 73 of this Act) in so far as it relates to any such ground; or
(b)   any ground of referral in the original application to which the application relates is established, he may proceed in accordance with section 68(10) of this Act.

(7)   Where the sheriff is satisfied as is mentioned in subsection (6)(a) above, he may—
(a)   order that any supervision requirement so mentioned shall terminate—
  (i)   immediately; or
  (ii)   on such date as he may specify; or
(b)   if he is satisfied that there is evidence sufficient to establish any ground of referral, being a ground which was not stated in the original application, find such ground established and proceed in accordance with section 68(10) of this Act in relation to that ground.

(8)   Where the sheriff specifies a date for the termination of a supervision requirement in accordance with subsection (7)(a)(ii) above, he may, before such termination, order a variation of that requirement, of any requirement imposed under subsection (6) of section 70 of this Act, or of any determination made under subsection (7) of that section; and such variation may take effect—
(a)   immediately; or
(b)   on such date as he may specify.

(9)   Where the sheriff orders the termination of a supervision requirement in accordance with subsection (7)(a) above, he shall consider whether, after such termination, the child concerned will still require supervision or guidance; and where he considers that such supervision or guidance will be necessary he shall direct a local authority to provide it in accordance with subsection (10) below.

(10)   Where a sheriff has given a direction under subsection (9) above, it shall be the duty of the local authority to comply with that direction; but that duty shall be regarded as discharged where they offer such supervision or guidance to the child and he, being a child of sufficient age and maturity to understand what is being offered, is unwilling to accept it.

CHAPTER 4
PARENTAL RESPONSIBILITIES ORDERS, ETC

[. . .]

Miscellaneous

90   Consent of child to certain procedures

Nothing in this Part of this Act shall prejudice any capacity of a child enjoyed by virtue of section 2(4) of the Age of Legal Capacity (Scotland) Act 1991 (capacity of child with sufficient understanding to consent to surgical, medical or dental procedure or treatment); and without prejudice to that generality, where a condition contained, by virtue of—

(a)   section 66(4)(a), section 67(2) or section 69(9)(a) of this Act, in a warrant; or

(b)   section 70(5)(a) of this Act, in a supervision requirement,

requires a child to submit to any examination or treatment but the child has the capacity mentioned in the said section 2(4), the examination or treatment shall only be carried out if the child consents.

91   Procedural rules in relation to certain applications etc

(1)   All proceedings to which this section applies are civil proceedings for the purposes of section 32 of the Sheriff Courts (Scotland) Act 1971 (power of Court of Session to regulate civil procedure in the sheriff court).

(2)   Any reference in this Part of this Act to regulation or prescription by rules in relation to any proceedings to which this section applies shall be construed, unless the context otherwise requires, as a reference to regulation or prescription by rules made under the said section 32.

(3)   Without prejudice to the generality of the said section 32, rules may make provision as to—

(a)   the functions of a person appointed by the sheriff under section 41(1) of this Act and any right of that person to information relating to the proceedings;

(b)   the circumstances in which any person who has been given notice in accordance with such rules of an application for a child assessment order, or any other person specified in the rules, may apply to the court to have that order varied or discharged;

(c)   the persons to whom notice of the making of a child protection order shall be given by the applicant for that order, and without prejudice to that generality may in making such provision require such notice to be given to either or both of the child and any relevant person in relation to that child;

(d)   the persons to whom notice of an application for an exclusion order or, under section 79(3) of this Act, for the recall or variation of such an order or of anything done under section 77(2) of this Act shall be given;

(e)   the period within which a hearing shall be held under subsection (5) of section 76 of this Act after the granting of an order under subsection (4) of that section;

(f)   the service of any exclusion order on the named person and the appropriate person within such period as may be specified in the rules.

(4)   In relation to any proceedings to which this section applies, rules may permit a party to such proceedings, in such circumstances as may be specified in the rules, to be represented by a person who is neither an advocate nor a solicitor.

(5)   This section applies to any application made to the sheriff, and any other proceeding before the sheriff (whether on appeal or otherwise), under any provision of this Part of this Act.

Interpretation of Part II

93   Interpretation of Part II

(1)   In this Part of this Act, unless the context otherwise requires,—

'accommodation' shall be construed in accordance with section 25(8) of this Act;

'chief social work officer' means an officer appointed under section 3 of the Social Work (Scotland) Act 1968;

'child assessment order' has the meaning given by section 55(1) of this Act;

'child protection order' has the meaning given by section 57(1) of this Act;

'children's hearing' shall be construed in accordance with section 39(3), but does not include a business meeting arranged under section 64, of this Act;

'compulsory measures of supervision' means, in respect of a child, such measures of supervision as may be imposed upon him by a children's hearing;

'constable' means a constable of a police force within the meaning of the Police (Scotland) Act 1967;

'contact order' has the meaning given by section 11(2)(d) of this Act;

'disabled' has the meaning given by section 23(2) of this Act;

['education authority' has the meaning given by section 135(1) of the Education (Scotland) Act 1980 (c 44);]

'exclusion order' has the meaning given by section 76(12) of this Act;

'family', in relation to a child, includes—

(a)   any person who has parental responsibility for the child; and

(b)   any other person with whom the child has been living;

'local authority' means a council constituted under section 2 of the Local Government etc (Scotland) Act 1994;

'local government area' shall be construed in accordance with section 1 of the said Act of 1994;

'parental responsibilities' has the meaning given by section 1(3) of this Act;

[. . .]

'parental rights' has the meaning given by section 2(4) of this Act;

'place of safety', in relation to a child, means—

(a)   a residential or other establishment provided by a local authority;

(b)   a community home within the meaning of section 53 of the Children Act 1989;

(c)   a police station;

[(d)   a hospital, or surgery, the person or body of persons responsible for the management of which is willing temporarily to receive the child;

(e)   the dwelling-house of a suitable person who is so willing; or

(f)   any other suitable place the occupier of which is so willing.]

'the Principal Reporter' means the Principal Reporter appointed under section 127 of the said Act of 1994 or any officer of the Scottish Children's Reporter Administration to whom there is delegated, under section 131(1) of that Act, any function of the Principal Reporter under this Act;

'relevant local authority', in relation to a child who is subject to a warrant granted under this Part of this Act or to a supervision requirement, means the local authority for whose area [there is established] the children's panel from which the children's hearing which granted the warrant or imposed the supervision requirement was [constituted];

'residence order' has the meaning given by section 11(2)(c) of this Act;

'residential establishment'—

(a)   in relation to a place in Scotland, means an establishment (whether managed by a local authority, by a voluntary organisation or by any other person) which provides residential accommodation for children for the purposes of this Act or the Social Work (Scotland) Act 1968;

(b)   in relation to a place in England and Wales, means a community home, voluntary home or [private] children's home (within the meaning of the Children Act 1989); and

(c) in relation to a place in Northern Ireland, means a home provided under Part VIII of the Children (Northern Ireland) Order 1995, or a voluntary home, or a registered children's home (which have respectively the meanings given by that Order);

'school age' shall be construed in accordance with section 31 of the Education (Scotland) Act 1980;

'secure accommodation' means accommodation provided in a residential establishment approved [by the Scottish Ministers in accordance with relations made under section 29(9)(a) of the Regulation of Care (Scotland) Act 2001 (asp 8) or] under [section 22(8)(a) of the Care Standards Act 2000], for the purpose of restricting the liberty of children;

'supervision requirement' has the meaning given by section 70(1) of this Act, and includes any condition contained in such a requirement or related to it;

'voluntary organisation' means a body (other than a public or local authority) whose activities are not carried on for profit; and

'working day' means every day except—

(a) Saturday and Sunday;

(b) December 25th and 26th; and

(c) January 1st and 2nd.

(2) For the purposes of—

(a) Chapter 1 and this Chapter (except this section) of this Part [and section 44], 'child' means a person under the age of eighteen years; and

(b) [Chapter 2 (except section 44) and Chapter 3 (except section 75A)] of this Part—

'child' means—

(i) a child who has not attained the age of sixteen years;

(ii) a child over the age of sixteen years who has not attained the age of eighteen years and in respect of whom a supervision requirement is in force; or

(iii) a child whose case has been referred to a children's hearing by virtue of section 33 of this Act;

and for the purposes of the application of those Chapters to a person who has failed to attend school regularly without reasonable excuse includes a person who is over sixteen years of age but is not over school age; and

'relevant person' in relation to a child means—

(a) any parent enjoying parental responsibilities or parental rights under Part I of this Act;

(b) any person in whom parental responsibilities or rights are vested by, under or by virtue of this Act;

[(ba) any person in whom parental responsibilities or parental rights are vested by, under or by virtue of a permanence order (as defined in section 80(2) of the Adoption and Children (Scotland) Act 2007); and]

(c) any person who appears to be a person who ordinarily (and other than by reason only of his employment) has charge of, or control over, the child.

(3) Where, in the course of any proceedings under Chapter 2 or 3 of this Part, a child ceases to be a child within the meaning of subsection (2) above, the provisions of those Chapters of this Part and of any statutory instrument made under those provisions shall continue to apply to him as if he had not so ceased to be a child.

(4) Any reference in this Part of this Act to a child—

(a) being 'in need', is to his being in need of care and attention because—

(i) he is unlikely to achieve or maintain, or to have the opportunity of achieving or maintaining, a reasonable standard of health or development unless there are provided for him, under or by virtue of this Part, services by a local authority;

(ii) his health or development is likely significantly to be impaired, or further impaired, unless such services are so provided;

(iii) he is disabled; or

(iv) he is affected adversely by the disability of any other person in his family;

(b) who is 'looked after' by a local authority, shall be construed in accordance with section 17(6) of this Act.

(5) Any reference to any proceedings under this Part of this Act, whether on an application or on appeal, being heard by the sheriff, shall be construed as a reference to such proceedings being heard by the sheriff in chambers.

. . .

PART IV
GENERAL AND SUPPLEMENTAL

99 Registration of births by persons who are themselves children

(1) In paragraph (a) of section 14(1) of the Registration of Births, Deaths and Marriages (Scotland) Act 1965 (duty of father and mother to give information of particulars of birth), for the words 'father or mother of the child' substitute 'child's father or mother (whether or not they have attained the age of sixteen years)'.

(2) Where, at any time after the coming into force of the Age of Legal Capacity (Scotland) Act 1991 but before the coming into force of subsection (1) above, a person mentioned in the said paragraph (a) who had not at that time attained the age of sixteen years purported to fulfil the duty mentioned in the said section 14(1), he shall be presumed to have had legal capacity to fulfil that duty.

(3) [amends Registration of Births, Deaths and Marriages (Scotland) Act 1965]

(4) Where, at any time after the coming into force of the Age of Legal Capacity (Scotland) Act 1991 but before the coming into force of subsection (3) above, a person who had not at that time attained the age of sixteen years made a request, declaration, statutory declaration or application mentioned in subsection (1) or (2) of the said section 18 in relation to a child in respect of whose birth an entry was consequently made under the said subsection (1) in a register of births, or as the case may be under the said subsection (2) in the Register of Corrections etc, the person shall be presumed to have had legal capacity to make the request, declaration, statutory declaration, or application in question.

100 [Amends Social Work (Scotland) Act 1968]

101 Panels for curators ad litem, reporting officers and safeguarders

[(1) The Scottish Ministers may by regulations make provision for the establishment of one or more of each of the following—

(a) a panel of persons from which curators ad litem may be appointed [by virtue of section 108 of the Adoption and Children (Scotland) Act 2007] or under section 87(4) of this Act;

(b) a panel of persons from which reporting officers may be appointed under either of those sections; and

(c) a panel of persons from which appointments may be made under section 41(1) of this Act.]

(2) Regulations under subsection (1) above may provide, without prejudice to the generality of that subsection—

(a) for the appointment, qualifications and training of persons who may be appointed to [those panels]; and

(b) for the management and organisation of persons available for appointment from [those panels].

[(3)   Regulations under subsection (1) above may provide—
(a)   for the defrayment by local authorities of expenses incurred by members of any panel established by virtue of that subsection; and
(b)   for the payment by local authorities of fees and allowances for such members.
(4)   Paragraphs 9 and 10(b) of Schedule 1 to this Act shall apply in relation to any panel established by virtue of subsection (1)(c) above as they apply in relation to children's panels.]

102   Removal of duty to report on operation of Children Act 1975
Section 105 of the Children Act 1975 (which among other things provides that every five years there shall be laid before Parliament by the Secretary of State a report on the operation of such sections of that Act as are for the time being in force) shall cease to have effect.

103   Interpretation, rules, regulations and Parliamentary control
(1)   Any reference in this Act, or in any enactment amended by this Act, to a person having, or to there being vested in him, parental responsibilities or parental rights shall, unless the context otherwise requires, be construed as a reference to his having, or to there being so vested, any of those rights or as the case may be responsibilities.
(2)   Any reference in this Act to something being 'prescribed' is, unless the context otherwise requires, a reference to its being prescribed by regulations; and any power conferred by this Act on the Secretary of State or the Lord Advocate to make rules or regulations shall be exercisable by statutory instrument which shall be subject to annulment in pursuance of a resolution of either House of Parliament.
(3)   Rules or regulations made under this Act—
(a)   may make different provision for different cases or classes of case; and
(b)   may exclude certain cases or classes of case.

104   Financial provision
There shall be paid out of money provided by Parliament—
(a)   any expenses of the Secretary of State incurred in consequence of the provisions of this Act; and
(b)   any increase attributable to this Act in the sums payable out of money so provided under any other enactment.

105   Extent, short title, minor and consequential amendments, repeals and commencement
(1)   This Act, which subject to subsections (8) to (10) below extends to Scotland only—
(a)   may be cited as the Children (Scotland) Act 1995; and
(b)   except for subsections (1), (2) and (6) to (10) of this section, shall come into force on such day as the Secretary of State may by order made by statutory instrument appoint;
and different days may be appointed under paragraph (b) above for different purposes.
(2)   An order under subsection (1)(b) above may contain such transitional and consequential provisions and savings as appear to the Secretary of State to be necessary or expedient in connection with the provisions brought into force.
(3)   The transitional provisions and savings contained in Schedule 3 to this Act shall have effect but are without prejudice to sections 16 and 17 of the Interpretation Act 1978 (effect of repeals).
(4)   Schedule 4 to this Act, which contains minor amendments and amendments consequential upon the provisions of this Act, shall have effect.
(5)   The enactments mentioned in Schedule 5 to this Act (which include spent

provisions) are hereby repealed to the extent specified in the third column of that Schedule.

(6) The Secretary of State may by order made by statutory instrument make such further amendments or repeals, in such enactments as may be specified in the order, as appear to him to be necessary or expedient in consequence of any provision of this Act.

(7) A statutory instrument containing an order under subsection (6) above shall be subject to annulment in pursuance of a resolution of either House of Parliament.

(8) Sections 18, 26(2), 33, 44, 70(4), 74, 82, 83, 93 and 104 of this Act and this section extend to England and Wales, and those sections and this section (except section 70(4)) also extend to Northern Ireland; but—

(a) subsection (4) of this section so extends—

(i) to England and Wales, only in so far as it relates to paragraphs 8, 10, 19, 31, 37, 41(1), (2) and (7) to (9), 48 to 52, 54 and 55 of Schedule 4; and

(ii) to Northern Ireland, only in so far as it relates to paragraphs 31, 37, 41(1); (2) and (7) to (9), 54, 55 and 58 of that Schedule; and

(b) subsection (5) of this section so extends—

(i) to England and Wales, only in so far as it relates to the entries in Schedule 5 in respect of Part V of the Social Work (Scotland) Act 1968, the Maintenance Orders (Reciprocal Enforcement) Act 1972, section 35(4)(c) of the Family Law Act 1986, the Children Act 1989, the Child Support Act 1991 and the Education Act 1993; and

(ii) to Northern Ireland, only in so far as it relates to the entries in that Schedule in respect of Part V of the Social Work (Scotland) Act 1968, the Maintenance Orders (Reciprocal Enforcement) Act 1972 and section 35(4)(c) of the Family Law Act 1986.

(9) This section, so far as it relates to the repeal of Part V of the Social Work (Scotland) Act 1968, also extends to the Channel Islands.

(10) Her Majesty may by Order in Council direct that any of the relevant provisions specified in the Order shall extend, with such exceptions, adaptations and modifications (if any) as may be specified in the Order, to any of the Channel Islands; and in this subsection 'the relevant provisions' means sections 74, 82, 83 and 93 of this Act and any regulations made under section 74 of this Act.

SCHEDULES

SCHEDULE 1
CHILDREN'S PANELS

Appointment

1. The Secretary of State shall, for each local government area, appoint such number of members of children's panels as he considers appropriate and from among that number appoint a chairman and a deputy chairman.

2. A member of a children's panel shall hold office for such period as is specified by the Secretary of State, but may be removed from office by the Secretary of State at any time.

Children's Panel Advisory Committees

3. Subject to paragraph 8 below, each local authority shall form a body (to be known as a 'Children's Panel Advisory Committee') consisting of two members nominated by the local authority and three members nominated by the Secretary of State.

4. The Secretary of State may at the request of the local authority provide for an increase in the membership of the Children's Panel Advisory Committee appointed under paragraph 3 above by such number, not exceeding five, of additional members as the authority specify in relation to their request, the additional members to be nominated as follows—

(a) the first, and any second or fourth additional member, by the Secretary of State;

(b) any third or fifth additional member, by the local authority.

5. The chairman of the Children's Panel Advisory Committee shall be appointed by the Secretary of State from among such of the members he has nominated as are resident in the local government area for which the panel is appointed.

6. It shall be the duty of the Children's Panel Advisory Committee—

(a) to submit names of possible panel members to the Secretary of State;

(b) to advise the Secretary of State, in so far as he requires advice, on the suitability of persons referred to him as potential panel members; and

(c) to advise the Secretary of State on such matters relating to the general administration of the panels as he may refer to them.

7. The Children's Panel Advisory Committee shall have power—

(a) to appoint sub-committees;

(b) to appoint to any such sub-committee a person who is not a member of the Children's Panel Advisory Committee; and

(c) to refer all or any of the duties set out in paragraph 6 above to any such sub-committee for their advice.

Joint Advisory Committees

8.—(1) Two or more local authorities may, instead of each acting under paragraph 3 above, make arrangements to form a Children's Panel Advisory Committee for their areas (a 'joint advisory committee').

(2) A joint advisory committee shall not be formed in pursuance of arrangements made under sub-paragraph (1) above unless the authorities concerned have obtained the consent in writing of the Secretary of State.

(3) The Secretary of State may give a direction, in any case where a joint advisory committee has not been formed, to two or more local authorities requiring them to form a joint advisory committee; and they shall comply with any such direction.

(4) Paragraphs 3 to 7, 10(a) and 11(b) of this Schedule shall apply to a joint advisory committee as they apply in respect of a Children's Panel Advisory Committee and, for the purposes of those paragraphs the local authorities acting under sub-paragraph (1) above shall be regarded as a single local authority.

Recruitment and training of panel members

9. The Secretary of State may make such arrangements as he considers appropriate—

(a) to recruit and train members, or possible members, of the children's panels; [and

[(b) to train members, or possible members, of the Children's Panel Advisory Committees (or of any sub-committees of any of those committees).]

10. Each local authority shall make such arrangements as they consider appropriate—

(a) to enable the Children's Panel Advisory Committee to obtain names for submission to the Secretary of State as potential panel members; and

(b) to train—

(i) panel members or potential panel members; and

(ii)   members or potential members of Children's Panel Advisory Committees (or of any sub-committees of any of those committees)]; and
(c)   to any person appointed under paragraph 7 above,
such allowances as may be determined by the Secretary of State; and he may determine differently in relation to different cases or different classes of case.

Publication of list of members of children's panel

12.   Each local authority shall publish a list of names and addresses of members of the children's panel for their area, and that list shall be open for public inspection at the principal offices of the local authority, and at any place where an electors list for the local government area is available for inspection.

[Schedule 2 amended the Adoption (Scotland) Act 1978]

SCHEDULE 3
TRANSITIONAL PROVISIONS AND SAVINGS

Section 105(3)

1.   Where, immediately before the day appointed for the coming into force of section 25 of this Act, a child is by virtue of section 15 of the 1968 Act (duty of local authority to provide for orphans, deserted children etc) in the care of a local authority, the child shall on and after that day be treated as if he had been provided with accommodation under (and within the meaning of) subsection (1) of the said section 25.

2.   Sections 29 and 30 of this Act shall apply in respect of a person who, at the time when he ceased to be of school age (as defined in section 31 of the Education (Scotland) Act 1980) or at any subsequent time, was—
(a)   in the care of a local authority by virtue of the said section 15 or of section 16 of the 1968 Act (assumption of parental rights and powers); or
(b)   subject to a supervision requirement (within the meaning of section 44(1) of the 1968 Act),
as they apply in respect of a person who at such time was looked after (within the meaning of Part II of this Act) by a local authority.

3.   Where the parental rights in respect of a child have, by a resolution under the said section 16 or under section 16A of the 1968 Act (duty of local authority in cases of necessity to assume parental rights and powers vested in a voluntary organisation), vested in a local authority and immediately before the day appointed for the coming into force of section 86 of this Act those rights remain so vested, the resolution shall on and after that day have effect as if it were a parental responsibilities order transferring the appropriate parental rights and responsibilities (as defined in subsection (3) of the said section 86) relating to the child to the authority; and any access order made under section 17B of the 1968 Act in relation to the child (with any order made under section 17C of that Act as respects the access order) being (in either case) an order which immediately before that day remains undischarged, shall on and after that day have effect as if it were an order made under section 88(3) of this Act as respects the child.

4.   Where the parental rights in respect of a child have, by a resolution under the said section 16, vested in a voluntary organisation (as defined in section 93 of this Act) and immediately before the day mentioned in paragraph 3 above those rights remain so vested, the resolution shall, notwithstanding the repeal by this Act of the said section 16, continue to have effect until one of the following occurs—
(a)   the child attains the age of eighteen years;
(b)   the resolution is rescinded by the local authority because it appears to them that their doing so would promote the child's welfare;

(c)   the period of six months commencing with that day expires;

(d)   an order is made by virtue of section 11(2)(b), or under section 86(1), of this Act in relation to the child;

[(e)   the making of an adoption order (as defined in section 28(1) of the Adoption and Children (Scotland) Act 2007) in respect of the child;

(f)   the making of a permanence order (as defined in subsection (2) of that Act) which includes provision such as is mentioned in paragraph (c) of that subsection in respect of the child.]

5.   Where the circumstance by virtue of which a resolution under the said section 16 ceases to have effect is that mentioned in sub-paragraph (c) of paragraph 4 above, the appropriate parental rights and responsibilities (defined as mentioned in paragraph 3 above) in relation to the child shall transfer forthwith to the local authority in whose area he resides; and for the purposes of sections 86(6) and 87 to 89 of this Act the transfer shall be deemed effected by a parental responsibilities order applied for by that authority.

6.   While a resolution continues to have effect by virtue of paragraph 4 above, sections 17(3A) and (6) to (10), 17A, 17B, 17D, 17E and 20(3) of the 1968 Act (together with the code of practice last published under subsection (5) of the said section 17E) shall continue to have effect in relation to the child in question notwithstanding the repeal by this Act of those sections.

7.   Where an order made under—

(a)   section 10 (power of court in actions of divorce etc to commit care of child to local authority) or 12 (power of court to provide for supervision of child) of the Matrimonial Proceedings (Children) Act 1958;

(b)   section 11 of the Guardianship Act 1973 (orders relating to care and custody of children); or

(c)   section 26 of the Adoption (Scotland) Act 1978 (provision for supervision or care where adoption order refused),

committed the care of the child to, or as the case may be placed the child under the supervision of, a local authority and immediately before the repeal by this Act of the section in question (the 'relevant repeal') that order remained undischarged, the order shall continue to have effect notwithstanding the relevant repeal until one of the following occurs—

(i)   the period of six months commencing with the date of the relevant repeal expires;

(ii)   the Court of Session direct, or the sheriff directs, that the order be discharged; or

(iii)   there is an event in consequence of which, but for the provisions (apart from this paragraph) of this Act, the order would have fallen to be discharged.

8.—(1)   Where relevant proceedings in relation to a child have been commenced and on the relevant date have not been concluded, the provisions of Part III of the 1968 Act shall continue to apply to those proceedings until the proceedings are concluded, notwithstanding the repeal of any of those provisions by this Act.

(2)   For the purposes of this paragraph, 'relevant proceedings' means any proceedings at a children's hearing under Part III of the 1968 Act, any application to the sheriff under that Part for a warrant or under section 42(2)(c) of that Act to establish any ground of referral, and any appeal under section 49 or 50 of that Act; and a reference to the commencement, or to the conclusion, of such proceedings shall be construed in accordance with sub-paragraph (3) or, as the case may be, (4) below.

(3)   Relevant proceedings are commenced when one of the following occurs—

(a)   a children's hearing is arranged under section 37(4) or section 39(3) of the 1968 Act;

(b)   an application under section 42(2)(c) of that Act is lodged;

(c)   an appeal to the sheriff under section 49 of that Act is lodged;

(d)   an application under section 50(2) of that Act is made.

(4)   Relevant proceedings are concluded when one of the following occurs—

(a)   the sheriff discharges the referral under section 42(5) of the 1968 Act;

(b)   a children's hearing discharge the referral under section 43(2) of that Act;

(c)   the period of three weeks after a children's hearing make a supervision requirement under section 44 of that Act or on remission to them under section 49(5) of that Act, expires provided that no appeal has been lodged within that period against that decision under section 49 of that Act;

(d)   subject, as respects a decision under section 49(5)(b) of that Act, to head (c) above, the period of twenty-eight days after the sheriff has disposed of an appeal under section 49(4), (5) or (6) of that Act expires provided that no application has been made within that period to him to state a case under section 50(2) of that Act;

(e)   the period of twenty-eight days after the sheriff has disposed of a case remitted to him under section 50(3) expires provided that no further application under the said section 50(2) has been made.

9.   Where a child has been taken to a place of safety, or is being detained in such a place, in accordance with section 37(2) of the 1968 Act before the relevant date, and the first lawful day for the purposes of subsection (4) of that section is on or after that date, the child's case shall be proceeded with as if that day had been before the relevant date.

CRIMINAL LAW (CONSOLIDATION) (SCOTLAND) ACT 1995
(1995, c 39)

PART I
SEXUAL OFFENCES

Incest and related offences

1   Incest

(1)   Any male person who has sexual intercourse with a person related to him in a degree specified in column 1 of the Table set out at the end of this subsection, or any female person who has sexual intercourse with a person related to her in a degree specified in column 2 of that Table, shall be guilty of incest, unless the accused proves that he or she—

(a)   did not know and had no reason to suspect that the person with whom he or she had sexual intercourse was related in a degree so specified; or

(b)   did not consent to have sexual intercourse, or to have sexual intercourse with that person; or

(c)   was married to that person, at the time when the sexual intercourse took place, by a marriage entered into outside Scotland and recognised as valid by Scots law.

Table
Degrees of Relationship

Column 1   Column 2

1. Relationships by consanguinity

Column 1	Column 2
Mother	Father
Daughter	Son
Grandmother	Grandfather
Grand-daughter	Grandson
Sister	Brother
Aunt	Uncle
Niece	Nephew
Great grandmother	Great grandfather
Great grand-daughter	Great grandson

2. Relationships by adoption

Column 1	Column 2
Adoptive mother or former adoptive mother.	Adoptive father or former adoptive father.
Adopted daughter or former adopted daughter.	Adopted son or former adopted son.

[*3. Relationships by virtue of Part 2 of the Human Fertilisation and Embryology Act 2008*

Column 1	Column 2
Mother	Father
Daughter	Son
Second female parent by virtue of section 42 or 43 of that Act.]	

(2)   For the purpose of this section, a degree of relationship exists in the case of a degree specified in paragraph 1 of the Table—

(a)   whether it is of the full blood or the half blood; and

(b)   even where traced through or to any person whose parents are not or have not been married to one another.

(3)   For the avoidance of doubt sexual intercourse between persons who are not related to each other in a degree referred to in subsection (1) above is not incest.

2   Intercourse with step-child

Any step-parent or former step-parent who has sexual intercourse with his or her step-child or former step-child shall be guilty of an offence if that step-child is either under the age of 21 years or has at any time before attaining the age of 18 years lived in the same household and been treated as a child of his or her family, unless the accused proves that he or she—

(a)   did not know and had no reason to suspect that the person with whom he or she had sexual intercourse was a step-child or former step-child; or

(b)   believed on reasonable grounds that that person was of or over the age of 21 years; or

(c)   did not consent to have sexual intercourse, or to have sexual intercourse with that person; or

(d)   was married to that person, at the time when the sexual intercourse took place, by a marriage entered into outside Scotland and recognised as valid by Scots law.

3 Intercourse of person in position of trust with child under 16

(1) Any person of or over the age of 16 years who—

(a) has sexual intercourse with a child under the age of 16 years;

(b) is a member of the same household as that child; and

(c) is in a position of trust or authority in relation to that child,

shall be guilty of an offence, unless the accused proves that subsection (2) below applies in his or her case.

(2) This subsection applies where the accused—

(a) believed on reasonable grounds that the person with whom he or she had sexual intercourse was of or over the age of 16 years; or

(b) did not consent to have sexual intercourse, or to have sexual intercourse with that person; or

(c) was married to that person, at the time when the sexual intercourse took place, by a marriage entered into outside Scotland and recognised as valid by Scots law.

[. . .]

Offences against children

5 Intercourse with girl under 16

(1) [Subject to section 205A of the Criminal Procedure (Scotland) Act 1995 (imprisonment for life on further conviction of certain offences)], any person who has unlawful sexual intercourse with any girl under the age of 13 years shall be liable on conviction on indictment to imprisonment for life.

(2) Any person who attempts to have unlawful sexual intercourse with any girl under the age of 13 years shall be liable on conviction on indictment to imprisonment for a term not exceeding [ten] years or on summary conviction to imprisonment for a term not exceeding three months.

(3) Without prejudice to sections 1 to 4 of this Act, any person who has, or attempts to have, unlawful sexual intercourse with any girl of or over the age of 13 years and under the age of 16 years shall be liable on conviction on indictment to imprisonment for a term not exceeding [ten] years or on summary conviction to imprisonment for a term not exceeding three months.

[. . .]

(5) It shall be a defence to a charge under subsection (3) above that the person so charged—

(a) had reasonable cause to believe that the girl was his wife; or

(b) being a man under the age of 24 years who had not previously been charged with a like offence, had reasonable cause to believe that the girl was of or over the age of 16 years.

(6) In subsection (5) above, 'a like offence' means an offence under—

(a) subsection (3) above; or

(b) section 4(1) or 10(1) of the Sexual Offences (Scotland) Act 1976 or section 5 or 6 of the Criminal Law Amendment Act 1885 (the enactments formerly creating the offences mentioned in subsection (3) above and section [9(1)] of this Act); or

(c) section 6 of the Sexual Offences Act 1956 (the provision for England and Wales corresponding to subsection (3) above), or with an attempt to commit such an offence; or

[(cc) any of sections 9 to 14 of the Sexual Offences Act 2003; or]

(d) section 9(1) of this Act.

[. . .]

6 Indecent behaviour towards girl between 12 and 16

Any person who uses towards a girl of or over the age of 12 years and under the age of 16 years any lewd, indecent or libidinous practice or behaviour which, if used towards a girl under the age of 12 years, would have constituted an offence at common law shall, whether the girl consented to such practice or behaviour or not, be liable on conviction on indictment to imprisonment for a term not exceeding [ten] years or on summary conviction to imprisonment for a term not exceeding three months.

Procuring, prostitution etc

7 Procuring

(1) Any person who procures or attempts to procure—

(a) any woman under 21 years of age or girl to have unlawful sexual intercourse with any other person or persons in any part of the world; or

(b) any woman or girl to become a common prostitute in any part of the world; or

(c) any woman or girl to leave the United Kingdom, with intent that she may become an inmate of or frequent a brothel elsewhere; or

(d) any woman or girl to leave her usual place of abode in the United Kingdom, with intent that she may, for the purposes of prostitution, become an inmate of or frequent a brothel in any part of the world,

shall be liable on conviction on indictment to imprisonment for a term not exceeding two years or on summary conviction to imprisonment for a term not exceeding three months.

(2) Any person who—

(a) by threats or intimidation procures or attempts to procure any woman or girl to have any unlawful sexual intercourse in any part of the world; or

(b) by false pretences or false representations procures any woman or girl to have any unlawful sexual intercourse in any part of the world; or

(c) applies or administers to, or causes to be taken by, any woman or girl any drug, matter or thing, with intent to stupefy or overpower so as thereby to enable any person to have unlawful sexual intercourse with such woman or girl,

shall be liable on conviction on indictment to imprisonment for a term not exceeding two years or on summary conviction to imprisonment for a term not exceeding three months.

(3) A man who induces a married woman to permit him to have sexual intercourse with her by impersonating her husband shall be deemed to be guilty of rape.

(4) A constable may arrest without a warrant any person whom he has good cause to suspect of having committed, or of attempting to commit, any offence under subsection (1) above.

10 Seduction, prostitution, etc, of girl under 16

(1) If any person having parental responsibilities (within the meaning of section 1(3) of the Children (Scotland) Act 1995), in relation to, or having charge or care of a girl under the age of 16 years causes or encourages—

(a) the seduction or prostitution of;

(b) unlawful sexual intercourse with; or

(c) the commission of an indecent assault upon,

her he shall be liable on conviction on indictment to imprisonment for a term not exceeding two years or on summary conviction to imprisonment for a term not exceeding three months.

(2) For the purposes of this section, a person shall be deemed to have caused or encouraged the matters mentioned in paragraphs (a) to (c) of subsection (1) above upon a girl who has been seduced or indecently assaulted, or who has had unlawful sexual intercourse or who has become a prostitute, if he has knowingly allowed her to consort with, or to enter or continue in the employment of, any prostitute or person of known immoral character.

(3) Subsections (1) and (2) above shall apply to a contravention of section 6 of this Act in like manner as they apply to an indecent assault, and any reference to

the commission of such an assault or to being indecently assaulted shall be construed accordingly.

(4)　Where on the trial of any offence under this Part of this Act it is proved to the satisfaction of the court that the seduction or prostitution of a girl under the age of 16 years has been caused, encouraged or favoured by her father, mother or guardian it shall be in the power of the court to divest such person of all authority over her, and to appoint any person or persons willing to take charge of such girl to be her guardian until she has attained the age of 21 years, or such lower age as the court may direct.

(5)　The High Court of Justiciary shall have the power from time to time to rescind or vary an order under subsection (4) above by the appointment of any other person or persons as such guardian, or in any other respect.

11　Trading in prostitution and brothel-keeping

(1)　Every male person who—

　(a)　knowingly lives wholly or in part on the earnings of prostitution; or

　(b)　in any public place persistently solicits or importunes for immoral purposes,

shall be liable on conviction on indictment to imprisonment for a term not exceeding two years or on summary conviction to imprisonment for a term not exceeding six months.

(2)　If it is made to appear to a court of summary jurisdiction by information on oath that there is reason to suspect that any house or any part of a house is used by a female for purposes of prostitution, and that any male person residing in or frequenting the house is living wholly or in part on the earnings of the prostitute, the court may issue a warrant authorising a constable to enter and search the house and to arrest that male person.

(3)　Where a male person is proved to live with or to be habitually in the company of a prostitute, or is proved to have exercised control, direction or influence over the movements of a prostitute in such a manner as to show that he is aiding, abetting or compelling her prostitution with any other person, or generally, he shall, unless he can satisfy the court to the contrary, be deemed to be knowingly living on the earnings of prostitution.

(4)　Every female who is proved to have, for the purposes of gain, exercised control, direction or influence over the movements of a prostitute in such a manner as to show that she is aiding, abetting or compelling her prostitution with any other person, or generally, shall be liable to the penalties set out in subsection (1) above.

(5)　Any person who—

　(a)　keeps or manages or acts or assists in the management of a brothel; or

　(b)　being the tenant, lessee, occupier or person in charge of any premises, knowingly permits such premises or any part thereof to be used as a brothel or for the purposes of habitual prostitution; or

　(c)　being the lessor or landlord of any premises, or the agent of such lessor or landlord, lets the same or any part thereof with the knowledge that such premises or some part thereof are or is to be used as a brothel, or is wilfully a party to the continued use of such premises or any part thereof as a brothel,

shall be guilty of an offence.

(6)　A person convicted of an offence under subsection (5) above shall be liable—

　(a)　in the sheriff court to a fine not exceeding level 4 on the standard scale or to imprisonment for a term not exceeding six months; and

　(b)　in the district court to a fine not exceeding level 3 on the standard scale or to imprisonment for a term not exceeding three months,

or, in either case, to both such fine and imprisonment.

12 Allowing child to be in brothel

(1) If any person having parental responsibilities (within the meaning of section 1(3) of the Children (Scotland) Act 1995), in relation to, or having charge or care of a child who has attained the age of four years and is under the age of 16 years, allows that child to reside in or to frequent a brothel, he shall be liable on conviction on indictment, or on summary conviction, to a fine not exceeding level 2 on the standard scale or alternatively, or in default of payment of such a fine, or in addition thereto, to imprisonment for a term not exceeding six months.

(2) Nothing in this section shall affect the liability of a person to be indicted under section 9 of this Act, but upon the trial of a person under that section it shall be lawful for the jury, if they are satisfied that he is guilty of an offence under this section, to find him guilty of that offence.

Homosexual offences

13 Homosexual offences

(1) Subject to the provisions of this section, a homosexual act in private shall not be an offence provided that the parties consent thereto and have attained the age of [16] years.

(2) An act which would otherwise be treated for the purpose of this Act as being done in private shall not be so treated if done— . . .

(b) in a lavatory to which the public have, or are permitted to have, access whether on payment or otherwise.

[. . .]

(4) In this section, 'a homosexual act' means sodomy or an act of gross indecency or shameless indecency by one male person with another male person.

(5) Subject to subsection (3) above, it shall be an offence to commit or to be party to the commission of, or to procure or attempt to procure the commission of a homosexual act—

(a) otherwise than in private;

(b) without the consent of [the] parties to the act; or

(c) with a person under the age of [16] years.

(6) It shall be an offence to procure or attempt to procure the commission of a homosexual act between two other male persons.

(7) A person who commits or is party to the commission of an offence under subsection (5) or subsection (6) above shall be liable on conviction on indictment to imprisonment for a term not exceeding two years or to a fine or to both and on summary conviction to imprisonment for a term not exceeding 3 months, or to a fine not exceeding the prescribed sum (within the meaning of section 225(8) of the Criminal Procedure (Scotland) Act 1995).

(8) It shall be a defence to a charge of committing a homosexual act under subsection (5)(c) above that the person so charged being under the age of 24 years who had not previously been charged with a like offence, had reasonable cause to believe that the other person was of or over the age of [16] years.

[(8A) A person under the age of 16 years does not commit an offence under subsection (5)(a) or (c) above if he commits or is party to the commission of a homosexual act with a person who has attained that age.]

(9) A person who knowingly lives wholly or in part on the earnings of another from male prostitution or who solicits or importunes any male person for the purpose of procuring the commission of a homosexual act within the meaning of subsection (4) above shall be liable—

(a) on summary conviction to imprisonment for a term not exceeding six months; or

(b) on conviction on indictment to imprisonment for a term not exceeding two years.

(10)   Premises shall be treated for the purposes of sections 11(1) and 12 of this Act as a brothel if people resort to it for the purposes of homosexual acts within the meaning of subsection (4) above in circumstances in which resort thereto for heterosexual practices would have led to its being treated as a brothel for the purposes of those sections.

(11)   No proceedings for—

(a)   the offences mentioned in subsections (5) and (6) above; and

(b)   any offence under subsection (9) above which consists of soliciting or importuning any male person for the purpose of procuring the commission of a homosexual act,

shall be commenced after the expiration of twelve months from the date on which that offence was committed.

[16B   Commission of certain sexual acts outside the United Kingdom

(1)   Subject to subsection (2) below, any act done by a person in a country or territory outside the United Kingdom which—

(a)   constituted an offence under the law in force in that country or territory; and

(b)   would constitute a listed sexual offence if it had been done in Scotland,

shall constitute that sexual offence.

(2)   No proceedings shall by virtue of this section be brought against any person unless he was at the commencement of this section, or has subsequently become, a British citizen or resident in the United Kingdom.

(3)   An act punishable under the law in force in any country or territory constitutes an offence under that law for the purposes of subsection (1) above, however it is described in that law.

(4)   Subject to subsection (5) below, the condition in subsection (1)(a) above shall be taken to be satisfied unless, not later than may be prescribed by Act of Adjournal, the accused serves on the prosecutor a notice—

(a)   stating that, on the facts as alleged with respect to the act in question, the condition is not in his opinion satisfied;

(b)   setting out the grounds for that opinion; and

(c)   requiring the prosecutor to prove that it is satisfied.

(5)   The court, if it thinks fit, may permit the accused to require the prosecutor to prove that the condition is satisfied without the prior service of a notice under subsection (4) above.

(6)   In proceedings on indictment, the question whether the condition is satisfied is to be decided by the judge alone.

[(6A)   A person may be proceeded against, indicted, tried and punished for any offence to which this section applies—

(a)   in any sheriff court district in Scotland in which he is apprehended or is in custody; or

(b)   in such sheriff court district as the Lord Advocate may determine,

as if the offence had been committed in that district; and the offence shall, for all purposes incidental to or consequential on trial or punishment, be deemed to have been committed in that district.

(6B)   In subsection (6A) above, 'sheriff court district' shall be construed in accordance with section 307(1) (interpretation) of the Criminal Procedure (Scotland) Act 1995 (c 46).]

(7)   Subject to subsection (8) below, in this section 'listed sexual offence' means any of the following—

(a)   rape of a girl under the age of 16;

(b)   indecent assault of a person under the age of 16;

(c)   lewd, indecent or libidinous behaviour or practices;

(d)   shamelessly indecent conduct involving a person under the age of 16;

(e)   sodomy with or against a boy under the age of 16;

(f)   an offence under section 5(1) or (2) of this Act (unlawful sexual intercourse with a girl under the age of 13);

(g)   an offence under section 5(3) of this Act (unlawful sexual intercourse with a girl under the age of 16);

(h)   an offence under section 6 of this Act (indecent behaviour towards a girl between the age of 12 and 16);

(i)   an offence under section 13(5) or (6) of this Act when the homosexual act involves a person under the age of 16 (prohibition on certain homosexual acts);

(j)   an offence under section 52 of the Civic Government (Scotland) Act 1982 (taking and distribution of indecent images of children);

[(k)   an offence under section 52A of that Act (possession of indecent images of children);

(l)   an offence under section 9 of the Protection of Children and Prevention of Sexual Offences (Scotland) Act 2005 (asp 9) (paying for sexual services of a child);

(m)   an offence under section 10 of that Act (causing or inciting provision by child of sexual services or child pornography);

(n)   an offence under section 11 of that Act (controlling a child providing sexual services or involved in pornography); and

(p)   an offence under section 12 of that Act (arranging or facilitating provision by child of sexual services or child pornography).]

(8)   'Listed sexual offence' includes—

(a)   any conspiracy or incitement to commit any such offence; and

(b)   any offence under section 293(2) of the Criminal Procedure (Scotland) Act 1995 (aiding and abetting etc the commission of statutory offences) relating to any offence mentioned in subsection (7)(f) to (j) above.]

PRIVATE INTERNATIONAL LAW (MISCELLANEOUS PROVISIONS) ACT 1995
(1995, c 42)

7   Validity and effect in Scots law of potentially polygamous marriages

(1)   A person domiciled in Scotland does not lack capacity to enter into a marriage by reason only that the marriage is entered into under a law which permits polygamy.

(2)   For the avoidance of doubt, a marriage valid by the law of Scotland and entered into—

(a)   under a law which permits polygamy; and

(b)   at a time when neither party to the marriage is already married,

has, so long as neither party marries a second spouse during the subsistence of the marriage, the same effects for all purposes of the law of Scotland as a marriage entered into under a law which does not permit polygamy.

PROTECTION FROM HARASSMENT ACT 1997
(1997, c 40)

Scotland

8   Harassment

(1)   Every individual has a right to be free from harassment and, accordingly, a person must not pursue a course of conduct which amounts to harassment of another and—

(a)   is intended to amount to harassment of that person; or

(b)   occurs in circumstances where it would appear to a reasonable person that it would amount to harassment of that person.

(2)   An actual or apprehended breach of subsection (1) may be the subject of a claim in civil proceedings by the person who is or may be the victim of the course of conduct in question; and any such claim shall be known as an action of harassment.

(3)   For the purposes of this section—

'conduct' includes speech;

'harassment' of a person includes causing the person alarm or distress; and

a course of conduct must involve conduct on at least two occasions.

(4)   It shall be a defence to any action of harassment to show that the course of conduct complained of—

    (a)   was authorised by, under or by virtue of any enactment or rule of law;

    (b)   was pursued for the purpose of preventing or detecting crime; or

    (c)   was, in the particular circumstances, reasonable.

(5)   In an action of harassment the court may, without prejudice to any other remedies which it may grant—

    (a)   award damages;

    (b)   grant—

        (i)   interdict or interim interdict;

        (ii)   if it is satisfied that it is appropriate for it to do so in order to protect the person from further harassment, an order, to be known as a 'non-harassment order', requiring the defender to refrain from such conduct in relation to the pursuer as may be specified in the order for such period (which includes an indeterminate period) as may be so specified,

but a person may not be subjected to the same prohibitions in an interdict or interim interdict and a non-harassment order at the same time.

(6)   The damages which may be awarded in an action of harassment include damages for any anxiety caused by the harassment and any financial loss resulting from it.

(7)   Without prejudice to any right to seek review of any interlocutor, a person against whom a non-harassment order has been made, or the person for whose protection the order was made, may apply to the court by which the order was made for revocation of or a variation of the order and, on any such application, the court may revoke the order or vary it in such manner as it considers appropriate.

(8)   In section 10(1) of the Damages (Scotland) Act 1976 (interpretation), in the definition of 'personal injuries', after 'to reputation' there is inserted ', or injury resulting from harassment actionable under section 8 of the Protection from Harassment Act 1997'.

9   Breach of non-harassment order

(1)   Any person who is found to be in breach of a non-harassment order made under section 8 is guilty of an offence and liable—

    (a)   on conviction on indictment, to imprisonment for a term not exceeding five years or to a fine, or to both such imprisonment and such fine; and

    (b)   on summary conviction, to imprisonment for a period not exceeding six months or to a fine not exceeding the statutory maximum, or to both such imprisonment and such fine.

(2)   A breach of a non-harassment order shall not be punishable other than in accordance with subsection (1).

[(3)   A constable may arrest without warrant any person he reasonably believes is committing or has committed an offence under subsection (1).

(4)   Subsection (3) is without prejudice to any power of arrest conferred by law apart from that subsection.]

11   Non-harassment order following criminal offence

After section 234 of the Criminal Procedure (Scotland) Act 1995 there is inserted the following section—

Non-harassment orders

234A   Non-harassment order

(1)   Where a person is convicted of an offence involving harassment of a person ('the victim'), the prosecutor may apply to the court to make a non-harassment order against the offender requiring him to refrain from such conduct in relation to the victim as may be specified in the order for such period (which includes an indeterminate period) as may be so specified, in addition to any other disposal which may be made in relation to the offence.

(2)   On an application under subsection (1) above the court may, if it is satisfied on a balance of probabilities that it is appropriate to do so in order to protect the victim from further harassment, make a non-harassment order.

(3)   A non-harassment order made by a criminal court shall be taken to be a sentence for the purposes of any appeal and, for the purposes of this sub-section 'order' includes any variation or revocation of such an order made under subsection (6) below.

(4)   Any person who is found to be in breach of a non-harassment order shall be guilty of an offence and liable—

(a)   on conviction on indictment, to imprisonment for a term not exceeding 5 years or to a fine, or to both such imprisonment and such fine; and

(b)   on summary conviction, to imprisonment for a period not exceeding 6 months or to a fine not exceeding the statutory maximum, or to both such imprisonment and such fine.

(5)   The Lord Advocate, in solemn proceedings, and the prosecutor, in summary proceedings, may appeal to the High Court against any decision by a court to refuse an application under subsection (1) above; and on any such appeal the High Court may make such order as it considers appropriate.

(6)   The person against whom a non-harassment order is made, or the prosecutor at whose instance the order is made, may apply to the court which made the order for its revocation or variation and, in relation to any such application the court concerned may, if it is satisfied on a balance of probabilities that it is appropriate to do so, revoke the order or vary it in such manner as it thinks fit, but not so as to increase the period for which the order is to run.

(7)   For the purposes of this section 'harassment' shall be construed in accordance with section 8 of the Protection from Harassment Act 1997.

PROTECTION FROM ABUSE (SCOTLAND) ACT 2001
(2001 asp 14)

1   Attachment of power of arrest to interdict

(1)   A person who is applying for, or who has obtained, an interdict for the pur-pose of protection against abuse may apply to the court for a power of arrest to be attached to the interdict under this Act.

[(1A)   In the case of an interdict which is—

(a)   a matrimonial interdict (as defined by section 14(2) of the Matrimonial Homes (Family Protection) (Scotland) Act 1981) which is ancillary to—

(i)   an exclusion order within the meaning of section 4(1) of that Act; or

(ii)   an interim order under section 4(6) of that Act; or

(b)   a relevant interdict (as defined by section 113(2) of the Civil Partnership Act 2004) which is ancillary to—

(i)   an exclusion order within the meaning of section 104(1) of that Act; or

(ii)   an interim order under section 104(6) of that Act,

the court must, on an application under subsection (1), attach a power of arrest to the interdict.]

(2) [In the case of any other interdict] the court must, on such application, attach a power of arrest to the interdict if satisfied that—

(a) the interdicted person has been given an opportunity to be heard by, or represented before, the court;

(b) [. . .] and

(c) attaching the power of arrest is necessary to protect the applicant from a risk of abuse in breach of the interdict.

(3) The court, on attaching a power of arrest, must specify a date of expiry for the power, being a date not later than three years after the date when the power is attached.

2 Duration, extension and recall

(1) A power of arrest comes into effect only when it has been served on the interdicted person along with such documents as may be prescribed.

(2) A power of arrest ceases to have effect—

(a) on the date of expiry specified by the court;

(b) when it is recalled by the court; or

(c) when the interdict to which the power is attached is varied or recalled, whichever is the earliest.

(3) The duration of a power of arrest must, on the application of the person who obtained it, be extended by the court, if satisfied that—

(a) the interdicted person has been given an opportunity to be heard by, or represented before, the court; and

(b) the extension is necessary to protect the applicant from a risk of abuse in breach of the interdict.

(4) The court, on extending the duration of a power of arrest, must specify a new date of expiry for the power, being a date not later than three years after the date when the extension is granted.

(5) Where the duration of a power of arrest has been extended—

(a) the extension comes into effect only when it has been served on the interdicted person along with such documents as may be prescribed; and

(b) subsection (2) applies as if the date referred to in paragraph (a) of that subsection were the new date of expiry specified by the court in granting the extension.

(6) Subsections (3), (4) and (5) apply to further extensions as they apply to an initial extension.

(7) A power of arrest must be recalled by the court if —

(a) the person who obtained it applies for recall; or

(b) the interdicted person applies for recall

and the court is satisfied that—

(i) the person who obtained the power has been given an opportunity to be heard by, or represented before, the court; and

(ii) the power is no longer necessary to protect that person from a risk of abuse in breach of the interdict.

3 Notification to police

(1) As soon as possible after—

(a) a power of arrest has been served;

(b) an extension of the duration of a power of arrest has been served;

(c) a recall of a power of arrest has been granted; or

(d) the relevant interdict has been varied or recalled,

the person who has obtained such power, extension, variation or recall, or such other person as may be prescribed, must deliver such documents as may be prescribed to the chief constable of any police area in which the relevant interdict has effect or (in the case of paragraph (d)) had effect before it was varied or recalled.

(2) In this section 'relevant interdict' means the interdict to which the power of arrest is or was attached.

4 Powers and duties of police

(1) Where a power of arrest attached to an interdict has effect a constable may arrest the interdicted person without warrant if the constable—

(a) has reasonable cause for suspecting that person of being in breach of the interdict; and

(b) considers that there would, if that person were not arrested, be a risk of abuse or further abuse by that person in breach of the interdict.

(2) A person who is arrested under subsection (1) must be informed immediately of the reason for the arrest and must thereafter be taken to a police station as quickly as is reasonably practicable and detained until—

(a) accused on petition or charged on complaint with an offence in respect of the facts and circumstances giving rise to the arrest; or

(b) brought before a court under section 5.

(3) A person who is detained under subsection (2) is entitled—

(a) to be informed immediately of the rights given by paragraphs (b) to (e);

(b) to have, on request, intimation of the detention and of the place of detention sent, without delay, to a solicitor and to one other person reasonably named by the detained person;

(c) to have, on request, intimation given to a solicitor that the solicitor's professional assistance is required;

(d) to have, on request, the solicitor informed, as soon as the information is available, of the court to which the detained person is to be taken and the date when that is to happen; and

(e) to have, on request, a private interview with the solicitor before any appearance in court under this Act.

(4) Where a person detained under subsection (2) appears to the officer in charge of the police station to be under 16 years of age the officer must where practicable, without delay and in addition to complying with subsection (3), send intimation of the detention and of the place of detention to any person known to have parental responsibilities and rights in relation to the detained person or to have care of that person; and any person to whom such intimation is given must be permitted reasonable access to the detained person.

(5) The following matters are to be recorded by the police in connection with the detention of a person under subsection (2)—

(a) the time at which the person was arrested;

(b) the police station to which the person was taken;

(c) the time when the person arrived at that police station;

(d) the address of any other place to which the person is, during the detention, thereafter taken;

(e) the time when the person was informed of the rights given by subsection (3);

(f) the time and nature of any request made by the person under subsection (3); and

(g) the time and nature of any action taken by a police officer under subsection (3) or (4).

(6) When a person has been arrested under this section the facts and circumstances giving rise to the arrest must be reported to the procurator fiscal as soon as is practicable.

5 Court appearance

(1) If the procurator fiscal decides that no criminal proceedings are to be taken in respect of the facts and circumstances which gave rise to the arrest, the detained person must wherever practicable be brought before the sheriff sitting as a court of summary criminal jurisdiction for the district in which the person was arrested not later than in the course of the first day after the arrest, such day not being a Saturday, a Sunday or a court holiday for that court.

(2)   Nothing in subsection (1) prevents the detained person from being brought before the sheriff on a Saturday, a Sunday or a court holiday if the sheriff is sitting on such a day for the disposal of criminal business.

(3)   When the detained person is brought before the sheriff under this section the procurator fiscal must present to the court a petition—

(a)   giving particulars of the detained person;

(b)   stating the facts and circumstances which gave rise to the arrest;

(c)   giving any information known to the procurator fiscal about the circumstances which gave rise to the interdict and the attachment of the power of arrest;

(d)   giving any other information known to the procurator fiscal and relevant to an assessment of the risk of abuse or further abuse in breach of the interdict; and

(e)   requesting the court to consider whether, on the information presented, a further period of detention is justified.

(4)   If it appears to the sheriff, after affording the detained person the opportunity to make representations, that—

(a)   the information presented to the court discloses a prima facie breach of the interdict by that person; and

(b)   there would, if further detention were not ordered, be a substantial risk of abuse or further abuse by that person in breach of the interdict, the sheriff may order that person to be detained for a further period not exceeding 2 days.

(5)   If the sheriff does not order further detention the detained person must, unless in custody in respect of any other matter, be released from custody.

[. . .]

7   Interpretation

In this Act, unless the context otherwise requires—

'abuse' includes violence, harassment, threatening conduct, and any other conduct giving rise, or likely to give rise, to physical or mental injury, fear, alarm or distress;

'conduct' includes—

(a)   speech; and

(b)   presence in a specified place or area;

'court' means the Court of Session or a sheriff;

'documents' includes documents in electronic form;

'interdict' includes interim interdict;

'interdicted person' means—

(a)   in section 1, the person against whom the power of arrest is sought (being the person or one of the persons prohibited by the interdict mentioned in subsection (1) of that section); and

(b)   in sections 2 and 4, the person against whom the power of arrest has been granted;

'parental responsibilities and rights' has the same meaning as in the Children (Scotland) Act 1995 (c 36);

'person' means natural person;

'power of arrest' means a power of arrest under this Act; and

'prescribed' means prescribed by rules of court.

8   Short title and commencement

(1)   This Act may be cited as the Protection from Abuse (Scotland) Act 2001.

(2)   This Act comes into force at the end of the period of three months beginning with the date of Royal Assent.

CRIMINAL JUSTICE (SCOTLAND) ACT 2003
(2003, asp 7)

PART 7
CHILDREN

51 Physical punishment of children

(1) Where a person claims that something done to a child was a physical punishment carried out in exercise of a parental right or of a right derived from having charge or care of the child, then in determining any question as to whether what was done was, by virtue of being in such exercise, a justifiable assault a court must have regard to the following factors—

(a) the nature of what was done, the reason for it and the circumstances in which it took place;

(b) its duration and frequency;

(c) any effect (whether physical or mental) which it has been shown to have had on the child;

(d) the child's age; and

(e) the child's personal characteristics (including, without prejudice to the generality of this paragraph, sex and state of health) at the time the thing was done.

(2) The court may also have regard to such other factors as it considers appropriate in the circumstances of the case.

(3) If what was done included or consisted of—

(a) a blow to the head;

(b) shaking; or

(c) the use of an implement,

the court must determine that it was not something which, by virtue of being in exercise of a parental right or of a right derived as is mentioned in subsection (1), was a justifiable assault; but this subsection is without prejudice to the power of the court so to determine on whatever other grounds it thinks fit.

(4) In subsection (1), 'child' means a person who had not, at the time the thing was done, attained the age of sixteen years.

(5) [amends Children and Young Persons (Scotland) Act 1937]

[52 Amends Children (Scotland) Act 1995]

53 Provision by Principal Reporter of information to victims

(1) Where the Principal Reporter has received information about a case in which it appears that an offence has been committed by a child, the Principal Reporter may provide any information about the case as is mentioned in subsection (2) to any person mentioned in subsection (3) if (and only if)—

(a) the information is requested by the person; and

(b) the Principal Reporter is satisfied that—

(i) the provision of the information would not be detrimental to the best interests of the child concerned in, or any other child connected (in any way) with, the case; and

(ii) it is appropriate in the circumstances of the case to provide the information.

(2) The information is information as to—

(a) what action the Principal Reporter has taken in the case; and

(b) any disposal of the case,

in so far as the information relates to the offence.

(3) The persons are—

(a) any person against whom the offence appears to have been committed or, where that person is a child, any relevant person; and

(b)   any other person or class of persons, subject to such conditions, as may be prescribed.

(4)   In this section—

'child' means a person who has not attained the age of eighteen years;

'the Principal Reporter' has the same meaning as it has in Part II of the Children (Scotland) Act 1995 (c 36);

'relevant person' in relation to a child means—

(a)   any parent enjoying parental responsibilities or parental rights under Part I of that Act;

(b)   any person in whom parental responsibilities or rights are vested by, under or by virtue of that Act; and

(c)   any person who appears to be a person who ordinarily (and other than by reason only of that person's employment) has charge of, or control over, the child.

COMMISSIONER FOR CHILDREN AND YOUNG PEOPLE (SCOTLAND) ACT 2003
(2003, asp 17)

The Commissioner

1   Establishment

(1)   There is to be a Commissioner for Children and Young People in Scotland.

(2)   Schedule 1 makes further provision about the Commissioner.

2   Appointment

(1)   The Commissioner is to be an individual appointed by Her Majesty on the nomination of the Parliament.

(2)   A person is disqualified from appointment as the Commissioner if that person is, at the date when the appointment is to take effect, or in the year prior to that date has been—

(a)   a member of the Parliament;

(b)   a member of the House of Commons; or

(c)   a member of the European Parliament.

(3)   The Commissioner is to be appointed for such period, not exceeding five years, as the Parliamentary corporation may determine.

(4)   A person who has been appointed for one period as the Commissioner may be appointed for a second period (whether or not consecutive) but not for any additional period.

3   Removal

(1)   The Commissioner may be removed from office by Her Majesty if—

(a)   the Commissioner so requests; or

(b)   the Parliament has passed a resolution for removal on the ground—

(i)   that the Commissioner has breached the terms of appointment; or

(ii)   that the Parliament has lost confidence in the Commissioner's willingness, ability or suitability to carry out the functions of the office.

(2)   A resolution for removal of the Commissioner, if passed on a division, must be voted for by not less than two thirds of those voting.

Functions

4   Promoting and safeguarding rights

(1)   The general function of the Commissioner is to promote and safeguard the rights of children and young people.

(2)   In exercising that general function the Commissioner is, in particular, to—

(a)   promote awareness and understanding of the rights of children and young people;

(b)   keep under review the law, policy and practice relating to the rights of children and young people with a view to assessing the adequacy and effectiveness of such law, policy and practice;

(c)   promote best practice by service providers; and

(d)   promote, commission, undertake and publish research on matters relating to the rights of children and young people.

5   United Nations Convention and equal opportunities

(1)   In exercising functions under this Act, the Commissioner must comply with subsections (2) to (4).

(2)   The Commissioner must have regard to any relevant provisions of the United Nations Convention on the Rights of the Child.

(3)   The Commissioner must, in particular—

(a)   regard, and encourage others to regard, the best interests of children and young people as a primary consideration; and

(b)   have regard to, and encourage others to have regard to, the views of children and young people on all matters affecting them, due allowance being made for age and maturity.

(4)   The Commissioner must act in a manner which encourages equal opportunities and, in particular, the observance of the equal opportunity requirements.

6   Involving children and young people

(1)   The Commissioner must encourage the involvement of children and young people in the work of the Commissioner.

(2)   The Commissioner must, in particular, take reasonable steps to—

(a)   ensure that children and young people are made aware of—

(i)   the functions of the Commissioner;

(ii)   the ways in which they may communicate with the Commissioner; and

(iii)   the ways in which the Commissioner may respond to any issues which they raise;

(b)   consult children and young people on the work to be undertaken by the Commissioner; and

(c)   consult organisations working with and for children and young people on the work to be undertaken by the Commissioner.

(3)   In carrying out the duties under subsections (1) and (2) the Commissioner must pay particular attention to groups of children and young people who do not have other adequate means by which they can make their views known.

(4)   The Commissioner must prepare and keep under review a strategy for involving children and young people in the work of the Commissioner in accordance with this section.

7   Carrying out investigations

(1)   The Commissioner may carry out an investigation into whether, by what means and to what extent, a service provider has regard to the rights, interests and views of children and young people in making decisions or taking actions that affect those children and young people.

(2)   The Commissioner may carry out such an investigation only if the Commissioner, having considered the available evidence on, and any information received about, the matter, is satisfied on reasonable grounds that—

(a)   the matter to be investigated raises an issue of particular significance to children and young people generally or to particular groups of children and young people; and

(b)   the investigation would not duplicate work that is properly the function of another person.

(3)   The Commissioner may not carry out an investigation—

(a)   if it would relate to a reserved matter;

(b)   if it would relate only to a particular child or young person; or

(c)   so far as it would relate to—

(i) the making of decisions or taking of action in particular legal proceedings before a court or tribunal; or

(ii) a matter which is the subject of legal proceedings before a court or tribunal.

8   Initiation and conduct of investigation

(1)   Before taking any steps in the conduct of an investigation, the Commissioner must—

(a)   draw up terms of reference for the investigation; and

(b)   publish notice of the investigation and its terms of reference in such manner as appears to the Commissioner appropriate to bring it to the attention of persons likely to be affected by it.

(2)   An investigation is to be conducted in public except to the extent that the Commissioner considers that the taking of evidence in private is necessary or appropriate.

9   Investigations: witnesses and documents

(1)   The Commissioner may require any person—

(a)   to give evidence on any matter within the terms of reference of an investigation; or

(b)   to produce documents in the custody or control of that person which have a bearing on any such matter.

(2)   The Commissioner may not impose such a requirement on any person whom the Parliament could not require, under section 23 of the Scotland Act, to attend its proceedings for the purpose of giving evidence or to produce documents.

(3)   Schedule 2 makes further provision with respect to witnesses and documents and the sanctions for non-compliance with a requirement under this section.

Reports

10   Annual report

(1)   The Commissioner must lay before the Parliament annually a report on the exercise of the Commissioner's functions.

(2)   The report must include—

(a)   a review of issues identified by the Commissioner in the period covered by the report as being relevant to children and young people;

(b)   a review of the Commissioner's activity in that period, including the steps taken to fulfil each of the Commissioner's functions;

(c)   any recommendations by the Commissioner arising out of such activity; and

(d)   an overview of work to be undertaken by the Commissioner in the year following the period covered by the report, including the strategy for involving children and young people in the work of the Commissioner.

11   Reports on investigations

(1)   The Commissioner must, at the conclusion of any investigation, lay before the Parliament a report of the investigation.

(2)   The report must contain any recommendations by the Commissioner arising out of the investigation.

(3)   A report of an investigation into the activities of a person named in, or identifiable from, the report may be laid before the Parliament only if that person has, where this is reasonable and practicable, been given a copy of the draft report and an opportunity to make representations on it.

12   Other reports to Parliament
The Commissioner may lay before the Parliament such other reports on the exercise of the Commissioner's functions as the Commissioner considers necessary or appropriate.

13   Anonymity for children and young people
The Commissioner must ensure that, so far as reasonable and practicable having regard to the subject matter, a report under this Act does not name or identify any child or young person, or group of children or young people, referred to in it.

14   Publication
(1)   The Commissioner must publish any report laid before the Parliament under this Act.

(2)   The Commissioner may publish any other report relating to the exercise of the Commissioner's functions.

(3)   Where the Commissioner publishes a report which is not specifically designed for children or young people the Commissioner must also publish a child friendly version of the report.

Defamation

15   Protection from actions of defamation
(1)   For the purposes of the law of defamation—

(a)   any statement made by the Commissioner or any of the Commissioner's staff—

(i)   in conducting an investigation under this Act;

(ii)   in communicating with any person for the purposes of such an investigation;

(iii)   in a report published under this Act,

has absolute privilege;

(b)   any other statement made by the Commissioner or any of the Commissioner's staff in pursuance of the purposes of this Act has qualified privilege; and

(c)   any statement made to the Commissioner or any of the Commissioner's staff in pursuance of those purposes has qualified privilege.

(2)   In subsection (1), 'statement' has the same meaning as in the Defamation Act 1996 (c 31).

Interpretation, commencement and short title

16   Interpretation
(1)   In this Act, unless the context otherwise requires—

'action' includes failure to act and related expressions are to be construed accordingly;

'best practice' means such practice in relation to the rights of children and young people as appears to the Commissioner to be desirable;

'child friendly version', in relation to a report, means a version or summary which is specifically designed to take account, so far as practicable, of the age, understanding and usual language of any children or young people by whom it is intended that the report should be read;

'children and young people' means natural persons in Scotland who are under the age of 18 years or, if they have at any time been in the care of, or looked after by, a local authority or Northern Ireland authority, under the age of 21 years; and related expressions have corresponding meanings;

'Commissioner' means the Commissioner for Children and Young People in Scotland;

'equal opportunities' and 'equal opportunity requirements' have the same meaning as in Section L2 of Part II of Schedule 5 to the Scotland Act;

'local authority' means any council of a county, city, town, burgh, borough, district, island or other local government area in Scotland, England or Wales;

'looked after', in relation to a local authority in Scotland, has the same meaning as in section 17(6) of the Children (Scotland) Act 1995 (c 36), in relation to a local authority in England and Wales, has the same meaning as in section 22(1) of the Children Act 1989 (c 41) and in relation to a Northern Ireland authority, has the same meaning as in article 25(1) of the Children (Northern Ireland) Order 1995 (SI 1995/755);

'Northern Ireland authority' means any authority (including any Health and Social Services Board or trust) in Northern Ireland;

'Scotland Act' means the Scotland Act 1998 (c 46);

'Scottish Law Officer' means the Lord Advocate or the Solicitor General for Scotland;

'service provider' means any person providing services for children and young people but does not include a parent or guardian exercising the responsibilities imposed or the rights conferred by sections 1 and 2 of the Children (Scotland) Act 1995 (c 36); and

'terms' includes conditions.

(2)   Any reference in this Act to the United Nations Convention on the Rights of the Child is to that Convention read subject to any reservations, objections or interpretative declarations by the United Kingdom for the time being in force.

17   Commencement and short title

(1)   The provisions of this Act, except for—
- (a)   sections 1 to 3 and section 16;
- (b)   schedule 1; and
- (c)   this section,

come into force at the end of the period of six months beginning with the date of Royal Assent.

(2)   This Act may be cited as the Commissioner for Children and Young People (Scotland) Act 2003.

SCHEDULES

SCHEDULE 1
THE COMMISSIONER FOR CHILDREN AND YOUNG PEOPLE IN SCOTLAND
(introduced by section 1)

Status

1.—(1)   Neither the Commissioner nor any member of the Commissioner's staff is to be regarded as a servant or agent of the Crown or as having any status, immunity or privilege of the Crown.

(2)   The Commissioner's property is not to be regarded as property of, or property held on behalf of, the Crown.

Independence

2.—(1)   The Commissioner is not, except as provided in the provisions of this Act listed in sub-paragraph (2), subject to the direction or control of—
- (a)   any member of the Parliament;
- (b)   any member of the Scottish Executive; or
- (c)   the Parliamentary corporation.

(2)   The listed provisions are sections 2(3) and 3(1)(b), paragraphs 4, 6(3), 7 and 10 of this schedule and paragraph 8 of schedule 2.

Validity of actings
3.   The validity of any actings of the Commissioner is not affected by—
(a)   any defect in the nomination by the Parliament for the Commissioner's appointment; or
(b)   any disqualification from appointment as Commissioner.

Remuneration and terms of appointment
4.—(1)   The Commissioner is entitled to—
(a)   a salary of such amount; and
(b)   such allowances,
as the Parliamentary corporation may determine.
(2)   The appointment of the Commissioner is otherwise on such terms as the Parliamentary corporation may determine.
(3)   The terms may include provision as to the circumstances in which the Commissioner may hold any other office or appointment.

Pensions etc
5.—(1)   The Parliamentary corporation may make arrangements for the payment of pensions, allowances and gratuities to, or in respect of, any person who has ceased to hold the office of Commissioner.
(2)   The Parliamentary corporation may, in particular—
(a)   make contributions or payments towards provision for such pensions, allowances or gratuities; and
(b)   establish and administer one or more pension schemes.

General powers
6.—(1)   The Commissioner has a general power to do anything necessary or expedient for the purposes of, or in connection with, the exercise of the Commissioner's functions.
(2)   In particular, the Commissioner may enter into contracts and acquire and dispose of property.
(3)   The Commissioner may charge for such services as may be specified by the Scottish Ministers, by order made by statutory instrument, as chargeable services for the purposes of this Act.
(4)   A statutory instrument containing an order under sub-paragraph (3) is subject to annulment in pursuance of a resolution of the Parliament.

Staff
7.—(1)   The Commissioner may, with the consent of the Parliamentary corporation as to numbers, appoint staff to assist in carrying out the Commissioner's functions.
(2)   The Commissioner may, with the consent of the Parliamentary corporation, determine the terms of appointment of such staff, including arrangements for the payment of pensions, allowances or gratuities to, or in respect of, any person who has ceased to be a member of staff of the Commissioner.

Delegation of authority
8.   The Commissioner may authorise any person to exercise functions on behalf of the Commissioner to the extent specified in the authorisation, but any such delegation of authority does not affect the responsibility of the Commissioner for the exercise of the functions.

Financial provision
9.   The Parliamentary corporation is to pay—
     (a)   the salary and allowances of the Commissioner; and
     (b)   any expenses properly incurred by the Commissioner in the exercise of
the Commissioner's functions.

Accountable officer
10.—(1)   The Parliamentary corporation is to designate the Commissioner or a
member of the Commissioner's staff as the accountable officer for the purposes of
this paragraph.
     (2)   The functions of the accountable officer are—
     (a)   signing the accounts of the expenditure and receipts of the Commis-
sioner;
     (b)   ensuring the propriety and regularity of the finances of the Com-
missioner;
     (c)   ensuring that the resources of the Commissioner are used economically,
efficiently and effectively; and
     (d)   where the accountable officer is not the Commissioner, the duty set out
in sub-paragraph (4).
     (3)   The accountable officer is answerable to the Parliament for the exercise of
those functions.
     (4)   The duty referred to in sub-paragraph (2)(d) is a duty, where the account-
able officer is required to act in some way but considers that to do so would be
inconsistent with the proper performance of the functions specified in sub-
paragraph (2)(a) to (c), to—
     (a)   obtain written authority from the Commissioner before taking the action;
and
     (b)   send a copy of that authority as soon as possible to the Auditor General
for Scotland.

Accounts and audit
11.—(1)   The Commissioner must keep proper accounts at all times and prepare
annual accounts in respect of each financial year.
     (2)   The Commissioner must send a copy of the annual accounts to the Auditor
General for Scotland for auditing.
     (3)   The financial year of the Commissioner is—
     (a)   the period beginning with the date on which the first Commissioner is
appointed and ending with the 31st of March next following that date; and
     (b)   each successive period of twelve months ending with the 31st of March.
     (4)   If requested by any person, the Commissioner must make available at any
reasonable time, and without charge, in printed or electronic form, the audited
accounts, so that they may be inspected by that person.

Appointment of acting Commissioner
12.—(1)   Where there is no Commissioner for the time being, or the Commissioner is unable to act, the Parliamentary corporation may appoint a person
(whether or not a member of the Commissioner's staff) to discharge the Commissioner's functions until a new Commissioner is appointed or the Commissioner is
again able to act; and a person so appointed is referred to in this Act as the 'acting
Commissioner'.
     (2)   A person who is disqualified from appointment as the Commissioner is
also disqualified from appointment as acting Commissioner.
     (3)   While holding office as such, the acting Commissioner is governed by the
provisions of this Act, other than paragraphs 3(a) and 5 of this schedule, applying
to the Commissioner.

SCHEDULE 2
INVESTIGATIONS: SUPPLEMENTARY PROVISIONS ON WITNESSES AND DOCUMENTS
(introduced by section 9)

Requirement to give evidence or produce documents

1.—(1)   A requirement under section 9 is imposed by the Commissioner giving the person in question notice in writing specifying—

(a)   the time and place at which the person is to attend before the Commissioner and the particular subjects concerning which that person is required to give evidence; or

(b)   the documents, or types of documents, which that person is to produce, the date by which that person is to produce them, and the particular subjects concerning which they are required.

(2)   Such notice must be given—

(a)   in the case of an individual, by sending it, by registered post or the recorded delivery service, addressed to that person at the person's usual or last known address or, where the person has given an address for service, at that address;

(b)   in any other case, by sending it, by registered post or the recorded delivery service, addressed to the person at the person's registered or principal office.

Privileges

2.—(1)   A person is not obliged under this Act to answer any question or to produce any document which that person would be entitled to refuse to answer or produce in proceedings in a court in Scotland.

(2)   A Scottish Law Officer or a procurator fiscal is not obliged under this Act to answer any question or to produce any document which that officer would be entitled to decline to answer or to produce in accordance with section 27(3) or, as the case may be, section 23(10) of the Scotland Act.

Evidence on oath

3.—(1)   The Commissioner may—

(a)   administer an oath to any person giving evidence to the Commissioner; and

(b)   require that person to take an oath.

(2)   Any person who refuses to take an oath when required to do so under this paragraph is guilty of an offence and liable on summary conviction to a fine not exceeding level 5 on the standard scale or to imprisonment for a period not exceeding three months.

Admissibility of statements in subsequent criminal proceedings

4.   Any statement made by a person in answer to any question which that person was obliged under this Act to answer is not admissible in any criminal proceedings against that person, except where the proceedings are in respect of perjury relating to that statement.

Offences

5.—(1)   Any person to whom a notice under paragraph 1 has been duly given who, not being privileged under paragraph 2—

(a)   refuses or fails to attend before the Commissioner as required by the notice;

(b)   refuses or fails, when attending before the Commissioner as required by the notice, to answer any question concerning the subjects specified in the notice;

(c)   deliberately alters, suppresses, conceals or destroys any document which that person is required to produce by the notice; or

(d)   refuses or fails to produce any such document,
is guilty of an offence.

(2)   It is a defence for a person charged with an offence under sub-paragraph (1)(a), (b) or (d) to prove that there was a reasonable excuse for the refusal or failure.

(3)   A person guilty of an offence under this paragraph is liable on summary conviction to a fine not exceeding level 5 on the standard scale or to imprisonment for a period not exceeding three months.

Offences by bodies corporate and partnerships

6.—(1)   Where an offence under paragraph 5 which has been committed by a body corporate is proved to have been committed with the consent or connivance of, or to be attributable to any neglect on the part of—

(a)   a director, manager, secretary or other similar officer of the body corporate; or

(b)   any person who was purporting to act in any such capacity,

that person, as well as the body corporate, is guilty of that offence and liable to be proceeded against accordingly.

(2)   Where the affairs of a body corporate are managed by its members, sub-paragraph (1) applies in relation to the acts or defaults of a member in connection with the member's functions of management as if the member were a director of the body corporate.

(3)   Where an offence under paragraph 5 which has been committed by a partnership is proved to have been committed with the consent or connivance of, or to be attributable to any neglect on the part of, a partner, the partner as well as the partnership is guilty of that offence and liable to be proceeded against accordingly.

Producing copies or extracts

7.   For the purposes of section 9 and this schedule a person complies with a requirement to produce a document if that person produces a copy of, or an extract of the relevant part of, the document.

Allowances and expenses

8.   The Commissioner may pay such allowances and expenses to persons giving evidence before the Commissioner or producing documents which they have been required or requested to produce as the Commissioner may, with the agreement of the Parliamentary corporation, determine.

GENDER RECOGNITION ACT 2004
(2004, c 7)

Applications for gender recognition certificate

1   Applications

(1)   A person of either gender who is aged at least 18 may make an application for a gender recognition certificate on the basis of—

(a)   living in the other gender, or

(b)   having changed gender under the law of a country or territory outside the United Kingdom.

(2)   In this Act 'the acquired gender', in relation to a person by whom an application under subsection (1) is or has been made, means—

(a)   in the case of an application under paragraph (a) of that subsection, the gender in which the person is living, or

(b)   in the case of an application under paragraph (b) of that subsection, the gender to which the person has changed under the law of the country or territory concerned.

(3)   An application under subsection (1) is to be determined by a Gender Recognition Panel.

(4)   Schedule 1 (Gender Recognition Panels) has effect.

2   Determination of applications

(1)   In the case of an application under section 1(1)(a), the Panel must grant the application if satisfied that the applicant—

(a)   has or has had gender dysphoria,

(b)   has lived in the acquired gender throughout the period of two years ending with the date on which the application is made,

(c)   intends to continue to live in the acquired gender until death, and

(d)   complies with the requirements imposed by and under section 3.

(2)   In the case of an application under section 1(1)(b), the Panel must grant the application if satisfied—

(a)   that the country or territory under the law of which the applicant has changed gender is an approved country or territory, and

(b)   that the applicant complies with the requirements imposed by and under section 3.

(3)   The Panel must reject an application under section 1(1) if not required by subsection (1) or (2) to grant it.

(4)   In this Act 'approved country or territory' means a country or territory prescribed by order made by the Secretary of State after consulting the Scottish Ministers and the Department of Finance and Personnel in Northern Ireland.

3   Evidence

(1)   An application under section 1(1)(a) must include either—

(a)   a report made by a registered medical practitioner practising in the field of gender dysphoria and a report made by another registered medical practitioner (who may, but need not, practise in that field), or

(b)   a report made by a chartered psychologist practising in that field and a report made by a registered medical practitioner (who may, but need not, practise in that field).

(2)   But subsection (1) is not complied with unless a report required by that subsection and made by—

(a)   a registered medical practitioner, or

(b)   a [registered] psychologist,

practising in the field of gender dysphoria includes details of the diagnosis of the applicant's gender dysphoria.

(3)   And subsection (1) is not complied with in a case where—

(a)   the applicant has undergone or is undergoing treatment for the purpose of modifying sexual characteristics, or

(b)   treatment for that purpose has been prescribed or planned for the applicant,

unless at least one of the reports required by that subsection includes details of it.

(4)   An application under section 1(1)(a) must also include a statutory declaration by the applicant that the applicant meets the conditions in section 2(1)(b) and (c).

(5)   An application under section 1(1)(b) must include evidence that the applicant has changed gender under the law of an approved country or territory.

(6)   Any application under section 1(1) must include—

(a)   a statutory declaration as to whether or not the applicant is married [or a civil partner],

(b)   any other information or evidence required by an order made by the Secretary of State, and

(c)   any other information or evidence which the Panel which is to determine the application may require, and may include any other information or evidence which the applicant wishes to include.

(7) The Secretary of State may not make an order under subsection (6)(b) without consulting the Scottish Ministers and the Department of Finance and Personnel in Northern Ireland.

(8) If the Panel which is to determine the application requires information or evidence under subsection (6)(c) it must give reasons for doing so.

4 Successful applications

(1) If a Gender Recognition Panel grants an application under section 1(1) it must issue a gender recognition certificate to the applicant.

(2) Unless the applicant is married [or a civil partner], the certificate is to be a full gender recognition certificate.

(3) If the applicant is married [or a civil partner], the certificate is to be an interim gender recognition certificate.

(4) Schedule 2 (annulment or dissolution of marriage after issue of interim gender recognition certificate) has effect.

(5) The Secretary of State may, after consulting the Scottish Ministers and the Department of Finance and Personnel in Northern Ireland, specify the content and form of gender recognition certificates.

5 [Issue of full certificates where applicant has been married]

(1) A court which—

(a) makes absolute a decree of nullity granted on the ground that an interim gender recognition certificate has been issued to a party to the marriage, or

(b) (in Scotland) grants a decree of divorce on that ground, must, on doing so, issue a full gender recognition certificate to that party and send a copy to the Secretary of State.

(2) If an interim gender recognition certificate has been issued to a person and either—

(a) the person's marriage is dissolved or annulled (otherwise than on the ground mentioned in subsection (1)) in proceedings instituted during the period of six months beginning with the day on which it was issued, or

(b) the person's spouse dies within that period,

the person may make an application for a full gender recognition certificate at any time within the period specified in subsection (3) (unless the person is again married [or is a civil partner).

(3) That period is the period of six months beginning with the day on which the marriage is dissolved or annulled or the death occurs.

(4) An application under subsection (2) must include evidence of the dissolution or annulment of the marriage and the date on which proceedings for it were instituted, or of the death of the spouse and the date on which it occurred.

(5) An application under subsection (2) is to be determined by a Gender Recognition Panel.

(6) The Panel—

(a) must grant the application if satisfied that the applicant [is neither married nor a civil partner], and

(b) otherwise must reject it.

(7) If the Panel grants the application it must issue a full gender recognition certificate to the applicant.

[5A Issue of full certificates where applicant has been a civil partner

(1) A court which—

(a) makes final a nullity order made on the ground that an interim gender recognition certificate has been issued to a civil partner, or

(b) (in Scotland) grants a decree of dissolution on that ground, must, on doing so, issue a full gender recognition certificate to that civil partner and send a copy to the Secretary of State.

(2)   If an interim gender recognition certificate has been issued to a person and either—

(a)   the person's civil partnership is dissolved or annulled (otherwise than on the ground mentioned in subsection (1)) in proceedings instituted during the period of six months beginning with the day on which it was issued, or

(b)   the person's civil partner dies within that period,

the person may make an application for a full gender recognition certificate at any time within the period specified in subsection (3) (unless the person is again a civil partner or is married).

(3)   That period is the period of six months beginning with the day on which the civil partnership is dissolved or annulled or the death occurs.

(4)   An application under subsection (2) must include evidence of the dissolution or annulment of the civil partnership and the date on which proceedings for it were instituted, or of the death of the civil partner and the date on which it occurred.

(5)   An application under subsection (2) is to be determined by a Gender Recognition Panel.

(6)   The Panel—

(a)   must grant the application if satisfied that the applicant is neither a civil partner nor married, and

(b)   otherwise must reject it.

(7)   If the Panel grants the application it must issue a full gender recognition certificate to the applicant.]

6   Errors in certificates

(1)   Where a gender recognition certificate has been issued to a person, the person or the Secretary of State may make an application for a corrected certificate on the ground that the certificate which has been issued contains an error.

(2)   If the certificate was issued by a court the application is to be determined by the court but in any other case it is to be determined by a Gender Recognition Panel.

(3)   The court or Panel—

(a)   must grant the application if satisfied that the gender recognition certificate contains an error, and

(b)   otherwise must reject it.

(4)   If the court or Panel grants the application it must issue a corrected gender recognition certificate to the applicant.

7   Applications: supplementary

(1)   An application to a Gender Recognition Panel under section 1(1), 5(2) [, 5A(2)] or 6(1) must be made in a form and manner specified by the Secretary of State after consulting the Scottish Ministers and the Department of Finance and Personnel in Northern Ireland.

(2)   The applicant must pay to the Secretary of State a non-refundable fee of an amount prescribed by order made by the Secretary of State unless the application is made in circumstances in which, in accordance with provision made by the order, no fee is payable; and fees of different amounts may be prescribed for different circumstances.

8   Appeals etc

(1)   An applicant to a Gender Recognition Panel under section 1(1), 5(2) [, 5A(2)] or 6(1) may appeal to the High Court or Court of Session on a point of law against a decision by the Panel to reject the application.

(2)   An appeal under subsection (1) must be heard in private if the applicant so requests.

(3)   On such an appeal the court must—
   (a)   allow the appeal and issue the certificate applied for,
   (b)   allow the appeal and refer the matter to the same or another Panel for reconsideration, or
   (c)   dismiss the appeal.
(4)   If an application under section 1(1) is rejected, the applicant may not make
another application before the end of the period of six months beginning with the
date on which it is rejected.
(5)   If an application under section 1(1), 5(2) [, 5A(2)] or 6(1) is granted but the
Secretary of State considers that its grant was secured by fraud, the Secretary of
State may refer the case to the High Court or Court of Session.
(6)   On a reference under subsection (5) the court—
   (a)   must either quash or confirm the decision to grant the application, and
   (b)   if it quashes it, must revoke the gender recognition certificate issued on
the grant of the application and may make any order which it considers appropriate in consequence of, or otherwise in connection with, doing so.

Consequences of issue of gender recognition certificate etc

9   General
(1)   Where a full gender recognition certificate is issued to a person, the person's gender becomes for all purposes the acquired gender (so that, if the acquired
gender is the male gender, the person's sex becomes that of a man and, if it is the
female gender, the person's sex becomes that of a woman).
(2)   Subsection (1) does not affect things done, or events occurring, before the
certificate is issued; but it does operate for the interpretation of enactments passed,
and instruments and other documents made, before the certificate is issued (as
well as those passed or made afterwards).
(3)   Subsection (1) is subject to provision made by this Act or any other enactment or any subordinate legislation.

10   Registration
(1)   Where there is a UK birth register entry in relation to a person to whom a
full gender recognition certificate is issued, the Secretary of State must send a copy
of the certificate to the appropriate Registrar General.
(2)   In this Act 'UK birth register entry', in relation to a person to whom a full
gender recognition certificate is issued, means—
   (a)   an entry of which a certified copy is kept by a Registrar General, or
   (b)   an entry in a register so kept,
containing a record of the person's birth or adoption (or, if there would otherwise
be more than one, the most recent).
(3)   'The appropriate Registrar General' means whichever of—
   (a)   the Registrar General for England and Wales,
   (b)   the Registrar General for Scotland, or
   (c)   the Registrar General for Northern Ireland,
keeps a certified copy of the person's UK birth register entry or the register containing that entry.
(4)   Schedule 3 (provisions about registration) has effect.

12   Parenthood
The fact that a person's gender has become the acquired gender under this Act
does not affect the status of the person as the father or mother of a child.

15   Succession etc
The fact that a person's gender has become the acquired gender under this Act
does not affect the disposal or devolution of property under a will or other instrument made before the appointed day.

16 Peerages etc

The fact that a person's gender has become the acquired gender under this Act—

(a)   does not affect the descent of any peerage or dignity or title of honour, and

(b)   does not affect the devolution of any property limited (expressly or not) by a will or other instrument to devolve (as nearly as the law permits) along with any peerage or dignity or title of honour unless an intention that it should do so is expressed in the will or other instrument.

17 Trustees and personal representatives

(1)   A trustee or personal representative is not under a duty, by virtue of the law relating to trusts or the administration of estates, to enquire, before conveying or distributing any property, whether a full gender recognition certificate has been issued to any person or revoked (if that fact could affect entitlement to the property).

(2)   A trustee or personal representative is not liable to any person by reason of a conveyance or distribution of the property made without regard to whether a full gender recognition certificate has been issued to any person or revoked if the trustee or personal representative has not received notice of the fact before the conveyance or distribution.

(3)   This section does not prejudice the right of a person to follow the property, or any property representing it, into the hands of another person who has received it unless that person has purchased it for value in good faith and without notice.

18 Orders where expectations defeated

(1)   This section applies where the disposition or devolution of any property under a will or other instrument (made on or after the appointed day) is different from what it would be but for the fact that a person's gender has become the acquired gender under this Act.

(2)   A person may apply to the High Court or Court of Session for an order on the ground of being adversely affected by the different disposition or devolution of the property.

(3)   The court may, if it is satisfied that it is just to do so, make in relation to any person benefiting from the different disposition or devolution of the property such order as it considers appropriate.

(4)   An order may, in particular, make provision for—

(a)   the payment of a lump sum to the applicant,

(b)   the transfer of property to the applicant,

(c)   the settlement of property for the benefit of the applicant,

(d)   the acquisition of property and either its transfer to the applicant or its settlement for the benefit of the applicant.

(5)   An order may contain consequential or supplementary provisions for giving effect to the order or for ensuring that it operates fairly as between the applicant and the other person or persons affected by it; and an order may, in particular, confer powers on trustees.

19 Sport

(1)   A body responsible for regulating the participation of persons as competitors in an event or events involving a gender-affected sport may, if subsection (2) is satisfied, prohibit or restrict the participation as competitors in the event or events of persons whose gender has become the acquired gender under this Act.

(2)   This subsection is satisfied if the prohibition or restriction is necessary to secure—

(a)   fair competition, or

(b)   the safety of competitors,

at the event or events.

(3) 'Sport' means a sport, game or other activity of a competitive nature.

(4) A sport is a gender-affected sport if the physical strength, stamina or physique of average persons of one gender would put them at a disadvantage to average persons of the other gender as competitors in events involving the sport.

(5) This section does not affect—

(a) section 44 of the Sex Discrimination Act 1975 (c 65) (exception from Parts 2 to 4 of that Act for acts related to sport), or

(b) Article 45 of the Sex Discrimination (Northern Ireland) Order 1976 (SI 1976/1042 (NI 15)) (corresponding provision for Northern Ireland).

20 Gender-specific offences

(1) Where (apart from this subsection) a relevant gender-specific offence could be committed or attempted only if the gender of a person to whom a full gender recognition certificate has been issued were not the acquired gender, the fact that the person's gender has become the acquired gender does not prevent the offence being committed or attempted.

(2) An offence is a 'relevant gender-specific offence' if—

(a) either or both of the conditions in subsection (3) are satisfied, and

(b) the commission of the offence involves the accused engaging in sexual activity.

(3) The conditions are—

(a) that the offence may be committed only by a person of a particular gender, and

(b) that the offence may be committed only on, or in relation to, a person of a particular gender,

and the references to a particular gender include a gender identified by reference to the gender of the other person involved.

21 Foreign gender change and marriage

(1) A person's gender is not to be regarded as having changed by reason only that it has changed under the law of a country or territory outside the United Kingdom.

(2) Accordingly, a person is not to be regarded as being married by reason of having entered into a foreign post-recognition marriage.

(3) But if a full gender recognition certificate is issued to a person who has entered into a foreign post-recognition marriage, after the issue of the certificate the marriage is no longer to be regarded as being void on the ground that (at the time when it was entered into) the parties to it were not respectively male and female.

(4) However, subsection (3) does not apply to a foreign post-recognition marriage if a party to it has entered into a later (valid) marriage [or civil partnership] before the issue of the full gender recognition certificate.

(5) For the purposes of this section a person has entered into a foreign post-recognition marriage if (and only if)—

(a) the person has entered into a marriage in accordance with the law of a country or territory outside the United Kingdom,

(b) before the marriage was entered into the person had changed gender under the law of that or any other country or territory outside the United Kingdom,

(c) the other party to the marriage was not of the gender to which the person had changed under the law of that country or territory, and

(d) by virtue of subsection (1) the person's gender was not regarded as having changed under the law of any part of the United Kingdom.

Supplementary

22 Prohibition on disclosure of information

(1) It is an offence for a person who has acquired protected information in an official capacity to disclose the information to any other person.

(2) 'Protected information' means information which relates to a person who has made an application under section 1(1) and which—

(a) concerns that application or any application by the person under section 5(2) [, 5A(2)] or 6(1), or

(b) if the application under section 1(1) is granted, otherwise concerns the person's gender before it becomes the acquired gender.

(3) A person acquires protected information in an official capacity if the person acquires it—

(a) in connection with the person's functions as a member of the civil service, a constable or the holder of any other public office or in connection with the functions of a local or public authority or of a voluntary organisation,

(b) as an employer, or prospective employer, of the person to whom the information relates or as a person employed by such an employer or prospective employer, or

(c) in the course of, or otherwise in connection with, the conduct of business or the supply of professional services.

(4) But it is not an offence under this section to disclose protected information relating to a person if—

(a) the information does not enable that person to be identified,

(b) that person has agreed to the disclosure of the information,

(c) the information is protected information by virtue of subsection (2)(b) and the person by whom the disclosure is made does not know or believe that a full gender recognition certificate has been issued,

(d) the disclosure is in accordance with an order of a court or tribunal,

(e) the disclosure is for the purpose of instituting, or otherwise for the purposes of, proceedings before a court or tribunal,

(f) the disclosure is for the purpose of preventing or investigating crime,

(g) the disclosure is made to the Registrar General for England and Wales, the Registrar General for Scotland or the Registrar General for Northern Ireland,

(h) the disclosure is made for the purposes of the social security system or a pension scheme,

(i) the disclosure is in accordance with provision made by an order under subsection (5), or

(j) the disclosure is in accordance with any provision of, or made by virtue of, an enactment other than this section.

(5) The Secretary of State may by order make provision prescribing circumstances in which the disclosure of protected information is not to constitute an offence under this section.

(6) The power conferred by subsection (5) is exercisable by the Scottish Ministers (rather than the Secretary of State) where the provision to be made is within the legislative competence of the Scottish Parliament.

(7) An order under subsection (5) may make provision permitting—

(a) disclosure to specified persons or persons of a specified description,

(b) disclosure for specified purposes,

(c) disclosure of specified descriptions of information, or

(d) disclosure by specified persons or persons of a specified description.

(8) A person guilty of an offence under this section is liable on summary conviction to a fine not exceeding level 5 on the standard scale.

23 Power to modify statutory provisions

(1) The Secretary of State may by order make provision for modifying the operation of any enactment or subordinate legislation in relation to—

(a)   persons whose gender has become the acquired gender under this Act, or

(b)   any description of such persons.

(2)   The power conferred by subsection (1) is exercisable by the Scottish Ministers (rather than the Secretary of State) where the provision to be made is within the legislative competence of the Scottish Parliament.

(3)   The appropriate Northern Ireland department may by order make provision for modifying the operation of any enactment or subordinate legislation which deals with a transferred matter in relation to—

(a)   persons whose gender has become the acquired gender under this Act, or

(b)   any description of such persons.

(4)   In subsection (3)—

'the appropriate Northern Ireland department', in relation to any enactment or subordinate legislation which deals with a transferred matter, means the Northern Ireland department which has responsibility for that matter,

'deals with' is to be construed in accordance with section 98(2) and (3) of the Northern Ireland Act 1998 (c 47), and

'transferred matter' has the meaning given by section 4(1) of that Act.

(5)   Before an order is made under this section, appropriate consultation must be undertaken with persons likely to be affected by it.

24   Orders and regulations

(1)   Any power of the Secretary of State [. . .] the Scottish Ministers or a Northern Ireland department to make an order under this Act includes power to make any appropriate incidental, supplementary, consequential or transitional provision or savings.

(2)   Any power of the Secretary of State [. . .] or the Scottish Ministers to make an order under this Act, and any power of the Registrar General for England and Wales or the Registrar General for Scotland to make regulations under this Act, is exercisable by statutory instrument.

(3)   No order may be made under section 2 [. . .] unless a draft of the statutory instrument containing the order has been laid before, and approved by a resolution of, each House of Parliament.

(4)   A statutory instrument containing an order made by the Secretary of State under section 7, 22 or 23 is subject to annulment in pursuance of a resolution of either House of Parliament.

(5)   A statutory instrument containing an order made by the Scottish Ministers under section 22 or 23 is subject to annulment in pursuance of a resolution of the Scottish Parliament.

(6)   Any power of a Northern Ireland department to make an order or regulations under this Act is exercisable by statutory rule for the purposes of the Statutory Rules (Northern Ireland) Order 1979 (SI 1979/1573 (NI 12)).

(7)   Orders and regulations made by a Northern Ireland department under this Act are subject to negative resolution (within the meaning of section 41(6) of the Interpretation Act (Northern Ireland) 1954 (c 33 (NI))).

25   Interpretation

In this Act—

'the acquired gender' is to be construed in accordance with section 1(2),

'approved country or territory' has the meaning given by section 2(4),

'the appointed day' means the day appointed by order under section 26,

[. . .]

'enactment' includes an enactment contained in an Act of the Scottish Parliament or in any Northern Ireland legislation,

'full gender recognition certificate' and 'interim gender recognition certificate' mean the certificates issued as such under section 4 [, 5 or 5A] and 'gender recognition certificate' means either of those sorts of certificate, 'gender dysphoria' means the disorder variously referred to as gender dys-phoria, gender identity disorder and transsexualism,

'Gender Recognition Panel' (and 'Panel') is to be construed in accordance with Schedule 1,

['registered psychologist' means a person registered in the part of the register maintained under the Health Professions Order 2001 which relates to practitioner psychologists,]

'subordinate legislation' means an Order in Council, an order, rules, regulations, a scheme, a warrant, bye-laws or any other instrument made under an enactment, and

'UK birth register entry' has the meaning given by section 10(2).

26 Commencement
Apart from sections 23 to 25, this section and sections 28 and 29, this Act does not come into force until such day as the Secretary of State may appoint by order made after consulting the Scottish Ministers and the Department of Finance and Personnel in Northern Ireland.

27 Applications within two years of commencement
(1) This section applies where applications are made under section 1(1)(a) during the period of two years beginning with the appointed day ('the initial period').

(2) Section 2(1)(a) has effect as if there were inserted at the end 'or has under-gone surgical treatment for the purpose of modifying sexual characteristics,'.

(3) In the case of an application which—
    (a)   is made during the first six months of the initial period, or
    (b)   is made during the rest of the initial period and is based on the applicant having undergone surgical treatment for the purpose of modifying sexual charac-teristics,
section 2(1)(b) has effect as if for 'two' there were substituted 'six'.

(4) Subsections (5) and (6) apply in the case of an application to which sub-section (3) applies and in the case of an application—
    (a)   made during the rest of the initial period,
    (b)   based on the applicant having or having had gender dysphoria, and
    (c)   including a statutory declaration by the applicant that the applicant has lived in the acquired gender throughout the period of six years ending with the date on which the application is made.

(5) Section 3 has effect as if for subsections (1) to (3) there were substituted—
    '(1)   An application under section 1(1)(a) must include either—
        (a)   a report made by a registered medical practitioner, or
        (b)   a report made by a [registered psychologist] practising in the field of gender dysphoria.
    (2)   Where the application is based on the applicant having or having had gender dysphoria—
        (a)   the reference in subsection (1) to a registered medical practitioner is to one practising in the field of gender dysphoria, and
        (b)   that subsection is not complied with unless the report includes details of the diagnosis of the applicant's gender dysphoria.
    (3)   Subsection (1) is not complied with in a case where—
        (a)   the applicant has undergone or is undergoing treatment for the purpose of modifying sexual characteristics, or
        (b)   treatment for that purpose has been prescribed or planned for the applicant, unless the report required by that subsection includes details of it.'

(6) Paragraph 4(2) of Schedule 1 has effect with the omission of paragraph (b).

28 Extent

(2) The following provisions extend only to Scotland—
  (a) section 24(5),
  (b) Part 2 of Schedule 2,
  (c) Part 2 of Schedule 3, and
  (d) Part 2 of Schedule 4.
(3) The following provisions extend only to England and Wales and Scotland—
  (a) paragraphs 12, 14 and 16 of Schedule 5, and
  (b) Part 1 of Schedule 6.

29 Short title

(1) This Act may be cited as the Gender Recognition Act 2004.
(2) Nothing in this Act shall impose any charge on the people or on public funds, or vary the amount or incidence of or otherwise alter any such charge in any manner, or affect the assessment, levying, administration or application of any money raised by any such charge.

SCHEDULES

SCHEDULE 1
GENDER RECOGNITION PANELS

Section 1

List of persons eligible to sit

1.—(1) [Subject to sub-paragraph (1A),] the Lord Chancellor must, after consulting the Scottish Ministers and the Department of Finance and Personnel in Northern Ireland, make appointments to a list of persons eligible to sit as members of Gender Recognition Panels.

[(1A) The Lord Chancellor may appoint a person under sub-paragraph (1) only with the concurrence of all of the following:—
  (a) the Lord Chief Justice of England and Wales;
  (b) the Lord President of the Court of Session;
  (c) The Lord Chief Justice of Northern Ireland.]

(2) The only persons who may be appointed to the list are persons who—
  (a) have a relevant legal qualification ('legal members'), or
  (b) are registered medical practitioners or [registered psychologists] ('medical members').

(3) The following have a relevant legal qualification—
  (a) a person who has a 7 year general qualification within the meaning of section 71 of the Courts and Legal Services Act 1990 (c 41),
  (b) an advocate or solicitor in Scotland of at least seven years' standing, and
  (c) a member of the Bar of Northern Ireland or solicitor of the Supreme Court of Northern Ireland of at least seven years' standing.

President

2.—(1) [Subject to sub-paragraph (1A),] the Lord Chancellor must, after consulting the Scottish Ministers and the Department of Finance and Personnel in Northern Ireland—
  (a) appoint one of the legal members to be the President of Gender Recognition Panels ('the President'), and
  (b) appoint another of the legal members to be the Deputy President of Gender Recognition Panels ('the Deputy President').

[(1A) The Lord Chancellor may appoint a person under sub-paragraph (1) only with the concurrence of all of the following:—
  (a) the Lord Chief Justice of England and Wales;
  (b) the Lord President of the Court of Session;

(c)   The Lord Chief Justice of Northern Ireland.]
(2)   The Deputy President has the functions of the President—
(a)   if the President is unavailable, and
(b)   during any vacancy in the office of President.

Tenure of persons appointed to list
3.   Persons on the list—
(a)   hold and vacate their appointments in accordance with the terms on which they are appointed, and
(b)   are eligible for re-appointment at the end of their period of appointment.

Membership of Panels
4.—(1)   The President must make arrangements for determining the membership of Panels.
(2)   The arrangements must ensure that a Panel determining an application under section 1(1)(a) includes—
(a)   at least one legal member, and
(b)   at least one medical member.
5.   The arrangements must ensure that a Panel determining an application under section 1(1)(b), 5(2) [, 5A(2)] or 6(1) includes at least one legal member.

Procedure
6.—(1)   Where a Panel consists of more than one member, either the President or Deputy President or another legal member nominated by the President must preside.
(2)   Decisions of a Panel consisting of more than one member may be taken by majority vote (and, if its members are evenly split, the member presiding has a casting vote).
(3)   Panels are to determine applications in private.
(4)   A Panel must determine an application without a hearing unless the Panel considers that a hearing is necessary.
(5)   The President may, after consulting the [Administrative Justice and Tribunals Council], give directions about the practice and procedure of Panels.
(6)   Panels must give reasons for their decisions.
(7)   Where a Panel has determined an application, the Secretary of State must communicate to the applicant the Panel's decision and its reasons for making its decision.

Staff and facilities
7.   The Secretary of State may make staff and other facilities available to Panels.

Money
8.—(1)   The Secretary of State may pay sums by way of remuneration, allowances and expenses to members of Panels.
(2)   The Secretary of State may pay compensation to a person who ceases to be on the list if the Secretary of State thinks it appropriate to do so because of special circumstances.

[Delegation
8A.—(1)   The Lord Chief Justice of England and Wales may nominate a judicial office holder (as defined in section 109(4) of the Constitutional Reform Act 2005) to exercise any of his functions under this Schedule.
(2)   The Lord President of the Court of Session may nominate a judge of the Court of Session who is a member of the First or Second Division of the Inner House of that Court to exercise his functions under this Schedule.

(3) The Lord Chief Justice of Northern Ireland may nominate any of the following to exercise his functions under this Schedule—

(a) the holder of one of the offices listed in Schedule 1 to the Justice (Northern Ireland) Act 2002;

(b) a Lord Justice of Appeal (as defined in section 88 of that Act).]

Disqualification

9. In Part 3 of Schedule 1 to the House of Commons Disqualification Act 1975 (c 24) (offices disqualifying person from membership of House of Commons), at the appropriate place insert—

'Person on the list of those eligible to sit as members of a Gender Recognition Panel.'

10. In Part 3 of Schedule 1 to the Northern Ireland Assembly Disqualification Act 1975 (c 25) (offices disqualifying persons from membership of Northern Ireland Assembly), at the appropriate place insert—

'Person on the list of those eligible to sit as members of a Gender Recognition Panel.'

SCHEDULE 3
REGISTRATION

Section 10

PART 2
SCOTLAND

Introductory

12. In this Part—

'the Registrar General' means the Registrar General for Scotland, and 'the 1965 Act' means the Registration of Births, Deaths and Marriages (Scotland) Act 1965 (c 49).

Gender Recognition Register

13.—(1) The Registrar General must maintain, in the General Register Office of Births, Deaths and Marriages in Scotland, a register to be called the Gender Recognition Register.

(2) In this Part 'the Gender Recognition Register' means the register maintained under sub-paragraph (1).

(3) The form in which the Gender Recognition Register is maintained is to be determined by the Registrar General.

(4) The Gender Recognition Register is not to be open to public inspection or search.

Entries in Gender Recognition Register

14.—(1) If the Registrar General receives under section 10(1) a copy of a full gender recognition certificate issued to a person, the Registrar General must—

(a) make an entry in the Gender Recognition Register containing such particulars as may be prescribed in relation to the person's birth and any other prescribed matter, and

(b) otherwise than by annotating in any way the birth register, make traceable the connection between the UK birth register entry and the entry in the Gender Recognition Register.

(2) Sub-paragraph (1) does not apply if the gender recognition certificate was issued after an application under section 6(1) and that sub-paragraph has already been complied with in relation to the person.

(3) Information kept by the Registrar General for the purposes of sub-paragraph (1)(b) is not to be open to public inspection or search.

(4) 'Prescribed' means prescribed by regulations made by the Registrar General with the approval of the Scottish Ministers.

Indexing of entries in Gender Recognition Register

15.—(1) The Registrar General must make arrangements for each entry made in the Gender Recognition Register to be included in an index of such entries kept in the General Register Office of Births, Deaths and Marriages in Scotland.

(2) Whenever the Registrar General causes a search to be made under sub-section (2)(a) of section 38 of the 1965 Act (search of indexes of entries in the registers of births, deaths and marriages) on behalf of any person, he must also, without payment of any fee additional to the fee or fees prescribed under that section—

(a) cause a search to be made of the index of entries in the Gender Recognition Register on behalf of that person, and

(b) issue to that person an extract of any such entry provided that (disregarding, for the purposes of subsection (4)(j) of section 22, this paragraph) disclosure of the entry to the person would not constitute an offence under that section.

Extracts of entries in Gender Recognition Register

16.—(1) This paragraph applies in respect of an extract issued under paragraph 15(2)(b).

(2) Except as regards the sex and name of the person to whom it relates, the extract must have the form and content it would have had had it been an extract from the register of births of the entry relating to that person.

(3) The extract must not disclose the fact that the entry is contained in the Gender Recognition Register.

Abbreviated certificates of birth compiled from Gender Recognition Register

17. Where an abbreviated certificate of birth under section [39E] of the 1965 Act is compiled from the Gender Recognition Register, the certificate must not disclose that fact.

Gender Recognition Register: correction, re-registration etc

18. Section 18A(2) (decrees of parentage and non-parentage), section 20(1) [. . .] (re-registration in certain cases), section 42(1) and (5) (correction of errors), section 43(1), (2) and (5) to (9) (recording change of name or surname) and section 44 (Register of Corrections etc) of the 1965 Act apply in relation to the Gender Recognition Register as they apply in relation to the register of births.

Revocation of gender recognition certificate etc

19.—(1) This paragraph applies if, after an entry has been made in the Gender Recognition Register in relation to a person, the High Court or the Court of Session makes an order under section 8(6) quashing the decision to grant the person's application under section 1(1) [, 5(2) or 5A(2)].

(2) The High Court or the Court of Session must inform the Registrar General.

(3) Subject to any appeal, the Registrar General must cancel the entry in the Gender Recognition Register.

Authentication and admissibility

20. [Sections 41 and 41A] of the 1965 Act (authentication of extracts etc and their admissibility as evidence) [apply] in relation to the Gender Recognition Register as in relation to the registers kept under the provisions of that Act.

ANTISOCIAL BEHAVIOUR ETC (SCOTLAND) ACT 2004
(2004, asp 8)

PART 9
PARENTING ORDERS

Applications

102 Applications

(1) The court may make a parenting order in respect of a parent of a child where—

(a) subsection (2) or (3) applies; and

(b) the Scottish Ministers have notified the court that the local authority for the area in which the parent ordinarily resides has made arrangements that would enable the order to be complied with.

(2) This subsection applies where—

(a) the application for the order is made by the appropriate local authority; and

(b) the court is satisfied that—

(i) the behaviour condition; or

(ii) the conduct condition,

is met.

(3) This subsection applies where—

(a) the application for the order is made by the Principal Reporter, and

(b) the court is satisfied that—

(i) the behaviour condition;

(ii) the conduct condition; or

(iii) the welfare condition,

is met.

(4) The behaviour condition is—

(a) that the child has engaged in antisocial behaviour; and

(b) that the making of the order is desirable in the interests of preventing the child from engaging in further such behaviour.

(5) The conduct condition is—

(a) that the child has engaged in criminal conduct; and

(b) that the making of the order is desirable in the interests of preventing the child from engaging in further such conduct.

(6) The welfare condition is that the making of the order is desirable in the interests of improving the welfare of the child.

(7) For the purposes of subsection (5), a child engages in criminal conduct if the child engages in conduct that constitutes a criminal offence (or would do so if the child had attained the age of 8 years).

(8) An application under this section shall be made by summary application to the sheriff of the sheriffdom where the parent ordinarily resides.

(9) Before an application is made under this section—

(a) by a local authority, it shall consult the Principal Reporter;

(b) by the Principal Reporter, the Principal Reporter shall consult the appropriate local authority.

(10) In this section, 'appropriate local authority' means the local authority for the area where the child ordinarily resides.

Parenting orders

103 Parenting orders

(1) A parenting order is an order requiring the specified person—

(a) to comply, during a specified period—

(i) beginning with the making of the order; and

      (ii)   not exceeding 12 months,
with such requirements as are specified; and
   (b)   subject to subsection (2), to attend, during a specified period—
      (i)   falling within the specified period mentioned in paragraph (a); and
      (ii)   not exceeding 3 months,
such counselling or guidance sessions as may be directed by a supervising officer appointed by the relevant local authority.

(2)   Where a parenting order has been made in respect of the person on a previous occasion in the interests of the child in whose interests the order is to be made, the order need not include a requirement under subsection (1)(b).

(3)   The Scottish Ministers may by order amend the number of months mentioned in—
   (a)   subsection (1)(a)(ii); and
   (b)   subsection (1)(b)(ii).

(5)   In subsection (1), 'specified' means specified in the order.

Matters following making of order

104   Notification of making of order

(1)   The clerk of the court by which a parenting order is made shall cause a copy of the order to be—
   (a)   given to the person specified in the order; or
   (b)   sent to the person so specified by registered post or the recorded delivery service.

(2)   A certificate of posting of a letter sent under subsection (1)(b) issued by the postal operator concerned shall be sufficient evidence of the sending of the letter on the day specified in such certificate.

(3)   In subsection (2), 'postal operator' has the meaning given by section 125(1) of the Postal Services Act 2000 (c 26).

105   Review of order

(1)   On the application of a relevant applicant the court that made a parenting order may, if it considers that it would be appropriate to do so—
   (a)   revoke the order; or
   (b)   vary the order by—
      (i)   deleting any of the requirements specified in the order;
      (ii)   adding a new requirement;
      (iii)   altering the period specified for the purpose of section 103(1)(b).

(2)   In subsection (1), 'relevant applicant' means—
   (a)   the person specified in the order;
   (b)   the child in respect of whom the order was made;
   (c)   the local authority for the area in which the person specified in the order ordinarily resides.

(3)   Before an application is made under subsection (1) by a local authority, it shall consult the Principal Reporter.

(4)   Where an application under subsection (1) for the revocation or, as the case may be, variation, of a parenting order is refused, another such application by the same applicant under that subsection for revocation or, as the case may be, variation, may be made only with the consent of the court that made the order.

(5)   Where the court that made a parenting order is satisfied that—
   (a)   the person specified in the order proposes to change, or has changed, the person's place of ordinary residence; and
   (b)   it is appropriate to make an order specifying the sheriff of another sheriffdom as the court that may entertain applications under subsection (1),
it may make such an order; and in such a case, this section shall be read as if references to the court that made the order were references to that sheriff.

106 Appeals

An interlocutor—

(a) varying, or refusing to vary a parenting order; or

(b) making a parenting order under section 13,

is an appealable interlocutor.

107 Failure to comply with order

(1) If the person specified in a parenting order fails without reasonable excuse to comply with—

(a) any requirement specified in the order; or

(b) any direction given under the order,

the person shall be guilty of an offence.

(2) A person guilty of an offence under subsection (1) shall be liable on summary conviction to a fine not exceeding level 3 on the standard scale.

(3) In determining the sentence to be imposed on a person guilty of an offence under subsection (1) a court shall take into consideration the welfare of any child in respect of whom the person is a parent.

General requirements

108 Procedural requirements

(1) Before making, varying or revoking a parenting order, a court shall—

(a) having regard to the age and maturity of the child, so far as practicable—

(i) give the child an opportunity to indicate whether the child wishes to express views; and

(ii) if the child so wishes, give the child an opportunity to express those views;

(b) give the parent the opportunity to be heard;

(c) obtain information about the family circumstances of the parent and the likely effect of the order on those circumstances.

(2) Before making a parenting order, the court shall explain in ordinary language—

(a) the effect of the order and of the requirements proposed to be included in it;

(b) the consequences of failing to comply with the order;

(c) the powers the court has under section 81; and

(d) the entitlement of the parent to appeal against the making of the order.

(3) Before varying or revoking a parenting order, the court shall explain in ordinary language the effect of the variation or, as the case may be, revocation.

(4) Subsections (1A) and (1B) apply only where the parent is present in court.

(5) Failure to comply with subsection (1A) or (1B) shall not affect the validity of the order made.

(6) Without prejudice to the generality of subsection (1)(a), a child who is at least 12 years of age shall be presumed to be of sufficient age and maturity to form a view.

109 General considerations relating to making, varying and revoking order

(1) Where a court is determining whether to make, vary or revoke a parenting order its paramount consideration shall be the welfare of the child.

(2) Where a court is determining whether to make a parenting order it shall have regard to—

(a) such views as the child has expressed in relation to that matter by virtue of paragraph (a) of subsection (1) of section 108;

(b) the information obtained in relation to that matter by virtue of paragraph (c) of that subsection;

(c) whether (and if so the extent to which) the parent has, at any time that appears to the court to be relevant, taken relevant voluntary steps; and

(d)   any other behaviour of the parent that appears to the court to be relevant.

(3)   Where a court is determining whether to vary or revoke a parenting order it shall have regard to—

(a)   such views as the child has expressed in relation to that matter by virtue of paragraph (a) of subsection (1) of section 108;

(b)   the information obtained in relation to that matter by virtue of paragraph (c) of that subsection; and

(c)   any behaviour of the parent that appears to the court to be relevant.

(4)   In subsection (2)(c) 'relevant voluntary steps' means—

(a)   where the court is determining whether to—

(i)   make a parenting order under section 13; or

(ii)   make a parenting order under subsection (1) of section 102 in respect of the condition mentioned in subsection (4) of that section,

voluntary steps intended to be in the interests of preventing the child from engaging in antisocial behaviour;

(b)   where the court is determining whether to make a parenting order under subsection (1) of section 102 in respect of the condition mentioned in subsection (5) of that section, voluntary steps intended to be in the interests of preventing the child from engaging in criminal conduct;

(c)   where the court is determining whether to make a parenting order under subsection (1) of section 102 in respect of the condition mentioned in subsection (6) of that section, voluntary steps intended to be in the interests of improving the welfare of the child.

110   Account to be taken of religion, work and education

(1)   A court shall ensure that the requirements of a parenting order made by it avoid, so far as practicable—

(a)   any conflict with the religious beliefs of the person specified in the order; and

(b)   any interference with times at which that person normally works (or carries out voluntary work) or attends an educational establishment.

(2)   The supervising officer appointed by a local authority in respect of a parenting order shall ensure that the directions given by the officer avoid, so far as practicable, the matters mentioned in subsection (1)(a) and (b).

Miscellaneous

111   Restriction on reporting proceedings relating to parenting orders

(1)   Subject to subsection (2), a person shall be guilty of an offence if the person publishes, anywhere in the world, any matter in respect of relevant proceedings which is intended, or likely to, identify—

(a)   the parent concerned in the proceedings (the 'person concerned');

(b)   any address as being that of the person concerned;

(c)   the child concerned in the proceedings;

(d)   any other child—

(i)   who is a member of the same household as the person concerned; or

(ii)   of whom the person concerned is a parent; or

(e)   any—

(i)   address; or

(ii)   school,

as being that of a child mentioned in paragraph (c) or (d).

(2)   In relevant proceedings, the court may, in the interests of justice, order that subsection (1) shall not apply to the proceedings to such extent as the court considers appropriate.

(3)   A person guilty of an offence under subsection (1) shall be liable on summary conviction to a fine not exceeding level 4 on the standard scale.

(4)   It shall be a defence for a person charged with an offence under subsection (1) to show that the person—

   (a)   did not know; and

   (b)   had no reason to suspect,

that the published matter was intended, or was likely, to identify the person concerned, child, address or school (as the case may be).

(5)   Section 46 of the Children and Young Persons (Scotland) Act 1937 (c 37) shall apply in relation to relevant proceedings only in respect of a person concerned in the proceedings as a witness.

(6)   A child in whose interests a parenting order has been made shall be regarded as a person who falls within subsection (1)(a) of section 47 of the Criminal Procedure (Scotland) Act 1995 (c 46) for the purposes of that section in its application to proceedings in respect of the commission of an offence under section 83(1) in respect of that order.

(7)   In this section—

'programme service' has the meaning given by section 201 of the Broadcasting Act 1990 (c 42);

'publishes' includes—

   (a)   causing to be published; and

   (b)   publishing in a programme service,

and 'published' shall be construed accordingly; and

'relevant proceedings' means—

   (a)   proceedings before a sheriff for the purpose of considering whether to make a parenting order under section 13(1);

   (b)   proceedings before a sheriff on an application for the making of a parenting order under section 102(1);

   (c)   proceedings before a sheriff on an application for the variation, or revocation, of a parenting order under section 105(1);

   (d)   proceedings before a sheriff for the purpose of considering whether to make an order under section 105(5);

   (e)   an appeal arising from proceedings such as are mentioned in paragraphs (a) to (d).

112   Conduct of proceedings by reporters

(1)   The Scottish Ministers may by regulations empower a reporter, whether or not the reporter is an advocate or solicitor, to conduct proceedings—

   (a)   before a sheriff—

      (i)   on an application by the Principal Reporter for the making of a parenting order;

      (ii)   on an application for the variation, or revocation, of a parenting order made on the application of the Principal Reporter, under section 105(1); or

      (iii)   for the purpose of considering whether to make an order under section 105(5) in respect of a parenting order made on the application of the Principal Reporter; or

   (b)   before a sheriff principal, on any appeal arising from proceedings such as are mentioned in paragraph (a).

(2)   Regulations under subsection (1) may prescribe such requirements as the Scottish Ministers think fit as to—

   (a)   qualifications;

   (b)   training; or

   (c)   experience,

necessary for a reporter to be so empowered.

(3)   In this section 'reporter' means—

   (a)   the Principal Reporter; and

   (b)   any officer of the Scottish Children's Reporter Administration to whom there is delegated, under section 131(1) of the Local Government etc (Scotland)

Act 1994 (c 39), any of the functions which the Principal Reporter has under any enactment.

113 Initial investigations by Principal Reporter

(1) For the purpose of determining whether to make an application for the making of a parenting order under section 102, the Principal Reporter may make such investigations as the Principal Reporter considers appropriate.

(2) On a request made by the Principal Reporter for the purpose mentioned in subsection (1), a local authority shall supply to the Principal Reporter a report on—

(a) the child in relation to whom the Principal Reporter is determining whether to make the application;

(b) the parent in relation to whom the Principal Reporter is determining whether to make the application; and

(c) such circumstances concerning—

(i) the child; and

(ii) the parent,

as appear to the Principal Reporter to be relevant.

114 Power of court to direct reporter to consider application for parenting order

Where, in any proceedings (other than proceedings under section 4 or 102), it appears to a court that it might be appropriate for a parenting order to be made in respect of a parent of a child, the court may require the Principal Reporter to consider whether to apply under section 102 for such an order.

115 Guidance about parenting orders

A person (other than a court) shall, in discharging functions by virtue of section 13 or this Part, have regard to any guidance given by the Scottish Ministers about—

(a) the discharge of those functions; and

(b) matters arising in connection with the discharge of those functions.

116 *[Amends Children (Scotland) Act 1995]*

Interpretation

117 Interpretation of Part 9

In this Part—

'child' means a person who is under the age of 16 years;

'parent' means any individual who is a relevant person as defined in section 93(2)(b) of the Children (Scotland) Act 1995 (c 36) (the references to a 'person' in that section being read as references to an individual);

'parenting order' has the meaning given by section 103(1).

CIVIL PARTNERSHIP ACT 2004
(2004, c 33)

PART 1
INTRODUCTION

1 Civil partnership

(1) A civil partnership is a relationship between two people of the same sex ('civil partners')—

(a) which is formed when they register as civil partners of each other—

(i) in England or Wales (under Part 2),

(ii) in Scotland (under Part 3),

(iii) in Northern Ireland (under Part 4), or

(iv) outside the United Kingdom under an Order in Council made under Chapter 1 of Part 5 (registration at British consulates etc or by armed forces personnel), or

(b)   which they are treated under Chapter 2 of Part 5 as having formed (at the time determined under that Chapter) by virtue of having registered an overseas relationship.

(2)   Subsection (1) is subject to the provisions of this Act under or by virtue of which a civil partnership is void.

(3)   A civil partnership ends only on death, dissolution or annulment.

(4)   The references in subsection (3) to dissolution and annulment are to dissolution and annulment having effect under or recognised in accordance with this Act.

(5)   References in this Act to an overseas relationship are to be read in accordance with Chapter 2 of Part 5.

PART 3
CIVIL PARTNERSHIP: SCOTLAND

CHAPTER 1
FORMATION AND ELIGIBILITY

85   Formation of civil partnership by registration

(1)   For the purposes of section 1, two people are to be regarded as having registered as civil partners of each other once each of them has signed the civil partnership schedule, in the presence of—

(a)   each other,
(b)   two witnesses both of whom have attained the age of 16, and
(c)   the authorised registrar,

(all being present at a registration office or at a place agreed under section 93).

(2)   But the two people must be eligible to be so registered.

(3)   Subsection (1) applies regardless of whether subsection (4) is complied with.

(4)   After the civil partnership schedule has been signed under subsection (1), it must also be signed, in the presence of the civil partners and each other by—

(a)   each of the two witnesses, and
(b)   the authorised registrar.

86   Eligibility

(1)   Two people are not eligible to register in Scotland as civil partners of each other if—

(a)   they are not of the same sex,
(b)   they are related in a forbidden degree,
(c)   either has not attained the age of 16,
(d)   either is married or already in civil partnership, or
(e)   either is incapable of—
(i)   understanding the nature of civil partnership, or
(ii)   validly consenting to its formation.

(2)   Subject to [subsection (3)], a man is related in a forbidden degree to another man if related to him in a degree specified in column 1 of Schedule 10 and a woman is related in a forbidden degree to another woman if related to her in a degree specified in column 2 of that Schedule.

(3)   A man and any man related to him in a degree specified in column 1 of paragraph 2 of Schedule 10, or a woman and any woman related to her in a degree specified in column 2 of that paragraph, are not related in a forbidden degree if—

(a)   both persons have attained the age of 21, and
(b)   the younger has not at any time before attaining the age of 18 lived in the same household as the elder and been treated by the elder as a child of the elder's family.

[(4)   Paragraph 2 of Schedule 10 has effect subject to the modifications specified in subsection (5) in the case of a person (here the 'relevant person') whose gender has become the acquired gender under the Gender Recognition Act 2004 (c 7).

(5)   The reference in that paragraph to—

(a)   a former wife of the relevant person includes any former husband of the relevant person, and

(b)   a former husband of the relevant person includes any former wife of the relevant person.]

[(5A)   This section and Schedule 10 have effect as if any reference in that Schedule to a mother within any of the degrees of relationship specified in either column included a woman who is a parent of a child by virtue of section 42 or 43 of the Human Fertilisation and Embryology Act 2008 (c 22).]

[. . .]

(8)   References in this section and in Schedule 10 to relationships and degrees of relationship are to be construed in accordance with section 1(1) of the Law Reform (Parent and Child) (Scotland) Act 1986 (c 9).

(9)   For the purposes of this section, a degree of relationship specified in paragraph 1 of Schedule 10 exists whether it is of the full blood or the half blood.

(10)   [Amends Adoption (Scotland) Act 1978.]

CHAPTER 2
REGISTRATION

87   Appointment of authorised registrars

For the purpose of affording reasonable facilities throughout Scotland for registration as civil partners, the Registrar General—

(a)   is to appoint such number of district registrars as he thinks necessary, and

(b)   may, in respect of any district for which he has made an appointment under paragraph (a), appoint one or more assistant registrars,

as persons who may carry out such registration (in this Part referred to as 'authorised registrars').

88   Notice of proposed civil partnership

(1)   In order to register as civil partners, each of the intended civil partners must submit to the district registrar a notice, in the prescribed form [. . .] of intention to enter civil partnership (in this Part referred to as a 'notice of proposed civil partnership').

(2)   [Each of the intended civil partners must also pay the prescribed fee and submit the following documents—

(a)   that person's birth certificate,]

(b)   if that person has previously been married or in civil partnership and—

(i)   the marriage or civil partnership has been dissolved, a copy of the decree of divorce or dissolution, or

(ii)   the other party to that marriage or civil partnership has died, the death certificate of that other party, and

(c)   if that person has previously ostensibly been married or in civil partnership but decree of annulment has been obtained, a copy of that decree.

(3)   If a person is unable to submit a certificate or decree required by subsection (2) he may instead make a declaration to that effect, stating what the reasons are; and he must provide the district registrar with such—

(a)   information in respect of the matters to which the certificate or document would have related, and

(b)   documentary evidence in support of that information, as the district registrar may require.

(4)   If a document submitted under subsection (2) or (3) is in a language other than English, the person submitting it must attach to the document a translation of it in English, certified by the translator as a correct translation.

(5)   A person submitting a notice under subsection (1) must make and [attest in the prescribed manner] the necessary declaration (the form for which must be included in any form prescribed for the notice).

[(5A)   Regulations prescribing the form of the notice of proposed civil partnership may make provision for the notice to be electronic rather than paper-based.]

(6)   The necessary declaration is a declaration that the person submitting the notice believes that the intended civil partners are eligible to be in civil partnership with each other.

89   Civil partnership notice book

(1)   On receipt of a notice of proposed civil partnership, the district registrar is to enter in a book (to be known as 'the civil partnership book') supplied to him for that purpose by the Registrar General such particulars, extracted from the notice, as may be prescribed and the date of receipt by him of that notice.

(2)   The form and content of any page of that book is to be prescribed.

90   Publicisation

(1)   Where notices of a proposed civil partnership are [received by] a district registrar, he must, as soon as practicable after [such receipt] (or, if the two documents are not [received] on the same day, after [the first is received]), publicise the relevant information and send it to the Registrar General who must also publicise it.

(2)   'The relevant information' means—
    (a)   the names of the intended civil partners, and
    (b)   the date on which it is intended to register them as civil partners of each other, being a date more than 14 days after publicisation by the district registrar under subsection (1).

(3)   Paragraph (b) of subsection (2) is subject to section 91.

(4)   The manner in which and means by which relevant information is to be publicised are to be prescribed.

91   Early registration

An authorised registrar who receives a request in writing from one or both of two intended civil partners that they should be registered as civil partners of each other on a date specified in the request (being a date 14 days or fewer after publicisation by the district registrar under subsection (1) of section 90) may, provided that he is authorised to do so by the Registrar General, fix that date as the date for registration; and if a date is so fixed, paragraph (b) of subsection (2) of that section is to be construed as if it were a reference to that date.

92   Objections to registration

(1)   Any person may at any time before the registration in Scotland of two people as civil partners of each other submit in writing an objection to such registration to the district registrar.

[(1A)   For the purpose of subsection (1), an objection which is submitted to the registrar by electronic means is to be treated as in writing if it is received in a form which is legible and capable of being used for subsequent reference.]

(2)   But where the objection is that the intended civil partners are not eligible to be in civil partnership with each other because either is incapable of—
    (a)   understanding the nature of civil partnership, or
    (b)   validly consenting to its formation,
it shall [not be treated as submitted until there has also been produced to the registrar] a supporting certificate [attested in the prescribed manner] by a registered medical practitioner.

(3)   A person claiming that he may have reason to submit such an objection may, free of charge and at any time when the registration office at which a notice of proposed civil partnership to which the objection would relate is open for public business, inspect any relevant entry in the civil partnership book.

(4)   Where the district registrar receives an objection in accordance with subsection (1) he must—

(a)   in any case where he is satisfied that the objection relates to no more than a misdescription or inaccuracy in a notice submitted under section 88(1)—

(i)   notify the intended civil partners of the nature of the objection and make such enquiries into the matter mentioned in it as he thinks fit, and

(ii)   subject to the approval of the Registrar General, make any necessary correction to any document relating to the proposed civil partnership, or

(b)   in any other case—

(i)   at once notify the Registrar General of the objection, and

(ii)   pending consideration of the objection by the Registrar General, suspend the completion or issue of the civil partnership schedule in respect of the proposed civil partnership.

(5)   If the Registrar General is satisfied, on consideration of an objection of which he has received notification under subsection (4)(b)(i) that—

(a)   there is a legal impediment to registration, he must direct the district registrar not to register the intended civil partners and to notify them accordingly, or

(b)   there is no such impediment, he must inform the district registrar to that effect.

(6)   For the purposes of this section and section 94, there is a legal impediment to registration where the intended civil partners are not eligible to be in civil partnership with each other.

93   Place of registration

(1)   Two people may be registered as civil partners of each other at a registration office or any other place which they and the local registration authority agree is to be the place of registration.

(2)   The place of registration may, if the approval of the Registrar General is obtained, be [—

(a)   in a registration district other than that of the authorised registrar carrying out the registration, or

(b)   in or on Scottish waters.]

(3)   But the place must not be in religious premises, that is to say premises which—

(a)   are used solely or mainly for religious purposes, or

(b)   have been so used and have not subsequently been used solely or mainly for other purposes.

(4)   'Local registration authority' has the meaning given by section 5(3) of the 1965 Act.

[(5)   'Scottish waters' has the meaning given by section 26(2) of the Marriage (Scotland) Act 1977 (c 15).]

94   The civil partnership schedule

Where—

(a)   the district registrar has received a notice of proposed civil partnership in respect of each of the intended civil partners and—

(i)   is satisfied that there is no legal impediment to their registration as civil partners of each other, or

(ii)   as the case may be, is informed under section 92(5)(b) that there is no such impediment,

(b)   the 14 days mentioned in paragraph (b) of section 90(2) have expired (or as the case may be the date which, by virtue of section 91, that paragraph is to be construed as a reference to has been reached), and

(c)   the period which has elapsed since the day of receipt of the notices by him (or, if the two notices were not received on the same day, since the day of receipt of the later) does not exceed 3 months, he is to complete a civil partnership schedule in the prescribed form.

95 Further provision as to registration

(1) Before the persons present sign in accordance with section 85 the authorised registrar is to require the intended civil partners to confirm that (to the best of their knowledge) the particulars set out in the civil partnership schedule are correct.

(2) As soon as practicable after the civil partnership schedule has been signed, the authorised registrar must cause those particulars to be entered in a register (to be known as the 'civil partnership register') supplied to him for that purpose by the Registrar General.

(3) The form and content of any page of that register is to be prescribed.

(4) A fee payable by the intended civil partners for their registration as civil partners of each other is to be prescribed.

[95A Validity following entry in civil partnership register

(1) Subsection (2) applies where the particulars set out in a civil partnership schedule signed in accordance with section 85 are entered in the civil partnership register in pursuance of section 95(2).

(2) The validity of the registration as civil partners to which the schedule relates is not to be questioned in any legal proceedings on the ground of failure to comply with a requirement or restriction imposed by or under this Part.

(3) Subsection (2)—

    (a) is subject to section 85(2), and

    (b) does not prejudice section 100.]

96 Civil partnership with former spouse

(1) Where an intended civil partner has a full gender recognition certificate issued under section 5(1) of the Gender Recognition Act 2004 (c 7) and the other intended civil partner was the other party in the proceedings in which the certificate was issued, the procedures for their registration as civil partners of each other may—

    (a) if they so elect, and

    (b) if each of them submits a notice under section 88(1) within 30 days after the certificate is issued,

be expedited as follows.

(2) The registration may take place on any of the 30 days immediately following—

    (a) that on which the notices are submitted, or

    (b) (if the two notices are not submitted on the same day) that on which the later is submitted.

(3) And accordingly there are to be disregarded—

    (a) in section 90—

        (i) in subsection (2)(b), the words from 'being' to the end, and

        (ii) subsection (3),

    (b) section 91, and

    (c) in section 94, paragraph (b).

97 Certificates of no impediment for Part 2 purposes

(1) This section applies where—

    (a) two people propose to register as civil partners of each other under Chapter 1 of Part 2, and

    (b) one of them ('A') resides in Scotland but the other ('B') resides in England or Wales.

(2) A may submit a notice of intention to register under section 88 as if A and B intended to register as civil partners in the district in which A resides.

(3) If the district registrar is satisfied (after consultation, if he considers it

necessary, with the Registrar General) that there is no impediment (in terms of section 92(6)) to A registering as B's civil partner, he must issue a certificate to A in the prescribed form that there is not known to be any such impediment.

(4) But the certificate may not be issued to A earlier than 14 days after the receipt (as entered in the civil partnership notice book) of the notice under subsection (2) unless—

(a)   the circumstances are as mentioned in section 96(1), and

(b)   A makes an election for the certificate to be issued as soon as possible.

(5) Any person may, at any time before a certificate is issued under subsection (3), submit to the district registrar an objection in writing to its issue.

(6) Any objection made under subsection (5) must be taken into account by the district registrar in deciding whether he is satisfied that there is no legal impediment to A registering as B's civil partner.

[98   Application of certain provisions to civil partnership

(1) The following sections of the 1965 Act apply in relation to the civil partnership register as they apply in relation to the registers of births, marriages and deaths—

(a)   section 34 (examination and transmission of registers),

(b)   section 38(1) and (2) (search of indexes kept by Registrar General),

(c)   section 39C (provision of information to district registrars), and

(d)   section 44 (Register of Corrections Etc).

[. . .].

99   Correction of errors in civil partnership register

(1) No alteration is to be made in the civil partnership register except as authorised by or under this or any other Act ('Act' including an Act of the Scottish Parliament).

(2) Any clerical error in the register or error in it of a kind prescribed may be corrected by the district registrar.

(3) The Registrar General may authorise district examiners ('district examiner' having the meaning given by section 2(1) of the 1965 Act) to correct any error in the register of a type specified by him which they discover during an examination under section 34 of the 1965 Act.

100   Offences

(1) A person ('A') commits an offence who registers in Scotland as the civil partner of another person ('B') knowing that either or both—

(a)   A is already married to or in civil partnership with a person other than B, or

(b)   B is already married to or in civil partnership with a person other than A.

(2) A person commits an offence who knowingly—

(a)   falsifies or forges any civil partnership document (that is to say, any document issued or made, or purporting to be issued or made, or required, under this Part),

(b)   uses, or gives or sends to any person as genuine, any false or forged civil partnership document,

(c)   being an authorised registrar, purports to register two people as civil partners of each other before any civil partnership schedule available to him at the time of registration has been duly completed,

(d)   not being an authorised registrar, conducts himself in such a way as to lead intended civil partners to believe that he is authorised to register them as civil partners of each other,

(e)   being an authorised registrar, purports to register two people as civil partners of each other without both of them being present, or

(f)   being an authorised registrar, purports to register two people as civil partners of each other in a place other than a registration office or a place agreed under section 93.

(3)   A person guilty of an offence under subsection (1) or (2) is liable—

(a)   on conviction on indictment, to imprisonment for a term not exceeding 2 years or to a fine (or both);

(b)   on summary conviction, to imprisonment for a term not exceeding 3 months or to a fine not exceeding level 3 on the standard scale (or both).

(4)   Summary proceedings for an offence under subsection (1) or (2) may be commenced at any time within 3 months after evidence sufficient in the opinion of the Lord Advocate to justify the proceedings comes to his knowledge or within 12 months after the offence is committed (whichever period last expires).

(5)   Subsection (3) of section 136 of the Criminal Procedure (Scotland) Act 1995 (c 46) (time limits) has effect for the purposes of this section as it has for the purposes of that section.

CHAPTER 3
OCCUPANCY RIGHTS AND TENANCIES

Occupancy rights

101   Occupancy rights

(1)   Where, apart from the provisions of this Chapter, one civil partner in a civil partnership is entitled, or permitted by a third party, to occupy a family home of the civil partnership (that civil partner being referred in this Chapter as an 'entitled partner') and the other civil partner is not so entitled or permitted (a 'non-entitled partner'), the non-entitled partner has, subject to the provisions of this Chapter, the following rights—

(a)   if in occupation, a right to continue to occupy the family home;

(b)   if not in occupation, a right to enter into and occupy the family home.

(2)   The rights conferred by subsection (1) to continue to occupy or, as the case may be, to enter and occupy the family home include, without prejudice to their generality, the right to do so together with any child of the family.

(3)   In subsection (1), an 'entitled partner' includes a civil partner who is entitled, or permitted by a third party, to occupy the family home along with an individual who is not the other civil partner only if that individual has waived a right of occupation in favour of the civil partner so entitled or permitted.

(4)   If the entitled partner refuses to allow the non-entitled partner to exercise the right conferred by subsection (1)(b), the non-entitled partner may exercise that right only with the leave of the Court of Session or the sheriff under section 103(3) or (4).

(5)   A non-entitled partner may renounce in writing the rights mentioned in paragraphs (a) and (b) of subsection (1) only—

(a)   in a particular family home, or

(b)   in a particular property which it is intended by the civil partners will become their family home.

(6)   A renunciation under subsection (5) has effect only if, at the time of making the renunciation, the non-entitled partner swears or affirms before a notary public that it is made freely and without coercion of any kind.

[(6A)   Subject to subsection (5), if—

(a)   there has been no cohabitation between an entitled partner and a non-entitled partner during a continuous period of two years, and

(b)   during that period the non-entitled partner has not occupied the family home, the non-entitled partner shall, on the expiry of that period, cease to have occupancy rights in the family home.

(6B)   A non-entitled partner who has ceased to have occupancy rights by virtue of subsection (6A) may not apply to the court for an order under section 103(1).]

(7)   In this Part—

'child of the family' means [any child or grandchild of either civil partner, and any person who has been brought up or treated by either civil partner as if the person were a child of that partner, whatever the age of such a child, grandchild or person], and

'family' means the civil partners in the civil partnership, together with any child [, grandchild or person so treated] by them.

(8)   In subsection (6), 'notary public' includes any person duly authorised, by the law of the country other than Scotland in which the swearing or affirmation takes place, to administer oaths or receive affirmations in that other country.

102   Occupancy: subsidiary and consequential rights

(1)   For the purpose of securing the occupancy rights of a non-entitled partner, that partner is, in relation to a family home, entitled without the consent of the entitled partner—

(a)   to make any payment due by the entitled partner in respect of rent, rates, secured loan instalments, interest or other outgoings (not being outgoings on repairs or improvements);

(b)   to perform any other obligation incumbent on the entitled partner (not being an obligation in respect of non-essential repairs or improvements);

(c)   to enforce performance of an obligation by a third party which that third party has undertaken to the entitled partner to the extent that the entitled partner may enforce such performance;

(d)   to carry out such essential repairs as the entitled partner may carry out;

(e)   to carry out such non-essential repairs or improvements as may be authorised by an order of the court, being such repairs or improvements as the entitled partner may carry out and which the court considers to be appropriate for the reasonable enjoyment of the occupancy rights;

(f)   to take such other steps, for the purpose of protecting the occupancy rights of the non-entitled partner, as the entitled partner may take to protect the occupancy rights of the entitled partner.

(2)   Any payment made under subsection (1)(a) or any obligation performed under subsection (1)(b) has effect in relation to the rights of a third party as if the payment were made or the obligation were performed by the entitled partner; and the performance of an obligation which has been enforced under subsection (1)(c) has effect as if it had been enforced by the entitled partner.

(3)   Where there is an entitled and a non-entitled partner, the court, on the application of either of them, may, having regard in particular to the respective financial circumstances of the partners, make an order apportioning expenditure incurred or to be incurred by either partner—

(a)   without the consent of the other partner, on any of the items mentioned in paragraphs (a) and (d) of subsection (1);

(b)   with the consent of the other partner, on anything relating to a family home.

(4)   Where both partners are entitled, or permitted by a third party, to occupy a family home—

(a)   either partner is entitled, without the consent of the other partner, to carry out such non-essential repairs or improvements as may be authorised by an order of the court, being such repairs or improvements as the court considers to be appropriate for the reasonable enjoyment of the occupancy rights;

(b)   the court, on the application of either partner, may, having regard in particular to the respective financial circumstances of the partners, make an order apportioning expenditure incurred or to be incurred by either partner, with or without the consent of the other partner, on anything relating to the family home.

(5)   Where one partner ('A') owns or hires, or is acquiring under a hire-purchase or conditional sale agreement, furniture and plenishings in a family home—

(a)   the other partner may, without the consent of A—

(i)   make any payment due by A which is necessary, or take any other step which A is entitled to take, to secure the possession or use of any such furniture and plenishings (and any such payment is to have effect in relation to the rights of a third party as if it were made by A), or

(ii)   carry out such essential repairs to the furniture and plenishings as A is entitled to carry out;

(b)   the court, on the application of either partner, may, having regard in particular to the respective financial circumstances of the partners, make an order apportioning expenditure incurred or to be incurred by either partner—

(i)   without the consent of the other partner, in making payments under a hire, hire-purchase or conditional sale agreement, or in paying interest charges in respect of the furniture and plenishings, or in carrying out essential repairs to the furniture and plenishings, or

(ii)   with the consent of the other partner, on anything relating to the furniture or plenishings.

(6)   An order under subsection (3), (4)(b) or (5)(b) may require one partner to make a payment to the other partner in implementation of the apportionment.

(7)   Any application under subsection (3), (4)(b) or (5)(b) is to be made within 5 years after the date on which any payment in respect of such incurred expenditure was made.

(8)   Where—

(a)   the entitled partner is a tenant of a family home,

(b)   possession of it is necessary in order to continue the tenancy, and

(c)   the entitled partner abandons such possession,

the tenancy is continued by such possession by the non-entitled partner.

(9)   In this section 'improvements' includes alterations and enlargement.

103   Regulation by court of rights of occupancy of family home

(1)   [Subject to section 101(6A),] where there is an entitled and a non-entitled partner, or where both partners are entitled, or permitted by a third party, to occupy a family home, either partner may apply to the court for an order—

(a)   declaring the occupancy rights of the applicant partner;

(b)   enforcing the occupancy rights of the applicant partner;

(c)   restricting the occupancy rights of the non-applicant partner;

(d)   regulating the exercise by either partner of his or her occupancy rights;

(e)   protecting the occupancy rights of the applicant partner in relation to the other partner.

(2)   Where one partner owns or hires, or is acquiring under a hire-purchase or conditional sale agreement, furniture and plenishings in a family home and the other partner has occupancy rights in that home, that other person may apply to the court for an order granting to the applicant the possession or use in the family home of any such furniture and plenishings; but, subject to section 102, an order under this subsection does not prejudice the rights of any third party in relation to the non-performance of any obligation under such hire-purchase or conditional sale agreement.

(3)   The court is to grant an application under subsection (1)(a) if it appears to the court that the application relates to a family home; and, on an application under any of paragraphs (b) to (e) of subsection (1) or under subsection (2), the court may make such order relating to the application as appears to it to be just and reasonable having regard to all the circumstances of the case including—

(a)   the conduct of the partners, whether in relation to each other or otherwise,

(b)   the respective needs and financial resources of the partners,

(c)   the needs of any child of the family,

(d)   the extent (if any) to which—

(i)   the family home, and

(ii)   in relation only to an order under subsection (2), any item of furniture and plenishings referred to in that subsection, is used in connection with a trade, business or profession of either partner, and

(e)   whether the entitled partner offers or has offered to make available to the non-entitled partner any suitable alternative accommodation.

(4)   Pending the making of an order under subsection (3), the court, on the application of either partner, may make such interim order as it considers necessary or expedient in relation to—

(a)   the residence of either partner in the home to which the application relates,

(b)   the personal effects of either partner or of any child of the family, or

(c)   the furniture and plenishings,

but an interim order may be made only if the non-applicant partner has been afforded an opportunity of being heard by or represented before the court.

(5)   The court is not to make an order under subsection (3) or (4) if it appears that the effect of the order would be to exclude the non-applicant partner from the family home.

(6)   If the court makes an order under subsection (3) or (4) which requires the delivery to one partner of anything which has been left in or removed from the family home, it may also grant a warrant authorising a [judicial officer] to enter the family home or other premises occupied by the other partner and to search for and take possession of the thing required to be delivered, (if need be by opening shut and lockfast places) and to deliver the thing in accordance with the order.

(7)   A warrant granted under subsection (6) is to be executed only after expiry of such period as the court is to specify in the order for delivery.

(8)   Where it appears to the court—

(a)   on the application of a non-entitled partner, that the applicant has suffered a loss of occupancy rights or that the quality of the applicant's occupation of a family home has been impaired, or

(b)   on the application of a partner who has been given the possession or use of furniture and plenishings by virtue of an order under subsection (3), that the applicant has suffered a loss of such possession or use or that the quality of the applicant's possession or use of the furniture and plenishings has been impaired, in consequence of any act or default on the part of the other partner which was intended to result in such loss or impairment, it may order that other partner to pay to the applicant such compensation as it considers just and reasonable in respect of that loss or impairment.

(9)   A partner may renounce in writing the right to apply under subsection (2) for the possession or use of any item of furniture and plenishings.

104   Exclusion orders

(1)   Where there is an entitled and non-entitled partner, or where both partners are entitled, or permitted by a third party, to occupy a family home, either partner, whether or not that partner is in occupation at the time of the application, may apply to the court for an order (in this Chapter referred to as 'an exclusion order') suspending the occupancy rights of the other partner ('the non-applicant partner') in a family home.

(2)   Subject to subsection (3), the court is to make an exclusion order if it appears to it that to do so is necessary for the protection of the applicant or any child of the family from any conduct, or threatened or reasonably apprehended

conduct, of the non-applicant partner which is or would be injurious to the physical or mental health of the applicant or child.

(3) The court is not to make an exclusion order if it appears to it that to do so would be unjustified or unreasonable—

(a) having regard to all the circumstances of the case including the matters specified in paragraphs (a) to (e) of section 103(3), and

(b) where the family home—

(i) is, or is part of, an agricultural holding within the meaning of section 1 of the Agricultural Holdings (Scotland) Act 1991 (c 55), or

(ii) is let, or is a home in respect of which possession is given, to the non-applicant partner or to both partners by an employer as an incident of employment,

having regard to any requirement that the non-applicant partner, or, as the case may be, both partners must reside in the family home and to the likely consequences of the exclusion of the non-applicant partner from the family home.

(4) In making an exclusion order the court is, on the application of the applicant partner—

(a) to grant a warrant for the summary ejection of the non-applicant partner from the family home unless the non-applicant partner satisfies the court that it is unnecessary for it to grant such a remedy,

(b) to grant an interdict prohibiting the non-applicant partner from entering the family home without the express permission of the applicant, and

(c) to grant an interdict prohibiting the removal by the non-applicant partner, except with the written consent of the applicant or by a further order of the court, of any furniture and plenishings in the family home unless the non-applicant partner satisfies the court that it is unnecessary for it to grant such a remedy.

(5) In making an exclusion order the court may—

(a) grant an interdict prohibiting the non-applicant partner from entering or remaining in a specified area in the vicinity of the family home;

(b) where the warrant for the summary ejection of the non-applicant partner has been granted in that partner's absence, give directions as to the preservation of that partner's goods and effects which remain in the family home;

(c) on the application of either partner, make the exclusion order or the warrant or interdict mentioned in paragraph (a), (b) or (c) of subsection (4) or paragraph (a) of this subsection subject to such terms and conditions as the court may prescribe;

(d) on the application of either partner, make such other order as it considers necessary for the proper enforcement of an order made under subsection (4) or paragraph (a), (b) or (c).

(6) Pending the making of an exclusion order, the court may, on the application of the applicant partner, make an interim order suspending the occupancy rights of the non-applicant partner in the family home to which the application for the exclusion order relates; and subsections (4) and (5) apply to such an interim order as they apply to an exclusion order.

(7) But an interim order may be made only if the non-applicant partner has been afforded an opportunity of being heard by or represented before the court.

(8) Without prejudice to subsections (1) and (6), where both partners are entitled, or permitted by a third party, to occupy a family home, it is incompetent for one partner to bring an action of ejection from the family home against the other partner.

105   Duration of orders under sections 103 and 104

(1) The court may, on the application of either partner, vary or recall any order made by it under section 103 or 104.

(2) Subject to subsection (3), any such order, unless previously so varied or recalled, ceases to have effect—

(a)   on the dissolution of the civil partnership,

(b)   subject to section 106(1), where there is an entitled and non-entitled partner, on the entitled partner ceasing to be an entitled partner in respect of the family home to which the order relates, or

(c)   where both partners are entitled, or permitted by a third party, to occupy the family home, on both partners ceasing to be so entitled or permitted.

(3)   Without prejudice to the generality of subsection (2), an order under section 103(3) or (4) which grants the possession or use of furniture and plenishings ceases to have effect if the furniture and plenishings cease to be permitted by a third party to be retained in the family home.

106   Continued exercise of occupancy rights after dealing

(1)   Subject to subsection (3)—

(a)   the continued exercise of the rights conferred on a non-entitled partner by the provisions of this Chapter in respect of a family home are not prejudiced by reason only of any dealing of the entitled partner relating to that home, and

(b)   a third party is not by reason only of such a dealing entitled to occupy that home or any part of it.

[(1A)   The occupancy rights of a non-entitled partner in relation to a family home shall not be exercisable in relation to the home where, following a dealing of the entitled partner relating to the home—

(a)   a person acquires the home, or an interest in it, in good faith and for value from a person other than the person who is or, as the case may be, was the entitled partner, or

(b)   a person derives title to the home from a person who acquired title as mentioned in paragraph (a).]

(2)   In this section and section 107—

'dealing' includes the grant of a heritable security and the creation of a trust but does not include a conveyance under section 80 of the Lands Clauses Consolidation Act 1845 (c 18);

'entitled partner' does not include a civil partner who, apart from the provisions of this Chapter—

(a)   is permitted by a third party to occupy a family home, or

(b)   is entitled to occupy a family home along with an individual who is not the other civil partner whether or not that individual has waived a right of occupation in favour of the civil partner so entitled, ('non-entitled partner' being construed accordingly).

(3)   This section does not apply in any case where—

(a)   the non-entitled partner in writing either—

(i)   consents or has consented to the dealing (any consent being in such form as the Scottish Ministers may, by regulations made by statutory instrument, prescribe), or

(ii)   renounces or has renounced occupancy rights in relation to the family home or property to which the dealing relates,

(b)   the court has made an order under section 107 dispensing with the consent of the non-entitled partner to the dealing,

(c)   the dealing occurred, or implements a binding obligation entered into by the entitled partner, before the registration of the civil partnership,

(d)   the dealing occurred, or implements a binding obligation entered into, before the commencement of this section,

(e)   the dealing comprises a [transfer for value] to a third party who has acted in good faith, if there is produced to the third party by the [transferor—

(i)   a written declaration signed by the transferor, or a person acting on behalf of the transferor under a power of attorney or as a guardian (within the meaning of the Adults with Incapacity (Scotland) Act 2000 (asp 4)), that the subjects of the transfer are not, or were not at the time of the dealing, a family home in relation to which a civil partner or the transferor has or had occupancy rights, or

(ii) a renunciation of occupancy rights or consent to the dealing which bears to have been properly made or given by the non-entitled partner or a person acting on behalf of the non-entitled partner under a power of attorney or as a guardian (within the meaning of the Adults with Incapacity (Scotland) Act 2000 (asp 4)).]

(f) the entitled partner has permanently ceased to be entitled to occupy the family home, and at any time after that a continuous period of [2] years has elapsed during which the non-entitled partner has not occupied the family home.

(4) For the purposes of subsection (3)(e), the time of the dealing, in the case of the sale of an interest in heritable property, is the date of delivery to the purchaser of the deed transferring title to that interest.

107 Dispensation with civil partner's consent to dealing

(1) [Subject to subsections (1A) and (1C),] the court may, on the application of an entitled partner or any other person having an interest, make an order dispensing with the consent of a non-entitled partner to a dealing which has taken place or a proposed dealing, if—

(a) such consent is unreasonably withheld,

(b) such consent cannot be given by reason of physical or mental disability, or

(c) the non-entitled partner cannot be found after reasonable steps have been taken to trace that partner.

[(1A) Subsection (1B) applies if, in relation to a proposed sale—

(a) negotiations with a third party have not begun, or

(b) negotiations have begun but a price has not been agreed.

(1B) An order under subsection (1) dispensing with consent may be made only if—

(a) the price agreed for the sale is no less than such amount as the court specifies in the order, and

(b) the contract for the sale is concluded before the expiry of such period as may be so specified.

(1C) Subsection (1D) applies if the proposed dealing is the grant of a heritable security.

(1D) An order under subsection (1) dispensing with consent may be made only if—

(a) the heritable security is granted for a loan of no more than such amount as the court specifies in the order, and

(b) the security is executed before the expiry of such period as may be so specified.]

(2) For the purposes of subsection (1)(a), a non-entitled partner has unreasonably withheld consent to a dealing which has taken place or a proposed dealing, where it appears to the court either—

(a) that the non-entitled partner—

(i) has led the entitled partner to believe that the non-entitled partner would consent to the dealing, and

(ii) would not be prejudiced by any change in the circumstances of the case since the conduct which gave rise to that belief occurred, or

(b) that the entitled partner has, having taken all reasonable steps to do so, been unable to obtain an answer to a request for consent.

(3) The court, in considering whether to make an order under subsection (1), is to have regard to all the circumstances of the case including the matters specified in paragraphs (a) to (e) of section 103(3).

[(3A) If the court refuses an application for an order under subsection (1), it may make an order requiring a non-entitled partner who is or becomes the occupier of the family home—

(a) to make such payments to the owner of the home in respect of that partner's occupation of it as may be specified in the order,

(b) to comply with such other conditions relating to that partner's occupation of the family home as may be so specified.]

(4) Where—

(a) an application is made for an order under this section, and

(b) an action is or has been raised by a non-entitled partner to enforce occupancy rights,

the action is to be sisted until the conclusion of the proceedings on the application.

108 Interests of heritable creditors

(1) The rights of a third party with an interest in the family home as a creditor under a secured loan in relation to the non-performance of any obligation under the loan are not prejudiced by reason only of the occupancy rights of the non-entitled partner; but where a non-entitled partner has or obtains occupation of a family home and—

(a) the entitled partner is not in occupation, and

(b) there is a third party with such an interest in the family home,

the court may, on the application of the third party, make an order requiring the non-entitled partner to make any payment due by the entitled partner in respect of the loan.

(2) This section does not apply to secured loans in respect of which the security was granted prior to the commencement of section 13 of the Law Reform (Miscellaneous Provisions) (Scotland) Act 1985 (c 73) unless the third party in granting the secured loan acted in good faith and there was produced to the third party by the entitled partner—

(a) [a written declaration signed] by the entitled partner declaring that there is no non-entitled partner, or

(b) a renunciation of occupancy rights or consent to the taking of the loan which bears to have been properly made or given by the non-entitled partner.

(3) This section does not apply to secured loans in respect of which the security was granted after the commencement of section 13 of the Law Reform (Miscellaneous Provisions) (Scotland) Act 1985 (c 73) unless the third party in granting the secured loan acted in good faith and there was produced to the third party by the grantor—

(a) [a written declaration signed] by the grantor declaring that the security subjects are not or were not at the time of the granting of the security a family home in relation to which a civil partner of the grantor has or had occupancy rights, or

(b) a renunciation of occupancy rights or consent to the granting of the security which bears to have been properly made or given by the non-entitled partner.

(4) For the purposes of subsections (2) and (3), the time of granting a security, in the case of a heritable security, is the date of delivery of the deed creating the security.

109 Provisions where both civil partners have title

(1) Subject to subsection (2), where, apart from the provisions of this Chapter, both civil partners are entitled to occupy a family home—

(a) the rights in that home of one civil partner are not prejudiced by reason only of any dealing of the other civil partner, and

(b) a third party is not by reason only of such a dealing entitled to occupy that home or any part of it.

(2) Sections 106(3) and 107 and the definition of 'dealing' in section 106(2)

apply for the purposes of subsection (1) as they apply for the purposes of section 106(1) but subject to the following modifications—

    (a)   any reference to the entitled partner and to the non-entitled partner is to be construed as a reference to a civil partner who has entered into, or as the case may be proposes to enter into, a dealing and to the other civil partner respectively, and

    (b)   in paragraph (b) of section 107(4) the reference to occupancy rights is to be construed as a reference to any rights in the family home.

110   Rights of occupancy in relation to division and sale

Where a civil partner brings an action for the division and sale of a family home owned in common with the other civil partner, the court, after having regard to all the circumstances of the case including—

    (a)   the matters specified in paragraphs (a) to (d) of section 103(3), and

    (b)   whether the civil partner bringing the action offers or has offered to make available to the other civil partner any suitable alternative accommodation,

may refuse to grant decree in that action or may postpone the granting of decree for such period as it considers reasonable in the circumstances or may grant decree subject to such conditions as it may prescribe.

111   Adjudication

(1)   Where a family home as regards which there is an entitled partner and a non-entitled partner is adjudged, the Court of Session, on the application of the non-entitled partner made within 40 days after the date of the decree of adjudication, may—

    (a)   order the reduction of the decree, or

    (b)   make such order as it thinks appropriate to protect the occupancy rights of the non-entitled partner,

if satisfied that the purpose of the diligence was wholly or mainly to defeat the occupancy rights of the non-entitled partner.

(2)   Section 106(2) applies in construing 'entitled partner' and 'non-entitled partner' for the purposes of subsection (1).

[111A   Effect of court action under section 103, 104 or 105 on reckoning of periods in sections 101 and 106

(1)   Subsection (2) applies where an application is made under section 103(1), 104(1) or 105(1).

(2)   In calculating the period of two years mentioned in section 101(6A)(a) or 106(3)(f), no account shall be taken of the period mentioned in subsection (3).

(3)   The period is the period beginning with the date on which the application is made and—

    (a)   in the case of an application under section 103(1) or 104(1), ending on the date on which—

        (i)   an order under section 103(3) or, as the case may be, 104(2) is made, or

        (ii)   the application is otherwise finally determined or abandoned,

    (b)   in the case of an application under section 105(1), ending on the date on which—

        (i)   the order under section 103(3) or, as the case may be, 104(2) is varied or recalled, or

        (ii)   the application is otherwise finally determined or abandoned.]

Transfer of tenancy

112   Transfer of tenancy

(1)   The court may, on the application of a non-entitled partner, make an order transferring the tenancy of a family home to that partner and providing, subject to subsection (12), for the payment by the non-entitled partner to the entitled partner

of such compensation as seems to it to be just and reasonable in all the circumstances of the case.

(2)   In an action—

(a)   for dissolution of a civil partnership, the Court of Session or the sheriff,

(b)   for declarator of nullity of a civil partnership, the Court of Session,

may, on granting decree or within such period as the court may specify on granting decree, make an order granting an application under subsection (1).

(3)   In determining whether to grant an application under subsection (1), the court is to have regard to all the circumstances of the case including the matters specified in paragraphs (a) to (e) of section 103(3) and the suitability of the applicant to become the tenant and the applicant's capacity to perform the obligations under the lease of the family home.

(4)   The non-entitled partner is to serve a copy of an application under subsection (1) on the landlord and, before making an order under subsection (1), the court is to give the landlord an opportunity of being heard by it.

(5)   On the making of an order granting an application under subsection (1), the tenancy vests in the non-entitled partner without intimation to the landlord, subject to all the liabilities under the lease (other than liability for any arrears of rent for the period before the making of the order).

(6)   The arrears mentioned in subsection (5) are to remain the liability of the original entitled partner.

(7)   The clerk of court is to notify the landlord of the making of an order granting an application under subsection (1).

(8)   It is not competent for a non-entitled partner to apply for an order under subsection (1) where the family home—

(a)   is let to the entitled partner by the entitled partner's employer as an incident of employment, and the lease is subject to a requirement that the entitled partner must reside there,

(b)   is or is part of an agricultural holding,

(c)   is on, or pertains to—

(i)   a croft,

(ii)   the subject of a cottar, or

(iii)   the holding of a landholder or of a statutory small tenant,

(d)   is let on a long lease, or

(e)   is part of the tenancy land of a tenant-at-will.

(9)   In subsection (8)—

'agricultural holding' has the same meaning as in section 1 of the Agricultural Holdings (Scotland) Act 1991 (c 55),

'cottar' has the same meaning as in section 12(5) of the Crofters (Scotland) Act 1993 (c 44),

'croft' has the same meaning as in that Act of 1993,

'holding', in relation to a landholder and a statutory small tenant,

'landholder' and 'statutory small tenant' have the same meanings respectively as in sections 2(1), 2(2) and 32(1) of the Small Landholders (Scotland) Act 1911 (c 49),

'long lease' has the same meaning as in section 28(1) of the Land Registration (Scotland) Act 1979 (c 33), and

'tenant-at-will' has the same meaning as in section 20(8) of that Act of 1979.

(10)   Where both civil partners are joint or common tenants of a family home, the court may, on the application of one of the civil partners, make an order vesting the tenancy in that civil partner solely and providing, subject to subsection (12), for the payment by the applicant to the other partner of such compensation as seems just and reasonable in the circumstances of the case.

(11)   Subsections (2) to (9) apply for the purposes of an order under subsection (10) as they apply for the purposes of an order under subsection (1) but subject to the following modifications—

(a)   in subsection (3), for 'tenant' there is substituted 'sole tenant';

(b)   in subsection (4), for 'non-entitled' there is substituted 'applicant';
(c)   in subsection (5), for 'non-entitled' there is substituted 'applicant',
(d)   in subsection (6), for 'liability of the original entitled partner' there is substituted 'joint and several liability of both partners';
(e)   in subsection (8)—
    (i)   for 'a non-entitled' there is substituted 'an applicant',
    (ii)   for paragraph (a) there is substituted—
    '(a)   is let to both partners by their employer as an incident of employment, and the lease is subject to a requirement that both partners must reside there;', and
    (iii)   paragraphs (c) and (e) are omitted.
(12)   Where the family home is a Scottish secure tenancy within the meaning of the Housing (Scotland) Act 2001 (asp 10), no account is to be taken, in assessing the amount of any compensation to be awarded under subsection (1) or (10), of the loss, by virtue of the transfer of the tenancy of the home, of a right to purchase the home under Part 3 of the Housing (Scotland) Act 1987 (c 26).

CHAPTER 4
INTERDICTS

113   Civil partners: competency of interdict
(1)   It shall not be incompetent for the Court of Session or the sheriff to entertain an application by one civil partner in a civil partnership for a relevant interdict by reason only that the civil partners are living together in civil partnership.
(2)   In subsection (1) [. . .] 'relevant interdict' means an interdict, including an interim interdict, which—
    (a)   restrains or prohibits any conduct of one civil partner towards the other civil partner or a child of the family, or
    (b)   [subject to subsection (3), prohibits a civil partner from entering or remaining in—
        (i)   a family home,
        (ii)   any other residence occupied by the applicant civil partner,
        (iii)   any place of work of the applicant civil partner,
        (iv)   any school attended by a child in the permanent or temporary care of the applicant civil partner.]
    [(3)   Subsection (4) applies if in relation to a family home the non-applicant civil partner—
        (a)   is an entitled partner, or
        (b)   has occupancy rights.
(4)   Except where subsection (5) applies, the court may not grant a relevant interdict prohibiting the non-applicant civil partner from entering or remaining in the family home.
(5)   This subsection applies if—
    (a)   the interdict is ancillary to an exclusion order, or
    (b)   by virtue of section 101(4), the court refuses leave to exercise occupancy rights.
(6)   In this section [. . .], 'applicant civil partner' means the civil partner who has applied for the interdict; and 'non-applicant civil partner' is to be construed accordingly.]

[. . .]

CHAPTER 5
DISSOLUTION, SEPARATION AND NULLITY

Dissolution and separation

117 Dissolution

(1)   An action for the dissolution of a civil partnership may be brought in the Court of Session or in the sheriff court.

(2)   In such an action the court may grant decree, if, but only if, it is established that—

(a)   the civil partnership has broken down irretrievably, or

(b)   an interim gender recognition certificate under the Gender Recognition Act 2004 (c 7) has, after the date of registration of the civil partnership, been issued to either of the civil partners.

(3)   The irretrievable breakdown of a civil partnership is taken to be established if—

(a)   since the date of registration of the civil partnership the defender has at any time behaved (whether or not as a result of mental abnormality and whether such behaviour has been active or passive) in such a way that the pursuer cannot reasonably be expected to cohabit with the defender,

[. . .]

(c)   there has been no cohabitation between the civil partners at any time during a continuous period of [one year] after the date of registration of the civil partnership and immediately preceding the bringing of the action and the defender consents to the granting of decree of dissolution of the civil partnership, or

(d)   there has been no cohabitation between the civil partners at any time during a continuous period of [two] years after that date and immediately preceding the bringing of the action.

(4)   Provision is to be made by act of sederunt—

(a)   for the purpose of ensuring that, in an action to which paragraph (c) of subsection (3) relates, the defender has been given such information as enables that civil partner to understand—

(i)   the consequences of consenting to the granting of decree, and

(ii)   the steps which must be taken to indicate such consent, and

(b)   as to the manner in which the defender in such an action is to indicate such consent, and any withdrawal of such consent,

and where the defender has indicated (and not withdrawn) such consent in the prescribed manner, that indication is sufficient evidence of such consent.

(5)   Provision is to be made by act of sederunt for the purpose of ensuring that, where in an action for the dissolution of a civil partnership the defender is suffering from mental illness, the court appoints a curator ad litem to the defender.

[. . .]

(8)   In an action for dissolution of a civil partnership the standard of proof required to establish the ground of action is on balance of probability.

118 Encouragement of reconciliation

(1)   At any time before granting decree in an action by virtue of paragraph (a) of section 117(2) for dissolution of a civil partnership, if it appears to the court that there is a reasonable prospect of a reconciliation between the civil partners it must continue, or further continue, the action for such period as it thinks proper to enable attempts to be made to effect such a reconciliation.

(2)   If during any such continuation the civil partners cohabit with one another, no account is to be taken of such cohabitation for the purposes of that action.

119 Effect of resumption of cohabitation

[. . .]

(3) In considering whether any period mentioned in paragraph (c) or (d) of section 117(3) has been continuous, no account is to be taken of any period or periods not exceeding 6 months in all during which the civil partners cohabited with one another; but no such period or periods during which the civil partners cohabited with one another is to count as part of the period of non-cohabitation required by any of those paragraphs.

120 Separation

(1) An action for the separation of the civil partners in a civil partnership may be brought in the Court of Session or in the sheriff court.

(2) In such an action the court may grant decree if satisfied that the circumstances set out in any of paragraphs (a) to (d) of section 117(3) are established.

121 Dissolution following on decree of separation

(1) The court may grant decree in an action for the dissolution of a civil partnership even though decree of separation has previously been granted to the pursuer on the same, or substantially the same, facts as those averred in support of that action; and in any such action the court may treat an extract decree of separation lodged in process as sufficient proof of the facts under which that decree was granted.

(2) Nothing in this section entitles a court to grant decree of dissolution of a civil partnership without receiving evidence from the pursuer.

122 Registration of dissolution of civil partnership

(1) The Registrar General is to maintain at the General Register Office a register of decrees of dissolution of civil partnership (a register which shall be known as the 'Register of Dissolutions of Civil Partnership').

(2) The Registrar General is to cause to be made and kept at the General Register Office an alphabetical index of the entries in that register.

(3) The register is to be in such form as may be prescribed.

(4) On payment to him of such fee or fees as may be prescribed, the Registrar General must, at any time when the General Register Office is open for that purpose—

(a) cause a search of the index to be made on behalf of any person or permit any person to search the index himself,

(b) issue to any person an extract of any entry in the register which that person may require.

(5) An extract of any entry in the register is to be sufficient evidence of the decree of dissolution to which it relates.

(6) The Registrar General may—

(a) delete,

(b) amend, or

(c) substitute another entry for,

any entry in the register.

[(7) Section 39C of the 1965 Act applies in relation to the Register of Dissolutions of Civil Partnership as it applies in relation to the Register of Divorces.]

Nullity

123 Nullity

[(1)] Where two people register in Scotland as civil partners of each other, the civil partnership is void if, and only if—

(a) they were not eligible to do so,

(b) though they were so eligible, either of them did not [. . .] consent to its formation, [or

(c) at the time of registration one of them who was capable of consenting to the formation of the civil partnership purported to give consent but did so by reason only of duress or error.]

[(2)   In this section 'error' means—

(a)   error as to the nature of civil partnership, or

(b)   a mistaken belief held by a person ('A') that the other person with whom A purported to register a civil partnership was the person with whom A had agreed to register a civil partnership.]

124   Validity of civil partnerships registered outside Scotland

(1)   Where two people register as civil partners of each other in England and Wales—

(a)   the civil partnership is void if it would be void in England and Wales under section 49, and

(b)   the civil partnership is voidable if it would be voidable there under section 50(1)(a), (b), (c) or (e).

(2)   Where two people register as civil partners of each other in Northern Ireland, the civil partnership is—

(a)   void, if it would be void in Northern Ireland under section 173, and

(b)   voidable, if it would be voidable there under section 174(1)(a), (b), (c) or (e).

(3)   Subsection (4) applies where two people register as civil partners of each other under an Order in Council under—

(a)   section 210 (registration at British consulates etc), or

(b)   section 211 (registration by armed forces personnel), ('the relevant section').

(4)   The civil partnership is—

(a)   void, if—

(i)   the condition in subsection (2)(a) or (b) of the relevant section is not met, or

(ii)   a requirement prescribed for the purposes of this paragraph by an Order in Council under the relevant section is not complied with, and

(b)   voidable, if—

(i)   the appropriate part of the United Kingdom is England and Wales and the circumstances fall within section 50(1)(a), (b), (c) or (e), or

(ii)   the appropriate part of the United Kingdom is Northern Ireland and the circumstances fall within section 174(1)(a), (b), (c) or (e).

(5)   The appropriate part of the United Kingdom is the part by reference to which the condition in subsection (2)(b) of the relevant section is met.

(6)   Subsections (7) and (8) apply where two people have registered an apparent or alleged overseas relationship.

(7)   The civil partnership is void if—

(a)   the relationship is not an overseas relationship, or

(b)   (even though the relationship is an overseas relationship), the parties are not treated under Chapter 2 of Part 5 as having formed a civil partnership.

(8)   The civil partnership is voidable if—

(a)   the overseas relationship is voidable under the relevant law,

(b)   where either of the parties was domiciled in England and Wales at the time when the overseas relationship was registered, the circumstances fall within section 50(1)(a), (b), (c) or (e), or

(c)   where either of the parties was domiciled in Northern Ireland at the time when the overseas relationship was registered, the circumstances fall within section 174(1)(a), (b), (c) or (e).

(9)   Section 51 or (as the case may be) section 175 applies for the purposes of—

(a)   subsections (1)(b), (2)(b) and (4)(b),

(b)   subsection (8)(a), in so far as applicable in accordance with the relevant law, and

(c)   subsection (8)(b) and (c).

(10)   In subsections (8)(a) and (9)(b) 'the relevant law' means the law of the

country or territory where the overseas relationship was registered (including its rules of private international law).

(11)   For the purposes of subsections (8) and (9)(b) and (c), references in sections 50 and 51 or (as the case may be) sections 174 and 175 to the formation of the civil partnership are to be read as references to the registration of the overseas relationship.

[Special destinations: revocation on dissolution or annulment

124A   Special destination: revocation on dissolution or annulment

(1)   Subsections (2) and (3) apply where—
  (a)   heritable property is held in the name of—
    (i)   a person ('A') and A's civil partner ('B') and the survivor of them,
    (ii)   A, B and another person and the survivor or survivors of them,
    (iii)   A with a special destination on A's death, in favour of B,
  (b)   A and B's civil partnership is terminated by dissolution or annulment, and
  (c)   after the dissolution or annulment A dies.

(2)   In relation to the succession to A's heritable property (or part of it) under the destination, B shall be deemed to have failed to survive A.

(3)   If a person has in good faith and for value (whether by purchase or otherwise) acquired title to the heritable property, the title so acquired shall not be challengeable on the ground that, by virtue of subsection (2), the property falls to the estate of A.

(4)   Subsection (2) shall not apply if the destination specifies that B is to take under the destination despite the termination of A and B's civil partnership by dissolution or annulment.]

Financial provision after overseas proceedings

125   Financial provision after overseas dissolution or annulment

Schedule 11 relates to applications for financial provision in Scotland after a civil partnership has been dissolved or annulled in a country or territory outside the British Islands.

CHAPTER 6
MISCELLANEOUS AND INTERPRETATION

Miscellaneous

126   Regulations

(1)   In this Chapter and in Chapters 2 and 5, 'prescribed' means prescribed by regulations made by the Registrar General.

(2)   Regulations so made may make provision (including provision as to fees) supplementing, in respect of the provision of services by or on behalf of the Registrar General or by local registration authorities (as defined by section 5(3) of the 1965 Act), the provisions of Chapter 2 of this Part.

(3)   Any power to make regulations under subsection (1) or (2) is exercisable by statutory instrument; and no such regulations are to be made except with the approval of the Scottish Ministers.

(4)   A statutory instrument containing regulations under subsection (1) or (2), or regulations under section 106(3)(a)(i), is subject to annulment in pursuance of a resolution of the Scottish Parliament.

127   Attachment

Where an attachment has been executed of furniture and plenishings of which the debtor's civil partner has the possession or use by virtue of an order under section 103(3) or (4), the sheriff, on the application of that civil partner made within 40 days after the execution of the attachment, may—

(a)   declare the attachment null, or
(b)   make such order as he thinks appropriate to protect such possession or
use by that civil partner,
if satisfied that the purpose of the attachment was wholly or mainly to prevent
such possession or use.

128   Promise or agreement to enter into civil partnership

No promise or agreement to enter into civil partnership creates any rights or obligations under the law of Scotland; and no action for breach of such a promise or
agreement may be brought in any court in Scotland, whatever the law applicable
to the promise or agreement.

[. . .]

130   Civil partner of accused a competent witness

(1)   The civil partner of an accused may be called as a witness—
(a)   by the accused, or
(b)   without the consent of the accused, by a co-accused or by the prosecutor.
(2)   But the civil partner is not a compellable witness for the co-accused or for
the prosecutor and is not compelled to disclose any communication made, while
the civil partnership subsists, between the civil partners.
(3)   The failure of a civil partner of an accused to give evidence is not to be
commented on by the defence or the prosecutor.

131   Succession: legal rights arising by virtue of civil partnership

(1)   Where a person dies survived by a civil partner then, unless the circumstance is as mentioned in subsection (2), the civil partner has right to half of the
moveable net estate belonging to the deceased at the time of death.
(2)   That circumstance is that the person is also survived by issue, in which case
the civil partner has right to a third of that moveable net estate and those issue
have right to another third of it.
(3)   In this section—
'issue' means issue however remote, and
'net estate' has the meaning given by section 36(1) (interpretation) of the Succession (Scotland) Act 1964 (c 41).
(4)   Every testamentary disposition executed after the commencement of this
section by which provision is made in favour of the civil partner of the testator
and which does not contain a declaration to the effect that the provision so made
is in full and final satisfaction of the right to any share in the testator's estate to
which the civil partner is entitled by virtue of subsection (1) or (2), has effect
(unless the disposition contains an express provision to the contrary) as if it contained such a declaration.
(5)   In section 36(1) of the Succession (Scotland) Act 1964 (c 41), in the definition
of 'legal rights', for 'and legitim' substitute 'legitim and rights under section 131 of
the Civil Partnership Act 2004'.

132   Assurance policies

Section 2 of the Married Women's Policies of Assurance (Scotland) Act 1880 (c 26)
(which provides that a policy of assurance may be effected in trust for a person's
spouse, children or spouse and children) applies in relation to a policy of assurance—
(a)   effected by a civil partner (in this section referred to as 'A') on A's own
life, and
(b)   expressed upon the face of it to be for the benefit of A's civil partner, or
of A's children, or of A's civil partner and children,
as it applies in relation to a policy of assurance effected as, and expressed upon
the face of it to be for such benefit as, is mentioned in that section.

134   General provisions as to fees

(1)   Subject to such exceptions as may be prescribed, a district registrar may refuse to comply with any application voluntarily made to him under this Part until the appropriate fee, if any, provided for by or under this Part is paid to him; and any such fee, if not prepaid, is recoverable by the registrar to whom it is payable.

(2)   Circumstances, of hardship or otherwise, may be prescribed in which fees provided for by or under this Part may be remitted by the Registrar General.

Interpretation

135   Interpretation of this Part

[(1)]   In this Part, unless the context otherwise requires—

'the 1965 Act' means the Registration of Births, Deaths and Marriages (Scotland) Act 1965 (c 49);

'authorised registrar' has the meaning given by section 87;

'caravan' means a caravan which is mobile or affixed to land;

'child of the family' has the meaning given by section 101(7);

'civil partnership book' has the meaning given by section 89;

'civil partnership register' has the meaning given by section 95(2);

'civil partnership schedule' has the meaning given by section 94;

'the court' means the Court of Session or the sheriff;

'district' means a registration district as defined by section 5(1) of the 1965 Act;

'district registrar' has the meaning given by section 7(12) of the 1965 Act;

'entitled partner' and 'non-entitled partner', subject to sections 106(2) and 111(2), have the meanings respectively assigned to them by section 101(1);

'exclusion order' has the meaning given by section 104(1);

'family' has the meaning given by section 101(7);

'family home' means [, subject to subsection (2),] any house, caravan, houseboat or other structure which has been provided or has been made available by one or both of the civil partners as, or has become, a family residence and includes any garden or other ground or building [. . .] usually occupied with, or otherwise required for the amenity or convenience of, the house, caravan, houseboat or other structure but does not include a residence provided or made available by [a person for one] civil partner to reside in, whether with any child of the family or not, separately from the other civil partner;

'furniture and plenishings' means any article situated in a family home of civil partners which—

(a)   is owned or hired by either civil partner or is being acquired by either civil partner under a hire-purchase agreement or conditional sale agreement, and

(b)   is reasonably necessary to enable the home to be used as a family residence,

but does not include any vehicle, caravan or houseboat or such other structure as is mentioned in the definition of 'family home';

'notice of proposed civil partnership' has the meaning given by section 88(1);

'occupancy rights' means the rights conferred by section 101(1);

'Registrar General' means the Registrar General of Births, Deaths and Marriages for Scotland;

'registration office' means a registration office provided under section 8(1) of the 1965 Act;

'tenant' includes—

(a)   a sub-tenant,

(b)   a statutory tenant as defined in section 3 of the Rent (Scotland) Act 1984 (c 58), and

(c)   a statutory assured tenant as defined in section 16(1) of the Housing (Scotland) Act 1988 (c 43),
and 'tenancy' is to be construed accordingly.
    [(2)   If—
        (a)   the tenancy of a family home is transferred from one civil partner to the other by agreement or under any enactment, and
        (b)   following the transfer, the civil partner to whom the tenancy was trans-ferred occupies the home but the other civil partner does not,
the home shall, on such transfer, cease to be a family home.]

136   The expression 'relative' in the 1965 Act
In section 56(1) of the 1965 Act (interpretation), in the definition of 'relative', at the end insert ', a civil partner and anyone related to the civil partner of the person as regards whom the expression is being construed'.

PART 5
CIVIL PARTNERSHIP FORMED OR DISSOLVED ABROAD ETC

Jurisdiction of Scottish courts

225   Jurisdiction of Scottish courts
    (1)   The Court of Session has jurisdiction to entertain an action for the dissolu-tion of a civil partnership or for separation of civil partners if (and only if)—
        (a)   the court has jurisdiction under section 219 regulations,
        (b)   no court has, or is recognised as having, jurisdiction under section 219 regulations and either civil partner is domiciled in Scotland on the date when the proceedings are begun, or
        (c)   the following conditions are met—
            (i)   the two people concerned registered as civil partners of each other in Scotland,
            (ii)   no court has, or is recognised as having, jurisdiction under section 219 regulations, and
            (iii)   it appears to the court to be in the interests of justice to assume jurisdiction in the case.
    (2)   The sheriff has jurisdiction to entertain an action for the dissolution of a civil partnership or for separation of civil partners if (and only if) the requirements of paragraph (a) or (b) of subsection (1) are met and either civil partner—
        (a)   was resident in the sheriffdom for a period of 40 days ending with the date when the action is begun, or
        (b)   had been resident in the sheriffdom for a period of not less than 40 days ending not more than 40 days before that date and has no known residence in Scotland at that date.
    (3)   The Court of Session has jurisdiction to entertain an action for declarator of nullity of a civil partnership if (and only if)—
        (a)   the Court has jurisdiction under section 219 regulations,
        (b)   no court has, or is recognised as having, jurisdiction under section 219 regulations and either of the ostensible civil partners—
            (i)   is domiciled in Scotland on the date when the proceedings are begun, or
            (ii)   died before that date and either was at death domiciled in Scotland or had been habitually resident in Scotland throughout the period of 1 year ending with the date of death, or
        (c)   the following conditions are met—
            (i)   the two people concerned registered as civil partners of each other in Scotland,
            (ii)   no court has, or is recognised as having, jurisdiction under section 219 regulations, and

(iii) it appears to the court to be in the interests of justice to assume jurisdiction in the case.

(4) At any time when proceedings are pending in respect of which a court has jurisdiction by virtue of any of subsections (1) to (3) (or this subsection) it also has jurisdiction to entertain other proceedings, in respect of the same civil partnership (or ostensible civil partnership), for dissolution, separation or (but only where the court is the Court of Session) declarator of nullity, even though that jurisdiction would not be exercisable under any of subsections (1) to (3).

226 Sisting of proceedings

(1) Rules of court may make provision in relation to civil partnerships corresponding to the provision made in relation to marriages by Schedule 3 to the Domicile and Matrimonial Proceedings Act 1973 (c 45) (sisting of Scottish consistorial actions).

(2) The rules may in particular make provision—

(a) for the provision of information by the pursuer and by any other person who has entered appearance in an action where proceedings relating to the same civil partnership (or ostensible civil partnership) are continuing in another jurisdiction, and

(b) for an action to be sisted where there are concurrent proceedings elsewhere in respect of the same civil partnership (or ostensible civil partnership).

227 Scottish ancillary and collateral orders

(1) This section applies where after the commencement of this Act an application is competently made to the Court of Session or the sheriff for the making, or the variation or recall, of an order which is ancillary or collateral to an action for—

(a) the dissolution of a civil partnership,

(b) the separation of civil partners, or

(c) declarator of nullity of a civil partnership.

(2) And the section applies whether the application is made in the same proceedings or in other proceedings and whether it is made before or after the pronouncement of a final decree in the action.

(3) If the court has or, as the case may be, had jurisdiction to entertain the action, it has jurisdiction to entertain the application unless—

(a) jurisdiction to entertain the action was under section 219 regulations, and

(b) to make, vary or recall the order to which the application relates would contravene the regulations.

(4) Where the Court of Session has jurisdiction by virtue of this section to entertain an application for the variation or recall, as respects any person, of an order made by it and the order is one to which section 8 (variation and recall by the sheriff of certain orders made by the Court of Session) of the Law Reform (Miscellaneous Provisions) (Scotland) Act 1966 (c 19) applies, then for the purposes of any application under that section for the variation or recall of the order in so far as it relates to the person, the sheriff (as defined in that section) has jurisdiction to exercise the power conferred on him by that section.

(5) The reference in subsection (1) to an order which is ancillary or collateral is to an order relating to children, aliment, financial provision or expenses.

PART 6
RELATIONSHIPS ARISING THROUGH CIVIL PARTNERSHIP

246 Interpretation of statutory references to stepchildren etc

(1) In any provision to which this section applies, references to a stepchild or step-parent of a person (here, 'A'), and cognate expressions, are to be read as follows—

A's stepchild includes a person who is the child of A's civil partner (but is not A's child);

A's step-parent includes a person who is the civil partner of A's parent (but is not A's parent);

A's stepdaughter includes a person who is the daughter of A's civil partner (but is not A's daughter);

A's stepson includes a person who is the son of A's civil partner (but is not A's son);

A's stepfather includes a person who is the civil partner of A's father (but is not A's parent);

A's stepmother includes a person who is the civil partner of A's mother (but is not A's parent);

A's stepbrother includes a person who is the son of the civil partner of A's parent (but is not the son of either of A's parents);

A's stepsister includes a person who is the daughter of the civil partner of A's parent (but is not the daughter of either of A's parents).

(2) For the purposes of any provision to which this section applies—

'brother-in-law' includes civil partner's brother,

'daughter-in-law' includes daughter's civil partner,

'father-in-law' includes civil partner's father,

'mother-in-law' includes civil partner's mother,

'parent-in-law' includes civil partner's parent,

'sister-in-law' includes civil partner's sister, and

'son-in-law' includes son's civil partner.

247 Provisions to which section 246 applies: Acts of Parliament etc

(1) Section 246 applies to—

(a) any provision listed in Schedule 21 (references to stepchildren, in-laws etc in existing Acts),

(b) except in so far as otherwise provided, any provision made by a future Act, and

(c) except in so far as otherwise provided, any provision made by future subordinate legislation.

(2) A Minister of the Crown may by order—

(a) amend Schedule 21 by adding to it any provision of an existing Act;

(b) provide for section 246 to apply to prescribed provisions of existing subordinate legislation.

(3) The power conferred by subsection (2) is also exercisable—

(a) by the Scottish Ministers, in relation to a relevant Scottish provision;

(b) by a Northern Ireland department, in relation to a provision which deals with a transferred matter;

(c) by the National Assembly for Wales, if the order is made by virtue of subsection (2)(b) and deals with matters with respect to which functions are exercisable by the Assembly.

(4) Subject to subsection (5), the power to make an order under subsection (2) is exercisable by statutory instrument.

(5) Any power of a Northern Ireland department to make an order under subsection (2) is exercisable by statutory rule for the purposes of the Statutory Rules (Northern Ireland) Order 1979 (SI 1979/1573 (NI 12)).

(6) A statutory instrument containing an order under subsection (2) made by a Minister of the Crown is subject to annulment in pursuance of a resolution of either House of Parliament.

(7) A statutory instrument containing an order under subsection (2) made by the Scottish Ministers is subject to annulment in pursuance of a resolution of the Scottish Parliament.

(8) A statutory rule containing an order under subsection (2) made by a Northern Ireland department is subject to negative resolution (within the meaning of section 41(6) of the Interpretation Act (Northern Ireland) 1954 (c 33 (NI))).

(9)   In this section—

'Act' includes an Act of the Scottish Parliament;

'existing Act' means an Act passed on or before the last day of the Session in which this Act is passed;

'existing subordinate legislation' means subordinate legislation made before the day on which this section comes into force;

'future Act' means an Act passed after the last day of the Session in which this Act is passed;

'future subordinate legislation' means subordinate legislation made on or after the day on which this section comes into force;

'Minister of the Crown' has the same meaning as in the Ministers of the Crown Act 1975 (c 26);

'prescribed' means prescribed by the order;

'relevant Scottish provision' means a provision that would be within the legislative competence of the Scottish Parliament if it were included in an Act of that Parliament;

'subordinate legislation' has the same meaning as in the Interpretation Act 1978 (c 30) except that it includes an instrument made under an Act of the Scottish Parliament;

'transferred matter' has the meaning given by section 4(1) of the Northern Ireland Act 1998 (c 47) and 'deals with' in relation to a transferred matter is to be construed in accordance with section 98(2) and (3) of the 1998 Act.

PART 7
MISCELLANEOUS

249   Immigration control and formation of civil partnerships

Schedule 23 contains provisions relating to the formation of civil partnerships in the United Kingdom by persons subject to immigration control.

253   Civil partners to have unlimited insurable interest in each other

(1)   Where two people are civil partners, each of them is to be presumed for the purposes of section 1 of the Life Assurance Act 1774 (c 48) to have an interest in the life of the other.

(2)   For the purposes of section 3 of the 1774 Act, there is no limit on the amount of value of the interest.

PART 8
SUPPLEMENTARY

258   Regulations and orders

(1)   This section applies to any power conferred by this Act to make regulations or an order (except a power of a court to make an order).

(2)   The power may be exercised so as to make different provision for different cases and different purposes.

(3)   The power includes power to make any supplementary, incidental, consequential, transitional, transitory or saving provision which the person making the regulations or order considers expedient.

259   Power to make further provision in connection with civil partnership

(1)   A Minister of the Crown may by order make such further provision (including supplementary, incidental, consequential, transitory, transitional or saving provision) as he considers appropriate—

(a)   for the general purposes, or any particular purpose, of this Act,

(b)   in consequence of any provision made by or under this Act, or

(c)   for giving full effect to this Act or any provision of it.

(2)   The power conferred by subsection (1) is also exercisable—

(a)   by the Scottish Ministers, in relation to a relevant Scottish provision;

(b)   by a Northern Ireland department, in relation to a provision which deals with a transferred matter;

(c)   by the National Assembly for Wales, in relation to a provision which is made otherwise than by virtue of subsection (3) and deals with matters with respect to which functions are exercisable by the Assembly.

(3)   An order under subsection (1) may—

(a)   amend or repeal any enactment contained in an Act passed on or before the last day of the Session in which this Act is passed, including an enactment conferring power to make subordinate legislation where the power is limited by reference to persons who are or have been parties to a marriage;

(b)   amend, repeal or (as the case may be) revoke any provision contained in Northern Ireland legislation passed or made on or before the last day of the Session in which this Act is passed, including a provision conferring power to make subordinate legislation where the power is limited by reference to persons who are or have been parties to a marriage;

(c)   amend, repeal or (as the case may be) revoke any Church legislation.

(4)   An order under subsection (1) may—

(a)   provide for any provision of this Act which comes into force before another such provision has come into force to have effect, until that other provision has come into force, with such modifications as are specified in the order;

(b)   amend or revoke any subordinate legislation.

(5)   The power to make an order under subsection (1) is not restricted by any other provision of this Act.

(6)   Subject to subsection (7), the power to make an order under subsection (1) is exercisable by statutory instrument.

(7)   Any power of a Northern Ireland department to make an order under this section is exercisable by statutory rule for the purposes of the Statutory Rules (Northern Ireland) Order 1979 (SI 1979/1573 (NI 12)).

(8)   An order under subsection (1) which contains any provision (whether alone or with other provisions) made by virtue of subsection (3) may not be made—

(a)   by a Minister of the Crown, unless a draft of the statutory instrument containing the order has been laid before, and approved by a resolution of, each House of Parliament;

(b)   by the Scottish Ministers, unless a draft of the statutory instrument containing the order has been laid before, and approved by a resolution of, the Scottish Parliament;

(c)   by a Northern Ireland department, unless a draft of the statutory rule containing the order has been laid before, and approved by a resolution of, the Northern Ireland Assembly.

(9)   A statutory instrument containing an order under subsection (1) to which subsection (8) does not apply—

(a)   if made by a Minister of the Crown, is subject to annulment in pursuance of a resolution of either House of Parliament;

(b)   if made by the Scottish Ministers, is subject to annulment in pursuance of a resolution of the Scottish Parliament.

(10)   A statutory rule made by a Northern Ireland department and containing an order to which subsection (8) does not apply is subject to negative resolution (within the meaning of section 41(6) of the Interpretation Act (Northern Ireland) 1954 (c 33 (NI))).

(11)   In this section—

'Act' includes an Act of the Scottish Parliament;

'Church legislation' has the same meaning as in section 255;

'Minister of the Crown' has the same meaning as in the Ministers of the Crown Act 1975 (c 26);

'relevant Scottish provision' means a provision that would be within the legislative competence of the Scottish Parliament if it were included in an Act of that Parliament;

'subordinate legislation' has the same meaning as in the Interpretation Act 1978 (c 30) except that it includes any instrument made under an Act of the Scottish Parliament and any instrument within the meaning of section 1(c) of the Interpretation Act (Northern Ireland) 1954 (c 33 (NI));

'transferred matter' has the meaning given by section 4(1) of the Northern Ireland Act 1998 (c 47) and 'deals with' in relation to a transferred matter is to be construed in accordance with section 98(2) and (3) of the 1998 Act.

260 Community obligations and civil partners

(1)   Subsection (2) applies where any person, by Order in Council or regulations under section 2(2) of the European Communities Act 1972 (c 68) (general implementation of Treaties)—

(a)   is making provision for the purpose of implementing, or for a purpose concerning, a Community obligation of the United Kingdom which relates to persons who are or have been parties to a marriage, or

(b)   has made such provision and it has not been revoked.

(2)   The appropriate person may by Order in Council or (as the case may be) by regulations make provision in relation to persons who are or have been civil partners in a civil partnership that is the same or similar to the provision referred to in subsection (1).

(3)   'Marriage' and 'civil partnership' include a void marriage and a void civil partnership respectively.

(4)   'The appropriate person' means—

(a)   if subsection (1)(a) applies, the person making the provision referred to there;

(b)   if subsection (1)(b) applies, any person who would have power to make the provision referred to there if it were being made at the time of the exercise of the power under subsection (2).

(5)   The following provisions apply in relation to the power conferred by subsection (2) to make an Order in Council or regulations as they apply in relation to the power conferred by section 2(2) of the 1972 Act to make an Order in Council or regulations—

(a)   paragraph 2 of Schedule 2 to the 1972 Act (procedure etc in relation to making of Orders in Council and regulations: general);

(b)   paragraph 15(3)(c) of Schedule 8 to the Scotland Act 1998 (c 46) (modifications of paragraph 2 in relation to Scottish Ministers and to Orders in Council made on the recommendation of the First Minister);

(c)   paragraph 3 of Schedule 2 to the 1972 Act (modifications of paragraph 2 in relation to Northern Ireland departments etc) and the Statutory Rules (Northern Ireland) Order 1979 (SI 1979/1573 (NI 12)) (treating the power conferred by subsection (2) as conferred by an Act passed before 1st January 1974 for the purposes of the application of that Order);

(d)   section 29(3) of the Government of Wales Act 1998 (c 38) (modifications of paragraph 2 in relation to the National Assembly for Wales).

261 *[Minor and consequential amendments, repeals and revocations]*

262 Extent

(2)   Part 3 (civil partnership: Scotland), including Schedules 10 and 11, extends to Scotland only.

(4)   In Part 5 (civil partnerships formed or dissolved abroad etc)—

(b)   sections 225 to 227 extend to Scotland only;

(5)   In Part 6—

(a)   any amendment made by virtue of section 247(1)(a) and Schedule 21 has the same extent as the provision subject to the amendment;

(8)   Schedule 28 extends to Scotland only.

263   *[Commencement]*

264   Short title

This Act may be cited as the Civil Partnership Act 2004.

SCHEDULE 10
FORBIDDEN DEGREES OF RELATIONSHIP: SCOTLAND
Section 86

Column 1	Column 2
1.—Relationships by consanguinity	
Father	Mother
Son	Daughter
Father's father	Father's mother
Mother's father	Mother's mother
Son's son	Son's daughter
Daughter's son	Daughter's daughter
Brother	Sister
Father's brother	Father's sister
Mother's brother	Mother's sister
Brother's son	Brother's daughter
Sister's son	Sister's daughter
Father's father's father	Father's father's mother
Father's mother's father	Father's mother's mother
Mother's father's father	Mother's father's mother
Mother's mother's father	Mother's mother's mother
Son's son's son	Son's son's daughter
Son's daughter's son	Son's daughter's daughter
Daughter's son's son	Daughter's son's daughter
Daughter's daughter's son	Daughter's daughter's daughter
2.—Relationships by affinity	
Son of former wife	Daughter of former husband
Son of former civil partner	Daughter of former civil partner
Former husband of mother	Former wife of father
Former civil partner of father	Former civil partner of mother
Former husband of father's mother	Former wife of father's father
Former civil partner of father's father	Former civil partner of father's mother
Former husband of mother's mother	Former wife of mother's father
Former civil partner of mother's father	Former civil partner of mother's mother
Son of son of former wife	Daughter of son of former husband
Son of son of former civil partner	Daughter of son of former civil partner
Son of daughter of former wife husband	Daughter of daughter of former
Son of daughter of former civil partner	Daughter of daughter of former civil partner
[. . .]	

SCHEDULE 11
FINANCIAL PROVISION IN SCOTLAND AFTER OVERSEAS PROCEEDINGS
Section 125

PART 1
INTRODUCTORY

1 (1)   This Schedule applies where—

(a)   a civil partnership has been dissolved or annulled in a country or territory outside the British Islands by means of judicial or other proceedings (here the 'overseas proceedings'), and

(b)   the dissolution or annulment (here the 'overseas determination') is entitled to be recognised as valid in Scotland.

(2)   This Schedule applies even if the date of the overseas determination is earlier than the date on which this Schedule comes into force.

PART 2
CIRCUMSTANCES IN WHICH COURT MAY ENTERTAIN APPLICATION FOR FINANCIAL PROVISION

2 (1)   Subject to sub-paragraph (4), if the jurisdictional requirements and the conditions set out in sub-paragraphs (2) and (3), respectively, are satisfied, the court may entertain an application by one of the former civil partners or former ostensible civil partners, (here 'A') for an order for financial provision.

(2)   The jurisdictional requirements are—

(a)   that A is domiciled or habitually resident in Scotland when the application is made,

(b)   that the other former civil partner, or former ostensible civil partner, (here 'B')—

(i)   is domiciled or habitually resident in Scotland when the application is made,

(ii)   was domiciled or habitually resident in Scotland when A and B last lived together in civil partnership, or

(iii)   when the application is made is an owner or tenant of, or has a beneficial interest in, property in Scotland which has at some time been a family home of A and B, and

(c)   where the court is the sheriff, that when the application is made either—

(i)   A or B is habitually resident in the sheriffdom, or

(ii)   property mentioned in sub-paragraph (2)(b)(iii) is wholly or partially in the sheriffdom.

(3)   The conditions are that—

(a)   B initiated the overseas proceedings,

(b)   the application is made within 5 years after the overseas determination takes effect,

(c)   the civil partnership (or ostensible civil partnership) had a substantial connection with Scotland,

(d)   A and B are alive when the application is made, and

(e)   (taking Part 3 of this Act to have been in force) a court in Scotland would have had jurisdiction to entertain an action for dissolution or annulment of the civil partnership, if such an action had been brought immediately before the overseas determination took effect.

(4)   Where the jurisdiction of the court to entertain proceedings under this Schedule would fall to be determined by reference to the jurisdictional requirements imposed by virtue of Part 1 of the Civil Jurisdiction and Judgments Act 1982 (c 27) (implementation of certain European conventions) or by virtue of Council Regulation (EC) No 44/2001 of 22nd December 2000 on jurisdiction and the recog-

nition and enforcement of judgments in civil and commercial matters [, as amended from time to time and as applied by the Agreement made on 19th October 2005 between the European Community and the Kingdom of Denmark on jurisdiction and the recognition and enforcement of judgments in civil and commercial matters (OJ No L 299 16.11.2005 at p 62)] then—

(a)   satisfaction of the jurisdictional requirements set out in sub-paragraph (2) does not obviate the need to satisfy those so imposed, and

(b)   satisfaction of those so imposed obviates the need to satisfy those set out in sub-paragraph (2).

PART 3
DISPOSAL OF APPLICATIONS

3 (1)   Subject to sub-paragraphs (2) to (5), Scots law applies in relation to an application made under paragraph 2 as it would apply were the application made in an action in Scotland for, as the case may be, dissolution or annulment of a civil partnership.

(2)   In disposing of an application made under paragraph 2 the court must exercise its powers so as to place A and B, in so far as it is reasonable and practicable to do so, in the financial position in which they would have been had that application been disposed of, in such an action in Scotland, on the date when the overseas determination took effect.

(3)   In determining what is reasonable and practicable for the purposes of sub-paragraph (2), the court must have regard in particular to—

(a)   A and B's respective resources, both present and foreseeable, at the date the application is disposed of,

(b)   any order made by a foreign court in or in connection with the overseas proceedings, being an order—

(i)   for the making of financial provision, in whatever form, by A for B or by B for A, or

(ii)   for the transfer of property from A to B or from B to A.

(4)   Subject to sub-paragraph (5), the court may make an order for an interim award of a periodical allowance where—

(a)   it appears from A's averments that in the disposal of the application an order for financial provision is likely to be made, and

(b)   the court considers that such an interim award is necessary to avoid hardship to A.

(5)   Where but for paragraph 2(2)(b)(iii) the court would not have jurisdiction to entertain the application, the court may make no order for financial provision other than an order—

(a)   relating to the former family home or its furniture and plenishings, or

(b)   that B must pay A a capital sum not exceeding the value of B's interest in the former family home and its furniture and plenishings.

PART 4
THE EXPRESSION 'ORDER FOR FINANCIAL PROVISION'

4   In this Schedule, 'order for financial provision' means any one or more of the orders specified in section 8(1) of the Family Law (Scotland) Act 1985 (c 37) or an order under section 111.

VULNERABLE WITNESSES (SCOTLAND) ACT 2004
(2004, asp 3)

PART 2
CIVIL PROCEEDINGS

Evidence of children and other vulnerable witnesses: special measures

11 Interpretation of this Part

(1)   For the purposes of this Part of this Act, a person who is giving or is to give evidence in or for the purposes of any civil proceedings is a vulnerable witness if—

(a)   the person is under the age of 16 on the date of commencement of the proceedings (such a vulnerable witness being referred to in this Part as a 'child witness'), or

(b)   where the person is not a child witness, there is a significant risk that the quality of the evidence to be given by the person will be diminished by reason of—

(i)   mental disorder (within the meaning of section 328 of the Mental Health (Care and Treatment) (Scotland) Act 2003 (asp 13)), or

(ii)   fear or distress in connection with giving evidence in the proceedings.

(2)   In considering whether a person is a vulnerable witness by virtue of subsection (1)(b) above, the court must take into account—

(a)   the nature and circumstances of the alleged matter to which the proceedings relate,

(b)   the nature of the evidence which the person is likely to give,

(c)   the relationship (if any) between the person and any party to the proceedings,

(d)   the person's age and maturity,

(e)   any behaviour towards the person on the part of—

(i)   any party to the proceedings,

(ii)   members of the family or associates of any such party,

(iii)   any other person who is likely to be a party to the proceedings or a witness in the proceedings, and

(f)   such other matters, including—

(i)   the social and cultural background and ethnic origins of the person,

(ii)   the person's sexual orientation,

(iii)   the domestic and employment circumstances of the person,

(iv)   any religious beliefs or political opinions of the person, and

(v)   any physical disability or other physical impairment which the person has,

as appear to the court to be relevant.

(3)   For the purposes of subsection (1)(a) above, proceedings are taken to have commenced when the petition, summons, initial writ or other document initiating the proceedings is served, and, where the document is served on more than one person, the proceedings shall be taken to have commenced when the document is served on the first person on whom it is served.

(4)   In subsection (1)(b), the reference to the quality of evidence is to its quality in terms of completeness, coherence and accuracy.

(5)   In this Part—

'child witness notice' has the meaning given in section 12(2),

'civil proceedings' includes, in addition to such proceedings in any of the ordinary courts of law, any proceedings to which section 91 (procedural rules in relation to certain applications etc) of the Children (Scotland) Act 1995 (c 36) applies,

'court' is to be construed in accordance with the meaning of 'civil proceedings', 'special measure' means any of the special measures set out in, or prescribed under, section 18,

'vulnerable witness application' has the meaning given in section 12(6)(a).

12 Orders authorising the use of special measures for vulnerable witnesses

(1) Where a child witness is to give evidence in or for the purposes of any civil proceedings, the court must, before the proof or other hearing at which the child is to give evidence, make an order—

(a) authorising the use of such special measure or measures as the court considers to be the most appropriate for the purpose of taking the child witness's evidence, or

(b) that the child witness is to give evidence without the benefit of any special measure.

(2) The party citing or intending to cite a child witness must lodge with the court a notice (referred to in this Part as a 'child witness notice')—

(a) specifying the special measure or measures which the party considers to be the most appropriate for the purpose of taking the child witness's evidence, or

(b) if the party considers that the child witness should give evidence without the benefit of any special measure, stating that fact,

and the court must have regard to the child witness notice in making an order under subsection (1) above.

(3) If a child witness notice specifies any of the following special measures, namely—

(a) the use of a live television link in accordance with section 20 where the place from which the child witness is to give evidence by means of the link is another part of the court building in which the court-room is located,

(b) the use of a screen in accordance with section 21, or

(c) the use of a supporter in accordance with section 22 in conjunction with either of the special measures referred to in paragraphs (a) and (b) above,

that special measure is, for the purposes of subsection (1)(a) above, to be taken to be the most appropriate for the purposes of taking the child witness's evidence.

(4) The court may make an order under subsection (1)(b) above only if satisfied—

(a) that the child witness has expressed a wish to give evidence without the benefit of any special measure and that it is appropriate for the child witness so to give evidence, or

(b) that—

(i) the use of any special measure for the purpose of taking the evidence of the child witness would give rise to a significant risk of prejudice to the fairness of the proceedings or otherwise to the interests of justice, and

(ii) that risk significantly outweighs any risk of prejudice to the interests of the child witness if the order is made.

(5) Subsection (6) below applies in relation to a person other than a child witness who is to give evidence in or for the purpose of any civil proceedings (referred to in this section as 'the witness').

(6) The court may—

(a) on an application (referred to in this Part as a 'vulnerable witness application') made to it by the party citing or intending to cite the witness, and

(b) if satisfied that the witness is a vulnerable witness,

make an order authorising the use of such special measure or measures as the court considers most appropriate for the purpose of taking the witness's evidence.

(7) In deciding whether to make an order under subsection (6) above, the court must—

(a) have regard to—

(i) the possible effect on the witness if required to give evidence without the benefit of any special measure, and

(ii) whether it is likely that the witness would be better able to give evidence with the benefit of a special measure, and

(b)   take into account the matters specified in section 11(2)(a) to (f).

13   Review of arrangements for vulnerable witnesses

(1)   In any civil proceedings in which a person who is giving or is to give evidence (referred to in this section as 'the witness') appears to the court to be a vulnerable witness, the court may at any stage in the proceedings (whether before or after the commencement of the proof or other hearing at which the witness is giving or is to give evidence or before or after the witness has begun to give evidence)—

(a)   on the application of the party citing or intending to cite the witness, or

(b)   of its own motion,

review the current arrangements for taking the witness's evidence and make an order under subsection (2) below.

(2)   The order which may be made under this subsection is—

(a)   where the current arrangements for taking the witness's evidence include the use of a special measure or combination of special measures authorised by an order under section 12 or under this subsection (referred to as the 'earlier order'), an order varying or revoking the earlier order, or

(b)   where the current arrangements for taking the witness's evidence do not include any special measure, an order authorising the use of such special measure or measures as the court considers most appropriate for the purpose of taking the witness's evidence.

(3)   An order under subsection (2)(a) above varying an earlier order may—

(a)   add to or substitute for any special measure authorised by the earlier order such other special measure as the court considers most appropriate for the purpose of taking the witness's evidence, or

(b)   where the earlier order authorises the use of a combination of special measures for that purpose, delete any of the special measures so authorised.

(4)   The court may make an order under subsection (2)(a) above revoking an earlier order only if satisfied that—

(a)   the witness has expressed a wish to give or, as the case may be, continue to give evidence without the benefit of any special measure and that it is appropriate for the witness so to give evidence, or

(b)   that—

(i)   the use, or continued use, of the special measure for the purpose of taking the witness's evidence would give rise to a significant risk of prejudice to the fairness of the proceedings or otherwise to the interests of justice, and

(ii)   that risk significantly outweighs any risk of prejudice to the interests of the witness if the order is made.

(5)   Subsection (7) of section 12 applies to the making of an order under subsection (2)(b) of this section as it applies to the making of an order under subsection (6) of that section but as if the references to the witness were to the witness within the meaning of this section.

(6)   In this section, 'current arrangements' means the arrangements in place at the time the review under this section is begun.

14   [Amends Court of Session Act 1988.]

15   Vulnerable witnesses: supplementary provision

(1)   Subsection (2) below applies where—

(a)   a party is considering for the purposes of a child witness notice or a vulnerable witness application which of the special measures is or are the most appropriate for the purpose of taking the evidence of the person to whom the notice or application relates, or

(b)   the court is making an order under section 12(1) or (6) or 13(2).

(2)   The party or, as the case may be, the court must—
(a)   have regard to the best interests of the witness, and
(b)   take account of any views expressed by—
(i)   the witness (having regard, where the witness is a child witness, to the witness's age and maturity), and
(ii)   where the witness is a child witness, the witness's parent.
(3)   For the purposes of subsection (2)(b) above, where the witness is a child witness—
(a)   the witness is to be presumed to be of sufficient age and maturity to form a view if aged 12 or older, and
(b)   in the event that any views expressed by the witness are inconsistent with any views expressed by the witness's parent, the views of the witness are to be given greater weight.
(4)   In this section—
'parent', in relation to a child witness, means any person having parental responsibilities within the meaning of section 1(3) of the Children (Scotland) Act 1995 (c 36) in relation to the child witness
'the witness' means—
(a)   in the case referred to in subsection (1)(a) above, the person to whom the child witness notice or vulnerable witness application relates,
(b)   in the case referred to in subsection (1)(b) above, the person to whom the order would relate.

16   Party to proceedings as a vulnerable witness
Where a child witness or other person who is giving or is to give evidence in or for the purposes of any civil proceedings (referred to in this section as 'the witness') is a party to the proceedings—
(a)   sections 12 and 13 have effect in relation to the witness as if references in those sections to the party citing or intending to cite the witness were references to the witness, and
(b)   section 15 has effect in relation to the witness as if—
(i)   in subsection (1), paragraph (a) were omitted, and
(ii)   in subsection (2), the words 'The party or, as the case may be,' were omitted.

17   Crown application and saving provision
(1)   Sections 11 to 15 of this Act apply to the Crown.
(2)   Nothing in section 12 or 13 of this Act affects any power or duty which a court has otherwise than by virtue of those sections to make or authorise any special arrangements for taking the evidence of any person in any civil proceedings.

18   The special measures
(1)   The special measures which may be authorised to be used by virtue of section 12 or 13 of this Act for the purpose of taking the evidence of a vulnerable witness are—
(a)   taking of evidence by a commissioner in accordance with section 19,
(b)   use of a live television link in accordance with section 20,
(c)   use of screen in accordance with section 21,
(d)   use of a supporter in accordance with section 22, and
(e)   such other measures as the Scottish Ministers may, by order made by statutory instrument, prescribe.
(2)   An order under subsection (1)(e) above is not to be made unless a draft of the statutory instrument containing the order has been laid before and approved by a resolution of the Scottish Parliament.

19   Taking of evidence by a commissioner
(1)   Where the special measure to be used is taking of evidence by a commis-

sioner, the court must appoint a commissioner to take the evidence of the vulnerable witness in respect of whom the special measure is to be used.

(2) Proceedings before a commissioner appointed under subsection (1) above must be recorded by video recorder.

(3) A party to the proceedings—

(a) must not, except by leave of the court, be present in the room where such proceedings are taking place, but

(b) is entitled by such means as seem suitable to the court to watch and hear the proceedings.

(4) The recording of the proceedings made in pursuance of subsection (2) above is to be received in evidence without being sworn to by witnesses.

20 Live television link

(1) Where the special measure to be used is a live television link, the court must make such arrangements as seem to it appropriate for the vulnerable witness in respect of whom the special measure is to be used to give evidence by means of such a link.

(2) Where—

(a) the live television link is to be used in proceedings in a sheriff court, but

(b) that court lacks accommodation or equipment necessary for the purpose of receiving such a link,

the sheriff may by order transfer the proceedings to any sheriff court in the same sheriffdom which has such accommodation or equipment available.

(3) An order may be made under subsection (2) above—

(a) at any stage in the proceedings (whether before or after the commencement of the proof or other hearing at which the vulnerable witness is to give evidence), or

(b) in relation to a part of the proceedings.

21 Screens

(1) Where the special measure to be used is a screen, the screen must be used to conceal the parties to the proceedings from the sight of the vulnerable witness in respect of whom the special measure is to be used.

(2) However, the court must make arrangements to ensure that the parties are able to watch and hear the vulnerable witness giving evidence.

(3) Subsections (2) and (3) of section 20 apply for the purposes of use of a screen under this section as they apply for the purposes of use of a live television link under that section but as if—

(a) references to the live television link were references to the screen, and

(b) the reference to receiving such a link were a reference to the use of a screen.

22 Supporters

(1) Where the special measure to be used is a supporter, another person ('the supporter') nominated by or on behalf of the vulnerable witness in respect of whom the special measure is to be used may be present alongside the witness for the purpose of providing support whilst the witness is giving evidence.

(2) Where the person nominated as the supporter is to give evidence in the proceedings, that person may not act as the supporter at any time before giving evidence.

(3) The supporter must not prompt or otherwise seek to influence the vulnerable witness in the course of giving evidence.

FAMILY LAW (SCOTLAND) ACT 2006
(2006, asp 2)

Marriage

3 Abolition of marriage by cohabitation with habit and repute

(1)   The rule of law by which marriage may be constituted by cohabitation with habit and repute shall cease to have effect.

(2)   Nothing in subsection (1) shall affect the application of the rule in relation to cohabitation with habit and repute where the cohabitation with habit and repute—

(a)   ended before the commencement of this section ('commencement');

(b)   began before, but ended after, commencement; or

(c)   began before, and continues after, commencement.

(3)   Nothing in subsection (1) shall affect the application of the rule in relation to cohabitation with habit and repute where—

(a)   the cohabitation with habit and repute began after commencement; and

(b)   the conditions in subsection (4) are met.

(4)   Those conditions are—

(a)   that the cohabitation with habit and repute was between two persons, one of whom, ('A'), is domiciled in Scotland;

(b)   that the person with whom A was cohabiting, ('B'), died domiciled in Scotland;

(c)   that, before the cohabitation with habit and repute began, A and B purported to enter into a marriage ('the purported marriage') outwith the United Kingdom;

(d)   that, in consequence of the purported marriage, A and B believed themselves to be married to each other and continued in that belief until B's death;

(e)   that the purported marriage was invalid under the law of the place where the purported marriage was entered into; and

(f)   that A became aware of the invalidity of the purported marriage only after B's death.

4 Extension of jurisdiction of sheriff

In subsection (1) of section 5 of the Sheriff Courts (Scotland) Act 1907 (c 51) (extension of jurisdiction), the words '(except declarators of marriage or nullity of marriage)' shall be repealed.

14 Collusion no longer to be bar to divorce

(1)   Any rule of law by which collusion between parties is a bar to their divorce shall cease to have effect.

(2)   [*Amends Divorce (Scotland) Act 1976.*]

Special destinations: revocation on divorce or annulment

19 Special destinations: revocation on divorce or annulment

(1)   Subsections (2) and (3) apply where—

(a)   heritable property is held in the name of—

(i)   a person ('A') and A's spouse ('B') and the survivor of them;

(ii)   A, B and another person and the survivor or survivors of them;

(iii)   A with a special destination on A's death, in favour of B;

(b)   A and B's marriage is terminated by divorce or annulment; and

(c)   after the divorce or annulment A dies.

(2)   In relation to the succession to A's heritable property (or part of it) under the destination, B shall be deemed to have failed to survive A.

(3)   If a person has in good faith and for value (whether by purchase or otherwise) acquired title to the heritable property, the title so acquired shall not be chal-

lengeable on the ground that, by virtue of subsection (2), the property falls to the estate of A.

(4)   Subsection (2) shall not apply if the destination specifies that B is to take under the destination despite the termination of A and B's marriage by divorce or annulment.

Domicile of persons under 16

22   Domicile of persons under 16

(1)   Subsection (2) applies where—

   (a)   the parents of a child are domiciled in the same country as each other; and

   (b)   the child has a home with a parent or a home (or homes) with both of them.

(2)   The child shall be domiciled in the same country as the child's parents.

(3)   Where subsection (2) does not apply, the child shall be domiciled in the country with which the child has for the time being the closest connection.

(4)   In this section, 'child' means a person under 16 years of age.

Cohabitation

25   Meaning of 'cohabitant' in sections 26 to 29

(1)   In sections 26 to 29, 'cohabitant' means either member of a couple consisting of—

   (a)   a man and a woman who are (or were) living together as if they were husband and wife; or

   (b)   two persons of the same sex who are (or were) living together as if they were civil partners.

(2)   In determining for the purposes of any of sections 26 to 29 whether a person ('A') is a cohabitant of another person ('B'), the court shall have regard to—

   (a)   the length of the period during which A and B have been living together (or lived together);

   (b)   the nature of their relationship during that period; and

   (c)   the nature and extent of any financial arrangements subsisting, or which subsisted, during that period.

(3)   In subsection (2) and section 28, 'court' means Court of Session or sheriff.

26   Rights in certain household goods

(1)   Subsection (2) applies where any question arises (whether during or after the cohabitation) as to the respective rights of ownership of cohabitants in any household goods.

(2)   It shall be presumed that each cohabitant has a right to an equal share in household goods acquired (other than by gift or succession from a third party) during the period of cohabitation.

(3)   The presumption in subsection (2) shall be rebuttable.

(4)   In this section, 'household goods' means any goods (including decorative or ornamental goods) kept or used at any time during the cohabitation in any residence in which the cohabitants are (or were) cohabiting for their joint domestic purposes; but does not include—

   (a)   money;

   (b)   securities;

   (c)   any motor car, caravan or other road vehicle; or

   (d)   any domestic animal.

27   Rights in certain money and property

(1)   Subsection (2) applies where, in relation to cohabitants, any question arises (whether during or after the cohabitation) as to the right of a cohabitant to—

(a)   money derived from any allowance made by either cohabitant for their joint household expenses or for similar purposes; or

(b)   any property acquired out of such money.

(2)   Subject to any agreement between the cohabitants to the contrary, the money or property shall be treated as belonging to each cohabitant in equal shares.

(3)   In this section 'property' does not include a residence used by the cohabitants as the sole or main residence in which they live (or lived) together.

28   Financial provision where cohabitation ends otherwise than by death

(1)   Subsection (2) applies where cohabitants cease to cohabit otherwise than by reason of the death of one (or both) of them.

(2)   On the application of a cohabitant (the 'applicant'), the appropriate court may, after having regard to the matters mentioned in subsection (3)—

(a)   make an order requiring the other cohabitant (the 'defender') to pay a capital sum of an amount specified in the order to the applicant;

(b)   make an order requiring the defender to pay such amount as may be specified in the order in respect of any economic burden of caring, after the end of the cohabitation, for a child of whom the cohabitants are the parents;

(c)   make such interim order as it thinks fit.

(3)   Those matters are—

(a)   whether (and, if so, to what extent) the defender has derived economic advantage from contributions made by the applicant; and

(b)   whether (and, if so, to what extent) the applicant has suffered economic disadvantage in the interests of—

(i)   the defender; or

(ii)   any relevant child.

(4)   In considering whether to make an order under subsection (2)(a), the appropriate court shall have regard to the matters mentioned in subsections (5) and (6).

(5)   The first matter is the extent to which any economic advantage derived by the defender from contributions made by the applicant is offset by any economic disadvantage suffered by the defender in the interests of—

(a)   the applicant; or

(b)   any relevant child.

(6)   The second matter is the extent to which any economic disadvantage suffered by the applicant in the interests of—

(a)   the defender; or

(b)   any relevant child,

is offset by any economic advantage the applicant has derived from contributions made by the defender.

(7)   In making an order under paragraph (a) or (b) of subsection (2), the appropriate court may specify that the amount shall be payable—

(a)   on such date as may be specified;

(b)   in instalments.

(8)   Any application under this section shall be made not later than one year after the day on which the cohabitants cease to cohabit.

(9)   In this section—

'appropriate court' means—

(a)   where the cohabitants are a man and a woman, the court which would have jurisdiction to hear an action of divorce in relation to them if they were married to each other;

(b)   where the cohabitants are of the same sex, the court which would have jurisdiction to hear an action for the dissolution of the civil partnership if they were civil partners of each other;

'child' means a person under 16 years of age;

'contributions' includes indirect and non-financial contributions (and, in particular, any such contribution made by looking after any relevant child or any house in which they cohabited); and

'economic advantage' includes gains in—

    (a)   capital;

    (b)   income; and

    (c)   earning capacity;

and 'economic disadvantage' shall be construed accordingly.

    (10)   For the purposes of this section, a child is 'relevant' if the child is—

    (a)   a child of whom the cohabitants are the parents;

    (b)   a child who is or was accepted by the cohabitants as a child of the family.

29 Application to court by survivor for provision on intestacy

    (1)   This section applies where—

    (a)   a cohabitant (the 'deceased') dies intestate; and

    (b)   immediately before the death the deceased was—

        (i)   domiciled in Scotland; and

        (ii)   cohabiting with another cohabitant (the 'survivor').

    (2)   Subject to subsection (4), on the application of the survivor, the court may—

    (a)   after having regard to the matters mentioned in subsection (3), make an order—

        (i)   for payment to the survivor out of the deceased's net intestate estate of a capital sum of such amount as may be specified in the order;

        (ii)   for transfer to the survivor of such property (whether heritable or moveable) from that estate as may be so specified;

    (b)   make such interim order as it thinks fit.

    (3)   Those matters are—

    (a)   the size and nature of the deceased's net intestate estate;

    (b)   any benefit received, or to be received, by the survivor—

        (i)   on, or in consequence of, the deceased's death; and

        (ii)   from somewhere other than the deceased's net intestate estate;

    (c)   the nature and extent of any other rights against, or claims on, the deceased's net intestate estate; and

    (d)   any other matter the court considers appropriate.

    (4)   An order or interim order under subsection (2) shall not have the effect of awarding to the survivor an amount which would exceed the amount to which the survivor would have been entitled had the survivor been the spouse or civil partner of the deceased.

    (5)   An application under this section may be made to—

    (a)   the Court of Session;

    (b)   a sheriff in the sheriffdom in which the deceased was habitually resident at the date of death;

    (c)   if at the date of death it is uncertain in which sheriffdom the deceased was habitually resident, the sheriff at Edinburgh.

    (6)   Any application under this section shall be made before the expiry of the period of 6 months beginning with the day on which the deceased died.

    (7)   In making an order under paragraph (a)(i) of subsection (2), the court may specify that the capital sum shall be payable—

    (a)   on such date as may be specified;

    (b)   in instalments.

    (8)   In making an order under paragraph (a)(ii) of subsection (2), the court may specify that the transfer shall be effective on such date as may be specified.

    (9)   If the court makes an order in accordance with subsection (7), it may, on an application by any party having an interest, vary the date or method of payment of the capital sum.

(10)   In this section—

'intestate' shall be construed in accordance with section 36(1) of the Succession (Scotland) Act 1964 (c 41);

'legal rights' has the meaning given by section 36(1) of the Succession (Scotland) Act 1964 (c 41);

'net intestate estate' means so much of the intestate estate as remains after provision for the satisfaction of—

(a)   inheritance tax;

(b)   other liabilities of the estate having priority over legal rights and the prior rights of a surviving spouse or surviving civil partner; and

(c)   the legal rights, and the prior rights, of any surviving spouse or surviving civil partner; and

'prior rights' has the meaning given by section 36(1) of the Succession (Scotland) Act 1964 (c 41).

Private international law

38   Validity of marriages

(1)   Subject to the Foreign Marriage Act 1892 (c 23), the question whether a marriage is formally valid shall be determined by the law of the place where the marriage was celebrated.

(2)   The question whether a person who enters into a marriage—

(a)   had capacity; or

(b)   consented,

to enter into it shall, subject to subsections (3) and (4) and to section 50 of the Family Law Act 1986 (c 55) (non-recognition of divorce or annulment in another jurisdiction no bar to remarriage), be determined by the law of the place where, immediately before the marriage, that person was domiciled.

(3)   If a marriage entered into in Scotland is void under a rule of Scots internal law, then, notwithstanding subsection (2), that rule shall prevail over any law under which the marriage would be valid.

(4)   The capacity of the person to enter into the marriage shall not be determined under the law of the place where, immediately before the marriage, the person was domiciled in so far as it would be contrary to public policy in Scotland for such capacity to be so determined.

(5)   If the law of the place in which a person is domiciled requires a person under a certain age to obtain parental consent before entering into a marriage, that requirement shall not be taken to affect the capacity of a person to enter into a marriage in Scotland unless failure to obtain such consent would render invalid any marriage that the person purported to enter into in any form anywhere in the world.

39   Matrimonial property

(1)   Any question in relation to the rights of spouses to each other's immoveable property arising by virtue of the marriage shall be determined by the law of the place in which the property is situated.

(2)   Subject to subsections (4) and (5), if spouses are domiciled in the same country, any question in relation to the rights of the spouses to each other's moveable property arising by virtue of the marriage shall be determined by the law of that country.

(3)   Subject to subsections (4) and (5), if spouses are domiciled in different countries then, for the purposes of any question in relation to the rights of the spouses to each other's moveable property arising by virtue of the marriage, the spouses shall be taken to have the same rights to such property as they had immediately before the marriage.

(4)   Any question in relation to—

(a)   the use or occupation of a matrimonial home which is moveable; or

(b)   the use of the contents of a matrimonial home (whether the home is moveable or immoveable),

shall be determined by the law of the country in which the home is situated.

(5)   A change of domicile by a spouse (or both spouses) shall not affect a right in moveable property which, immediately before the change, has vested in either spouse.

(6)   This section shall not apply—

(a)   in relation to the law on aliment, financial provision on divorce, transfer of property on divorce or succession;

(b)   to the extent that spouses agree otherwise.

(7)   In this section, 'matrimonial home' has the same meaning as in section 22 of the 1981 Act.

40   Aliment

Subject to the Maintenance Orders (Reciprocal Enforcement) Act 1972 (c 18), a court in Scotland shall apply Scots internal law in any action for aliment which comes before it.

41   Effect of parents' marriage in determining status to depend on law of domicile

Any question arising as to the effect on a person's status of—

(a)   the person's parents being, or having been, married to each other; or

(b)   the person's parents not being, or not having been, married to each other,

shall be determined by the law of the country in which the person is domiciled at the time at which the question arises.

Declarator of freedom and putting to silence: action no longer competent

42   Action for declarator of freedom and putting to silence to cease to be competent

It shall not be competent to raise an action for declarator of freedom and putting to silence.

General

43   Interpretation

In this Act—

'the 1976 Act' means the Divorce (Scotland) Act 1976 (c 39); and

'the 1981 Act' means the Matrimonial Homes (Family Protection) (Scotland) Act 1981 (c 59).

44   Ancillary provision

(1)   The Scottish Ministers may by order made by statutory instrument make such consequential, transitional or saving provision as they consider appropriate for the purposes of, in consequence of or for giving full effect to this Act or any provision of it.

(2)   An order under subsection (1) may modify any enactment (including this Act).

(3)   The power conferred by subsection (1) on the Scottish Ministers to make orders may be exercised so as to make different provision for different purposes.

(4)   A statutory instrument containing an order under subsection (1) shall, subject to subsection (5), be subject to annulment in pursuance of a resolution of the Scottish Parliament.

(5)   A statutory instrument containing an order under subsection (1) which includes provision modifying an Act or an Act of the Scottish Parliament shall not be made unless a draft of the instrument has been laid before, and approved by resolution of, the Scottish Parliament.

45 *[Minor and consequential amendments and repeals]*

46 Short title and commencement
  (1) This Act may be cited as the Family Law (Scotland) Act 2006.
  (2) The provisions of this Act (except this section) shall come into force on such day as the Scottish Ministers may by order made by statutory instrument appoint.
  (3) An order under subsection (2) may—
    (a) appoint different days for different purposes; and
    (b) include such transitional or saving provision as the Scottish Ministers consider necessary or expedient in connection with the coming into force of the provisions brought into force.

ADOPTION AND CHILDREN (SCOTLAND) ACT 2007
(2007, asp 4)

PART 1
ADOPTION

Chapter 1
The Adoption Service

The adoption service

1 Duty of local authority to provide adoption service
  (1) Each local authority must—
    (a) to the extent that it already provides an adoption service in its area, continue to do so, and
    (b) to the extent that it does not provide such a service in its area, provide such a service there.
  (2) In this Act, 'adoption service' means services designed to meet the needs, in relation to adoption, of persons mentioned in subsection (3).
  (3) Those persons are—
    (a) children who may be adopted,
    (b) persons who have been adopted,
    (c) parents and guardians of children mentioned in paragraph (a),
    (d) natural parents of persons who have been adopted,
    (e) persons who, before the placing of a child for adoption or the adoption of a child, treated the child as their child,
    (f) siblings (whether of the whole-blood or half-blood), natural grandparents and former guardians of—
      (i) children mentioned in paragraph (a), or
      (ii) persons mentioned in paragraph (b),
    (g) persons who may adopt a child,
    (h) persons who have adopted a child,
    (i) in relation to persons mentioned in paragraph (g) or (h), children of, or children treated as children of, such persons, and
    (j) any other persons who are—
      (i) affected by the placing, or proposed placing, of a child for adoption, or
      (ii) affected by an adoption.
  (4) An adoption service includes, in particular, services consisting of or including—
    (a) arrangements for assessing children who may be adopted,
    (b) arrangements for assessing prospective adopters,
    (c) arrangements for placing children for adoption,
    (d) the provision of information about adoption to any of the persons mentioned in subsection (3), and

(e)   adoption support services.

(5)   In this Act, 'adoption support services' means services consisting of or including the provision of—

    (a)   counselling to any of the persons mentioned in subsection (3),

    (b)   guidance about adoption to such persons,

    (c)   any other assistance in relation to the adoption process that the local authority providing an adoption service in a particular case considers appropriate in the circumstances of that case.

2   Carrying out of duties imposed by section 1

(1)   For the purpose of carrying out the duties imposed by section 1(1) efficiently and effectively, a local authority must have regard to—

    (a)   the other services that it provides in its area in carrying out the functions of a local authority under any of the enactments mentioned in section 5(1B) of the Social Work (Scotland) Act 1968 (c 49) (power of the Scottish Ministers to issue certain directions) including, in particular, those functions in so far as they relate to children, and

    (b)   any registered adoption service provided there.

(2)   A local authority may carry out the duties imposed by section 1(1) by securing the provision of its adoption service by a registered adoption service.

(3)   In this section, 'registered adoption service' means an adoption service provided as mentioned in section 2(11)(b) of the Regulation of Care (Scotland) Act 2001 (asp 8) and registered under Part 1 of that Act.

3   Adoption service: regulations

The Scottish Ministers may by regulations—

    (a)   amend subsection (4) or (5) of section 1 by—

        (i)   adding further services,

        (ii)   modifying the services mentioned in those subsections,

    (b)   make further provision about adoption services.

4   Local authority plans

(1)   Before the expiry of such period as the Scottish Ministers may direct, each local authority must prepare and publish a plan for the provision of the adoption service which it is required by section 1(1) to continue to provide, or to provide, in its area.

(2)   Each local authority—

    (a)   must from time to time review the plan published by it under subsection (1), and

    (b)   may, having regard to any such review, prepare and publish—

        (i)   modifications of the plan, or

        (ii)   a plan in substitution for the plan.

(3)   In preparing a plan, or carrying out a review, under this section a local authority must consult—

    (a)   each Health Board constituted under section 2 of the National Health Service (Scotland) Act 1978 (c 29) which provides services under that Act in the area of the local authority,

    (b)   such voluntary organisations as appear to the authority to represent the interests of persons who use, or are likely to use, the adoption service in that area,

    (c)   such voluntary organisations as appear to the authority to provide services in that area which, were they to be provided by the authority, might be an adoption service, and

    (d)   such other persons as may be prescribed by regulations made by the Scottish Ministers.

(4)   A local authority may incorporate a plan published under subsection (1) in

any plan published by the authority under section 19(1) of the 1995 Act (local authority plans for services for children).

(5)   Where a local authority incorporates a plan as mentioned in subsection (4), it need not separately publish a plan under subsection (1).

(6)   Subsections (2) and (5) apply to a plan modified or substituted under subsection (2) as they apply to a plan published under subsection (1).

(7)   The Scottish Ministers may give a local authority directions as to the carrying out of its functions under subsection (2).

(8)   The Scottish Ministers may vary or revoke any direction given under subsection (7).

5   Guidance

(1)   Subsection (2) applies where a local authority is carrying out its function under section 1 to continue to provide, or to provide, an adoption service or to secure the provision of such a service.

(2)   The local authority must have regard to any guidance given by the Scottish Ministers.

(3)   Guidance such as is mentioned in subsection (2) may, in particular, contain provision in relation to—

(a)   how a local authority should assess (or reassess) the needs of a person for adoption support services,

(b)   how the power conferred by section 9(1)(b) should be exercised,

(c)   the classes of person in relation to whom that power should be exercised,

(d)   how responsibility for the provision of an adoption service should be transferred from one local authority to another.

(4)   The Scottish Ministers may vary or revoke any guidance such as is mentioned in subsection (2).

6   Assistance in carrying out functions under sections 1 and 4

(1)   Where it appears to a local authority that an appropriate person could assist the authority in carrying out any of its functions under section 1 or 4, it may require the person to assist the authority in the way specified in the requirement.

(2)   An appropriate person need not comply with a requirement made by virtue of subsection (1) if—

(a)   it would not be reasonably practicable to do so,

(b)   doing so would be incompatible with the person's functions (whether statutory or otherwise), or

(c)   where the person is not a natural person, doing so would unduly prejudice the carrying out of such functions.

(3)   For the purposes of this section, a person is 'appropriate' if the person is—

(a)   another local authority,

(b)   a Health Board constituted under section 2 of the National Health Service (Scotland) Act 1978 (c 29),

(c)   such other person as may be prescribed by regulations made by the Scottish Ministers.

7   [Amends Regulation of Care (Scotland) Act 2001.]

8   Adoption agencies: regulations about carrying out of functions

(1)   The Scottish Ministers may make regulations for any purpose relating to the carrying out of its functions by a registered adoption service.

(2)   The Scottish Ministers may make regulations with respect to the carrying out by local authorities of their functions in relation to adoption.

(3)   Regulations under this section may in particular make provision for or in connection with—

(a)   specifying circumstances in which a local authority proposing to make arrangements for the adoption of a child must apply for a permanence order which includes provision granting authority for the child to be adopted,

(b)   requiring such an application to be made within a period specified in the regulations.

9   Assessment of needs for adoption support services

(1)   A local authority—

(a)   must, on the request of a person mentioned in any of paragraphs (a) to (i) of subsection (3) of section 1, make an assessment of the needs of the person for adoption support services,

(b)   may, on the request of a person mentioned in paragraph (j) of that subsection, make an assessment of the needs of the person for such services.

(2)   Where a local authority makes an assessment of the needs of a person for adoption support services under subsection (1), the authority must decide whether the needs of the person call for the provision of such services.

(3)   A local authority making an assessment of needs under subsection (1) must—

(a)   do so in such manner as may be prescribed by regulations made by the Scottish Ministers, and

(b)   have regard to such matters as may be so prescribed.

10   Provision of services

(1)   On the request of a person mentioned in subsection (3) of section 1, a local authority must provide [. . .] services of a type mentioned in paragraph (d) of subsection (4) of that section to the person.

(2)   On the request of a person mentioned in paragraph (a), (c) or (g) of subsection (3) of section 1, a local authority—

(a)   must provide [. . .] services of a type mentioned in paragraphs (a) to (c) of subsection (4) of that section to the person, and

(b)   may, without prejudice to subsection (4)(a), provide adoption support services to the person.

(3)   For the purposes of subsection (2), it is immaterial whether the local authority has made an assessment of the needs of the person under section 9(1)(a).

(4)   Where a local authority decides under section 9(2) that the provision of adoption support services is called for in respect of—

(a)   a person mentioned in any of paragraphs (a) to (i) of subsection (3) of section 1, the authority must provide the services to the person,

(b)   a person mentioned in paragraph (j) of that subsection, the authority may provide the services to the person.

11   Urgent provision

(1)   If in the opinion of a local authority a person mentioned in subsection (3) of section 1 requires adoption support services as a matter of urgency, nothing in section 9 prevents the authority from providing, or arranging for the provision of, those services for the person without first carrying out an assessment under that section of the person's needs for adoption support services.

(2)   If by virtue of subsection (1) a local authority provides, or arranges for the provision of, adoption support services the authority must, as soon as is reasonably practicable after such provision, make an assessment of the person's needs for adoption support services.

12   Power to provide payment to person entitled to adoption support service

(1)   Subsection (2) applies where a local authority—

(a)   has, in respect of a person, an obligation to provide, or secure the provision of, an adoption support service under this Part, or

(b)   has a power so to provide and determines it should provide.

(2)   Subject to subsection (4), the authority may, after having regard to the

matters mentioned in subsection (3), provide the person with a payment instead of the service.

(3) Those matters are—

(a) the person's eligibility for assistance from any other body,

(b) where the person is so eligible, the availability to the person of that assistance at the time when the service might have been provided to the person by the authority,

(c) the ability of the authority to provide, or secure the provision of, the service, and

(d) the person's need for the service.

(4) A payment under subsection (2) may be made subject to such conditions (including conditions as to repayment) as the authority considers reasonable.

(5) In imposing conditions under subsection (4), the authority must have regard to the person's eligibility for assistance from any other body.

Regulations

13 Regulations

(1) The Scottish Ministers may by regulations make provision for or in connection with—

(a) determining in circumstances specified in the regulations which local authority is, or may become, responsible for—

(i) the provision of an adoption service,

(ii) the making of an assessment of needs under section 9(1)(a),

(b) determining the time at which, and the circumstances in which, a local authority's duty to provide an adoption service ends,

(c) specifying the circumstances in which a local authority may continue to provide an adoption service after the time determined by virtue of paragraph (b) has passed,

(d) specifying the arrangements a local authority may make when a person in respect of whom the authority provides, or has a power or a duty to provide, an adoption service moves outwith the authority's area,

(e) specifying the persons with whom such arrangements may be made,

(f) assessing the needs for adoption support services of persons who have moved or who intend to move—

(i) from one local authority area to another,

(ii) from outwith Scotland to Scotland.

(2) The power conferred by subsection (1) may be exercised so as to make different provision for different adoption services.

Chapter 2
The Adoption Process

Preliminary

14 Considerations applying to the exercise of powers

(1) Subsections (2) to (4) apply where a court or adoption agency is coming to a decision relating to the adoption of a child.

(2) The court or adoption agency must have regard to all the circumstances of the case.

(3) The court or adoption agency is to regard the need to safeguard and promote the welfare of the child throughout the child's life as the paramount consideration.

(4) The court or adoption agency must, so far as is reasonably practicable, have regard in particular to—

(a) the value of a stable family unit in the child's development,

(b)   the child's ascertainable views regarding the decision (taking account of the child's age and maturity),

(c)   the child's religious persuasion, racial origin and cultural and linguistic background, and

(d)   the likely effect on the child, throughout the child's life, of the making of an adoption order.

(5)   Where an adoption agency is placing a child for adoption it must have regard, so far as is reasonably practicable, to the views of the parents, guardians and other relatives of the child.

(6)   In carrying out the duties imposed on it by subsections (2) to (4) an adoption agency must, before making any arrangements for the adoption of a child, consider whether adoption is likely best to meet the needs of the child or whether there is some better practical alternative for the child.

(7)   If an adoption agency concludes that there is an alternative such as is mentioned in subsection (6), it must not make arrangements for the adoption of the child.

(8)   Without prejudice to the generality of subsection (4)(b), a child who is aged 12 or over is presumed to be of sufficient age and maturity to form a view for the purposes of that subsection.

Pre-adoption requirements

15   Child to live with adopters before adoption order made

(1)   Where—

(a)   subsection (2) applies, an adoption order may not be made in relation to a child unless the conditions in subsection (3) are met,

(b)   subsection (2) does not apply, an adoption order may not be made in relation to the child unless the condition in subsection (4) is met.

(2)   This subsection applies if—

(a)   the person applying for the adoption order (the 'applicant'), or one of the applicants, is a parent, step-parent or relative of the child, or

(b)   the child was placed with the applicant, or applicants, by an adoption agency.

(3)   The conditions are—

(a)   that the child is at least 19 weeks old, and

(b)   that at all times during the period of 13 weeks immediately preceding the making of the order the child's home was with the applicants.

(4)   The condition is that at all times during the period of 12 months immediately preceding the making of the order the child's home was with the applicants.

(5)   In relation to—

(a)   an adoption proposed to be effected by a Convention adoption order, or

(b)   an adoption of a child habitually resident outwith the British Islands which is proposed to be effected by an adoption order other than a Convention adoption order, subsection (3)(b) has effect as if the reference to a period of 13 weeks were a reference to a period of 6 months.

16   Home visits

(1)   Where a child was placed for adoption with the applicants by an adoption agency, an adoption order may not be made unless the appropriate court is satisfied that the condition in subsection (2) is met.

(2)   The condition is that sufficient opportunities to see the child with the applicant or, in the case of an application by two applicants, both of them together in the home environment have been given to the agency.

(3)   Where the child was not placed for adoption with the applicants by an adoption agency, an adoption order may not be made unless the appropriate court is satisfied that the condition in subsection (4) is met.

(4)   The condition is that sufficient opportunities to see the child with the appli-

cant or, in the case of an application by two applicants, both of them together in the home environment have been given—

(a)   where the home is in Scotland, to the local authority within whose area the home is situated,

(b)   where the home is outwith Scotland, to any local authority.

17   Reports where child placed by agency

(1)   Subsection (2) applies where an application for an adoption order relates to a child placed for adoption by an adoption agency.

(2)   The agency must—

(a)   submit to the court a report on—

(i)   the suitability of the applicants, and

(ii)   any other matters relevant to the operation of section 14, and

(b)   assist the court in any manner the court directs.

18   Notification to local authority of adoption application

(1)   Subsection (2) applies where a child was not placed for adoption with the applicants by an adoption agency.

(2)   An adoption order may not be made in relation to the child unless the applicants have, at least 3 months before the date of the order, given notice to the appropriate local authority of their intention to apply for the order.

(3)   In subsection (2), 'appropriate local authority' means—

(a)   where the applicants have their home in Scotland, the local authority within whose area the home is situated,

(b)   where they have their home outwith Scotland, any local authority.

19   Notice under section 18: local authority's duties

(1)   This section applies where a local authority receives a notice under section 18 in respect of a child.

(2)   On receipt of the notice the authority must—

(a)   investigate the matter, and

(b)   submit to the court a report of the investigation.

(3)   The local authority must in particular investigate—

(a)   so far as is reasonably practicable, the suitability of the applicants and any other matters relevant to the operation of section 14 in relation to the application,

(b)   whether there has been a contravention of section 75 in relation to the child, and

(c)   whether there has been a failure to comply with section 76(2) in relation to the child.

(4)   If the authority knows that the child is being looked after by another local authority, it must, before the expiry of the period of 7 days beginning with the day on which it receives the notice, give the other authority a copy of the notice.

Restrictions on removal of children placed for adoption

20   Restrictions on removal: child placed for adoption with consent

(1)   Subsection (2) applies where—

(a)   an adoption agency has placed a child for adoption with persons ('prospective adopters'), and

(b)   each parent or guardian of the child has, in accordance with such provision as may be made by regulations by the Scottish Ministers, consented to the placement (whether or not each parent or guardian knows the identity of the prospective adopters).

(2)   A parent or guardian of the child must not remove the child from the care of the prospective adopters without the leave of—

(a)   the adoption agency, or

(b)   the appropriate court.

(3) A person who removes a child in contravention of this section commits an offence and is liable on summary conviction to imprisonment for a term not exceeding 3 months or a fine not exceeding level 5 on the standard scale or both.

21 Restrictions on removal: notice of intention to adopt given

(1) Subsection (2) applies where—

(a) persons ('prospective adopters') give notice under section 18(2) in relation to a child, and

(b) during the period of 5 years immediately preceding the giving of notice, the child's home has been with the prospective adopters.

(2) Except where subsection (3) applies, a person may not remove the child from the care of the prospective adopters during the period beginning with the giving of notice and ending with the relevant act.

(3) This subsection applies if—

(a) the prospective adopters consent to the removal,

(b) a court having jurisdiction to make adoption orders grants leave for the removal,

(c) the child is arrested, or

(d) the removal is authorised by virtue of any enactment.

(4) For the purposes of subsection (2), 'relevant act' means—

(a) where before the expiry of the 3 month period the prospective adopters apply for an adoption order in relation to the child to whom the notice relates, the making of the application for the adoption order,

(b) where the prospective adopters do not apply for an adoption order before the expiry of that period, the expiry of that period.

(5) In this section, '3 month period' means the period of 3 months beginning with the day on which the local authority receives the notice.

(6) If during—

(a) the 3 month period, or

(b) the period of 28 days beginning with the expiry of the 3 month period, the prospective adopters give a further notice under section 18(2) to a local authority in respect of the same child, subsection (2) does not apply.

(7) A person who removes a child in contravention of this section commits an offence and is liable on summary conviction to imprisonment for a term not exceeding 3 months or a fine not exceeding level 5 on the standard scale or both.

22 Restrictions on removal: application for adoption order pending

(1) Subsection (2) applies where—

(a) an application for an adoption order in relation to a child has been made to, but not determined by, the appropriate court, and

(b) during the period of 5 years immediately preceding the making of the application, the child's home has been with the persons applying for the order (the 'prospective adopters').

(2) Except where subsection (3) applies, a person may not remove the child from the care of the prospective adopters.

(3) This subsection applies if—

(a) the prospective adopters consent to the removal,

(b) the court determining the application grants leave for the removal,

(c) the child is arrested, or

(d) the removal is authorised by virtue of any enactment.

(4) A person who removes a child in contravention of this section commits an offence and is liable on summary conviction to imprisonment for a term not exceeding 3 months or a fine not exceeding level 5 on the standard scale or both.

23 Restrictions on removal of child looked after by local authority

(1) Subsection (2) applies where—

(a) section 21(1) or 22(1) applies,

(b) before the child's home came to be with the prospective adopters, the child was looked after by a local authority, and

(c) the child continues to be looked after by a local authority.

(2) Except where subsection (3) applies, the local authority must not remove the child from the care of the prospective adopters.

(3) This subsection applies if—

(a) the removal is made in accordance with section 25 or 26,

(b) an appropriate court grants leave for the removal, or

(c) the removal is authorised by virtue of Chapter 2 or 3 of Part II of the 1995 Act.

Return of children

24 Return of child removed in breach of certain provisions

(1) The relevant court may, on the application of a person from whose care a child has been removed in breach of any of the relevant provisions, order the person who has so removed the child to return the child to the applicant.

(2) The relevant court may, on the application of a person who has reasonable grounds for believing that another person is intending to remove a child from the applicant's care in breach of any of the relevant provisions, by order direct that other person not to remove the child from the applicant's care in breach of the provision concerned.

(3) The 'relevant court' is—

(a) if there is pending in respect of the child an application for an adoption order or a permanence order, the court in which the application is pending,

(b) in any other case—

(i) the Court of Session, or

(ii) the sheriff court of the sheriffdom within which the applicant resides.

(4) The relevant provisions are—

(a) sections 20, 21, 22 and 23,

(b) sections 30, 34, 35 and 36 of the 2002 Act,

(c) Articles 28 and 29 of the Northern Ireland Order.

25 Return of child placed for adoption by adoption agency

(1) This section applies where—

(a) in pursuance of arrangements made by an adoption agency or a registered adoption society for the adoption of a child by persons (the 'prospective adopters'), the child has been placed with the prospective adopters, and

(b) no adoption order has been made in relation to the child on the application of the prospective adopters.

(2) The prospective adopters may give notice to the agency or society of their intention not to retain the care of the child.

(3) The agency or society may give notice to the prospective adopters of its intention not to allow the child to remain in the care of the prospective adopters.

(4) If an application for an adoption order in relation to the child has been made by the prospective adopters, notice under subsection (3) may be given only with leave of the court which is hearing the application.

(5) Subsection (6) applies where—

(a) notice is given by virtue of subsection (2) or (3), or

(b) an application for an adoption order made by the prospective adopters is refused or withdrawn.

(6) The prospective adopters must, before the expiry of the relevant period, return the child to—

(a) the agency or, as the case may be, society, or

(b) a person nominated by the agency or, as the case may be, society for the purposes of this section.

(7) In subsection (6), 'relevant period' means—

    (a)   in the case mentioned in paragraph (a) of subsection (5), the period of 7
days beginning with the day on which notice was given,
    (b)   in the case mentioned in paragraph (b) of that subsection—
        (i)   the period of 7 days beginning with the day on which the application
    was refused or withdrawn, or
        (ii)   if, before the expiry of the period mentioned in sub-paragraph (i), the
    court makes an order extending that period for a period (not exceeding 6
    weeks) specified in the order, the period so specified.
    (8)   A person who fails to return a child in contravention of this section com-
mits an offence and is liable on summary conviction to imprisonment for a term
not exceeding 3 months or a fine not exceeding level 5 on the standard scale or
both.
    (9)   The court by which a person is convicted by virtue of subsection (8) may
order that the child in respect of whom the offence is committed be returned to the
child's parent or guardian or, as the case may be, the adoption agency or registered adoption society.

Adoption not proceeding: arrangements

26   Looked after children: adoption not proceeding

    (1)   This section applies where—
    (a)   persons ('prospective adopters') give notice under section 18(2) in re-
lation to a child,
    (b)   the child has a home with the prospective adopters,
    (c)   the child was not placed with the prospective adopters in pursuance of
arrangements made by an adoption agency or a registered adoption society for
the adoption of the child by the prospective adopters, and
    (d)   the child is being looked after by a local authority (the 'relevant local
authority').
    (2)   The prospective adopters may give notice to the relevant local authority of
their intention not to retain the care of the child.
    (3)   The authority may give notice to the prospective adopters of its intention
not to allow the child to remain in the care of the prospective adopters.
    (4)   Where notice is given by virtue of subsection (2) or (3) the prospective
adopters must, before the expiry of the period of 7 days beginning with the day on
which notice is given, deliver the child to—
    (a)   the authority, or
    (b)   person nominated by the authority for the purposes of this section.
    (5)   If an application for an adoption order in relation to the child has been
made by the prospective adopters, notice under subsection (3) may be given only
with leave of the court which is hearing the application.
    (6)   If an application for an adoption order in relation to the child is refused or
withdrawn, the child—
    (a)   must be delivered to the relevant local authority only if the authority re-
quires it, and
    (b)   where such a requirement is made, must be delivered before the expiry
of the period of 7 days beginning with the day on which the requirement is
made.
    (7)   Where an application by the prospective adopters for an adoption order in
relation to the child has been made but not disposed of, any right of the relevant
local authority to require the child to be delivered otherwise than by virtue of this
section is suspended.
    (8)   A person who fails to deliver a child in contravention of this section com-
mits an offence and is liable on summary conviction to imprisonment for a term
not exceeding 3 months or a fine not exceeding level 5 on the standard scale or
both.

(9) The court by which a person is convicted by virtue of subsection (8) may order that the child in respect of whom the offence is committed be delivered to the child's parent or guardian or, as the case may be, the relevant local authority.

[. . .]

Contravention of sections 30 to 36 of 2002 Act

27   Contravention of sections 30 to 36 of 2002 Act

(1) A person who contravenes any of the provisions of the 2002 Act mentioned in subsection (2) commits an offence and is liable on summary conviction to imprisonment for a term not exceeding 3 months or a fine not exceeding level 5 on the standard scale or both.

(2) Those provisions are—

(a)   section 30(1), (2) and (3) (removal of child placed or who may be placed for adoption),

(b)   sections 32(2)(b), 33(2) and 35(2) (return of child by prospective adopters),

(c)   section 34(1) (removal of child in contravention of placement order),

(d)   section 36(1) (removal of child in non-agency case), and

(e)   section 36(5) (return of child to parent or guardian).

The making of adoption orders

28   Adoption orders

(1) An adoption order is an order made by the appropriate court on an application under section 29 or 30 vesting the parental responsibilities and parental rights in relation to a child in the adopters or adopter.

(2) The court must not make an adoption order unless it considers that it would be better for the child that the order be made than not.

(3) An adoption order may contain such terms and conditions as the court thinks fit.

(4) An adoption order may be made in respect of a person aged 18 or over if the application for the order was made when the person was under 18.

(5) An adoption order may be made in respect of a child who is subject to a permanence order.

(6) An adoption order may be made even if the child to be adopted is already an adopted child.

(7) An adoption order may not be made in respect of a person who is or has been—

(a)   married, or

(b)   a civil partner.

29   Adoption by certain couples

(1) Where—

(a)   each member of a relevant couple is aged 21 or over,

(b)   neither member of the couple is a parent of the child to be adopted, and

(c)   one of the conditions in subsection (2) is met,

an adoption order may be made on the application of the couple.

(2) Those conditions are—

(a)   that a member of the couple is domiciled in a part of the British Islands,

(b)   that each member of the couple has been habitually resident in a part of the British Islands for a period of at least one year ending with the date of the application.

(3) A couple is 'relevant' for the purposes of this section if its members are—

(a)   persons who are married to each other,

(b)   persons who are civil partners of each other,
(c)   persons who are living together as if husband and wife in an enduring family relationship, or
(d)   persons who are living together as if civil partners in an enduring family relationship.
(4)   In this section 'parent', in relation to the child to be adopted, means a parent who has any parental responsibilities or parental rights in relation to the child.

30   Adoption by one person

(1)   An adoption order may be made on the application of a person ('A') if—
(a)   A is aged 21 or over,
(b)   subsection (2), (3), (4) or (5) applies,
(c)   one of the conditions in subsection (6) is met, and
(d)   where A is a natural parent of the child to be adopted, subsection (7) applies.
(2)   This subsection applies if A is not a member of a relevant couple.
(3)   This subsection applies if—
(a)   A and another person ('B') are a relevant couple,
(b)   B is aged 18 or over,
(c)   B is a parent of the child to be adopted, and
(d)   B—
(i)   is domiciled in a part of the British Islands, or
(ii)   has been habitually resident in a part of the British Islands for a period of at least one year ending with the date of the application.
(4)   This subsection applies if—
(a)   A and B are—
(i)   married to each other, or
(ii)   civil partners of each other,
(b)   B is not a parent of the child to be adopted, and
(c)   the court is satisfied that—
(i)   B cannot be found,
(ii)   A and B have separated and are living apart and the separation is likely to be permanent, or
(iii)   B is by reason of ill-health (whether physical or mental) incapable of making an application for an adoption order.
(5)   This subsection applies if—
(a)   A and B are a relevant couple by virtue of being members of a couple falling within paragraph (c) or (d) of subsection (3) of section 29,
(b)   B is not a parent of the child to be adopted, and
(c)   the court is satisfied that B is by reason of ill-health (whether physical or mental) incapable of making an application for an adoption order.
(6)   Those conditions are—
(a)   that A is domiciled in a part of the British Islands,
(b)   that A has been habitually resident in a part of the British Islands for a period of at least one year ending with the date of the application.
(7)   This subsection applies if the court is satisfied that—
(a)   the other natural parent is dead,
(b)   the other natural parent cannot be found,
(c)   by virtue of [the provisions specified in subsection (7A), there is no other parent], or
(d)   the exclusion of the other natural parent from the application for adoption is justified on some other ground.
[(7A)   The provisions referred to in subsection (7)(c) are—
(a)   section 28 of the Human Fertilisation and Embryology Act 1990 (disregarding subsections (5A) to (5I) of that section), or

(b)   sections 34 to 47 of the Human Fertilisation and Embryology Act 2008 (disregarding sections 39, 40 and 46 of that Act).]

(8)   In subsections (3)(c), (4)(b) and (5)(b), 'parent' has the meaning given by section 29(4).

31   Parental etc consent

(1)   An adoption order may not be made unless one of the five conditions is met.

(2)   The first condition is that, in the case of each parent or guardian of the child, the appropriate court is satisfied—

(a)   that the parent or guardian understands what the effect of making an adoption order would be and consents to the making of the order (whether or not the parent or guardian knows the identity of the persons applying for the order), or

(b)   that the parent's or guardian's consent to the making of the adoption order should be dispensed with on one of the grounds mentioned in sub-section (3).

(3)   Those grounds are—

(a)   that the parent or guardian is dead,

(b)   that the parent or guardian cannot be found or is incapable of giving consent,

(c)   that subsection (4) or (5) applies,

(d)   that, where neither of those subsections applies, the welfare of the child otherwise requires the consent to be dispensed with.

(4)   This subsection applies if the parent or guardian—

(a)   has parental responsibilities or parental rights in relation to the child other than those mentioned in sections 1(1)(c) and 2(1)(c) of the 1995 Act,

(b)   is, in the opinion of the court, unable satisfactorily to—

(i)   discharge those responsibilities, or

(ii)   exercise those rights, and

(c)   is likely to continue to be unable to do so.

(5)   This subsection applies if—

(a)   the parent or guardian has, by virtue of the making of a relevant order, no parental responsibilities or parental rights in relation to the child, and

(b)   it is unlikely that such responsibilities will be imposed on, or such rights given to, the parent or guardian.

(6)   In subsection (5)(a), 'relevant order' means a permanence order which does not include provision granting authority for the child to whom the order relates to be adopted.

(7)   The second condition is that a permanence order granting authority for the child to be adopted is in force.

(8)   The third condition is that each parent or guardian of the child has con-sented under section 20 of the 2002 Act (advance consent to adoption), has not withdrawn the consent and does not oppose the making of the adoption order.

(9)   The fourth condition is that—

(a)   the child has been placed for adoption by an adoption agency (within the meaning of section 2(1) of the 2002 Act) with the prospective adopters in whose favour the adoption order is proposed to be made,

(b)   the child was placed for adoption—

(i)   under section 19 of the 2002 Act (placing children with parental con-sent) with the consent of each parent or guardian and the consent of the mother was given when the child was at least 6 weeks old, or

(ii)   under an order made under section 21 of the 2002 Act (placement orders) and the child was at least 6 weeks old when the order was made, and

(c)   no parent or guardian of the child opposes the making of the adoption order.

(10)   The fifth condition is that an order under Article 17(1) or 18(1) of the Northern Ireland Order (orders declaring children free for adoption) is in force in relation to the child.

(11)   Consent is ineffective for the purposes of subsection (2)(a) if given by the mother less than 6 weeks after the child's birth.

(12)   A parent or guardian may not oppose the making of an adoption order under subsection (8) or (9) without leave of the court.

(13)   The court must not give leave under subsection (12) unless satisfied that there has been a change of circumstances since the consent of the parent or guardian was given or, as the case may be, the order under section 21 of the 2002 Act was made.

(14)   The withdrawal of—

(a)   any consent to the placement of a child for adoption under section 19, or under an order under section 21, of the 2002 Act, or

(b)   any consent given under section 20 of that Act,

is ineffective if the consent is given after an application for an adoption order is made.

(15)   In subsections (2) and (3), 'parent', in relation to the child to be adopted, means—

(a)   a parent who has any parental responsibilities or parental rights in relation to the child, or

(b)   a parent who, by virtue of a permanence order which does not include provision granting authority for the child to be adopted, has no such responsibilities or rights.

32   Consent of child aged 12 or over

(1)   Except where subsection (2) applies, an adoption order may not be made in respect of a child who is aged 12 or over unless the child consents.

(2)   This subsection applies where the court is satisfied that the child is incapable of consenting to the order.

33   Restrictions on making orders

(1)   Except where subsection (2) applies, the court may not hear an application for an adoption order in relation to a child where a previous application falling within subsection (3) made in relation to the child by the same persons was refused by any court.

(2)   This subsection applies where—

(a)   in refusing the previous application, the court directed that this section should not apply, or

(b)   it appears to the court that, because of a change in circumstances, or for any other reason, it is proper to hear the application.

(3)   An application falls within this subsection if it is an application for—

(a)   an adoption order,

(b)   an adoption order as defined in section 46(1) of the 2002 Act,

(c)   an order made, or having effect as if made, under Article 12 of the Northern Ireland Order,

(d)   an order for adoption made in the Isle of Man,

(e)   an order for adoption made in any of the Channel Islands.

34   Contravention of section 72 no bar to making order

The court may make an adoption order in relation to a child even where it is found that the applicants have, as respects the child, contravened section 72.

Effect of order on existing rights etc

35   Effect of order on existing rights etc

(1)   Where an adoption order is made on the application of a member of a relevant couple by virtue of subsection (3) of section 30, the making of the order—

(a)   does not affect any parental responsibilities and parental rights which immediately before the making of the order were vested in the other member of the relevant couple,

(b)   does not extinguish any duty owed to the child by that other member—

(i) to pay or provide aliment in respect of any period occurring after the making of the order,

(ii) to make any payment arising out of parental responsibilities and parental rights in respect of such a period.

(2)   Otherwise, the making of an adoption order—

(a)   extinguishes any parental responsibilities and parental rights relating to the child which immediately before the making of the order were vested in any person,

(b)   subject to subsection (3), extinguishes any duty owed to the child immediately before the making of the order—

(i) to pay or provide aliment in respect of any period occurring after the making of the order,

(ii) to make any payment arising out of parental responsibilities and parental rights in respect of such a period.

(3)   The making of an adoption order does not extinguish a duty arising under a deed or agreement—

(a)   which constitutes a trust, or

(b)   which expressly provides that the duty is not to be extinguished by the making of an adoption order.

(4)   An adoption order does not affect parental responsibilities and parental rights so far as they relate to any period before the making of the order.

Revocation of supervision requirement

36   Revocation of supervision requirement

(1)   Subsection (2) applies where—

(a)   the child to be adopted is subject to a supervision requirement, and

(b)   the appropriate court is satisfied that, were it to make an adoption order in relation to the child, compulsory measures of supervision in respect of the child would no longer be necessary.

(2)   The court must make an order providing that, on the making of the adoption order, the supervision requirement ceases to have effect.

Adoption records

37   Information to be kept about adoptions

The Scottish Ministers may make regulations for or in connection with specifying—

(a)   the information which an adoption agency must keep in relation to adoptions, and

(b)   the form and manner in which it must keep the information.

38   Disclosure of information kept under relevant enactment

(1)   The Scottish Ministers may by regulations make provision for or in connection with the disclosure by adoption agencies to adopted persons and other persons of a description or descriptions specified in the regulations of information kept by virtue of a relevant enactment.

(2)   Regulations under subsection (1) may in particular include provision—

(a)   in circumstances specified in the regulations, conferring discretion on adoption agencies as to whether to disclose or withhold information,

(b)   specifying conditions which are to apply in relation to the disclosure of information, or information of a type so specified, to adopted persons of a description or descriptions so specified,

(c)   specifying circumstances in which information should not be disclosed to adopted persons of a description or descriptions so specified,

(d)   about the review of decisions of adoption agencies in connection with—

(i)   the disclosure of information,

(ii)   the conditions applicable to such disclosure.

(3)   In this section, 'relevant enactment' means—

(a)   section 37, or

(b)   any other enactment (whether or not in force) which imposes a requirement (however expressed) to keep records relating to adoptions.

Chapter 3
Status of Adopted Children

39 Meaning of 'adoption' in Chapter 3

(1)   In this Chapter, 'adoption' means—

(a)   adoption by an adoption order,

(b)   adoption by an adoption order as defined in section 46(1) of the 2002 Act,

(c)   adoption by an order made, or having effect as if made, under Article 12 of the Northern Ireland Order,

(d)   adoption by an order made in the Isle of Man or any of the Channel Islands,

(e)   a Convention adoption,

(f)   an overseas adoption, or

(g)   an adoption recognised by the law of Scotland and effected under the law of any other country;

and related expressions are to be interpreted accordingly.

(2)   References in this Chapter to adoption do not include an adoption effected before the day on which this chapter comes into force.

(3)   Any reference in an enactment to an adopted person within the meaning of this Chapter includes a reference to an adopted child within the meaning of Part IV of the Adoption (Scotland) Act 1978 (c 28).

40 Status conferred by adoption

(1)   An adopted person is to be treated in law as if born as the child of the adopters or adopter.

(2)   If an adopted person is adopted—

(a)   by a relevant couple, or

(b)   by virtue of section 30(3), by a member of a relevant couple, the adopted person is to be treated as the child of the couple concerned.

(3)   An adopted person adopted by virtue of section 30(3) by a member of a relevant couple is to be treated in law as not being the child of any person other than the adopter and the other member of the couple.

(4)   Otherwise, an adopted person is to be treated in law as not being the child of any person other than the adopters or adopter.

(5)   Subsections (3) and (4) do not affect any reference in this Act to a person's natural parent or to any other natural relationship.

(6)   Subsection (7) applies where, in the case of a person adopted under a Convention adoption, the Court of Session is satisfied, on an application under this section—

(a)   that under the law of the country in which the adoption was effected the adoption is not a full adoption,

(b)   that—

(i)   the consents mentioned in Article 4(c) and (d) of the Convention have not been given for a full adoption, or

(ii)   the United Kingdom is not the receiving State (within the meaning of Article 2 of the Convention), and (c)　that it would be more favourable to the person for a direction to be given under that subsection.

(7)　The court may direct that subsection (4)—

(a)　is not to apply, or

(b)　is not to apply to such extent as may be specified in the direction.

(8)　In subsection (6), 'full adoption' means an adoption by virtue of which the person falls to be treated in law as if the person were not the child of any person other than the adopters or adopter.

(9)　This section has effect from the date of the adoption.

(10)　Subject to the provisions of this Chapter, this section—

(a)　applies for the interpretation of enactments or instruments passed or made before as well as after the adoption and so applies subject to any contrary indication, and

(b)　has effect as respects things done, or events occurring, on or after the adoption.

41　Miscellaneous enactments

(1)　Subject to subsection (2), section 40 does not apply—

(a)　for the purposes of determining the forbidden degrees of consanguinity and affinity in respect of the law relating to marriage or to the eligibility of persons to register as civil partners of each other, or

(b)　in respect of the crime of incest.

(2)　On the making of an adoption order, the adopter and the person adopted are deemed, for all time coming, to be within the forbidden degrees in respect of the law relating to marriage, to such eligibility and to incest.

(3)　Section 40 does not apply for the purposes of any provision of—

(a)　the British Nationality Act 1981 (c 61),

(b)　the Immigration Act 1971 (c 77),

(c)　any instrument having effect under either of those Acts, or

(d)　any other law for the time being in force which determines British citizenship, British overseas territories citizenship or British Overseas Citizenship.

42　Pensions

Section 40 does not affect entitlement to a pension which is payable to or for the benefit of a person and is in payment at the time of the person's adoption.

43　Insurance

(1)　Subsections (2) and (3) apply where a child is adopted whose natural parent has effected an insurance with—

(a)　a friendly society,

(b)　a collecting society, or

(c)　an industrial insurance company,

for the payment on the death of the child of money for funeral expenses.

(2)　The rights and liabilities under the policy are by virtue of the adoption transferred to the adoptive parents.

(3)　For the purposes of the enactments relating to such societies and companies, the adoptive parents are to be treated as the person who took out the policy.

(4)　Where the adoption is effected by an order made by virtue of section 30(3), the references in subsections (2) and (3) to the adoptive parents are to be read as references to the adopter and the other member of the relevant couple.

44　Succession and inter vivos deeds

Section 40 does not affect the law relating to adopted persons in respect of—

(a)　succession to an intestate or testate estate, and

(b)　the disposal of property by virtue of an inter vivos deed.

Chapter 4
Adoption Support Plans

Adoption support plans

45   Adoption support plans

(1)   This section applies where—

(a)   a local authority has, by virtue of section 9(1), assessed the needs of a person for adoption support services and decides that the provision of such services is called for in respect of the person, and

(b)   the person is a member of a relevant family.

(2)   Subject to subsection (4), the authority must prepare an adoption support plan in respect of each member of the relevant family.

(3)   An adoption support plan must, in relation to the person it concerns ('the person') —

(a)   specify the needs of the person identified as a result of an assessment carried out by virtue of section 9(1),

(b)   record details of the adoption support services the provision of which the authority decides is called for by virtue of section 9(2),

(c)   specify any other needs of the person identified by the authority,

(d)   set out how the needs mentioned in paragraphs (a) and (c) may be met by the provision of adoption support services,

(e)   record details of any previous assessment of needs in respect of the person carried out by virtue of section 9(1),

(f)   record details of any assessment of needs in respect of the person made under section 12A(1) of the Social Work (Scotland) Act 1968 (c 49),

(g)   where the person has been adopted, record details of any care plan prepared by a local authority in respect of the person under regulations made under section 17 of the 1995 Act,

(h)   record details of any adoption support services which—

(i)   were provided to the person before the plan was prepared, or

(ii)   are being provided to the person when the plan is prepared,

(i)   specify any other matter which, in the opinion of the local authority preparing the plan, is relevant to the provision of adoption support services to the person, and

(j)   where there is no information to be included in the plan under any of paragraphs (a) to (i), record that fact.

(4)   The authority may, with the consent of each member of the relevant family aged 12 or over, prepare a single adoption support plan in respect of all members of the relevant family instead of preparing adoption support plans in respect of each of them.

(5)   Subsection (3) applies to a single adoption support plan prepared under subsection (4) as if—

(a)   for the words 'the person it concerns ("the person")' there were substituted 'each member of the relevant family it concerns',

(b)   for the words 'the person' in paragraphs (a), (c), (e), (f), (h) and (i) there were substituted 'each member',

(c)   for the words 'the person' in paragraph (g), where they first occur, there were substituted 'a member of the relevant family', and

(d)   for the words 'the person' in that paragraph, where they second occur, there were substituted 'that member'.

(6)   If in the opinion of the authority a member of the relevant family aged 12 or over is incapable of giving consent under subsection (4), the requirement to obtain such consent does not apply in relation to the member.

(7)   In this section, 'relevant family' means—

(a)   a child who is placed for adoption,

(b)	the person or persons with whom a child is placed for adoption,

(c)	a child who has been adopted,

(d)	the person who has, or persons who have, adopted that child,

(e)	any—

(i)	child of a person or persons mentioned in paragraph (b) or (d),

(ii)	other child who has been treated by the person or persons as a child of the person or persons, living in the same household as the person or persons.

## 46	Duration

(1)	An adoption support plan ceases to have effect on the occurrence of whichever of the events in subsection (2) first occurs.

(2)	Those events are—

(a)	the preparation of a further adoption support plan in respect of the member or, as the case may be, members of the relevant family in relation to whom the adoption support plan was prepared,

(b)	the date on which an appropriate child reaches the age of 18.

(3)	In this section, 'appropriate child' means a child—

(a)	who has been placed for adoption, or

(b)	who has been adopted,

and who is a member of the relevant family in relation to which, or to any members of which, the adoption support plan was prepared.

## 47	Family member's right to require review of plan

(1)	This section applies where an adoption support plan is in force in respect of a member of a relevant family or, as the case may be, a relevant family.

(2)	Subject to subsection (4), the person to whom the plan relates or, as the case may be, a member of the relevant family to which the plan relates (in either case, the 'relevant member') may, if the relevant member believes the local authority is not complying with any of its obligations mentioned in the plan, require the authority to review the plan.

(3)	The authority may, in reviewing the plan, carry out a reassessment of the needs of the relevant member for adoption support services.

(4)	A relevant member (other than the person or persons with whom the child has been placed for adoption or the person who has, or persons who have, adopted the child) may not make a requirement under subsection (2) unless, in the opinion of the local authority, the member is capable of understanding the need for adoption support services.

(5)	After reviewing the plan, the local authority must vary the plan to reflect any changes in—

(a)	the needs of any relevant member for adoption support services identified as a result of a reassessment of needs made under subsection (3),

(b)	the adoption support services the local authority will provide.

(6)	In this section, any references to a reassessment of needs of a person include, where no assessment has been carried out by virtue of section 9(1)(a) in relation to the person, references to an assessment of needs of the person.

## 48	Other cases where authority under duty to review plan

(1)	This section applies where an adoption support plan is in force.

(2)	The local authority must review the plan—

(a)	from time to time, and

(b)	at any time when the authority becomes aware of a change in the circumstances of a relevant member.

(3)	In reviewing the plan, the authority may make a reassessment of the needs of any relevant member.

(4)	After reviewing the plan, the authority must vary the plan to reflect any changes in—

(a) the needs of any relevant member for adoption support services identified as a result of a reassessment of needs made under subsection (3),

(b) the adoption support services the local authority will provide.

(5) In this section—

(a) any references to a reassessment of needs of a person are to be construed in accordance with subsection (6) of section 47,

(b) 'relevant member' has the same meaning as in that section.

Reassessment

49 Reassessment of needs for adoption support services

(1) This section applies where an adoption support plan is in force.

(2) Any relevant member aged 12 or over may require the local authority which prepared the plan to make a reassessment of the member's needs for adoption support services.

(3) The authority, having regard to the results of that reassessment, must decide whether the needs of the member call for the provision of such services.

(4) Where the authority decides, by virtue of subsection (3), that the provision of adoption support services is called for, the authority must provide the services.

(5) Where the authority provides adoption support services under subsection (4), it must vary the adoption support plan to reflect any changes in the services the authority will provide.

(6) A relevant member (other than the person or persons with whom the child has been placed for adoption or the person who has, or persons who have, adopted the child) may not require a reassessment to be made under subsection (2) unless, in the opinion of the local authority, the member is capable of understanding the need for adoption support services.

(7) Where a local authority is making a reassessment of needs under this section, it must—

(a) do so in such manner as may be prescribed by regulations made by the Scottish Ministers, and

(b) have regard to such matters as may be so prescribed.

(8) In this section—

(a) any references to a reassessment of needs of a person are to be construed in accordance with subsection (6) of section 47,

(b) 'relevant member' has the same meaning as in that section.

Directions

50 Implementation of plans: directions

(1) The Scottish Ministers may give directions of a general or specific nature to a local authority as to the implementation of adoption support plans.

(2) A direction under subsection (1) may not require an authority—

(a) to provide or, as the case may be, continue to provide, or

(b) withhold provision of,

a particular adoption support service.

(3) The Scottish Ministers may vary or revoke any direction under subsection (1).

Guidance

51 Guidance

(1) In preparing or reviewing adoption support plans, a local authority must have regard to any guidance issued by the Scottish Ministers.

(2) The Scottish Ministers may vary or revoke any such guidance.

Regulations

52 Regulations about reviews of adoption support plans

The Scottish Ministers may by regulations make provision for or in connection with specifying the way in which reviews of adoption support plans are to be carried out.

Chapter 5
Registration

53 Adopted Children Register and index

(1) The Registrar General must continue to maintain—
    (a) a register to be called the Adopted Children Register, and
    (b) an index of the Adopted Children Register.

(2) No entries may be made in the Adopted Children Register other than entries—
    (a) directed to be made in it by adoption orders, or
    (b) required to be made under schedule 1.

(3) The provisions of the Registration of Births, Deaths and Marriages (Scotland) Act 1965 (c 49) with regard to the correction of errors in entries apply in relation to entries in the Adopted Children Register as they apply in relation to entries in any register of births.

(4) Schedule 1 (which makes provision about registration of adoptions and the amendment of adoption orders) has effect.

54 Searches and extracts

(1) The terms, conditions and regulations as to payment of fees, form and authentication of documents and otherwise applicable under the Registration of Births, Deaths and Marriages (Scotland) Act 1965 (c 49) in respect of—
    (a) searches in indexes kept by virtue of that Act by the Registrar General, and
    (b) the supply from the General Register Office of extracts of entries in the registers of births, deaths and marriages, apply in respect of searches in the index of the Adopted Children Register and supplies of extracts of entries in the Adopted Children Register.

(2) Where a person makes a request in accordance with those terms, conditions and regulations (including paying such fee as may be prescribed by those regulations), the Registrar General is, if the General Register Office is open for the purpose, to—
    (a) search (or permit the person to search) the index of the Adopted Children Register, and
    (b) issue to the person an extract of an entry in the register.

55 Connections between the register and birth records

(1) The Registrar General must make traceable the connection between any entry in the register of births which, by virtue of paragraph 2(2) of schedule 1 or any enactment at the time in force, has been marked 'Adopted' and any corresponding entry in the Adopted Children Register.

(2) Information kept by the Registrar General for the purposes of subsection (1) is not to be open to public inspection or search.

(3) The Registrar General may disclose any such information only in accordance with subsection (4).

(4) Information is disclosed in accordance with this subsection if disclosed—
    (a) under an order of the Court of Session or a sheriff,
    (b) to an adopted person who is aged 16 or over and to whom the information relates, or
    (c) to a local authority, Board, registered adoption society or relevant adoption society which is providing counselling for any such adopted person.

(5)　Where the Registrar General discloses information in accordance with subsection (4)(b), the Registrar must inform the adopted person that counselling services are available for the person—

    (a)　if the person is in Scotland, from any local authority in Scotland,

    (b)　if the person is in England and Wales, from any local authority in England and Wales,

    (c)　if the person is in Northern Ireland, from any Board,

    (d)　if the person is in the United Kingdom and the person's adoption was arranged by—

        (i)　a registered adoption service, from that service,

        (ii)　a registered adoption society, from that society, or

        (iii)　relevant adoption society, from that society.

(6)　Where—

    (a)　in accordance with subsection (4) information is disclosed to an adopted person who is in Scotland, or

    (b)　such a person applies for information under—

        (i)　Schedule 2 to the 2002 Act, or

        (ii)　Article 54 of the Northern Ireland Order,

any body mentioned in subsection (7) from which the adopted person requests counselling must provide counselling for the person.

(7)　Those bodies are—

    (a)　any local authority in Scotland,

    (b)　any registered adoption service, or

    (c)　any registered adoption society or relevant adoption society in so far as (by virtue of section 76(2)) that society is acting as an adoption society in Scotland.

(8)　In this section—

'Board' means a Health and Social Services Board established under Article 16 of the Health and Personal Social Services (Northern Ireland) Order 1972 (SI 1972/1265),

'local authority', in relation to England and Wales, means—

    (a)　any unitary authority, or

    (b)　any county council so far as it is not a unitary authority, 'relevant adoption society'means an adoption society registered under Article 4 of the Northern Ireland Order.

56　Admissibility of extracts as evidence

(1)　An extract of an entry in the Adopted Children Register issued by virtue of section 54(2)(b) is sufficient evidence of the adoption to which it relates.

(2)　Where an entry in the Adopted Children Register contains a record of—

    (a)　the date of birth, or

    (b)　the country of the birth,

of the adopted person, an extract of the entry issued by virtue of that section is sufficient evidence of that date or, as the case may be, country.

57　Interpretation of Chapter 5

(1)　In this Chapter, 'Registrar General' means the Registrar General of Births, Deaths and Marriages for Scotland.

(2)　Any register, index or record maintained by virtue of section 53 or 55 or schedule 1 may be maintained in any form that the Registrar General considers appropriate.

(3)　References (however expressed) to entries in such a register, or to their amendment, cancellation or marking, are to be read accordingly.

Chapter 6
Adoptions With a Foreign Element

Restrictions on movement of children

58   Restriction on bringing children into the United Kingdom

(1)   This section applies where a person who is habitually resident in the British Islands (the 'British resident')—

(a)   brings, or causes another to bring, a child who is habitually resident outwith the British Islands into the United Kingdom for the purpose of adoption by the British resident, or

(b)   at any time brings, or causes another to bring, into the United Kingdom a child adopted by the British resident under an external adoption effected within the period of 12 months ending with that time.

(2)   In subsection (1), the references to adoption, or a child adopted, by the British resident include a reference to adoption, or a child adopted, by the British resident and another person.

(3)   This section does not apply if the child is intended to be adopted under a Convention adoption order.

(4)   An external adoption means an adoption, other than a Convention adoption, of a child effected under the law of any country or territory outwith the British Islands, whether or not the adoption is—

(a)   an adoption within the meaning of Chapter 3, or

(b)   a full adoption (as defined in section 40(8)).

(5)   Regulations may require a person intending to bring, or to cause another to bring, a child into the United Kingdom in circumstances where this section applies—

(a)   to apply to an adoption agency in the prescribed manner for an assessment of the person's suitability to adopt the child, and

(b)   to give the agency any information it may require for the purpose of the assessment.

(6)   Regulations may require prescribed conditions to be met in respect of a child brought into the United Kingdom in circumstances where this section applies.

(7)   In relation to a child brought into the United Kingdom for adoption in circumstances where this section applies, regulations may provide for any provision of Chapter 2 to apply with modifications or not to apply.

(8)   Regulations may provide for this section not to apply if—

(a)   the adopters or, as the case may be, prospective adopters of the child in question are—

(i)   natural parents,

(ii)   natural relatives, or

(iii)   guardians,

of the child (or one of them is), or

(b)   the British resident in question is a step-parent of the child,

and any prescribed conditions are met.

(9)   On the occasion of the first exercise of the power to make regulations under subsection (8)—

(a)   the regulations must not be made unless a draft of the regulations has been approved by a resolution of the Scottish Parliament, and

(b)   accordingly section 117(4) does not apply to the statutory instrument containing the regulations.

(10)   In this section, 'prescribed' means prescribed by regulations and 'regulations' means regulations made by the Scottish Ministers.

59   Preliminary order where child to be adopted abroad

(1)   The appropriate court may, on an application by persons ('the prospective

adopters') who the court is satisfied intend to adopt a child under the law of a country or territory outwith the British Islands, make an order vesting parental responsibilities and parental rights in relation to the child in the prospective adopters.

(2) If the court is satisfied that the prospective adopters would meet the requirements as to domicile, or habitual residence, in Scotland which they would require to meet if an adoption order were to be made on their application, the court may not make an order under this section.

(3) An order under this section may not be made unless any requirements prescribed by regulations by the Scottish Ministers are satisfied.

(4) An application for an order under this section may not be made unless at all times during the period of 10 weeks immediately preceding the application the child's home was with the prospective adopters.

(5) Section 35 has effect in relation to an order under this section as it has effect in relation to adoption orders.

(6) The Scottish Ministers may by regulations provide for any provision of this Act which relates to adoption orders to apply, with or without modifications, to orders under this section.

60 Restriction on removal of children for adoption outwith Great Britain

(1) A person who takes or sends a protected child out of Great Britain to any place outwith the British Islands with a view to the adoption of the child by any person commits an offence.

(2) A person who makes or takes part in any arrangements for transferring the care of a protected child to another person, knowing that the other person intends to take or send the child out of Great Britain in circumstances which would constitute an offence under subsection (1), commits an offence.

(3) No offence is committed under subsection (1) if the child is taken or sent out of Great Britain under the authority of an order under—
  (a)   section 59,
  (b)   section 84 of the 2002 Act, or
  (c)   Article 57 of the Northern Ireland Order.

(4) A person is deemed to take part in arrangements for transferring the care of a child to another person for the purpose mentioned in subsection (2) if the person—
  (a)   facilitates the placing of the child in the care of the other person,
  (b)   initiates or takes part in negotiations the purpose or effect of which is—
      (i)   the making of such arrangements, or
      (ii) the conclusion of an agreement to transfer the care of the child,
  for the purpose mentioned in that subsection, or
  (c)   causes any person to initiate or take part in any such negotiations.

(5) The Scottish Ministers may by regulations provide for subsections (1) to (3) to apply with modifications, or not to apply, if—
  (a)   the prospective adopters are—
      (i)   parents,
      (ii) relatives, or
      (iii) guardians,
  of the child (or one of them is), or
  (b)   the prospective adopter is a step-parent of the child,
and any conditions prescribed by the regulations are met.

(6) On the occasion of the first exercise of the power to make regulations under subsection (5)—
  (a)   the regulations must not be made unless a draft of the regulations has been approved by a resolution of the Scottish Parliament, and
  (b)   accordingly section 117(4) does not apply to the statutory instrument containing the regulations.

(7) In any proceedings under this section—

(a) a report by a British consular officer or a deposition made before, and authenticated under the signature of, such an officer is (if proved that the officer or deponent cannot be found in the United Kingdom) sufficient evidence of the matters stated in the report or deposition, and

(b) it is not necessary to prove the signature or official character of the person who bears to have signed the report or deposition.

(8) A person who commits an offence under this section is liable on summary conviction to imprisonment for a term not exceeding 3 months or a fine not exceeding level 5 on the standard scale or both.

(9) In subsections (1) and (2), 'protected child' means a child who is—

(a) habitually resident in the United Kingdom, or

(b) a Commonwealth citizen.

61 Regulations under section 58: offences

(1) If a person brings, or causes another to bring, a child into the United Kingdom at any time in circumstances where section 58 applies, the person commits an offence—

(a) if the person has not complied with any requirement imposed by virtue of subsection (5) of that section, or

(b) if the person has not met any condition which the person is required to meet by virtue of subsection (6) of that section, before that time, or before any later time which may be prescribed by regulations made by the Scottish Ministers.

(2) A person who commits an offence under subsection (1) is liable—

(a) on summary conviction to imprisonment for a term not exceeding 6 months or a fine not exceeding the statutory maximum or both,

(b) on conviction on indictment to imprisonment for a term not exceeding 12 months, or a fine or both.

Adoptions from abroad: special restrictions

62 Declaration of special restrictions on adoptions from abroad

(1) This section applies if the Scottish Ministers have reason to believe that, because of practices taking place in a country or territory outwith the British Islands (the 'relevant country') in connection with the adoption of children, it would be contrary to public policy to further the bringing of children into the United Kingdom in the cases mentioned in subsection (2).

(2) Those cases are—

(a) that a British resident wishes to bring, or cause another to bring, a child who is not a British resident into the United Kingdom for the purpose of adoption by the British resident and, in connection with the proposed adoption, there have been, or would have to be, proceedings in the relevant country or dealings with authorities or agencies there, or

(b) that a British resident wishes to bring, or cause another to bring, into the United Kingdom a child adopted by the British resident under an adoption effected, within the period of 12 months ending with the date of the bringing in, under the law of the relevant country.

(3) The Scottish Ministers may by order declare, in relation to any relevant country, that special restrictions are to apply for the time being in relation to the bringing in of children in the cases mentioned in subsection (2).

(4) The Scottish Ministers must, as respects each relevant country in relation to which such a declaration has effect for the time being (a 'restricted country'), publish reasons for making the declaration in relation to the country.

(5) The Scottish Ministers must publish a list of restricted countries ('the restricted list') and keep the list up to date.

(6) The reasons and the restricted list are to be published in whatever way the

Scottish Ministers think appropriate for bringing them to the attention of adoption agencies and members of the public.

(7) In this section, 'British resident' means a person habitually resident in the British Islands.

(8) Any reference in this section to adoption by a British resident includes adoption by a British resident and another person.

63 Review

(1) The Scottish Ministers must keep under review, in relation to each restricted country, whether it should continue to be a restricted country.

(2) If the Scottish Ministers determine, in relation to a restricted country, that there is no longer a reason to believe what is mentioned in subsection (1) of section 62, they must by order revoke the order containing the declaration made in relation to it under subsection (3) of that section.

(3) In this section, 'restricted country' has the same meaning as in section 62.

64 The special restrictions

(1) The special restrictions mentioned in subsection (3) of section 62 are that the Scottish Ministers are not to take any step which they might otherwise have taken in connection with furthering the bringing of a child into the United Kingdom in the cases mentioned in subsection (2) of that section (whether or not that step is provided for by virtue of any enactment).

(2) Nothing in subsection (1) prevents the Scottish Ministers from taking those steps if, in any particular case, the prospective adopters or, as the case may be, the adopters satisfy the Scottish Ministers that they should take those steps despite the special restrictions.

(3) The Scottish Ministers may make regulations providing for—

(a) the procedure to be followed by them in determining whether or not they are satisfied as mentioned in subsection (2),

(b) matters which they are to take into account when making such a determination (whether or not they also take other matters into account).

65 Imposition of extra conditions in certain cases

(1) The Scottish Ministers may make regulations providing—

(a) for them to specify in the restricted list, in relation to any restricted country, a step which is not otherwise provided for by virtue of any enactment but which, by virtue of the arrangements between the United Kingdom and that country, the Scottish Ministers normally take in connection with the bringing in of a child where that country is concerned, and

(b) that, if such a step has been so specified in relation to a restricted country, one or more conditions specified in the regulations are to be met in respect of a child brought into the United Kingdom in either of the cases mentioned in section 62(2) (reading the reference there to the 'relevant country' as being to the restricted country in question).

(2) Those conditions are in addition to any provided for by virtue of—

(a) section 58, or

(b) any other enactment.

(3) A person who brings, or causes another to bring, a child into the United Kingdom commits an offence if the person has not met any condition which the person is required to meet by virtue of subsection (1)(b).

(4) Subsection (3) does not apply if the step specified in the restricted list in relation to any country had already been taken before the publication of the restricted list.

(5) A person who commits an offence under subsection (3) is liable—

(a) on summary conviction to imprisonment for a term not exceeding 6 months or a fine not exceeding the statutory maximum or both,

(b)   on conviction on indictment to imprisonment for a term not exceeding 12 months or a fine or both.

(6)   In this section, 'restricted country' and 'restricted list' have the same meanings as in section 62.

Charging

66   Power to charge

(1)   This section applies to adoptions to which—

(a)   section 58 applies, or

(b)   regulations made under section 1 of the Adoption (Intercountry Aspects) Act 1999 (c 18) apply.

(2)   The Scottish Ministers may charge a fee to adopters for services provided or to be provided by them in relation to adoptions to which this section applies.

(3)   The Scottish Ministers may determine the level of fee as they see fit and may, in particular—

(a)   charge a flat fee or charge different fees in different cases or descriptions of case,

(b)   in any case or description of case, waive a fee.

(4)   The Scottish Ministers must secure that, taking one financial year with another, the income from fees under this section does not exceed the total cost to them of providing the services in relation to which the fees are imposed.

(5)   In this section, 'financial year' means a period of 12 months ending with 31 March.

(6)   Any references in this section—

(a)   to adoptions include prospective adoptions, and

(b)   to adopters include prospective adopters.

Overseas adoptions etc

67   Meaning of 'overseas adoption'

(1)   In this Act, 'overseas adoption'—

(a)   means an adoption of a description specified in regulations made by the Scottish Ministers (being a description of adoptions effected under the law of any country or territory outwith the British Islands), but

(b)   does not include a Convention adoption.

(2)   The Scottish Ministers may by regulations prescribe the requirements that ought to be met by an adoption of any description effected after the coming into force of the regulations for it to be an overseas adoption for the purposes of this Act.

(3)   At any time when regulations under subsection (2) are in force, the Scottish Ministers must exercise their power under subsection (1) so as to secure that adoptions of any description effected after the coming into force of the regulations are not overseas adoptions for the purposes of this Act if they consider that such adoptions are not likely, within a reasonable time, to meet the requirements prescribed under subsection (2).

(4)   Regulations under subsection (1) may contain provision as to the manner in which evidence of any overseas adoption may be given.

(5)   In this section, 'adoption' means the adoption of a child or of a person who was a child at the time the adoption was applied for.

68   Annulment and recognition

(1)   The Court of Session may, on an application under this subsection, by order annul a Convention adoption or a Convention adoption order on the ground that the adoption or, as the case may be, order is contrary to public policy.

(2)   The Court of Session may, on an application under this subsection—

(a)   order that an overseas adoption or a determination is to cease to be valid in Great Britain on the ground that the adoption or, as the case may be, determination is contrary to public policy or that the authority which purported to authorise the adoption or make the determination was not competent to entertain the case,

(b)   decide the extent, if any, to which a determination has been affected by a subsequent determination.

(3)   The Court of Session may, in any proceedings in that court, decide that an overseas adoption or a determination is, for the purposes of those proceedings, to be treated as invalid in Great Britain on either of the grounds mentioned in subsection (2)(a).

(4)   An order or decision of the High Court on an application under section 89(2) of the 2002 Act is to be recognised and to have effect as if it were an order or decision of the Court of Session on an application under subsection (2).

(5)   Except as provided by this section, the validity of a Convention adoption, a Convention adoption order, an overseas adoption or a determination is not to be questioned in proceedings in any court in Scotland.

(6)   In this section 'determination' means such a determination as is mentioned in section 70.

69   Section 68: supplementary provision

(1)   Any application for—

(a)   an order under section 68, or

(b)   a decision under subsection (2)(b) of that section, is to be made in the manner prescribed in regulations made by the Scottish Ministers and within such period as may be so prescribed.

(2)   No application is to be made under section 68(1) in respect of an adoption unless immediately before the application is made—

(a)   the person adopted was habitually resident in Scotland, or

(b)   the persons on whose application the adoption order was made were habitually resident there.

(3)   In deciding in pursuance of section 68 whether such an authority as is mentioned in section 70 was competent to hear a particular case, a court is to be bound by any finding of fact made by the authority and stated by the authority to be so made for the purpose of determining whether the authority was competent to hear the case.

70   Effect of determinations and orders made outwith Scotland

(1)   Subsection (2) applies where—

(a)   an authority of a Convention country (other than the United Kingdom) having power under the law of that country—

(i)   to authorise, or review the authorisation of, a Convention adoption, or

(ii)   to give or review a decision revoking or annulling such an adoption or a Convention adoption order, or

(b)   an authority of a relevant territory having power under the law of that territory—

(i)   to authorise, or review the authorisation of, a Convention adoption or an adoption effected in that territory, or

(ii)   to give or review a decision revoking or annulling such an adoption or a Convention adoption order, makes a determination ('the relevant determination') in the exercise of that power.

(2)   Subject to section 68 and any subsequent determination having effect under this subsection, the relevant determination has effect in Scotland for the purpose of effecting, confirming or terminating the adoption in question or confirming its termination as the case may be.

(3)   In subsection (1), 'relevant territory' means—

(a)   any of the Channel Islands,

(b)   the Isle of Man, or

    (c)   any British overseas territory (within the meaning of the British Nationality Act 1981 (c 61)).

(4)   Section 35 applies in relation to an order under Article 17 (freeing child for adoption with parental agreement) or 18 (freeing child for adoption without parental agreement) of the Northern Ireland Order as if it were an adoption order.

(5)   Sections 35(2) and (3) and 43 apply in relation to a child who is the subject of an order which—

    (a)   is similar to an order under section 59, and

    (b)   is made (whether before or after this Act has effect) in a part of the British Islands,

as those sections apply in relation to a child who is the subject of an adoption order.

Chapter 7
Miscellaneous

Adoption allowances

71 Adoption allowances schemes

(1)   Subject to subsection (3), an adoption agency which is—

    (a)   a local authority must, within such period after the coming into force of this section as the Scottish Ministers may by order direct, prepare an adoption allowances scheme,

    (b)   a registered adoption service may prepare such a scheme.

(2)   An adoption allowances scheme is a scheme for or in connection with the payment by the agency of allowances to any person who has adopted, or intends to adopt, a child in any case where arrangements for the adoption were made or, as the case may be, are to be made by the agency.

(3)   The Scottish Ministers may by regulations make provision for or in connection with adoption allowances schemes.

(4)   Regulations under subsection (3) may in particular make provision for or in connection with specifying—

    (a)   the procedure to be followed by an agency in determining whether a person should be paid an allowance,

    (b)   the circumstances in which an allowance may be paid,

    (c)   the factors to be taken into account in determining the amount of an allowance,

    (d)   the procedure for review, variation and termination of allowances,

    (e)   the information about allowances which is to be supplied by an agency to a person who intends to adopt a child, and

    (f)   the procedure to be followed by an agency in preparing, modifying or revoking an adoption allowances scheme.

Prohibited payments

72 Prohibition of certain payments

(1)   This section applies to any payment (other than an excepted payment) which is made to any person for or in consideration of—

    (a)   the adoption by that person of a child,

    (b)   the giving by that person of any consent required in connection with the adoption of a child,

    (c)   the transfer by that person of the care of a child with a view to the adoption of the child, or

    (d)   the making by that person of any arrangements for the adoption of a child.

(2)   Any person who—

    (a)   makes any payment to which this section applies,

(b)   agrees or offers to make any such payment,

(c)   receives, or agrees to receive, any such payment, or

(d)   attempts to obtain any such payment,

commits an offence.

(3)   A person who commits an offence under subsection (2) is liable on summary conviction to imprisonment for a term not exceeding 3 months or a fine not exceeding level 5 on the standard scale or both.

(4)   Where a person is convicted of an offence under subsection (2), the court may, without prejudice to any power which it has to make any other order in relation to the child as respects whom the offence was committed, order the child to be removed to a place of safety until—

(a)   the child can be returned to the child's parent or guardian, or

(b)   other arrangements can be made for the child.

(5)   In this section—

'payment' includes reward,

'place of safety' has the meaning given by section 93(1) of the 1995 Act.

73   Excepted payments

(1)   A payment is an excepted payment if it is made by virtue of, or in accordance with, provision made by virtue of this Act, the 2002 Act or the Northern Ireland Order.

(2)   A payment is an excepted payment if—

(a)   it is made to an adoption agency by—

(i)   a parent or guardian of the child, or

(ii)   a person who adopts, or proposes to adopt, a child,

in respect of expenses reasonably incurred by the agency in connection with the adoption, or proposed adoption, of the child,

(b)   it is made in respect of any legal or medical expenses incurred or to be incurred by any person in connection with an application which the person has made, or proposes to make, for an adoption order or an order under section 59,

(c)   it is authorised by the court to which an application for an adoption order is made,

(d)   it is made by an adoption agency to another adoption agency in consideration of placing the child for adoption,

(e)   it is made by an adoption agency to a voluntary organisation for the time being approved for the purposes of this paragraph by the Scottish Ministers as a fee for the services of the organisation in putting the agency in touch with another adoption agency with a view to the making of arrangements between the adoption agencies for the adoption of a child.

(3)   In this section, 'payment' includes reward.

Disclosure of medical information about parents

74   Disclosure of medical information about parents

(1)   The Scottish Ministers may by regulations make provision for or in connection with disclosure of information about the health of the natural parents of a child who is to be, may be or has been adopted ('the relevant child').

(2)   In making regulations under subsection (1), the Scottish Ministers must secure that a person to whom information is disclosed by virtue of the regulations has a duty of confidentiality in relation to the information.

(3)   Notwithstanding subsection (2), regulations under subsection (1)may include provision enabling a person to whom information is disclosed by virtue of the regulations, in such circumstances and to such an extent as may be specified in the regulations, to disclose the information to—

(a)   the relevant child,

(b)   persons who are to or may adopt, or have adopted, the relevant child.

(4)   Regulations under subsection (1) may, in particular, include provision for or in connection with specifying—
   (a)   the descriptions of person by whom, and to whom, information may be disclosed,
   (b)   the circumstances in which information may be disclosed,
   (c)   the type of information which may, or may not, be disclosed,
   (d)   the circumstances in which consent to disclosure of information need not be obtained,
   (e)   the processing of information by a person to whom information is disclosed.
(5)   In subsection (4)(e), 'processing' has the same meaning as in section 1(1) of the Data Protection Act 1998 (c 28).

Restrictions on arranging adoptions and placing for adoption

75   Restriction on arranging adoptions and placing children
(1)   Subject to subsection (2), a person other than an adoption agency who—
   (a)   makes arrangements for the adoption of a child, or
   (b)   places a child for adoption,
commits an offence.
(2)   Subsection (1) does not apply if the person proposing to adopt the child or, as the case may be, the person with whom the child is placed is—
   (a)   a parent of the child,
   (b)   any other relative of the child, or
   (c)   where a parent of the child is a member of a relevant couple, the other member of the couple.
(3)   A person who receives a child placed in contravention of subsection (1) knowing that the placement is with a view to the person's adopting the child commits an offence.
(4)   A person who takes part in the management or control of a body of persons—
   (a)   which exists wholly or partly for the purpose of making arrangements for the adoption of children, and
   (b)   which is not an adoption agency,
commits an offence.
(5)   A person who commits an offence under this section is liable on summary conviction to imprisonment for a term not exceeding 3 months or a fine not exceeding level 5 on the standard scale or both.
(6)   In any proceedings for an offence under subsection (4), proof of—
   (a)   things done, or
   (b)   words written, spoken or published,
by any person taking part in the management or control of the body of persons, or in making arrangements for the adoption of children on behalf of the body, is sufficient evidence of the purpose for which that body exists.
(7)   It is immaterial whether the actions mentioned in paragraphs (a) and (b) of subsection (6) are carried out in the presence of a party to the proceedings.

76   Adoption societies which are not registered adoption services
(1)   Subsection (2) applies where—
   (a)   an adoption society is—
     (i)   a registered adoption society, or
     (ii)   registered as respects Northern Ireland under Part III of the Health and Personal Social Services (Quality, Improvement and Regulation) (Northern Ireland) Order 2003 (SI 2003/431), and
   (b)   the society is not a registered adoption service.
(2)   Except to the extent that the society considers it necessary to do so in the interests of a person mentioned in section 3(1) of [the 2002] Act or, as the case may

be, Article 3 of the Northern Ireland Order, it must not act as an adoption society in Scotland.

Effect of orders, and placing for adoption, under 2002 Act

77 Effect of certain orders made in England and Wales

(1) An adoption order (within the meaning of section 46(1) of the 2002 Act) has effect in Scotland as it has in England and Wales but as if any reference to the parental responsibility for the child were to the parental responsibilities and parental rights in relation to the child.

(2) An order made under section 21 of that Act (placement orders), and the variation or revocation of such an order under section 23 or 24 of that Act, have effect in Scotland as they have in England and Wales but as if any reference to the parental responsibility for the child were to the parental responsibilities and parental rights in relation to the child.

78 Effect of placing for adoption etc under 2002 Act

(1) If—

(a) a child is placed for adoption under section 19 of the 2002 Act (placing children with parental consent), or

(b) an adoption agency is authorised to place a child for adoption under that section,

sections 25 (parental responsibility) and 28(2) to (4) (further consequences of placement) of that Act have effect in Scotland as they have in England and Wales but with the modifications specified in subsection (2).

(2) Those modifications are—

(a) in section 25, any reference to the parental responsibility for the child is to be read as a reference to the parental responsibilities and parental rights in relation to the child, and

(b) in section 28(2), the reference to the court is to be read as a reference to the appropriate court.

79 Further consequences of placement and placement orders

(1) Subsection (2) applies where—

(a) a child is placed for adoption under section 19 of the 2002 Act (placing children with parental consent), or

(b) an adoption agency is authorised to place a child for adoption under that section.

(2) No order under subsection (1) of section 11 of the 1995 Act (court orders relating to parental responsibilities etc) of a kind mentioned in subsection (2)(c) (residence orders) of that section may be made in respect of the child.

(3) On the making of an order under section 21 of the 2002 Act (a 'placement order') in respect of a child, any order under subsection (1) of section 11 of the 1995 Act of a kind mentioned in subsection (2)(c) to (f) (residence orders, contact orders, specific issue orders and interdicts in relation to parental responsibilities) of that section in respect of the child ceases to have effect.

(4) Where a placement order is in force—

(a) no such order as is mentioned in subsection (3) of this section, and

(b) no order under section 55 of the 1995 Act (child assessment orders),

may be made in respect of the child.

PART 2
PERMANENCE ORDERS

The making of permanence orders

80 Permanence orders

(1) The appropriate court may, on the application of a local authority, make a permanence order in respect of a child.

(2) A permanence order is an order consisting of—

(a) the mandatory provision,

(b) such of the ancillary provisions as the court thinks fit, and

(c) if the conditions in section 83 are met, provision granting authority for the child to be adopted.

(3) In making a permanence order in respect of a child, the appropriate court must secure that each parental responsibility and parental right in respect of the child vests in a person.

81 Permanence orders: mandatory provision

(1) The mandatory provision is provision vesting in the local authority for the appropriate period—

(a) the responsibility mentioned in section 1(1)(b)(ii) of the 1995 Act (provision of guidance appropriate to child's stage of development) in relation to the child, and

(b) the right mentioned in section 2(1)(a) of that Act (regulation of child's residence) in relation to the child.

(2) In subsection (1) 'the appropriate period' means—

(a) in the case of the responsibility referred to in subsection (1)(a), the period beginning with the making of the permanence order and ending with the day on which the child reaches the age of 18,

(b) in the case of the right referred to in subsection (1)(b), the period beginning with the making of the permanence order and ending with the day on which the child reaches the age of 16.

82 Permanence orders: ancillary provisions

(1) The ancillary provisions are provisions—

(a) vesting in the local authority for the appropriate period—

(i) such of the parental responsibilities mentioned in section 1(1)(a), (b)(i) and (d) of the 1995 Act, and

(ii) such of the parental rights mentioned in section 2(1)(b) and (d) of that Act,

in relation to the child as the court considers appropriate,

(b) vesting in a person other than the local authority for the appropriate period—

(i) such of the parental responsibilities mentioned in section 1(1) of that Act, and

(ii) such of the parental rights mentioned in section 2(1)(b) to (d) of that Act,

in relation to the child as the court considers appropriate,

(c) extinguishing any parental responsibilities which, immediately before the making of the order, vested in a parent or guardian of the child, and which—

(i) by virtue of section 81(1)(a) or paragraph (a)(i), vest in the local authority, or

(ii) by virtue of paragraph (b)(i), vest in a person other than the authority,

(d) extinguishing any parental rights in relation to the child which, immediately before the making of the order, vested in a parent or guardian of the child, and which—

(i) by virtue of paragraph (a)(ii), vest in the local authority, or

(ii) by virtue of paragraph (b)(ii), vest in a person other than the authority,

(e) specifying such arrangements for contact between the child and any other person as the court considers appropriate and to be in the best interests of the child, and

(f) determining any question which has arisen in connection with—

(i) any parental responsibilities or parental rights in relation to the child, or

(ii) any other aspect of the welfare of the child.

(2) In subsection (1), 'the appropriate period' means—

(a) in the case of the responsibility mentioned in section 1(1)(b)(ii) of the 1995 Act, the period beginning with the making of the permanence order and ending with the day on which the child reaches the age of 18,

(b) in any other case, the period beginning with the making of the permanence order and ending with the day on which the child reaches the age of 16.

83 Order granting authority for adoption: conditions

(1) The conditions referred to in section 80(2)(c) are—

(a) that the local authority has, in the application for the permanence order, requested that the order include provision granting authority for the child to be adopted,

(b) that the court is satisfied that the child has been, or is likely to be, placed for adoption,

(c) that, in the case of each parent or guardian of the child, the court is satisfied—

(i) that the parent or guardian understands what the effect of making an adoption order would be and consents to the making of such an order in relation to the child, or

(ii) that the parent's or guardian's consent to the making of such an order should be dispensed with on one of the grounds mentioned in subsection (2),

(d) that the court considers that it would be better for the child if it were to grant authority for the child to be adopted than if it were not to grant such authority.

(2) Those grounds are—

(a) that the parent or guardian is dead,

(b) that the parent or guardian cannot be found or is incapable of giving consent,

(c) that subsection (3) or (4) applies,

(d) that, where neither of those subsections applies, the welfare of the child otherwise requires the consent to be dispensed with.

(3) This subsection applies if the parent or guardian—

(a) has parental responsibilities or parental rights in relation to the child other than those mentioned in sections 1(1)(c) and 2(1)(c) of the 1995 Act,

(b) is, in the opinion of the court, unable satisfactorily to—

(i) discharge those responsibilities, or

(ii) exercise those rights, and

(c) is likely to continue to be unable to do so.

(4) This subsection applies if—

(a) the parent or guardian has, by virtue of the making of a permanence order which does not include provision granting authority for the child to be adopted, no parental responsibilities or parental rights in relation to the child, and

(b) it is unlikely that such responsibilities will be imposed on, or such rights given to, the parent or guardian.

(5) In subsections (1)(c) and (2), 'parent', in relation to the child in respect of whom the permanence order is to be made, means—

(a) a parent who has any parental responsibilities or parental rights in relation to the child, or

(b) a parent who, by virtue of a permanence order which does not include provision granting authority for the child to be adopted, has no such responsibilities or rights.

84 Conditions and considerations applicable to making of order

(1) Except where subsection (2) applies, a permanence order may not be made in respect of a child who is aged 12 or over unless the child consents.

(2) This subsection applies where the court is satisfied that the child is incapable of consenting to the order.

(3) The court may not make a permanence order in respect of a child unless it considers that it would be better for the child that the order be made than that it should not be made.

(4) In considering whether to make a permanence order and, if so, what provision the order should make, the court is to regard the need to safeguard and promote the welfare of the child throughout childhood as the paramount consideration.

(5) Before making a permanence order, the court must—

(a) after taking account of the child's age and maturity, so far as is reasonably practicable—

(i) give the child the opportunity to indicate whether the child wishes to express any views, and

(ii) if the child does so wish, give the child the opportunity to express them,

(b) have regard to—

(i) any such views the child may express,

(ii) the child's religious persuasion, racial origin and cultural and linguistic background, and

(iii) the likely effect on the child of the making of the order, and

(c) be satisfied that—

(i) there is no person who has the right mentioned in subsection (1)(a) of section 2 of the 1995 Act to have the child living with the person or otherwise to regulate the child's residence, or

(ii) where there is such a person, the child's residence with the person is, or is likely to be, seriously detrimental to the welfare of the child.

(6) A child who is aged 12 or over is presumed to be of sufficient age and maturity to form a view for the purposes of subsection (5)(a).

85 Child in respect of whom order may be made

(1) A permanence order may be made in respect of a child who is an adopted child.

(2) A permanence order may not be made in respect of a child who is or has been—

(a) married,

(b) a civil partner.

86 Representations

(1) In any proceedings relating to an application for a permanence order, the appropriate court must permit any person mentioned in subsection (2) who wishes to make representations to the court to do so.

(2) Those persons are—

(a) the local authority making the application,

(b) the child or the child's representative,

(c) any person who has parental responsibilities or parental rights in relation to the child,

(d) any other person who claims an interest.

Effect of order

87 Effect of order on existing parental right

The making of a permanence order extinguishes the parental right mentioned in subsection (1)(a) of section 2 of the 1995 Act of—

(a)   a parent of the child in respect of whom the order is made,

(b)   guardian of such a child,

which, immediately before the making of the order, vested in the parent or, as the case may be, guardian.

88 Effect of order on existing orders

(1)   This section applies where—

(a)   parental responsibilities or parental rights in relation to a child vest in a person by virtue of—

(i)   a permanence order, or

(ii)   an order under section 11 of the 1995 Act (court orders relating to parental responsibilities etc),

('the existing order'), and

(b)   the appropriate court intends to make a permanence order ('the new order') as respects the child.

(2)   On the making of the new order, the existing order is revoked.

(3)   In making the new order, the court must secure that the parental responsibilities or parental rights vesting by virtue of the existing order vest in a person under the new order.

Revocation of supervision requirement

89 Revocation of supervision requirement

(1)   Subsection (2) applies where—

(a)   the child in respect of whom a permanence order is to be made is subject to a supervision requirement, and

(b)   the appropriate court is satisfied that, were it to make a permanence order in respect of the child, compulsory measures of supervision in respect of the child would no longer be necessary.

(2)   The court must make an order providing that, on the making of the permanence order, the supervision requirement ceases to have effect.

Precedence

90 Precedence of court orders and supervision requirements over order

(1)   Subsection (2) applies where a local authority has, by virtue of a permanence order, parental responsibilities or parental rights in relation to a child.

(2)   The local authority must not act in any way which would be incompatible with—

(a)   any other court order of which the authority is aware relating to the child or the child's property,

(b)   any supervision requirement to which the child is subject.

Exercise of parental right under order

91 Exercise of parental right under order

(1)   Subsection (2) applies where—

(a)   two or more persons have a parental right in relation to a child, and

(b)   by virtue of paragraph (a) or (b) of subsection (1) of section 82, the right vests in one of them or, as the case may be, two or more of them.

(2)   Each of the persons mentioned in subsection (1)(a) may exercise the right without the consent of the other or, as the case may be, any of the others.

(3) Subsection (2) does not apply where an order vesting the right, or regulating its exercise, provides otherwise.

Variation

92 Variation of ancillary provisions in order

(1) This section applies where a permanence order which includes ancillary provisions is in force.

(2) The appropriate court may, on an application by a person mentioned in subsection (3), vary such of the ancillary provisions as the court considers appropriate.

(3) Those persons are—

(a) the local authority on whose application the permanence order was made,

(b) if the child in respect of whom the order was made is—

(i) aged 12 or over, or

(ii) under the age of 12 but, in the court's opinion (taking account of the child's age and maturity), capable of understanding the effect of the order, that child,

(c) any person in whom parental responsibilities and parental rights are vested by virtue of the order,

(d) any person in whom were vested, immediately before the making of the order, any parental responsibilities or parental rights which, by virtue of the making of the order, vest in another person,

(e) any person in whom were vested, immediately before a variation by virtue of this section of the order, parental responsibilities or parental rights which, by virtue of the variation, vest in another person,

(f) any other person who claims an interest.

(4) Subsection (5) applies where the court exercises its power under subsection (2) to vary the ancillary provisions so as to vest, by virtue of paragraph (a) or (b) of subsection (1) of section 82, in a person a parental responsibility or a parental right which, immediately before the variation, vested in another person.

(5) The court may include in the order as varied provision extinguishing the responsibility or right of that other person.

(6) Subsections (4), (5)(a) and (b) and (6) of section 84 apply to the variation of a permanence order under this section as they apply to the making of such an order.

(7) In subsections (1) and (2), 'ancillary provisions' has the same meaning as in section 82.

(8) In this section, 'vary' includes add to, omit, or amend; and 'variation' is to be construed accordingly.

93 Amendment of order to grant authority for child to be adopted

(1) This section applies where—

(a) a permanence order in respect of a child is in force, and

(b) the order does not include provision granting authority for the child to be adopted.

(2) On the application of the local authority on whose application the order was made, the appropriate court may amend the order so as to include provision granting authority for the child to be adopted if (and only if)—

(a) the court is satisfied that the child has been placed for adoption, or is likely to be placed for adoption,

(b) the court is satisfied that the condition in subsection (3) or subsection (4) is met, and

(c) the court considers that it would be better for the child that authority for the child to be adopted is granted than that it should not be granted.

(3) The condition is that each parent or guardian of the child understands what

the effect of making an adoption order would be and consents to the making of such an order in relation to the child.

(4)   The condition is that the consent of each parent or guardian should be dispensed with on any of the grounds mentioned in section 83.

(5)   Subsections (4), (5)(a) and (b) and (6) of section 84 apply to the amendment of a permanence order under this section as they apply to the making of such an order.

(6)   In subsections (3) and (4)—

'guardian', in relation to a child in respect of whom a permanence order to which this section applies is in force, means a guardian—

(a)   who has any parental responsibilities or parental rights in relation to the child, or

(b)   who, by virtue of the making of a previous such order, no longer has any such responsibilities or rights,

'parent', in relation to a child in respect of whom a permanence order to which this section applies is in force, means a parent—

(a)   who has any parental responsibilities or parental rights in relation to the child, or

(b)   who, by virtue of the making of a previous such order, no longer has any such responsibilities or rights.

94   Proceedings

(1)   In any proceedings for variation of a permanence order by the local authority on whose application the order was granted, the appropriate court must permit any person who is affected by the order, and who wishes to make representations to the court, to do so.

(2)   In any proceedings for variation of a permanence order by a person other than the local authority on whose application the order was granted, the appropriate court must permit any person mentioned in subsection (3) who wishes to make representations to the court to do so.

(3)   Those persons are—

(a)   the local authority on whose application the permanence order was made,

(b)   if the child in respect of whom the original order was made is—

(i)   aged 12 or over, or

(ii)   under the age of 12 but, in the court's opinion (taking account of the child's age and maturity), is capable of understanding the effect of the order, that child,

(c)   any person who has parental responsibilities or parental rights in relation to the child,

(d)   any person on whom a duty was imposed, or power conferred, by the order,

(e)   any person in whom were vested, immediately before the making of the order, any parental responsibilities or parental rights which, by virtue of the making of the order, vest in another person,

(f)   any person in whom were vested, immediately before a variation by virtue of section 92 of the order, parental responsibilities or parental rights which, by virtue of the variation, vest in another person, and

(g)   any other person who claims an interest.

(4)   A person other than the local authority on whose application a permanence order was granted may not apply to the court for a variation of the order without first obtaining the leave of the court.

(5)   If the court is satisfied—

(a)   that there has been a material change in the circumstances directly relating to any of the order's provisions, or

(b)   that for any other reason it is proper to allow the application to be made, it must grant that leave.

(6)   In determining whether there has been a material change in circumstances, the court must have regard, in particular, to any aspect of—

(a)   the welfare of the child in respect of whom the permanence order was made, and

(b)   the circumstances of—

(i)   a parent, or the parents, of the child,

(ii)   the child's guardian, or

(iii)   any person mentioned in paragraph (e) or (f) of subsection (3).

(7)   In subsection (1), the reference to variation of a permanence order includes a reference to amendment of the order to include provision granting authority for the child to whom the order relates to be adopted.

Orders and supervision requirements

95   Duty of children's hearing to prepare report for court

(1)   Subsection (2) applies where—

(a)   an application is made for a permanence order, or variation of such an order, in respect of a child,

(b)   the application has not been determined (or, as the case may be, withdrawn or abandoned), and

(c)   a children's hearing proposes to—

(i)   make a supervision requirement in respect of the child, or

(ii)   modify, under paragraph (c) or (d) of subsection (9) of section 73 of the 1995 Act, a supervision requirement that has been made in respect of the child.

(2)   The children's hearing must prepare for the court to which the application has been made a report containing such information as the Scottish Ministers may by regulations prescribe.

(3)   In subsection (1)(a), the reference to variation of a permanence order includes a reference to amendment of the order to include provision granting authority for the child to whom the order relates to be adopted.

96   Application: effect on supervision requirement

(1)   Subsection (2) applies where an application is made for a permanence order, or variation of such an order, in respect of a child.

(2)   A supervision requirement in respect of the child may not be—

(a)   made, or

(b)   modified under paragraph (c) or (d) of subsection (9) of section 73 of the 1995 Act,

until the application is determined (or, as the case may be, withdrawn or abandoned).

(3)   Subsection (2) does not apply if the court to which the application is made refers the child's case to the Principal Reporter (whether following receipt of a report under section 95 or otherwise).

(4)   In subsection (1), the reference to variation of a permanence order includes a reference to amendment of the order to include provision granting authority for the child to whom the order relates to be adopted.

(5)   In subsection (3), 'Principal Reporter' has the same meaning as in Part II of the 1995 Act.

97   Interim orders and revocation of supervision requirement

(1)   Subsection (2) applies where an application is made for a permanence order, or variation of such an order, in respect of a child.

(2)   The appropriate court may make such interim order as it thinks fit.

(3)   Subsection (4) applies where—

(a)   the child in respect of whom an interim order is to be made is subject to a supervision requirement, and

(b)   the court is satisfied that, were it to make an interim order in relation to the child, compulsory measures of supervision in respect of the child would no longer be necessary.

(4)   The court must make an order providing that, on the making of the interim order, the supervision requirement ceases to have effect.

(5)   If—

(a)   the child in respect of whom an interim order is made is subject to a supervision requirement, and

(b)   the provisions of the order conflict, or are otherwise inconsistent, with the requirement,

the provisions of the order prevail.

(6)   In subsection (1), the reference to variation of a permanence order includes a reference to amendment of the order to include provision granting authority for the child to whom the order relates to be adopted.

Revocation and variation

98   Revocation

(1)   The appropriate court may, on an application by a person mentioned in subsection (2), revoke a permanence order if satisfied that it is appropriate to do so in all the circumstances of the case, including, in particular—

(a)   a material change in the circumstances directly relating to any of the order's provisions,

(b)   any wish by the parent or guardian of the child in respect of whom the order was made to have reinstated any parental responsibilities or parental rights vested in another person by virtue of the order.

(2)   Those persons are—

(a)   the local authority on whose application the order was made,

(b)   any other person affected by the order who has obtained the leave of the court to apply for revocation of the order.

(3)   Subsections (4), (5)(a) and (b) and (6) of section 84 apply to the revocation of a permanence order under this section as they apply to the making of such an order.

99   Duty of local authority to apply for variation or revocation

(1)   Subsection (2) applies where a local authority on whose application a permanence order was made determines that—

(a)   there has been a material change in the circumstances directly relating to any of the order's provisions, and

(b)   in consequence of that change, the order ought to be varied or revoked.

(2)   The authority must, as soon as is reasonably practicable, apply to the appropriate court for variation or, as the case may be, revocation of the order.

(3)   In this section, 'variation', in relation to the permanence order, includes amendment of the order so as to include provision granting authority for the child to whom the order relates to be adopted; and 'varied' is to be construed accordingly.

100   Revocation: order under section 11 of 1995 Act

(1)   Subsection (2) applies where the appropriate court revokes a permanence order in respect of a child.

(2)   The court must consider whether to make an order under section 11of the 1995 Act—

(a)   imposing on a person specified in the order parental responsibilities in relation to the child, and

(b)   giving to such a person parental rights in relation to the child.

Notification requirements

101 Local authority to give notice of certain matters

(1) This section applies where—

(a) a permanence order includes provision granting authority for the child to be adopted,

(b) after the order is made or, as the case may be, amended under section 93(2) so as to include that provision, an event mentioned in subsection (2) occurs, and

(c) the order has not been revoked under section 98(1).

(2) Those events are—

(a) the child is placed for adoption,

(b) an adoption order is made in respect of the child,

(c) the child ceases to be placed for adoption otherwise than on the making of an adoption order.

(3) As soon as is reasonably practicable after the occurrence of the event, the local authority on whose application the permanence order was made must give notice of the event to any person falling within subsection (4).

(4) A person falls within this subsection if—

(a) the person consented under section 83(1)(c)(i) or 93(3) to the making of the order,

(b) the person's consent to the making of the order was dispensed with under section 83(1)(c)(ii) or 93(4).

(5) The local authority need not comply with the requirement imposed by subsection (3) in relation to a person if the person has given notice to that effect to the authority.

Effect of subsequent adoption order on permanence order

102 Effect of subsequent adoption order on permanence order

(1) Subsection (2) applies where—

(a) a permanence order is in force in respect of a child, and

(b) an adoption order is made in respect of the child.

(2) The permanence order ceases to have effect on the making of the adoption order.

Restriction on making certain orders under 1995 Act

103 [Amends Children (Scotland) Act 1995]

Rules of procedure

104 Permanence orders: rules of procedure

(1) Provision may be made by rules of court in respect of—

(a) applications for permanence orders,

(b) applications for variation, or revocation, of permanence orders,

(c) applications for leave to apply for such variation or revocation.

(2) In the case of an application for a permanence order containing a request that the order include provision granting authority for the child to be adopted, or an application made by virtue of section 93(2), rules must require—

(a) any person mentioned in subsection (3)(a) to be notified of the matters mentioned in subsection (4), and

(b) the person mentioned in subsection (3)(b) (if he can be found) to be notified of the matters mentioned in paragraphs (a) and (b) of subsection (4).

(3) Those persons are—

(a) every person who can be found and whose consent to the making of the order is required to be given or dispensed with under this Act or, if no such person can be found, any relative prescribed by the rules who can be found,

(b) if the father of the child in relation to whom the order is to be made does not have, and has never had, parental responsibilities or parental rights in relation to the child, the father of the child.

(4) Those matters are—
  (a) that the application has been made,
  (b) the date on which, and place where, the application will be heard,
  (c) the fact that the person is entitled to be heard on the application,
  (d) the fact that, unless the person wishes, or the court requires, the person need not attend the hearing.

(5) In subsection (1), any references to an application for variation of a permanence order include references to an application to amend the order to include provision granting authority for the child to whom the order relates to be adopted.

PART 3

MISCELLANEOUS

Provisions applicable to adoption orders and permanence orders

105 Notification of proposed application for order

(1) Subsection (2) applies where—
  (a) a local authority—
    (i) proposes to make an application for a permanence order in respect of a child, or
    (ii) becomes aware that an application for an adoption order in respect of a child in its area has been, or is to be, made,
  (b) the father of the child is not married to the mother of the child on the relevant date,
  (c) the father, never having had parental responsibilities or parental rights in relation to the child, does not have such responsibilities or rights on the relevant date, and
  (d) the authority—
    (i) knows the identity and whereabouts of the father, or
    (ii) can, by taking such reasonable and practicable steps as are appropriate in the circumstances of the case, ascertain that information.

(2) The local authority must, on or after the relevant date—
  (a) give notice to the father that—
    (i) it proposes to apply for a permanence order,
    (ii) an application for an adoption order has been made, or
    (iii) an application for an adoption order is to be made,
  as the case may be, and
  (b) provide the father with prescribed information relating to the processes for applying for the order in question.

(3) Where a local authority is required to give notice under subsection (2)(a)(i), it must give the notice at least 4 weeks before the application for the permanence order is made.

(4) Where a local authority is required to give notice under sub-paragraph (ii) or (iii) of subsection (2)(a), it must give the notice as soon as is reasonably practicable after it becomes aware that the application for an adoption order has been or, as the case may be, is to be made.

(5) In this section—
  (a) 'relevant date' means—
    (i) the date on which the local authority determines it will make the application mentioned in sub-paragraph (i) of subsection (1)(a), or
    (ii) the date on which the authority becomes aware of the application mentioned in sub-paragraph (ii) of that subsection,
  as the case may be,

(b) 'prescribed' means prescribed by regulations made by the Scottish Ministers.

106 Child subject to supervision requirement: duty to refer to Principal Reporter

(1) Subsection (2) applies where—

    (a) a child is subject to a supervision requirement,

    (b) a registered adoption service is satisfied that the best interests of the child would be served by placing the child for adoption, and

    (c) it intends to place the child for adoption.

(2) The registered adoption service must refer the child's case to the Principal Reporter.

(3) The Scottish Ministers may make regulations specifying by reference to the occurrence of an event or events described in the regulations the period of time during which a referral under this section is to be made.

(4) In subsection (2), 'Principal Reporter' has the same meaning as in Part II of the 1995 Act.

107 [Amends Children (Scotland) Act 1995]

108 Rules: appointment of curators ad litem and reporting officers

(1) In the case of an application for a relevant order in relation to a child, rules of court must provide for the appointment, in such cases as are prescribed by the rules—

    (a) of a person to act as curator ad litem of the child on the hearing of the application, with the duty of safeguarding the interests of the child in such manner as may be so prescribed,

    (b) of a person to act as reporting officer for the purpose of witnessing agreements to adoption and performing such other duties as may be so prescribed.

(2) Rules may in particular make provision—

    (a) enabling the reporting officer to be appointed before the application is made,

    (b) enabling the court to appoint the same person to be curator ad litem and reporting officer.

(3) Rules may not make provision for—

    (a) the appointment of a person who is employed by an adoption agency which has placed a child for adoption to act as curator ad litem or reporting officer for the purposes of an application for an adoption order in respect of the child,

    (b) the appointment of a person who is employed by a local authority which is making (or has made) an application for a permanence order to act as curator ad litem or reporting officer for the purposes of the application.

(4) A relevant order means—

    (a) an adoption order,

    (b) a permanence order, or

    (c) an order under section 59.

109 Proceedings to be in private

(1) Any proceedings before the court relating to applications under any of the provisions mentioned in subsection (2) must be heard and determined in private unless the court otherwise directs.

(2) Those provisions are—

    (a) section 24,

    (b) section 29,

    (c) section 30,

    (d) section 59,

    (e) section 80,

    (f) section 92,

(g)   section 93,
[(ga)   section 98, and]
(h)   section 99.

Care allowances: regulations

110   Allowances for care of certain children: regulations

(1)   The Scottish Ministers may by regulations make provision about payments by a local authority in respect of a child who falls within subsection (2).

(2)   A child falls within this subsection if—

(a)   the child is placed by the authority under section 26(1)(a) of the 1995 Act,

(b)   the child is required by virtue of section 70(3)(a) of that Act to reside with a person other than a parent of the child, or

(c)   were the child not residing with a relative, the authority would be required by section 25(1) of that Act to provide accommodation for the child.

(3)   Regulations under subsection (1) may in particular include provision for or in connection with—

(a)   specifying descriptions of person to whom payments may be made,

(b)   specifying circumstances in which payments may be made,

(c)   specifying rates of payment to be payable in such circumstances as may be specified in the regulations,

(d)   where a rate is so specified—

(i)   requiring local authorities to pay at least that rate in the circumstances so specified,

(ii)   recommending that local authorities pay at least that rate ('the recommended rate') in the circumstances so specified,

(e)   where a recommended rate is payable, requiring local authorities which pay less than that rate to publish, in such manner as may be so specified, their reasons for doing so.

(4)   A child does not cease to fall within paragraph (a) of subsection (2) by reason only of the making of a permanence order vesting parental responsibilities in a person who is a member of the family with whom the child was placed.

(5)   A child does not fall within paragraph (c) of subsection (2) if the relative is a guardian of the child.

(6)   It is immaterial for the purposes of paragraph (c) of subsection (2) whether the relative has any parental rights or parental responsibilities in relation to the child.

Evidence and notices

111   Evidence of consent

(1)   If a document signifying any consent which is required by this Act to be given is witnessed in accordance with rules of court, it is sufficient evidence of the signature of the person by whom it was executed.

(2)   A document signifying any such consent which purports to be witnessed in accordance with rules is to be presumed to be so witnessed and to have been executed and witnessed on the date and at the place specified in the document unless the contrary is shown.

112   Service of notices etc

Any notice or information required to be given under this Act may be given by post.

113   Admissibility of certain documents as evidence

Any document which is receivable as evidence of any matter—

(a)   in England and Wales under section 77(4) and (5) of the 2002 Act, or

(b)   in Northern Ireland under Article 63(1) of the Northern Ireland Order, is sufficient evidence in Scotland of the matter to which it relates.

PART 4
GENERAL

114 Rules of procedure

(1) Provision may be made by rules of court in respect of any matter to be pre-scribed by rules made by virtue of this Act and dealing generally with all matters of procedure.

(2) In the case of an application for an adoption order, the rules must require—

(a) any person mentioned in subsection (3) to be notified of the matters men-tioned in subsection (4), and

(b) the person mentioned in subsection (5) (if he can be found) to be notified of the matters mentioned in paragraphs (a) and (b) of subsection (4).

(3) Those persons are—

(a) every person who can be found and whose consent to the making of the order is required to be given or dispensed with under this Act or, if no such person can be found, any relative prescribed by rules who can be found,

(b) every person who has consented to the making of the order under section 20 of the 2002 Act (and has not withdrawn the consent) unless the person has given a notice under subsection (4)(a) of that section which has effect,

(c) every person who, if leave were given under section 31(12), would be entitled to oppose the making of the order.

(4) Those matters are—

(a) that the application has been made,

(b) the date on which, and place where, the application will be heard,

(c) the fact that the person is entitled to be heard on the application, and

(d) the fact that, unless the person wishes, or the court requires, the person need not attend the hearing.

(5) The person is the father of the child to be adopted if he does not have, and has never had, parental responsibilities or parental rights in relation to the child.

(6) In the case of an application under section 59, rules of court must require every person who can be found, and whose consent to the making of the order would be required if the application were for an adoption order (other than a Con-vention adoption order) to be notified of the matters mentioned in subsection (4).

115 Offences by bodies corporate and partnerships

(1) Where an offence under this Act committed by a body corporate is proved to have been committed with the consent or connivance of, or to be attributable to any neglect on the part of, a relevant person, the relevant person as well as the body corporate is guilty of the offence and is liable to be proceeded against and punished accordingly.

(2) Where the affairs of a body corporate are managed by its members, sub-section (1) applies in relation to the acts and defaults of a member in connection with the member's functions of management as if the member were a relevant person.

(3) Where an offence under this Act committed by a partnership is proved to have been committed with the consent or connivance of, or to be attributable to any neglect on the part of, a partner, the partner as well as the partnership is guilty of the offence and is liable to be proceeded against and punished accord-ingly.

(4) In this section, 'relevant person', in relation to a body corporate, means a director, manager, secretary or other similar officer of the body, or a person pur-porting to act in any such capacity.

116 Ancillary provision

(1) The Scottish Ministers may by order make such incidental, supplementary, consequential, transitory, transitional or saving provision as they consider neces-

sary for the purposes of, in consequence of or for giving full effect to this Act or any provision of it.

(2) An order under subsection (1) may modify any enactment (including this Act).

117 Orders and regulations

(1) Any power conferred by this Act on the Scottish Ministers or the Registrar General to make orders or regulations is exercisable by statutory instrument.

(2) Any power conferred by this Act on the Scottish Ministers or the Registrar General to make orders or regulations—

(a) may be exercised so as to make different provision for different purposes,

(b) includes power to make such incidental, supplementary, consequential, transitory, transitional or saving provision as the Scottish Ministers consider appropriate or, as the case may be, the Registrar General considers appropriate.

(3) Any power conferred by this Act on the Scottish Ministers to make orders or regulations (as well as being exercisable in relation to all cases to which it extends) may be exercised in relation to—

(a) those cases subject to specified exceptions, or

(b) a particular case or class of case.

(4) Subject to subsection (5), a statutory instrument containing an order or regulations made under this Act (other than an order under section 121) is subject to annulment in pursuance of a resolution of the Scottish Parliament.

(5) A statutory instrument containing—

(a) regulations under—

(i) section 3 which includes provision amending subsection (4) or (5) of section 1,

(ii) section 38(1),

(iii) section 74(1),

(b) an order under section 116(1) which includes provision modifying an Act or an Act of the Scottish Parliament,

is not to be made unless a draft of the instrument has been laid before, and approved by resolution of, the Scottish Parliament.

(6) In this section, 'Registrar General' has the meaning given by section 57(1).

118 Meaning of 'appropriate court'

(1) In this Act, 'appropriate court', as respects any application made by virtue of this Act, is to be construed as follows.

(2) If the application relates to a child who is in Scotland when the application is made, the appropriate court is—

(a) the Court of Session, or

(b) the sheriff court of the sheriffdom within which the child is.

(3) If—

(a) the application is for—

(i) an adoption order, or

(ii) a permanence order seeking provision granting authority for the child to whom the order relates to be adopted, and

(b) the child is not in Scotland when the application is made,

the appropriate court is the Court of Session.

119 Interpretation

(1) In this Act, unless the context otherwise requires—

'the 1995 Act' means the Children (Scotland) Act 1995 (c 36),

'the 2002 Act' means the Adoption and Children Act 2002 (c 38),

'the Northern Ireland Order' means the Adoption (Northern Ireland) Order 1987 (SI 1987/2203),

'adoption agency'—

   (a) means—
      (i) a local authority, or
      (ii) a registered adoption service, and
   (b) in sections 15, 17, 18, 20, 58 and 75 includes—
      (i) an adoption agency within the meaning of section 2(1) of the 2002 Act (adoption agencies in England and Wales), and
      (ii) an adoption agency within the meaning of Article 3 of the Northern Ireland Order (adoption agencies in Northern Ireland),

'adoption order' has the meaning given by section 28(1),

'adoption society' means a body of persons whose functions consist of or include the making of arrangements for or in connection with the adoption of children,

'adoption support services' has the meaning given by section 1(5),

'applicant', in sections 16 to 19 and 34, has the meaning given by section 15(2),

'British Islands' means the United Kingdom, the Channel Islands and the Isle of Man,

'child' means a person who is under the age of 18,

'compulsory measures of supervision' has the same meaning as in Part II of the 1995 Act,

'the Convention' means the Convention on Protection of Children and Co-operation in respect of Intercountry Adoption, concluded at the Hague on 29th May 1993,

'Convention adoption' means an adoption effected under the law of a Convention country outwith the British Islands and certified in pursuance of Article 23(1) of the Convention,

'Convention adoption order' means an adoption order which, by virtue of regulations under section 1 of the Adoption (Intercountry Aspects) Act 1999 (c 18), is made as a Convention adoption order,

'Convention country' means any country or territory in which the Convention is in force,

'guardian', in relation to a child, means a person appointed by deed or will or by a court of competent jurisdiction to be the guardian of the child,

'local authority' means a council constituted under section 2 of the Local Government etc. (Scotland) Act 1994 (c 39),

'notice' means notice in writing,

'overseas adoption' has the meaning given by section 67,

'parental responsibilities' and 'parental rights' have the meanings respectively given by sections 1(3) and 2(4) of the 1995 Act (analogous expressions being construed accordingly),

'permanence order' has the meaning given by section 80(2),

'registered adoption service' has the meaning given by section 2(3),

'registered adoption society' has the meaning given by section 2(2) of the 2002 Act,

'relative', in relation to a child, means a grandparent, brother, sister, uncle or aunt of the child (in each case, whether or not by affinity, and in the cases of a brother, sister, uncle or aunt, whether of the full-blood or half-blood); and includes a civil partner of any such grandparent, brother, sister, uncle or aunt,

'relevant family' has the meaning given by section 45(7); and 'member', in relation to a relevant family, is to be construed accordingly,

'supervision requirement' has the meaning given by section 93(1) of the 1995 Act,

'voluntary organisation' means a body other than a public or local authority the activities of which are not carried on for profit.

   (2) In this Act, unless the context otherwise requires, references to adoption are to the adoption of children, wherever they may be habitually resident, effected under the law of any country or territory, whether within or outwith the British Islands.

(3)   In this Act, references to an adoption service include references to part of such a service.

(4)   In this Act, references, in relation to a child, to being looked after by a local authority are to be construed in accordance with section 17(6) of the 1995 Act.

(5)   In this Act, references to a relevant couple are to be construed in accordance with section 29(3).

(6)   Subject to subsection (7), for the purposes of this Act, a person is deemed to make arrangements for the adoption of a child if—

(a)   the person enters into or makes any agreement or arrangement for, or for facilitating, the adoption of the child by any other person (whether the adoption is effected or intended to be effected in Great Britain or elsewhere),

(b)   the person initiates or takes part in any negotiations the purpose or effect of which is the conclusion of any such agreement or the making of any such arrangement, or

(c)   the person causes another person to act as mentioned in paragraph (a) or (b).

(7)   The making under section 70 of the 1995 Act by a children's hearing of a supervision requirement which, in respect that it provides as to where the child is to reside, facilitates an adoption agency's placing the child for adoption does not constitute the making of such arrangements.

120   Minor and consequential amendments and repeals

(1)   Schedule 2 (which contains minor amendments and amendments consequential on the provisions of this Act) has effect.

(2)   The enactments mentioned in the first column in schedule 3 (which include enactments that are spent) are repealed to the extent set out in the second column.

121   Short title and commencement

(1)   This Act may be cited as the Adoption and Children (Scotland) Act 2007.

(2)   The provisions of this Act (except this section and sections 116 and 117) come into force on such day as the Scottish Ministers may by order appoint.

(3)   An order under subsection (2) may appoint different days for different purposes.

SCHEDULE 1

REGISTRATION OF ADOPTIONS

(introduced by section 53(4))

Registration of adoption orders

1—(1)   Every adoption order must contain a direction to the Registrar General to make in the Adopted Children Register an entry in the form prescribed by regulations made by the Registrar General with the approval of the Scottish Ministers.

(2)   For the purposes of compliance with the requirements of sub-paragraph (1)—

(a)   where the precise date of the child's birth is not proved to the satisfaction of the court—

(i)   the court is to determine the probable date of the child's birth, and

(ii)   the date so determined is to be specified in the adoption order as the date of the child's birth,

(b)   where the country of birth of the child is not proved to the satisfaction of the court—

(i)   if it appears probable that the child was born in a part of the British Islands, the child is to be treated as having been born in Scotland,

(ii)   in any other case, the particulars of the country of birth may be omitted from the adoption order and from the entry in the Adopted Children Register,

(c)   where—

(i)   the application for the adoption order specifies a name (or names) and surname as being those of the child, that name (or those names) and surname are to be recorded in the adoption order as the name (or names) and surname of the child,

(ii)   no name (or names) or surname is so specified, the original name (or names) of the child and the surname of the applicant are to be recorded in the adoption order as the name (or names) and surname of the child.

2—(1)   Sub-paragraph (2) applies where—

(a)   on an application to the appropriate court for an adoption order in respect of a child, the identity of the child with a child to whom an entry in the register of births relates is proved to the satisfaction of the court, and

(b)   the child has not previously been the subject of an adoption order made by a court in Scotland under this Act or any enactment at the time in force.

(2)   Any adoption order made in pursuance of the application must contain a direction to the Registrar General to secure that the entry in the register of births is marked with the word "Adopted".

3   Where an adoption order is made in respect of a child who has previously been the subject of an adoption order made by a court in Scotland under this Act or any enactment at the time in force, the order must contain a direction to the Registrar General to secure that the previous entry in the Adopted Children Register is marked with the word "Re-adopted".

4—(1)   Where an adoption order is made, the clerk of the court which made the order must secure that the order is communicated to the Registrar General.

(2)   As soon as is reasonably practicable after receipt of the communication, the Registrar General must secure that the direction contained in the order is complied with.

Registration of adoptions in other parts of the British Islands

5—(1)   Sub-paragraphs (2) and (3) apply where the Registrar General is notified by the authority maintaining a register of adoptions in a part of the British Islands outwith Scotland that an order has been made in that part authorising the adoption of a child.

(2)   If an entry in the register of births (and no entry in the Adopted Children Register) relates to the child, the Registrar General must secure that the entry is marked with the word "Adopted" followed by the name, in brackets, of the part of the British Islands in which the order was made.

(3)   If an entry in the Adopted Children Register relates to the child, the Registrar General must mark the entry with the word "Re-adopted" followed by the name, in brackets, of the part of the British Islands in which the order was made.

(4)   Where, after an entry in either of the registers mentioned in sub-paragraphs (2) and (3) has been so marked, the Registrar General is notified by the authority concerned that—

(a)   the order has been quashed,

(b)   an appeal against the order has been allowed, or

(c)   the order has been revoked,

the Registrar General must secure that the marking is cancelled.

(5)   Where the marking of an entry in a register is cancelled under sub-paragraph (4), an extract of the entry is not to be treated as accurate unless both the marking and the cancellation are omitted from it.

(6)   This paragraph applies in relation to orders corresponding to orders under section 59 as it applies in relation to orders authorising the adoption of a child except that any marking of an entry required by virtue of this sub-paragraph is to consist of the words "proposed foreign adoption" or, as the case may require,

"proposed foreign re-adoption" followed by the name, in brackets, of the part of the British Islands in which the order was made.

Registration of other adoptions

6—(1) If the Registrar General is satisfied, on an application under this paragraph, that the Registrar General has sufficient particulars relating to a child adopted under a registrable foreign adoption to enable an entry to be made in the Adopted Children Register for the child, the Registrar General must make the entry accordingly.

(2) If the Registrar General is also satisfied that an entry in the register of births relates to the child, the Registrar General must secure that the entry in that register is marked "Adopted" or "Re-adopted", as the case may be, followed by the name, in brackets, of the country in which the adoption was effected.

(3) An application under this paragraph must be made in the prescribed manner by a prescribed person and the applicant must provide the prescribed particulars.

(4) An entry made in the Adopted Children Register by virtue of this paragraph must be made in the prescribed form.

(5) In this paragraph—

"prescribed" means prescribed by regulations made by the Registrar General with the approval of the Scottish Ministers,

"registrable foreign adoption" means an adoption which satisfies prescribed requirements and which is—

(a)   a Convention adoption, or

(b)   an overseas adoption.

Amendment of orders and rectification of registers

7—(1) The court by which an adoption order has been made may, on the application of the adopter or the adopted person, amend the order by the correction of any error in the particulars contained in it.

(2) The court by which an adoption order has been made may, if satisfied on the application of the adopter or the adopted person that before the expiry of the period of one year beginning with the date of the order any new name—

(a)   has been given to the adopted person (whether in baptism or otherwise), or

(b)   has been taken by the adopted person,

in place of or in addition to a name specified in the particulars required to be entered in the Adopted Children Register in pursuance of the order, amend the order by substituting or, as the case may be, adding that name in those particulars.

(3) The court by which an adoption order has been made may, if satisfied on the application of any person concerned that a direction for the marking of an entry in the register of births or the Adopted Children Register included in the order in pursuance of paragraph 2 or 3 was wrongly so included, revoke that direction.

(4) Where an adoption order is amended or a direction revoked under subparagraphs (1) to (3), the clerk of the court must secure that the amendment is communicated in the prescribed manner to the Registrar General.

(5) As soon as is reasonably practicable after receipt of the communication, the Registrar General must secure that—

(a)   the entry in the Adopted Children Register is amended accordingly, or

(b)   the marking of the entry in the register of births or the Adopted Children Register is cancelled,

as the case may be.

(6) Where an adoption order is quashed or an appeal against an adoption

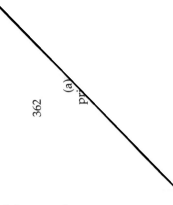

order allowed by any court, the court must give directions to to secure that—

(a) any entry in the Adopted Children Register, and

(b) any marking of an entry in that register or, as the c the register of births, which was effected in pursuance of the

(7) Where an adoption order has been amended, any e entry in the Adopted Children Register which may be is section 54 must be a copy of the entry as amended, without t

(a) any note or marking relating to the amendment, or

(b) any matter cancelled in pursuance of it.

(8) Where the marking of an entry is cancelled, an extract of the entry is not to be treated as accurate unless both the marking and the cancellation are omitted from it.

(9) If the Registrar General is satisfied—

(a) that a registrable foreign adoption (as defined in sub-paragraph (5) of paragraph 6) has ceased to have effect (whether on annulment or otherwise), or

(b) that any entry or mark was erroneously made in pursuance of that paragraph in the Adopted Children Register or the register of births,

the Registrar General may secure that such alterations are made in those registers as the Registrar General considers are required in consequence of the adoption ceasing to have effect or to correct the error.

(10) Where an entry in such a register is amended in pursuance of sub-paragraph (9), an extract of the entry is not to be treated as accurate unless it shows the entry as amended but without indicating that it has been amended.

(11) In this paragraph, "prescribed" means prescribed by regulations made by the Registrar General with the approval of the Scottish Ministers.

Marking of entries on re-registration of birth

8 Without prejudice to any other provision of this Act, where—

(a) an entry in the register of births has been marked in accordance with paragraph 5 or 6, and

(b) the birth is re-registered under section 20(1) of the Registration of Births, Deaths and Marriages (Scotland) Act 1965 (c 49),

the entry made on re-registration must be marked in the same way.

CHILD MAINTENANCE AND OTHER PAYMENTS ACT 2008
(2008, c 8)

PART 1
THE CHILD MAINTENANCE AND ENFORCEMENT COMMISSION

1 The Child Maintenance and Enforcement Commission

(1) There shall be a body corporate to be known as the Child Maintenance and Enforcement Commission (referred to in this Act as 'the Commission').

(2) Schedule 1 (which makes further provision about the Commission) has effect.

2 Objectives of the Commission

(1) The Commission's main objective is to maximise the number of those children who live apart from one or both of their parents for whom effective maintenance arrangements are in place.

(2) The Commission's main objective is supported by the following subsidiary objectives—

to encourage and support the making and keeping by parents of appropriate voluntary maintenance arrangements for their children;

(b) to support the making of applications for child support maintenance under the Child Support Act 1991 (c 48) and to secure compliance when appropriate with parental obligations under that Act.

(3) The Commission shall aim to pursue, and to have regard to, its objectives when exercising a function that is relevant to them.

3 Functions of the Commission: general

(1) The Commission has—

(a) the functions relating to child support transferred to it from the Secretary of State by virtue of this Act, and

(b) such other functions as are conferred by, or by virtue of, this or any other enactment.

(2) The Secretary of State may by regulations provide for the Commission to have an additional function if it appears to the Secretary of State that it is necessary or expedient for the Commission to have the function in relation to any of its objectives.

(3) The Commission must exercise its functions effectively and efficiently.

4 Promotion of child maintenance

The Commission must take such steps as it thinks appropriate for the purpose of raising awareness among parents of the importance of—

(a) taking responsibility for the maintenance of their children, and

(b) making appropriate arrangements for the maintenance of children of theirs who live apart from them.

5 Provision of information and guidance

(1) The Commission must provide to parents such information and guidance as it thinks appropriate for the purpose of helping to secure the existence of effective maintenance arrangements for children who live apart from one or both of their parents.

(2) The Commission may provide information for other purposes in the course of exercising its function under subsection (1).

6 Fees

(1) The Secretary of State may by regulations make provision about the charging of fees by the Commission in connection with the exercise of its functions.

(2) Regulations under subsection (1) may, in particular, make provision—

(a) about when a fee may be charged;

(b) about the amount which may be charged;

(c) for the supply of information needed for the purpose of determining the amount which may be charged;

(d) about who is liable to pay any fee charged;

(e) about when any fee charged is payable;

(f) about the recovery of fees charged;

(g) about waiver, reduction or repayment of fees.

(3) The power conferred by subsection (1) includes power to make provision for the charging of fees which are not related to costs.

(4) The Secretary of State may by regulations provide that the provisions of the Child Support Act 1991 (c 48) with respect to—

(a) the collection of child support maintenance,

(b) the enforcement of any obligation to pay child support maintenance,

shall apply equally (with any necessary modifications) to fees payable by virtue of regulations under subsection (1).

(5) The Secretary of State may by regulations make provision for a person affected by a decision of the Commission under regulations under subsection (1) to have a right of appeal against the decision to an appeal tribunal.

(6)   Subsections (3) to (5), (7) and (8) of section 20 of the Child Support Act 1991 (appeals to appeal tribunals) apply to appeals under regulations under subsection (5) as they apply to appeals under that section.

(7)   The Commission shall pay into the Consolidated Fund any amount which it receives in respect of fees charged by it under regulations under this section.

7   Agency arrangements and provision of services

(1)   Arrangements may be made between the Commission and any relevant authority for—

(a)   any functions of one of them to be exercised on their behalf by, or by members of staff of, the other;

(b)   the provision of administrative, professional or technical services by one of them for the other.

(2)   The reference in subsection (1)(a) to functions does not include functions of making, confirming or approving subordinate legislation.

(3)   The Commission may make arrangements under this section on such terms and conditions as it thinks fit.

(4)   In this section 'relevant authority' means—

(a)   any Minister of the Crown or department of the Government of the United Kingdom;

(b)   a public body specified in regulations made by the Secretary of State for the purposes of this section.

8   Contracting out

(1)   Any function of the Commission may be exercised by, or by employees of, such person (if any) as the Commission may authorise for the purpose.

(2)   An authorisation given by virtue of subsection (1) may authorise the exercise of the function concerned—

(a)   either wholly or to such extent as may be specified in the authorisation,

(b)   either generally or in such cases or areas as may be so specified, and

(c)   either unconditionally or subject to the fulfilment of such conditions as may be so specified.

(3)   An authorisation given by virtue of subsection (1)—

(a)   may specify its duration,

(b)   may be revoked at any time by the Commission, and

(c)   shall not prevent the Commission or any other person from exercising the function to which the authorisation relates.

(4)   Where a person is authorised to exercise any function by virtue of subsection (1), anything done or omitted to be done by or in relation to that person (or an employee of that person) in, or in connection with, the exercise or purported exercise of the function shall be treated for all purposes as done or omitted to be done by or in relation to the Commission.

(5)   Subsection (4) shall not apply—

(a)   for the purposes of so much of any contract made between the authorised person and the Commission as relates to the exercise of the function, or

(b)   for the purposes of any criminal proceedings brought in respect of anything done or omitted to be done by the authorised person (or an employee of that person).

(6)   Where—

(a)   a person is authorised to exercise any function by virtue of subsection (1), and

(b)   the authorisation is revoked at a time when a relevant contract is subsisting,

the authorised person shall be entitled to treat the relevant contract as repudiated by the Commission (and not as frustrated by reason of the revocation).

(7)   In subsection (6), the reference to a relevant contract is to so much of any

contract made between the authorised person and the Commission as relates to the exercise of the function.

9 Annual report to Secretary of State

(1) The Commission must prepare a report for each financial year.

(2) Each report under this section must—

(a) deal with the activities of the Commission in the financial year for which it is prepared, including the matters mentioned in subsection (3),

(b) include the report prepared under paragraph 20(5) of Schedule 1 by the committee established under that paragraph.

(3) The matters referred to in subsection (2)(a) are—

(a) the strategic direction of the Commission and the manner in which it has been kept under review;

(b) the Commission's objectives and targets, the steps taken to meet them and the extent to which they have been met;

(c) the steps taken to monitor the performance of the Commission in ensuring that its functions are exercised effectively and efficiently;

(d) the extent to which the Commission has relied on sections 7(1) and 8(1).

(4) The Commission must—

(a) send each report to the Secretary of State as soon as practicable after the end of the financial year for which it is prepared, and

(b) publish the report in such manner as the Commission considers appropriate.

(5) The Secretary of State must lay before Parliament a copy of every report received under this section.

(6) In this section, 'financial year' means—

(a) the period beginning with the date on which the Commission is established and ending with the next following 31st March, and

(b) each successive period of 12 months.

10 Directions and guidance

(1) The Secretary of State may give the Commission—

(a) guidance as to the exercise of its functions;

(b) general or specific directions as to the exercise of its functions.

(2) In exercising its functions, the Commission must—

(a) have regard to any guidance under subsection (1)(a), and

(b) comply with any directions under subsection (1)(b).

(3) Guidance or directions under this section must be in writing.

(4) Power under this section to give guidance or directions includes power to vary or revoke guidance or directions given in previous exercise of the power.

(5) The Secretary of State must lay before Parliament a copy of any direction given under subsection (1)(b).

(6) The Secretary of State may exclude from what is laid before Parliament—

(a) any information which the Secretary of State considers to be against the commercial interests of any person;

(b) any information which relates to an individual who can be identified from that information.

11 Review of the status of the Commission

(1) The Secretary of State must review the status of the Commission as a Crown body.

(2) The review under subsection (1) must be conducted as soon as reasonably practicable after the end of the initial period.

(3) The Secretary of State may review the status of the Commission as a Crown body at any other time after the end of the initial period, if the Secretary of State considers it appropriate to do so.

(4)   The Secretary of State must prepare a report of any review under subsection (1) or (3).

(5)   The Secretary of State must lay before Parliament a copy of the report.

(6)   If, on a review under this section, it appears to the Secretary of State appropriate to do so, the Secretary of State may by order made by statutory instrument provide that the Commission is to cease to be a Crown body.

(7)   An order under subsection (6) may—

(a)   make any amendment to Schedule 1 that appears to the Secretary of State to be necessary or expedient in consequence of the Commission ceasing to be a Crown body;

(b)   provide for the Transfer of Undertakings (Protection of Employment) Regulations 2006 to apply, subject to such modifications and exceptions as may be prescribed, as if, on the Commission ceasing to be a Crown body, there were a transfer of an undertaking or business which is a relevant transfer.

(8)   In this section—

'Crown body' means a body whose functions are to be exercised on behalf of the Crown;

'initial period' means the period of 3 years beginning with the day on which section 13 comes into force.

12   Supplementary provisions

(1)   In this Part, 'child' has the same meaning as in the Child Support Act 1991 (c 48).

(2)   The Secretary of State may by regulations make provision about when a child is, or is not, to be regarded for the purposes of this Part as living apart from a parent.

HUMAN FERTILISATION AND EMBRYOLOGY ACT 2008
(2008, c 22)

PART 2
PARENTHOOD IN CASES INVOLVING ASSISTED REPRODUCTION

Meaning of 'mother'

33   Meaning of 'mother'

(1)   The woman who is carrying or has carried a child as a result of the placing in her of an embryo or of sperm and eggs, and no other woman, is to be treated as the mother of the child.

(2)   Subsection (1) does not apply to any child to the extent that the child is treated by virtue of adoption as not being the woman's child.

(3)   Subsection (1) applies whether the woman was in the United Kingdom or elsewhere at the time of the placing in her of the embryo or the sperm and eggs.

Application of sections 35 to 47

34   Application of sections 35 to 47

(1)   Sections 35 to 47 apply, in the case of a child who is being or has been carried by a woman (referred to in those sections as 'W') as a result of the placing in her of an embryo or of sperm and eggs or her artificial insemination, to determine who is to be treated as the other parent of the child.

(2)   Subsection (1) has effect subject to the provisions of sections 39, 40 and 46 limiting the purposes for which a person is treated as the child's other parent by virtue of those sections.

Meaning of 'father'

35   Woman married at time of treatment

(1)   If—

(a)   at the time of the placing in her of the embryo or of the sperm and eggs or of her artificial insemination, W was a party to a marriage, and

(b)   the creation of the embryo carried by her was not brought about with the sperm of the other party to the marriage,

then, subject to section 38(2) to (4), the other party to the marriage is to be treated as the father of the child unless it is shown that he did not consent to the placing in her of the embryo or the sperm and eggs or to her artificial insemination (as the case may be).

(2)   This section applies whether W was in the United Kingdom or elsewhere at the time mentioned in subsection (1)(a).

36   Treatment provided to woman where agreed fatherhood conditions apply

If no man is treated by virtue of section 35 as the father of the child and no woman is treated by virtue of section 42 as a parent of the child but—

(a)   the embryo or the sperm and eggs were placed in W, or W was artificially inseminated, in the course of treatment services provided in the United Kingdom by a person to whom a licence applies,

(b)   at the time when the embryo or the sperm and eggs were placed in W, or W was artificially inseminated, the agreed fatherhood conditions (as set out in section 37) were satisfied in relation to a man, in relation to treatment provided to W under the licence,

(c)   the man remained alive at that time, and

(d)   the creation of the embryo carried by W was not brought about with the man's sperm,

then, subject to section 38(2) to (4), the man is to be treated as the father of the child.

37   The agreed fatherhood conditions

(1)   The agreed fatherhood conditions referred to in section 36(b) are met in relation to a man ('M') in relation to treatment provided to W under a licence if, but only if,—

(a)   M has given the person responsible a notice stating that he consents to being treated as the father of any child resulting from treatment provided to W under the licence,

(b)   W has given the person responsible a notice stating that she consents to M being so treated,

(c)   neither M nor W has, since giving notice under paragraph (a) or (b), given the person responsible notice of the withdrawal of M's or W's consent to M being so treated,

(d)   W has not, since the giving of the notice under paragraph (b), given the person responsible—

(i)   a further notice under that paragraph stating that she consents to another man being treated as the father of any resulting child, or

(ii)   a notice under section 44(1)(b) stating that she consents to a woman being treated as a parent of any resulting child, and

(e)   W and M are not within prohibited degrees of relationship in relation to each other.

(2)   A notice under subsection (1)(a), (b) or (c) must be in writing and must be signed by the person giving it.

(3)   A notice under subsection (1)(a), (b) or (c) by a person ('S') who is unable to sign because of illness, injury or physical disability is to be taken to comply with the requirement of subsection (2) as to signature if it is signed at the direction of S,

in the presence of S and in the presence of at least one witness who attests the signature.

38 Further provision relating to sections 35 and 36

(1)   Where a person is to be treated as the father of the child by virtue of section 35 or 36, no other person is to be treated as the father of the child.

(2)   In England and Wales and Northern Ireland, sections 35 and 36 do not affect any presumption, applying by virtue of the rules of common law, that a child is the legitimate child of the parties to a marriage.

(3)   In Scotland, sections 35 and 36 do not apply in relation to any child who, by virtue of any enactment or other rule of law, is treated as the child of the parties to a marriage.

(4)   Sections 35 and 36 do not apply to any child to the extent that the child is treated by virtue of adoption as not being the man's child.

39 Use of sperm, or transfer of embryo, after death of man providing sperm

(1)   If—

(a)   the child has been carried by W as a result of the placing in her of an embryo or of sperm and eggs or her artificial insemination,

(b)   the creation of the embryo carried by W was brought about by using the sperm of a man after his death, or the creation of the embryo was brought about using the sperm of a man before his death but the embryo was placed in W after his death,

(c)   the man consented in writing (and did not withdraw the consent)—

(i)   to the use of his sperm after his death which brought about the creation of the embryo carried by W or (as the case may be) to the placing in W after his death of the embryo which was brought about using his sperm before his death, and

(ii)   to being treated for the purpose mentioned in subsection (3) as the father of any resulting child,

(d)   W has elected in writing not later than the end of the period of 42 days from the day on which the child was born for the man to be treated for the purpose mentioned in subsection (3) as the father of the child, and

(e)   no-one else is to be treated—

(i)   as the father of the child by virtue of section 35 or 36 or by virtue of section 38(2) or (3), or

(ii)   as a parent of the child by virtue of section 42 or 43 or by virtue of adoption,

then the man is to be treated for the purpose mentioned in subsection (3) as the father of the child.

(2)   Subsection (1) applies whether W was in the United Kingdom or elsewhere at the time of the placing in her of the embryo or of the sperm and eggs or of her artificial insemination.

(3)   The purpose referred to in subsection (1) is the purpose of enabling the man's particulars to be entered as the particulars of the child's father in a relevant register of births.

(4)   In the application of this section to Scotland, for any reference to a period of 42 days there is substituted a reference to a period of 21 days.

40 Embryo transferred after death of husband etc who did not provide sperm

(1)   If—

(a)   the child has been carried by W as a result of the placing in her of an embryo,

(b)   the embryo was created at a time when W was a party to a marriage,

(c)   the creation of the embryo was not brought about with the sperm of the other party to the marriage,

(d)   the other party to the marriage died before the placing of the embryo in W,

(e)   the other party to the marriage consented in writing (and did not withdraw the consent)—

(i)   to the placing of the embryo in W after his death, and

(ii)   to being treated for the purpose mentioned in subsection (4) as the father of any resulting child,

(f)   W has elected in writing not later than the end of the period of 42 days from the day on which the child was born for the man to be treated for the purpose mentioned in subsection (4) as the father of the child, and

(g)   no-one else is to be treated—

(i)   as the father of the child by virtue of section 35 or 36 or by virtue of section 38(2) or (3), or

(ii)   as a parent of the child by virtue of section 42 or 43 or by virtue of adoption,

then the man is to be treated for the purpose mentioned in subsection (4) as the father of the child.

(2)   If—

(a)   the child has been carried by W as a result of the placing in her of an embryo,

(b)   the embryo was not created at a time when W was a party to a marriage or a civil partnership but was created in the course of treatment services provided to W in the United Kingdom by a person to whom a licence applies,

(c)   a man consented in writing (and did not withdraw the consent)—

(i)   to the placing of the embryo in W after his death, and

(ii)   to being treated for the purpose mentioned in subsection (4) as the father of any resulting child,

(d)   the creation of the embryo was not brought about with the sperm of that man,

(e)   the man died before the placing of the embryo in W,

(f)   immediately before the man's death, the agreed fatherhood conditions set out in section 37 were met in relation to the man in relation to treatment proposed to be provided to W in the United Kingdom by a person to whom a licence applies,

(g)   W has elected in writing not later than the end of the period of 42 days from the day on which the child was born for the man to be treated for the purpose mentioned in subsection (4) as the father of the child, and

(h)   no-one else is to be treated—

(i)   as the father of the child by virtue of section 35 or 36 or by virtue of section 38(2) or (3), or

(ii)   as a parent of the child by virtue of section 42 or 43 or by virtue of adoption,

then the man is to be treated for the purpose mentioned in subsection (4) as the father of the child.

(3)   Subsections (1) and (2) apply whether W was in the United Kingdom or elsewhere at the time of the placing in her of the embryo.

(4)   The purpose referred to in subsections (1) and (2) is the purpose of enabling the man's particulars to be entered as the particulars of the child's father in a relevant register of births.

(5)   In the application of this section to Scotland, for any reference to a period of 42 days there is substituted a reference to a period of 21 days.

41   Persons not to be treated as father

(1)   Where the sperm of a man who had given such consent as is required by paragraph 5 of Schedule 3 to the 1990 Act (consent to use of gametes for purposes of treatment services or non-medical fertility services) was used for a

purpose for which such consent was required, he is not to be treated as the father of the child.

(2) Where the sperm of a man, or an embryo the creation of which was brought about with his sperm, was used after his death, he is not, subject to section 39, to be treated as the father of the child.

(3) Subsection (2) applies whether W was in the United Kingdom or elsewhere at the time of the placing in her of the embryo or of the sperm and eggs or of her artificial insemination.

Cases in which woman to be other parent

42   Woman in civil partnership at time of treatment

(1) If at the time of the placing in her of the embryo or the sperm and eggs or of her artificial insemination, W was a party to a civil partnership, then subject to section 45(2) to (4), the other party to the civil partnership is to be treated as a parent of the child unless it is shown that she did not consent to the placing in W of the embryo or the sperm and eggs or to her artificial insemination (as the case may be).

(2) This section applies whether W was in the United Kingdom or elsewhere at the time mentioned in subsection (1).

43   Treatment provided to woman who agrees that second woman to be parent

If no man is treated by virtue of section 35 as the father of the child and no woman is treated by virtue of section 42 as a parent of the child but—

(a) the embryo or the sperm and eggs were placed in W, or W was artificially inseminated, in the course of treatment services provided in the United Kingdom by a person to whom a licence applies,

(b) at the time when the embryo or the sperm and eggs were placed in W, or W was artificially inseminated, the agreed female parenthood conditions (as set out in section 44) were met in relation to another woman, in relation to treatment provided to W under that licence, and

(c) the other woman remained alive at that time,

then, subject to section 45(2) to (4), the other woman is to be treated as a parent of the child.

44   The agreed female parenthood conditions

(1) The agreed female parenthood conditions referred to in section 43(b) are met in relation to another woman ('P') in relation to treatment provided to W under a licence if, but only if,—

(a) P has given the person responsible a notice stating that P consents to P being treated as a parent of any child resulting from treatment provided to W under the licence,

(b) W has given the person responsible a notice stating that W agrees to P being so treated,

(c) neither W nor P has, since giving notice under paragraph (a) or (b), given the person responsible notice of the withdrawal of P's or W's consent to P being so treated,

(d) W has not, since the giving of the notice under paragraph (b), given the person responsible—

(i) a further notice under that paragraph stating that W consents to a woman other than P being treated as a parent of any resulting child, or

(ii) a notice under section 37(1)(b) stating that W consents to a man being treated as the father of any resulting child, and

(e) W and P are not within prohibited degrees of relationship in relation to each other.

(2) A notice under subsection (1)(a), (b) or (c) must be in writing and must be signed by the person giving it.

(3)   A notice under subsection (1)(a), (b) or (c) by a person ('S') who is unable to sign because of illness, injury or physical disability is to be taken to comply with the requirement of subsection (2) as to signature if it is signed at the direction of S, in the presence of S and in the presence of at least one witness who attests the signature.

45   Further provision relating to sections 42 and 43

(1)   Where a woman is treated by virtue of section 42 or 43 as a parent of the child, no man is to be treated as the father of the child.

(2)   In England and Wales and Northern Ireland, sections 42 and 43 do not affect any presumption, applying by virtue of the rules of common law, that a child is the legitimate child of the parties to a marriage.

(3)   In Scotland, sections 42 and 43 do not apply in relation to any child who, by virtue of any enactment or other rule of law, is treated as the child of the parties to a marriage.

(4)   Sections 42 and 43 do not apply to any child to the extent that the child is treated by virtue of adoption as not being the woman's child.

46   Embryo transferred after death of civil partner or intended female parent

(1)   If—

(a)   the child has been carried by W as the result of the placing in her of an embryo,

(b)   the embryo was created at a time when W was a party to a civil partnership,

(c)   the other party to the civil partnership died before the placing of the embryo in W,

(d)   the other party to the civil partnership consented in writing (and did not withdraw the consent)—

(i)   to the placing of the embryo in W after the death of the other party, and

(ii)   to being treated for the purpose mentioned in subsection (4) as the parent of any resulting child,

(e)   W has elected in writing not later than the end of the period of 42 days from the day on which the child was born for the other party to the civil partnership to be treated for the purpose mentioned in subsection (4) as the parent of the child, and

(f)   no one else is to be treated—

(i)   as the father of the child by virtue of section 35 or 36 or by virtue of section 45(2) or (3), or

(ii)   as a parent of the child by virtue of section 42 or 43 or by virtue of adoption,

then the other party to the civil partnership is to be treated for the purpose mentioned in subsection (4) as a parent of the child.

(2)   If—

(a)   the child has been carried by W as the result of the placing in her of an embryo,

(b)   the embryo was not created at a time when W was a party to a marriage or a civil partnership, but was created in the course of treatment services provided to W in the United Kingdom by a person to whom a licence applies,

(c)   another woman consented in writing (and did not withdraw the consent)—

(i)   to the placing of the embryo in W after the death of the other woman, and

(ii)   to being treated for the purpose mentioned in subsection (4) as the parent of any resulting child,

(d)   the other woman died before the placing of the embryo in W,

(e)   immediately before the other woman's death, the agreed female parent-hood conditions set out in section 44 were met in relation to the other woman in relation to treatment proposed to be provided to W in the United Kingdom by a person to whom a licence applies,

(f)   W has elected in writing not later than the end of the period of 42 days from the day on which the child was born for the other woman to be treated for the purpose mentioned in subsection (4) as the parent of the child, and

(g)   no one else is to be treated—

(i)   as the father of the child by virtue of section 35 or 36 or by virtue of section 45(2) or (3), or

(ii)   as a parent of the child by virtue of section 42 or 43 or by virtue of adoption,

then the other woman is to be treated for the purpose mentioned in subsection (4) as a parent of the child.

(3)   Subsections (1) and (2) apply whether W was in the United Kingdom or elsewhere at the time of the placing in her of the embryo.

(4)   The purpose referred to in subsections (1) and (2) is the purpose of enabling the deceased woman's particulars to be entered as the particulars of the child's other parent in a relevant register of births.

(5)   In the application of subsections (1) and (2) to Scotland, for any reference to a period of 42 days there is substituted a reference to a period of 21 days.

47   Woman not to be other parent merely because of egg donation

A woman is not to be treated as the parent of a child whom she is not carrying and has not carried, except where she is so treated—

(a)   by virtue of section 42 or 43, or

(b)   by virtue of section 46 (for the purpose mentioned in subsection (4) of that section), or

(c)   by virtue of adoption.

Effect of sections 33 to 47

48   Effect of sections 33 to 47

(1)   Where by virtue of section 33, 35, 36, 42 or 43 a person is to be treated as the mother, father or parent of a child, that person is to be treated in law as the mother, father or parent (as the case may be) of the child for all purposes.

(2)   Where by virtue of section 33, 38, 41, 45 or 47 a person is not to be treated as a parent of the child, that person is to be treated in law as not being a parent of the child for any purpose.

(3)   Where section 39(1) or 40(1) or (2) applies, the deceased man—

(a)   is to be treated in law as the father of the child for the purpose men-tioned in section 39(3) or 40(4), but

(b)   is to be treated in law as not being the father of the child for any other purpose.

(4)   Where section 46(1) or (2) applies, the deceased woman—

(a)   is to be treated in law as a parent of the child for the purpose mentioned in section 46(4), but

(b)   is to be treated in law as not being a parent of the child for any other purpose.

(5)   Where any of subsections (1) to (4) has effect, references to any relationship between two people in any enactment, deed or other instrument or document (whenever passed or made) are to be read accordingly.

(6)   In relation to England and Wales and Northern Ireland, a child who—

(a)   has a parent by virtue of section 42, or

(b)   has a parent by virtue of section 43 who is at any time during the period

beginning with the time mentioned in section 43(b) and ending with the time of the child's birth a party to a civil partnership with the child's mother,
is the legitimate child of the child's parents.

(7) In relation to England and Wales and Northern Ireland, nothing in the provisions of section 33(1) or sections 35 to 47, read with this section—

(a) affects the succession to any dignity or title of honour or renders any person capable of succeeding to or transmitting a right to succeed to any such dignity or title, or

(b) affects the devolution of any property limited (expressly or not) to devolve (as nearly as the law permits) along with any dignity or title of honour.

(8) In relation to Scotland—

(a) those provisions do not apply to any title, coat of arms, honour or dignity transmissible on the death of its holder or affect the succession to any such title, coat of arms or dignity or its devolution, and

(b) where the terms of any deed provide that any property or interest in property is to devolve along with a title, coat of arms, honour or dignity, nothing in those provisions is to prevent that property or interest from so devolving.

References to parties to marriage or civil partnership

49 Meaning of references to parties to a marriage

(1) The references in sections 35 to 47 to the parties to a marriage at any time there referred to—

(a) are to the parties to a marriage subsisting at that time, unless a judicial separation was then in force, but

(b) include the parties to a void marriage if either or both of them reasonably believed at that time that the marriage was valid; and for the purposes of those sections it is to be presumed, unless the contrary is shown, that one of them reasonably believed at that time that the marriage was valid.

(2) In subsection (1)(a) 'judicial separation' includes a legal separation obtained in a country outside the British Islands and recognised in the United Kingdom.

50 Meaning of references to parties to a civil partnership

(1) The references in sections 35 to 47 to the parties to a civil partnership at any time there referred to—

(a) are to the parties to a civil partnership subsisting at that time, unless a separation order was then in force, but

(b) include the parties to a void civil partnership if either or both of them reasonably believed at that time that the civil partnership was valid; and for the purposes of those sections it is to be presumed, unless the contrary is shown, that one of them reasonably believed at that time that the civil partnership was valid.

(2) The reference in section 48(6)(b) to a civil partnership includes a reference to a void civil partnership if either or both of the parties reasonably believed at the time when they registered as civil partners of each other that the civil partnership was valid; and for this purpose it is to be presumed, unless the contrary is shown, that one of them reasonably believed at that time that the civil partnership was valid.

(3) In subsection (1)(a), 'separation order' means—

(a) a separation order under section 37(1)(d) or 161(1)(d) of the Civil Partnership Act 2004,

(b) a decree of separation under section 120(2) of that Act, or

(c) a legal separation obtained in a country outside the United Kingdom and recognised in the United Kingdom.

Further provision about registration by virtue of section 39, 40 or 46

51 Meaning of 'relevant register of births'

For the purposes of this Part a 'relevant register of births', in relation to a birth, is whichever of the following is relevant—

    (a) a register of live-births or still-births kept under the Births and Deaths Registration Act 1953,

    (b) a register of births or still-births kept under the Registration of Births, Deaths and Marriages (Scotland) Act 1965, or

    (c) a register of live-births or still-births kept under the Births and Deaths Registration (Northern Ireland) Order 1976.

52 Late election by mother with consent of Registrar General

    (1) The requirement under section 39(1), 40(1) or (2) or 46(1) or (2) as to the making of an election (which requires an election to be made either on or before the day on which the child was born or within the period of 42 or, as the case may be, 21 days from that day) is nevertheless to be treated as satisfied if the required election is made after the end of that period but with the consent of the Registrar General under subsection (2).

    (2) The Registrar General may at any time consent to the making of an election after the end of the period mentioned in subsection (1) if, on an application made to him in accordance with such requirements as he may specify, he is satisfied that there is a compelling reason for giving his consent to the making of such an election.

    (3) In this section 'the Registrar General' means the Registrar General for England and Wales, the Registrar General of Births, Deaths and Marriages for Scotland or (as the case may be) the Registrar General for Northern Ireland.

Interpretation of references to father etc where woman is other parent

53 Interpretation of references to father etc

    (1) Subsections (2) and (3) have effect, subject to subsections (4) and (6), for the interpretation of any enactment, deed or any other instrument or document (whenever passed or made).

    (2) Any reference (however expressed) to the father of a child who has a parent by virtue of section 42 or 43 is to be read as a reference to the woman who is a parent of the child by virtue of that section.

    (3) Any reference (however expressed) to evidence of paternity is, in relation to a woman who is a parent by virtue of section 42 or 43, to be read as a reference to evidence of parentage.

    (4) This section does not affect the interpretation of the enactments specified in subsection (5)(which make express provision for the case where a child has a parent by virtue of section 42 or 43).

    (5) Those enactments are—

    (a) the Legitimacy Act (Northern Ireland) 1928,

    (b) the Schedule to the Population (Statistics) Act 1938,

    (c) the Births and Deaths Registration Act 1953,

    (d) the Registration of Births, Deaths and Marriages (Special Provisions) Act 1957,

    (e) Part 2 of the Registration of Births, Deaths and Marriages (Scotland) Act 1965,

    (f) the Congenital Disabilities (Civil Liability) Act 1976,

    (g) the Legitimacy Act 1976,

    (h) the Births and Deaths Registration (Northern Ireland) Order 1976,

    (i) the British Nationality Act 1981,

    (j) the Family Law Reform Act 1987,

    (k) Parts 1 and 2 of the Children Act 1989,

(l)   Part 1 of the Children (Scotland) Act 1995,

(m)   section 1 of the Criminal Law (Consolidation)(Scotland) Act 1995, and

(n)   Parts 2, 3 and 14 of·the Children (Northern Ireland) Order 1995.

(6)   This section does not affect the interpretation of references that fall to be read in accordance with section 1(2)(a) or (b) of the Family Law Reform Act 1987 or Article 155(2)(a) or (b) of the Children (Northern Ireland) Order 1995 (references to a person whose father and mother were, or were not, married to each other at the time of the person's birth).

Parental orders

54   Parental orders

(1)   On an application made by two people ('the applicants'), the court may make an order providing for a child to be treated in law as the child of the applicants if—

(a)   the child has been carried by a woman who is not one of the applicants, as a result of the placing in her of an embryo or sperm and eggs or her artificial insemination,

(b)   the gametes of at least one of the applicants were used to bring about the creation of the embryo, and

(c)   the conditions in subsections (2) to (8) are satisfied.

(2)   The applicants must be—

(a)   husband and wife,

(b)   civil partners of each other, or

(c)   two persons who are living as partners in an enduring family relationship and are not within prohibited degrees of relationship in relation to each other.

(3)   Except in a case falling within subsection (11), the applicants must apply for the order during the period of 6 months beginning with the day on which the child is born.

(4)   At the time of the application and the making of the order—

(a)   the child's home must be with the applicants, and

(b)   either or both of the applicants must be domiciled in the United Kingdom or in the Channel Islands or the Isle of Man.

(5)   At the time of the making of the order both the applicants must have attained the age of 18.

(6)   The court must be satisfied that both—

(a)   the woman who carried the child, and

(b)   any other person who is a parent of the child but is not one of the applicants (including any man who is the father by virtue of section 35 or 36 or any woman who is a parent by virtue of section 42 or 43),

have freely, and with full understanding of what is involved, agreed unconditionally to the making of the order.

(7)   Subsection (6) does not require the agreement of a person who cannot be found or is incapable of giving agreement; and the agreement of the woman who carried the child is ineffective for the purpose of that subsection if given by her less than six weeks after the child's birth.

(8)   The court must be satisfied that no money or other benefit (other than for expenses reasonably incurred) has been given or received by either of the applicants for or in consideration of—

(a)   the making of the order,

(b)   any agreement required by subsection (6),

(c)   the handing over of the child to the applicants, or

(d)   the making of arrangements with a view to the making of the order,

unless authorised by the court.

(9)   For the purposes of an application under this section—

(a)   in relation to England and Wales, section 92(7) to (10) of, and Part 1 of Schedule 11 to, the Children Act 1989 (jurisdiction of courts) apply for the purposes of this section to determine the meaning of 'the court' as they apply for the purposes of that Act and proceedings on the application are to be 'family proceedings' for the purposes of that Act,

(b)   in relation to Scotland, 'the court' means the Court of Session or the sheriff court of the sheriffdom within which the child is, and

(c)   in relation to Northern Ireland, 'the court' means the High Court or any county court within whose division the child is.

(10)   Subsection (1)(a) applies whether the woman was in the United Kingdom or elsewhere at the time of the placing in her of the embryo or the sperm and eggs or her artificial insemination.

(11)   An application which—

(a)   relates to a child born before the coming into force of this section, and

(b)   is made by two persons who, throughout the period applicable under subsection (2) of section 30 of the 1990 Act, were not eligible to apply for an order under that section in relation to the child as husband and wife,

may be made within the period of six months beginning with the day on which this section comes into force.

55   Parental orders: supplementary provision

(1)   The Secretary of State may by regulations provide—

(a)   for any provision of the enactments about adoption to have effect, with such modifications (if any) as may be specified in the regulations, in relation to orders under section 54, and applications for such orders, as it has effect in relation to adoption, and applications for adoption orders, and

(b)   for references in any enactment to adoption, an adopted child or an adoptive relationship to be read (respectively) as references to the effect of an order under section 54, a child to whom such an order applies and a relationship arising by virtue of the enactments about adoption, as applied by the regulations, and for similar expressions in connection with adoption to be read accordingly.

(2)   The regulations may include such incidental or supplemental provision as appears to the Secretary of State to be necessary or desirable in consequence of any provision made by virtue of subsection (1)(a) or (b).

(3)   In this section 'the enactments about adoption' means—

(a)   the Adoption (Scotland) Act 1978,

(b)   the Adoption and Children Act 2002,

(c)   the Adoption and Children (Scotland) Act 2007, and

(d)   the Adoption (Northern Ireland) Order 1987.

Amendments of enactments

56   Amendments relating to parenthood in cases involving assisted reproduction

Schedule 6 contains amendments related to the provisions of this Part.

General

57   Repeals and transitional provision relating to Part 2

(1)   Sections 33 to 48 have effect only in relation to children carried by women as a result of the placing in them of embryos or of sperm and eggs, or their artificial insemination (as the case may be), after the commencement of those sections.

(2)   Sections 27 to 29 of the 1990 Act (which relate to status) do not have effect in relation to children carried by women as a result of the placing in them of embryos or of sperm and eggs, or their artificial insemination (as the case may be), after the commencement of sections 33 to 48.

(3)   Section 30 of the 1990 Act (parental orders in favour of gamete donors) ceases to have effect.

(4)   Subsection (3) does not affect the validity of any order made under section 30 of the 1990 Act before the coming into force of that subsection.

58   Interpretation of Part 2

(1)   In this Part 'enactment' means an enactment contained in, or in an instrument made under—

   (a)   an Act of Parliament,

   (b)   an Act of the Scottish Parliament,

   (c)   a Measure or Act of the National Assembly for Wales, or

   (d)   Northern Ireland legislation.

(2)   For the purposes of this Part, two persons are within prohibited degrees of relationship if one is the other's parent, grandparent, sister, brother, aunt or uncle; and in this subsection references to relationships—

   (a)   are to relationships of the full blood or half blood or, in the case of an adopted person, such of those relationships as would subsist but for adoption, and

   (b)   include the relationship of a child with his adoptive, or former adoptive, parents,

but do not include any other adoptive relationships.

(3)   Other expressions used in this Part and in the 1990 Act have the same meaning in this Part as in that Act.

PART II

INTERNATIONAL CONVENTIONS

EUROPEAN CONVENTION FOR THE PROTECTION OF HUMAN RIGHTS AND FUNDAMENTAL FREEDOMS (1950)

Article 6

1. In the determination of his civil rights and obligations or of any criminal charge against him, everyone is entitled to a fair and public hearing within a reasonable time by an independent and impartial tribunal established by law. Judgment shall be pronounced publicly but the press and public may be excluded from all or part of the trial in the interests of morals, public order or national security in a democratic society, where the interests of juveniles or the protection of the private life of the parties so require, or to the extent strictly necessary in the opinion of the court in special circumstances where publicity would prejudice the interests of justice.

2. Everyone charged with a criminal offence shall be presumed innocent until proved guilty according to law.

3. Everyone charged with a criminal offence has the following minimum rights:

(a) to be informed promptly, in a language which he understands and in detail, of the nature and cause of the accusation against him;

(b) to have adequate time and facilities for the preparation of his defence;

(c) to defend himself in person or through legal assistance of his own choosing or, if he has not sufficient means to pay for legal assistance, to be given it free when the interests of justice so require;

(d) to examine or have examined witnesses against him and to obtain the attendance and examination of witnesses on his behalf under the same conditions as witnesses against him;

(e) to have the free assistance of an interpreter if he cannot understand or speak the language used in court.

Article 8

1. Everyone has the right to respect for his private and family life, his home and his correspondence.

2. There shall be no interference by a public authority with the exercise of this right except such as is in accordance with the law and is necessary in a democratic society in the interests of national security, public safety or the economic well-being of the country, for the prevention of disorder or crime, for the protection of health or morals, or for the protection of the rights and freedoms of others.

Article 12

Men and women of marriageable age have the right to marry and to found a family, according to the national laws governing the exercise of this right.

Article 14

The enjoyment of the rights and freedoms set forth in this Convention shall be secured without discrimination on any ground such as sex, race, colour, language, religion, political or other opinion, national or social origin, association with a national minority, property, birth or other status.

UNITED NATIONS CONVENTION ON THE RIGHTS OF THE CHILD
(1989)

Article 1
For the purposes of the present Convention, a child means every human being below the age of eighteen years unless, under the law applicable to the child, majority is attained earlier.

Article 2
1. States Parties shall respect and ensure the rights set forth in the present Convention to each child within their jurisdiction without discrimination of any kind, irrespective of the child's or his or her parent's or legal guardian's race, colour, sex, language, religion, political or other opinion, national, ethnic or social origin, property, disability, birth or other status.
2. States Parties shall take all appropriate measures to ensure that the child is protected against all forms of discrimination or punishment on the basis of the status, activities, expressed opinions, or beliefs of the child's parents, legal guardians, or family members.

Article 3
1. In all actions concerning children, whether undertaken by public or private social welfare institutions, courts of law, administrative authorities or legislative bodies, the best interests of the child shall be a primary consideration.
2. States Parties undertake to ensure the child such protection and care as is necessary for his or her well-being, taking into account the rights and duties of his or her parents, legal guardians, or other individuals legally responsible for him or her, and to this end, shall take all appropriate legislative and administrative measures.
3. States Parties shall ensure that the institutions, services and facilities responsible for the care or protection of children shall conform with the standards established by competent authorities, particularly in the areas of safety, health, in the number and suitability of their staff, as well as competent supervision.

Article 6
1. States Parties recognise that every child has the inherent right to life.
2. States Parties shall ensure to the maximum extent possible the survival and development of the child.

Article 7
1. The child shall be registered immediately after birth and shall have the right from birth to a name, the right to acquire a nationality and, as far as possible, the right to know and be cared for by his or her parents.
2. States Parties shall ensure the implementation of these rights in accordance with their national law and their obligations under the relevant international instruments in this field, in particular where the child would otherwise be stateless.

Article 9
1. States Parties shall ensure that a child shall not be separated from his or her parents against their will, except when competent authorities subject to judicial review determine, in accordance with applicable law and procedures, that such separation is necessary for the best interests of the child. Such determination may be necessary in a particular case such as one involving abuse or neglect of the child by the parents, or one where the parents are living separately and a decision must be made as to the child's place of residence.
2. In any proceedings pursuant to paragraph 1 of the present article, all interested parties shall be given the opportunity to participate in the proceedings and make their views known.
3. States Parties shall respect the right of the child who is separated from one

or both parents to maintain personal relations and direct contact with both parents on a regular basis, except if it is contrary to the child's best interests.

4. Where such separation results from any action initiated by a State Party, such as the detention, imprisonment, exile, deportation or death (including death arising from any cause while the person is in the custody of the State) of one or both parents or of the child, that State Party shall, upon request, provide the parents, the child or, if appropriate, another member of the family with the essential information concerning the whereabouts of the absent member(s) of the family unless the provision of the information would be detrimental to the well-being of the child. States Parties shall further ensure that the submission of such a request shall of itself entail no adverse consequences for the person(s) concerned.

Article 10

1. In accordance with the obligation of States Parties under article 9, paragraph 1, applications by a child or his or her parents to enter or leave a State Party for the purposes of family reunification shall be dealt with by States Parties in a positive, humane and expeditious manner. States Parties shall further ensure that the submission of such a request shall entail no adverse consequences for the applicants and for the members of their family.

2. A child whose parents reside in different States shall have the right to maintain on a regular basis, save in exceptional circumstances, personal relations and direct contacts with both parents. Towards that end and in accordance with the obligation of States Parties under article 9, paragraph 1, States Parties shall respect the right of the child and his or her parents to leave any country, including their own, and to enter their own country. The right to leave any country shall be subject only to such restrictions as are prescribed by law and which are necessary to protect the national security, public order (*ordre public*), public health or morals or the rights and freedoms of others and are consistent with the other rights recognised in the present Convention.

Article 12

1. States Parties shall assure to the child who is capable of forming his or her own views the right to express those views freely in all matters affecting the child, the views of the child being given due weight in accordance with the age and maturity of the child.

2. For this purpose, the child shall in particular be provided the opportunity to be heard in any judicial and administrative proceedings affecting the child, either directly, or through a representative or an appropriate body, in a manner consistent with the procedural rules of national law.

Article 18

1. States Parties shall use their best efforts to ensure recognition of the principle that both parents have common responsibilities for the upbringing and development of the child. Parents or, as the case may be, legal guardians, have the primary responsibility for the upbringing and development of the child. The best interests of the child will be their basic concern.

2. For the purpose of guaranteeing and promoting the rights set forth in the present Convention, States Parties shall render appropriate assistance to parents and legal guardians in the performance of their child-rearing responsibilities and shall ensure the development of institutions, facilities and services for the care of children.

3. States Parties shall take all appropriate measures to ensure that children of working parents have the right to benefit from child-care services and facilities for which they are eligible.

Article 22

1. States Parties shall take appropriate measures to ensure that a child who is seeking refugee status or who is considered a refugee in accordance with appli-

cable international or domestic law and procedures shall, whether unaccompanied or accompanied by his or her parents or by any other person, receive appropriate protection and humanitarian assistance in the enjoyment of applicable rights set forth in the present convention and in other international human rights or humanitarian instruments to which the said States are Parties.

2.   For this purpose, States Parties shall provide, as they consider appropriate, co-operation in any efforts by the United Nations and other competent inter-governmental organisations or non-governmental organisations co-operating with the United Nations to protect and assist such a child and to trace the parents or other members of the family of any refugee child in order to obtain information necessary for reunification with his or her family. In cases where no parents or other members of the family can be found, the child shall be accorded the same protection as any other child permanently or temporarily deprived of his or her family environment for any reason, as set forth in the present Convention.

Article 40

1.   States Parties recognise the right of every child alleged as, accused of, or recognised as having infringed the penal law to be treated in a manner consistent with the promotion of the child's sense of dignity and worth, which reinforces the child's respect for the human rights and fundamental freedoms of others and which takes into account the child's age and the desirability of promoting the child's reintegration and the child's assuming a constructive role in society.

2.   To this end, and having regard to the relevant provisions of international instruments, States Parties shall, in particular, ensure that:

(a)   No child shall be alleged as, be accused of, or recognised as having infringed the penal law by reason of acts or omissions that were not prohibited by national or international law at the time they were committed;

(b)   Every child alleged as or accused of having infringed the penal law has at least the following guarantees:

(i)   To be presumed innocent until proven guilty according to law;

(ii)   To be informed promptly and directly of the charges against him or her, and, if appropriate, through his or her parents or legal guardians, and to have legal or other appropriate assistance in the preparation and presentation of his or her defence;

(iii)   To have the matter determined without delay by a competent, independent and impartial authority or judicial body in a fair hearing according to law, in the presence of legal or other appropriate assistance and, unless it is considered not to be in the best interest of the child, in particular, taking into account his or her age or situation, his or her parents or legal guardians;

(iv)   Not to be compelled to give testimony or to confess guilt; to examine or have examined adverse witnesses and to obtain the participation and examination of witnesses on his or her behalf under conditions of equality;

(v)   If considered to have infringed the penal law, to have this decision and any measures imposed in consequence thereof reviewed by a higher competent, independent and impartial authority or judicial body according to law;

(vi)   To have the free assistance of an interpreter if the child cannot understand or speak the language used;

(vii)   To have his or her privacy fully respected at all stages of the proceedings.

3.   States Parties shall seek to promote the establishment of laws, procedures, authorities and institutions specifically applicable to children alleged as, accused of, or recognised as having infringed the penal law, and, in particular:

(a)   The establishment of a minimum age below which children shall be presumed not to have the capacity to infringe the penal law;

(b)   Whenever appropriate and desirable, measures for dealing with such children without resorting to judicial proceedings, providing that human rights and legal safeguards are fully respected.

4.   A variety of dispositions, such as care, guidance and supervision orders; counselling; probation; foster care; education and vocational training programmes and other alternatives to institutional care shall be available to ensure that children are dealt with in a manner appropriate to their well-being and proportionate both to their circumstances and the offence.

INDEX OF STATUTES